UNDERSTANDING

NEGRO

HISTORY

UNDERSTANDING

NEGRO

HISTORY

EDITED WITH COMMENTARY BY

DWIGHT W. HOOVER

CHICAGO

QUADRANGLE BOOKS

Library of Congress Catalog Card Number: 68-26441

Designed by Vincent Torre

Grateful acknowledgment is made to publishers, journals, and individuals for permission to reprint copyrighted materials, as noted herein.

Preface

This book is not intended to be a general history of the Negro in the United States; other historians have devoted themselves to the task of writing a comprehensive Negro history with vigor and enthusiasm. Nor is it designed to probe in depth any particular aspect of Negro history, exhausting all available scholarship in that attempt. Rather, this book considers the major problems in studying and writing Negro history, the compelling questions that are being asked by discerning contemporary scholars, and the areas of exploration that seem to hold the most interest for the future. It also provides a structure so that both laymen and historians not usually involved with Negro history can categorize the rapidly increasing data. Finally, it is meant to serve as a guide to further ideas about the possibilities of Negro history.

One factor complicating this kind of book is the recent intrusion of white scholars into a field previously the domain of Negroes. As Frenise A. Logan indicated in 1959 in the Journal of Negro History, white scholars from white institutions are rapidly replacing Negro scholars from Negro institutions in the writing of Negro history. Some of the later converts have the tendency to assume that the ground has never been explored, that the material is all very fresh. In fact, often the material is new only to the researcher; one is struck by how much Negro scholars in the past anticipated the present. One of the questions implicit in this anthology is, How new is new? I have taken the middle ground here and included material that has been worked through before, if such material reveals fresh insights or is exceedingly well written.

Most of the selections herein were written within the last ten years and are drawn predominantly from journals. I have made no attempt to strike a balance from the sources. Because of their continuing interest in Negro history, the Journal of Negro History and the Journal of Southern History are probably used more than any other journals. Given the choice, I have taken articles rather than chapters of books in the belief that articles are more likely to be self-contained. When an author has written an article which has later been incorporated or enlarged into a book, I have taken the original article.

Because of the quantity of material to select from and the limited topics and space, many areas of investigation and many competent historians have been excluded. I chose those selections which best illustrate the problems that seemed to me most important; I did this without regard for any other criteria.

Inevitably, the study of history involves controversy, and Negro history is no exception. This book does not attempt to present both sides of an issue. There are no balancing essays on each topic; rather, newer interpretations are stressed. I have assumed that the reader, because of his immersion in American society, already has an acquaintance with American history in the form of conventional knowledge. In addition, I recognize the tentative nature of historical knowledge. To say that historical knowledge is temporal is, in part, to define the historian's task.

No section of this book concerns the Negro outside the United States. An excellent case can be made for studying the effect of seventeenth-century African backgrounds on the institutional forms of slavery in the Western hemisphere. A comprehensive history of the Negro would surely include this, but it is beyond the scope of this collection. The basic assumption here is that the history of the Negro in the United States is inextricably tied to the history of American society, and that the major question is therefore the role the Negro is to play in that society.

The arrangement of the book is topical rather than chronological, but most of the selections concern the nineteenth century. This concentration reflects the search for a usable past, the availability of sources, and the crucial nature of decisions made at that time. More recent events are not included for two reasons. First, historians are notoriously reluctant to come to grips with the immediate past, and the contemporary scene is perhaps better explained by the behavioral scientist. Second, the availability and wide dissemination of information about recent events makes them less desirable in a book designed to explore the unfamiliar.

Contents

PREFACE   5

PART I
THE USES OF NEGRO HISTORY

CREATING AND MAINTAINING AN HISTORICAL
TRADITION   17
   by Charles H. Wesley
A TRAGIC CONCEPTION OF NEGRO HISTORY   27
   by Samuel DuBois Cook
THE NEGRO REVOLUTION AND THE INTELLECTUALS   46
   by William B. Hixson, Jr.

PART II
PROBLEMS IN WRITING NEGRO HISTORY

The Nature of the Evidence
   MODERN TENSIONS AND THE ORIGINS OF AMERICAN
   SLAVERY   61
      by Winthrop D. Jordan
   THE VESEY PLOT: A RECONSIDERATION   74
      by Richard C. Wade
The Historians Blinded
   JAMES FORD RHODES AND THE NEGRO: A STUDY IN
   THE PROBLEM OF OBJECTIVITY   95
      by Robert Cruden

ON TURNER, BEARD AND SLAVERY   106
by Staughton Lynd

PART III
MAJOR TRENDS IN NEGRO HISTORY

Racism, Implicit and Explicit

THE NEGRO IN CINCINNATI, 1800-1830   126
by Richard C. Wade

THE ABOLITIONIST DILEMMA: THE ANTISLAVERY
MOVEMENT AND THE NORTHERN NEGRO   138
by Leon F. Litwack

THE NORTHWEST AND THE RACE ISSUE, 1861-1862   159
by Jacque Voegoli

CULTURAL HISTORY WRITTEN WITH LIGHTNING:
THE SIGNIFICANCE OF *THE BIRTH OF A NATION*   176
by Everett Carter

Reaction and Protest

TURNER'S SAFETY VALVE AND FREE NEGRO WESTWARD
MIGRATION   189
by George R. Woolfolk

NEGRO PROSCRIPTION, PROTESTS, AND PROPOSED
SOLUTIONS IN GEORGIA, 1880-1908   200
by Clarence A. Bacote

THE REACTION OF THE NEGRO TO THE
MOTION PICTURE *BIRTH OF A NATION*   224
by Thomas R. Cripps

The Negro Effort

THE LIBERTY LINE: REMINISCENCE AND ROMANCE   241
by Larry Gara

THE SABLE ARM   266
by Dudley Cornish

THE GENESIS OF THE FIRST WISCONSIN
CIVIL RIGHTS ACT   294
by Leslie H. Fishel, Jr.

The Unbalanced Scales

THE FEDERAL GOVERNMENT AND THE FREE
NEGRO, 1790-1860   312
by Leon F. Litwack

NEGROES AND THE SEMINOLE WAR, 1835-1842   328
by Kenneth Wiggins Porter

ENFORCING THE FIFTEENTH AMENDMENT, 1870-1877   352
    by Everette Swinney
WOODROW WILSON AND FEDERAL SEGREGATION   369
    by Kathleen Wolgemuth
THE CIVILIAN CONSERVATION CORPS AND THE
NEGRO   383
    by John A. Salmond

Undiscovered Possibilities

SIMON GRAY, RIVERMAN: A SLAVE WHO WAS
ALMOST FREE   401
    by John Hebron Moore
THE NEGRO COWBOY   413
    by Philip Durham

INDEX   425

PART I

THE USES
OF NEGRO HISTORY

F or the historian, historical knowledge is an end in itself, and any addition to knowledge is welcome. But the historian's resources are limited and the reconstruction of the entire past is impossible, so he must set priorities and study that history that offers the greatest reward in insight and explanation. In this sense, Negro history competes with other histories as well as with other disciplines. The question the historian must ask himself is, Why study Negro history rather than the history of the South or any other history? If he is interested in American society, the historian will probably decide that the study of Negro history in America offers the best clues to the nature of that society. Within the historian's frame of reference, this is the most compelling reason.

But history is not for the historian alone; it also serves a public. At first glance, Negro history would seem to fit the pattern of ethnic history, designed to acquaint present generations with the moral courage and strength of past generations. In this sense, the historian is a secular theologian, explaining ways of society to man. Typically, ethnic history is immigrant history, which traces the arrival of a group in the New World, the vicissitudes suffered in the struggle for existence, and the insularity and cohesiveness that enable that group to survive. The second generation experiences forces tugging in two different cultural directions. Later generations, after a longer or shorter time of travail, assimilate into American society and become virtually indistinguishable from other, *earlier immigrant groups. The history is a history of success, the Americanization of another disparate group.*

The Negro past, however, does not fit into this mold. In the first place, the circumstances of immigration are different: the first Negro immigrants date back almost to the beginnings of the Virginia colony. In the second place, the conflict between Negro and white is not couched in terms of two cultures, alien and American. Both Negro and white, for the most part, proclaim the same values of liberty and equality, and their visions of the ideal society are identical. In the third place, and most important, the place of the Negro in American society is still in doubt. Negro history does not end as immigrant history does with the middle-class descendant of the immigrant grandparent.

Perhaps the history of the Indian and the Negro in the United States have much more in common. Both peoples share a common failure to be fully accepted into American life. Indeed, the Indian is even more isolated than the Negro, but he has not suffered the total cultural impact of slavery. More than the Negro, the Indian, at the cost of isolation, has been permitted to retain cultural values of his own past.

The major problem in Negro history, then, is how to explain failure. Historians of American life have not often been called upon to explain failure; their orientation is toward success. If certain movements have failed, certain elements of these movements have not. Thus, the historian of the Populist movement commonly ends with the triumphant assertion that Populist principles have become Republican and Democratic ones. To admit otherwise would be to admit failure of ideas too valuable to fail. The criterion of success is all ·pervasive in Americans, in historians as well as in nonhistorians. Because of this powerful value orientation, one of the major problems with Negro history is how to fit it into a framework of progress and success.

In the following selections three authors speculate about the use of Negro history, each handling the problem of failure differently and each addressing a different public. Charles H. Wesley, speaking primarily to Negroes, argues the instrumental use of Negro history. Using Jewish history as an example, Wesley claims that a knowledge of past triumphs, often achieved in the face of almost hopeless odds, will instill group pride in the present generation. Failure is caused by the strength of the opposition; even limited success shows the courage and persistence of heroic individuals. Surely Wesley is correct here; the drive to teach Negro history in elementary and high schools reflects the same basic assumption. No one can quarrel with his thesis, for without a past no racial group can hope to attain pride and social cohesiveness. But there is a weakness in the approach which has plagued those who see Negro history as the instrument of Negro liberation. Without a real appreciation of the barriers in the past, the championing of certain individuals seems to elevate them beyond their actual position. It becomes too easy to claim too much, especially to those whose knowledge of past restrictions is sketchy. Nonetheless, the teaching of Negro history as a tool for building pride surely would be justification enough.

The second article, by Samuel DuBois Cook, has consequences for all Americans, white and Negro alike. Cook accepts as given the failure of the Negro to achieve full equality in American life; but rather than explaining it away, he seizes upon this failure to supply an ingredient in short supply in American society—tragedy. Harking back to classical historical views, Cook sees Negro history as a corrective to American optimism. There is no reason why history should not be tragic; a tragic view of life may be nearer reality than any other. Nor is failure less instructive than success. Cook challenges the basic assumptions of American historians who have unconsciously accepted the values of their own society. If his view of the use of Negro history is correct, that history's greatest lesson may be moral or spiritual. One might also assume that Negro history ought to be more useful to whites than to Negroes, for the former lack tragic experience. Cook's idea is in the tradition of Western historiography, but it also poses problems. Those most in need of a tragic sense are unlikely to become acquainted with Negro history, and those best acquainted with Negro history perhaps need the corrective least. Further, a moral example is likely to be cold comfort to those caught in the grip of the ghetto.

William B. Hixson, Jr., in the last article in this section, views the impact of Negro experience, hence Negro history, upon an elite—white intellectuals. Negro history provides an effective counterargument to the consensus view of American society as being devoid of serious conflict. For Hixson, the presence of an unassimilated group, regardless of the moral drawn from the failure to assimilate, is of paramount importance. Negro history provides a severe critique of American society and forms the basis for a reconstruction of that society. Implicit in Hixson's view is a belief that the intellectuals can reform society, that the key to any change lies with the intellectuals. The aim of Negro history is to impress the white intellectual. Hixson's critique is a radical one, looking to the transformation of society. It goes beyond Cook's and sees the seeds of future success in present failure. Hixson would use Negro experience to change ideas and then society. Carried too far, this view ends up exploiting the Negro past for the benefit of a larger, predominantly white society.

All three scholars represented in this section assign high value to

Negro history, each for his own reasons. If only a small part of what they desire were to be accomplished, the study of Negro history will have been worth the effort expended. If, in the end, the Negro becomes a full partner in American life, Negro history may have played a part in that achievement and may then parallel other ethnic histories.

CREATING AND MAINTAINING

AN HISTORICAL TRADITION

Charles H. Wesley

Historical traditions have been associated with the building of nationalism and group pride. They have been the creators of ideals for many peoples. Whether oral, written, or historically unsound, they have had influence on history. They are parts of the historical sources which are transmitted from one generation to another. Worthy traditions have been translated from opinions, legends, and doctrines into symbols and have been used for stimulation of group development. In the ancient world, the glory that was Greece and the grandeur that was Rome grew out of traditions. Their traditions of history and culture made them what they seemed to be. In later periods, nationalism was developed mainly by group allegiances to common traditions. Valuable traditions produced a group consciousness in a people through the creation of a rich inheritance of memories and the desire to maintain them. Groups of peoples developed a spiritual unity through common triumphs, common failures, similar traditions, and similar hopes. This has been a fact of history; as Thomas Carlyle has exclaimed, "What an enormous magnifier is tradition." Even in Ireland, through the youth groups as they struggled to create an Irish tradition of value, there was developed a basis of opposition to British dominance and power for Irish containment. A worthy tradition was created out of their unsatisfactory historical experiences. The American Irish Historical Society and the Irish Historical Review have continued this historical tradition.

Charles H. Wesley, "Creating and Maintaining an Historical Tradition," *Journal of Negro History*, XLIX, No. 1 (January, 1964), 13-33. This article has been slightly abridged.

The Irish had constituted a minority in the British realm who refused to accept the traditions of the group defects imposed upon them
by British historians. On the contrary, their language, literature, dress,
songs, and customs were employed to create a worthy tradition for
them. The custodians of their tradition were the Irish historians and
writers who wrote and rewrote historical events with heroic emphasis.
Although generally defeated, the bravery of the "Fighting Irish" became the glorious tradition of Ireland. Their historians, authors and
publicists, and organizations have given the highlights of tradition to
Irish history and have built a worthy tradition in spite of defeats of
Irish armies and British opposition until the picture has appeared that
the Irish in spite of their weaknesses were the victors in their centuries-
old struggle for freedom.

The Jewish people have had a remarkable record in this respect.
When the Jews went out from slavery in Egypt, they had no common
literature or history, no common background for belief in themselves
or for others to believe in them; but the prophetic historians of these
people began to dig into legendary and traditional history and to bring
up worthy facts from hidden and forgotten records. They constructed
genealogies, hitherto unknown. They drew up family and individual
histories. They assembled their traditions, and when they returned to
Jerusalem they had their Old Testament story and their history, which
they had created out of their past. This consolidation of their past and
its relationship to their present helped to unite Jews, scattered as they
were, and out of this collection of fact and fiction came the colossal
idea of belonging to a "chosen" people, and a people with a destiny.

The most important fact about these incidents is that these people
believed that they were predestined for achievement in spite of their
despised past. Jews scattered over the world believed this idea and it
was woven into their minds and hearts. Jewish parents sacrificed that
their children might go to school and college. It became a part of their
tradition, and almost their religion—to go to school and college and to
achieve. Parents had their youth believe in themselves as Jews and be
loyal to themselves—not ashamed of themselves, despite centuries of
oppression and unnumbered discriminations. They concentrated their
energies upon an accentuation of the positive. The tradition of their
greatness so lived that it was basic in Western life and culture, and the
founding of our democracy. Whenever great names were called in literature, science, philosophy, art, and all cultural fields, Jewish names were
among them. They themselves, with their friends, struck the blows
against their chains of racial and religious prejudice, and they continue
these programs as opposition to them continues.

The experience of the Jewish people in history is not too different from our own. The great difference is in their attitude and reactions. They did not turn away from themselves. They did not spurn or reject history, nor their prophets, priests, and kings, as weak as they were. They praised their leaders who became heroes even in the long years of slavery, and their historians and authors were inspired to create and build their traditions.

One of these historians, Simon Wolf, in describing Jewish defenses against that which he termed "the public vilifications of the Jewish people," wrote that their "writers and thinkers carried on their polemics in the domain of idealism, in poetry and philosophy, and their thoughts were soon re-echoed in the outgivings of the succeeding generations of scientists, students, and statesmen." [1] The American Jewish Historical Society, the American Jewish Committee, and the *Jewish Encyclopedia* have continued this historical tradition.

Other minorities in the United States have had experiences of like character and are deeply concerned that they should create traditions of value to themselves so that they would be worthy of respect from others. The main obstacle to this creation is characterized by Louis Adamic in his *A Nation of Nations*. He states:

> There are two ways of looking at our history:
>
> One is this: that the United States is an Anglo-Saxon country with a white-Protestant-Anglo-Saxon civilization struggling to preserve itself against infiltration and adulteration by other civilizations brought here by Negroes and hordes of "foreigners."
>
> The second is this: that the pattern of the United States is not essentially Anglo-Saxon, although her language is English. Nor is the pattern Anglo-Saxon with a motley addition of darns and patches. The pattern of America is all of one piece; it is a blend of cultures from many lands, woven of threads from many corners of the world. Diversity is the pattern, is the stuff and color of the fabric.[2]

As one of the minorities in American life, Negroes have experienced the creation of a doctrine of inferiority as a tradition which has been accepted in thought and in their relationships with other American people. This result has grown out of dogmatic conclusions which have been drawn from differences in color, physique, opportunity, and characteristics of their inescapable background. While the Jim Crow system is primarily a product of the latter half of the nineteenth century and the early part of the twentieth century, the concept of Negro inferiority is older, and now the two are associated.[3] Surface differences became the basis of segregation and discrimination, and the feelings and atti-tudes of many white Americans were concepts fixed traditionally from generation to generation.

Negro Americans have created and maintained defenses against the negative traditions which have characterized American life and thought, but they were slow in creating a worthy tradition. The first of these endeavors was protest against their use in the adoption of resolutions by assembled groups denying these charges, but beyond such action little of lasting value was accomplished. The second of the endeavors to combat these allegations took the form of individual denials in speech. These two avenues of defensive approach to the problem of historical tradition were followed by a third one, the organization of historical societies—and this was primarily a positive offensive approach.

The earliest collective endeavors by Negroes to combat allegations of inferiority and to substitute facts were in the Negro conventions which were national, state, and local in their representation. The first of these conventions was held in Philadelphia, at Bethel A. M. E. Church, with Richard Allen serving as its chairman, from September 20–24, 1830. This was an organization convention which looked forward to a later larger convention. Resolutions were adopted unifying their thinking and purpose. One of these resolutions declared that "the purpose of our enemies is to show our inferiority in the scale of human beings." [4]

This convention of 1830 led to a second convention, June 6–11, 1831, at Philadelphia, with fifteen delegates from New York, Pennsylvania, Delaware, Maryland, and Virginia. One of the resolutions again pro-tested the efforts made by "our enemies to show our inferiority in the scale of human beings." [5] The third convention assembled in Philadel-phia, June 3–13, 1833. The main objective of the convention was de-clared to be the immediate emancipation of slaves and the moral and intellectual improvement of free Negroes. [6] The succeeding convention was held in New York in 1834. The cause of abolition was the major purpose of its call, and to secure for free Negroes "equal civil and polit-ical rights and privileges with the whites." [7] The last of this series of conventions was held in 1837. Irregular and periodic state, city, and inter-state conventions were then convened in subsequent years.

State conventions of Negro representatives assembled occasionally after 1840, and with regularity in infrequent sessions after 1850. The addresses and resolutions were directed toward mistreatment as citizens, in education and employment. Again and again the point was raised, "The Constitution makes no distinction as to color." Further defense was made of this fact by reference to property owned, schools maintained, and cultural interest of Negroes. These facts were presented with the hope that state legislatures and officials would be considerate and grant the requested relief. The Declaration of Independence was also quoted and the participation of Negroes in the Republic was described. They seemed to say that because of these services, "we should be given our rights."

The values in history and in creating and maintaining a tradition had not yet appeared in their thought. The *Cleveland Leader* characterized these conventions with the statement: "Speech making occupied the time, pretty much as is usual in the conventions of white folks." [8] There was no concept of history expressed or adopted in these early sessions, for these convention representatives knew of no historical facts upon which they could build their pride. References were made to Africa, but they were always of benighted Africa. The main job to be done in this period concerned the termination of slavery and the oppression of their citizenship through civil and political disabilities.

The first mention of history and the evidence of a historical concept came in the largest pre–Civil War convention held in Rochester, New York, July 6–8, 1853, with James W. C. Pennington presiding and attended by 114 delegates. The convention declared that:

> By birth, we are American citizens—by the facts of history and the admission of American statesmen. We are American citizens—by the courage and fidelity displayed by our ancestors in defending the liberties and in achieving the independence of our land, we are American citizens. Among the colored people, we can point, with pride and hope, to men of education and refinement, who have become such despite the most unfavorable influence. We can point to mechanics, farmers, merchants, teachers, ministers, doctors, lawyers, editors, and authors against whose progress the concentrated energies of American prejudice have proved quite unavailing.

Another important resolution called for a committee on publication to "collect all facts, statistics and statements, all laws and historical records and biographies of colored people and all books by colored authors. They shall have, for the safekeeping of these documents, a library, with a reading room and museum. . . ." [9]

The inevitable consequence of these contributions has been that old traditions are passing, and a new one has come into reality. These teachers and students of Negro history know that men, women, and events become great in history, not only because they occurred, but because historians made them great. Sometimes a poet can accomplish this task, as was the case with Longfellow's account of Paul Revere's ride, which had been overlooked by historians of the early nineteenth century until Longfellow brought it into the light, and it became rapidly not only a fact but a tradition.

Obviously, toward the goal of an historical tradition, we are in need of the continued search for documents and historical materials, with their presentation in the tradition of Leopold von Ranke, of Germany, whose celebrated statement of history's purpose was that, "it merely undertakes to show how things really took place." This is needed among us, but the creation of an historical tradition demands more. Such a tradition will have solid historical foundations and there must be no lack of authenticity, nor any unreliability. The traditions must have the support of documents, primary and secondary sources, and there should be no uncertainty concerning the facts. We need historians trained in the method of producing pages and pages filled with printed words, statistics, and figures. At the same time, we need interpretations, portraitures, brilliant narration. There must be no mythical or legendary bases unless supported by fact. This concept of the fabulous and mythical caused Stopford Brooke, Irish author, to inquire of the epic poem, *Beowulf*, "Is it entirely mythical and legendary, or is there any actual history contained in it?" In similar vein, a professor of English literature criticized Lytton Strachey's *Elizabeth and Essex*, in a phrase, "What was the use of his writing on that topic? All the facts were known." [10]

As we face the future, there are two major needs which now are challenges in the continued creation of an historical tradition in Negro history: One concerns the writing of history, and the second the teaching of history. We need the literary historian, who will be, withal, not an inaccurate, injudicious, misrepresenting writer. We have had more of this than our share before and after the Civil War, and on our contemporary scene. We have had enough of the concepts of "Uncle Tom," "Aunt Mandy," and "Sambo," the stereotypes in the comic books, and the concept of "the Negro" as the humorous, slovenly, lazy, incompetent, and inferior individual. The patronizing, moral, and sentimental concepts, then and now, should all be replaced with a realism basic to a tradition of value. [11]

Our materials of history should fall into the hands of those who are historians and teachers, and those who are inspired with the sense of history as literature, as well as the style of the academic and pedantic specialist writing for other specialists. There should be poets, philosophers, dramatists, novelists, artists, and devotees of the cultural life who will make contributions to this cause. The use of imagination under the control of comprehensive minds has value for an historical tradition, just as does the result of the cold analysis of events by the scientific historian. Says George Trevelyan, "Let the science and research of the historian find the fact and let his imagination and art make clear its significance."

We are moved and made the more convinced that we in the association are on the road when a littérateur such as Langston Hughes, who once worked as a youth with Carter G. Woodson, turns to history and brings out *The Pictorial History of the Negro in America, The First Book of American Negroes,* and *Fight for Freedom: The Story of the NAACP.* The same reaction comes with the dramatic proposals of Lorraine Hansberry, which are to be based upon history. This is art added to history. It is imagination viewing the fact. Obviously, such persons may write without documentation and can be corrected by the scholarly inclined. In the meantime, the realism, even the comedy, is refreshing to the public after the dry-as-dust, run-of-the-mill historian's writing. The results may at times leave much to be desired by us, for the technique of the historian is different from that of the imaginative writer, but both can have value in capturing the interest of youths and adults, and in creating a worthy tradition.

The *second* need is for teaching materials in elementary and secondary schools. We now have four steps in Negro history, ranging from elementary school to college, which are being used widely. They are: (1) *Child's Story of the Negro;* (2) *Negro Makers of History;* (3) *The Story of the Negro Retold;* and (4) *The Negro in Our History.* These books have been purchased by individual teachers and ordered through textbook committees, parent-teacher associations, faculties, and school libraries.

There is the larger field of public education already occupied by textbook publishers, with almost exclusive controls. However, there have been criticisms of groups of textbooks now in use, as a result of our current Negro revolution and the publication of historical facts brought to light through this association. These publishers are at this time hurriedly revising and rewriting their texts in order to keep their monopolies of this lucrative field.

In New York City, Mrs. Edwina Chavers Johnson, a teacher in Queens, chairman of the Interborough Negro History Committee, has criticized the New York school textbooks and answered those who have said that there are no materials, by saying, "There is no paucity of material. There has been failure to recognize the positive contributions of Negroes, as shown in fifty years of research done by the Association for the Study of Negro Life and History." Pressed by "Operation Heritage," sponsored by our New York branch, with Miss Gertrude Parthenia McBrown as program director, the Board of Education has responded to these appeals and has an appointed Curriculum Committee drawing up proposals under the title "The Negro in Our History and Culture." The Brooklyn branch has also been active in this area. Detroit is adding to its teaching in history the use of a fifty-two-page booklet entitled *The Struggle for Freedom and Rights*. This is a supplement to the textbook *Our United States* now in use there. Other cities are experimenting with similar plans.

Such proposals are not going to be satisfactory, whether they are hastily thrown together textbooks revised by publishers or supplements drawn up by teachers-on-the-job. This challenge can be met best by our association. Let us then rise to the demands of this occasion. We propose that we who are active in this association undertake the preparation of thirty units of study in United States history, which shall be for use in integrated school systems with textbooks already adopted, and these units could also be used in areas with currently separate schools. Even when efforts of these types are placed in action, much of the history taught will be forgotten as the boy or girl leaves the elementary school and the high school, and has to learn history again in college. Nevertheless, there will be retained a general concept of a valuable tradition, a comprehensive overtone, an imaginative overview. These gains can be increased with factual knowledge as time moves on. The tradition created in the school and the home can have grandeur and a liberating spirit.

The present Negro revolution needs this support, for while this revolution owes its origin in part to the spread of the concept of non-violence as a weapon of protest and progress, at the base of this movement there are the long-time teachings of this association: that among dark men and women there are talented persons who have achieved in spite of handicaps, social barriers, and public opinion; that group self-respect is the foundation of group advancement even with legal victories; that our folk are not a simple, childlike, ignorant people who must wait to be treated equal after they are ready; that the books of America tell a false, ugly story and illustrate an all-white America instead of the integrated people that we are. Our Negro revolution is now based upon a background of sound history. Negroes say: We are not afraid because our fathers and mothers in their day were not afraid. They won their freedom in 1863 and 1865 and we shall win ours one hundred years later. Lord Macaulay, English historian, emphasizes this idea on the basis of the historical tradition of the English people, when he writes, "A people that takes no pride in the noble achievements of remote ancestors will never achieve anything to be remembered by remote posterity."

A people's knowledge of facts can free them from ignorance but by itself it has never inspired a crusade. The revolution needs history and it needs valued traditions. Backed by a worthy historical tradition and supported by reaffirmations of the American promise as a firm foundation, we can march forward and break the chains of public opinion which maintains contempt, derision, and second-class citizenship. On the foundation of our history, we can continue to build a lasting temple of self-respect and self-esteem, as other population groups have done. In the meantime, we shall work at this challenging tradition still to be created and seek to replace the bad image of other years. Let us resolve to maintain, expand, and build it by our individual and collective endeavors, for this temple of history built by us can last while the ages roll. The decision in this respect is ours!

NOTES

1. Dagobert D. Runes, *The Hebrew Impact on Western Civilization* (New York, 1951), p. 13; Simon Wolf, *The American Jew as Patriot, Soldier and Citizen* (New York, 1895), p. 489; Charles H. Wesley, "Background and Achievement," *The Crisis*, LXVII, No. 3, 142.

2. New York, 1945, p. 6.

3. C. Vann Woodward, *The Strange Career of Jim Crow* (New York, 1957), pp. 7, 47, 53, and *passim;* W. S. Jenkins, *Pro-Slavery Thought in the Old South* (Gloucester, Mass., 1960), p. 243; Charles H. Wesley, "The Concept of Negro Inferiority in American Thought," *Journal of Negro History*, XXV (1940), 540-560.

4. "The First Colored Convention," *Anglo-African Magazine*, I, No. 10 (October, 1859); Bella Gross, "The First National Negro Convention," *Journal of Negro History*, XXXI, No. 4 (October, 1946), 435-443; *The Liberator*, October 22, 1831; Charles H. Wesley, *Richard Allen: Apostle of Freedom* (Washington, D.C., 1935), pp. 235-236.

5. John W. Cromwell, "Early Negro Convention Movement in America," Occasional Papers, No. 6, The Negro Academy (Washington, D.C., 1921). John W. Cromwell, "Early Convention Movement," *The Negro in American History* (Washington, D.C., 1914), pp. 27-46.

6. *Minutes and Proceedings of the Third Annual Convention for the Improvement of the Free People of Color* (Philadelphia, 1833).

7. *Minutes of the Fourth Annual Convention for the Improvement of the Free People of Color* (New York, 1834).

8. Quoted by J. Reuben Sheeler, "The Struggle of the Negro in Ohio for Freedom," *The Journal of Negro History*, XXXI, No. 2 (April, 1946), 224.

9. *Proceedings of the Colored Convention, Held in Rochester, July 6th, 7th, and 8th, 1853;* John W. Cromwell, *The Negro in American History,* pp. 38, 41; Leon F. Litwack, *North of Slavery: The Negro in the Free States* (Chicago, 1961), p. 265.

10. Emery Neff, *The Poetry of History, the Contribution of Literature and Literary Scholarship to the Writing of History Since Voltaire* (New York, 1946), p. 199.

11. Lorenzo D. Turner, *Anti-Slavery Sentiment in American Literature Prior to 1865* (Washington, D.C., 1929), p. 120.

A TRAGIC CONCEPTION

OF NEGRO HISTORY

Samuel DuBois Cook

INTRODUCTION

The final problem of human existence is to make it meaningful, to make
sense of the human enterprise. History is, it seems, the order of temporal succession, causation, evolution, correlation, or priority. The ultimate problem of historiography is to make the order of time intelligible.
It is to make meaningful the intricate web and multitudinous mass of
historical events—to make sense of man's journey in the flow and flux
of time.[1] Time, with all of its mystery, is a primal category of historical
thought. "The drama of history is played upon the stage of time. All
historical actions take place against the background of an inexorable
forward movement from past to present." [2]

For a variety of reasons, it is true, we speak of historical inquiry as
being concerned with the data of the "past." Pragmatically, this is understandable and necessary. The object inquiry must be reduced to manageable terms. But we cannot draw a precise line between past, present,
and future. Continuity seems to be a quality of time. It flows unbrokenly
even as we, for various purposes, are compelled to try to organize its
happenings into eras, epochs, ages, periods, decades, centuries, etc. The
"no longer," the "now" and the "not yet" are integrally related in the
historical continuum.[3] The study of time and history is always different
from the endless flow and drama of time and history.

Samuel DuBois Cook, "A Tragic Conception of Negro History," *Journal
of Negro History*, XLV, No. 4 (October, 1960), 219-240.

Aware of the essential "oneness" of the sequence of time, some thinkers deny the categories of the past and future and insist, instead, on an all-inclusive "eternal present." This, too, is understandable. It is a special reminder of the ultimate peril of all easy and neat systems of historical classification. Yet this viewpoint discloses only one dimension of the problem. For not only ordinary common-sense experience but also rational inquiry, while recognizing no exact division in the order of time, insists upon distinctions within the continuous flow of the historical and temporal stream. Therefore, even within the "eternal present," the categories of memory and anticipation must be distinguished, if not separated, from the "existential" moment. Time, like "being" and "becoming," change and stability, must be viewed dialectically—in terms of both unity and difference, depending upon the level of analysis, the nature of the discourse, and the purpose of particular inquiry. Time is at once one-dimensional and three-dimensional.

In these terms, then, we approach "Negro history." The ultimate purpose of the historiography of the Negro is not merely to investigate, verify, and record facts about the temporal reality of Negroes. True, such is necessary. In fact, it would be sheer folly to deny or even to minimize the importance of specific and detailed empirical inquiries dealing with various eras, facets, nuances, and relations of the history of the American Negro. But equally relevant and urgent is the need to make facts meaningful and significant from a broad perspective. Facts in themselves are an undifferentiated and silent mass—discrete, atomic, meaningless. Does Negro history make sense? If Toynbee is right in the observation that "Mankind does not do very much of its historical thinking in easy and prosperous times," [4] then the contemporary tragic plight of the Negro invites him to give sober and sustained thought to his history and destiny.

To raise the question of the *meaning* and *implications* of Negro history is the primary purpose of this paper. Even the assumption that it has no meaning entails a cognitive claim: that there is a way of knowing the vast meaninglessness of the Negro's journey and of the consequent futility of inquiry into it. We may, indeed, we will, disagree on the answer. But even a skeptic or a cynic can hardly deny that the problem of the meaning of Negro history is fraught with significance and is worthy of our best, though puny and frail, efforts. To subordinate conclusions and results to the spirit and process of inquiry is the hallmark of a liberal mind.

Let us, then, probe and brood over the Negro's island in the big American sea and, in brief and preliminary fashion, try to suggest how and why the Negro has come to be what he is, along with the meaning of that process. Imperative is the need to seek to dig into the very roots of our national being and to winnow therefrom at least a modicum of meaning and validity. We should not be discouraged by the inability to give the problem either exhaustive consideration or final answers. Finality eludes man.

Events by themselves are amorphous, anonymous, and blind. They take on meaning as they are connected both to one another and to a broad and inclusive framework or principle of meaning. Out of the relationships and interaction of events come their meaning and intelligibility. Unless we are committed to the positivistic claim of a "value-free" historiography, the crucial problem is the selection of a perspective which best illumines the facts under consideration. But in spite of the contention of positivism, history, like other disciplines, is value-laden,[5] and value judgments are worse when they are uncritically and tacitly assumed. "Sober reflection shows," as Cohen observed, "that what we call historic facts are the results of our interpretation of certain fragmentary data or remains. Our implicitly assumed principles determine the character of our interpretation."[6] Value judgments affect the choice of a problem for investigation, the selection, meaning, organization, and presentation of the "facts," and the categories of interpretation as well.[7] Thus conceived, history intrinsically involves preconceptions or predilections which determine the total process of selection or abstraction.

This paper is written from the standpoint of human tragedy. Our conceptual scheme, however, recognizes both the importance of alternative approaches and its own limited applicability. For, although our principle of interpretation is necessary to a proper understanding of the complex facets of the history of the American Negro, it is not sufficient. It should be supplemented, for example, by economic and sociopsychological orientations. But without a profound sense of tragedy, it is impossible to comprehend, in their fulness and power, the antinomies, the disappointments, the sad and hopeless strivings, the frightening frustrations, ambiguities, and contradictions, the gnawing predicaments; in a word, the grim and grinding realities of Negro history. Dissociated from a framework of tragedy, there are, in the stream of Negro history, countless series and concatenations of unintelligible events. With a profound sense of tragedy, a deep and intense feeling of the agony of boundless longing without fulfilment, these events are not buried in the already teeming cemetery of meaninglessness. Of the validity of our approach, the test is whether it helps to illumine the Negro's pilgrimage in the ebb and flow of American history, whether it opens our eyes to a realm of meaning and possibility otherwise hidden and obscure. About this, there is little room for doubt; indeed, we are seeking to interpret an embarrassing wealth of obvious historical phenomena.

True enough, the category of tragedy does not exhaust the meaning and rich variety of Negro history. On the part of both a white minority (the abolitionists and their spiritual descendants) and the Negro himself, the history of the Negro is interspersed with moments of glory and creativity. A hunger for meaning and justice has animated the Negro; consequently, he sought desperately and endlessly to eke out from existence elements of fulfilment. In this regard, his spirituals and historic religion are revealing. They disclose, in large measure, an attempt to substitute the infinite values of eternity for the finite goods of time. On the edge of the abyss of meaninglessness, the Negro tried to discover in a transcendent and imperishable realm the affirmations and fulfilments which history negates and repels. Consider, for example, the spiritual about "climbing Jacob's ladder." Symbolic and expressive of the Negro's craving, it is largely a compensatory substitute for the Negro's inability to ascend the social, economic, political, and cultural pyramid of power. Frustrated at every turn in time, the Negro looked for a redress of his grievances in a realm beyond time. His imagination, therefore, was creative and consoling if not redemptive.

In many other adventures of the mind and spirit, moreover, the Negro has aspired, sometimes frantically, to build islands of satisfaction and to wrest from existence various degrees of meaning and self-realization. In this sense, even great tragedy was not altogether barren. The very effort to come to grips with pathos and futility, with deep and sustained longing without fulfilment is inspiring and heartwarming; for it is a mighty testament to the vitality of the human spirit. Therefore, from the Negro's tragic predicament have come, occasionally, creative and glorious fragments of value. But, even so, tragedy has been the keystone of the arch of the Negro's sojourn and the bedrock of his experiences. The sheer unique need for him, in comparison with his fellow human beings, to squeeze from life outlets of individuality and particles of meaning and satisfaction is itself a reflection of the tragic dimension of his history. For even his most moving achievements—and they have been many and varied—have been built on the scaffold of a broken heart and disconsolate spirit.

These unflattering observations will, no doubt, provoke much disagreement. We are not accustomed to think in terms of the category of tragedy. Nevertheless, these conclusions are, it seems to us, inescapable. An ineradicable part of our past, they are an inexpugnable factor in our prospects. The reader has only to reflect upon slavery and the almost century of promised and suspended "freedom and equality." Paradoxically, the Negro has won and has yet to win the "equal justice" of the human estate. Before legal manumission, there was, because of his spirit and will, a degree of freedom in his slavery; since the Emancipation Proclamation, there has been, because of a network of imposed restraints, a large measure of slavery in his freedom.

THE TRAGIC FRAMEWORK OF NEGRO HISTORY

Meaning

Tragedy is, of course, a term of multiple meaning.[8] The history of ideas speaks with many tongues on its meaning, elements, and implications. Into mind come Greek,[9] Shakespearean,[10] and Christian [11] as well as various minor notions.[12] We, however, do not seek to force the facts of Negro history into these conceptual schemes, particularly the technical forms of the dramatists.

For us, tragedy is an action or situation in which evil is pursued for the sake of an alleged good. In the social and political spheres, tragedy means the negation of the essential values and meanings of some individuals or groups—a denial of the essence of their selfhood and crucial equality as human beings—for the sake of the supposed good of others or of a supposed larger good. The banner of the good is waved even as human personalities are stunted and crushed. A tragic situation emits, as Aristotle suggested, the emotions of "pity and fear" and terror.

By the tragic conception of Negro history, then, we mean an interpretation which seeks to grasp the full dimensions and naked depths of the systematic, persistent, and institutionalized negation of the Negro's meanings and values on grounds of *ethical desirability and necessity*. Estrangement of the Negro from the substance of American culture has been held to be desirable and necessary for him and for all others—as a condition of consensus, order, wisdom, power, progress, and virtue. Indeed, alienation and subordination of the Negro have been perceived by some as a divine imperative. Here one understands the awful significance of Rauschenbusch's observation that the "idealization of evil is an indispensable means for its perpetuation and transmission." [13] Subjection and domination of the Negro, then, have been reinforced by pious pretensions to high morality. Ethical and intellectual resources have been utilized primarily for the justification, not the rectification, of injustice.

The question, therefore, is not simply one of contradiction between ideal and reality.[14] More deeply, it is a denial of that contradiction. Evil has been pursued for the sake of an alleged good. That is why so much injustice has been inflicted upon the Negro not only with an easy conscience but with a sense of pride and moral duty. "All suffering is bitter," Brunner observes, "but unjust suffering is doubly bitter." [15] If that is true, then unjust suffering in the name of justice for the sufferer is ineffably bitter.

The deepest tragedy of the South today is that it makes existing institutional arrangements normative. It takes seriously Pope's dictum that "whatever is, is right" and therefore ought to be. The South sanctifies and absolutizes the status quo and hence forecloses rational inquiry into its merit. The desperation of the South in closing schools and threatening to close them *en masse* is a symbol of a much deeper malady. It indicates its tortuous willingness to apply the discredited doctrines of "interposition," "nullification," and "massive resistance" to civilization itself. For education is vital to civilized society and *a fortiori* to a civilization which prides itself on freedom of the mind and spirit and which boasts of its scientific and technological genius. Educationally retarded, the South should be the last section of the country even to imagine arresting educational growth and development.

The problem, then, cuts much deeper than educational issues and constitutional issues. The South is attempting to apply "nullification," "interposition," and "massive resistance" to reason, justice, progress, and to the solidarity of the human commonwealth. And all this is done in the name of justice and the good. In making the prevailing system of rights and responsibilities normative, the typical Southern argument never gets beyond obvious circular reasoning: "Our way of life is good and must be preserved because it is our way of life." But what of the nation, the American Constitution, the ethics of democracy, simple justice, and the Negro? What of *humanity?* Defending social injustice in the name of justice, advocating lawlessness in the name of law, and pretending that the Supreme Court renders the impossible—unconstitutional decisions, Southern public officials, power-seekers, and opinion-molders are consistently blind to the larger, deeper, and inclusive interests of a just common life.[16] And the few dissenting voices are hardly a ripple in the water.

To be sure, all societies tend to make the status quo normative and to identify existing patterns of social organization with a "higher" order of reality: God, natural law, historical wisdom, nature, accumulated and hallowed experience, evolution, etc. This is the basic reason why social change is so difficult—the moral conceit and pretensions of "power structures" and privileged groups. They always predict that any disturbance of the status quo will bring in its train all forms of consuming evil. The recognition of this property of privileged classes, however, neither justifies it nor explains the uniqueness of the South in this regard. After all, the South is a "national minority" in a country committed to democracy. Beyond this, rapid changes are taking place in the country and the world community. Of special interest are the revolts against oppression in Asia and Africa.

But if what is, is right, why change? This is the tragic assumption of the South. It moralizes injustice. And, even worse, this idealization of evil is buttressed and cushioned by the powerful forces of coercion, habit, custom, inertia, and the natural resistance to, and fear of, social change. The "is" has many unmerited props on which to lean.

Ideological Foundation

Obviously the ideological root of the tragic character of Negro history is that of race. A difference of color and historical exposure has been elaborated into a difference of essence, so that the Negro's very *power to be* is separate and distinct. Superficial and arbitrary differences are developed into a *doctrine of man*, from which issues a bifurcation of essence, value, and existence along racial lines. The Negro's intellectual, psychological, emotional, moral, and cultural capacities are, according to this view, unique and inferior. In the very scale of being and value, therefore, the Negro is given a lower rank. Inevitably, numerous schemes, allegedly representing science, ethics, religion, history, and common sense, were advanced to substantiate this initial bias—what logicians call the fallacy of initial predication.[17]

The total structure and content of the Negro's experience (both conceptual and perceptual), then, are held to be of an intrinsically separate order, on the basis of which institutional and cultural differentiations are erected and justified.[18]

All of this is, of course, a legacy for which men, including the ingenious and mighty Aristotle (who thought that some men are, regardless of race, slaves by nature), always have to invent reasons to justify. Indeed, every social order based on hierarchy and subordination—alleged superiority and inferiority—finds it necessary and convenient to create majestic justifications. These "rationalizations" serve a double purpose: an ideological prop for the pretensions of the privileged classes so that they are blind to injustice and a tranquilizer for the oppressed groups so that they will not protest and rebel.

Our thesis, it should be noted, is concerned with the overriding ethos of American culture. It does not imply that all members of the dominant group have shared this a priori and authoritarian presupposition. Nor does it deny differences of kind, degree, or form of expression (for example, between the North and the South) of the legacy of race relations. These differences are significant. Yet the ideology of race cuts much deeper into the heart and nerve center of the substance of culture than is generally assumed. It wears many masks and finds numerous outlets—including some very subtle and sophisticated forms.

The Major Consequence: Creature and Object of Action

Probably the best way to understand the depth and magnitude of the tragic dimension of the Negro is to grasp his paradoxical significance in the drama of American history. One will find difficulty overestimating the importance and vitality of the Negro as a *creature* and *object of action*. This can be apprehended from many perspectives. Consider him economically as a source of cheap and manageable labor. But if, on the other hand, the Negro is conceived of as a *creator, subject,* or *agent* of action, then economically, as in other facets of American culture, the tragic element is clear.

The dramatic significance of the Negro as a creature and object of action is best illustrated in the realm of politics where he has been a veritable and perpetual "center of attraction." Consider, for example, the lengthy debates over slavery in the Constitutional Convention, the provisions of the Constitution itself relating to the Negro, the great compromises of 1820 and 1850, fugitive slave laws, and special legislation dealing with free Negroes in the pre–Civil War period. Also consider various controversies over the admission of new states to the Union and extension of slavery, the Lincoln-Douglas debates, the politically-laden Dred Scott decision, the Civil War, national Reconstruction, and the staggering mass of civil rights bills introduced and debated in Congress for almost a century. On all these occasions, the Negro was a mere creature and object of action, not a creative participant. Of the many symbols of the Negro as creature and object of action, the history of the Senate filibuster is one of the most graphic. Again, consider the history of political campaigns, national political conventions, party platforms, registration and election laws, and legislative apportionment. The

Negro has been a pawn in "the great game of politics." But he has been an animating pawn.

Perhaps as good as any interpretation of the course of Southern history is one that envisions it from the standpoint of actions, reactions, memories, and anticipations based on the presence of the Negro. In the context of a variety of schemes designed to exclude him from the process of power and social control, the Negro has been, in the profoundest sense, a mere creature and object of action and domination.

True, from the final standpoint of historical interpretation, man is always a creature as well as creator of the historical process; he bears a dual and paradoxical relation to it.[19] Man is always profoundly influenced by the sequences and relations of history. He is a product of the very matrix of events which he helps to create. But the Negro's existence in the drama of American history has been virtually exhausted in his "creature-lines"—in being an object of action and control. Unlike his fellow Americans, he has been denied the power to be an architect and engineer of the destiny of America, including his own destiny in the American scheme of things. Toynbee points out that man's capacity for intellectual detachment enables him to be a spectator of historical happenings.[20] The Negro, however, has been an unusual spectator. He has been an observer of an endless series of events in which his own *destiny has been manipulated and controlled by others*. His existence has been governed externally, by foreign capitals of meaning and value, and largely arbitrarily. The content of experience, along with the range and depth of his choices, has been, in the main, determined from without— by remote control. In consequence, the very integrity and creativity of the Negro's mind and spirit have been shipwrecked by virtue of an alleged difference of essence. His power to be a creator of the historical process has been prematurely arrested, and, it should be remembered, this blockage of the Negro's equal opportunity to affect the course of history in the realization of freedom and selfhood was accomplished under the direction, prestige, and power of an alleged good. Herein lies the deep tragedy.[21]

Even briefly, we cannot attempt to catalogue or adumbrate the various sad implications and consequences of the Negro's role in the American scheme of things as a mere object of thought and action. Suffice it to say that the adverse impact on his mind, personality, will, and spirit has been great and far-reaching. Chief among these consequences were the thwarting of his desire for self-fulfilment, the dulling of his nerve of striving, the crushing of his aspiration, and the minimizing of his self-esteem and appreciative awareness. It has been extremely difficult, almost impossible, for the Negro to grasp the full dimensions of his selfhood and his full stature as a person. It has been well said that to "break down a man's sense of his own worth murders his aspirations. It chokes the God in him. . . ." [22]

THE CURRENT SITUATION
PROGRESS AND TRADITION: A PARADOX

The Negro has made obvious and sweeping progress—educational, economic, political, and cultural. His giant strides should gladden the heart of every lover of mankind as well as stir the Negro's hope and faith in American democracy. This should quicken his pulses and kindle his imagination. But this mountain of progress, like all mountains, has another side. The Negro's progress abounds in baffling paradoxes and contradictions—brilliant triumphs and frightening setbacks. Of his present predicament, the newer dimensions are rooted in the fact and psychology of his very achievements in juxtaposition to a bitter, fanatical, angry and desperate South and a reluctant, oscillating, and bewildered country.

The pressure of facing a desperate South and of evaluating, adjusting, and making judgments in the crisis of battle is aggravated by the far-reaching consequences and implications of the Negro's actions. He knows that history contains a crucial element of irreversibility. In a real sense, the Negro is, for the first time, in a genuine position to be a creator as well as creature of the historical process. Reconstruction was too close to the Scylla of slavery and the Charybdis of the Civil War for him to be enduringly creative—though we are not unmindful of DuBois' *Black Reconstruction*. Today, the Negro has no mean power of initiative and action. He has alternatives. He cannot avoid choosing; for the refusal to choose is itself a choice—a choice to do nothing—for which he is responsible. But obviously his choices may be destructive as well as creative, and they, while intending the good, might foster evil. He, like all centers of power, will have to answer to the judgment of history for his choices. The South today is under historical judgment from which it has tried (and is still trying) desperately to escape.

Equally significant is the fact that the Negro, perhaps, will have occasion to be compelled to sacrifice one good for another. Conflicting values contribute to the tragic character of the human drama. Sometimes men have to surrender even a highly cherished value for an equivalent or a higher one. For example, both public education and integrated public schools rank high in the hierarchy of the Negro's value system. But what of the awful choice between the two? If that occasion should arise, what would be the criterion of choice? *Who* would evaluate and decide? There is no easy method of determining the duration of incompatible objects of value.

In a sense, the Negro's very progress tends to magnify his frustrations, insecurities, anxieties, tensions, and pathetic dilemmas. For his unsatisfied desires expand, his longings intensify, his expectations are greater, his level of aspiration soars, and his imagination and vision are more lucid, inspired, and vivid. Accordingly, disappointments are more bitter, roadblocks more intolerable, barriers more baffling and gnawing, and suffering more poignant. Success aggravates failure. Failure erodes success.

The Negro achieves giant successes only to have them partly annulled by onrushing opposing forces before which he seems pitifully helpless. So Congress, for the first time in almost ninety years, enacts two Civil Rights laws. These laws are modest indeed, being designed primarily to secure the most elementary right of citizenship, that of the right to participate via suffrage in the process of government. From Aristotle to the present, men have recognized that the sharing of political power is a condition of citizenship. But in certain Southern states, these voting laws have been met with all forms of resistance: intimidation, economic reprisals, and even threats to life and limb. As these pages are being written, Negroes in Fayette and Haywood counties in Tennessee, because they desire to register and vote, face an economic boycott so severe that, according to published reports, they cannot even buy gasoline, oil, and other supplies for their agricultural machines, or secure bank credit for their crops. It is so difficult even to purchase necessities like food, household commodities, and clothing that organizations are importing food there in order to avert mass starvation.

Again, the Supreme Court invalidates segregation in public education. In the wake of that decision, however, the Negro encounters a multitude of evasive schemes, retaliatory legislation and administration, economic pressure, political deprivations, and various forms of psychical and emotional coercion. Beyond all this, integration of some school systems has produced (though by no means justly and inevitably) unemployed Negro teachers.[23] This is a tragic paradox. Then, too, in virtually every Southern state, money from Negro taxpayers is being spent to thwart desegregation—to subsidize, in other words, the continuation of the practice of raping Negroes of their constitutional rights.

Moreover, even where there is no defiance or circumvention of the Supreme Court's desegregation decision, the impact of that decision is partly voided by residential segregation and discrimination. In fact, this has long been a thorny problem for Negroes outside the South where integration of schools is the public policy but also where "restrictive covenants," among other things, sometimes make for segregated schools as well as residential ghettos. All of this illustrates the multiplicity of our problems as well as the way in which these problems are related.

The current school situation is not without a touch of irony. It is sadly ironic that some public schools have been closed—and in all probability there will be many others—in order to avoid desegregation when, in the period of Reconstruction, the Negro made a considerable contribution to the establishment of state-supported education in the South for white and Negro children alike.[24]

Consider another pathetic dilemma: that of federal aid to education. Without federal aid, Negro children, like others, will suffer. But should there be federal aid at the cost of perpetuating segregation? With the "Powell amendment," Congress is likely to defeat the bill; without that amendment, the government itself will be a party to the support of segregation in violation of the spirit of the Supreme Court's decision of May, 1954. In either case, therefore, the Negro is likely at once to be helped and hurt.

Still another aspect of the Negro's predicament is in the realm of economics. Economic power is vital to other forms of power—political, educational, cultural, etc. But consider the Negro's rate of economic growth as well as his starting-point in proportion to the total population. Consider, again, the doors closed to him in matters of employment and promotion. This lack of economic power cancels out many opportunities and exposes some of the pretensions of "phenomenal progress." The psychological, emotional, and educational fruit of this deprivation is not far to seek.

Since our discussion of progress and tragedy can be easily misunderstood, a word of caution is necessary. The fact that the Negro's progress is the bearer of new perplexities and perils is by no means an argument for the termination or reversal of the process of social change. Such an assumption is simply a *non sequitur*. That civilization creates its own particular pitfalls is no argument for a return to barbarism. Modern technical and industrial culture breeds its own special perils, but few would argue for a restoration of feudalism or for a cessation of technological advance. What we are suggesting is that each level of the Negro's progress, like historical progress in general, brings in its train novel pitfalls, dangers, and woes.

It has been well said that progress involves a collision of contradictions, a dramatic dialectic encounter of opposites rather than a natural evolution of higher stages or a continually ascending scale of cumulative creative achievements. Destruction and construction, decay and growth, tragedy and triumph are often mixed on the stage of history. There is no escape from the inner contradictions of life and the aches and pains of human finitude. Nor is there any escape from the grim paradox of progress and tragedy. Belief in the constancy and the inevitability of progress may be a comfortable illusion, but history has a way of doing havoc even with our most cherished illusions.

Of late, there has been much talk about the inevitability of integration and other universal values. But this is a dangerous seed to sow. The achievement of a social order institutionalizing justice, freedom, and equality for all does not depend upon the certainty and power of the alleged imperatives and inevitables of the progressive development of history. Rather, it depends upon a variety of variables, among which are human intelligence, skill, will, organization, leadership, and resources as well as historical accidents. Integration and equality, therefore, are not inevitable. They must be won by human effort.

CONCLUSION: THE SIGNIFICANCE OF A TRAGIC VIEW OF NEGRO HISTORY

Of the many mysteries of Negro history, the greatest is the absence of a deep sense of tragedy.[25] In spite of the degrading and harrowing character of his odyssey, the Negro has been, in the main, consistently optimistic about his historic destiny. In view of his unique experiences, the general optimism of modern culture, especially American, is not very instructive. Neither the agony of slavery nor the frustrations of fragmentary and somewhat suspended freedom have, for the most part, struck a tragic note in the depths of his being and consciousness. Somehow, he has clung tenaciously to an optimistic *Weltanschauung*. Even when some Negroes lost faith in the possibilities of American justice, they exuded robust confidence in the redemptive character of simple panaceas such as colonization and expatriation.

There does not seem to be any evidence that the Negro's optimistic outlook is grounded in presuppositions of historical inevitability, i.e., belief that history is on his side. Some have maintained that this optimism is "inherent," or "natural." But clearly this argument is a *petitio principii;* it begs the very point at issue. Is the historic optimism of the Negro based on religion? [26] Is it anchored in a compensatory psychology, so that flight from reality serves as a philosophy and technique of adjustment and survival? [27] Has life been so tragic for the Negro that he has sought desperately to deny its negations? Or does the Negro's historic optimism reflect inadequate appreciation of the intrinsic dignity and significance of his own selfhood? Has he always taken seriously his status as a moral and rational being? Does today's Negro inhabit a world of fantasy? [28]

In any event, the Negro should develop a sense and appreciation of the tragic dimension of history. Born of sorrow, he must gird himself to encounter deep sorrow for a long and indefinite period; for such is likely to be his destiny. True enough, no mortal can penetrate the dark mystery of the future. All we can do is to calculate possibilities and probabilities, and have the humility to recognize that even our best and most careful prediction may well be wrong. Sober analysis of the present situation, however, suggests that psychological, emotional, spiritual, and cultural estrangement from the substantive and positive roots, flowers, and sunlight of American culture will probably govern the Negro's foreseeable future. Even with the removal of customary barriers and the consequent expansion of opportunities for growth and development, the tragedy of isolation will not necessarily recede. As John Dewey observed, "the full freedom of the human spirit and of individuality can be achieved only as there is effective opportunity to share in the cultural resources of civilization." [29] Without freedom of mind and spirit, without an intimate feeling of belonging, and without an ethos of genuine and creative participation in the common life and the shared values of culture, the Negro cannot be truly and fully free. Hence the overcoming of cultural estrangement and social isolation is indispensable to his becoming a free participant in the great dialogue of American thought and culture. Equality must be *felt* as well as recognized by all participants.

Undoubtedly, there will be various forms and degrees of alleviation and amelioration of the Negro's troubles and woes. But a millennium is beyond his present field of intelligent and responsible vision. It is an illusion.

But today, some of our leaders and spokesmen are advancing time-tables, target dates, and even predicting the exact year that Negroes will gain "complete freedom and equality." As a spur and guide to action, they may well be important. But the wisdom of history counsels against the opening of false doors of hope and expectation. Unless prognostications and strategems are grounded in a healthy recognition of the complexities, variables, accidents, and risks of the process of social change, they will fade into bitter ashes and haunting gloom.

What, then, are the virtues of a tragic conception of Negro history? First, it helps to illuminate the unflattering and heartrending maze of events and interactions in which the Negro has been involved. It makes his desolation and misery more intelligible. Because of the absence of a sense of tragedy, the Negro has not always fully understood the magnitude, depths, and meaning of his pilgrimage in the magnificent drama of American history.

Second, a framework of tragedy makes the Negro's struggles and sufferings ethically significant. This is the deep, inner beauty of tragedy. For it is, in part, in the encounter with tragedy and triumph over it, in various degrees and ways, that strength and nobility of spirit are disclosed. Without proper appreciation of what is involved, we cannot adequately understand efforts and achievements. All great tragedy purges the spirit.[30] "Of all the arts," Russell observes, "tragedy is the proudest, the most triumphant; for it builds its shining citadel in the very centre of the enemy's country. . . ."[31]

Finally, a sense of the tragic character of Negro history is a way of relating that history to the historical process itself, to human history in general. In the final analysis, history, like nature (we are all subject to the laws of decay and mortality, and death is the final proof of man's finitude), has no favorites. History has a tragic dimension. It is, "among other things, the cemetery of human hopes."[32] Or, as Royce puts it: "All finite life is a struggle with evil."[33] As the Negro realizes, then, the tragic element of history, he will see his own history in perspective. This can be ethically sustaining; for he will discover anew that he is an integral part of mankind. Since frustrations, failures, and sorrows are expressive of human finitude, they are ineradicable facets of the human heritage.

There are, of course, numerous objections to the conception whose barest outlines have been suggested. Let us indicate what our rejoinder would be to three of them. Is it true that Negro history has been tragic? The answer to this question involves historical imagination, reconstruction, and re-enactment as well as definition. With sympathetic understanding and imagination, we must try to get inside the Negro slave and the "free" Negro and share the fullness of their experiences. Having attempted this, we cannot avoid the conclusion that the drama of Negro history is tragic indeed. But each interpreter will have to answer this question for himself.

Does the tragic conception of human history justify the evils of history, especially the Negro past? There is, to be sure, no guarantee against the use of any perspective for partisan purposes; even science itself is often given partisan overtones and applications. This is the perennial problem of man as a bearer of values as well as a seeker of knowledge. However, it is one thing to try to *understand* the phenomena of history; it is quite another to seek to *justify* those phenomena. Knowledge of the tragic dimension of history is no more a justification of tragedy than knowledge of the brevity of human life is a justification of death.

Does the conception of tragedy petrify courage, gnaw away zest, and undermine the nerve of striving? Such is possible, but it is not inevitable. Recognition of the tragic sector of history should contribute to the liberation of the mind and will. A realistic appreciation of the tragic element of history is a better safeguard against despair and cynicism than a simple and sentimental optimism blind to the perennial pitfalls and risks of the human enterprise. Despair is more often a product of exaggerated and false hopes than of sober ones.[34] A sense of tragedy need not imply either the futility of effort or the impotence of hope. On the contrary, it is a perspective for coming to terms and doing our best with the imperfections of existence both without falling into the abyss of despair and without failing to take life seriously.

We live in a very challenging and fertile era which abounds in creative as well as destructive opportunities. Despite the legacy of cultural estrangement and denial, we have come, in a significant degree and in the words of James Weldon Johnson, "to the place for which our fathers sighed." Always but especially in this period of "transition" (and who can speak with finality of its course and duration), the Negro's efforts will be more meaningful, his triumphs more rewarding, and his failures more bearable if he will remember the sobering words of Sophocles' Chorus:

> Tomorrow and for all time to come,
> As in the past,
> This law is immutable;
> For mortals greatly to live is greatly to suffer.[35]

NOTES

1. Cf. R. G. Collingwood, *The Idea of History* (Oxford, 1946), Part V. "We study history," he asserts, "in order to attain self-knowledge" (*ibid.*, p. 315).

2. Reinhold Niebuhr, *Faith and History* (New York, 1949), p. 35.

3. On the unity of time, see Morris R. Cohen, *The Meaning of Human History* (LaSalle, Illinois, 1947), and Josiah Royce, *The World and the Individual* (New York, 1901), I, 407-421, and II, 127.

4. Arnold J. Toynbee, *Greek Historical Thought* (Mentor ed.; New York, 1952), p. xxvii.

5. See Charles M. Wiltse, "History as Social Philosophy," *Ethics*, XLVI (1935), 49-63; Immanuel Lewy, "Valuation in Fact-Finding," *Journal of Philosophy*, XLIV (1947), 575-578; George H. Sabine, *Social Studies and Objectivity* (Berkeley, 1941); and the series of articles by Lewy, Hartung, *et al.* in *Philosophy of Science*, XV (1948).

6. Cohen, *op. cit.*, pp. 4-5. Also see the same author's *Reason and Nature* (Rev. ed.; New York, 1953), pp. 342-351, and *A Preface to Logic* (New York, 1944), pp. 163-166.

7. Cohen, *The Meaning of Human History*, p. 80.

8. Perhaps the most famous definition of tragedy was given by Aristotle in *Poetics*. "A tragedy, then, is the imitation of an action that is serious and also, as having magnitude, complete in itself; in language with pleasurable accessories, each kind brought in separately in the parts of the work; in a dramatic, not in a narrative form; with incidents arousing pity and fear, wherewith to accomplish its catharsis of such emotions." Richard McKeon (ed.), *The Basic Works of Aristotle* (New York, 1941), p. 1460.

9. See Edith Hamilton, *The Greek Way to Western Civilization* (Mentor ed.; New York, 1948), chap. 11.

10. A. C. Bradley, *Shakespearean Tragedy* (Meridian ed.; New York, 1955).

11. In addition to Augustine's *City of God*, see the various writings of Reinhold Niebuhr, and Karl Lowith, *Meaning in History* (Chicago, 1949).

12. Cf. Fred B. Millett and Gerald E. Bentley, *The Art of Drama* (New York, 1935), chap. 2.

13. Walter Rauschenbusch, *A Theology for the Social Gospel* (New York, 1917), p. 66.

14. Cf. Gunnar Myrdal, *An American Dilemma* (2 Vols.; New York, 1944). In this monumental work, Myrdal builds on the contradiction between norm

and practice. The historic treatment of the Negro is, no doubt, incompatible with the ethics of democracy. But Myrdal's insights notwithstanding, no context of contradiction can explain the easy conscience of so many whites relative to the Negro; and, indeed, the fact that some have a sense of moral righteousness about that status is partial proof of the denial of the contradiction. A feeling of moral contradiction gives rise to a perplexed and panged conscience. Per contra, a considerable number of whites, especially Southerners, view the special status and disabilities of the Negro as "natural," "inevitable," "just," or "right."

15. Emil Brunner, *Justice and the Social Order*, trans. Mary Hottinger (London, 1945), p. 13. "The suffering which is fate unites men; unjust suffering breeds strife. . . . Unjust suffering does not merely thwart man's desire for happiness; it also destroys an established order; it deprives me of my due. Unjust suffering arouses indignation; it affects the life of the spirit; it eats into personality." *Ibid.*

16. See Ralph McGill, *A Church, A School* (Nashville, 1959).

17. One of the crudest efforts to establish the Negro's exclusion from the bonds of humanity was recorded by Rauschenbusch, *op. cit.*, n. 1, pp. 185-186.

18. This tradition transcends sectional boundaries. It is easy to forget the historic guilt of the North. See Rayford Logan, *The Negro in American Life and Thought* (New York, 1954), p. 6, and Elsie G. Hobson, *Educational Legislation and Administration in the State of New York, 1777-1850* (private ed.; Chicago, 1918), esp. pp. 108, 110.

19. See Reinhold Niebuhr, *The Self and the Dramas of History* (New York, 1955), pp. 41-43, and *Faith and History*, pp. 55-58.

20. Arnold J. Toynbee, *The New Opportunity for Historians* (Minneapolis, 1955), p. 3.

21. The bulk of human history, it is true, consists of groups whose plight, in part, paralleled that of the Negro—groups outside the pale of the process of power and social control. But, unlike most "outside" groups in history, the Negro's position has been compounded and aggravated by the color of his skin.

22. Walter Rauschenbusch, *Christianizing the Social Order* (New York, 1912), p. 418.

23. Consider, for example, the state of Oklahoma. In a heartwarming account of integration of public schools there, former governor Raymond Gary observes: "Integration has, however, created one really disturbing problem. Only about ten Negro teachers are working in integrated schools, and 344 Negro teachers have lost their jobs, since individual school boards, with rare exceptions, have not yet seen fit to hire Negro teachers." "The South Can Integrate Its Schools," *Look*, March 31, 1959, p. 21.

24. See Arthur M. Schlesinger, *Political and Social History of the United States* (New York, 1925), p. 243.

"The first great mass movement for public education at the expense of the state, in the South, came from Negroes. . . . Public education for all at public

expense, was, in the South, a Negro idea." W. E. B. DuBois, *Black Reconstruction in America* (New York, 1935), p. 638.

25. What of Negro spirituals? "It must not be overlooked," Mrs. Butcher
observes, "that the comic 'jig-song and dance' and the serious, almost tragic
'spirituals' were plantation contemporaries." Margaret J. Butcher, *The Negro
in American Culture* (New York, 1956), p. 26.

26. Cf. Benjamin E. Mays, *The Negro's God* (Boston, 1938).

27. Cf. Butcher, *op. cit.*, pp. 37-39.

28. Cf. E. Franklin Frazier, *The Black Bourgeoisie* (Glencoe, 1957), pp.
23-26, 153-238.

29. *Problems of Men* (New York, 1946), p. 140.

30. See Cohen, *The Meaning of Human History*, pp. 294-295, and his *The
Faith of a Liberal* (New York, 1946), pp. 79-84.

31. Bertrand Russell, *Mysticism and Logic* (Anchor ed.; New York, 1957),
p. 51.

32. Cohen, *The Meaning of Human History*, p. 294.

33. Royce, *op. cit.*, II, p. 397.

34. The pilgrimage of John Milton illustrates this point. "We cannot measure the depth of Milton's later pessimism unless we appreciate the fervid and
unrealistic optimism of his youth and early manhood." Douglas Bush, *English
Literature in the Earlier Seventeenth Century* (Oxford, 1945), p. 369.

Also compare the optimism of the nineteenth century with the pessimism
of recent decades.

35. "Antigone," in Sophocles, *The Theban Plays*, trans. E. F. Watling
(Penguin ed.; London, 1947), pp. 142-143.

THE NEGRO REVOLUTION

AND THE INTELLECTUALS

William B. Hixson, Jr.

Seldom has the idea of revolution been held in greater disfavor among Americans than in the years since the end of the Second World War. In a world in which men seize the power of the modern state in order to mold entire populations into their ideological patterns, such a revulsion is hardly surprising. Among American intellectuals, the erosion of any hopes they had placed in the Soviet "experiment" had developed, by the 1950's, into a distrust of systematic thought, social planning, and revolutionary tactics. Instead, they began increasingly to find virtue and wisdom embodied in the pragmatism, pluralism, and conservatism of the American political tradition. One wonders what would happen if a movement appeared that found this tradition so deeply flawed that it wanted to start on new foundations? If Hannah Arendt is correct in saying that the distinguishing characteristic of modern revolution is its sense of novelty, then surely such a movement would be "revolutionary."

This attitude is increasingly the position of the American Negro: his demands for equality are still framed in the rhetoric of American democratic idealism; he still wants what the rest of his fellow citizens want. But that is not the issue. The American Negro is becoming aware, not only that his demands have so often been rejected in the past, but that they cannot now be achieved within our society as it is presently constituted. Thus the sources of potential conflict may lie not only in irrational white resistance to his demands for equality. "White Americans impress me," James Baldwin has written, "as being far more hopeful,

William D Hixson, Jr., "The Negro Revolution and the Intellectuals," *American Scholar,* XXXIII, No. 4 (Autumn, 1964), 581-593.

far more innocent, far more irresponsible, far less aware of the terrible black, ugly facts of life than black people can afford to be." Could it be that the real crisis will come in the Negro's challenge of the image that white America has of itself? If so, could it also be that the intellectuals' current interpretation of American history and society may be partly to blame for this mistaken image?

The American intellectual community has not reinforced the educated public's racial prejudice; that it has consistently challenged. But it has reinforced their conservatism. Insofar as the intellectual mood of the last two decades has been "conservative," it has inevitably created a barrier between intellectuals and the "revolutionary" Negro movement. "Conservative" theories emphasizing consensus, pluralism, and human fallibility, although by no means maintained by all intellectuals, have been held by the most influential thinkers in the period since World War II. They began their interpretation with an attempt to explain the "uniqueness" of America in avoiding the apparent old-world cycle of revolution and despotism. First, they explained, we had avoided the social misery that had provoked total conflict in Europe; and, because of this, we had been able to develop a "consensus" both on our economic objectives (equality of opportunity in a capitalist economy) and on our political procedures (universal suffrage and representative government). American political argument had appealed to the same values and institutions; no successful political party in America had challenged either the economic objectives or the political procedures.

American society, they believed, had been a successful experiment, not only because all the interest groups competing for control of the government had abided by the procedural rules, but because all actual or potential interest groups had been given the chance to control it. Dominant economic and social groups had not, in our society, been allowed to monopolize political power and restrict the fluidity of the entire system. Business interests had dominated economic policy, and white Anglo-Saxon Protestant prejudice had limited ethnic and religious tolerance in the nineteenth century. But, this "theory of balance" maintained, recent political movements (notably the New Deal) had given the labor movement, the farmers, and minority groups the institutional power to counteract those forces.

It was to those areas of political action where their "theory of balance" did not apply that intellectuals turned their attention in the fifties. For, in foreign policy and civil liberties, there are few, if any, interest groups preventing a frustrated mass public from either attacking dissenters within or railing at the world outside. Contemporary intellectuals have therefore challenged some earlier assumptions about the degree of intelligence, interest, and tolerance of the average citizen. However strange it might seem to some of their predecessors, today's still nominally liberal intellectuals have given their loyalties to such "undemocratic" institutions as a professional diplomatic corps and the Federal court system. In both cases, they argue, only such barriers can prevent public hysteria from destroying the framework for intellectual debate within the country, and from seriously damaging, through bellicose policies, America's position of strength within the world.

A society composed from its beginnings of "middling orders," a society devoted to reform within the limits of democratic procedure and a capitalist economy, a society with "countervailing power" among interest groups and some institutional protection against waves of hysteria—this, I suggest, is the composite portrait of America that her most representative intellectuals have portrayed in the last fifteen years. It is a conservative view, although most of the men adhering to it consider themselves liberals. In their devotion to social reform and civil liberties they are "liberal"; their view is certainly not "conservative" in the sense of Barry Goldwater or the *National Review*. Their view is conservative in the traditional sense; like the newly appreciated Edmund Burke and John Adams, they tend to favor social order and a dispassionate governing class, and acknowledge the limits of majority rule and of any attempt to reform society. The reasons for the rapprochement between so many American intellectuals and the Kennedy Administration, I would suggest, was that policy makers (even those without intellectual backgrounds) shared so many of the same values. Unfortunately, the "conservative" mood of the intellectuals tended to provide the perfect justification for any administrator who identified his particular Congressional gadfly with the principle of representative government and his own mental sluggishness with the metaphysical limits of social reform. It was not a matter, as some of their less influential colleagues charged, of these intellectuals being bought off: they were simply reaping the harvest of their ideas. If Henry George anticipated the angry agrarianism of the Populists, and Charles Beard the iconoclasm of the New Dealers, these men foreshadowed the cautious reform of the New Frontier.

If the Negro movement of today can be defined as a "revolt" against white liberal leadership, it should not be surprising that it also rejects the interpretations offered by white liberal intellectuals. American Negroes are increasingly aware that theirs is a unique position in our society. Although he has been here from the beginning, the Negro has never been accepted as a full participant in the "American way of life." White immigrant groups, now largely assimilated, also met long and bitter prejudice in their drive for equality; but even in exclusion they had a coherent culture, a common language and religion, to give them security. But the Negro, uprooted from his native Africa, was given only an imposed culture—part of the white man's religion and none of his education—in his years of slavery. And having denied him the possibility of a family, of an education, and of self-advancement for 250 years, white America has accused him of promiscuity, stupidity, and shiftlessness ever since emancipation.

For a long time the American Negro was left out of the democratic process. Alone among Americans, he was born neither free nor equal, and the condition that most of his countrymen claim as a birthright was granted him only by the grace of the majority. Our reform movements have usually passed him by. The Revolution did bring about emancipation in the North, but gave the Negro few, if any, of the political and civil rights that accompany freedom. Rather, some of the most sensitive minds of the time thought the solution to lie in sending free Negroes back to Africa. Confronted by the new profitability of slavery made possible by the cotton gin, emancipation halted; as of 1861, only 12 per cent of American Negroes could be considered "free." The North incorporated the Negro in its Civil War idealism, formally liberated him, and then, with little more than the language of three Constitutional amendments to protect him, abandoned him to his former masters. In the Age of Reform, the Negro was attacked by embittered Populists and patronized by the Progressives; not until the New Deal could he regard government as having a personal interest in his welfare, and even then he was often faced with discrimination in relief administration and agricultural policies. Many of the compromises of the American "consensus" have been made at his expense; American Negroes have difficulty in not regarding the Civil War as fought between one side that wanted to keep them enslaved, and another that didn't want them at all. Negro attempts to find white allies, whether in middle-class "civil rights" organizations or in lower-class economic movements, from the days of Abolitionism to those of the Student Nonviolent Coordinating Committee, have been met with the white majority's acquiescence in the campaigns of terror and fraud against them. The American consensus that the Negro has known has been that of hostility.

Intellectuals would be the first to admit the truth of this indictment; much of their recent effort has been to show the pervasive racism of earlier American thinkers and politicians. They would insist, however, that the gains of the last twenty years indicate major progress toward racial equality, mainly due to the political power of the Northern Negro and the liberalism of the Federal judiciary. It took the snarling dogs and the fire hoses of Birmingham to thrust the Negro before the

American conscience, and make the educated public and intellectuals realize what progress had *not* been made. The Southern Negro will be the beneficiary of the most sweeping Civil Rights Act in history. But for the Northern Negro, already surrounded by a battery of egalitarian statutes, liberal judges and politicians eager for his vote, the Civil Rights Act of 1964 will do little good at all. The Northern Negro is losing faith in both the ability of his "interest group" to accomplish much through political channels, and in the ability of nonpolitical administrative institutions to enforce the law effectively and objectively. For in the North, where agencies have been set up, the Negro's condition is only partially improved. Not only is he faced with the usual bureaucratic inefficiencies, but with the long, slow, expensive process of investigation and injunctive relief. Faced with any massive resistance on the part of the white community, governmental efforts on his behalf are often nullified, as the protracted battle with the construction unions should prove. The good things of life, as America defines them, cannot be enjoyed without money—and a job to earn it. But the rate of Negro unemployment remains twice as high as among whites.

The American Negro remains somewhat cynical about the idea of an America with a wide diffusion of power. His belief in a "power structure," if nothing else, means for the Negro that he has been excluded for so long that conflicts within the system seem less real to him than the overriding white hostility. He has never fared well in the cross-pressures of interest groups, and not only because he alone among Americans has had his constitutional rights subject to the vagaries of factional pressure. The "theory of balance" implies a certain give-and-take among competing interests, with compromise depending upon the parties' respective strengths; the result, in economic terms, has been evolving policies toward collective bargaining, control of agricultural production, business organization, and so on. But so oppressed has the Negro been that his "group rights" are the basic conditions that other Americans take for granted: among other things, the right to eat, sleep, and go to the bathroom without having to make it a major project, full of danger and difficulty. Given the differences between such Negro demands and those of economic interest groups, compromise reaches absurdity. And with the memory of his abandonment after Reconstruction, the Negro does not need to be reminded that what the majority grants, it can also take away.

If, to the Negro, legislation has meant compromise at his expense; administrative commissions, vacillation; the courts, lengthy litigation; and law enforcement, the blows of a policeman's club—it is not surprising that he turns to the direct action techniques of civil disobedience. When Thoreau refused to pay his poll tax and went to jail, he helped set the three criteria of civil disobedience: he had broken the law, he had done so publicly as an affirmation of specific values (the participant in civil disobedience does not reserve the right to break any law he pleases), and he had done so nonviolently. He also accepted his punishment; for, unlike the rebel, the civil disobedient does not challenge the authority of the state. Thoreau's was an individual refusal to perpetuate injustice, however, not a collective demand for justice. Social groups, unlike individuals, have the power to precipitate a crisis in institutions, even through nonviolent action. At the same time, an objective change in the unjust situation must result, and not, as with an individual, merely moral satisfaction. The demands this places upon the Negro leadership are almost intolerable: they must direct the activism of their members toward attainable goals, and try to prevent demonstrations for demonstrations' sake; but when specific results are not achieved, bitterness is all the greater. In the South, the Negro campaign of nonviolence has to contend with overt hostility, but, as Birmingham proved, it can appeal to a wider national audience. In the North, however, it can only appeal to the same apathetic majority that has already allowed its legislative gains to be frustrated.

The "revolutionary" demands of the Negro movement, revolutionary not in their rejection of American ideals but in their opposition to the structure of American society, raise more than the obvious political and social issues. Their demands also create an important intellectual issue, for they involve an implicit rejection of the prevailing interpretations of "consensus" and "balance," and the values of order and moderation. It is true that in the last year intellectuals themselves have been revising many of their attitudes. The world itself has changed since the 1950's. When the two major powers possess "overkill" capacity, when centrifugal tendencies disrupt both the Soviet bloc and the Western alliance, and when the underdeveloped South of the world becomes increasingly assertive, the defense of American institutions must be perceived in different terms than a decade ago. The recent discovery that there are between thirty-two and fifty million Americans who are trying to live on a family income of twenty-five hundred dollars a year or less has at least qualified the idea of an "affluent society"; their number, in a society already unable to achieve full employment, will almost certainly grow as the effects of automation make themselves felt. The past year has brought Senator Fulbright's "thinking unthinkable thoughts" about our foreign policy, Michael Harrington's dissection of American poverty,

the brashness of *Dr. Strangelove*, and the Ad Hoc Committee on the
Triple Revolution—all nearly impossible to imagine in the America of
ten or fifteen years ago.

If all these events are indications of changing attitudes in the intellectual community, what, then, is the problem? In its crucial aspects,
the prevailing interpretation of the fifties has not been changed, and
our intellectual history shows that major changes in thought are necessary to achieve even moderate political reform. Progressivism and the
New Deal were made possible partly by the destruction of the Darwin-
ist and formalist intellectual edifice by Dewey, Veblen, Boas, Beard,
Holmes, and a whole generation of thinkers. Today, instead, the intellectuals' cautious expression of their commitments, their pursuit of
"qualitative liberalism" and reluctance to consider structural reform
as relevant, has undoubtedly contributed to the state of mind Walter
Lippmann described several years ago. "We talk about ourselves these
days as if we are a completed society," he wrote in 1960, "one which
has achieved its purposes and has no further business to transact." Those
intellectuals who have regarded poverty, discrimination, and violence
as somehow exceptions in an otherwise moderate and affluent America
are confronted with a Negro movement that has arisen precisely as a
protest against all three conditions. As the Negro revolution uncovers
the brutality in American society, intellectuals will be less and less able
to describe our society accurately either to the policymakers or to the
educated public.

There are several fruitful approaches, it seems to me, for intellectuals
to take to come to an understanding of the Negro movement. The description of American history in terms of "consensus," as it was re-
fracted from one level to another, tended to "convert a vibrant, dynamic,
and violent society, in which men have fought out with all available
weapons the crucial issues of their times," in John P. Roche's words, "into
a peaceful, even somnolent process of brotherhood and compromise, an
extended Quaker meeting." During the fifties, furthermore, few intellectuals ever bothered to define what they meant by "consensus." A definition, not without current relevance, was once made by Horace Kallen.
"Every consensus is a won agreement," he said, and in it "the parties
to the initiating conflict presumably enjoy parity. The confronted interests are alike in freedom and importance. The issues between them get
joined not by exclusion and antagonistic imposition but by reciprocal
interpenetration."

Consensus, for Kallen, is thus differentiated from conformity and
coercion; in neither of the latter are the interests "alike in freedom and
importance. . . . Agreement by conformity comes about through the

voluntary adjustment to a social environment over which the conformer has no control. Coerced agreements, per contra, are involuntary." His definition has much to say about the American experience. Leaving aside the place of the Negro in the American "consensus," who can deny the coercion of the American Indian? Or is the American "consensus" firmer than the South African, simply because the suppressed aborigines are less numerous? The polite rhetoric of the "melting pot" aside, what about the cultural Procrustean bed into which we have put our non-Anglo-Saxon, non-Protestant immigrants?

Similarly, the "theory of balance," with its image of competing and approximately equal groups, needs to be modified. Edmond Cahn has pointed out the distinction between the perspective of those who measure the administration of justice by its ability to keep the system running smoothly, and those who view it "according to its concussions on human lives." Intellectuals have tended to use the first, the "imperial," perspective. Political scientists, sociologists, and economists have for too long regarded the political conflicts of the last twenty years as taking place between the two Americas that possess power. One America feels that the country is no longer "theirs," and is fighting a rearguard action to repeal the changes of the last several decades; another accepts these changes, but, in its new affluence, favors only a few supplementary reforms (such as urban renewal and federal aid to education). It is now evident that these intellectuals have ignored the "other" America, the unskilled, the migrant workers, the tenant farmers, the victims of regional depression—and this "other" America includes the majority of American Negroes—who, without economic or political power to protect themselves, have been the victims of discrimination, economic exploitation, and brutality. Having automatically included these groups under those aided by the welfare state, intellectuals have overlooked the violence that still meets the efforts of the really dispossessed to organize themselves. With a perspective regarding the Negro and his suffering as somehow peripheral to the main issues of American society, it is not surprising that Negro intellectuals have responded with the themes of *Invisible Man* and *Nobody Knows My Name*.

Since it indirectly raises the question of violence, the Negro movement challenges not only the intellectuals' analysis but their moral commitments. As we have seen, the chronic instability of European governments and their succumbing to totalitarian revolutions impressed intellectuals with the benefits of social order. In their view, revolution was not only linked with despotism, but was unproductive of social gains. Peter Viereck expressed the "new conservative" mood: "He who irresponsibly incites some minor abuse within a good tradition, may bring the whole house crashing down on his head and find himself back in the jungle—or its ethical equivalent, the police-state." American Negroes, however, find it difficult to call their treatment in our society "a minor abuse"; for them our tradition inevitably remains deeply flawed. So when the Negro movement claims that racial justice is *the* issue in American life, it is not only challenging intellectuals' priorities but offering a completely different perspective.

No concept of the intellectuals has reached a wider audience than the idea of a neutral framework of "law and order" to which all, as parties to the continuing American consensus, must adhere. In the demagogic atmosphere of McCarthyism, and today with Southern resistance to desegregation, the concept is still useful. But in respect to the Negro movement, "law and order" long ago lost its clarity. In the first place, although the Negro movement may have been forced outside the institutional structure to accomplish its purposes, as Loren Miller, a prominent Negro attorney, has pointed out, "the Negro is outraged at being called an extremist. Since he takes the position that the Constitution confers complete equality on all citizens, he must rest his case on the proposition that there is only one side: his side, the constitutional side." In the North, Negro demands do not challenge the laws but rather (as in demonstrations before construction sites) are on behalf of stricter enforcement of existing antidiscrimination statutes. In the South, most of the laws in this field are *ipso facto* discriminatory, and unconstitutional; if both sides had "obeyed" the law, there would have been no integration movement. And in the South, violence and disobedience are embodied in the institutions themselves: the Negro cannot forget that when he violates a local trespassing ordinance he is mowed down by fire hoses, that when the Governor of Alabama defies federal court orders he runs for President.

It is not clear that "law" is synonymous with "order." The plain fact, perceived mainly by right-wing extremists, is that the Supreme Court (in its desegregation, reapportionment, and criminal procedure cases) is the greatest instrument of social change in America. If the Court is interpreting the Constitution correctly (and most intellectuals undoubtedly believe it is), then they are faced with the question of why, in a democratic society with a "balance" of interest groups, it is the courts that have to equalize suffrage and abolish discrimination. In attempting to explain the origins of the Radical Right, intellectuals have tended to ignore the significance of these changes in our legal institutions. Unlike their successors, nineteenth-century conservatives had no need to attack either courts or law enforcement agencies: both performed their duties admirably in the Pullman strike of 1894. Today, faced with a greatly changed judicial and administrative outlook, those who would defend the status quo roundly denounce the Supreme Court and the Department of Justice. Conservatives today, in other words, far from being "pseudo" conservative in challenging governmental authority, are behaving in a typically American fashion, once they are cornered, and fighting with every means at their disposal.

The possibility that widespread violence will result from opposition to civil rights reaches the foundations of our democratic society. In the Deep South the ugly face of violence has already appeared this summer in opposition to voter registration drives. Today America cannot say, as it did in 1877, "Let the South handle its own problems," for Mississippi Negroes are as surely Southerners as Mississippi whites, and *they* are demanding justice. But in spite of the progress in the border states and the liberalism of Atlanta, the Deep South still says "never." Every state may have accepted desegregated education in principle, but ten years after the 1954 Court decision only 1.18 per cent of Negroes in the states of the Old Confederacy were in desegregated schools. After Little Rock in 1957, after Oxford in 1962, and after Birmingham and Tuscaloosa in 1963, Southern liberals predicted that extremism was making a last-ditch stand. Not only does it continue; its advocates are stumping the North. And the nomination of Senator Goldwater has made too many Southerners regard racial justice as no longer "inevitable." Will any civil rights legislation ever be accepted peacefully in the Alabama of George Wallace, the Louisiana of Leander Perez, or the Mississippi of Ross Barnett? Would a second military reconstruction accomplish any more than the first? Or do we have to wait for a change of heart on the part of the Deep South majority? White Americans seem never to have decided whether the liberation of four million slaves was worth the death of six hundred thousand white men in the Civil War. It is at least worth asking again to what degree "social order" and the protection of civil rights are reconcilable, and whether acquiescence in oppression is necessary for the continuation of a "free" society.

It has been my contention here that contemporary American intellectuals, in their interpretation of American society as one of "consensus" and "balance," have necessarily left the Negro out of their considerations. But the relationship of the Negro to their general interpretations would remain an academic matter, were it not for the demands of the Negro movement. Those demands not only challenge the intellectuals' analysis but the values implicit in it, and present the intellectuals with a dilemma. Most intellectuals sincerely regard themselves as sympathetic to the Negro cause: they have attacked biased interpretations of earlier scholars, and have taken the lead in supporting governmental efforts to secure civil rights. But their theories are now leading in an antiliberal direction. Insofar as they have reinforced their public's devotion to order, they have aided militant white racists in the South, who by standing firm can establish the terms of the conflict, and vacillating administrators in the North. By attacking those earlier movements in American history sympathetic to the Negro—Abolitionism, Reconstruction, the Populists—they undercut the moral authority of today's Negro movement. Insofar as they have portrayed America as an orderly society, with a high degree of equality and pluralism, they have made the Negro's task of articulating his aims to the educated public more difficult. A Negro writer, John Oliver Killens, has written, "The Negro loves America enough to criticize her fundamentally. Most of white America can't be bothered." Unless intellectuals themselves begin such a fundamental criticism, by re-evaluating their present interpretations, their public, faced with increasingly "revolutionary" demands, will regard the Negro movement as challenging everything "American." In such a conflict that common commitment to American ideals which her Negroes, her white public, and her intellectuals still share will surely be destroyed.

PART II

PROBLEMS IN WRITING

NEGRO HISTORY

The Nature
of the Evidence

This section contains two selections which illustrate various problems of sources in the writing of Negro history. Both articles concern the Negro in slavery; one deals with seventeenth-century origins and the other with nineteenth-century resistance. For the period before the Civil War, the sources are most scanty and the evidence is quite often inferential, particularly when it involves slavery. Legal records, the standby of many historians, prove unsatisfactory because of either their lack of conclusiveness or their omissions. Forbidden by law to testify in cases not involving other slaves, the bond servant is a shadowy figure in court cases. Lacking means of communication and denied those of the power structure, the slave remains mainly inarticulate in the written records.

Winthrop D. Jordan discusses two questions that have aroused considerable interest in historical circles. The first concerns the origin of slavery in Virginia: Were the first Negroes slaves or indentured servants? The second explores the relationship between slavery and prejudice: Were Negroes considered inferior because they were slaves or were they slaves because they were considered inferior? Reviewing briefly the historiography of the case, Jordan concludes that there is insufficient evidence to derive an unequivocal answer to these questions. Despite the failure to provide answers, Jordan's article shows how contemporary pressures affect historians looking at the past and how one view of the past can have greater utility than another. If slavery did create prejudice that had no prior existence, then the burial of slavery ought also to be the burial of prejudice. If slavery is a product of prejudice, the question of the origin of prejudice remains unanswered. Jordan's article offers an excellent example of the continuing revision that is the task of the historian as he works his way toward a closer approximation of historical truth.

Richard C. Wade's article shows that documentary evidence may be misleading. Wade, a student of cities and slavery, and author, among other works, of Slavery in the Cities, (1964), makes a very strong case for the view that the Vesey plot was largely a product of the tensions of South Carolina society in the 1820's. He casts doubt on the reliability of the testimony of witnesses and points to the lack of hard evidence of guilt. The fact that Vesey and others were executed, and the report that grandiose plans were purportedly made, have convinced many students that Vesey was indeed about to spark a massive uprising. If Wade is correct, surely there is an ironic humor—if any humor can be derived from human misery—in the utilization of Vesey's story. The original purpose of showing the white citizens of South Carolina the danger hidden in both free and enslaved Negroes has faded into the dim historic past. The story is now used to show Negro citizens of the United States Vesey's resistance to an oppressive society. But beyond this irony is the dilemma of achieving historical knowledge. How can the historian go behind the words of witnesses to discover their intent? In a sophisticated way, Wade attempts to understand the pressures of the system upon those individuals involved in the trial and tries to trace the logic of the final verdict. The selection demonstrates the hazards of conventional knowledge and points out the possible exceptions to it.

Both Jordan and Wade consider extreme cases, and extreme cases make bad law. Other problems in Negro history have more reliable sources, and the solutions to these problems seem much more clear-cut. But the demurrers of Jordan and Wade ought to serve as a warning to those who believe that earlier historical judgments need not be reexamined, and that historians are value free.

MODERN TENSIONS AND THE
ORIGINS OF AMERICAN SLAVERY

Winthrop D. Jordan

Thanks to John Smith we know that Negroes came to the British continental colonies in 1619.[1] What we do not know is exactly when Negroes were first enslaved there. This question has been debated by historians for the past seventy years, the critical point being whether Negroes were enslaved almost from their first importation or whether they were at first simply servants and only later reduced to the status of slaves. The long duration and vigor of the controversy suggest that more than a simple question of dating has been involved. In fact certain current tensions in American society have complicated the historical problem and greatly heightened its significance. Dating the origins of slavery has taken on a striking modern relevance.

During the nineteenth century historians assumed almost universally that the first Negroes came to Virginia as slaves. So close was their acquaintance with the problem of racial slavery that it did not occur to them that Negroes could ever have been anything but slaves. Philip A. Bruce, the first man to probe with some thoroughness into the early years of American slavery, adopted this view in 1896, although he emphasized that the original difference in treatment between white servants and Negroes was merely that Negroes served for life. Just six years later, however, came a challenge from a younger, professionally trained historian, James C. Ballagh. His *A History of Slavery in Virginia* appeared in the "Johns Hopkins University Studies in Historical and Political Science," an aptly named series which was to usher in the new era of

Winthrop D. Jordan, "Modern Tensions and the Origins of American Slavery," *Journal of Southern History*, XXVIII, No. 1 (February, 1962), 18-32.

scholarly detachment in the writing of institutional history. Ballagh offered a new and different interpretation; he took the position that the first Negroes served merely as servants and that enslavement did not begin until around 1660, when statutes bearing on slavery were passed for the first time.[2]

There has since been agreement on dating the statutory establishment of slavery, and differences of opinion have centered on when enslavement began in actual practice. Fortunately there has also been general agreement on slavery's distinguishing characteristics: service for life and inheritance of like obligation by any offspring. Writing on the free Negro in Virginia for the Johns Hopkins series, John H. Russell in 1913 tackled the central question and showed that some Negroes were indeed servants but concluded that "between 1640 and 1660 slavery was fast becoming an established fact. In this twenty years the colored population was divided, part being servants and part being slaves, and some who were servants defended themselves with increasing difficulty from the encroachments of slavery."[3] Ulrich B. Phillips, though little interested in the matter, in 1918 accepted Russell's conclusion of early servitude and transition toward slavery after 1640. Helen T. Catterall took much the same position in 1926. On the other hand, in 1921 James M. Wright, discussing the free Negro in Maryland, implied that Negroes were slaves almost from the beginning, and in 1940 Susie M. Ames reviewed several cases in Virginia which seemed to indicate that genuine slavery had existed well before Ballagh's date of 1660.[4]

All this was a very small academic gale, well insulated from the outside world. Yet despite disagreement on dating enslavement, the earlier writers—Bruce, Ballagh, and Russell—shared a common assumption which, though at the time seemingly irrelevant to the main question, has since proved of considerable importance. They assumed that prejudice against the Negro was natural and almost innate in the white man. It would be surprising if they had felt otherwise in this period of segregation statutes, overseas imperialism, immigration restriction, and full-throated Anglo-Saxonism. By the 1920's, however, with the easing of these tensions, the assumption of natural prejudice was dropped unnoticed. Yet only one historian explicitly contradicted that assumption: Ulrich Phillips of Georgia, impressed with the geniality of both slavery and twentieth-century race relations, found no natural prejudice in the white man and expressed his "conviction that Southern racial asperities are mainly superficial, and that the two great elements are fundamentally in accord."[5]

Only when tensions over race relations intensified once more did the older assumption of natural prejudice crop up again. After World War II

American Negroes found themselves beneficiaries of New Deal politics and reforms, wartime need for manpower, world-wide repulsion at racist excesses in Nazi Germany, and growingly successful colored anticolonialism. With new militancy Negroes mounted an attack on the citadel of separate but equal, and soon it became clear that America was in for a period of self-conscious reappraisal of its racial arrangements. Writing in this period of heightened tension (1949) a practiced and careful scholar, Wesley F. Craven, raised the old question of the Negro's original status, suggesting that Negroes had been enslaved at an early date. Craven also cautiously resuscitated the idea that white men may have had natural distaste for the Negro, an idea which fitted neatly with the suggestion of early enslavement. Original antipathy would mean rapid debasement.[6]

In the next year (1950) came a sophisticated counterstatement, which contradicted both Craven's dating and implicitly any suggestion of early prejudice. Oscar and Mary F. Handlin in "Origins of the Southern Labor System" offered a case for late enslavement, with servitude as the status of Negroes before about 1660. Originally the status of both Negroes and white servants was far short of freedom, the Handlins maintained, but Negroes failed to benefit from increased freedom for servants in mid-century and became less free rather than more.[7] Embedded in this description of diverging status were broader implications: Late and gradual enslavement undercut the possibility of natural, deep-seated antipathy toward Negroes. On the contrary, if whites and Negroes could share the same status of half freedom for forty years in the seventeenth century, why could they not share full freedom in the twentieth?

The same implications were rendered more explicit by Kenneth M. Stampp in a major reassessment of Southern slavery published two years after the Supreme Court's 1954 school decision. Reading physiology with the eye of faith, Stampp frankly stated his assumption "that innately Negroes *are*, after all, only white men with black skins, nothing more, nothing less."[8] Closely following the Handlins' article on the origins of slavery itself, he almost directly denied any pattern of early and inherent racial antipathy: ". . . Negro and white servants of the seventeenth century seemed to be remarkably unconcerned about their visible physical differences." As for "the trend toward special treatment" of the Negro, "physical and cultural differences provided handy excuses to justify it."[9] Distaste for the Negro, then, was in the beginning scarcely more than an appurtenance of slavery.

These views squared nicely with the hopes of those even more directly concerned with the problem of contemporary race relations, sociologists and social psychologists. Liberal on the race question almost to a man, they tended to see slavery as the initial cause of the Negro's current degradation. The modern Negro was the unhappy victim of long association with base status. Sociologists, though uninterested in tired questions of historical evidence, could not easily assume a natural prejudice in the white man as the cause of slavery. Natural or innate prejudice would not only violate their basic assumptions concerning the dominance of culture but would undermine the power of their new Baconian science. For if prejudice was natural there would be little one could do to wipe it out. Prejudice must have followed enslavement, not vice versa, else any liberal program of action would be badly compromised. One prominent social scientist suggested in a UNESCO pamphlet that racial prejudice in the United States commenced with the cotton gin.[10]

Just how closely the question of dating had become tied to the practical matter of action against racial prejudice was made apparent by the suggestions of still another historian. Carl N. Degler grappled with the dating problem in an article frankly entitled "Slavery and the Genesis of American Race Prejudice." [11] The article appeared in 1959, a time when Southern resistance to school desegregation seemed more adamant than ever and the North's hands none too clean, a period of discouragement for those hoping to end racial discrimination. Prejudice against the Negro now appeared firm and deep-seated, less easily eradicated than had been supposed in, say, 1954. It was Degler's view that enslavement began early, as a result of white settlers' prejudice or antipathy toward the first Negroes. Thus not only were the sociologists contradicted but the dating problem was now overtly and consciously tied to the broader question of whether slavery caused prejudice or prejudice caused slavery. A new self-consciousness over the American racial dilemma had snatched an arid historical controversy from the hands of an unsuspecting earlier generation and tossed it into the arena of current debate.

Ironically there might have been no historical controversy at all if every historian dealing with the subject had exercised greater care with facts and greater restraint in interpretation. Too often the debate entered the realm of inference and assumption. For the crucial early years after 1619 there is simply not enough evidence to indicate with any certainty whether Negroes were treated like white servants or not. No historian has found anything resembling proof one way or the other. The first Negroes were sold to the English settlers, yet so were other Englishmen. It can be said, however, that Negroes were set apart from white men by the word *Negroes,* and a distinct name is not attached to a group unless it is seen as different. The earliest Virginia census reports plainly distinguished Negroes from white men, sometimes giving Negroes

no personal name; and in 1629 every commander of the several plantations was ordered to "take a generall muster of all the inhabitants men
woemen and Children as well Englishe as Negroes." [12] Difference, however, might or might not involve inferiority.

The first evidence as to the actual status of Negroes does not appear
until about 1640. Then it becomes clear that *some* Negroes were serving
for life and some children inheriting the same obligation. Here it is
necessary to suggest with some candor that the Handlins' statement to
the contrary rests on unsatisfactory documentation.[13] That some Negroes
were held as slaves after about 1640 is no indication, however, that
American slavery popped into the world fully developed at that time.
Many historians, most cogently the Handlins, have shown slavery to
have been a gradual development, a process not completed until the
eighteenth century. The complete deprivation of civil and personal rights,
the legal conversion of the Negro into a chattel, in short slavery as
Americans came to know it, was not accomplished overnight. Yet these
developments practically and logically depended on the practice of
hereditary lifetime service, and it is certainly possible to find in the
1640's and 1650's traces of slavery's most essential feature.[14]

The first definite trace appears in 1640 when the Virginia General
Court pronounced sentence on three servants who had been retaken
after running away to Maryland. Two of them, a Dutchman and a Scot,
were ordered to serve their masters for one additional year and then the
colony for three more, but "the third being a negro named John Punch
shall serve his said master or his assigns for the time of his natural
life here or else where." No white servant in America, so far as known,
ever received a like sentence.[15] Later the same month a Negro was again
singled out from a group of recaptured runaways; six of the seven were
assigned additional time while the Negro was given none, presumably
because he was already serving for life.[16] After 1640, too, county court
records began to mention Negroes, in part because there were more of
them than previously—about 2 per cent of the Virginia population in
1649.[17] Sales for life, often including any future progeny, were recorded
in unmistakable language. In 1646 Francis Pott sold a Negro woman and
boy to Stephen Charlton "to the use of him . . . forever." Similarly, six
years later William Whittington sold to John Pott "one Negro girle
named Jowan; aged about Ten yeares and her Issue and produce duringe
her (or either of them) for their Life tyme. And their Successors forever"; and a Maryland man in 1649 deeded two Negro men and a
woman "and all their issue both male and Female." The executors of a
York County estate in 1647 disposed of eight Negroes—four men, two
women, and two children—to Captain John Chisman "to have hold

occupy posesse and inioy and every one of the afforementioned Negroes forever(.)" [18] The will of Rowland Burnham of "Rapahanocke," made in 1657, dispensed his considerable number of Negroes and white servants in language which clearly differentiated between the two by specifying that the whites were to serve for their "full terme of tyme" and the Negroes "for ever." [19] Nor did anything in the will indicate that this distinction was exceptional or novel.

In addition to these clear indications that some Negroes were owned for life, there were cases of Negroes held for terms far longer than the normal five or seven years.[20] On the other hand, some Negroes served only the term usual for white servants, and others were completely free.[21] One Negro freeman, Anthony Johnson, himself owned a Negro.[22] Obviously the enslavement of some Negroes did not mean the immediate enslavement of all.

Further evidence of Negroes serving for life lies in the prices paid for them. In many instances the valuations placed on Negroes (in estate inventories and bills of sale) were far higher than for white servants, even those servants with full terms yet to serve. Since there was ordinarily no preference for Negroes as such, higher prices must have meant that Negroes were more highly valued because of their greater length of service. Negro women may have been especially prized, moreover, because their progeny could also be held perpetually. In 1645, for example, two Negro women and a boy were sold for fifty-five hundred pounds of tobacco. Two years earlier William Burdett's inventory listed eight servants (with the time each had still to serve) at valuations ranging from four hundred to eleven hundred pounds, while a "very anntient" Negro was valued at three thousand and an eight-year-old Negro girl at two thousand pounds, with no time-remaining indicated for either. In the late 1650's an inventory of Thomas Ludlow's large estate evaluated a white servant with six years to serve at less than an elderly Negro man and only one-half of a Negro woman.[23] The labor owned by James Stone in 1648 was evaluated as follows:

	lb tobo
Thomas Groves, 4 yeares to serve	1300
Francis Bomley for 6 yeares	1500
John Thackstone for 3 yeares	1300
Susan Davis for 3 yeares	1000
Emaniell a Negro man	2000
Roger Stone 3 yeares	1300
Mingo a Negro man	2000 [24]

Besides setting a higher value on the two Negroes, Stone's inventory, like Burdett's, failed to indicate the number of years they had still to serve. It would seem safe to assume that the time remaining was omitted in this and similar documents simply because the Negroes were regarded as serving for an unlimited time.

The situation in Maryland was apparently the same. In 1643 Governor Leonard Calvert agreed with John Skinner, "mariner," to exchange certain estates for seventeen sound Negro "slaves," fourteen men and three women between sixteen and twenty-six years old. The total value of these was placed at twenty-four thousand pounds of tobacco, which would work out to one thousand pounds for the women and fifteen hundred for the men, prices considerably higher than those paid for white servants at the time.[25]

Wherever Negro women were involved, however, higher valuations may have reflected the fact that they could be used for field work while white women generally were not. This discrimination between Negro and white women, of course, fell short of actual enslavement. It meant merely that Negroes were set apart in a way clearly not to their advantage. Yet this is not the only evidence that Negroes were subjected to degrading distinctions not directly related to slavery. In several ways Negroes were singled out for special treatment which suggested a generalized debasing of Negroes as a group. Significantly, the first indications of debasement appeared at about the same time as the first indications of actual enslavement.

The distinction concerning field work is a case in point. It first appeared in the written record in 1643, when Virginia pointedly recognized it in her taxation policy. Previously tithable persons had been defined (1629) as "all those that worke in the ground of what qualitie or condition soever." Now the law stated that all adult men and *Negro* women were to be tithable, and this distinction was made twice again before 1660. Maryland followed a similar course, beginning in 1654.[26] John Hammond, in a 1656 tract defending the tobacco colonies, wrote that servant women were not put to work in the fields but in domestic employments, "yet som wenches that are nasty, and beastly and not fit to be so imployed are put into the ground." [27] Since all Negro women were taxed as working in the fields, it would seem logical to conclude that Virginians found them "nasty" and "beastly." The essentially racial nature of this discrimination was bared by a 1668 law at the time slavery was crystallizing on the statute books: "Whereas some doubts, have arisen whether negro women set free were still to be accompted tithable according to a former act, *It is declared by this grand assembly* that negro women, though permitted to enjoy their ffreedome yet ought not in all respects to be admitted to a full fruition of the exemptions and impunities of the English, and are still lyable to payment of taxes." [28]

Virginia law set Negroes apart in a second way by denying them the important right and obligation to bear arms. Few restraints could indicate more clearly the denial to Negroes of membership in the white community. This action, in a sense the first foreshadowing of the slave codes, came in 1640, at just the time when other indications first appear that Negroes were subject to special treatment.[29]

Finally, an even more compelling sense of the separateness of Negroes was revealed in early distress concerning sexual union between the races. In 1630 a Virginia court pronounced a now famous sentence: "Hugh Davis to be soundly whipped, before an assembly of Negroes and others for abusing himself to the dishonor of God and shame of Christians, by defiling his body in lying with a negro." [30] While there were other instances of punishment for interracial union in the ensuing years, fornication rather than miscegenation may well have been the primary offense, though in 1651 a Maryland man sued someone who he claimed had said "'that he had a black bastard in Virginia." [31] There may have been nothing racial about the 1640 case by which Robert Sweet was compelled "to do penance in Church according to laws of England, for getting a negroe woman with child and the woman whipt." [32] About 1650 a white man and a Negro woman were required to stand clad in white sheets before a congregation in Lower Norfolk County for having had relations, but this punishment was sometimes used in ordinary cases of fornication between two whites.[33]

It is certain, however, that in the early 1660's when slavery was gaining statutory recognition, the colonial assemblies legislated with feeling against miscegenation. Nor was this merely a matter of avoiding confusion of status, as was suggested by the Handlins. In 1662 Virginia declared that "if any christian shall committ ffornication with a negro man or woman, hee or shee soe offending" should pay double the usual fine. Two years later Maryland prohibited interracial marriages: ". . . forasmuch as divers freeborne English women forgettfull of their free Condicon and to the disgrace of our Nation doe intermarry with Negro Slaves by which alsoe divers suites may arise touching the Issue of such woemen and a great damage doth befall the Masters of such Negros for prevention whereof for deterring such freeborne women from such shamefull Matches. . . ," strong language indeed if the problem had only been confusion of status. A Maryland act of 1681 described marriages of white women with Negroes as, among other things, "always to the Satisfaccon of theire Lascivious & Lustfull desires, & to the disgrace not only of the English butt allso of many other Christian Nations." When Virginia finally prohibited all interracial liaisons in 1691, the assembly vigorously denounced miscegenation and its fruits as "that abominable mixture and spurious issue." [34]

One is confronted, then, with the fact that the first evidences of enslavement and of other forms of debasement appeared at about the same time. Such coincidence comports poorly with both views on the causation of prejudice and slavery. If slavery caused prejudice, then invidious distinctions concerning working in the fields, bearing arms, and sexual union should have appeared only after slavery's firm establishment. If prejudice caused slavery, then one would expect to find such lesser discriminations preceding the greater discrimination of outright enslavement.

Perhaps a third explanation of the relationship between slavery and prejudice may be offered, one that might fit the pattern of events as revealed by existing evidence. Both current views share a common starting point: they predicate two factors, prejudice and slavery, and demand a distinct order of causality. No matter how qualified by recognition that the effect may in turn react upon the cause, each approach inevitably tends to deny the validity of its opposite. But what if one were to regard both slavery and prejudice as species of a general debasement of the Negro? Both may have been equally cause and effect, constantly reacting upon each other, dynamically joining hands to hustle the Negro down the road to complete degradation. Mutual causation is, of course, a highly useful concept for describing social situations in the modern world.[35] Indeed it has been widely applied in only slightly altered fashion to the current racial situation: racial prejudice and the Negro's lowly position are widely accepted as constantly reinforcing each other.

This way of looking at the facts might well fit better with what we know of slavery itself. Slavery was an organized pattern of human relationships. No matter what the law might say, it was of different character than cattle ownership. No matter how degrading, slavery involved human beings. No one seriously pretended otherwise. Slavery was not an isolated economic or institutional phenomenon; it was the practical facet of a general debasement without which slavery could have no rationality. (Prejudice, too, was a form of debasement, a kind of slavery in the mind.) Certainly the urgent need for labor in a virgin country guided the direction which debasement took, molded it, in fact, into an institutional framework. That economic practicalities shaped the external form of debasement should not tempt one to forget, however, that slavery was at bottom a social arrangement, a way of society's ordering its members in its own mind.

NOTES

1. "About the last of August came in a dutch man of warre that sold us twenty Negars." Smith was quoting John Rolfe's account. Edward Arber and A. G. Bradley (eds.), *Travels and Works of Captain John Smith* . . . (2 vols.; Edinburgh, 1910), II, 541.

2. Philip A. Bruce, *Economic History of Virginia in the Seventeenth Century* (2 vols.; New York, 1896), II, 57-130; James C. Ballagh, *A History of Slavery in Virginia* (Baltimore, 1902), pp. 28-35.

3. *The Free Negro in Virginia, 1619-1865* (Baltimore, 1913), p. 29.

4. *Ibid.*, pp. 23-39; Ulrich B. Phillips, *American Negro Slavery* (New York, 1918), pp. 75-77, and *Life and Labor in the Old South* (Boston, 1929), p. 170; Helen T. Catterall (ed.), *Judicial Cases Concerning American Slavery and the Negro* (5 vols.; Washington, 1926-1937), I, 54-55, 57-63; James M. Wright, *The Free Negro in Maryland, 1634-1860* (New York, 1921), pp. 21-23; Susie M. Ames, *Studies of the Virginia Eastern Shore in the Seventeenth Century* (Richmond, 1940), pp. 100-106. See also T. R. Davis, "Negro Servitude in the United States," *Journal of Negro History,* VIII (July, 1923), 247-283, and Edgar T. Thompson, "The Natural History of Agricultural Labor in the South" in David K. Jackson (ed.), *American Studies in Honor of William Kenneth Boyd* (Durham, N.C., 1940), pp. 127-146.

5. Phillips, *American Negro Slavery,* p. viii.

6. Wesley F. Craven, *The Southern Colonies in the Seventeenth Century, 1607-1689* (Baton Rouge, 1949), pp. 217-219, 402-403.

7. *William and Mary Quarterly,* ser. 3, VII (April, 1950), 199-222.

8. Kenneth M. Stampp, *The Peculiar Institution: Slavery in the Ante-Bellum South* (New York, 1956), pp. vii-viii, 3-33.

9. *Ibid.*, pp. 21-22.

10. Arnold Rose, "The Roots of Prejudice" in UNESCO, *The Race Question in Modern Science* (New York, 1956), p. 224. For examples of the more general view see Frederick G. Detweiler, "The Rise of Modern Race Antagonisms," *American Journal of Sociology,* XXXVII (March, 1932), 743; M. F. Ashley Montagu, *Man's Most Dangerous Myth: The Fallacy of Race* (New York, 1945), pp. 10-11, 19-20; Gunnar Myrdal, *An American Dilemma: The Negro Problem and Modern Democracy* (New York, 1944), pp. 83-89, 97; Paul Kecskemeti, "The Psychological Theory of Prejudice; Does It Underrate the Role of Social History?" *Commentary,* XVIII (October, 1954), 364-366.

11. *Comparative Studies in Society and History,* II (October, 1959), 49-66. See also Degler, *Out of Our Past: The Forces That Shaped Modern America* (New York, 1959), pp. 26-39.

12. H. R. McIlwaine (ed.), *Minutes of the Council and General Court of Colonial Virginia, 1622-1632, 1670-1676* (Richmond, 1924), p. 196. See the lists and musters of 1624 and 1625 in John C. Hotten (ed.), *The Original Lists of Persons of Quality* . . . (New York, 1880), pp. 169-265.

13. "The status of Negroes was that of servants; and so they were identified and treated down to the 1660's." ("Origins," p. 203.) The footnote to this statement reads, "For disciplinary and revenue laws in Virginia that did not discriminate Negroes from other servants, see Hening, *Statutes*, I (1631-1645), 174, 198, 200, 243, 306." But pp. 200 and 243 of William Waller Hening (ed.), *The Statutes at Large; Being a Collection of All the Laws of Virginia* . . . (2nd ed. of vols. I-IV; New York, 1823), I, in fact contain nothing about either servants or Negroes, while a tax provision on p. 242 specifically discriminates against Negro women. The revenue act on p. 306 lists the number of pounds of tobacco levied on land, cattle, sheep, horses, etc., and on tithable persons, and provides for collection of lists of the above so that the colony can compute its tax program; nothing else is said of servants and tithables. To say, as the Handlins did in the same note, that Negroes, English servants, and horses, etc., were listed all together in some early Virginia wills, with the implication that Negroes and English servants were regarded as alike in status, is hardly correct unless one is to assume that the horses were sharing this status as well. (For complete bibliographical information on Hening [ed.], *Statutes*, see E. G. Swem, *Virginia Historical Index* [2 vols.; Roanoke, Va., 1934-1936], I, xv-xvi.)

14. Latin-American Negroes did not lose all civil and personal rights, did not become mere chattels, yet we speak of "slavery" in Latin America without hesitation. See Frank Tannenbaum, *Slave and Citizen: The Negro in the Americas* (New York, 1947), and Gilberto Freyre, *The Masters and the Slaves: A Study in the Development of Brazilian Civilization* (New York, 1946).

15. "Decisions of the General Court," *Virginia Magazine of History and Biography*, V (January, 1898), 236. Abbot Emerson Smith in the standard work on servitude in America, *Colonists in Bondage: White Servitude and Convict Labor in America, 1607-1776* (Chapel Hill, 1947), p. 171, says that "there was never any such thing as perpetual slavery for any white man in any English colony." There were instances in the seventeenth century of white men sold into "slavery," but this was when the meaning of the term was still indefinite and often equated with servitude.

16. "Decisions of the General Court," pp. 236-237.

17. *A Perfect Description of Virginia* . . . (London, 1649), reprinted in Peter Force (ed.), *Tracts* . . . (4 vols.; Washington, 1836-1846), II.

18. These four cases may be found in Northampton County Deeds, Wills & c. (Virginia State Library, Richmond), No. 4 (1651-1654), pp. 28 (misnumbered 29), p. 124; *Archives of Maryland* (69 vols.; Baltimore, 1883-1961), XLI, 261-262; York County Records (Virginia State Library), No. 2 (Transcribed Wills & Deeds, 1645-1649), pp. 256-257.

19. Lancaster County Loose Papers (Virginia State Library), Box of Wills, 1650-1719, Folder 1656-1659.

20. For examples running for as long as thirty-five years, see *William and Mary Quarterly*, ser. 1, XX (October, 1911), 148; Russell, *Free Negro in Virginia*, pp. 26-27; Ames, *Eastern Shore*, p. 105. Compare the cases of a Negro and an Irish servant in *Calendar of Virginia State Papers* . . . (11 vols.; Richmond, 1875-1893), I, 9-10, and *Maryland Archives*, XLI, 476-478; XLIX, 123-124.

21. Russell, *Free Negro in Virginia*, pp. 24-41. See especially the cases in *Virginia Magazine of History and Biography*, V (July, 1897), 40; York County Deeds, Wills, Orders, etc. (Virginia State Library), No. 1 (1653-1657, 1691-1694), pp. 338-339.

22. John H. Russell, "Colored Freemen As Slave Owners in Virginia," *Journal of Negro History*, I (July, 1916), 234-237.

23. York County Records, No. 2, p. 63; Northampton County Orders, Deeds, Wills, &c., No. 2 (1640-1645), p. 224; York County Deeds, Orders, Wills, &c. (1657-1662), pp. 108-109.

24. York County Records, No. 2, p. 390.

25. Apparently Calvert's deal with Skinner was never consummated. *Maryland Archives*, IV, vii, 189, 320-321. For prices of white servants see *ibid.*, pp. 31, 47-48, 74, 78-79, 81, 83, 92, 98, 108-109, 184, 200, 319.

26. Hening (ed.), *Statutes*, I, 144, 242, 292, 454. The Handlins erroneously placed the "first sign of discrimination" in the matter in 1668 ("Origins," p. 217n). For Maryland, see *Maryland Archives*, I, 342; II, 136, 399, 538-539; XIII, 538-539.

27. John Hammond, *Leah and Rachel, or, the Two Fruitfull Sisters Virginia, and Maryland: Their Present Condition, Impartially Stated and Related* . . . (London, 1656), reprinted in Force (ed.), *Tracts*, II.

28. Hening (ed.), *Statutes*, II, 267. The distinction between white and colored women was neatly described at the turn of the century by Robert Beverley, *The History and Present State of Virginia*, ed. Louis B. Wright (Chapel Hill, 1947), pp. 271-272.

29. Hening (ed.), *Statutes*, I, 226, and for the same act in more detail see *William and Mary Quarterly*, ser. 2, IV (July, 1924), 147. The Handlins discounted this law: "Until the 1660's the statutes on the Negroes were not at all unique. Nor did they add up to a decided trend." ("Origins," p. 209.) The note added to this statement reads, "That there was no trend is evident from the fluctuations in naming Negroes slaves or servants and in their right to bear arms. See Hening, *Statutes*, I, 226, 258, 292, 540; Bruce, *Institutional History*, II, 5ff., 109ff. For similar fluctuations with regard to Indians, see Hening, *Statutes*, I, 391, 518." But since the terms "servants" and "slaves" did not have precise meaning, as the Handlins themselves asserted, fluctuations in naming Negroes one or the other cannot be taken to mean that their status itself was fluctuating. Of the pages cited in Hening, p. 258 is an act encouraging Dutch traders and contains nothing about Negroes, servants, slaves, or arms. Page 292 is an act providing that fifteen tithable persons should support one soldier; Negroes were among those tithable, but nothing was said of allowing them to arm. Page 540 refers to "any negro

slaves" and "said negro," but mentions nothing about servants or arms. In the pages dealing with Indians, p. 391 provides that no one is to employ Indian servants with guns, and p. 518 that Indians (not "Indian servants") are to be allowed to use their own guns; the two provisions are not contradictory. Philip A. Bruce, *Institutional History of Virginia in the Seventeenth Century* (2 vols.; New York, 1910), II, 5 ff., indicates that Negroes were barred from arming in 1639 and offers no suggestion that there was any later fluctuation in this practice.

30. Hening (ed.), *Statutes,* I, 146. "Christianity" appears instead of "Christians" in McIlwaine (ed.), *Minutes of the Council,* p. 479.

31. *Maryland Archives,* X, 114-115.

23. Hening (ed.), *Statutes,* I, 552; McIlwaine, *Minutes of the Council,* p. 477.

33. Bruce, *Economic History of Virginia,* II, 110.

34. Hening (ed.), *Statutes,* II, 170; III, 86-87; *Maryland Archives,* I, 533-534; VII, 204. Opinion on this matter apparently was not unanimous, for a petition of several citizens to the Council in 1699 asked repeal of the inter-marriage prohibition. See H. R. McIlwaine (ed.), *Legislative Journals of the Council of Colonial Virginia* (3 vols., Richmond, 1918-1919), I, 262. The Handlins wrote ("Origins," p. 215), "Mixed marriages of free men and servants were particularly frowned upon as complicating status and therefore limited by law." Their citation for this, Hening (ed.), *Statutes,* II (1661-62), 114, and Marcus W. Jernegan, *Laboring and Dependent Classes in Colonial America, 1607-1783* (Chicago, 1931), pp. 55, 180, gives little backing to the statement. In Virginia secret marriages or bastardy between whites of different status got the same punishment as such between whites of the same status. A white servant might marry any white if his master consented. See Hening (ed.), *Statutes,* I, 252-253, 438-439; II, 114-115, 167; III, 71-75, 137-140. See also James C. Ballagh, *White Servitude in the Colony of Virginia* (Baltimore, 1895), p. 50. For Maryland, see *Maryland Archives,* I, 73, 373-374, 441-442; II, 396-397; XIII, 501-502. The Handlins also suggested that in the 1691 Virginia law, "spurious" meant simply "illegitimate," and they cited Arthur W. Calhoun, *A Social History of the American Family from Colonial Times to the Present* (3 vols.; Cleveland, Ohio, 1917-1919), I, 42, which turns out to be one quotation from John Milton. However, "spurious" was used in colonial laws with reference only to unions between white and black, and never in bastardy laws involving whites only. Mulattoes were often labeled "spurious" offspring.

35. For example, George C. Homans, *The Human Group* (New York, 1950).

THE VESEY PLOT:

A RECONSIDERATION

Richard C. Wade

On May 25, 1822, two slaves stood alongside the fish wharf in Charleston harbor chatting idly about the ships that lay at anchor nearby. William Paul asked Devany Prioleau if he knew that "something serious is about to take place." Then, more precisely, he said that "many of us are determined to right ourselves" and "shake off our bondage." Devany had not heard of the plot. "Astonished and horror-struck," he quickly broke off the conversation and hurried away.[1] After a few agitated days he confided the news to a free Negro, George Pencil, and asked what to do. Pencil told him to tell his owner. On May 30 at three o'clock Devany gave the fateful information to Mrs. Prioleau.[2]

Two hours later the mayor of Charleston called the city council into extraordinary session. The police picked up both Devany and William; officials began an intensive inquiry. For a week they kept William in solitary confinement in the "black hole of the Work House," interrogating him every day. Finally he gave them the names of Mingo Harth and Peter Poyas. These Negroes were questioned but disclosed nothing. In fact, they "behaved with so much composure and coolness, and treated the charges . . . with so much levity" that the officials were "completely deceived" and released them both.[3] Later William implicated others, but they too claimed no knowledge. The authorities were further baffled when Ned Bennett, a slave of Governor Thomas Bennett of South Carolina, came in voluntarily to clear himself of suspicion.[4]

Having turned up nothing—but suspicious of everything—the mayor

Richard C. Wade, "The Vesey Plot: A Reconsideration," *Journal of Southern History*, XXX, No. 2 (May, 1964), 143-161.

strengthened his patrols, armed his men for extensive action, and waited. On June 14 the break came. Another slave corroborated William Paul's testimony, disclosing that the uprising originally set for July 2 was now moved up to June 16. For the first time the public knew that danger threatened. A strong guard surrounded the city; the police appeared in force. Still nothing happened. On June 16, ten slaves were arrested; and, two days later, a hastily assembled court of freeholders began hearing secret testimony. On June 21 the police brought in Denmark Vesey. And eleven days later, on July 2, the bodies of Vesey and five other Negroes swung from the gallows at the edge of town.

The uprising now seemed quashed. But, as word of it spread in the city, public shock turned into hysteria. No master could be sure his bondsmen were not involved; whites who owned no slaves had little more assurance. Every Negro became a possible enemy, indeed assassin; every action by a black could be construed as a prelude to violence. Since slaves lived in the same yard with their masters, it was not even possible to lock out the intruder.

As the terror spread, so too did the presumed magnitude of the conspiracy. The letters of Ana Hayes Johnson, daughter of a respected judge and a niece of the governor, describe the fears and rumors that were current. "Their plans were simply these," she wrote late in June: "They were to set fire to the town and while the whites were endeavoring to put it out they were to commence their horrid depredations." Then in more detail: "It seems that the Governor, Intendant [i.e., mayor], and my poor father were to have been the first victims—the men and Black women were to have been indiscriminately murdered—& we poor devils were to have been removed to fill their—Harams—horrible—I have a very beautiful cousin who was set apart for the wife or more properly, the 'light of the Haram' of one of their chiefs." [5]

Panic gripped the colored community, too, after the executions. As more and more blacks disappeared into prison, as rumors widened, and as the newspapers announced new arrests, the alarm deepened. Was someone informing on his neighbor? Had the police picked up so many that some had to be housed in a nearby county? Were white irregulars about to take things into their own hands because the court was too slow? In the awful uncertainty the Negroes found an uneasy unity. Most of those questioned by municipal officials professed no knowledge of any plot; others wore armbands of crepe in mourning for the dead until officials forbade demonstrations of sympathy. [6]

Outwardly, the normal deference to whites increased. "There was a wonderful degree of politeness shown to us," a white recalled, "bows and politeness, and—'give way for the gentlemen and ladies,' met you at every turn and corner." [7] Before long the crisis waned. The first six executions seemed to have ripped the heart out of the rebellion. "We thought it was ended," Miss Johnson wrote on July 18; "the court had been dismissed and the town was again sinking into its wonted security when information was given that another attempt would be made." The tip came from a Negro who later became a key witness. The court reassembled, the patrol returned to its stations, and more Negroes were jailed.

A new excitement swept the city, and the court, working rapidly, ordered more executions. "In all probability the executed will not end under 100," Miss Johnson estimated, and others asserted that "even should there be 500 executed there would still be enough" conspirators to pull off the scheme. "How far the mischief has extended heaven only knows," she lamented fearfully.[8] A later letter reported morbid details: "22 unfortunate wretches were at one fatal moment sent to render their account, 29 had been sentenced but 7 had their sentences commuted to perpetual banishment—but on Tuesday 6 more are to be executed . . . gracious heavens to what will all this lead . . . and I am told that there are an awful number yet to be tried." Miss Johnson had more knowledge than most, but she could observe on the street that "there is a look of horror in every countenance." "I wish I could act for myself," she added; "I would not stay in this city another day . . . my feelings have been so lacerated of late that I can hardly speak or act." [9]

From the beginning municipal authorities had been no less frightened, but they were compelled to act. The five freeholders who comprised the court appointed on June 18 were chosen because they possessed "in an eminent degree the confidence of the community." The tribunal quickly drew up its rules: no slave could be tried without the presence of his owner or the owner's counsel; "the testimony of one witness unsupported by additional evidence, or by circumstances, should lead to no conviction of a *capital* nature"; witnesses would confront the accused except "where testimony was given under a solemn pledge that the name . . . would not be divulged" because the judges feared the informant might be "murdered by the blacks"; a master or free Negro could have counsel if asked for, and "the statements of defenses of the accused should be heard, in every case, and they be permitted themselves to examine any witness they thought proper." [10] The freeholders worked in complete secrecy because of the "peculiar nature of the investigations" and because "it was also morally certain that no coloured witness would have ventured to incur the resentment of his comrades, by voluntarily disclosing his testimony in a public court." [11]

During its sittings, from the first outbreak in June until July 26, the court heard over 130 cases.[12] It divided the conspirators into two groups. The first comprised those "who exhibited energy and activity"; they were executed. The other included those "who did little (if any more) than yield their acquiescence to the proposal to enter the plot"; they were deported. The judges later confided to the governor that the distinction did not wholly meet the facts, but "the terror of example we thought would be sufficiently operative by the number of criminals sentenced to death" that "without any injury to the community . . . a measure might be adopted . . . which would save the necessity of more numerous executions than policy required." [13]

The court found it difficult to get conclusive evidence. Vesey and the first five went to the gallows without confessing—indeed asserting their innocence. During the second trial, however, three men under the sentence of death implicated, under a promise of leniency, scores of other blacks. In asking the governor to pardon Monday Gell, Charles Drayton, and Harry Haig, the judges described the conditions of their testimony: "Under the impression that they could ultimately have their lives spared they made . . . disclosures not only important in the detection of the general plan of the conspiracy but enabling the court to convict a number of principal offenders." Like "the terror of example," the officials wanted deportation in place of the hangman so that "negroes should know that even their principal advisers and ringleaders cannot be confided in and that under the temptations of exemption from capital punishment they will betray the common cause." [14]

Despite the difficulty of acquiring sufficient evidence, the court moved energetically and decisively. Of the 131 picked up, 35 were executed, 31 transported, 27 tried and acquitted, and 38 questioned but discharged.[15] Throughout July the gallows was kept busy. On "the Line," which separated the city from the Neck, the neighborhood numbly watched the public display.

Most of the condemned died without admitting guilt, and some with almost defiant contempt. Bacchus Hammett, who had "confessed," "went to the gallows *laughing and bidding his acquaintances in the streets* 'good bye'; on being hung, owing to some mismanagement in the fall of the trap, he was not thrown off, but the board canted, he slipped; yet he was so hardened that he *threw himself forward, and as he swung back he lifted his feet, so that he might not touch the board!*" [16] Others were dispatched more expertly, and the bodies left to dangle for hours to make certain that no colored resident could mistake the point of the punishment.

Constable Belknap, the executioner, later complained that the frequency of the hangings had caused him great "personal inconvenience"

and had "deranged" his "private business." At the height of the crisis
he had spent "all his time and services" in the "call of the public, both
by night and by day, in assisting at the preparation of the Gallows, the
digging of the graves and various other offices connected with the execution." [17] The city's budget too felt the strain. In December the
council asked the state to reimburse it for the unusual expenses surrounding the plot and trial. The bill came to $2,284.84¼, including costs
of confinement, a payment of $200 to "Col. Prioleau's man Peter for
secret services rendered," and the expenses of "erecting a Gallows" and
procuring "carts to carry the criminals to the place of execution." [18]

A second court, which included Robert Y. Hayne and Joel Poinsett,
was appointed August 1 "for the trial of sundry persons of color, apprehended for attempting to raise an insurrection." [19] Though it sat
only a week, it sentenced one man to death and directed six others to
be transported out of the state. These new cases, however, were connected with the events of May and June.[20]

As the court wound up its grim business, the city tried to recover
something of its old composure. In the second week of August the
Courier closed the books on the episode. "The legal investigations of
crime have ceased. The melancholy requisitions of Justice, as painful
to those who inflicted, as to those who suffered them, have been complied with; and an awful but a necessary, and, it is hoped, an effectual
example has been afforded to deter from further occasions of offense
and punishment." [21] The editor then called on the council for a day of
thanksgiving to God for "his preserving care" and because "he has
watched and guarded the tranquillity of our city" and "endowed our
magistrates with firmness and wisdom, rendered necessary by an alarming crisis." [22]

This brief narrative includes the essential facts about the Vesey uprising generally accepted by historians today. The standard source is a
long pamphlet containing the court's record of the trial, published by
the city in 1822 under the title of *An Official Report of the Trials of
Sundry Negroes* and edited by two members of the court. This document conveyed a special authenticity because the testimony and confessions purported to be as "originally taken, without even changing
the phraseology, which was generally in the very words used by the
witnesses." Indeed, the court had instructed the editors "*not to suppress
any part of it.*" [23] Scholars had few other sources to turn to. Charleston
newspapers imposed a nearly perfect blackout on the details of the episode throughout the summer, confining themselves to a simple recording
of sentences and executions. And contemporaries left only a few scat-

tered items to help fill out the slight skeleton provided by the council's publication.

Hence, historians accepted the facts available and drew their accounts from the official record. They did not question the court's findings but rather dwelt on certain aspects of the episode. Some, like Carter G. Woodson and Ulrich B. Phillips, emphasized the extent and precision of the planning.[24] Others centered on the extraordinary quality of the rebels, especially their leader. Dwight Dumond found Denmark Vesey a "brilliant man," familiar with the Bible, and acquainted with the debates in Congress over the admission of Missouri to the Union. He concluded that "few men were better informed . . . in the history of race relations." John Hope Franklin characterized Vesey as "a sensitive, liberty-loving person" who believed in equality for everyone and resolved "to do something for his slave brothers." Still others were impressed with the unity of the Negroes which made the plot possible. Herbert Aptheker, for example, quoted the report of two Negroes who said they "never spoke to any person of color on the subject, or knew of any who had been spoken to by the other leaders, who had withheld his assent." [25]

More important was the broader meaning of the conspiracy. Most authors viewed it in the context of the resistance of Negroes to the institution of slavery. Along with Nat Turner, they placed Denmark Vesey at the head of the list of colored rebels. For some his plot demonstrated the latent urge for freedom that lay beneath the regime of bondage; for others it revealed an ugly layer of hatred and revenge contained only by stringent laws and alert policemen.

But all accepted the official version: that a widespread conspiracy existed and only a last-minute betrayal rescued the city from insurrection and civil war. Whether the author was Negro or white, Northerner or Southerner, opponent of or apologist for slavery, there was no quarrel on this point. Historians who otherwise disagreed on many issues did not question the conventional story. Hence there was little incentive for reappraisal.[26]

Yet, in spite of the apparent agreement of most contemporaries and the consensus of subsequent historians, there is persuasive evidence that no conspiracy in fact existed, or at most that it was a vague and unformulated plan in the minds or on the tongues of a few colored townsmen. No elaborate network had been established in the countryside; no cache of arms lay hidden about the city; no date for an uprising had been set; no underground apparatus, carefully organized and secretly maintained, awaited a signal to fire Charleston and murder the whites.

What did exist were strong grievances on one side and deep fears on the other. Combined with a number of somewhat unrelated circumstances, they made it possible for many people, both white and Negro, to believe in the existence of a widespread scheme to overturn the institution of slavery.

The first note of skepticism came from a respected judge, a long-time resident of Charleston. Watching the mounting excitement in June, and privy to the proceedings of the court, he warned in a newspaper letter against the "Melancholy Effect of Popular Excitement." In an oblique parable he recounted an episode "within the recollection of thousands" when a freeholders' court had hastily hanged a slave, Billy, for sounding a false alarm to the patrols by blowing a horn. Although "no evidence was given whatever as to a motive for sounding the horn, and the horn was actually found covered and even filled with cobwebs, they condemned that man to die the next day!" The only testimony had been provided by another slave who "was first whipped severely to extort a confession, and then, with his eyes bound, commanded to prepare for instant death from a sabre" if he would not divulge the needed information. Many of the worthiest men in the area protested and asked for "a more deliberate hearing." It did no good, however. "Billy was hung amidst crowds of execrating spectators," the "popular demand for a victim" being so great that it was doubtful whether even a governor's pardon could have saved him.[27]

The letter was unsigned, but everyone knew its author was of "commanding authority." Moreover, published at the time of the newspaper blackout, it obviously came from someone close to those involved in the trial. In fact, its author was William Johnson, a judge and brother-in-law of the governor. His daughter observed that when the article appeared, the freeholders "took up the cudgels, supposing it was a slur at them—guilty conscience you know" and "threatened their anathemas at him." Johnson responded with a pamphlet, which his daughter characterized as asserting the "entire innocence of the slaves" and in which he pointed out that the charge against Billy had been "an attempt to raise an insurrection."[28] The moral could hardly be clearer: he feared the court would bend to the popular hysteria and find guilt where there was none.[29]

His daughter, too, soon took this view. Her letters spanning the two months of the crisis moved from frenzy to skepticism. At the beginning of the trouble she wrote that the conspirators spoke of "rapine and murder" with "the coolness of demons" and that "the plot is computed to be about 30,000—the children were to have been spiked and murdered &c." [30] A few weeks later the tone became more measured, the numbers involved much fewer, and she could "thank God none of our slaves have been found in the plot, though there are twenty of them in the yard." [31]

Still later some deeper doubts crept in. "You know," Miss Johnson wrote, "that the leading characteristic of our state is our impetuosity and ardency of feeling which unavoidably lays them [the people] open to deception and consequently leads them on to error in action." Not much, however, could be done about it: "you might as well attempt to 'fetter tides with silken bands' as to make them listen to reason when under this excitement." Yet she concluded that in a few days "the unfortunate creatures are to be hung—it is most horrible—it makes my blood curdle when I think of it, but they are guilty most certainly." [32] Her final letter mentions no plot at all and is obsessed with "the most awful tragedy in this . . . city that comes within the recollection of man"—the mass executions. "Certainly," she added, the whole affair "will throw our city back at least ten years." [33] By the end, Miss Johnson, if she believed a conspiracy existed at all, thought it surely had not extended far enough to justify the massive retaliation of the courts.

The criticism by Governor Thomas Bennett was much more precise. The court should not have "closed its doors upon the community" in its secret proceedings and "shut out those accidental rays which occasionally illuminate the obscurity." Moreover, he found the testimony gathered by the judges "equivocal, the offspring of treachery or revenge, and the hope of immunity." "Nor should it be less a source of embarrassment and concern," he continued, contesting the official version of the city, "that the testimony should be received under pledges of inviolable secrecy" and "that the accused should be convicted, and sentenced to death, without seeing the persons, or hearing the voices of those who testified to their guilt." [34]

The governor noted particularly that the decisive information came from three witnesses "while they were under the impression that they would have their life spared." Their testimony not only facilitated "the detection of the general plan of conspiracy, but enabled the court to convict a number of the principal offenders." While questioned, "two of them were sometimes closeted together," achieving a uniformity of evidence. In one case William, "the slave of Mr. Palmer," was convicted "exclusively on the testimony of two of the persons under sentence of death." He protested his innocence, claimed he had attended no meetings and never talked about a plot, and demonstrated his high reputation in many ways. Worse still, Charles Drayton "predicated his claim of escape [from the gallows] on the number of convictions he could make" with his story. "Nothing," Governor Bennett asserted, "could exceed the chilling depravity of this man."

Though the governor probably believed in a plot of some kind, he could not take the one described by the city very seriously. "It is scarcely possible to imagine one, more crude or imperfect," he said. "They were unprovided with arms," and except for a few pennies that had been subscribed, "no effort was used to procure them." The leaders showed "no confidence in each other"; in fact, they were "in many instances unknown to each other." They had "no definite plans of attack concerted; nor place of rendezvous fixed." Yet the city represented the danger as "mature and within a few hours of consummation."

He went on to say that the idea of an insurrection itself seemed unlikely, although some of the reasons he gave are less convincing. "The liberal and enlightened humanity of our Fellow Citizens, produce many attachments, that operate as checks on the spirit of insubordination." Indeed, there were "unsurmountable obstacles"—the "habitual respect" of the slaves "for an obedience to the authority of their owners; their natural indolence, and want of means and opportunities to form combinations; their characteristic cowardice and treachery, excited by a knowledge of the positive ability of the state to crush in an instant their boldest enterprise." The governor's view of the episode was plain. "The public mind had been raised to a pitch of excitement" over the rumor of a slave revolt and "sought relief in an exhibition of truth." [35] Instead, the action of the city created further panic and confusion.

A close examination of the published record of the trial tends to confirm the governor's doubts. Though the testimony seems at first reading to suggest a ripe plan, the important evidence is missing at the critical points. For example, the transcript stated that "the whole numbers engaged" were nine thousand, "partly from the country and partly from the city." But, it added, "it is true that the witness who had made these assertions did not see the lists [of accomplices] himself; but he heard from one who was in daily communication with Peter, . . . and as Peter wrote a good hand and was active throughout the whole affair, it is impossible to doubt that he had such lists." To be sure, the judges then contended that the larger figure was "greatly exaggerated, and perhaps designedly so." [36] Yet not a single roster of names ever turned up.

If the numbers were conjectural, the extent of the conspiracy was even more so. The report estimated the infected area covered not only the regions around the city but neighboring parishes as well. All through the crisis, however, no one detected any activity in the rural sections.[37]

The charge that some of the central figures had acquaintances in the surrounding area was not accompanied by any evidence of complicity. Indeed, one black testified that Pierre Lewis told him "something serious would happen" but that "I was country born, and he was afraid to trust me." [38]

On the matter of weapons the official record reveals the same ambivalence. A blacksmith was supposed to have made some long pikes, six of which a few witnesses claimed existed. But the pikes were never located, thereby forcing the court into a curious logic: "as those six pike heads have not been found, there is no reason for disbelieving the testimony of there hav[ing] been many more made." Later the transcript mentions that "one hundred [pike heads and bayonets] were said to have been made at an early day, and by the 16th June, as many as two or three hundred, and between three and four hundred daggers." And there was still more. "Besides the above mentioned, it was proved that Peter had a sword; that Charles Drayton had a gun & sword; that John Henry had a sword; that Pharo Thompson a scythe converted into a sword; that Adam Yates had a knife . . . that Monday had a sword"; and that Bacchus Hammett gave a sword and a gun to others. Yet, except for these few individual weapons, no arms cache was uncovered. "To presume that the Insurgents had no arms because none were seized," the judges concluded, "would be drawing an inference in direct opposition to the whole of the evidence." [39] Since the city published the full text to allay suspicions both in Charleston and in the North that some injustice had been done, the inconclusiveness of the case at the crucial points is significant. [40]

Equally important is the fact that the printed transcript is at odds in both wording and substance with manuscript records of the witnesses. For example, the confessions of Bacchus Hammett and John Enslow, among the few surviving original documents, have been carefully edited in the authorized version. Some passages were omitted; facts not mentioned in the original interrogation were added; even the tone of the narrative was changed with the alterations. [41]

For example, while Bacchus Hammett is reported to have testified, "At Vesey's they wanted to make a collection to make pikes for the country people, but the men had no money," [42] the manuscript suggests something different: "Denmark told me in March, he was getting arms fast, about 150 to 200 pikes made, and there was a great deal of money placed in his hands for the purpose." [43] Again the *Official Report* lists names of accomplices. "Bellisle Yates I have seen at meetings, and Adam Yates and Napham Yates and Dean Mitchell, and Caesar Smith, and George a Stevidore [sic]." It also includes Jack McNeil,

Prince Righton, Jerry Cohen. None appear in the original confession.[44]

At some points the manuscript included material not found at all in the printed version. To use but a single instance, the confession of Bacchus is quite explicit on a rebellion in Georgetown which would precede the Charleston uprising. "I also heard them say that they were well informed in Georgetown. That they would let the principal Men know the time of the attack, being a short distance from Charleston, would commence a day or two before." The plan was simple. "Kill all the whites between there and Charleston, make their way through the woods and be in time to assist these people in town. It is also said by them that the Population in Georgetown could be killed in one half hour." Yet the city's account contains no mention of this extraordinary dimension of the plot.

The discrepancies seem deliberate since the preface of the pamphlet went to great pains to say that "the whole evidence has been given in each particular case, in the order of its trial, and wherever any additional, or incidental testimony has been disclosed against any criminal subsequently to his conviction, sentence or execution, it has been noticed." "In most cases," the judges contended, "it was as originally taken, without even changing the phraseology" and using "the very words" of the witnesses.[45] Yet these two depositions indicate that little confidence can be placed in the authenticity of the official account.[46]

Strangely, historians have received it less skeptically than some contemporaries. While many newspapers outside the state approved the silence of the Charleston press during the trial, some also looked forward to a "succinct account of the whole transaction" that had been promised by the court. When it arrived, however, there was disappointment. "We doubt the policy of the present publication," wrote a reader of the Boston *Daily Advertiser.* "If intended to awe the blacks, it would seem the executions and banishments *silently* made, would be more terrible, but if really designed as an appeal, and a justification to the American people and to the world, as to the justice of the sentences, it appears either too much or too little." The "historical part," he concluded, "is too loose." [47]

In fact, the explanation of the whole episode lay in the "historical part." If a genuine conspiracy was lacking, tension between the races was not. In the years before the "plot," several developments had worsened relations that always were uneasy. The census figures conveniently summed up white fears. Officially Negroes outnumbered whites 14,127 to 10,653.[48] During the summer when many families left the city to escape the heat, the colored majority was even larger. Thomas Pinckney, in an extended post-mortem on the grim event, expressed the consequent anxiety. He called the imbalance "the principal encouragement to the late attempt, for without it, mad and wild as they appear to have been, they would not have dared to venture on a contest of force." In a word, numerical superiority was the "*sine qua non* of insurrection." [49]

Numbers alone, however, would not have produced panic. Some rural areas had a higher percentage of slaves than the city without the same alarm. It was the kind of colored population, not its mere predominance, that frightened white leaders. Charleston's Negroes, like urban blacks elsewhere, were a far different lot than their country brothers. They were more advanced, engaged in higher tasks, more literate, more independent, and less servile than those on plantations. Not confined to the field or the big house, many found employment as draymen, porters, fishermen, hucksters, butchers, barbers, carpenters, and even as clerks and bookkeepers. Their work took these slaves away from the constant surveillance of their masters and generated a measure of self-reliance not usually found in the "peculiar institution." Added to this was an urban environment that provided churches, livery stables, cook houses, and grog shops as centers of informal community life.

Even the domestics who comprised the bulk of urban bondsmen in Charleston afforded slight comfort, though they were popularly believed to be loyally attached to the families of their owners.[50] In fact, Pinckney thought them "certainly the most dangerous" because they had an "intimate acquaintance with all circumstances relating to the interior of the dwellings," because of "the confidence reposed in them," and because of "information they unavoidably obtain, from hearing the conversation, and observing the habitual transactions of their owners." Having "the amplest means for treacherous bloodshed and devastation," this group would comprise the core of a conspiracy. Yet these slaves, he complained, had been "so pampered" by "indulgencies," even "being taught to read and write," that the "considerable control" embodied in ordinances and state laws had been frustrated by the "weakness of many proprietors." [51]

Nearly all those believed to be ringleaders by the court came from one or another of these areas of colored life. Denmark Vesey, who "stood at the head of this conspiracy" according to the court's report, was a successful carpenter who had bought his freedom with money won in a lottery in 1801. Since he was the only free Negro executed (six others were questioned and dismissed), officials assumed "the idea undoubtedly originated with him" and that he concocted the plot. His house and shop became the rendezvous of the rebels and he the moving genius. For several years before he "disclosed his intentions to anyone," the court declared, "he appears to have been constantly and assiduously engaged in endeavoring to embitter the minds of the coloured population against the white." He "rendered himself perfectly familiar" with the Bible and used whatever parts "he could pervert to his purpose; and would readily quote them, to prove that slavery was contrary to the laws of God." Moreover, he distributed "inflammatory pamphlets" among the bondsmen. He even "sought every opportunity" to "introduce some bold remark on slavery" into conversations with whites while in the presence of other Negroes.[52]

His associates were no less impressive. Monday Gell not only hired his own time but kept a shop on Meeting Street where he made harness; his owner entrusted arms as well as money to him. Governor Bennett once called him "the projector of the plot" and "its most active partisan."[53] Peter Poyas was a "first rate ship carpenter" who had an excellent reputation and the implicit confidence of his master. Two others belonged to the governor of the state, and one of them tended the family's business when his owner was at the capital. Only Gullah Jack, who claimed to be a sorcerer with mysterious powers, seemed irregular.

White fears fixed on this colored urban elite, on those who managed to "succeed" a little in bondage. To the whites of Charleston, the character of the city's Negro population made an uprising seem possible, indeed, reasonable. The Negroes were, as a group of residents put it, the "most condensed and most intelligent."[54] Moreover, the extent of literacy brought the "powerful operation of the Press" on "their uninformed and easily deluded minds" and, more precisely, made them privy to events outside the city and the South. The example of Santo Domingo, where the blacks had risen successfully against the whites, and the debate over the Missouri Compromise were thought to have "directly or indirectly" heightened the unrest and encouraged insurrectionary activity.[55] In sum, both the quality and the quantity of Charleston slaves rendered the whites uneasy.

The Negroes, too, were edgy, for things had not gone well for them in the preceding months. New state legislation had made manumission more difficult, nearly closing the door on those who hoped to get their freedom either by purchase or the generosity of their masters.[56] Such "uncivilized laws," "A Colored American" recalled, were "a great and intolerable hindrance" to the slaves' "peace and happiness," since some had already made arrangements to buy their liberty.[57]

Another cause of controversy was the closing of an independent Methodist church established for colored people. In this sanctuary many blacks had found both spiritual consolation and brief relief from servitude. When it was closed down in 1821, the Negro community became embittered. Bible-class leaders especially felt aggrieved because it deprived them of one of the few positions of modest status open to bondsmen. The resentment of this articulate group was scarcely a secret. In fact, the city later charged that almost all the ringleaders were connected with this church.[58]

The atmosphere, then, was charged with fears and grievances. No doubt conversations among whites turned often, if hesitantly, to the topic; and certainly in the grog shops, in Negro quarters, and on the job, the slaves talked about their difficulties. The gap between the races was great, calculatedly so, and was quickly filled by gossip and rumor. Blacks heard the whites were going to "thin out" the colored population, that a false alarm would bring out the militia and volunteers to butcher the slaves on the spot, that new restraints were under consideration in city hall and the state legislature. Circulating among the whites were equally hair-raising notions: a servile uprising, the seizure of the city, the carrying off of women after all males had been exterminated.

Under these circumstances anything specific—names, places, target dates—seemed to give substance to the rumor, suggesting that a plot not only existed but was ripe. Prudence dictated preventive action and a withering show of force by the city. Not only the ringleaders but even those remotely connected had to be swiftly seized, tried, and punished. Hence, the chance encounter of Devany Prioleau with William Paul on the wharf on May 25, 1822, with its garbled but ominous portent, set off a chain of events that did not end until thirty-five had been executed, still more deported, and a town frozen in terror for almost a summer.

Thus Charleston stumbled into tragedy. The "plot" was probably never more than loose talk by aggrieved and embittered men. Curiously, its reputation as a full-scale revolt has endured, in part, because both sides in the slavery controversy believed insurrections to be essential to their broader argument. Apologists for the "peculiar institution" contended that the stringent laws against Negroes in the South were needed to protect whites from violence; opponents of slavery asserted that the urge for freedom was so embedded in human nature that none would passively remain enchained. In either event the Denmark Vesey uprising became a convenient illustration of a larger view of bondage. No closer examination seemed necessary. What *both* Aptheker and Phillips could accept as fact, it was assumed, must necessarily be true.

But the very agreement tended to obscure the important reality. For a concerted revolt against slavery was actually less likely in a city than in the countryside. The chances for success anywhere, of course, were never very good, but ordinary circumstances favored a Nat Turner over a Denmark Vesey. The reasons for this are clear. Nowhere, not even in Charleston, did the blacks have the numerical superiority that was present on many plantations. Moreover, police forces in the towns, large and well organized, constituted a more powerful deterrent than the vigilante patrol system characteristic of places with scattered populations. And ironically, the urban environment proved inhospitable to conspiracies because it provided a wider latitude to the slave, a measure of independence within bondage, and some relief from the constant surveillance of the master. This comparative freedom deflected the discontent, leading Negroes to try to exploit measures.

The white community, however, could see only the dangers. The Negroes in Charleston were not only numerous but quite different from the imbruted field hands of the cane and cotton country. Many mastered skills, learned to read and write, joined churches, and in every way tried to comport themselves as free men. This was the source of the fear. They seemed capable both of resenting their bondage and organizing an insurrection against it. It was not difficult to translate a few rumors into a widespread conspiracy. Indeed, it was so easy that historians, too, have done so for nearly a century and a half.

NOTES

1. Lionel H. Kennedy and Thomas Parker, *An Official Report of the Trials of Sundry Negroes, Charged with an Attempt to Raise an Insurrection in the State of South-Carolina: Preceded by an Introduction and Narrative; and in an Appendix, a Report of the Trials of Four White Persons, on Indictments for Attempting to Excite the Slaves to Insurrection. Prepared and Published at the Request of the Court* (Charleston, 1822), p. 50.

2. A postscript to the publication revised this original version slightly, asserting that Devany told his young master before he did Pencil, but the free Negro advised him to go directly to his master. Since Mr. Prioleau was not available he told Mrs. Prioleau. The editor concluded that this added information "places the fidelity of the slave . . . on much higher ground." "Extracts," *Official Report*, p. 4. The state rewarded both Devany and Pencil with a $50 annuity for life. In 1837, when Devany turned seventy, the state raised it to $150. Memorial of the City Council of Charleston to the Senate of South

Carolina, 1822 (South Carolina Archives Division); Petition of Peter Devany for Increase of Annual Bounty Conferred upon Him by the Act of Assembly, Anno Domini, 1822 for Meritorious Services in the Disturbances of That Year, October, 1837 (South Carolina Archives Division). Devany had also been manumitted for his role in uncovering the plot.

3. *Official Report*, p. 51.

4. *Ibid.*, p. 3ff.

5. Ana Hayes Johnson to Elizabeth E. W. Haywood, Charleston, June 23, 1822, in Ernest Haywood Papers (Southern Historical Collection, University of North Carolina Library).

6. "A Colored American," *The Late Contemplated Insurrection in Charleston, S.C., with the Execution of Thirty-Six of the Patriots, Etc.* (New York, 1850), p. 7.

7. *Southern Patriot and Commercial Advertiser* (Charleston), September 12, 1822.

8. Ana Hayes Johnson to Elizabeth E. W. Haywood, Charleston, July 18, 1822, in Ernest Haywood Papers.

9. *Ibid.*, July 27, 1822.

10. *Official Report*, p. vi.

11. *Ibid.*, pp. iii, vii.

12. The court sat in "arduous session for five weeks and three days" and probably had some contact with more than this number. *Southern Patriot and Commercial Advertiser* (Charleston), July 27, 1822.

13. L. Kennedy, Thomas Parker, William Drayton, Nathaniel Heyward, J. R. Pringle, H. Deos, and Robert J. Turnbull to Governor Thomas Bennett, July 24, 1822 (South Carolina Archives Division).

14. Petition for the Pardon of Monday Gell, Charles Drayton, and Harry Haig to the Governor of South Carolina, July 24, 1822 (South Carolina Archives Division).

15. *Official Report*, p. 183.

16. Bacchus, the Slave of Benjamin Hammett, "Confession," in William and Benjamin Hammett Papers (Duke University Library).

17. Petition of B. Belknap of the City of Charleston to the Senate and House of Representatives, November 14, 1822 (South Carolina Archives Division).

18. "Report of the Committee on the Memorial of the City of Charleston," Senate Committee, December 14, 1822 (South Carolina Archives Division).

19. *Southern Patriot and Commercial Advertiser* (Charleston), August 2, 1822.

20. *Ibid.*, August 8, 1822. The prisoner who was executed, William Garner, had earlier escaped from the city. His death brought the total to thirty-six and explains the confusion in secondary sources concerning the precise number of executions. H. M. Henry, *The Police Control of the Slave in South Carolina* (Emory, Va., 1914), p. 152.

21. *Charleston Courier*, August 12, 1822.

22. *Ibid.*, August 24, 1822.

23. *Official Report,* p. iii.

24. Carter G. Woodson, *The Negro in Our History* (Washington, 1927), p. 180; Ulrich B. Phillips, "The Slave Labor Problem in the Charleston District," *Political Science Quarterly,* XXII (September, 1907), 429-430.

25. Dwight Lowell Dumond, *Antislavery: The Crusade for Freedom in America* (Ann Arbor, Mich., 1961), p. 114; John Hope Franklin, *From Slavery to Freedom: A History of American Negroes* (New York, 1956), p. 210; Herbert Aptheker, *American Negro Slave Revolts* (New York, 1943), p. 270.

26. In a paper delivered to the Southern Historical Association meeting in 1957 Thomas T. Hamilton of the University of Wichita evidently developed some doubts about the case from "irregularities in the trials and testimony." Presumably this skepticism stemmed from a close reading of the text. *Journal of Southern History,* XXIV (February, 1958), 71. Standard accounts of the Vesey plot include Anne King Gregorie, "Denmark Vesey," *Dictionary of American Biography,* XIX, 258-259; John Lofton, "Negro Insurrectionist," *Antioch Review,* XVIII (Summer, 1958), 183-196; and John M. Lofton, Jr., "Denmark Vesey's Call to Arms," *Journal of Negro History,* XXXIII (October, 1948), 395-417.

27. *Charleston Courier,* June 21, 1822.

28. Ana Hayes Johnson to Elizabeth E. W. Haywood, Charleston, July 24, 1822, in Ernest Haywood Papers. For the court's reply see *Charleston Courier,* June 29, 1822.

29. "If it was intended as it would seem to be to make this moral, and the story which accompanies applicable to a supposed existing state of things in our community . . ." wrote the mayor (intendant), "I have only to remark that the *discretion* of the writer is altogether equal to the unjust libel he has insinuated against his fellow citizens." The mayor contended that the measures adopted were taken in a spirit of the most perfect justice and moderation. *Southern Patriot and Commercial Advertiser* (Charleston), June 22, 1822.

30. Ana Hayes Johnson to Elizabeth E. W. Haywood, Charleston, June 23, 1822, Ernest Haywood Papers.

31. *Ibid.,* July 18, 1822.

32. *Ibid.,* July 24, 1822.

33. *Ibid.,* July 27, 1822.

34. Message of Governor Thomas Bennett to the Senate and House of Representatives of the State of South Carolina, November 28, 1822 (South Carolina Archives Division). The Charleston delegation thought the governor's message was too harsh on the city's handling of the episode. *Mercury* (Charleston), December 18, 1822.

35. Message of Governor Thomas Bennett.

36. *Official Report,* pp. 25-26.

37. Nonetheless, a prominent planter explained, "the orderly conduct of the Negroes in any district within 40 miles of Charleston, is no evidence that they were ignorant of the intended attempt. A more orderly gang than my own is not to be found in this state—and one of Denmark Vesey's directives

was, that they should assume the most implicit obedience." *Official Report*, pp. 28n-31n. The plot presumably stretched as far as seventy or eighty miles from the city. *Ibid.*, p. 31.

38. *Ibid.*, p. 159.

39. *Ibid.*, p. 32.

40. The Washington *Daily National Intelligencer* of August 3, 1822, noted that the Charleston *City Gazette* promised that "a succinct account of the whole transaction shall be given to the world. It will bring to view a scheme of wildness and of wickedness, enough to make us smile at the folly, did we not shudder at the indiscriminate mischief of the plan and its objects. Those (they were but few) who at first thought we had no cause for alarm, must be overwhelmed with conviction to the contrary."

41. Bacchus, the Slave of Benjamin Hammett, "Confession," and "The Confession of Mr. Enslow's Boy John," 1822, in William and Benjamin Hammett Papers.

42. *Official Report*, p. 146.

43. Bacchus, the Slave of Benjamin Hammett, "Confession," and "The Confession of Mr. Enslow's Boy John."

44. *Official Report*, pp. 146, 147.

45. *Ibid.*, p. iii.

46. Indeed, a close reading of the report suggests that the object of the trials was not to discover the extent of the plot but rather to awe the Negroes by a show of force. "The object of punishment being effectually attained by these examples, and the ring leaders being convicted," the court explained, "the arrests stopped here." *Ibid.*, pp. 48, 59.

47. *Daily Advertiser* (Boston), October 8, 1822.

48. *Census for 1820, Published by Authority of an Act of Congress, Under the Direction of the Secretary of State* (Washington, 1821), p. 26.

49. Achates (Thomas Pinckney), *Reflections Occasioned by the Late Disturbances in Charleston* (Charleston, 1822), p. 10.

50. The *Official Report* contained the conventional view. "Few if any domestic servants were spoken to (by the leaders), as *they* were distrusted." *Ibid.*, p. 26. Pinckney's appraisal of the domestics suggests that he did not wholly trust the analysis of the court even though he believed in the existence of the plot.

51. Pinckney, *Reflections*, pp. 6-9.

52. *Official Report*, pp. 17-19. Later in the testimony, however, the court contended that Vesey "enjoyed so much the confidence of the whites, that when he was accused, the charge was not only discredited, but he was not even arrested for several days after, and not until proof of his guilt had become too strong to be doubted." This does not square well with the previous description of years of agitation and bold confrontation with whites.

53. Message of Governor Thomas Bennett.

54. *Southern Patriot and Commercial Advertiser* (Charleston), August 21, 1822.

55. Pinckney, *Reflections*, p. 9.

56. *Acts and Resolutions of the General Assembly of the State of South-Carolina Passed in December, 1820* (Columbia, 1821), pp. 22-24.

57. "A Colored American," *Late Contemplated Insurrection,* p. 5.

58. The church included both slaves and free blacks. Though some accounts emphasize the petition of free Negroes to the legislature for the privilege of conducting their own worship, the report of the trial asserts that nearly all the bondsmen involved also belonged to the African church and that many were class leaders.

The Historians Blinded

T he act of writing history involves two ingredients: the available past and the historian. We have seen some of the problems of reaching the available past; in these selections we see some of the problems of the historian himself—problems that are a direct consequence of his own history. His personal experiences and his cultural surroundings cause him to see certain events and ignore others, to ask one kind of question and therefore fail to ask another. As the history we know is a product of historians and is filtered through these second persons, the assumptions of historians unconsciously become our own. The more influential the historian, the more widespread the assumptions become, both to the general public and to students who follow and emulate their teacher. In the two following selections, three of the historians who have probably had the greatest impact on the recent American public are examined for their views on the Negro and on slavery. James Ford Rhodes's multivolume work, The History of the United States from the Compromise of 1850 (1893-1906), achieved wide circulation here and abroad. Frederick Jackson Turner and Charles A. Beard quite possibly have had more influence upon members of the historical profession than anyone else in the twentieth century.

Robert Cruden's consideration of James Ford Rhodes shows that it is possible for an individual who places a high value on objectivity to fail to be objective. He also shows how the climate of opinion affects even a person unsympathetic to Southern views, one who defends the Union in the Civil War. Perhaps in the long run, for a man of Rhodes's sympathies to ignore the Negro or accept a lower position for him does much greater damage to the public's conception of the past than the same ideas from an obviously biased person. If Rhodes's standards are higher than those of others of his time, the distortion of the Negro's past is indeed great.

Lynd's discussion of the views of Turner and Beard on slavery centers on the institution of slavery and the conception of the farmer. Believing the pioneer and the farmer to be gallant heroes, the two giants of American history overlooked the farmer as slaveowner and the frontier as the Southwest. Captured by their own preconceptions of the important issues in the past—for Turner the frontier as the agent of democracy, for Beard the struggle between "capitalism" and "agrarianism"—these two historians conceived of slavery as a weaker and less consequential institution than it actually was. Thus, the explanation of the keys to American experience left out one of the crucial elements, that of slavery. Indeed Lynd argues that slavery is one of the two or three distinctive themes in American experience. If he is correct, the shift of attention to slavery surely must bring the object of the institution into the brighter light of historical scholarship.

Gradually, works specifically in Negro history are beginning to merge into the whole context of American history. This results from the present interest in Negro rights and from a recognition that the history of the past has been singularly white. As historians become better educated, perhaps an integrated history will result and the older lines of division will become meaningless.

JAMES FORD RHODES AND THE NEGRO: A STUDY IN THE PROBLEM OF OBJECTIVITY

Robert Cruden

The continuing debate among historians as to the scientific nature of their discipline involves, as a basic element, the problem of objectivity. Is it possible for history to be objective in the sense that the physical and biological sciences are objective: namely, that its findings "do not depend in any important sense on the personal idiosyncrasies or private feelings of those who reach them, but are marked by a process in which complete abstraction is made from these"? [1] If so, by what standards may we determine its objectivity? The purpose of this article is to examine some of the factors involved in these questions as they emerge from a study of the work of one of America's most noted historians, James Ford Rhodes. To pinpoint the issue, discussion is limited to that aspect of Rhodes's writings in which the problems are most clearly delineated: namely, Rhodes's treatment of the role of the Negro in the period of which he wrote, 1850 to 1877.

Rhodes, it may be recalled, was the prosperous Cleveland business-man (one of his partners was his brother-in-law, Mark Hanna) who, in middle age, turned to the writing of history with such success that his interpretations of the Civil War and Reconstruction strongly influenced American thought in the generation prior to World War I. Even today, two of the most eminent of American historians, Samuel Eliot Morison and Henry Steele Commager, believe that his seven-volume *History of*

Robert Cruden, "James Ford Rhodes and the Negro," *Ohio History*, LXXI, No. 2 (July, 1962), 129-137.

the United States from the Compromise of 1850 to the Final Restoration of Home Rule at the South in 1877 [2] "is still the best detailed history of that period although shot full of holes by the research of the last fifty years." They commend his treatment of Reconstruction as "notably impartial." [3]

That phrase admirably sums up Rhodes's own appraisal of his work. Although he thought of himself as a literary rather than scientific historian, he insisted that in writing his *History* he sought "to get rid so far as possible of all preconceived notions and theories," for, as he said,

> such is the constitution of the human mind, or at any rate my own, that as I went through the mass of my material I would have seized upon all the facts that made for my theory and marshalled them in its support while those that told against it I would have unconsciously and undoubtedly quite honestly neglected.[4]

He was persuaded that in dealing with the Negro, he was, as he put it, "an earnest seeker after truth, . . . trying to hold a judicial balance and to tell the story without fear, favor or prejudice." [5]

In this belief Rhodes was confirmed by the almost unanimous verdict of his contemporaries, both lay and scholarly. When Albert Shaw, editor of the *Review of Reviews*, praised Rhodes's work as "like finality itself" he summarized similar comments by such diverse figures as Theodore Roosevelt, Gamaliel Bradford, and Justice Oliver Wendell Holmes, Jr., and by such disparate publications as *The World's Work* and the *International Socialist Review*.[6] Woodrow Wilson's judgment that Rhodes's *History* was "perhaps the finest piece of historical writing yet done by an American" represented, in extreme degree, the conclusions of other historians, including Albert Bushnell Hart, Edward Channing, William E. Dodd, and Frederic L. Paxson.[7] The awesome confidence of the American public in Rhodes's fairness, objectivity, and integrity is demonstrated with almost embarrassing frankness in a letter to Rhodes from John T. Morse, Jr., the editor of the "American Statesmen" series:

> You are absolutely the most fair-minded man who ever dealt with matters of controversy. . . . Of course you manage to infuse a certain kindliness and gentle mercy into your justice, as we are told that God does—(though I would rather trust you than him).[8]

Much the same opinion of Rhodes's work was entertained by such distinguished English historians as Samuel R. Gardiner, W. E. H. Lecky, and Charles Harding Firth.[9]

Yet Rhodes it was who set it down as "scientific truth" that Negroes

constituted "one of the most inferior races of mankind." [10] Capable of
only limited mental development, they early in life turned aside from
intellectual to sensual pursuits; incapable of love or affection, they
showed that a lack of chastity was "a natural inclination of the African
race." [11] Much of the horror of slavery was mitigated by the fact that
the griefs of the Negro were transient.[12] As to public morality, wherever
the Negro had been given political freedom he had shown himself
"greedy for office and emolument," while demonstrating both indifference to movements for political reform and incapacity for matters of
government.[13] The history of the race indicated that it had contributed
little to human progress.[14]

It followed, then, that Reconstruction was not only a failure but also
"an attack upon civilization," for it was essentially an effort to impose
upon a highly developed Anglo-Saxon culture the rule of this "ignorant
mass of an alien race," a rule made all the worse because it embraced
also "knavish white natives and the vulturous adventurers who flocked
from the North." [15] As Rhodes saw it, "Intelligence and property stood
bound and helpless under Negro-carpet-bag rule" while Negro legislators and their depraved white allies wrote a "sickening tale of extravagance, waste, corruption and fraud." [16] Despite the frequently devious
and violent means used by the enemies of the Reconstruction governments, the eventual overthrow of such governments was a development
at which "all lovers of good government must rejoice." [17] This interpretation became almost standard among historians, and, as has been noted,
even in our own day some historians find it "notably impartial."

Use of the racial formula led Rhodes to quite different conclusions
about Anglo-Saxons. American greatness, he wrote, was due basically to
the energetic and independent character of the people, deriving from
their Protestant Anglo-Saxon forebears.[18] During the Civil War, northern Democrats showed the Anglo-Saxon sense of political responsibility;
the Union troops at Gettysburg displayed Anglo-Saxon zeal in defense
of the homeland.[19] The Anglo-Saxon spirit of resistance to oppression
helped explain why the Confederacy fought so courageously.[20] Anglo-
Saxon respect for law, on the other hand, was symbolized in the career
of Abraham Lincoln.[21] Lincoln's plan for reconstruction displayed Anglo-
Saxon practicality, while that of Senator Sumner "smacked of the logic
of the French." [22] As for southern Anglo-Saxons, Rhodes fully endorsed
the description of them by Senator George F. Hoar of Massachusetts:

They are a noble race. . . . Their love of home; their chivalrous
respect for women; their courage; their delicate sense of honor;
their constancy . . . are things by which the people of the more

mercurial North may take a lesson. And there is another thing—
covetousness, corruption, the low temptation of money has not yet
found any place in our Southern politics.[23]

So much for the racial content of Rhodes's *History.* Let us briefly examine Rhodes's use of sources.

First, he relied almost entirely on white sources for his treatment of
the role of the Negro: white scientists, white magazines (particularly
The Nation), and white newspapers. To be sure, the Negro press of
the day was not the extensive enterprise that it is today, but there were
some Negro newspapers available for the period, and certainly after
1870 there was a steady growth in the number of such newspapers.[24]
Rhodes showed no familiarity with them at all. Likewise, he paid no
attention to the proceedings of the various public bodies of the Reconstruction governments, preferring to rely on second-hand accounts by
unsympathetic white observers.[25] When Negro sources were called to
his attention, such as the works of John R. Lynch and Kelly Miller, he
refused to read them on the grounds that they were partisan and
controversial.[26]

Second, Rhodes chose to accept only certain types of white testimony.
Thus in the conflict between the reports of U. S. Grant and Carl
Schurz on conditions in the postwar South, he believed Grant rather
than Schurz because the general "possessed one of those minds which
often attain to correct judgments without knowing the how and the
why." [27] Likewise, in the conflict between the majority and minority
reports of the Ku Klux Klan committee he chose to accept that of the
Democratic minority, for, as he put it,

> the minority report comes nearer to the truth. At many points the
> Republican document halts and boggles. . . . Consciousness of a
> bad cause may be read between the lines. . . . While the Demo-
> crats attempt to prove too much, . . . they are straightforward
> and aggressive with the consciousness of a cause based on the
> eternal principles of nature and justice.[28]

Much of Rhodes's treatment of Reconstruction in South Carolina was
based on *The Prostrate State* by James S. Pike, although one might expect an historian "trying to hold a judicial balance" to exercise caution
in accepting uncritically the reports of a newspaperman who believed
that "a large majority of all the voting citizens of the state are habitually
guilty of thieving and of concubinage." [29] Also, had Rhodes been more
careful, he might have discovered that Pike, a year before he set foot
in South Carolina, had written for the *New York Tribune* an article

which "made practically every major point he made" in his book, which, of course, purported to be a first-hand eyewitness account.[30] In any case, Pike's testimony was flatly contradicted by General Oliver O. Howard, head of the freedmen's bureau and a man with some experience in the postwar South. Rhodes, however, rejected Howard's testimony as "another of these extraordinary apologies for ignorance when covered by a black skin." [31] Perhaps the same reasoning explains his passing over James G. Blaine's tribute to the integrity of Negro congressmen and senators, although otherwise he drew heavily upon Blaine for his discussion of postwar politics.[32]

These examples have been cited, not to discredit Rhodes, but to point up the problems raised in this article: How could an historian who honestly strove to tell the story without fear, favor, or prejudice have fallen so far short of what we conceive to be basic standards of objectivity? And perhaps even more important, how can one account for the tribute paid to his work by historical scholars on the grounds that it was almost godlike in its objectivity?

There are many explanations why Rhodes fell short of his own ideal of objectivity. He lacked professional historical training, and indeed, apparently believed that if a person possessed such attributes as diligence, accuracy, love of truth, and impartiality, training was not really necessary.[33] It is not surprising, then, that he showed only dim awareness of problems of methodology and interpretation.

Also, and perhaps more important, Rhodes did not possess a keen, inquiring mind. Study of his work, as well as the testimony of those who knew him personally, shows that he shrank from analysis of the personal feelings and attitudes of people, including his own.[34] It is hardly to be wondered at, then, that he did not succeed as well as he believed in divesting himself of "preconceived notions and theories," particularly since he did not fully appreciate the various influences which shaped his conscious thought.

Paramount among these was his father, Daniel P. Rhodes, who played a decisive role in determining James's upbringing, education, and choice of business vocation.[35] Daniel was a militant Democrat in the Civil War period, a political campaigner for Clement L. Vallandigham, a man who objected to Mark Hanna because, in his view, young Hanna was "a damned screecher for freedom." [36] James said he drank in his father's opinions "eagerly." [37] In this context it is easy to understand why young James, on a trip to the South in 1872, had only to look at the "faces and manners" of the Negroes to understand why southern whites were fearful of "robbery, killing, burning and rape." [38]

On a more conscious level, Rhodes, like most middle-class Americans of his day, was deeply influenced by Herbert Spencer. He himself explained that he was not "emancipated" from Spencer until he was in his forties, but Rhodes's emancipation was more fancied than real.[39] He accepted Spencer's basic concepts of survival of the fittest and of racial evolution which produced superior and inferior varieties of the human race, and in his *History* he frequently cited Spencer as an authority.[40]

Of equal significance, perhaps, was the influence of Edwin L. Godkin, editor of *The Nation*, a journal which Rhodes read religiously from youth to old age.[41] As Rhodes put it, "his influence was abiding. . . . Godkin preached to us every week a timely and cogent sermon." [42] For his treatment of Reconstruction, Rhodes relied heavily upon *The Nation*, which, he said, provided "excellent historical material." [43] Godkin's attitudes may be gathered from his reference to leaders of Reconstruction governments as "rogues" and "ignorant thieves" and his endorsement of segregation in schools, together with his recommendation to Negroes that they earn the respect of white men while reconciling themselves to the fact that "most of the work has to be done by the lower class." [44]

Apart from such specific influences, Rhodes's approach to matters of race was deeply colored by the accepted opinion of his own day, that period which Rayford Logan has so aptly named the nadir of the Negro in American life and thought. Rhodes matured in a society the dominant cultural theme of which he himself outlined: "It was an age of science—the era of Darwin and Spencer, of Huxley and Tyndall. The influence of heredity and the great fact of race was better understood than ever before." [45] Rhodes was especially impressed by the arguments of Louis Agassiz, who testified that "from the very character of the negro race" social equality with whites was a "natural impossibility." Historically, wrote Agassiz, the Negroes had remained at a low sensual level: they "groped in barbarism and *never originated a regular organization among themselves.*" [46] To this Rhodes added: "What the whole country has only learned through years of costly and bitter experience was known to this leader of scientific thought before we ventured on the policy of trying to make Negroes intelligent by legislative acts." [47]

Such attitudes explain in part Rhodes's cavalier treatment of sources favorable to the Negro; it must be added that his treatment also sprang from his conception of the historian as judge rather than inquiring scholar. In his opinion, the most important quality of the historian was the judicial, not the inquiring, mind.[48] As judge, the historian evaluated the evidence placed before him—and in Rhodes's case this was literally true, for much of his research was done by others.[49] Evidence which the judge deemed false or prejudiced, he rejected; the honest testimony of honest men, he accepted. It did not occur to him that such testimony, when rooted in preconceptions as to race shared by the judge, might also be false or prejudiced or only partly true.

Further, the historian, as judge, was not to go beyond the *valid* testimony presented; he was under no obligation to scour the most unlikely places for data without considerations of race or color. Since it was generally agreed that the Negro was the most inferior of human beings, responsive only to sensual stimuli, why should his testimony be admitted in a court governed by the rules of reason? As to white sources favorable to the Negro, it was obvious to Rhodes that they were tainted by either interest or emotion, and were thus inadmissible. In short, just as Rhodes believed that the antislavery historian could best write objective history of the Civil War,[50] so he assumed that the white historian with Anglo-Saxon sympathies could best write objective history of the Reconstruction period.

Finally, it should be noted that Rhodes believed that history had a didactic purpose: quoting Tacitus, he declared that purpose to be "to let no worthy action be uncommemorated, and to hold out the reprobation of posterity as a terror to evil words and deeds."[51] Within the framework of American history, the purpose was to inculcate patriotism and to encourage the young to "follow in the path of the distinguished."[52] It is indicative of the unreflective character of Rhodes's mind that he saw no apparent contradiction between such attitudes and his avowal that he tried to write history without fear, favor, or prejudice.

So much for Rhodes himself. How are we to explain his reputation among historians for sound, critical scholarship?

First, so far as scholars of his day checked his sources they found them generally to be accurately cited. Indeed, this was a source of considerable praise by scholarly reviewers.[53] As to his use of purely white sources, and then only white sources unsympathetic with the Negro, Rhodes's judgments seemed so consonant with obvious "truths" in relation to race that the issue of bias rarely arose. Belief in his fairness was strengthened also by his frequent avowal that there was room for difference of opinion and by his stated willingness to make corrections of fact in future editions of his work.[54] His failure to include Negro opinion within this framework naturally elicited little objection from a scholarly community predominantly Anglo-Saxon in origin and attitude which shared the general belief in Negro inferiority.

Acceptance of Rhodes as a model of objectivity rested also on the fact that he and his public, lay and scholarly, shared a set of assumptions about race which they believed to be scientific truths. Rhodes's effort to buttress the accepted notion of Negro inferiority with the weight of scientific opinion seemed to prove once again his conscientious effort to be fair and objective. His exclusion of testimony favorable to the Negro, whether from white or Negro sources, seemed so much in the nature of things as to pass almost unnoticed. In this respect, Rhodes differed little from other historians of the early part of the twentieth century, as may be seen from examination of the works on Reconstruction which appeared at that time.[55]

Finally, Rhodes, in his role of didactic historian, handed down not only historical but also moral judgments. These judgments, stated explicitly throughout the seven volumes which appeared in the fateful period between 1892 and 1906, validated the traditional middle-class virtues of hard work, thrift, and sobriety; and the traditional beliefs in "hard money," laissez faire, and Anglo-Saxon supremacy.[56] To a middle class shaken by the panic of 1893 and its consequences, such as the Pullman strike and the Populist revolt, the intoning of the ancient litanies in the calm, authoritative accents of the historian brought comfort and reassurance. To the reawakened spirit of nationalism which marked the sectional reconciliation of the 1890's, Rhodes supplied reinterpretations of the Civil War and Reconstruction which brought a glow of satisfaction to readers in both North and South. To the confident, expansive America of the early twentieth century, Rhodes carried the message that the American people were sound at the core, representing, indeed, one of the foremost civilizing influences of the period. Scholars as well as laymen responded warmly to such genial assurance. As John T. Morse, Jr., put it: "Precisely such a book had been keenly desired, but by whom it should be written no one had been able to suggest. Now this secret was made known. . . . There was one universal acclaim of praise." [57]

What does all this have to do with discussion of the scientific nature of history?

It has been shown that Rhodes strove to write objectively and indeed quite honestly believed that he had done so. It has been noted that the scholarly critics of his day shared the opinion that he was a model of objectivity. It has also been indicated that from the vantage point of our own day it appears that Rhodes fell far short of that ideal. This study of an individual historian, therefore, suggests the following conclusion:

That until we have devised some means whereby the historian may isolate his judgments as historian from the influence of his own past and his own cultural milieu; and, perhaps more importantly, some means whereby the community of historical scholars may abstract its critical judgments from the unexamined assumptions which it makes about the nature of knowledge, of man, and of society, it seems premature to talk of history as a genuinely scientific discipline. Until that happy day, the historian will have to continue to beware of the lies of honest men—including his own.

NOTES

1. William H. Walsh, *An Introduction to Philosophy of History* (London, 1951), p. 96.

2. Published in New York from 1892 to 1906. It will be referred to hereafter as *History*.

3. Samuel Eliot Morison and Henry Steele Commager, *The Growth of the American Republic* (New York, 1950), I, 780; II, 829.

4. Rhodes to Charles Francis Adams, Jr., March 19, 1907, Rhodes Papers (Massachusetts Historical Society, Boston).

5. Rhodes to George A. Myers, April 19, 1916, in John A. Garraty (ed.), "The Correspondence of George A. Myers and James Ford Rhodes, 1910-1923," *Ohio Historical Quarterly*, LXIV (1955), 148.

6. Theodore Roosevelt to Rhodes, November 29, 1904, in Elting E. Morison (ed.), *The Letters of Theodore Roosevelt* (Cambridge, Mass., 1951-54), IV, 1049; Gamaliel Bradford to Rhodes, May 18, 1921, in Letterbooks of Gamaliel Bradford (Houghton Library, Harvard University); Oliver Wendell Holmes, Jr., to Mrs. Mark Hanna, March 31, 1919, and Albert Shaw to Rhodes, February 14, 1907, Rhodes Papers; *World's Work*, XIII (1906-7), 8378-8379; *International Socialist Review*, V (1905), 572; VII (1907), 635-636.

7. Woodrow Wilson, *Division and Reunion, 1829-1909* (New York, 1909), p. xi; Albert Bushnell Hart, *Slavery and Abolition* (New York, 1906), Dedication; Edward Channing, *The United States of America, 1765-1865* (New York, 1896), pp. vii-viii; Frederic L. Paxson, *The Civil War* (New York, 1911), p. x; William E. Dodd to Rhodes, February 22, 1907, Rhodes Papers.

8. John T. Morse, Jr., to Rhodes, February 7, 1920, Rhodes Papers.

9. Charles H. Firth to Rhodes, January 28, 1900, December 29, 1904, January 31, 1907; W. E. H. Lecky to Rhodes, August 25, 1895, November 11, 1899; Samuel R. Gardiner to Rhodes, October 13, 1895; Rhodes Papers.

10. Rhodes, *History*, I, 370; V, 556.

11. *Ibid.*, I, 318; V, 556; VI, 37-39.

12. *Ibid.*, I, 319-322.

13. *Ibid.*, VII, 169-170.

14. *Ibid.*, VI, 38.

15. *Ibid.*, VI, 35-36; VII, 168, 171.

16. *Ibid.*, VII, 104, 168. The citations refer to specific state governments, but they summarize Rhodes's overall view.

17. *Ibid.*, VI, 309; VII, 140.

18. *Ibid.*, III, 15-16.

19. *Ibid.*, IV, 228, 286.

20. *Ibid.*, III, 117, 402.

21. *Ibid.*, IV, 213.

22. *Ibid.*, V, 55-56.

23. *Ibid.*, VII, 173.

24. Gunnar Myrdal, *An American Dilemma: The Negro Problem and Modern Democracy* (New York, 1944), p. 913; Rayford Logan, *The Negro in American Life and Thought: The Nadir, 1877-1901* (New York, 1954) p. 322.

25. Rhodes, *History*, VI, VII, *passim.*

26. Rhodes to George A. Myers, October 7, 1910, April 19, 1916, in Garraty, "The Correspondence of George A. Myers and James Ford Rhodes," pp. 16-17, 148.

27. Rhodes, *History*, V, 551-552.

28. *Ibid.*, VI, 323-324.

29. Quoted in *ibid.*, VII, 149.

30. Robert F. Durden, *James Shepherd Pike: Republicanism and the American Negro, 1850-1882* (Durham, N.C., 1957), p. 187.

31. Rhodes, *History*, VII, 151.

32. James G. Blaine, *Twenty Years of Congress from Lincoln to Garfield* (Norwich, Conn., 1885-86), II, 448-449, 515.

33. James Ford Rhodes, *Historical Essays* (New York, 1909), pp. 18, 20.

34. Personal interviews with Mrs. Bertha H. Rhodes and Mrs. Lucia McBride; Jacob E. Cooke, *Frederic Bancroft, Historian* (Norman, Okla., 1957), pp. 48-49.

35. "James Ford Rhodes," an autobiographical sketch quoted in full in Mark A. DeWolfe Howe, *James Ford Rhodes: American Historian* (New York, 1929), pp. 17-29.

36. *Ibid.*, pp. 18-19; *Cleveland Leader*, March 9, 1859, June 13, 25, 26, 1863; William C. Cochrane, *The Western Reserve and the Fugitive Slave Law: A Prelude to the Civil War* (Cleveland, 1920), p. 140; Herbert Croly, *Marcus Alonzo Hanna: His Life and Work* (New York, 1912), pp. 47, 49-50.

37. Quoted in Howe, *James Ford Rhodes*, pp. 18-19.

38. Rhodes, *History*, VII, 104.

39. Rhodes, *Historical Essays*, p. 293.

40. Rhodes, *History*, I, 322, 358-362; II, 141; III, 17, 98-99.

41. Rhodes, *Historical Essays*, pp. 280-282; Rhodes to Sir George Otto Trevelyan, August 30, 1914, Rhodes Papers.

42. Rhodes, *Historical Essays*, pp. 279-280.

43. *Ibid.*, p. 95.

44. *The Nation*, X (1870), 50; XIV (1872), 114, 116.

45. Rhodes, *History*, VI, 36.

46. Quoted in *ibid.*, pp. 37-38. The italics are Agassiz'.

47. *Ibid.*, p. 39.

48. Rhodes, *Historical Essays*, p. 18.

49. Foremost among these assistants was David M. Matteson. Others included the historians Edward G. Bourne and Henry E. Bourne. *Ibid.*, pp. 197-198. See also Rhodes to Henry E. Bourne, August 10, 13, 1890, and Rhodes to Charles H. Firth, December 16, 1902, Rhodes Papers.

50. Rhodes, *History*, I, 152.

51. Rhodes, *Historical Essays*, pp. 9, 43.

52. *Ibid.*, p. 22. See also Rhodes to Sir George Otto Trevelyan, March 3, 1921, Rhodes Papers.

53. Among numerous testimonials to Rhodes's use of sources may be cited H. Morse Stephens, "Some Living American Historians," *World's Work*, IV (1902), 2321; William Garrott Brown, review of Rhodes's fifth volume, *American Historical Review*, XI (1905-6), 183-184; J. G. deRoulhac Hamilton, "A Notable Achievement in Historical Writing," *South Atlantic Quarterly*, VI (1907), 87-91.

54. Rhodes Papers, XI, *passim;* Rhodes to George A. Myers, April 22, 1917, quoted in Howe, *James Ford Rhodes*, pp. 277-278; Rhodes to Daniel W. Howe, February 13, 1915, Rhodes Papers.

55. Outstanding examples are John W. Burgess, *Reconstruction and the Constitution, 1866-1876* (New York, 1905), and William A. Dunning, *Reconstruction, Political and Economic, 1865-1877* (New York, 1907).

56. Rhodes, *History*, I, 19, 143, 156, 160-161, 215, 370; II, 21, 51, 175, 502; III, 4, 14, 31-33, 100; V, 243; VI, 410; VII, 291.

57. "Memoir of James Ford Rhodes," *Proceedings of the Massachusetts Historical Society*, LX (1927), 179.

ON TURNER, BEARD AND SLAVERY

Staughton Lynd

The significance of slavery in American history is a largely unexplored theme. Despite the recent increase of interest in such topics as Abolitionism, prejudice, and the plantation as a social system, these subjects tend to be kept separated (one might almost say, segregated) from the rest of American history. We have not yet begun to view slavery as a key to the meaning of our national experience.

The thesis of this essay is that the significance of slavery in American history has been obscured partly because the twin giants of modern American historiography, Frederick Jackson Turner and Charles Beard, systematically minimized its importance. Believing that a sentimental memory of the Civil War was being used to veil an emerging conflict between the capitalist and the common man, these two great historians went to an opposite extreme. Turner, I shall argue, attempted to shift attention from slavery to the frontier, and in so doing tended to forget that there was a Southwestern as well as a Northwestern frontier [1] and that Simon Legree was a frontier farmer. Beard, similarly, portrayed slavery both in the era of the Revolution and at the time of the Civil War as merely a form of "agrarianism." Thereby Beard blurred the fact that the Constitution was not a victory of capitalism over slavery, but a compromise between capitalism and slavery, and accomplished the difficult feat of presenting the Civil War as a revolution, while deftly moving offstage the Abolitionist revolutionaries who made it. By minimizing the significance of slavery, Turner and Beard inevitably also minimized the significance of Abolitionism, and paved the way for the revisionist view of the Abolitionist as an impractical fanatic.

For both Turner and Beard, the characteristic social struggle in

Staughton Lynd, "On Turner, Beard and Slavery," *Journal of Negro History*, XLVIII, No. 4 (October, 1963), 235-250.

American history was that between the Eastern financier and the Western farmer. "We may trace the contest between the capitalist and the democratic pioneer from the earliest colonial days," Turner wrote; and Beard set this quotation at the beginning of his *Economic Origins of Jeffersonian Democracy.*[2] Both were heavily influenced by the Populist Revolt of the 1890's, and tended to use the Populist analogy in interpreting earlier American history. Thus Beard entitled the chapter of his *Rise of American Civilization* which dealt with the 1780's, "Populism and Reaction." Turner, likewise, said in an introduction to Orin Libby's path-breaking study of the vote on the United States Constitution: [3]

the present Populistic agitation finds its stronghold in those western and southern regions whose social and economic conditions are in many respects strikingly like those existing in 1787 in the areas that opposed the ratification of the Constitution.

The Populist analogy led both historians to believe that throughout American history "the democratic party was the agrarian element." [4] And in their histories those aristocratic agrarians, the slaveholders of the South, quietly drop out of sight.

The ironic result was that although Turner and Beard called for a new history written from the standpoint of "the fourth estate, the great mass of the people," [5] they ended in directing attention away from the most exploited group in our history: the Negroes. In their indifference to the Negro, Turner and Beard were typical of Northern liberals at the turn of the century. This attitude was also common among historians. Turner, as will appear, followed his University of Wisconsin colleague Ulrich Phillips' appraisal of slavery, and Beard's views on Reconstruction were akin to those of his fellow-Columbians, Burgess and Dunning. Yet there was special irony in the fact that as Turner and Beard were neglecting the Negro and exalting the frontier Populist, many real Populists in the South were building a new, if fleeting, unity between white and Negro tenants. Equally paradoxical was the fact that the Negro's betrayal by the Republican Party had been engineered by the same force which Turner and Beard denounced: capitalist finance.[6] In their neglect of the Negro, therefore, Turner and Beard reflected the viewpoint of a social group which they opposed and ignored the efforts of a group which they championed; in this aspect of their writings, they stood not with the farmer but with the financier.

I

In "The Significance of the Frontier in American History," Turner made it quite clear that he sought to displace a view of American history which stressed the struggle over slavery, a view symbolized at that time by the writing of Edward Von Holst. "When American history comes to be rightly viewed," Turner said, "it will be seen that the slavery question is an incident." [7] Earlier, in an essay called "Problems in American History," Turner had developed this idea as follows:

> In commenting upon the constitutional history of a recent American writer, Professor Von Holst remarks that the work is the play of *Hamlet* with Hamlet omitted, because the slavery struggle is not brought into prominence. Future historians may say of Professor Von Holst's great work on the same subject that it also is the play of *Hamlet* with the title role left out, because in his attention to slavery he has lost sight of the fundamental, dominating fact in United States history, the expansion of the United States from the Alleghenies to the Pacific.

"The struggle over slavery," Turner went on, "is a most important incident in our history, but it will be seen, as the meaning of events unfolds, that the real lines of American development, the forces dominating our character, are to be studied in the history of westward expansion"; and in his more famous essay, Turner repeated much the same thought in much the same language.[8] For a generation since 1861, slavery had been cast as the central character of the historical drama. Now, in the belief that he expressed the new needs of a new day, Turner brought the frontier forward in its stead.

The most troublesome obstacle to Turner's frontier thesis was the Southwestern frontier with its plantation pioneers. Here the covered wagons had been followed by long lines of slaves; here, as Jefferson Davis observed in 1861, it was slaves not freemen who had made farms out of the wilderness; here the structure of power was aristocratic not egalitarian; [9] here the effect of frontier life was to coarsen and brutalize the peculiar institution, not to humanize it. Great historian that he was,

Turner sensed this contradiction in his argument. His answer was that there had originally existed in the Southern uplands a democratic frontier society similar to that in the Northwest, but that the advance of slavery had overlaid and destroyed it. Very briefly mentioned in "The Significance of the Frontier" as first delivered, this important corollary was expanded at no less than three points in the text when Turner revised it for subsequent publication.[10] Again and again in later writings Turner repeated the thought that originally, before "the fall" as it were, the Southern frontier like the Northern frontier had been a place of democracy and freedom.[11]

The belief that slavery was a late-coming and transitional force in the Southern interior underlay Turner's conception of Andrew Jackson, a key to the whole of Turner's thought. For Turner, Jackson was the personification of frontier ideals of "human rights" and "democracy," and Jacksonian Democracy "was based on the good fellowship and genuine social feeling of the frontier, in which classes and inequalities of fortune played little part." [12] This view of Jackson assumed a late dating of the moment when slavery overwhelmed the original Piedmont democracy and set the stamp of the plantation on the whole of the South. It presupposed that the transition (in Professor Abernethy's words) "from frontier to plantation in Tennessee" had not been consummated in 1828, when Jackson was elected to the Presidency. Throughout his life Turner vigorously defended the proposition that as late as 1830 the small farmer was the dominant social type of the Southwest, his "persistent contest against slavery" still in doubt.[13]

Turner's picture of the Southwest in Jackson's day is not convincing. Professor Abernethy has recently summed up a lifetime of research on the problem with the statement that by 1820 "the slave-owning planter was now the pioneer." [14] During Turner's lifetime, Edward Channing suggested that Jackson was a slaveholder who represented not frontier farmers but a solid slave South. In his last book Turner, with uncharacteristic passion, was still attacking Channing's thesis. "There was no 'solid South' in 1828," Turner declared and continued: [15]

The Mississippi Valley's psychology and politics were shaped by its pioneering experience to such an extent that it had a sectional attitude of its own. It would be impossible to understand the events of Jackson's administration if we regarded that portion of the Mississippi Valley which lies south of the Ohio River, reinforced by the slaveholding state of Missouri, as a part of a 'solid South,' dominated by slaveholding cotton planters in 1828.

Hence, Turner concluded, Andrew Jackson "was not so much a cotton planter and slaveholder as a personification of Western wishes and Western will." In the evaluation of Jackson, Turner's desire to center attention on Westward expansion met head-on with the fact of slavery which he wished to ignore. Turner was much more willing to recognize the influence on Jacksonian Democracy of the Eastern workingman [16] and the capitalist entrepreneur [17] than he was to concede the influence of the Southern slaveholder.[18]

Turner's conception of a diversified South wore a more unpleasant aspect as he applied it to the South of his own day. The old division of the South into democratic upland and aristocratic Black Belt still revealed itself, said Turner, in primary elections "in which the Negro issue is eliminated," although that division had been "obliterated in large measure in the era of civil war and reconstruction and in the later Solid South under the influence of the Negro problem." [19] Is it merely hyper-sensitiveness that makes the reader today perceive in these words a wish that not only "the Negro problem" but the Negro himself could, somehow, be "eliminated" from the American scene? Perhaps not; for coincidentally with the founding of the National Association for the Advancement of Colored People, Turner was writing: [20]

> the negro is still the problem of the South and while he remains there will be a Southern sectionalism. If the negro were removed, it seems not unlikely that the unity of the Mississippi Valley would once more have free play.

Turner went so far as to perceive in the triumph of the red neck and Jim Crow a victory for frontier egalitarianism. "Along the Southern Atlantic and the Gulf Coast," he wrote in 1914,[21]

> in spite of the preservative influence of the Negro, whose presence has always called out resistance to change on the part of the whites, the forces of social and industrial transformation are at work. The old tidewater aristocracy has surrendered to the up-country democrats.

Only a man profoundly insensitive to the experience of one-fifth of his fellow citizens could have spoken, in 1904, of "the wonderful development of the nation since the Reconstruction period," or could have called the generation 1889-1924 "these marvelous years." [22]

Tolerance toward the institution of slavery and intolerance toward the abolitionist movement are attitudes usually found together, for they support and supplement each other. So it was with Turner. As early as 1906, Turner accepted the authority of Ulrich Phillips on slavery; and almost a generation later, at the end of his life, the historian of democracy still shared Phillips' conception of "the presence of the Negro" and "slavery as the mode of dealing with the Negro" (the phrases are Turner's).[23] Most explicitly, Turner wrote: [24]

> It would seem that Northern men, in their conclusion that the slave was unhappy, tended to attribute to him their own feelings and reactions to the conditions under which he lived. In general, he was sufficiently fed, with a coarse diet, adequately clothed, but poorly housed (though not to such a degree as to produce discontent in the slave's mind), and allowed opportunity for expressing the natural joyousness of the African temperament; and hardship was felt rather by individuals than by the mass of slaves.

Abolitionism, accordingly, was mentioned by Turner (on the rare occasions when he mentioned it at all) as a diversion of the energies of American reform from its proper ends. Thus he wrote in his last book of "the diversion of the reformers to the abolition issue," as earlier he had insisted that the struggle over slavery and Reconstruction was "only one of the interests" of the years 1850-1870.[25]

It would have been difficult for any historian who identified himself so completely with the advance of the white settler across the continent to avoid insensitivity toward the victims of this process. Though he departed from the emphasis on Teutonic institutions prominent in the late nineteenth century, Turner did not altogether escape the biological presuppositions of the "germ" theory. "American colonization," he wrote in the early 1890's, "is part of a great historic movement—the Aryan migrations." [26] The American Indian was for Turner an obstacle in the path: Red Cloud of the Sioux, for example, was described by Turner as one who resisted "the march of civilization." [27] Most flagrant, perhaps because Turner's hero Jackson was involved, was Turner's attitude toward the removal of the Cherokees from Georgia. His account of the expulsion of this civilized nation, possessed of an alphabet, a newspaper, and a written constitution, began as follows: "From the beginning of the nation, the Indians on the borders of the settled area of Georgia were a menace and an obstacle to her development." [28] Turner was, in fact, very much a believer in Manifest Destiny. Thus he wrote: [29]

> De Tocqueville exclaimed, with reason, in 1833: "This gradual and continuous progress of the European race toward the Rocky

Mountains has the solemnity of a providential event. It is like a deluge of men, rising unabatedly, and driven daily onward by the hand of God."

Such blindness was not the whole of Frederick Jackson Turner's vision. But it restricted Turner's range as a historian. It confined his sympathies to those of his countrymen who were also white, and cut him off from the new viewpoints toward American history suggested by the experience of "the fugitive slave, and the Mexican prisoner on parole, and the Indian come to plead the wrongs of his race." [30]

II

Charles Beard did not share the quasi-racist attitude toward the Negro expressed by the older, more provincial Turner. He did view the Negro's role in American history as altogether passive: thus he characterized the attitude of slaves during the Civil War as a blend of contentment, affection for their owners, inertia, and helplessness.[31] But Beard's essential disservice to the effort to grasp what American slavery means for American history lay in his view of slavery as an economic system. Beard's approach to slavery, whether in the era of the American Revolution or in the period of the Civil War, was characterized above all by a tendency to regard slavery as merely a form of "agrarianism." In analyzing the social conflicts of both these American revolutions, Beard was inclined to lump together three very different groups: Frontier subsistence farmers, Northern commercial farmers, and Southern plantation owners.

One of the confusions resulting from Beard's use of the term "agrarianism" was a blurring of the distinction between subsistence and commercial farmers. Orin G. Libby had labored to make this distinction in his work on the ratification of the Constitution, concluding that farmers who lived near cities or near navigable rivers were for the most part Federalists. Beard's insistence on the conflict of "capitalism" and "agrarianism" (or as he put it in An Economic Interpretation of the Constitution, "personalty" and "realty") left little place for the commercial farmer, whose importance had recently to be re-emphasized by

Jackson Main.[32] In the era of the Civil War, too, many farmers, far from opposing capitalism, "saw their futures linked" with industrial and commercial development.[33]

More fundamental was Beard's failure to distinguish the freehold farmer with his two hundred acres from the slaveholding planter. The *locus classicus* for Beard's attitude is his analysis of the Civil War in *The Rise of American Civilization*. Describing the irrepressible conflict as one between Northern capitalism and Southern agrarianism, Beard argued that "the institution of slavery was not the fundamental issue" on the ground that no major political party, including the Republican Party of 1860, put the abolition of slavery in its platform.[34] This was strange reasoning for a historian whose stock-in-trade was to discern the economic motives which underlay men's declared intentions. And why did Beard take at face value the planks on tariffs, railroads, and homesteads in the platform of the Republican Party, but disregard the equally explicit statements of Alexander Stephens and Jefferson Davis that slavery was the cornerstone of the Confederacy?

What is at issue here is not economic interpretation as such. Obviously an economic interpretation is possible which stresses slavery, rather than minimizing it. As Thomas Pressly observes,[35] no less an economic interpreter than Karl Marx poured scorn on the belief that the tariff caused the war; Marx, unlike Beard, regarded the abolitionists as heroes, and considered the war's central issue to be the survival of democracy (albeit "bourgeois democracy") in America and all over the world.[36] Thus Beard did not propose an analysis which followed inevitably from an emphasis on economics. Beard's theory of the Civil War, like Turner's theory of the frontier, was distinctive not so much because it was economic, as because it attacked a previously prevailing theory based on slavery.

If for Beard the Civil War was a bloodbath inspired by sordid motives, Reconstruction was an equally self-interested attempt by Northern capitalists to ensure the fruits of victory. Don Fehrenbacher comments that "by disparaging the outcome of the war and the motives of Radical Republicanism, the Beard thesis tended to merge with the Dunning interpretation of Reconstruction."[37] Particularly noteworthy is Beard's remark about Negro suffrage in the Reconstruction period, that it "was tried with results which, to a large degree, would have been ludicrous if they had not been pitiable."[38] Beard's shallow and essentially uninterested attitude toward the adventure of Black Reconstruction is another illustration of the point made earlier, that to minimize the significance of slavery is to miss the meaning of the struggle against slavery, too.

Less obvious is the fact that Beard also neglected the impact of slavery in his most famous historical analysis, *An Economic Interpretation of the Constitution of the United States*. Here Beard's self-alienation from the Abolitionist tradition cost him dearly, for he neglected entirely the Abolitionist critique of the Constitution as a covenant with death and an agreement with hell because of its compromise with slavery. Beard noted the clauses of the Constitution protecting slavery; but slavery as an independent force in the shaping and ratification of the document escaped him, because it could not be fitted into the conflict of capitalism and agrarianism which, in this connection as in others, he considered quintessential.

Precise in so much else, Beard's famous book is strangely vague and confused in its handling of slavery. Was property in slaves "personalty" or "realty"? Beard wavered. In the chapter on "The Economic Interests of the Members of the Convention," Beard listed fifteen members of the Convention who owned "personalty in slaves." [39] But in the earlier chapter on "A Survey of Economic Interests in 1787," Beard classed "the slaveholders of the south" as "real property holders," and did not include slaveholding among the various "groups of personal property interests." [40]

This ambiguity in the economic analysis of slavery led to confusion in Beard's treatment of the politics of the slaveholders in the ratification struggle. Indeed, it would be more accurate to say that Beard nowhere squarely confronted the question of whether the Southern slaveholders were Federalists or Anti-Federalists. In surveying the ratification process in the several states, Beard built on Libby's conclusion that voters favoring the Constitution were concentrated near the coast; but, following Libby, he chose to consider Tidewater Virginia as "the region of the large towns, and where commercial interests were predominant" rather than as the region of densest slaveholding, and to characterize coastal South Carolina by saying, "its mercantile and commercial interests were important." [41] Libby's map should have made clear to Beard what has since been demonstrated in detail, that the great slaveholders were for the most part Federalists,[42] but when two years later he committed himself on the matter in *The Economic Origins of Jeffersonian Democracy* Beard came down on the wrong side.

Critics of Beard's work on the Constitution have made inadequate use of *The Economic Origins*, at the end of which Beard summarized the conclusions of both his books on the foundation of our national government. In this summary, Beard began by presenting the familiar capitalist-agrarian dualism: [43]

It is established upon a statistical basis that the Constitution of the United States was the product of a conflict between capitalistic and agrarian interests. The support for the adoption of the Constitution came principally from the cities and regions where the commercial, financial, manufacturing, and speculative interests were concentrated and the bulk of the opposition came from the small farming and debtor classes, particularly those back from the sea board.

From this opening statement Beard went on in subsequent paragraphs to reiterate his view that the core of both the Anti-Federalists of 1788 and the Jeffersonian Republicans of 1800 was made up of "backwoods agrarians" and "farmers." But then came a new thought, evidently the fruit of grappling with the role of Jefferson: the idea of "the agrarian masses led by an aristocracy of slave-owning planters." [44] At this point Beard finally brought into the structure of his analysis the slaveholding planters of the South.

Beard analyzed the relations of frontier farmers to plantation owners at one other place in *The Economic Origins*. Turner, we recall, had set these two groups in fiercest opposition, and Beard himself conceded that antagonism between them was "natural." But, Beard went on, "in a conflict with capitalism, the agrarians rallied around that agrarian class which had the cultural equipment for dominant direction," and so, by "a curious freak of fortune," the most aristocratic group in the nation became the spokesman for frontier democracy.[45] This was a suggestive formulation. It helped to explain how slaveowning Andrew Jackson had become a spokesman for the hill farmers of Tennessee. But it did *not* explain why the Southern slaveholders, enemies of Hamiltonian Federalism in 1800, had worked with the Federalists to make the Constitution in 1788. Beard wrongly supposed that the clash of 1800 was a continuation of the alignment of 1788, whereas in fact the party battles of the 1790's represented a breaking-up of the coalition which drafted and promoted the Constitution.

Adequately to explain the forces behind the Constitution, Beard would have had to jettison his fundamental dichotomy of "personalty" and "realty," and to recognize that men of wealth, rural as well as urban, had joined to make a stronger national government. This would have been just as "economic" an interpretation as the interpretation Beard proposed.[46] But Beard like Turner was wedded to a particular economic interpretation which aligned all agrarians, rich or poor, freehold-farming or plantation-owning, against capitalism. And so, Beard failed to see that the Constitution was a compromise between capitalists and slaveholders, the product as much of James Madison and the South Carolina Pinckneys as of Hamilton, Gouverneur Morris, and James Wilson.

Two scraps of evidence suggest that Beard was uneasy with his resolution of the role of slavery in early American politics, and might have modified his thinking. In a footnote to *The Economic Origins,* Beard promised that "a fuller review of the political economy of the Republicans after the inaugural of Jefferson will be given in a forthcoming volume on agrarianism and slavocracy." [47] Twenty years later, in a Preface to the second edition of *An Economic Interpretation,* Beard demonstrated his flexibility by acknowledging that the great landlords of the Hudson valley, whom in 1913-1915 he classified as Anti-Federalists, had in fact supported the Constitution. But a similar confrontation with the politics of the plantation-owners never took place. Two years after the publication of his book on Jeffersonian Democracy, Beard resigned from Columbia University on the issue of free speech and never returned to original research on the early national period.

III

In summary, it is clear that Turner and Beard sought to turn the attention of historians away from slavery toward the struggle of "capitalism" with "agrarianism." Much was gained thereby; but any sharply-defined insight must throw some things into shadow as it illuminates others, and the effect of the neglect of slavery by Turner and Beard has been to postpone the day when slavery will be recognized as one of the two or three distinctive themes of the American experience. When that day comes, it will seem grotesque that historians of the 1950's proposed "equality" as the concept which best enclosed the meaning of American history, or found the uniqueness of the American story in the absence of feudalism, while forgetting the presence of slavery.

It is past time for American historians to expose themselves to the presence of slavery, to the full force and the pain of it. Only then can they begin to understand the meaning for all American history of the great and terrible reality which the Founding Fathers of this country did not hesitate to call its original sin.

NOTES

1. Avery Craven has commented on Turner's tendency to assume that his native Middle West was typical: "Professor Turner's chief weaknesses lay in an uneven knowledge of the varied units which made up and contributed to American life." (Introduction to Frederick Jackson Turner, *The United States, 1830-1850: The Nation and Its Sections* [New York, 1935], p. vii.)

2. Turner used this phrase in his "Social Forces in American History" (1911), *The Frontier in American History* (New York, 1920), p. 325.

3. Orin G. Libby, *The Geographical Distribution of the Vote of the Thirteen States on the Federal Constitution, 1787-8* (Madison, 1894), pp. vi-vii.

4. Charles A. Beard, *An Economic Interpretation of the Constitution of the United States* (New York, 1913), p. 258.

5. Turner, "The Significance of History" (1891), *The Early Writings of Frederick Jackson Turner,* ed. Everett E. Edwards and Fulmer Mood (Madison, 1938), p. 47. See also in the same essay, Turner's description of his own time as "the age of socialistic inquiry" which requires historians to be concerned with "the economic basis of society in general" (*ibid.,* pp. 51-52).

6. The most recent study concludes: "Far from being the exclusive work of social and intellectual forces, the sectional realignment of the last quarter of the nineteenth century was largely the product of powerful economic forces. More than any other Northern groups, merchants engaged in Southern trade and Eastern industrialists frustrated Republican attempts to stress the war issues" (Stanley P. Hirshson, *Farewell to the Bloody Shirt: Northern Republicans and the Southern Negro, 1877-1893* [Bloomington, 1962], p. 252).

7. "The Significance of the Frontier in American History" (1893), *Early Writings,* p. 213.

8. "Problems in American History" (1892), *ibid.,* pp. 71-72. In "The Significance of the Frontier," Turner designates the period in which slavery had "primary but far from exclusive importance" as "the period from the end of the first half of the present century to the close of the Civil War": that is, merely the fifteen years 1850-1865 (*ibid.,* p. 213).

9. For a recent, well-documented exposition on this point, see Stanley Elkins and Eric McKitrick, "A Meaning for Turner's Frontier. Part II: The Southwest Frontier and New England," *Political Science Quarterly,* LXIX (1954), 565-583.

10. These additions are presented in an appendix to Turner's *Early Writings,* pp. 283, 285-286, 289-290.

11. See "Problems in American History" (1904), *The Significance of Sec-*

tions in American History (New York, 1932), pp. 12-13; "Is Sectionalism
Dying Away?" (1908), *ibid.*, pp. 293-295; "The Problem of the West" (1896),
The Frontier in American History, pp. 216-217; "The Old West" (1908), *ibid.*,
pp. 91 ff., 114 ff.; "Dominant Forces in Western Life" (1897), *ibid.*, p. 241;
The Rise of the New West, 1819-1829 (New York, 1906), pp. 52-53, 183;
The United States, 1830-1850, pp. 18, 30-31.

12. "Contributions of the West to American Democracy" (1903), *The
Frontier*, pp. 252-254; "The West and American Ideals" (1914), *ibid.*, pp.
302-303; "Western State-Making in the Revolutionary Era" (1895-1896),
Sections, p. 138; *The United States, 1830-1850*, p. 30.

13. *The United States, 1830-1850*, p. 18; "The Old West" (1908), *The
Frontier*, p. 122.

14. Thomas Perkins Abernethy, *The South in the New Nation, 1789-1819*
(Baton Rouge, 1961), p. 475. See also Abernethy, *From Frontier to Plantation in Tennessee* (Chapel Hill, 1932), p. 208:

Slaves had been brought out by Robertson and the earliest settlers and
figured in the life of the frontier stations. . . . A traveler in 1802
reported that plantations along the Knoxville road as far east as the
Cumberland crossing at Cairo were within a mile or two of each other.
. . . In 1795 the slave population of Middle Tennessee was more than
20 per cent of the whole, whereas in East Tennessee it was not more
than 12½ per cent.

Andrew Jackson bought a Negro girl shortly after his arrival in Tennessee
in 1788, and in the early 1820's the city of Nashville purchased fifty slaves
to keep its streets in repair (*ibid.*, pp. 123, 278).

Everett Dick, in his *The Dixie Frontier* (New York, 1948), presents similar evidence regarding Kentucky: "The first Kentucky settlers brought with
them their slaves. . . . In 1777, when a census of the inhabitants of
Harrodsburg, Kentucky, was taken, 10 per cent of the population was
slave" (p. 87; see also p. 17).

In 1820, there were more than 350,000 slaves in the states and territories of the frontier South (Kentucky, Tennessee, Alabama, Mississippi,
Louisiana, Arkansas, Missouri, and western Georgia). In none were slaves
less than 10 per cent of the total population; in Mississippi and Louisiana
they were more than 40 per cent. (For these statistics, see Bureau of the
Census, *A Century of Population Growth* . . . [Washington, 1909], pp. 82,
133, 222.) Wagon trains moving west with their slaves about 1820 are
described, e.g., by Abernethy, *The Formative Period in Alabama, 1815-1828*
(Montgomery, 1922), p. 26, and by Timothy Flint, *Recollections of the Last
Ten Years* (New York, 1932), pp. 194-195.

15. *The United States, 1830-1850*, pp. 31-32.

16. As early as 1896, Turner followed his famous statement that American
democracy "came, stark and strong and full of life, from the American forest,"
with the sentence: "But the triumph of this Western democracy revealed also
the fact that it could rally to its aid the laboring classes of the coast, then just
beginning to acquire self-consciousness and organization" ("The Problem of

the West" [1896], *The Frontier*, p. 216). Turner never lost sight of the workingman; see "Social Forces in American History" (1911), *ibid.*, pp. 326-327; "The West and American Ideals" (1914), *ibid.*, p. 303; "Middle Western Pioneer Democracy" (1918), *ibid.*, pp. 347-348; *The United States, 1830-1850*, pp. 578-579.

17. Turner discussed the conception that Jacksonian Democracy was essentially a movement of "expectant capitalists" in "Middle Western Pioneer Democracy" (1918), *The Frontier*, pp. 342-343, and in *The United States, 1830-1850*, p. 20.

18. Compare Arthur Schlesinger, Jr.'s brilliant but essentially unsuccessful attempt to explain away the ties between Jacksonian Democracy and the slave South in his *The Age of Jackson* (Boston, 1946), e.g., pp. 407-410, 424-427, 490-492, 505-507.

19. "Geographical Influences in American Political History" (1914), *Sections*, p. 190.

20. "Is Sectionalism in America Dying Away?" (1908), *ibid.*, p. 307.

21. "The West and American Ideals" (1914), *The Frontier*, p. 295.

22. "Problems in American History" (1904), *Sections*, p. 19; "Since the Foundations" (1924), *ibid.*, p. 215.

23. *Rise of the New West*, p. xvii; *The United States, 1830-1850*, pp. 149 n., 209.

24. *Ibid.*, p. 167.

25. *Ibid.*, p. 589; "Social Forces in American History" (1911), *The Frontier*, p. 330.

26. Introduction to extension lectures (1891), quoted in *Early Writings*, p. 33 n.

27. "The Middle West," *The Frontier*, p. 144.

28. See the combined excerpts from Turner's writings on the Cherokee removal in *The Removal of the Cherokee Nation*, ed. Louis Filler and Allen Guttmann (Boston, 1962), pp. 102-105.

29. "The Middle West," *The Frontier*, p. 153.

30. The quoted phrase is, of course, from Henry David Thoreau's *Essay on Civil Disobedience*.

31. Charles and Mary Beard, *The Rise of American Civilization* (New York, 1940), II, 116. At the same point Beard says of the slaves before the Civil War: "At any rate they had made no striking development in intelligence."

32. Jackson T. Main, *The Antifederalists: Critics of the Constitution, 1781-1787* (Chapel Hill, 1961), pp. 270-274.

33. Eugene D. Genovese, "The Significance of the Slave Plantation for Southern Economic Development," *Journal of Southern History*, XXVIII (1962), 427.

34. Beard, *Rise of American Civilization*, II, 40.

35. Thomas J. Pressly, *Americans Interpret Their Civil War* (Princeton, 1954), p. 216.

36. See Karl Marx and Friedrich Engels, *The Civil War in the United States* (New York, 1961), pp. 13, 58-59, 202-206, 255, 258, 279.

37. Don E. Fehrenbacher, "Disunion and Reunion," *The Reconstruction of American History*, ed. John Higham (New York, 1962), p. 110.

38. *American Government and Politics* (New York, 1910), p. 86.

39. *Economic Interpretation*, p. 151.

40. *Ibid.*, pp. 29-30.

41. These phrases are Libby's, quoted by Beard, *Economic Interpretation*, pp. 285, 288.

42. See Main, *Antifederalists*, pp. 219 n., 232, 245.

It is possible that Beard picked up the idea that Southern slaveholders largely opposed the Constitution from Federalist polemics of the 1790's. Thus Fisher Ames wrote to George Richards Minot, Nov. 30, 1791, that "the men of weight in the four southern States (Charleston City excepted) were more generally *antis*" (*Works of Fisher Ames* . . . , ed. Seth Ames [Boston, 1954], I, 103).

43. *The Economic Origins of Jeffersonian Democracy* (New York, 1915), pp. 464-465.

44. *Economic Origins*, pp. 466-467.

45. *Ibid.*, pp. 398-399. Schlesinger repeats this formulation in his *Age of Jackson*, p. 20: "Only in the planting South did agriculture possess concentrated holdings, alert leadership and a compulsion to run the state. To the Southern planters thus fell the main responsibility of opposing the Hamiltonian tendencies in the government." Beard himself quotes Richard Hildreth, *History of the United States* (New York, 1856), IV, 348-350.

46. E. James Ferguson, for example, interprets the Constitution from an economic standpoint but sharply disavows Beard's dichotomy of "personalty" and "realty" ("The Forces Behind the Constitution," *William and Mary Quarterly*, ser. 3, XIX [1962], 436).

47. *Economic Origins*, p. 440 n.

PART III

MAJOR TRENDS
IN NEGRO HISTORY

Racism,
Implicit and Explicit

I*f the history of the Negro in the United States is intertwined with that of the white majority, the points at which the two histories engage are the image of the Negro held by the white majority and the treatment resulting from that image. When slavery was legal, the image was quite clear. The slave occupied a degraded position; the Negro was degraded. Which belief came first is, as we have seen in Part II, a matter of dispute; nevertheless, the equation remained the same until the Civil War. But what about the image of the free Negro before the Civil War, or of the emancipated Negro after the war? Answering this question is one of the major contributions of Negro history to the understanding of American history. Racism is seen to be pervasive in the life of the Republic and the amount of prejudice is only now being discerned.*

Why this racism has not been obvious is a question best answered by C. Vann Woodward in his essay-review, "The Antislavery Myth." For Negroes the racism has always been there; but the white majority, including historians of that majority, blinded themselves to prejudice by viewing the Civil War as a struggle for human dignity and freedom, a fight to free the slaves. This polarization of the conflict led to a kind of treasury of virtue in the North, where only goodness, equality, and mercy existed. Thus, antislavery became synonymous with equality for the Negro, and the Negro could easily be ignored because of the presumed favor of freedom.

The following four selections all touch on the problem of racism, each in a different area and in a different way. The first essay, by Richard C. Wade, portrays the lot of the free Negro in Cincinnati, a border city, from 1800 to 1830, in the face of a growing resistance to increasing Negro settlement. While Wade concludes that the position of the Negro improved by the end of the period—an argument not necessarily convincing in light of his evidence—his picture of the daily life of the free Negro is indeed grim. Prejudice, segregation, and all the other attributes of third-class citizenship appear in Cincinnati in the early nineteenth century. While Cincinnati cannot be said to be typical of all Northern cities, the study of other cities —New York and Pittsburgh—reveals similar prejudices. It has been argued that the violence directed against the Irish in cities during the same period may very well be compared with the Cincinnati riot of 1829. There are, however, two important differences. In the first-place, the anti-Irish riots did not drastically reduce the Irish population; in the second place, the Negro did not seize a political opportunity to control the cities as did the Irish. One of Wade's books, Slavery in the Cities, *provides a further insight. Urban slavery in the South came to resemble the segregated status of the free Negro in the North. Carrying Wade's point to its logical extension, one finds little difference between the more mobile free Negro of Northern cities and the legally bound slave of the South.*

Leon Litwack's perceptive article demonstrates quite convincingly that even among the most outspoken white supporters of abolition there was considerable discussion about the social role of the Negro. Although these abolitionists argued for equal rights and succeeded in lifting some of the legal and institutional barriers to equal treatment, they also reflected prejudice and uncertainty in at least some of their attitudes. To that extent they shared the stereotypes of those who argued that slavery was a positive good. It should come as no shock to anyone of historical sophistication that the equalitarian assumptions of the mid-twentieth century were not shared by people in the nineteenth; still the depth of the prejudice is startling.

Jacque Voegoli attacks another myth in the pantheon which supports the moral superiority of the North in promoting Negro equality. He examines the positions of the Democratic and Republican parties in the Northwest during the critical years 1861-1862, largely through the printed accounts of party representatives. The older interpretation still found in standard textbooks of American history is that this area strongly supported both the Civil War and civil rights. The evidence usually cited is the participation of the Northwest in the war and the political success of the Republican Party there. Voegoli, however, shows that the Northwest was sympathetic to white superiority, and that the Republicans, in answering the charges of the Democrats, took a position reflecting considerable antipathy. Voegoli's article shows that the extent of prejudice was not noticeably less than that in Cincinnati thirty years earlier.

The last selection, written by Everett Carter, takes us into the twentieth century and marks the sad conjunction of an old prejudice with a new art form. The Southern views expressed in the first modern movie are depressingly similar to those seen in earlier essays. The film presents a slanted appraisal of slavery and Reconstruction, in a manner charged with sexual overtones and an exceedingly romantic view of the Southern past. This combination had an awesome impact upon an audience which had not become inured to the propagandizing of the mass media. Thus the prejudices of the nineteenth century became the first emotions conveyed by the communications revolution engendered by the movies, and the myth goes on.

The four selections which follow suggest a major theme in American cultural history brought to light by a close look at the Negro. The history of the United States shows that the majority of Americans have believed in the myth of racial inferiority, that even the most liberal were unable to shake loose from this conviction. In addition, the history shows an unwillingness to face racism directly and an ability to clothe the ugly belief in fitting garments.

THE NEGRO IN CINCINNATI,

1800-1830

Richard C. Wade

The Negro of the first decades of the nineteenth century had two images of Cincinnati. One image presented the city as a refuge from bondage; the other revealed the tough struggle of the free blacks for a respected place in white society. John Malvin caught both of these images in his flight from Virginia to Cincinnati in 1827. "I thought upon coming to a free state like Ohio that I would find every door thrown open to receive me, but from the treatment I received by the people generally, I found it little better than in Virginia." [1]

The colored population in Cincinnati grew only slowly in the first two decades of the nineteenth century. The first census in 1801 does not mention any Negroes at all,[2] and in 1810 the official total was only 80.[3] Four years later a fire marshal's count added 100 more "free blacks" [4] and by 1816 another listing numbered 247 "blacks and mulattoes" out of a population of 6,493.[5] In 1821 Thomas Dugan's census noted only 135 "people of color," but even the author was not satisfied with its accuracy.[6] Indeed, there is reason to believe that these figures are inexact at almost each instance,[7] but they convey the total picture. Negroes made up about 2 per cent of Cincinnati's population in 1820.

The next decade, however, found Cincinnati's colored population expanding rapidly. By 1829 the *Cincinnati Directory* listed 2,258 "blacks and mulattoes" living in the city, comprising almost 10 per cent of its people.[8] Though freed Negroes constituted most of this increase, many slaves found sanctuary in Cincinnati. The newspapers complained continually that the local colored community harbored runaways, and even

Richard C. Wade, "The Negro in Cincinnati, 1800-1830," *Journal of Negro History*, XXXIX, No. 1 (January, 1954), 43-57.

accused Cincinnatians of kidnapping them from ships passing down the Ohio.[9] But escaped slaves accounted for only a small proportion of the city's increasing Negro population, and the question of the rights of free blacks would have been raised even if this problem had not been present.

Not much is known of colored life in early Cincinnati, though enough evidence remains to sketch its outlines. In the twenties most Negroes lived in the first and fourth wards—known as "Little Africa"—where they were cut off, though not segregated, from the white population.[10] Some were well-housed, especially before the great influx.[11] But their increase strained available facilities, and more and more they crowded into wooden shacks and shanties along Columbia Street and Western Row.[12] By 1827 frame tenements ten or twelve feet high covered the entire district, creating health and fire hazards. In one instance two families converted a blacksmith's shop into a combined dwelling and grocery store where at least a dozen people lived.[13] In 1830 a fire raged through the area, graphically portraying the congestion and warning the town of the consequences of continued neglect.

Whites owned most of this housing, renting on leases running from three to five years. The property brought good returns and the owners resisted the attempt of the city council to prohibit the further erection of wooden buildings in the center of town. "Heaven preserve the shanties," an editor sarcastically observed, "and supply the proprietors with tenants from whom the rent can be screwed, without respect to color or character." [14] The ordinance finally passed, but it restricted only future construction, and did not disturb existing dwellings.[15] "We cannot drive the black population from the city in the summary way of pulling down the houses over their heads," lamented local officials.[16] Though a few Negroes moved out of the ghetto, most were too poor to escape to the better parts of the city.[17]

Cincinnati's colored people had to take employment where they could find it, since few had the skill that could demand preference, and trade unions denied them membership. They were "generally disciplined to laborious occupations," Daniel Drake observed, finding them "prone to the performance of light and menial drudgery." [18] Some became porters, vendors, shoeblacks, and messengers, and women often hired out as domestics.[19] Mostly, however, blacks found employment on the construction of roads and canals, or as laboring hands in the expanding commerce and manufacturing of the city. Bad employment situations tended to aggravate this problem,[20] but opportunities in Cincinnati were far better than in the surrounding country, especially in the twenties. Indeed, the great increase of Negroes in that decade reflected the growing prosperity that followed the depression of 1819.

Irregular employment in legitimate pursuits led some into less useful activity. In fact, underneath Negro life in Cincinnati lay an ugly layer of vice, crime, and violence. Of course, this was true of white society in the river town as well, but colored low living was more easily identified and gained greater attention. In 1821 a visitor commented that "the first thing that struck my attention after arriving in this city, was the crowds of negroes, parading the streets after night." [21] Whites lodged constant complaints about gambling houses and the "night walkers, lewd persons, and those who lounge about without any visible means of support." [22] As early as 1808 an ordinance sought to curb "black and mulatto persons of idle lives and vicious habits" and the "Riots, quarrels and disturbances" they created. [23] In the previous year Charles Britton committed the most celebrated crime of the period when, in league with a white, he stole $47,000 from the Receiver of Public Monies. [24] Negroes were responsible for only a small part of the lawlessness in this frontier metropolis, but their enemies never ceased to level every kind of charge against them. Drake observed that though a large portion of the blacks "are reputed" to be petty thieves, "no more than one individual has been punished corporally . . . since the settlement of the town." [25]

Fortunately, the growing colored community had stabilizing as well as disorganizing elements. Schools and churches tried to provide the rudiments of learning to the younger generation, while less formalized agencies joined religious organizations to aid adults in finding areas of useful work. Here, however, a pattern of segregation emerged. Though whites often lent support to Negro institutions, they carefully sealed blacks off from participation in nearly all of the town's activities. [26] Since the churches restricted membership, the colored people established two of their own, the African Methodist and Methodist Episcopal. Little is known of their labors until they split over the question of the repeal of the "black laws" of Ohio in 1829.

Schools followed the same exclusive practices, and in 1815 the Cincinnati Lancaster Seminary made the segregation policy official by erecting a separate Negro institution. [27] Fourteen years later, when the city established a common school system, special provision was made for colored children. Religious education embodied the same custom. In 1817 two white ladies, anxious to do something for the "unfortunate children of Africa," founded the first Sunday school for Negroes in the town. [28] Within three years it had between 70 and 80 students instructed by more than a dozen teachers, all of whom were white. By the 1820's the social life of the Queen City sanctioned the increasing separation of the colored community from the rest of society. At just the time when the black population expanded most rapidly, contacts between the two groups lessened markedly.

The response of the white majority in Cincinnati to the growing colored population was a mixture of sympathy, fear, and hostility. This ambivalence is nowhere better illustrated than in the constitution adopted by the state of Ohio in 1803. Here the Negro was given his freedom, from both slavery and indenture; but he was also consigned to a clearly inferior status. He could not vote, hold office, or serve in the militia. The convention which drew up these provisions displayed a highly unsettled attitude, and the vote on limitations was close. The Hamilton County (Cincinnati) delegation took a liberal view on questions concerning the status of Negroes, supporting nine to one a motion to extend suffrage to colored citizens, and heavily opposing a move to strip them of all civil rights.[29]

The first session of the Ohio legislature drew the lines tighter, decreeing that no Negro could settle in the state unless he produced a certificate of freedom from some court, and requiring all colored residents to register and pay a fee of twelve and a half cents. The burden of freedom thus fell on the blacks. In addition, laws prohibited anyone from hiring Negroes without certificates, fining the employer up to fifty dollars. Even harsher were the statutes regarding aid to runaway slaves which involved penalties as high as one thousand dollars. All of these regulations embodied provisions which awarded half the fine to the informer, a system which later played into the hands of the unscrupulous.[30]

Three years later the state stiffened these laws. Now a black coming into Ohio had to find two bondsmen to pledge five hundred dollars for the "good behavior of such Negro or mulatto" and who agreed to pay for his support if he could not find employment. In addition, the legislature doubled the fine for hiring colored people who did not have the proper papers, and created a new category of discrimination which prohibited Negroes from testifying against whites in court.[31] By 1807, the legal system had created a lower order of citizenship for black men. The legislators, at least, considered them a disturbing element, and took care to ring them about with a group of restrictions which came to be known as the "black laws."

This code, however, represented a greater crystallization in attitude than was general in Cincinnati. Many considered the legislation unconstitutional and no attempt was made to register Negroes or require the certificates of freedom.[32] The regulations caused no comment in the newspapers, and the city never raised the issue in the stark form of the state provisions. However, the problem of the runaway remained, and as early as 1803 local officials instructed the constables to watch for slaves who "pass . . . the River Ohio and spend the Sabbath and nights" in the corporation.[33] Five years later the council again took notice of the "many black and mulatto persons . . . who resort to the Town of Cincinnati under the pretext that they are free, and thus impose on the public, to the great damage of town and society." [34] But when, in 1820, five Kentuckians crossed over to capture a Negro who had lived in the city for five years an editor called it an "insulting outrage." [35] Unlike Ohio's state legislators, most Cincinnatians in the first decades of the century had no fixed idea of the place of free colored people in a white society.

However, as the Negro population grew in the twenties signs of hostility appeared. The editor of *Liberty Hall* warned that "the rapid increase of our black population, to say nothing of slavery, is of itself a great evil." [36] The formation in 1826 of the Cincinnati Colonization Society with 120 members, including many prominent citizens, reflected the growing anxiety of some whites.[37] Two years later the city council appointed a committee to look into a citizens' petition which asked the city "to take measures to prevent the increase of the negro population within the city." [38] This new concern derived in part from the discussion of the general question of slavery, but its intensity stemmed from the emergence of a significant Negro population in Cincinnati. By 1829 one out of ten people in the city was colored. Some feared that "we shall be overwhelmed by an emigration at once wretched in its character and destructive in its consequences." [39] Hostility fed on this fear—and soon that hostility spilled over into violence.

The "riot of 1829" is well known. A demand grew up in the city in that year to have the "black laws" of 1804-7 enforced; some Negroes fled to Canada, and white sorties into the colored section followed. Carter Woodson wrote of this later phase, "Bands of ruffians held sway in the city for three days, as the police were unable or unwilling to restore order. Negroes were insulted on the streets, attacked in their homes, and even killed. About a thousand or twelve hundred of them found it advisable to leave for Canada, where they established the settlement known as Wilberforce." [40] Francis Weisenburger pictured the episode in the same dark tones. "Mob rule . . . broke out for three days and nights and resulted in many casualties. . . . Between one and two thousand Negroes . . . left for Canada with the aid of private funds." [41] Other historians have recorded the disorders of 1829 in similar terms.[42]

Yet a study of contemporary sources fails to disclose any mob rule or three-day riot. To be sure there was an effort to drive the Negroes from Cincinnati, sporadic fighting ensued, and over half the black population fled the city in that year. But they left to escape the enforcement of the "black laws" and not in fear of violence. The physical attacks on the colored community were only incidental to the exodus, much of which took place before the outbreaks. The episode is important not so much because of the bloodshed—which was common in western towns—but for the issue it dramatized. The growing Negro population in Cincinnati posed the problem of the place of the free black in white society. For two decades this question had not been raised directly, except as a part of the general argument over slavery and its abolition. But by the late twenties a crisis developed which many people thought required solution. As the black influx increased white anxiety mounted. In the discussion which followed, racial fear mingled with a concern for justice, laying bare the deep conflict within this young urban community.

The issue was drawn in July, 1829, when the trustees of the township, acting as Overseers of the Poor, announced that they would enforce the "black laws" of 1804-7 which had lain dormant for better than twenty years.[43] All Negroes were directed to register, present their certificates of freedom, and enroll the names of their bondsmen within thirty days or leave the city. Behind this decision was not only the growing uncertainty of many whites, but the results of a ward election which had centered on this proposal.[44] Debate, which had been submerged for many years, immediately came to the surface. The editor of the *Daily Gazette* charged the township officials with hasty action. "Have the Trustees and the citizens who call upon them to act well considered what they are about to undertake?" he asked. "Negroes and mulattoes are men, and have, at least, some of the rights of men under the laws. The proposition to drive fifteen hundred to two thousand persons from their homes, is one that ought not be made or attempted" without full deliberation.[45] Indeed, many questions were raised. Where could the blacks be sent? Most came from southern states and could not legally return. If they were to be moved elsewhere, who would pay for the mass deportation?[46]

In addition to doubts of expediency, there were also problems of constitutionality and justice. "Our Constitution was framed and adopted by white people, and for their own benefit," "Wilberforce" stated bluntly, "and they of course had a right to say on what terms they would admit black emigrants." He further noted that Negroes were streaming into the areas around Cincinnati, and he warned that soon "we shall be overwhelmed."[47] "Blackstone" countered by declaring the laws to be unconstitutional because they singled out one group and were not for general application. "We are, by straining the construction of the Constitution, paving the way for the destruction of our own liberties," he observed. "It is just as constitutional to proscribe a man for the size of his head, as for the color of his skin."[48] Many others joined the debate emphasizing the legal issue raised by either the laws or the trustees' action.

Some grew impatient with the constitutional question. "I would not wish to complain of the law or presume to judge of its injustice," wrote one citizen, "but will call upon humanity to exert her influence in their [the Negroes'] case." [49] "Jefferson" contended that no matter what the legality of "black laws" they were so "odious" that humane people would "never stand for their enforcement." [50] Equally exasperated was the editor of the *Chronicle*, who thought the time had come to stop talking and get down to business. "There is but one way—we must remove that population from our territory, while the power is still in our hands." [51] No local issue in Cincinnati had ever received the extended public debate that surrounded the demand to evict the city's colored residents.

While the argument raged the Negroes tried to delay the thirty-day deadline. Leading colored citizens called a meeting which drew up a petition to the state legislature asking for the repeal of "those obnoxious black laws." [52] Signatures of many prominent Cincinnatians, including such people as Nicholas Longworth and Wykoff Piatt, gave the document broad support.[53] But the Negroes themselves were split over tactics. The powerful Methodist Episcopal Church disassociated itself from the petition, declaring that "all we ask is a continuation of the smiles of the white people as we have hitherto enjoyed them." [54] Meanwhile, Israel Lewis and Thomas Cressup went to Canada to find a place for resettlement. "If the act is enforced, we, the poor sons of Aethiopia, must take shelter where we can find it. . . . If we cannot find it in America, where we were born and spent all our days, we must beg it 'elsewhere." [55]

The drive against the colored population continued, however, with support coming from many sources and from every stratum in society. Among the most fanatic were the town's transients—boatmen, wagoners, and adventurers—who had no roots and little interest in Cincinnati, and who could be counted on to join a frolic no matter what its objectives. They constituted the shock troops of any disorder since police action did not frighten or restrain them. In addition, some unskilled workers feared Negro competition on the job, and they hoped that the removal of the blacks would bring higher wages.[56] These groups were leaderless and inarticulate and by themselves could not have acted decisively.

Crucial in the drive against the Negroes was the activity of the Cincinnati Colonization Society. Founded in 1826, this branch of the national association quickly attracted great public attention and recruited for its leaders some of the city's most influential people. Though organizationally weak in the Queen City, its propaganda found many outlets. Newspapers carried long articles on possible homesites for the blacks, and editorials expounded its program. Many churches devoted one Sunday annually to a collection of funds for its support, and ministers lent their names to the idea. Though the Cincinnati group had a membership of only 120 in 1829, its list of officers read like the social register.

The Colonization Society not only sought to solve the slavery question by removing bonded Negroes from the country, but it applied the same doctrine to free blacks. "We consider this class of people a serious evil among us. . . . The only remedy afforded is, to colonize them in their mother country." [57] This notion—that people could be easily moved from one place to another—provided the rationale for the attempt to drive the colored population from Cincinnati. What was cruel was thus made to seem reasonable.[58] In addition to furnishing a philosophical justification to the aggressors, members of the local organization lent respectability to the movement. "Now is the time for the Colonization Societies 'to be up and doing,'" wrote one of them in the midst of the crisis.[59]

With this support the tension grew. The exact order of events is hard to establish. The first ultimatum was given the Negroes about July 1 and extensions placed the deadline at the beginning of September. But raids into the colored section took place during the interim, reaching a climax on the weekend of August 22 when "some two or three hundred of the lowest canaille" descended on the blacks bent on terror and pillage. By Saturday evening the Negroes, despairing of official protection, armed to defend themselves. Fighting broke out around midnight, and in the scuffle that followed Eli Herick, one of the raiders, was killed and two others were injured. The police rounded up ten blacks and seven whites. After a hearing the Mayor released all the Negroes, declaring they had acted in self-defense, and at the same time he fined the others a total of seven hundred dollars.[60]

This was the episode often referred to as the "riot of 1829." Such violence was not unusual in western cities.[61] Indeed, only one of the five daily newspapers reported the event, and memoirs of the period are silent on the incident. There was no mob rule and no reign of terror. Nevertheless, the raids on the colored community were important because they sharpened the issue and threw into bold relief the grim tendency of events. Public sympathy, for a long time mixed and confused, went out to the Negroes, leading many whites to review the situation and re-examine their position.

Before this reassessment could take place, however, over half the colored population had fled the city. Lewis and Cressup located some land near York in Canada, later called Wilberforce, where many of the refugees settled. The land "beats all for beauty and fertility," they boasted. "Our rights here as freemen will be respected. We shall be as free as the atmosphere we breathe." [62] The Quakers donated some money to facilitate the migration, and other large contributions came from New York and Pennsylvania. Some Cincinnatians suggested that public money be used for "the voluntary removal of the blacks from the state," but nothing ever came of the idea.[63] Most of the funds, however, were raised among Negroes in the Queen City.

By winter the crisis had passed. Though there is no way of knowing exactly how many colored people left Cincinnati, the number was certainly no less than 1,100 and probably higher. Among these displaced persons were many of the most industrious, stable, and prosperous members of the Negro community. They had the financial resources and social energy needed for movement, while the less successful and weaker stayed behind. Some leadership remained in the city, but the cream was skimmed off. The editor of the *Gazette*, who had earlier supported the enforcement of the "black laws," appraised the episode and spoke for a chastened town.

It has driven away the sober, honest, industrious, and useful portion of the colored population. The vagrant is unaffected by it. The effect is to lessen much of the moral restraint, which the presence of respectable persons of their own colour, imposed on the idle and indolent, as well as the profligate. It has exposed employers of coloured persons to suits by common informers, where no good or public motive was perceptible. It has reduced honest individuals to want and beggary, in the midst of plenty and employment; because employers were afraid to employ them. It has subjected men of colour who own property to great sacrifices. It has furnished an occasion for the oppressor and the common informer to exhibit themselves, and commence their depredations on the weak and defenceless, under cover of law. It has demonstrated the humiliating fact, that cruelty and injustice, the rank oppression of a devoted people, may be consummated in the midst of us, without exciting either sympathy, or operative indignation.[64]

The attempt to enforce the "black laws" was the critical point in the early life of Cincinnati's Negroes. Success would have removed the Queen City as the central link in the life line which brought so many slaves and free blacks to northern safety. The riots of the thirties, though more spectacular, never carried this same implication, for white abolitionists absorbed as much of the punishment as the colored people. Martyrdom had won friends for the Negroes, and they never again had to stand alone without outside support. By 1830 they had earned the right to live in Cincinnati; the next struggles were over the right to a better life.

NOTES

1. John Malvin, *Autobiography of John Malvin* (Cleveland, 1879), p. 11.

2. *Western Spy*, May 6, 1801.

3. *Ibid.*, November 31, 1810.

4. *Liberty Hall*, February 15, 1814.

5. *Ibid.*, February 19, 1816.

6. *Ibid.*, January 6, 1821.

7. There were Negroes in Cincinnati before 1800, but not in large numbers. See *Northwest Sentinel*, April 19, 1794.

8. *The Cincinnati Directory for the Year 1829* (Cincinnati, 1829), n.p.

9. For example see *Liberty Hall*, May 8, 1815; also Malvin, *op. cit.*, pp. 14-15.

10. *Cincinnati Advertiser*, August 18, 1830.

11. *Cincinnati Tax List, 1818*, MSS (Historical and Philosophical Society of Ohio, Cincinnati). Some Negroes owned land, and Anthony Thompson, John Harrison, and others had houses assessed at $100 and $200.

12. *Cincinnati Sentinel*, quoted in the *Western Star* (Lebanon, Ohio), August 29, 1829.

13. Cincinnati City Council, *Minutes*, August 22, 1827.

14. *Daily Gazette*, October 28, 1830.

15. Cincinnati City Council, *Minutes*, September 19, 1827. For background see also June 8 and June 29, 1825.

16. *Ibid.*, August 29, 1827.

17. In 1829 one Negro built a house valued between $200 and $300. *Daily Gazette*, July 28, 1929.

18. Daniel Drake, *Natural and Statistical View*, or *Picture of Cincinnati* (Cincinnati, 1815), p. 172.

19. *Liberty Hall*, July 9, 1829.

20. During the depression of 1819 the Overseers of the Poor threatened to invoke the "black laws" to get the Negroes off the pauper lists. *Ibid.*, September 3, 1819.

21. *Ibid.*, August 8, 1821.

22. *Ibid.*, August 25, 1825.

23. Town of Cincinnati, *Ordinances*, March 22 and September 20, 1808.

24. It is interesting to note that Britton was the key witness in the trial,

though a state law made it illegal for Negroes to testify against white men. Nicholas Longworth, the defendant's lawyer, tried to keep Britton from testifying, but after a long discussion the judge admitted the evidence. "Two Gentlemen of Law Knowledge," *The Trial of Charles Vattier* (Cincinnati, 1807), pp. 30ff., 56-65, 131ff.

25. Drake, *op. cit.*, p. 172.

26. The Cincinnati Haytian Union had many white members, though its leadership was colored. It sought to encourage Negro emigration to the new Caribbean republic.

27. Drake, *op. cit.*, p. 157.

28. *Liberty Hall*, September 30, 1820.

29. Charles J. Wilson, "The Negro in Early Ohio," Ohio Archeological and Historical Society, *Publications*, XXXIX (1930), 746, 751.

30. *Acts of the State of Ohio*, 1803, 2nd Session, Chap. ii, Sec. 1, 2, 3, 4, 5, 7.

31. *Ibid.*, 1806, 1st Session, Chap. vii, Sec. 1, 3, 4.

32. Drake, *op. cit.*, p. 171.

33. Cincinnati, *Ordinances*, March 22, 1803.

34. *Ibid.*, September 20, 1808.

35. *Liberty Hall*, January 28, 1820.

36. *Ibid.*, June 28, 1825.

37. Cincinnati Colonization Society, *Proceedings* (Cincinnati, 1833), p. 3.

38. Cincinnati City Council, *Minutes*, November 19, 1828.

39. *Daily Gazette*, July 24, 1829.

40. Carter G. Woodson, "The Negroes of Cincinnati Prior to the Civil War," *Journal of Negro History*, I (1916), 6-7.

41. Francis Weisenburger, *Passing of the Frontier, 1825-50* (Columbus, 1941), p. 42.

42. For example see John Hope Franklin, *From Slavery to Freedom* (New York, 1947), pp. 231-232; Herbert Aptheker, *A Documentary History of the Negro People in the United States* (New York, 1951), p. 102; Alvin F. Harlow, *Serene Cincinnatians* (New York, 1950), p. 207.

43. *Daily Gazette*, July 4, 1829.

44. *Cincinnati Advertiser*, March 27, 1829.

45. *Daily Gazette*, July 4, 1829.

46. *Ibid.*

47. *Ibid.*, July 24, 1829.

48. *Ibid.*, July 27 1829.

49. *Ibid.*, July 17, 1829.

50. *Ibid.*, July 28, 1829.

51. *Cincinnati Chronicle and Literary Gazette*, July 4, 1829.

52. Malvin, *op. cit.*, p. 13.

53. *Ibid.*

54. *Daily Gazette*, July 4, 1829.

55. *Cincinnati Advertiser*, March 27, 1829.

56. *Western Star* (Lebanon, Ohio), August 29, 1829.

57. *The African Repository and Colonial Journal,* V (1830), 185.

58. Alvin Harlow lays the blame for the "riot" on the abolitionists whom he claims darkened counsel and intensified bitterness (*op. cit.,* p. 207). Actually the abolitionists had not become very important in Cincinnati, and their strength was not comparable to that of the Colonization Society.

59. *Hamilton Intelligencer* (Hamilton, Ohio), July 21, 1829.

60. The best description of the weekend is in the *Western Star* (Lebanon, Ohio), August 19, 1829. Some property damage resulted because shortly afterward, C. Foote, "a coloured man," petitioned the city council for damages done "to his house during the late riott" (Cincinnati City Council, *Minutes,* September 2, 1829).

61. Violence of this kind was so frequent that many grew callous. Charles Hammond, the editor of the *Cincinnati Gazette,* wrote to an acquaintance in 1824 that "our friend Sam Richardson has had an affray at Louisville and stabbed a man—it is supposed dangerously—But such things are always expected—If death ensues it is, at best, a case of manslaughter" (Charles Hammond to John C. Wright, May 3, 1824, Hammond MSS [Ohio Archeological and Historical Society, Columbus]).

62. *Cincinnati Gazette,* July 30, 1829.

63. *Ibid.,* September 17, 1829.

64. *Ibid.,* August 17, 1829.

THE ABOLITIONIST DILEMMA:

THE ANTISLAVERY MOVEMENT

AND THE NORTHERN NEGRO

Leon F. Litwack

Consistency demanded that abolitionists move against racial oppression in both the North and the South. Slaveholders and their spokesmen repeatedly defended the "peculiar institution" on the ground that Negroes were unfit to enjoy the rights and privileges exercised by whites, and they pointed to northern treatment of the free Negro as substantial proof of the real benevolence of slavery and the hypocrisy of antislavery arguments.[1] Abolitionists did not ignore the plight of northern Negroes; indeed, they contended that slaves and free Negroes shared a similar plight. After surveying the condition of Negroes in northern states and cities, they could come to no other conclusion.

Although fundamental differences existed between a condition of legal servitude and freedom, municipal, state, and federal statutes relegated northern Negroes to a position of legal inferiority, while custom and prejudice reduced them to a subservient economic and social status. Disfranchised in nearly every state, denied the right to settle in some, confined to a diminishing list of menial employments, northern Negroes found themselves systematically separated from the white community. They were either excluded altogether from railway cars, omnibuses, stage coaches, and steamboats, or assigned to special "Jim Crow" sections; they sat in secluded and remote corners of theaters; they could enter

Leon F. Litwack, "The Abolitionist Dilemma: The Antislavery Movement and the Northern Negro," *New England Quarterly*, XXXIV, No. 1 (March, 1961), 50-73.

most hotels, restaurants, and resorts only as servants; and they prayed in "Negro pews" in white churches. Moreover, they were educated in segregated schools, punished in segregated prisons, nursed in segregated hospitals, and buried in segregated cemeteries. The public burying ground or "Potter's Field" in Cincinnati symbolized the tragic plight of the Negro—even in death. White bodies were laid east to west; Negroes north to south.[2]

As long as northern laws, institutions, and customs rendered "the freedom of the colored people but an empty name—but the debasing mockery of true freedom," abolitionists confessed that it would be difficult indeed to condemn the practices of the South. Abolitionists, in short, must strike at the roots of slavery, show the Negro's capacity for self-improvement, and demonstrate the sincerity of their own professed sympathy for his plight.[3] Improving the condition of northern Negroes thus formed an integral part of the antislavery movement. In the first issue of *The Liberator*, William Lloyd Garrison advised his "free colored brethren" that the struggle for equal rights in the North constituted "a leading object" of abolitionism.[4] In no other way, agreed James Russell Lowell, could abolitionists more effectively serve "their holy cause."[5]

By 1860 the antislavery societies could point to some important achievements in the North. What made them especially noteworthy was not only the existence of the powerful public hostility but dissension and prejudice within the abolitionist movement itself.

I

While deploring racial prejudice and endorsing the Negro's claim to full citizenship, many white abolitionists hesitated to carry their views to the point of social intercourse with their Negro brethren. Since racial mixing flouted the prevailing social code and might easily lead to mob action, antislavery advocates faced a real dilemma. If an abolitionist fought for equal rights, some argued, it did not necessarily follow that he must also consort with Negroes socially. Indeed, such an act might endanger the effectiveness of the antislavery cause. "May we not find it more efficient to go for their improvement in . . . civil privileges," James Birney asked, "leaving their introduction to social privileges out of the public discussion? Would it not be better to leave this . . . matter rather more at rest for the present time than to press it upon the whole community? May not urging it now be throwing too much in our way the prejudice against it, and defeat the elevation of the Col'd people to civil privileges?" [6]

Although several Negroes actively participated in the organization and activities of the antislavery societies, white abolitionists continued to disagree on the expediency of Negro membership. In 1835, for example, Garrison criticized William Ellery Channing, an antislavery sympathizer, for expressing the belief that "we ought never to have permitted our colored brethren to unite with us in our associations." [7] The following year Charles Follen admitted before the Massachusetts Anti-Slavery Society that abolitionists had been advised "not unnecessarily to shock the feelings, though they were but prejudices, of the white people, by admitting colored persons to our Anti-Slavery meetings and societies. We have been told that many who would otherwise act in union with us, were kept away by our disregard of the feelings of the community in this respect." However, Follen added, excluding Negroes would not only deprive the movement of some effective workers but it would comply with "inhuman prejudice," sanction the principle of slavery, and "give the lie to our own most solemn professions." While abolitionists should select their social friends according to their own principles, "how can we have the effrontery to expect the white slaveholder of the South to live on terms of civil equality with his colored slave, if we, the white abolitionists of the North, will not admit colored freemen as members of our Anti-Slavery Societies?" [8]

But such liberal sentiments did not always prevail. When abolitionist leaders met in New York on March 9, 1836, to arrange a program for the anniversary meeting of the American Anti-Slavery Society, Lewis Tappan proposed that a Negro minister be invited to deliver one of the addresses. However, considerable opposition thwarted such a bold plan. "This is a ticklish point," Tappan wrote that night. "I insisted upon it as we must act out our principles, but it was said the time has not come to mix with people of color in public. So to prevent disunion I submitted." [9] A month later an even more heated discussion occurred at a meeting of the executive committee of the Society, and one member threatened to resign if "true abolitionism" required social intercourse betwen Negroes and whites. "I have observed," Tappan wrote after the meeting, "that when the subject of acting out our profound principles in treating men irrespective of color is discussed heat is always produced. I anticipate that the battle is to be fought here, & if ever there is a split in our ranks it will arise from collision on this point." [10]

The meetings of a Philadelphia antislavery society vividly demonstrated the division in abolitionist ranks on the questions of Negro membership and social intercourse. Organized in 1836, this society dedicated itself to arrest the progress of slavery and to strive for eventual abolition. One year after its formation, however, the organization found itself spending five sessions to discuss the question, "Is it expedient for colored persons to join our Anti-Slavery Societies?" After hearing speakers on both sides, the members finally decided in the affirmative by a margin of two votes. Subsequent meetings discussed such questions as, "Ought Abolitionists to encourage colored persons in joining Anti-Slavery Societies?" and "Is it expedient for Abolitionists to encourage social intercourse between white and colored families?" While resolving at its 1837 quarterly meeting to remove public prejudice and encourage the intellectual, moral, and religious improvement of Negroes, the members debated and eventually tabled a resolution which declared that social intercourse with Negroes would strengthen the bitterness of public prejudice, retard the acquisition of civil and religious privileges, and fasten the chains of bondage even tighter, and which condemned "the conduct of those who feel it their duty to encourage such intercourse, as a necessary consequence of their profession of Anti-Slavery principles." Instead, the convention resolved that it was neither "our object, or duty, to encourage social intercourse between colored and white families." However, they agreed by a margin of ten votes that it would be expedient to accept Negroes as members of antislavery societies.[11]

Such problems apparently confronted foreign as well as American antislavery societies. Edward Abdy, a staunch English abolitionist who visited the United States in the years 1833-1834, later wrote to an American friend, "We cannot, I am ashamed to say, claim exemption from the prejudice of color. . . . [Gustave?] De Beaumont, when asked why Bisette was not a member of the Committee of the French abolition society replied—'Why! he is a colored man.' Here we have a religious man and a liberal expressing sentiments opposed to every rational idea of what we owe to God and humanity. Thus it is that Benevolence is employed to foster Pride—we humiliate while we relieve. . . . It really seems as if many considered an African . . . as entitled to the same sort of sympathy and subscribed to the anti-slavery society as they subscribe to the society for the prevention of cruelty to animals."[12]

While abolitionists searched their consciences for a way out of these perplexing problems, Lewis Tappan engaged in a bitter controversy with the revivalist leader and antislavery sympathizer Charles S. Finney, over the wisdom of mixing Negroes and whites in public functions. When, for example, Negro and white choirs shared the same platform at the first-anniversary meeting of the American Anti-Slavery Society in May, 1835, some abolitionist sympathizers, including Finney, apparently intimated that such intercourse had helped to provoke the July anti-Negro riots in New York City. But "the choirs sat separately in the orchestra," Tappan explained, "the whites on one side and the colored on the other!" Having "been cruelly slandered about attempts to mix black and white people," Tappan asserted that the seating of the two choirs was "the only attempt I ever made to mix up the two colors in any public assembly or elsewhere," and "this I did by order of a committee of which I was chairman." However, Tappen admitted that he had once dined with two Negro members of the executive committee of the American Anti-Slavery Society and occasionally with "a few colored 'gentlemen'" but this constituted "the [head] and front of my offending. . . . And yet many abolitionists have talked about the efforts at amalgamation, etc." [13]

Acting as an intermediary in the Tappan-Finney dispute, Theodore Weld, the leading western abolitionist, expressed his own views on the delicate subject of social intercourse. "Take more pains to treat with attention, courtesy, and cordiality a colored person than a white," Weld advised, "from the fact that he is colored." But in mixing the two races on a social basis, abolitionists should first ask whether its effect on the general public would be "a blessing or a curse to the Colored people"? Weld felt that his own feelings toward Negroes had been sufficiently demonstrated by his actions while attending the Lane Seminary in Cincinnati. "If I attended parties," he declared, "it was theirs—weddings—theirs—Funerals—theirs—Religious meetings—theirs—Sabbath schools—Bible classes—theirs." It did not necessarily follow, however, that he would walk arm-in-arm with a Negro woman at midday down the main street of Cincinnati. Such an act "would bring down a storm of vengeance upon the defenceless people of Color, throw them out of employ, drive them out homeless, and surrender them up victims to popular fury"; indeed, such "an ostentatious display of superiority to prejudice and a blistering bravado defiance" would misconstrue the true motives and objectives of abolitionists and turn public attention from their major goal—the destruction of slavery—to a "collateral" point. While it would be sinful to manifest any unkindness toward Negroes, abolitionists must realize, Weld concluded, that "there are times when we may refrain from making public visible demonstrations of feelings about differences of color in practical exhibitions, when such demonstrations would bring down persecutions on them." [14]

Charges of racial mixing also deeply annoyed Arthur Tappan. Defending his conduct as late as 1863, the New York abolitionist leader and philanthropist wrote to an English friend regarding his past views and actions. While Christian conduct had bound him to treat Negroes without respect to color, Tappan explained that he had always felt that public sentiment on the subject required "great prudence" on the part of abolitionists. Although he had consistently shown his willingness "publicly" to associate with "a well educated and refined colored person," he considered it best to refrain from social intercourse until "the public mind and conscience were more enlightened on the subject." It was thus a "malignant falsehood" to accuse him of "any gross assault on the fastidiousness of the age." As to charges that he or any member of his family "have ever put arms into the hands of colored men or women in New York or anywhere else, it is without the slightest foundation." [15]

The problems of Negro membership and social intercourse also aroused considerable discussion among the women's anti-slavery organizations. When two Quaker women formed a Female Anti-Slavery Society in Fall River, Massachusetts, and invited several interested Negroes to join, it "raised such a storm among some of the leading members that for a time, it threatened the dissolution of the Society." Although the opposition denied any objections to Negroes attending their meetings, they considered it improper to invite them to become members of the Society, "thus putting them on an equality with ourselves." [16] While the Fall River group finally decided in favor of admission, "wicked prejudices about colour" prevented Negro membership in the New York women's anti-slavery society.[17] Delegates to the national convention of anti-slavery women approved, although not unanimously, a resolution by Sarah M. Grimke calling upon abolitionists to associate with their oppressed brethren, to sit with them in churches, to appear with them on the streets, to grant them equal rights in steamboats and stages, and to visit them in their homes and receive them "as we do our white fellow citizens." [18] Less than a month after the convention, two Philadelphia abolitionists wrote that the recently passed resolution had "greatly alarmed" some of our "timid friends" who unsuccessfully attempted to expunge it from the published convention report. Not content with this setback, these "pseudo-abolitionists" endeavored to induce leading Philadelphia Negroes to deny publicly any desire to mix socially with whites; only such a disavowal, they warned, would avert "destruction and bloodshed." [19] In Cincinnati, meanwhile, several of the women teachers at the Negro school complained to Weld that some "halfhearted" abolitionist co-workers expressed alarm "if perchance we lay our hands on a curly head, or kiss a coloured face." Since such actions seemed to "offend their nice taste," it became increasingly difficult to work with these prejudiced women in the company of Negroes. "Dear Br. [other]," they pleaded, "do pray the Lord to send us co-workers instead of anti-workers." [20]

Regardless of public opposition and personal doubts, some abolitionists considered social intercourse with Negroes a demonstration of true devotion to the cause. While admitting that one could advocate "the civil emancipation of those whom he would still be unwilling to associate with," the American Anti-Slavery Society warned in its 1837 annual report that its members yielded too readily to prejudice. If color or public opinion alone explained an abolitionist's reluctance to associate with Negroes, then "he wrongs the cause in which he is engaged." [21] When abolitionists did mix with Negroes, it became almost fashionable to tell others about this novel experience, treating it as a personal triumph over the amassed forces of prejudice and evil. Weld, for example, related at great length his daily intercourse with Negroes in Cincinnati. When Negro ministers and friends mixed with whites at the Weld-Grimke wedding, the new bride explained, "They were our invited guests, and we thus had an opportunity to bear our testimony against the horrible prejudice which prevails against colored persons." [22] Both Negroes and whites attended the funeral of James Forten, a prominent Philadelphia Negro leader, and one white participant proudly described it as "a real amalgamation funeral." [23]

But such intercourse was, after all, novel and often dangerous in the ante bellum United States. In facing this annoying problem, many abolitionists did, indeed, appear hesitant, careful, apprehensive—but always curious. "I hear that Mrs. [Lydia] Child has had a party lately," a Massachusetts woman abolitionist wrote, "and invited colored persons, do write me about it." [24]

II

The aversion to social relations with Negroes might be ascribed in part to the fact that most whites, whether abolitionists or not, acknowledged the existence of vast differences—physical and mental—between the two races. Some abolitionists, for example, failed to question the validity of commonly accepted stereotypes of the Negro character; they contended instead that these peculiar racial qualities constituted no just grounds for denying Negroes freedom or equal political rights. On the other hand, abolitionists such as William Lloyd Garrison argued that the Negro could unfortunately do nothing about the color of his skin and this alone perpetuated prejudice. "The black color of the body, the woolly hair, the thick lips, and other peculiarities of the African," Garrison's *Liberator* remarked, "form so striking a contrast to the Caucasian race, that they may be distinguished at a glance. . . . They are branded by the hand of nature with a perpetual mark of disgrace." [25]

Nevertheless, abolitionist literature contributed its share to the popular conception of the Negro, frequently referring to his meek, servile, comical, minstrel-like qualities. For example, William Ellery Channing, writing in an antislavery tract, described the Negro as "among the mildest, gentlest of men"; his nature is "affectionate, easily touched" and therefore more open to religious impression than the white man's; the European races manifest "more courage, enterprise, invention" but the Negro "carries within him, much more than we, the germs of a meek, long-suffering, loving virtue"; if civilized, the African would undoubtedly show less energy, courage, and intellectual originality than the Caucasian but would surpass him in "amiableness, tranquillty, gentleness and content"; he may never equal the white man "in outward condition" but he would probably be "a much happier race." [26] The Ohio Anti-Slavery Society found that Negroes "endure with more patience the scorn and wrong under which they are pressed down— are more grateful for the favors which they receive—more tractable than persons of like information and intelligence among the whites." [27] Abolitionist author Charles Stuart reported that Negroes were guilty of fewer "atrocious crimes" because they were "less ferocious, less proud, and passionate and revengeful, than others." [28] Accepting this composite picture of the Negro character, abolitioinsts might well argue that social intercourse with the blacks not only seemed impolitic but unnatural.

Negro efforts to break away from this stereotype did not always win acclaim within the abolitionist movement. Frederick Douglass, for example, proved to be a formidable antislavery orator. But some abolitionists became concerned over Douglass' rapid intellectual development; perhaps people would no longer believe that he had ever been a slave. "The public have itching ears to hear a colored man speak," antislavery agent John A. Collins pointed out to Garrison, "and particularly a slave. Multitudes will flock to hear one of this class speak. . . . It would be a good policy to employ a number of colored agents, if suitable ones can be found." By 1841, however, Douglass' suitability seemed to be in question. "People won't believe you ever was a slave, Frederick, if you keep on this way," one abolitionist told Douglass. Collins added, "Better have a little of the plantation speech than not; it is not best that you seem too learned." [29]

In battling prejudice while at the same time accepting certain popular notions about the Negro, abolitionists frequently exhibited a curious racial attitude. They might, for example, refer to their African brethren —innocently or otherwise—as "niggers" or emphasize some alleged physical or mental characteristic. At times they seemed to sense this dual attitude. When a prominent Massachusetts woman abolitionist described a recent antislavery fund-raising fair in New Bedford, she wrote to her sister, "All the fashionables of the town were there and all the 'nigers' (don't let this letter get into the Mass ab.[olitionist])." [30] Usually, however, abolitionists appeared unaware that they might be using offensive language in describing Negroes. Arnold Buffum, a New England antislavery leader, thus informed Garrison about his activities in behalf of a school "where honors may be dispensed to woolly heads." [31] Abolitionist James W. Alvord, after visiting a school in Clifton, Connecticut, wrote to Weld that one Negro girl sat with the white students. "Cant tell how it will go," he remarked. "Should not be surprised if some of the white parents should smell her very bad, tho I could not perceive the girls on either side were at all aware of her niggerly odour." At the same time, however, Alvord asked Weld what more he could do for "the salvation" of the Negro. "To this object," he declared, "I would dedicate my life." [32]

III

While Negroes demonstrated their appreciation of the efforts and accomplishments of the antislavery societies, they did not hesitate to condemn prejudice within the abolitionist movement. "Even our professed friends have not yet rid themselves of it," a Negro teacher lamented; "to some of them it clings like a dark mantle obscuring their many virtues and choking up the avenues to higher and nobler sentiments." As an example, she cited the comment of "one of the best and least prejudiced men" in the antislavery cause: " 'Ah,' said he, 'I can recall the time when in walking with a colored brother, the darker the night, the better Abolitionist was I.' " While this person no longer expressed such feelings, she feared that similar sentiments "oftentimes" manifested themselves among the white friend of the Negro. However, she added, "when we recollect what great sacrifices to public sentiment they are called upon to make, we cannot wholly blame them. Many, very many anxious to take up the cross, but how few are strong enough to bear it." [33]

Several Negro leaders complained that white abolitionists devoted so much time to fiery condemnations of southern slavery that they tended to overlook the plight of northern Negroes. One Negro newspaper charged in 1839 that making "abolition in the North" an objective of secondary importance clearly constituted "a primordial defect" in the antislavery movement.[34] Even when white abolitionists turned their attention to the condition of northern Negroes, it appeared to some that they stressed only political rights and education. Was it not "strange," a Negro leader asked, that the Constitution of the American Anti-Slavery Society failed to mention social equality as an objective? [35]

But while some Negro leaders criticized the apathy of white abolitionists, others contended that Negroes had placed too much reliance on the efforts of outside forces, thus actually hampering the struggle for equal rights. The antislavery societies, Martin R. Delany charged, have always "presumed to think for, dictate to, and know better what suited colored people, than they know for themselves." While he applauded the constructive work of these societies, he felt that Negroes placed too much faith in the "miracle" of abolition and demonstrated too little confidence in their own efforts. After the appearance of some white abolitionists at the 1831 national Negro convention to propose a manual labor college, it seemed to Delany that Negroes suddenly ceased their independent activities, "and with their hands thrust deep in their breeches-pockets, and their mouths gaping open, stood gazing with astonishment, wonder, and surprise, at the stupendous moral colossal statues of our Anti-Slavery friends and brethren, who in the heat and zeal of honest hearts, . . . promised a great deal more than they have ever been able half to fulfill, in thrice the period in which they expected it." Awaiting a practical application of abolitionist dogma, Negroes had been disappointed. Instead, "we find ourselves occupying the very same position in relation to our Anti-Slavery friends, as we do in relation to the pro-slavery part of the community—a mere secondary, underling position, in all our relations to them, and anything more than this, is not a matter of course . . . but . . . by mere sufferance." [36]

In assessing the weaknesses of the antislavery movement, Negro critics referred particularly to the economic depression of their people and the failure of abolitionists to offer Negroes decent jobs in their business establishments or even in the anti-slavery offices.[37] After all, abolitionist speeches and editorials could not correct the prevailing prejudices of white society—this required a demonstration of Negro economic improvement. "Our white friends are deceived," a Negro newspaper charged, "when they imagine they are free from prejudice against color, and yet are content with a lower standard of attainments for colored youth, and inferior exhibitions of talent on the part of colored men." [38] Abolitionists possessed the means to assist Negro laborers, these critics maintained, and yet few of them showed any willingness to train or hire Negroes. This prompted one Negro delegate to a convention of the American and Foreign Anti-Slavery Society to charge that attempts to induce members of the executive committee to admit Negroes into their commercial houses or into the anti-slavery offices had met with no success. Replying to a specific charge that he used Negroes only in menial employment, delegate Arthur Tappan, owner of a large New York City department store, claimed that he had recently hired a Negro porter but that this person had left his job before being qualified for a clerical position. In any case, Tappan declared, he would not ask "an Irishman sawing wood in the street, and covered with sweat" to dine with his family; neither would he ask a Negro in a similar condition. He only required that his associates be gentlemen, irrespective of color. While regretting that erroneous stories had been circulated among Negroes concerning his conduct, he was still pleased that delegates had alluded to them for this should "put all abolitionists on their guard, and induce them to act out, at all times, the principles they professed." [39]

IV

In view of the prevailing economic outlook among abolitionists, Negro expectations of substantial economic progress under the impetus of the antislavery movement were unwarranted. Abolitionists gave no indication of encouraging Negro workers to combine among themselves or with white workers for economic gains. Inasmuch as Garrison and other reformers had expressed no sympathy with the efforts of white workers to organize into trade unions, this attitude is not surprising.

However, abolitionists did consider the economic plight of the northern Negro. In their appeals to the Negro community, antislavery leaders stressed the importance of economic advancement and independence.

Accumulate money, Garrison told a Negro audience in 1831, for "money begets influence, and influence respectability." [40] This became standard abolitionist advice throughout the ante bellum period. "A colored man who makes a thousand dollars," a Unitarian clergyman and abolitionist declared in 1859, "does more to put down prejudice, or wrote a thousand pretty fair articles against it. No race in this country will be despised which makes money. If we had in Boston or New York ten orang-outangs worth a million dollars each, they would visit in the best society, we should leave our cards at their doors, and give them snug little dinner-parties." [41]

Antislavery organizations encouraged a program of economic uplift. They cheered Negro efforts to shift from menial to agricultural and mechanical employments and called upon sympathetic merchants and master mechanics to hire Negro apprentices.[42] In Pennsylvania, abolitionists established a register of Negro mechanics available for work, and in New England they moved to establish a manual labor college to train Negro youths.[43] Gerrit Smith, an antislavery leader and philanthropist, decided to promote the Negro drive for economic independence by distributing approximately 140,000 acres of his land in northern New York (much of which was poor and unfit for cultivation) to 3,000 Negroes.[44]

But abolitionist efforts consisted largely of advice and encouragement and failed to achieve any measurable economic advance. This partly stemmed from the abolitionists' adherence to orthodox middle-class economics. Garrison, for example, believed that an employer's sense of profit would override his racial prejudices. "Place two mechanics by the side of each other—one colored, and the other white," and "he who works the cheapest and best, will get the most custom. In making a bargain, the color of a man will never be consulted." [45] In a similar vein, an antislavery New England journal declared that Negro merchants would attract customers when they sold goods cheaper than their white neighbors, and Negro mechanics would be more frequently employed when they showed a willingness to work for lower wages than whites. The voice of interest, the journal concluded, speaks "louder and more to purpose than reason or philanthropy." [46]

In 1851 three prominent antislavery sympathizers—Cassius M. Clay, Horace Mann, and Benjamin Wade—communicated their recommendations to a convention of Ohio Negroes. Clay advised the delegates to sacrifice social equality, which he considered impossible to attain even in the free states, and immediate political rights in order to concentrate on the accumulation of wealth. "The blacks should 'get money,'" he declared. "Let them go into the trades—become farmers—manufacturers

—where capital and employment are wanting—let them combine, and thus diminish the expense of living, and increase their productive power." According to Mann, however, Negroes could advance economically only by forming separate communities apart from the whites where they could "rise from domestic labor and mere chance-service, from being ditchers and delvers, into farmers, mechanics, artizans, shopkeepers, printers, editors or professional men." Separation would afford all Negroes an equal opportunity to compete for the highest political and economic offices. Wade arrived at almost an identical conclusion; he advised Negroes to withdraw from all menial employments, form separate communities, cultivate the soil, enter the mechanical arts, and thereby attain economic independence. "While scattered about among the white people," this objective could not be realized. Independence, however, would compel whites to grant them respect and recognition, thus forever destroying the doctrine of racial superiority. "The colored skin is nothing," Wade concluded: "When was it ever known that virtue, industry and intelligence were not respected?" [47]

However, abolitionist moral encouragement did not break down the economic barriers confronting northern Negroes. As a result, the Negro entered the Civil War period as an unorganized and unskilled worker competing with newly arrived immigrants for the menial employments.

V

Economic orthodoxy and the aversion of some abolitionists to intimate social relations with Negroes did not prevent the antislavery movement from registering some important victories in the realm of equal rights. Perhaps the most spectacular of these was the successful integration of Negro and white students in the public schools of Boston.

Education constituted the foremost aspiration of the northern Negro. But the possibility of Negroes mixing with white children in the same classroom aroused even greater fears and prejudices than those that consigned them to an inferior place in the church, theater, and railroad car. This, indeed, was virtual amalgamation. Although Negroes sometimes gained admittance to white schools, most northern states either excluded them altogether from the public schools or established separate schools for them.[48]

Excluded from white schools, Negroes endeavored to establish their own educational institutions and enlisted the support of abolitionists. The education of the emancipated slave had formed a major goal of the early abolition societies, particularly in New York and Pennsylvania.[49] After 1831 the revived abolitionist movement sought to assist Negro education. The constitution of the American Anti-Slavery Society urged the encouragement of the "intellectual, moral, and religious improvement" of Negroes, and Garrison praised Negro efforts to improve their condition through education.[50] Convinced "that faith without works is death," Cincinnati abolitionists provided instruction for the Negro community. Other antislavery societies moved to duplicate the achievements of the Cincinnati group.[51]

However, even exclusively Negro schools frequently encountered strong opposition from the white community. The identification of abolitionism with the cause of Negro education provided whites with a convenient excuse for resisting such institutions. In New Haven, Connecticut, for example, Garrisonian abolitionists failed to establish a Negro manual labor college in the face of strenuous local opposition. Such an institution, city officials declared, would propagate antislavery sentiments, prove incompatible with the existence and prosperity of Yale and other notable schools, and be "destructive to the best interests of this city." Attempts to establish a Negro girls' school in Canterbury, Connecticut, and to enroll Negro students in a Canaan, New Hampshire, academy met even more violent resistance, and failed.

White abolitionists joined Negroes in assailing school segregation, and soon questioned their own efforts to establish exclusively Negro institutions. When some white colleges indicated a willingness to admit Negroes, an abolitionist leader asked Garrison in 1834 if it would not be preferable to patronize those institutions rather than build new ones since "the object we aim at, the destruction of caste, will be the sooner gained." [52] Two years later an abolitionist convention confirmed this opinion by resolving henceforth to oppose separate schools.[53]

Boston was the major focal point of the Negro-abolitionist attack on segregated schools. In Massachusetts, Negroes achieved virtual political and legal equality by 1845, and their children were admitted to public schools, without discrimination, in Salem, New Bedford, Nantucket, Worcester, and Lowell. Only Boston maintained a policy of separation, and it was there that Negroes launched the most concerted and successful attack on "caste" schools in the North. White abolitionists, convinced that local segregation practices were incompatible with their antislavery efforts, joined the campaign. "It is useless for us to prate of the conduct of South Carolina," a segregation foe declared in 1845, "so long as we maintain—illegally maintain—a practice here which at least incidentally sanctions it." [54] The following year the Massachusetts Anti-Slavery Society resolved that "the friends of the cause" residing in those communities which provided separate educational facilities should immediately inform Negroes of their legal rights, and "afford them all possible aid in securing the full and equal enjoyment of the public schools." [55]

While Garrison's *Liberator* assailed the Boston school committee, local Negroes met regularly to prepare new appeals and methods of attack.[56] Rejected by the school committee and the courts, they turned to legislative action and secured in 1855 the enactment of a bill to prohibit distinctions based on race, color, or religious opinions in determining the qualification of students to be admitted into any of the public schools.[57] Negroes and white abolitionists celebrated their triumph for equal rights in a mass meeting.[58] The foes of integration appeared disappointed and fearful. "Now the blood of the Winthrops, the Otises, the Lymans, the Endicotts, and the Eliots, is in a fair way to be amalgamated with the Sambos, the Catos, and the Pompeys," one newspaper declared. "The North is to be Africanized. Amalgamation has commenced. New England heads the column. God save the Commonwealth of Massachusetts!" [59]

The Boston victory encouraged Negroes and abolitionists in other states to increase their agitation, but they had less success. Some small and scattered communities consented to admit both races to the same schoolhouse, but the larger cities, such as Philadelphia, New York, Cincinnati, Providence, and New Haven, held firmly to a segregated school system and hoped to stem increasing agitation by promises to correct existing abuses and provide separate but equal facilities for Negro and white children.

In addition to their efforts on behalf of the economic and educational advancement of the northern Negro, abolitionists supported Negro attempts to secure equal political and legal rights with whites and to break down the segregation barrier in public places. The Garrisonian abolitionists, for example, achieved phenomenal success in Massachusetts as they combined with Negroes to secure the repeal of the ban on interracial marriages, the abandonment of "Jim Crow" seating in railroad cars, and the organization of integrated lyceums, as well as the integration of Boston's public schools.

By 1860 the antislavery societies could point to some noteworthy achievements. In assessing the weaknesses and inconsistencies of the abolitionist movement, historians must not overlook these important contributions to the cause of human freedom in the North. Abolitionists did indeed suffer from factionalism, extreme partisanship, narrow class attitudes, prejudice, and even hypocrisy, but they shared these weaknesses with nearly every organized movement and political party in ante bellum America. The fact that abolitionists did not allow these weaknesses to interfere materially with their struggle for civil rights is a tribute to their sincerity. Forced at times to endure mob violence, severe public censure, frustration and defeat, these dedicated agitators displayed an ability to apply theoretical arguments about equal rights to concrete situations. Although frequently hesitant and uncertain in their own social relations with Negroes, abolitionists nevertheless attempted to demonstrate to a hostile public that environmental factors, rather than any peculiar racial traits, largely accounted for the degradation of the northern Negro.

NOTES

1. See, for example, Register of Debates, 21st Congress, 1st Session, 47, 215; *Congressional Globe*, 30th Congress, 1st Session, p. 602; *Appendix to the Congressional Globe*, 29th Congress, 2nd Session, p. 349.

2. Edward S. Abdy, *Journal of Residence and Tour in the United States of North America, from April, 1833, to October, 1834* (London, 1835), III, 7.

3. For examples of this sentiment, see the address of William Goodell before the Lewis County Anti-Slavery Convention, January 10, 1837, in *Human Rights*, February, 1837; *Second Annual Report of the American Anti-Slavery Society . . .1835* (New York, 1835), pp. 6, 69; *Proceedings of the First Annual Meeting of the New York Anti-Slavery Society . . . 1836* (Utica, 1836), p. 57; address of Gerrit Smith before the second annual convention of the New York Anti-Slavery Society, in *The Friend of Man*, October 11, 1837; Sophia Davenport to Anne Warren Weston, June 30, 1838, Weston Papers (Boston Public Library).

4. *The Liberator*, January 1, 1831. See also issues of January 15 and May 28, 1831.

5. James Russell Lowell, *The Anti-Slavery Papers of James Russell Lowell* (Boston, 1902), I, 21-22.

6. James G. Birney to Theodore Weld, July 26, 1834, in Gilbert H. Barnes and Dwight L. Dumond (eds.), *Letters of Theodore Dwight Weld, Angelina Grimké Weld, and Sarah Grimké, 1822-1844* (New York, 1934), I, 163.

7. William Lloyd Garrison to Lewis Tappan, December 16, 1835, quoted in Charles H. Wesley, "The Negro's Struggle for Freedom in Its Birthplace," *Journal of Negro History*, XXX (1945), 74.

8. *Fourth Annual Report of the Board of Managers of the Massachusetts Anti-Slavery Society . . . January 20, 1836* (Boston, 1836), p. 50.

9. MSS Diary of Lewis Tappan, February 23, 1836 to August 29, 1838, Papers of Lewis Tappan (Library of Congress); Lewis Tappan to Theodore Weld, March 15, 1836, in Barnes and Dumond, *op. cit.*, I, 276-277.

10. Tappan Diary, *loc. cit.*

11. Minutes of the Junior Anti-Slavery Society of Philadelphia, 1836-1846, Historical Society of Pennsylvania (Philadelphia).

12. Edward Strutt Abdy to Maria (Weston) Chapman, May 24, 1844, Weston Papers (Boston Public Library).

13. Lewis Tappan to Theodore Weld, March 15, 1836, in Barnes and Dumond, *op. cit.*, I, 275-276. References to this dispute are also included in Weld to Tappan, November 17, 1835, March 9, April 5, October 24, 1836, *ibid.*, I, 242-243, 270-274, 289, 345; Tappan Diary, February 23, 1836 to August 29, 1838, especially the entries for February 25 and March 19, 1836. "I am satisfied CSF [Charles S. Finney] is wrong," Tappan wrote in his diary, "and has unjust suspicions of me. Last year, in another matter, he accused me of 'pious fraud' wh I thot wholly unmerited."

14. Theodore Weld to Lewis Tappan, March 9, 1836, Barnes and Dumond, *op. cit.*, I, 270, 272-274.

15. Arthur Tappan to A. F. Stoddard, August 27, 1863, quoted in Lewis Tappan, *The Life of Arthur Tappan* (New York, 1870), pp. 201-202.

16. Malcolm R. Lovell (ed.), *Two Quaker Sisters. From the Original Diaries* (New York, 1937), pp. 119-120. (Elizabeth Buffum Chace and Lucy Buffum Lovell)

17. Anne Warren Weston to Deborah Weston, October 22, 1836, Weston Papers. "Everybody has their own troubles and the New York brethren have theirs. Mrs. Cox is the life and soul of the New York Society and she is in a very sinful state of wicked prejudices about colour; they do not allow any coloured woman to join their society. . . . The Tappans have none of this prejudice therefore they and Mrs. Cox are hardly on speaking terms."

18. *Proceedings of the Anti-Slavery Convention of American Women, . . . 1838* (Philadelphia, 1838), p. 8. For additional sentiments on this question, see *Proceedings of the Third Anti-Slavery Convention of American Women, . . . 1839* (Philadelphia, 1839), pp. 22, 24; *Proceedings of the Anti-Slavery Convention of American Women, . . . 1837* (New York, 1937), pp. 13, 17.

19. James and Lucretia Mott to Anne Warren Weston, June 7, 1838, Weston Papers. "[I]t is only our half-way Abolitionists," Mrs. Mott explained, "and some timid ones like Dr. Parrish who have never joined our societies and who are now quaking with fear—These it is to be regretted are not well understood by the colored people whom they attempt to influence. They think them wholly identified with us and confiding in them as their best advisers they are in danger of being led astray." See also Lucretia Mott to Edward M. Davis, June 18, 1838, in Anna Davis Hallowell, *James and Lucretia Mott: Life and Letters* (Boston, 1884), p. 130.

20. Phebe Mathews, Emeline Bishop, Susan Lowe, and Lucy Wright to Theodore Weld, March, 1835, in Barnes and Dumond, *op. cit.*, I, 217.

21. *Fourth Annual Report of the American Anti-Slavery Society, . . . 1837* (New York, 1837), p. 107. For similar abolitionist criticism, see *Proceedings of a Meeting To Form the Broadway Tabernacle Anti-Slavery Society* (New York, 1838), p. 28, and *The [9th] Annual Report of the American and Foreign Anti-Slavery Society, . . . 1849* (New York, 1849), p. 68.

22. Sarah Grimké to Elizabeth Pease, May 20[?], 1838, Barnes and Dumond, *op. cit.*, II, 679.

23. Lucretia Mott to Richard and Hannah Webb, February 25, 1842, in Hallowell, *op. cit.*, p. 232.

24. Sophia Davenport to Caroline Weston, June 5, 1836, Weston Papers.

25. *Liberator*, January 22, 1831.

26. William Ellery Channing, "The African Character," in John A. Collins (ed.), *The Anti-Slavery Picknick: A Collection of Speeches, Poems, Dialogues and Songs; Intended for Use in Schools and Anti-Slavery Meetings* (Boston, 1842), pp. 56-58. See also Edward Abdy's interview with Channing in Abdy, *op. cit.*, III, pp. 217-237.

27. Ohio Anti-Slavery Society, *Condition of the People of Color in the State of Ohio* (Boston, 1839), p. 4.

28. Charles Stuart, "On the Colored People of the United States," *The Quarterly Anti-Slavery Magazine*, II (October, 1836), 16.

29. Frederick Douglass, *Life and Times of Frederick Douglass* (Hartford, Conn., 1884), pp. 269-270.

30. Deborah Weston to Mary Weston, January 5, 1840, Weston Papers. The "Mass Ab" refers to a weekly abolitionist newspaper edited by Elizur Wright, Jr., which generally disagreed with the Garrisonian position, especially concerning political action. Deborah Weston was a Garrisonian.

31. Arnold Buffum to William Lloyd Garrison, October 23, 1832, in Francis and Wendell P. Garrison, *William Lloyd Garrison, 1805-1879* (Boston, 1894), I, 327.

32. James W. Alvord to Theodore Weld, August 29, 1838, Barnes and Dumond, *op. cit.*, II, 697.

33. Sarah Forten to Angelina Grimké, April 15, 1837, *ibid.*, I, 380.

34. *Colored American*, May 18, 1839. "They [the American Anti-Slavery Society] make secondary and collateral what ought to have been the primary object of all their efforts. . . . At this moment more is known among abolitionists of slavery in the Carolinas, than of the deep and damning thralldom which grinds to the dust, the colored inhabitants of New York. And more efforts are made by them to rend the physical chains of Southern slaves, than to burst the soul-crushing bondage of the Northern states."

35. James McCune Smith to Gerrit Smith, March 1, 1855, quoted in Howard Holman Bell, "A Survey of the Negro Convention Movement, 1830-1861" (Ph.D. dissertation, Northwestern University, 1953), p. 41.

36. Martin R. Delany, *The Condition, Elevation, Emigration, and Destiny*

of the Colored People of the United States (Philadelphia, 1852), pp. 10, 24-25, 27.

37. See, for example, *Delany, op. cit.,* pp. 26-28. "It is true," the author remarked, "that the 'Liberator' office, in Boston has got . . . a colored youth, at the cases—the 'Standard,' in New York, a young colored man, and the 'Freeman,' in Philadelphia, . . . another, in the publication office, as 'packing clerk'; yet these are but three out of the hosts that fill these offices in their various departments, all occupying places that could have been, and as we once thought, would have been, easily enough, occupied by colored men. Indeed, we can have no other idea about anti-slavery in this country, than that the legitimate persons to fill any and every position about an anti-slavery establishment are colored persons." In addition to this criticism, a delegate to a meeting of the National Council of the Colored People in 1855 charged that "those who professed to be the strongest abolitionists have refused to render colored people anything but sympathy. . . . They might employ a colored boy as a porter or packer, but would as soon put a hod-carrier to the clerk's desk as a colored boy, ever so well educated though he be." *Frederick Douglass' Paper,* May 18, 1855.

38. *Colored American,* November 4, 1837, July 28, 1838.

39. *The [12th] Annual Report of the American and Foreign Anti-Slavery Society, . . . 1852* (New York, 1852), pp. 29-30.

40. William Lloyd Garrison, *An Address Delivered before the Free People of Color, in Philadelphia, New York, and Other Cities, during the Month of June, 1831* (Boston, 1831), p. 10.

41. James Freeman Clarke, "Condition of the Free Colored People of the United States," *The Christian Examiner,* LXVI, ser. 5, IV (1859), 263-264.

42. *The Fifth Annual Report of the American Anti-Slavery Society, . . . 1838* (New York, 1838), p. 127; *Proceedings of the Third Anti-Slavery Convention of American Women,* p. 8; Executive Committee of the American Anti-Slavery Society, *Address to the People of Color, in the City of New York* (New York, 1834), p. 5; Theodore Weld to Lewis Tappan, February 22, 1836, Barnes and Dumond, *op. cit.,* I, 264-265.

43. Minutes of the Committee for Improvement of the Colored People, Pennsylvania Abolition Society, 1837-1853, Historical Society of Pennsylvania, pp. 24-25; *Liberator,* September 29, 1832.

44. Several factors, however, resulted in the failure of this project. In addition to the poor quality of the land, the cost of moving, settling, seeding, and waiting for the first crops compelled many Negroes to abandon their grants. In 1848, two years after the inauguration of the plan, less than thirty Negro families had settled on the new lands. See *An Address to the Three Thousand Colored Citizens of New York, who are the owners of one hundred and twenty thousand acres of land, in the State of New York, given to them by Gerrit Smith, Esq. of Peterboro, September 1, 1846* (New York, 1846); *North Star,* January 7, February 18, 1848, January 5, March 2, June 1, 1849; Ralph V. Harlow, *Gerrit Smith* (New York, 1939), pp. 244-245, 250-252.

45. Garrison, *Address Delivered before the Free People of Color,* p. 10.

46. *New England Magazine*, January, 1832, quoted in *Liberator*, January 21, 1832.

47. *Proceedings of the Convention of the Colored Freemen of Ohio, . . . Cincinnati, . . . 1852* (Cincinnati, 1852), pp. 15-25. For the reaction of the Negro community to these recommendations, see *Frederick Douglass' Paper*, October 22, 1852, and *Liberator*, November 26, 1852.

48. The means by which Negroes were excluded from white schools varied only slightly from state to state. In New England, local school committees usually assigned Negro children to separate institutions, regardless of the district in which they resided. Pennsylvania and Ohio, although extending their public school privileges to all children, required district school directors to establish separate facilities for Negro students whenever twenty or more could be accommodated. The New York Legislature authorized any school district, upon the approval of a town's school commissioners, to provide for segregation. The newer states also consented to separate instruction. In the absence of legal restrictions, custom and popular prejudices prevented Negroes from entering white schools. For a general survey of state policies regarding Negro education, see U. S. Commissioner of Education, *Special Report of the Commissioner of Education on the Condition and Improvement of Public Schools in the District of Columbia, Submitted to the Senate, June, 1868, and to the House, with additions, June 13, 1870* (Washington, 1871), Part II: "Legal Status of the Colored Population in Respect to Schools and Education in the Different States," pp. 301-400; and Carter G. Woodson, the *Education of the Negro Prior to 1861* (New York, 1915), pp. 307-335.

49. Minutes of the Committee for Improving the Condition of Free Blacks, Pennsylvania Abolition Society, 1790-1803, Historical Society of Pennsylvania, pp. 1-2, 113, 219-220; Edward Needles, *An Historical Memoir of the Pennsylvania Society for Promoting the Abolition of Slavery, the Relief of Free Negroes Unlawfully Held in Bondage, and for Improving the Condition of the African Race* (Philadelphia, 1848), pp. 40, 43, 68, 69-70, 104-105; Charles C. Andrews, *The History of the New-York African Free Schools, from their establishment to the present time* (New York, 1830).

50. *The Declaration of Sentiments and Constitution of the American Anti-Slavery Society* (New York, 1835), p. 8; *First Annual Report of the Board of Managers of the New-England Anti-Slavery Society, presented January 9, 1833* (Boston, 1833), p. 7.

51. Barnes and Dumond, *op. cit.*, I, 132-135, 178-180, 211-218; Abdy, *op. cit.*, II, 388-389.

52. Elizur Wright, Jr., to William Lloyd Garrison, June 30, 1834, Garrison Papers (Boston Public Library), and Wright Papers (Library of Congress). A New Bedford, Massachusetts abolitionist wrote in 1837 that "it is hardly desirable that there should be an exclusively coloured school established, for the public schools are all open, and black children admitted on terms of the most perfect equality." Deborah Weston to Maria (Weston) Chapman, April, 1837, Weston Papers.

53. *Liberator*, November 19, 1836.

54. *Ibid.*, June 27, 1845.

55. *Fourteenth Annual Report presented to the Massachusetts Anti-Slavery Society, by its Board of Managers, January 28, 1846* (Boston, 1846), pp. 91-92.

56. *Liberator*, August 21, 1846, August 10, September 7, November 9, December 14, 1849; February 8, 1850.

57. *House Report*, Massachusetts House of Representatives, No. 167 (March 17, 1855).

58. *Triumph of Equal School Rights in Boston. Proceedings of the Presentation Meeting held in Boston, December 17, 1855; including addresses by John T. Hilton, Wm. C. Nell, Charles W. Slack, Wendell Phillips, Wm. Lloyd Garrison, Charles Lenox Remond* (Boston, 1856). "The best thing learned by these struggles," Wendell Phillips declared, "is, how to prepare for another. . . . He should never think Mass. a State fit to live in, until he saw one man, at least, as black as the ace of spades, a graduate of Harvard College. . . . (Cheers) When they had high schools and colleges to which all classes and colors were admitted on equal terms, then he should think Mass. was indeed the noblest representative of the principles that planted her."

59. New York *Herald*, quoted in *Liberator*, May 4, 1855. Subsequent testimony of Boston school officers and teachers praised the results of integration. Although a few white parents withdrew their children and some Negroes suffered insults, integrated schools resulted in neither racial violence nor amalgamation.

THE NORTHWEST AND THE

RACE ISSUE, 1861-1862

Jacque Voegoli

In a recent essay, C. Vann Woodward wrote critically of those writers—"myth-makers" he called them—who have created "the legend that the Mason and Dixon Line not only divided slavery from freedom in ante bellum America," but also "set apart racial inhumanity in the South from benevolence, liberality and tolerance in the North." In this "North Star Legend," the pre–Civil War North emerges as the practicing champion of racial equality.[1] This myth is related to and becomes, in fact, a part of a current interpretation of the Civil War. In this interpretation, which emphasizes the moral conflict, slavery appears not primarily as a political or emotional issue but as a thing of evil against which men must fight. Since the evil was sectional, the forces of good and evil appear divided along sectional lines. "Human dignity and freedom" as well as "democracy" were to be restored to the South. The North thus went to war in 1861 fighting for human dignity, freedom, and democracy.[2] Yet how deeply committed to human dignity and democracy for the Negro was the North? How deeply was it committed to equality for the Negro?

The northern commitment to equality cannot be measured by the amount of antislavery sentiment. Outrage over slavery and belief in white supremacy were two seemingly discordant strains of thought that were often harmonized in the antislavery intellect. In the section of the country then popularly called the Northwest, the coexistence of these two strains was perhaps most apparent. In that portion of the North, at any rate, humanitarian pity for the slaves did not always

Jacque Voegoli, "The Northwest and the Race Issue, 1861-1862," *Mississippi Valley Historical Review*, L, No. 2 (September, 1963) 235-251.

spring from a desire to confer equal rights on all men. Antislavery men did not necessarily understand that equality for the Negro would inexorably follow emancipation. In that section, when war broke out, opposition to the evil of slavery did not carry with it a commitment to equality for the Negro.

The Northwest comprised the seven states of Ohio, Indiana, Illinois, Michigan, Wisconsin, Minnesota, and Iowa. In 1861 it was a stronghold of white supremacy. As the nation girded for war, state constitutions and statutes reflected the racism that flourished in the region. The severity of the discriminatory legislation varied, but every state imposed legal disabilities upon its black residents. All seven states limited service in the militia to white males and barred Negroes from the suffrage. In Illinois and Indiana there were no provisions for the education of colored children, and Negroes were not recognized as competent witnesses in court trials when a white person was a party to the case. Iowa and Ohio excluded Negroes from jury service. Interracial marriages were forbidden in Michigan, Ohio, Indiana, and Illinois. Ohio denied Negroes the benefits of poor relief and provided for racially segregated public schools. Exclusion laws carrying severe penalties prohibited Negroes from settling in Indiana, Illinois, and Iowa.

Early in the war, the fate of the Negro race became a source of great concern to the Northwest. Armed conflict brought the realization that war could loosen the bonds of slavery and this in turn raised the question: What can be done with the freed slaves? This was not a new question; it had, of course, long troubled the friends of emancipation, both North and South. Now, with slavery in jeopardy for the first time, the most disturbing aspect of this problem in the Northwest was the apprehension that the freedmen would throng into the area and become social, economic, and political competitors of the whites.[3]

Apprehension became alarm as a result of legislation of the second session of the Thirty-seventh Congress, for by the time of adjournment on July 17, 1862, Republican party members had pushed through a series of measures designed to shatter the cornerstone of the Confederacy. Both houses approved a joint resolution offering financial aid to slave states that would adopt gradual emancipation. Bondsmen in the District of Columbia and in the territories were declared free. The use of military power in returning fugitive slaves to their masters was prohibited, and a militia act liberated Union slave-soldiers and their families owned by rebels. Climaxing this program, the Confiscation Act of July 17, 1862, provided that slaves owned by persons supporting the rebellion should be forever free.[4] If enforced, this law would have freed practically every slave in the Confederacy. The congressional drive

toward emancipation stirred violent partisan conflict, in and out of
Congress, as Democrats and Republicans debated the consequences of
freeing the slaves and plumbed the depths of the race problem. The
northwestern attitude toward the Negro now received its fullest
exposition.

Among the most implacable foes of emancipation were the northwestern Democrats. Although they had many constitutional and political
objections to slave liberation, much of their resistance to the assault on
slavery sprang from the fear that emancipation would deluge the Northwest with Negroes and challenge white supremacy there. These Democrats attacked every proposal to free the slaves or improve the lot of the
free Negro. They did not defend slavery as a positive good, but they
seemed ready to tolerate the institution rather than to increase the number of Negroes in the Northwest. Their attitude was that expressed by
an Iowa newspaperman. He opposed "slavery per se"; yet he was confident that slaves would not benefit from freedom and that there was
"little doubt of the demoralizing effect it will have upon the white
race in the North . . . to have these emancipated blacks introduced
among them." Representative Samuel S. Cox of Ohio observed, "If
slavery is bad, the condition of . . . Ohio, with an unrestrained black
population, only double what we now have, partly subservient, partly
slothful, partly criminal, and all disadvantageous and ruinous, will be
far worse." [5]

Skillfully exploiting the dread of a Negro invasion of the Northwest,
Democrats protested that slave confiscation and emancipation would send
the freed slaves surging into the Northwest, and that ruin and degradation would follow in their wake. They argued, in part, from reasons of
economic interest. The withdrawal of the southern laboring force would
destroy the prosperity of the South, thereby depriving the Northwest of
its market for surplus goods. Bills calling for federal compensation to
slave states which would adopt emancipation were scored as projects for
taxing the whites to build black communities in the North. Negro immigrants, they said, would drain the northern economy because they
were thieves and chronic paupers.[6] Wage earners were warned that
hordes of unskilled competitors would inundate the Northwest to degrade society, reduce wages, and drive the whites from their jobs.[7]

Professing to believe that the Republicans intended to "equalize" the
races, Democrats assailed the specter of racial equality with an appeal
to white superiority. Because the Negro was inherently inferior, said
the Democrats, equality for the black man would contaminate northwestern society and politics and debase the American people.[8] A Republican bill authorizing the exchange of diplomatic representatives

with Haiti and Liberia drew a stream of abuse from alarmed Democrats who suspected that this was an instrument for forcing equality. Representative Cox objected to receiving colored diplomats in Washington, he said, because history taught that "these Commonwealths and this Union were made for white men; that this Government is a Government of white men; and the men who made it never intended by anything they did to place the black race upon an equality with the white." To Representative William A. Richardson of Illinois, the Republicans were mocking the Almighty: "God made the white man superior to the black, and no legislation will undo or change the decrees of Heaven . . . and unlike the abolition equalizationists I find no fault and utter no complaint against the wisdom of our Creator." [9]

While the Democrats protested emancipation and vilified the Negro, Republicans slowly pushed their antislavery program through Congress. When Congress convened in December, 1861, there was no consensus on slavery within the Republican party. A deep gulf separated those abolitionists who interpreted the war as a divine command to destroy slavery from the moderate and conservative men, most of whom advanced haltingly to the position that the confiscation of slaves could sap the strength of the rebels. Emancipationists from the Northwest presented an appealing case for confiscating Confederate slaves. Confiscation and emancipation, they maintained, would cripple or crush the southern war effort, save the Union, insure future national unity, and punish the South.[10] Seldom, however, was the plight of the enslaved given as the chief justification for emancipation.

Many considerations determined this approach to the slavery problem. To most Republican congressmen in 1862 the war was being waged for the restoration of the Union, with or without slavery. Besides this, sound political tactics demanded that "Union," not "abolition," be the cry to unify the North. The party in power was especially sensitive to Democratic accusations that rabid abolitionists had caused the South to secede, seized control of the Republican party, and were forcing unconstitutional abolition measures upon Congress. The plea that slave liberation was the price of military victory was partially designed to overcome the constitutional scruples of those strict constructionists who doubted the constitutionality of the slave confiscation proposals. There was still another reason for not converting the war into an avowed abolition crusade: Republicans of every persuasion knew that the Northwest would not shed blood solely in behalf of a race it despised. Excessive emphasis upon the humanitarian objectives of emancipation would have lent truth to the Democratic complaint that the Republicans were fighting a war to free the Negro. Consequently, although they denounced slavery as a crime against God, humanity, morality, and natural rights, northwestern Republicans made it clear that they were primarily concerned with restoring the Union.[11]

The Democratic outcry that emancipation would inundate the Northwest with Negroes gravely disturbed the Republicans, for they knew of the deep-seated opposition in the Northwest to the entry of colored persons. Republican members of Congress warned of this feeling. When Senator Jacob M. Howard of Michigan was told by a colleague that if the slaves were freed and distributed among the various states in proportion to the white population, Michigan would have about 123,000 blacks instead of the 6,800 it then had, Howard retorted, "Canada is very near us, and affords a fine market for 'wool.'" Senator Lyman Trumbull of Illinois candidly told the Senate, "There is a very great aversion in the West—I know it to be so in my state—against having free Negroes come among us. Our people want nothing to do with the Negro." [12] Time and time again Republicans voiced these sentiments.[13] Some party leaders arraigned the section for its hostility toward Negroes, but no one questioned the prevalence or intensity of this feeling.

This Negrophobia impeded and imperiled the passage of slave confiscation and emancipation measures in 1862. Senator Trumbull, who was himself the chief draftsman of the confiscation bill, discerned that hostility to Negroes posed one of the most potent objections to his proposal. The people of the Northwest, Trumbull said, were asking the supporters of confiscation: "What will you do with them [slaves]; we do not want them set free to come in among us; we know it is wrong that the rebels should have the benefit of their services to fight us; but what do you propose to do with them?" An Ohio congressman put it more bluntly. Incensed by the slow progress of confiscation proposals, he cried: "The nation has been led astray quite long enough by the miserable partisan war cry that emancipation means 'to turn the niggers loose.'" [14]

To overcome these objections, a number of Republican leaders—both radicals and conservatives—brought forth a theory destined to become a Republican panacea for all the ills of emancipation. According to this theory, slave liberation would not only remove slavery from the South but would take the Negro from the Northwest. It was slavery, both the Republican press and politicians emphasized, that caused the flight of blacks from the cotton kingdom. Free the slaves, they said, and a warm climate, abundant land, a demand for their labor, a sentimental attachment to the South, and northern race prejudice would induce the freedmen to stay on Southern soil.[15] Furthermore, the same forces would send northern Negroes rushing southward.[16] Republicans from the middle states joined their northwestern brethren in this refrain. Two sanguine emancipationists, George W. Julian of Indiana and Albert G. Riddle of Ohio, expected freedom in the South to drain both the North and Canada of their colored residents.[17]

To what extent these Republicans actually believed that northern Negroes would go South to freedom is difficult to ascertain. But such pronouncements were certainly more than Machiavellian utterances fashioned to deceive the people of the North. The idea that the Negro was a creature of the tropics was a part of the stereotype of the black race. In private correspondence as well as in public statements, antislavery men declared their belief that slavery alone prevented northern Negroes from moving to the South. David Noggle, a Wisconsin judge who boasted of his radicalism, censured Senator James R. Doolittle for espousing the colonization of the slaves. "With all due deference to your wild notions of colonization," he wrote, "I think you can't but believe that [by] abolishing Slavery in the Southern States the Northern States would be speedily cleared of their present free colored population." This same belief led Secretary of the Treasury Salmon P. Chase of Ohio to advocate military emancipation in the Deep South. In a letter to Major General Benjamin F. Butler, then the Union Commander of the Department of the Gulf, Chase wrote that "many honest men really think they [Negroes] are not to be permitted to reside permanently in the Northern States." While he said he had no objection to the presence of colored people in his state, Chase felt that they would prefer the southern climate. "Let, therefore, the South be opened to Negro emigration by emancipation along the Gulf, and it is easy to see that the blacks of the North will slide southward, and leave behind them no question to quarrel about as far as they are concerned." [18]

Although many Republicans expressed such views, the party adhered officially to colonization as the answer to the problems which would be created by emancipation. The slaves that were to be freed were to be colonized in foreign lands. In the vanguard of the deportation movement were prominent northwestern Republicans—President Abraham Lincoln, Senators John Sherman of Ohio, James R. Doolittle of Wisconsin, Trumbull and Orville H. Browning of Illinois, and Henry S. Lane of Indiana.

These men were convinced that physical differences between the races created racial antagonism that would not be dispelled by emancipation. Senator Doolittle, a chief advocate of colonization, wrote that "the question of race is a more troublesome one than the question of condition." The colonizationists urged—since history and evidence on every hand indicated that white Americans would not admit black men to the equality to which all men aspired—that emancipation be followed by removal of the freedman from the United States. Such a course would benefit both races. The whites would profit from the departure of an alien race, and the blacks would escape from domination and oppression. The most concise statement of the philosophy of colonization came from President Lincoln. On August 14, 1862, shortly after Congress adjourned, Lincoln addressed a deputation of colored men and pointed out that both humanitarianism and racial antipathy nourished the colonization movement. Lincoln stated that the broad physical difference between the two races was disadvantageous to both. "I think your race suffer very greatly, many of them by living among us," he said, "while ours suffer from your presence. . . . If this is admitted, it affords a reason at least why we should be separated." He reminded his audience that freedom did not bring equality to the Negro; for "on this broad continent, not a single man of your race is made the equal of a single man of ours." [19]

Similar pleas for deportation were advanced by Republican congressmen from the Northwest. They emphasized the point that as long as the Negro race resided in the United States, it was doomed to subordination and ostracism. In bestowing freedom upon a proscribed people, the nation was obligated to resettle the outcasts in foreign lands where they could enjoy equal rights and govern themselves.[20] Many congressmen, especially those from New England, protested that colonization was inhumane, impractical, uneconomic, and un-Christian. With the strong support of the Northwest and the middle states, Congress overrode these objections. It incorporated into both the confiscation act and the District of Columbia emancipation act provisions for colonizing those slaves, liberated by that legislation, who were willing to leave the United States.[21]

There were also stern political exigencies that turned the Republican party to colonization in 1862. Some Republican strategists, including Lincoln, hoped that the adoption of deportation would persuade the loyal states to move toward emancipation. But it was the political situation in the North that insured Republican support for colonization. In the Northwest, Pennsylvania, and New Jersey, insistent voices clamored for positive action to shield the North from a Negro invasion. Colonization became a key part of the program to make slave confiscation and emancipation more palatable to the free states. Deportation would blunt the threat of a Negro ingress and thus would relieve emancipation of a dreaded burden.

Republicans, in fact, openly avowed that deportation was designated to keep the freedmen out of the North. When Senator Trumbull placed a confiscation measure before the Senate, he said that the colonization proposal in the bill would answer those northwesterners who wanted the slaves freed but objected to having them brought into their section. Republican Senator John C. Ten Eyck of New Jersey, a member of the committee which considered the confiscation bill, announced that the committee thought the colonization section to be "of the utmost importance." He contended that the North's opposition to an influx of Negroes called for a declaration of the government's policy on colonization.[22] After Congress had passed the acts containing provisions for voluntary colonization, assistant secretary of the interior John P. Usher of Indiana pressed President Lincoln to accept a plan for colonizing the freedmen in Chiriqui. On August 2, 1862, Usher advised the President that such action would allay apprehensions that the North was going to be overrun by free Negroes. Twelve days later, at his widely publicized conference with the colored men, the President noted that hopes for freedom would be greatly enhanced if some free Negroes would accept colonization. "There is an unwillingness on the part of our people, harsh as it may be, for you free colored people to remain with us," he said. "Now, if you could give a start to the white people, you would open a wide door for many to be made free." [23]

Throughout the congressional discussion of colonization and other measures relating to the condition of the Negro, it was apparent that northwestern Republicans were not advocating racial equality. If any of them were egalitarians, they pondered their principles in silence. They had joined with other Republicans in enacting legislation intended to improve the lot of the black man, particularly in the District of Columbia.[24] They were, in this respect, considerate of the humanity of the black man; but at the same time they disclaimed any goal of racial equality. They agreed that political and social rights were outside the province of federal law; only the states could confer political privileges, and each individual could regulate his own social relations.[25] Charity and humanity, not equality, were their watchwords. Sympathy for the victims of slavery, a spirit of *noblesse oblige,* and an urge to do justice to the oppressed inspired their benevolence. Representative John Hutchins of Ohio said: "These measures have no relation to political or social equality. . . . Because we are willing to do justice to the humblest in society, does it follow that we are bound to extend to them the same social and political privileges which we enjoy?" To Senator James Harlan, an Iowa Republican, civilized society was obligated to protect the Negroes, "another feeble people," but their freedom would neither bring nor require equality with the whites.[26]

Meanwhile, Republicans at home in the Northwest displayed much the same attitude. Although the Ohio state legislature Republicans withstood the demand for Negro-exclusion legislation, discriminatory laws continued to prevail. Republican-dominated legislatures in Iowa and Ohio met and adjourned without altering the anti-Negro laws on their statute books. The heavily Republican Iowa legislature amended its militia law, but continued to limit the enrollment to white males.[27]

There were some northwesterners who wished to grant equal political rights to the Negro. The referendum on a new state constitution for Illinois indicated the size of this minority in that state. In a direct vote on the franchise, the people of Illinois, by a majority of over five to one, chose to continue its ban on Negro suffrage and office holding.[28] In such an atmosphere, no political party and few, if any, politicians could admit egalitarian principles and survive.

As they talked at home and in Congress, many northwestern Republican stalwarts spoke the language of white supremacy. Governor William Dennison, a founder of the Republican party in Ohio, referred to the "superior [white] race." Because of the Negro's "kindly and affectionate" nature, remarked the Chicago *Tribune,* he is "rarely agitated by the profound passions which belong to his superiors." [29] Republican Senators Sherman, Browning, Doolittle, and Harlan were certain that a higher law transcended man-made rules and governed race relations. They stressed that natural instincts implanted by the Creator forbade equality of the races. God and nature, not prejudice, accounted for racial antipathy, and what God had decreed they did not propose to deny. The law of caste, asserted Sherman, was the unchangeable "law of God. . . . The whites and the blacks will always be separate, or where they are brought together, one will be inferior to the other." [30] According to Browning and Doolittle, human instincts caused white resistance to social and political equality. Doolittle stated that "in the temperate zone, the Caucasian race has always been dominant, and always will be. In the torrid zone the colored man dominates and will forever. . . . The Creator has written it upon the earth and upon the race." [31] Responding to a query about the possibility of interracial marriages, Senator Harlan asked, "Has the hand of nature fixed no barrier to such loathsome associations?" [32]

Events in the summer of 1862 warned of intensifying hostility toward the black race. In a June referendum on a new state constitution, Illinois voters refused to ratify the proposed constitution, but they overwhelmingly approved an article that prohibited Negroes from settling in the state and denied suffrage and public office to Negroes and mulattoes. Voting on these two provisions separately, the people endorsed the exclusion section by a vote of 171,896 to 71,806. Since the defeat of the constitution, reputedly a Democratic party document, was hailed as a Republican victory, the vote for the anti-Negro article was obviously drawn from both parties.[33] Later that summer anti-Negro sentiment became even more apparent, when in July and August serious race riots flared in New Albany (Indiana), Chicago, Toledo, and Cincinnati. [34]

The campaign which began in the summer of 1862 for the fall congressional elections found both emancipation and the status of the Negro as major political issues in the Northwest. Militant Democratic state conventions drafted caustic resolutions condemning emancipation as an unconstitutional, impractical measure that portended ruin for the region. The Iowa Democrats resolved that "this is a Government of white men, and was established exclusively for the white race; that the negroes are not entitled to, and ought not to be admitted to political or social equality with the white race." To halt economic competition between the races, the Democrats of Ohio opposed emancipation and demanded a ban on Negro immigration into the Buckeye State.[35] Excoriating slave liberation, the Illinois and Indiana Democratic conventions demanded enforcement of their exclusion laws on the grounds that white men alone were suited to the free institutions of their states. Wisconsin Democrats adopted and published an address which asserted that social equality of the races was contrary to the laws of nature: "Nature never placed the races together; when brought together the servitude of the inferior is the best condition for both races." [36]

Standing upon these party platforms, Democratic candidates and newspapers fired their familiar barrage of social, political, and economic objections at emancipation. If the slaves were liberated, they would fly to the North where their contact with a superior race would degrade white society, their economic rivalry would reduce wages, and their political competition would contaminate politics. Democrats spied the spirit of "equalization" lurking within every scheme of the Republicans. The preliminary proclamation of emancipation, issued by Lincoln on September 22, 1862, served as a prime target for the Democrats. In order to preserve white supremacy and repel the black invaders, the Democrats argued, the Republican party should be turned out of power before the President could execute his emancipation proclamation.[37]

On the emancipation and Negro issues, the campaign strategy of the Republican and Union party organizations in the Northwest usually followed a well-established line: slave confiscation and emancipation were desperately needed to win the war and restore the Union. Humanitarian goals were generally shunted aside while the voters were reassured that Union, not abolition, was the object of the war. On one point the Republicans concurred with the Democrats—Negroes were not wanted in the Northwest. Instead of extending an invitation to the slaves to seek their freedom in the free states, they made it clear that they neither desired nor expected any increase in the colored population of the area. From the press, pulpit, and political rostrum radicals and conservatives sounded the familiar cliche: slavery was driving southern Negroes into the Northwest, but emancipation in the Confederate states would hold the freedmen in the land of their labor and lure northern Negroes to the congenial South. Colonization, too, was offered as a means of reducing the Negro population.[38] Democratic charges of Republican egalitarianism were either ignored or dismissed as malicious slander. Irritated by the allegation that Republican policies would lead to equality of the races and that "our volunteers are periling their lives to make niggers the equal of whites," the Indianapolis *Journal* exclaimed, "what a monstrous and villainous lie." [39]

In the elections of October and November, 1862, the Democrats swept to victory in the Northwest. They carried Ohio, Illinois, and Indiana, and registered impressive gains in Michigan and Wisconsin. For the federal House of Representatives, the Democrats elected fourteen out of nineteen members from Ohio, seven of eleven in Indiana, nine of fourteen in Illinois, and divided six Wisconsin seats with their rivals. The next Congress would contain thirty-four Democrats out of a total of sixty-four northwestern representatives, a gain of eighteen seats for the resurgent party.[40]

Many factors inspired the political revolt against the party of Lincoln in the 1862 elections. In the Northwest, arbitrary arrests by federal authorities, suspension of the habeas corpus privilege, the emancipation proclamation, and a disappointing military situation plagued the nominees of the Republican and Union parties.[41] The emancipation issue with its many ramifications played a leading role in the Democratic victory. Many northwestern Republicans conceded its impact. Senator Browning informed Lincoln that the proclamation suspending the writ of habeas corpus and the emancipation edict had defeated the party. John Sherman wrote that the "ill timed proclamation contributed to the general result." According to Unionist Thomas Ewing, a former United States senator, Lincoln had ruined the Union party in Ohio by issuing the proclamations. A clarion of radical Republicanism, the Cleveland *Leader*, asserted that Ohio and Illinois had voted against emancipation.[42]

This opposition to emancipation was primarily the product of Negrophobia aggravated by the threat of a massive influx of Negroes. H. S. Bundy, an unsuccessful Union party aspirant for Congress from Ohio, wrote Salmon P. Chase that the emancipation proclamation had been delivered just in time to defeat him and many other Union candidates in the Indiana and Ohio elections. "I had thought until this year the cry of 'nigger' & 'abolitionism,' were played out but they never had as much power & effect in this part of the state as at the recent elections." [43] The disgruntled Chicago *Tribune* interpreted the political reverses as a signal for the Republican party to re-emphasize its devotion to the "white race." It counseled fellow Republicans to justify the emancipation proclamation in terms of its effect upon "the happiness, the freedom and the prosperity of the white men of the North. . . . We need not go beyond that; if we do we bring the prejudices of caste and races into full play, and by weakening the efforts of the North, impair the good the proclamation promises." [44]

Elated Democrats hailed the elections of 1862 as a repudiation of the emancipation heresy. To the Democratic Columbus *Crisis* the elections, a contest of "black *vs.* white," had resolved that Ohio would never become the refuge for southern Negroes. Representative Cox said the victory of his party had brought forth a new commandment, "Thou shalt not degrade the white race by such intermixtures as emancipation would bring." "The people," an Illinois Democrat told the House of Representatives, "are sick and tired of this eternal talk upon the Negro, and they have expressed their disgust unmistakably in the recent elections." [45]

Impressed by the North's persistent hostility toward the free Negro, President Lincoln strove to assuage the fears of the people. In his annual message to Congress in December, 1862, he contended that liberation and deportation of the slaves would benefit northern white men. He strongly recommended the adoption of a constitutional amendment calling for compensated emancipation and voluntary colonization of the freedmen. The claim that liberated Negroes would displace white labor the President termed "largely imaginary, if not sometimes malicious." If the freedmen should remain where they were, "they jostle no white laborers; if they leave their old places, they leave them open to white laborers." Emancipation alone would probably improve the wages of whites, and the deportation of colored workers would certainly increase the earnings of white men.

The President then turned to the fear "that the freed people will swarm forth, and cover the whole land":

Equally distributed among the whites of the whole country . . .
there would be but one colored to seven whites. Could the one,
in any way, greatly disturb the seven? . . . But why should emanci-

pation south, send the free people north? People, of any color, seldom run, unless there be something to run from. Heretofore colored people, to some extent, have fled north from bondage; and now, perhaps, from both bondage and destitution. But if gradual emancipation and deportation be adopted, they will have neither to flee from. Their old masters will give them wages . . . till new homes can be found for them in congenial climes, and with people of their own blood and race. . . . And, in any event, cannot the north decide for itself, whether to receive them?[46]

Under the skillful pen of Lincoln, emancipation, colonization, and exclusion became deterrents to a Negro invasion of the North.

By the end of 1862, the Northwest had amply demonstrated that ultimate equality for the Negro had not been a war aim when the conflict began.[47] The concept of the innate superiority of the "white race" cut across party lines and pervaded the mind of the Northwest. Moral opposition to slavery helped kindle the "irrepressible conflict," but moral principle had not abated the Northwest's determination to preserve white supremacy.

NOTES

1. C. Vann Woodward, "The Antislavery Myth," *American Scholar*, XXXI (Spring, 1962), 316.

2. Arthur M. Schlesinger, Jr., "The Causes of the Civil War: A Note on Historical Sentimentalism," *Partisan Review*, XVI (October, 1949), 968-981.

3. *Crisis* (Columbus, Ohio), July 11 and August 22, 1861; *Free Press* (Detroit), June 28, 1861; *Times* (Chicago), October 8 and November 28, 1861. The most complete work on the treatment of the Negro in the North is by Leon F. Litwack, *North of Slavery: The Negro in the Free States, 1790-1860* (Chicago, 1961). An excellent study of the same subject in a single state is in Emma Lou Thornbrough, *The Negro in Indiana: A Study of a Minority* (Indianapolis, 1957), pp. 1-182. See also Henry C. Hubbart, *The Older Middle West, 1840-1880* (New York, 1936), pp. 11, 13, 28, 45-51, 151-152.

4. James G. Randall and David Donald, *The Civil War and Reconstruction* (2nd ed.; Boston, 1961), pp. 372-375. It is not the purpose of this article to trace the course of this session of Congress, but, rather, to be concerned with the Northwest's views of the Negro, with some consideration of the influence of these attitudes on political policies.

5. *Herald* (Dubuque), April 13 and 29, 1862; *Congressional Globe*, 37th

Congress, 2nd Session, Appendix, pp. 244-245. See also *Times* (Chicago), March 18, 1862. In 1860 the number and percentage of Negroes in each state were as follows: Illinois, 7,628 (0.4); Indiana, 11,428 (0.93); Ohio, 36,673 (1.3); Wisconsin, 1,171 (0.2); Minnesota, 259 (0.1); Michigan, 6,799 (0.9); and Iowa, 333 (0.2). *Negro Population: 1790-1915* (Washington, 1918), pp. 44, 51.

6. *Herald* (Dubuque), April 29, 1862; *News* (Milwaukee), cited in *Herald* (Dubuque), April 20, 1862; *Free Press* (Detroit), December 10, 1861, and April 13, 1862; *Gazette* (Cairo), April 19, 1862; *Times* (Chicago), May 22, 1862; *Congressional Globe*, 37th Congress, 2nd Session, p. 1647 (April 11, 1862) and Appendix, pp. 247-248. For more information on the Democrats' use of Negrophobia as a political weapon in 1861 and 1862, see Wood Gray, *The Hidden Civil War: The Story of the Copperheads* (New York, 1942), pp. 23, 29, 30, 79, 89, 90, 97-100; Frank L. Klement, *The Copperheads in the Middle West* (Chicago, 1960), pp. 12-17, 25, 45; and Emma Lou Thornbrough, "The Race Issue in Indiana Politics during the Civil War," *Indiana Magazine of History*, XLVII (June, 1951), 169-180.

7. *Gazette* (Cairo), April 3, 1862; *Times* (Chicago), April 8 and 18, 1862; *Crisis* (Columbus), January 29, 1862; *Times* (Portsmouth, Ohio), cited in *Crisis* (Columbus), May 7, 1862; *Enquirer* (Cincinnati), cited in *Herald* (Dubuque), June 26, 1862; *Herald* (Dubuque), April 16, 19, and June 1, 13, and 22, 1862; *Free Press* (Detroit), June 15, 1862; *Sentinel* (Indianapolis), April 29, 1862, cited in Thornbrough, *The Negro in Indiana*, p. 189; *Congressional Globe*, 37th Congress, 2nd Session, p. 573 (January 30, 1862), p. 1436 (April 1, 1862), and Appendix, pp. 120, 240, 243-248, 285.

8. *Free Press* (Detroit), June 14, 1862; *Gazette* (Cairo), April 3, 1862; *Congressional Globe*, 27th Congress, 2nd Session, Appendix, p. 245.

9. *Crisis* (Columbus), May 7, 1862; *Congressional Globe*, 37th Congress, 2nd Session, p. 60 (December 11, 1861), p. 2207 (May 19, 1862), p. 2502 (June 2, 1862).

10. *Ibid.*, p. 195 (January 6, 1862), pp. 327-328 (January 14, 1862), pp. 858-859 (February 17, 1862), and Appendix, pp. 319-320.

11. *Ibid.*, p. 76 (December 12, 1861), pp. 194-195 (January 6, 1862), pp. 327-332 (January 14, 1862), pp. 348-349 (January 15, 1862), pp. 858-859 (February 17, 1862); p. 1816 (April 24, 1862).

12. *Ibid.*, p. 1780 (April 23, 1862), p. 944 (February 25, 1862).

13. *Ibid.*, p. 1357 (March 25, 1862), p. 1491 (April 2, 1862), p. 1606 (April 10, 1862), p. 2243 (May 20, 1862), p. 2923 (June 25, 1862), and Appendix, pp. 84, 297. See also J. M. Burgess to John Fox Potter, April 16, 1862, John Fox Potter Papers (Wisconsin State Historical Society, Madison).

14. *Congressional Globe*, 37th Congress, 2nd Session, p. 944 (February 23, 1862), and Appendix, p. 118. See also *ibid.*, p. 2301 (May 22, 1862).

15. *Sentinel* (Milwaukee), December 11, 1861, and June 28, 1862; *Illinois State Journal* (Springfield), April 26, 1862; *Transcript* (Peoria), cited in *Tribune* (Chicago), April 22, 1862; *Congressional Globe*, 37th Congress, 2nd Ses-

sion, p. 332 (January 14, 1862), p. 2243 (May 20, 1862), and Appendix, pp. 212, 327.

16. *Tribune* (Chicago), March 24 and April 22, 1862; *Sentinel* (Milwaukee), February 27 and May 10, 1862; *Congressional Globe*, 37th Congress, 2nd Session, p. 441 (January 22, 1862), p. 1107 (March 6, 1862), p. 1495 (April 2, 1862), p. 2301 (May 22, 1862).

17. *Ibid.*, p. 332 (January 14, 1862), p. 2243 (May 20, 1862).

18. David Noggle to James R. Doolittle, May 30, 1862, James R. Doolittle Papers (Wisconsin State Historical Society); Saimon P. Chase to Benjamin F. Butler, July 31, 1862, Jessie Ames Marshall (ed.), *Private and Official Correspondence of General Benjamin F. Butler during the Period of the Civil War* (5 vols.; Norwood, Mass., 1917), II, 132-133. The same belief was expressed by J. T. Worthington, an Ohio Unionist of unknown party affiliation, in Worthington to Rufus King, June, 1862, Rufus King Papers (Historical and Philosophical Society of Ohio, Cincinnati).

19. Doolittle to Mary Doolittle, April 19, 1862, Doolittle Papers; "Address on Colonization to a Deputation of Negroes," August 14, 1862, Roy P. Basler (ed.), *The Collected Works of Abraham Lincoln* (9 vols.; New Brunswick, 1953), V, 371-372. Lincoln's interest in colonization has been elaborately discussed. See Richard N. Current, *The Lincoln Nobody Knows* (New York, 1958), pp. 221-222; James G. Randall, *Lincoln the President: Springfield to Gettysburg* (2 vols.; New York, 1945), II, 137-141; Walter L. Fleming, "Deportation and Colonization: An Attempted Solution of the Race Problem," J. G. de Roulhac Hamilton (ed.), *Studies in Southern History and Politics Inscribed to William Archibald Dunning* (New York, 1914), pp. 3-30; Warren A. Beck, "Lincoln and Negro Colonization in Central America," *Abraham Lincoln Quarterly*, VI (September, 1950), 162-183; Paul J. Scheips, "Lincoln and the Chiriqui Colonization Project," *Journal of Negro History*, XXXVII (October, 1952), 418-453; Frederic Bancroft, "The Colonization of American Negroes, 1801-1865," in Jacob E. Cooke, *Frederic Bancroft, Historian* (Norman, 1957), pp. 186-187, 193, 196-197, 202-203, 209, 211-213.

20. *Congressional Globe*, 37th Congress, 2nd Session, p. 332 (January 14, 1862), pp. 1491-1492 (April 2, 1862), p. 1520 (April 3, 1862), p. 1604 (April 10, 1862), p. 2923 (June 25, 1862), and Appendix, pp. 83-84, 297.

21. *Ibid.*, Appendix, pp. 348, 412-413. In a key vote in the Senate, Republicans from the Northwest, New York, Pennsylvania, and New Jersey voted thirteen to three for colonization while New England senators voted against it, six to five. *Ibid.*, pp. 1522-23 (April 3, 1862).

22. *Ibid.*, pp. 944-946 (February 25, 1862). See also *ibid.*, Appendix, p. 297.

23. John P. Usher to Lincoln, August 2, 1862, Robert Todd Lincoln Collection (Manuscript Division, Library of Congress); "Address on Colonization . . ." The timing of this interview seems to indicate that Lincoln publicly reaffirmed his faith in colonization at this time to allay northern fears of a Negro influx.

24. *Congressional Globe*, 37th Congress, 2nd Session, Appendix, pp. 356-357, 361, 397.

25. *Ibid.*, p. 3131 (July 5, 1862), and Appendix, pp. 156, 322.

26. *Ibid.*, p. 1359 (March 25, 1862), p. 3131 (July 5, 1862), and Appendix, p. 322.

27. George H. Porter, *Ohio Politics During the Civil War Period* (New York, 1911), pp. 96-97; *Crisis* (Columbus), April 30, 1862; *Acts and Resolutions Passed at the Regular Session of the Ninth General Assembly of the State of Iowa* (Des Moines, 1862), p. 231.

28. *Illinois State Journal* (Springfield), August 16, 1862.

29. *Ohio State Journal* (Columbus), January 7, 1862; *Tribune* (Chicago), March 24, 1862.

30. *Congressional Globe*, 37th Congress, 2nd Session, p. 3199 (July 9, 1862).

31. *Ibid.*, p. 1521 (April 3, 1862), and Appendix, pp. 83-84.

32. *Ibid.*, Appendix, p. 321.

33. *Illinois State Journal* (Springfield), August 5, 1862; Arthur C. Cole, *The Era of the Civil War, 1848-1870* (*The Centennial History of Illinois*, Vol. III; Springfield, 1919), pp. 268-272.

34. *Times* (Chicago), July 15, 1862; *Tribune* (Chicago), August 10, 1862; *Crisis* (Columbus), July 16, 1862; Thornbrough, *The Negro in Indiana*, pp. 185-186; Charles R. Wilson, "Cincinnati's Reputation during the Civil War," *Journal of Southern History*, II (November, 1936), 478-479.

35. *Herald* (Dubuque), July 22, 1862; *Crisis* (Columbus), July 9, 1862.

36. *Illinois State Journal* (Springfield), September 11, 1862; *Journal* (Indianapolis), July 31, 1862. *Address to the People by the Democracy of Wisconsin, Adopted in State Convention at Milwaukee, Sept. 3d, 1862* (pamphlet; Madison, 1862), p. 3, in Moses M. Strong Papers (Wissconsin State Historical Society).

37. For examples, see *Free Press* (Detroit), September 28, October 23, 28, 31, and November 2, 1862; *Times* (Chicago), September 23, 25, 27, and October 3, 1862; *Gazette* (Cairo), August 21, September 27, and October 20, 1862; *Crisis* (Columbus), August 13, 27, September 3, 24, and October 15, 1862; *Herald* (Dubuque), September 20, and October 3, 7, 8, 10, 11, 12, and 14, 1862.

38. A number of Republicans and Unionist newspaper editors contented themselves with the observation that the emancipation proclamation was a "war measure," and then ignored it until after the elections. But the majority followed the course indicated above. See Joseph A. Wright Papers (Indiana Division, Indiana State Historical Library, Indianapolis); *Express* (Terre Haute), September 16, 1862; *Ohio State Journal* (Columbus), September 4 and October 8, 1862; *Sentinel* (Milwaukee), October 10, 21, and November 3, 1862; *Times* (Dubuque), August 21, and September 2, 3, and 6, 1862; *Tribune* (Howard, Ind.), August 21, 1862; *Tribune* (Chicago), August 7, September 21, 23, and October 8 and 19, 1862. In a sermon at Terre Haute on September 7, 1862, Lyman Abbott declared that emancipation

would turn the tide of Negro immigration southward (*Express* [Terre Haute], September 16, 1862).

39. *Journal* (Indianapolis), October 6, 1862.

40. Gray, *Hidden Civil War*, p. 108.

41. The issues and the elections of 1862 are treated in *ibid.*, pp. 97-112; Hubbart, *Older Middle West, 1840-1880*, chap. xi; Thornbrough, "The Race Issue in Indiana Politics," *Indiana Magazine of History*, XLVII, 176-179; Porter, *Ohio Politics during the Civil War Period*, pp. 101-109, 139-144; Cole, *Era of the Civil War, 1848-1870*, pp. 296-298, 334-335; Allan Nevins, *The War for the Union: War Becomes Revolution (The Ordeal of the Union, Vol. VI; New York, 1960)*, pp. 299-322.

42. Theodore C. Pease and James G. Randall (eds.), *The Diary of Orville Hickman Browning* (2 vols.; Springfield, 1927-1933), I, 588-589; John Sherman to William T. Sherman, November 16, 1862, W. T. Sherman Papers (Manuscript Division, Library of Congress); *Leader* (Cleveland), November 10, 1862.

43. H. S. Bundy to Chase, October 18, 1862, Salmon P. Chase Papers (Manuscript Division, Library of Congress).

44. *Tribune* (Chicago), November 3, 1862.

45. *Crisis* (Columbus), October 22 and 29, 1862; *Congressional Globe*, 37th Congress, 3rd Session, p. 95 (December 15, 1862), and Appendix, p. 39.

46. "Annual Message to Congress," December 1, 1862, Basler (ed.), *Collected Works of Lincoln*, V, 533-537.

47. A study of the continuing pattern of prejudice against the Negro can be found in Thornbrough, *The Negro in Indiana*.

CULTURAL HISTORY WRITTEN

WITH LIGHTNING: THE

SIGNIFICANCE OF

THE BIRTH OF A NATION

Everett Carter

On February 20, 1915, David Wark Griffith's long film, *The Clansman*, was shown in New York City. One of the spectators was Thomas Dixon, the author of the novel from which it was taken, who was moved by the power of the motion picture to shout to the wildly applauding spectators that its title would have to be changed. To match the picture's greatness, he suggested, its name should be *The Birth of a Nation*.[1] Only by a singular distortion of meaning could the film be interpreted as the story of a country's genesis; the birth it did herald was of an American industry and an American art; any attempt to define the cinema and its impact upon American life must take into account this classic movie. For with the release of *The Birth of a Nation* "significant motion picture history begins."[2] Its prestige became enormous. It was the first picture to be played at the White House, where Woodrow Wilson was reported to have said: "it is like writing history with lightning."[3] By January 1916 it had given 6,266 performances in the area of greater New York alone.[4] If we conservatively estimate that five

Everett Carter, "Cultural History Written with Lightning: The Significance of *The Birth of a Nation*," *American Quarterly*, XII, No. 3 (Fall, 1960), 347-357.

hundred patrons saw each performance, we arrive at the astounding total of over three million residents of and visitors to New York who saw the picture, and forever viewed themselves and their country's history through its colorations. And not only significant motion picture history begins, but most of the problems of the art's place in our culture begin too. The picture projects one of the most persistent cultural illusions; it presents vividly and dramatically the ways in which a whole people have reacted to their history; its techniques in the narrowest sense are the fully realized techniques of the pictorial aspects of the motion picture; in the widest sense, its techniques are a blend of the epical and the symbolically realistic, and each part of this mixture has developed into a significant genre of cinematic art.

Griffith was a Kentuckian, a devout believer in Southern values; and these values, he was certain, were embodied in *The Clansman*, a sentimental novel of the Reconstruction which had appeared in 1905, had been widely read, had been seen in dramatic form throughout the South, and whose author had dedicated it "To the memory of a Scotch-Irish leader of the South, my Uncle, Colonel Leroy McAfee, Grand Titan of the Invisible Empire Ku Klux Klan." [5] In his introduction, Dixon went on to describe his theme: "How the young South, led by the reincarnated souls of the Clansmen of Old Scotland, went forth under this cover and against overwhelming odds, daring exile, imprisonment, and a felon's death, and saved the life of a people, forms one of the most dramatic chapters in the history of the Aryan race." [6] This strong suggestion that the South's struggle is a racial epic, involving all the people of one blood in their defense against a common ancestral enemy, became, as we shall see, a major influence upon Griffith's conception of his cinematic theme. And, in addition, the novel in so many ways served as what would later be called a "treatment" from which the story would be filmed, that we must examine the book closely before we can understand the significance of the film.

The Clansman told the story of "Thaddeus Stevens' bold attempt to Africanize the ten great states of the American Union. . . ." It interpreted the history of the Reconstruction as the great Commoner's vengeance, motivated partly by economics: the destruction of his Pennsylvania iron mills by Lee's army; [7] partly by religion: in his parlor there was "a picture of a nun . . . he had always given liberally to an orphanage conducted by a Roman Catholic sisterhood"; [8] but mainly by lust: his housekeeper was "a mulatto, a woman of extraordinary animal beauty . . ." who became, through her power over Austin Stoneman (the fictional name for Stevens) "the presiding genius of National legislation." [9] Stoneman was shown in private conference with Lincoln, whose words in his Charleston debate with Douglas were directly quoted: "I believe there is a physical difference between the white and black races which will forever forbid their living together on terms of political and social equality." [10] Stoneman's instruments in the South were all described as animals, demonstrating that the Civil War was fought to defend civilization against the barbaric and bestial. Silas Lynch, the carpetbagger, "had evidently inherited the full physical characteristics of the Aryan race, while his dark yellowish eyes beneath his heavy brows glowed with the brightness of the African jungle." [11] The Negro leader, Aleck, had a nose "broad and crushed flat against his face," and jaws "strong and angular, mouth wide, and lips thick, curling back from solid teeth set obliquely. . . ." [12] The Cameron family of the Old South were the principal victims; Gus, a renegade Negro, ravished Marion Cameron, the sixteen-year-old "universal favourite" who embodied "the grace, charm, and tender beauty of the Southern girl. . . ." [13] Silas Lynch attempted to violate Elsie Stoneman, the betrothed of Ben Cameron. The actual rape was a climax of a series of figurative violations of the South by the North, one of which was the entry of Stoneman into the black legislature, carried by two Negroes who made "a curious symbolic frame for the chalk-white passion of the old Commoner's face. No sculptor ever dreamed a more sinister emblem of the corruption of a race of empire-builders than this group. Its black figures, wrapped in the night of four thousand years of barbarism, squatted there the 'equal' of their master, grinning at his forms of Justice, the evolution of forty centuries of Aryan genius." [14] These figurative and literal ravishments provoked the formation of the Ku Klux Klan, whose like "the world had not seen since the Knights of the Middle Ages rode on their Holy Crusades." [15] The Klan saved Elsie, revenged Marion, brought dismay to the Negro, the carpetbagger, and the scalawag; and, in the final words of the book, "Civilisation has been saved, and the South redeemed from shame." [16]

The picture followed the book faithfully in plot, character, motivation, and theme, and became a visualization of the whole set of irrational cultural assumptions which may be termed the "Plantation Illusion." The Illusion has many elements, but it is based primarily upon a belief in a golden age of the ante bellum South, an age in which feudal agrarianism provided the good life for wealthy, leisured, kindly, aristocratic owner and loyal, happy, obedient slave. The enormous disparity between this conception and the reality has been the subject of Gaines' *The Southern Plantation* [17] and Stampp's *The Peculiar Institution.*[18] But our concern is not with the reality but with what people have thought and felt about that reality; this thinking and feeling is the

Illusion, and the stuff of the history of sensibility. The Illusion was embodied in Kennedy's *Swallow Barn* (1832), developed through Carruthers' *The Cavaliers of Virginia* (1834), and firmly fixed in the national consciousness by Stephen Foster's "Old Folks at Home" (1851), "My Old Kentucky Home" and "Massa's in the Cold, Cold Ground" (1852), and "Old Black Joe," songs which nostalgically describe a "longing for the old plantation. . . ." In 1905 Dixon summarized it in the assertion that the South before the Civil War was ruled by an "aristocracy founded on brains, culture, and blood," the "old fashioned dream of the South" which "but for the Black curse . . . could be today the garden of the world."

This was the image realized almost immediately at the beginning of *The Birth of a Nation*. A scene of Southern life before the Civil War is preceded by the title: "In the Southland, life runs in a quaintly way that is no more." A primitive cart is shown trundling up a village street, filled with laughing Negroes; there is further merriment as a few children fall from the cart and are pulled into it; then appears a scene of a young aristocrat helping his sister into a carriage; she is in white crinoline and carries a parasol; the young Southerner helps her gallantly from the carriage, and the title reads: "Margaret Cameron, daughter of the old South, trained in manners of the old school." With the two levels of feudal society established, the scene is then of the porch of the plantation house. Dr. and Mrs. Cameron are rocking; he has a kitten in his arms, and puppies are shown playing at his feet. A pickaninny runs happily in and out among the classic columns while the Camerons look indulgently on; a very fat and very black servant claps her hands with glee.

A corollary of this aspect of the Southern Illusion, one might even say a necessary part of it, is the corresponding vision of the North as the land of coldness, harshness, mechanical inhumanity; expressed most generously, it is the description of the North as "head" and the South as the warm human "heart" which was Sidney Lanier's major metaphor in his Reconstruction poems. Although Lanier had called for the reunion of the heart and head, a modern Southerner, John Crowe Ransom, has scolded Lanier for preaching reconciliation when, Ransom said, what should have been preached was the "contumacious resistance" of the warm, agrarian South against the harsh industrialism and rationalism of the North.[19] *The Clansman* had emphasized the contrast between warm South and cold North by rechristening Thaddeus Stevens, "Austin Stoneman"—the man of stone; the radical Republican who is the obdurate villain of the picture. He has a clubfoot and moves angularly and mechanically; his house, his dress, are gloomy, dark, and cold, as opposed to the warmth and lightness of the Southern plantation garments and scene. In the novel, Dixon had identified him as the owner of Pennsylvania iron mills, and Griffith took the hint, giving him clothes to wear and expressions to assume which, in their harshness and implacability, suggest the unyielding metal. The sense of commercialism, combined with rigidity and pious hypocrisy, is identified with the North, too, by showing the presumed beginnings of slavery in America. We see a Puritan preacher sanctimoniously praying while two of the elect arrange the sale of a cringing slave; the following scene is of Abolitionists demanding the end of slavery; the grouping of the two scenes, the dress and features of the characters in both, make the point strongly that these are the same people; the montage is a dramatization of Ben Cameron's assertion in the novel, that "our slaves were stolen from Africa by Yankee skippers. . . . It was not until 1836 that Massachusetts led in Abolition—not until all her own slaves had been sold to us at a profit. . . .[20]

In these opening scenes, too, we have the complete cast of characters of the Plantation Ideal. The Camerons are shown as they go down to the fields to mingle with the happy and trusting slaves. A title tells us that "in the two hour interval for dinner given in their working day from six to six the slaves enjoy themselves"; then appears a view of slaves clapping hands and dancing. Ben Cameron places his hand paternally upon the shoulder of one, and shakes hands with another who bobs in a perfect frenzy of grateful loyalty: in several seconds a wonderful summary of a hundred years of romantic tradition in which "a beautiful felicity of racial contact has been presented, not as occasional but as constant; an imperious kindness on the part of the whites, matched by obsequious devotion on the part of the blacks." [21]

The Plantation Ideal had to explain the obvious fact that during the war and Reconstruction, many Negroes fought with the Union and greeted Emancipation with joy. The Illusion protected itself by explaining that the true, southern, full-blooded Negro remained loyal throughout and after the war. It expanded the truth of individual instances of this kind into a general rule. In the Civil War sequences of The Birth of a Nation, the Camerons' slaves are shown cheering the parade of the Confederate soldiers as they march off to defend them against their freedom. The fat Negro cook and the others of the household staff are described as "The Faithful Souls"; they weep at Southern defeat and Northern triumph; they rescue Dr. Cameron from his arrest by Reconstruction militia.

While the Illusion persistently maintained the loyalty of the true slave, it premised the disaffection of other Negroes upon several causes, all of them explicable within the framework of the Plantation Ideal. The major explanation was the corruption of the Negro by the North. The freed Negro, the Union soldier, is a monster of ingratitude, a renegade from the feudal code, and only evil can be expected of him. The picture shows The Faithful Soul deriding one such abolitionist; the title reads, "You northern black trash, don't you try any of your airs on me." And a little later, we see her lips saying, and then read on the screen, "Those free niggers from the north sho' am crazy." The second explanation was that the mulatto, the person of mixed blood, was the arch-villain in the tragedy of the South. Stoneman, the radical Republican leader, is shown, as he was in the novel, under the spell of his mulatto housekeeper. A scene of Stoneman lasciviously fondling his mistress is preceded by the title: "The great leader's weakness that is to blight a nation." The mistress, in turn, has as a lover another mulatto, Silas Lynch, who is described as the principal agent in Stoneman's plans to "Africanize" the South. This dark part of the Plantation Illusion is further represented in the twin climaxes of the picture, both of which are attempted sexual assaults on blond white girls, one by a Northern Negro, and the other by the mulatto, Silas Lynch.

The sexual terms into which this picture translated the violation of the Southern Illusion by the North underscore the way in which the film incorporates one of the most vital of the forces underlying the Illusion— the obscure, bewildering complex of sexual guilt and fear which the Ideal never overtly admits, but which is, as Stampp and Cash and Myrdal [22] have pointed out, deeply woven into the Southern sensibility. The mulatto, while he occasionally would be the offspring of the lowest class of white woman and the Negro, much more commonly was the result of the debasement of the Negro woman by the white man, and, not infrequently, by the most aristocratic of the characters in the plantation conception.[23] At the very least, then, the deep convictions of the Protestant South about the nature of sin would cause the Southern Illusion to regard the living, visible evidence of a parent's lust as evil in itself, and at the most, and worst, and most debilitating, as a reminder of the burden of guilt the white must bear in the record of sexual aggression against the Negro. The Birth of a Nation gives all aspects of these sexual fears and guilts full expression. Typically, the burden of guilt is discharged by making the mulatto the evil force in the picture, evincing both the bestial, animal sensuality of the unrestrained Negro, and the perverted intellectual powers of the white. And the full-blooded, but renegade, black justifies any excess of the Klan, by accomplishing that final, most dreaded act of the sexual drama, the violation of the blond "little sister." The book had made the rape actual:

"A single tiger-spring," it narrated, "and the black claws of the beast sank into the soft white throat." [24] The picture shows us the little sister as she jumps off a cliff to escape dishonor; but a scene of Gus, kneeling blackly over the white-clad, broken body, makes the sexual point without the overt act. And this point is further reinforced by a description of Lynch's attempts to possess Elsie Stoneman, by a portrayal of the passage of the first law of the black Reconstruction legislature legalizing miscegenation, and by a scene of Negroes who carry signs reading "Equal rights, equal marriage."

The descriptions of Gus as "tiger-like" and of Stoneman's mistress as a leopard, bring us to the last element of the Plantation Illusion—the defense of the system on the basis of the essential non-humanity of the Negro. The book had been blatant in its statement of this position; the picture projects this attitude by its shots of the eyes of mulatto and Negro displaying animal lust and ferocity, and by its view of Gus as a slinking animal, waiting, crouching, springing.

As the record of a cultural illusion, then, *The Birth of a Nation* is without equal. Furthermore, it is the film to which, as the historian of the art declares, "much of subsequent filmic progress owes its inspiration." In order to understand its significance, one has to remind oneself of the nature of the motion picture art. It is not an art of external events and the people who perform them; it is an art of the camera and the film. Before Griffith, the camera was treated as a fixed object, much like the spectator of the drama. The interpretation was by the actors, by their bodies, by their faces, by physical objects, and by the settings before which these performed. Griffith made the ordering and interpretation—the art, in brief—one of the location, the angle, the movement of the camera, and of the juxtaposition of the images the camera records by means of cutting and arranging these images to bring out their significance. An example of the first technique—camera position—was the famous scene of Sherman's march to the sea. The camera shows the serpentine line of Union troops in the distance, winding over the landscape. War is distant; it is simply a move of masses over territory; the camera turns slowly until it includes, in the left foreground, the figures of a weeping mother and child. Immediately a perspective is achieved; what was remote and inhuman becomes close and humanized; the human implications of such mass movements are illustrated clearly, sharply, and poignantly, simply by the perspective of the camera.

An example of the second aspect of the purely filmic technique was Griffith's juxtaposition of the two parallel scenes in the introduction to the Plantation Ideal: Negro cart and white carriage. Alone the first shot would be at worst meaningless, at best a bit of atmosphere; the second would serve merely to introduce two characters who might have been presented in an infinite variety of ways. Placed together, both scenes become significant forms because of the two elements they have in common: means of transportation, and the perfect fitness of each group of characters to that means; the juxtaposition thus serves to summarize the feudal theory—the rightness of each part of society in its place.

A second aspect of this editorial technique—the cutting and arranging of images—was also brought to its fullness of possibility in *The Birth of a Nation* after Griffith had experimented with it in earlier films. This was the intercutting of parallel scenes occurring at different locations in space, but at the same location in time, each of which has a bearing upon the other, with the meanings of both carefully interwoven, and with the tensions of either relieved only when the two are finally brought together. The famous example of this, an example which has been followed faithfully from then on, was the intercutting of shots of Lynch's attempted forced marriage to Elsie Stoneman with shots of the gathering of the Klan which will effect her rescue. A series of six shots of Lynch and Elsie is superseded by seven shots of the gathering of the Klan; then two single shots of the Klan and two of the attempted ravishment are quickly alternated; fourteen shots of Lynch and Elsie are followed by one of the Klan; a shot of long duration during which the Elsie-Lynch struggle becomes more intense is then followed by seven shots of the Klan's ride to the rescue; and so it goes until both sequences are joined in space when the Klan finally reaches Elsie. As an early critic described the meaning of this achievement: "Every little series of pictures . . . symbolizes a sentiment, a passion, or an emotion. Each successive series, similar yet different, carries the emotion to the next higher power, till at last, when both of the parallel emotions have attained the nth power, so to speak, they meet in the final swift shock of victory and defeat." [25] To these epoch-making achievements of camera placement, significant juxtaposition and intercutting, Griffith added the first uses of night photography, of soft-focus photography, and of moving camera shots, and the possibilities of film art were born.

And with it were born most of the problems of those of us who wish to take the art seriously. For what can we make of so awkward a combination of sentimental content and superb technique? We must admit, first of all, that the effect of the film's detachable content was pernicious. It served the ugliest purposes of pseudo-art, giving people a reflection of their own prejudices—sentimental at best, vicious at worst—and a restatement of their easy explanations of the terrible complexities of their history as Americans. It demonstrated how easily and how successfully the art could pander to the sentimentality of the public, how effectively and profitably it could transfer melodrama from the stage and false values from the novel. The enormous commercial success of the film at a time when men like Louis B. Mayer, later to become the head of the greatest studio, were starting their careers as exhibitors, cannot but have fixed the melodramatic, the cheap and obviously emotional, as the index to the potential economic success of a film.

But it showed, as well, two directions in which the film would move: one is in the direction of the epic, and the other in what may be termed "symbolic realism." Its move in the first direction, of course, was an immense and shocking perversion. Griffith apparently sensed the truth that great epics are involved with the destiny of whole races and nations, and had seized upon Dixon's hint that the South's struggle was part of an "Aryan" saga. The Klan was described in the book, and on the screen, as part of an "Aryan" tradition. The term is used again at a crucial point in the screen narrative, when a mob of Negro soldiers attack the embattled whites. The battle of the Caucasians, the title on the screen tells us, is "in defense of their Aryan birthright." Griffith improved upon Dixon in emphasizing the "epical" quality of the story: before they ride, the Klansmen are shown partaking of a primitive barbaric rite; they dip a flag into the blood of the blond white virgin before they go out to destroy.

The picture is no epic, but rather an epic manqué: partial, fragmentary, and therefore necessarily inartistic; in its attempt to be the saga of a shattered fragment of a nation, in its attempt to erect upon false premises a series of racial responses reputedly instinctive, it was immediately self-defeating. An epic is justified in its radical simplification, its stereotypes, its primitive terms, by its appeal to a real national unity of belief, and by its power to reinforce that unity. The oversimplifications of *The Birth of a Nation,* however, are not the controlled and ordering images of an art based upon a set of beliefs to which an entire people subscribe, images which emotionally order and control the world of that people's experience; instead it is the projection of images of disorder, an attack upon cultural and moral unity; the images of the film are the debilitating images of a false myth, a pseudo-epic.

The picture did, however, provide another cinematic genre with many of its basic situations. In 1908, with the "Bronco Billie" series, the Western setting had begun to be realized as particularly suitable to the enactment of the drama of simple primitive faith and national aspirations. After *The Birth of a Nation,* its images of elemental struggle and black and white moral values, and its techniques for making these exciting and significant, were transferred to the "Western." The epic qualities of *The Birth of a Nation* were false and vicious because they impinged upon contemporary reality and oversimplified both actual history and contemporary social circumstances; transferred to a realm of pure mythology—the Western scene of Richard Dix, *Stagecoach* and *High Noon*—and to the moral blackness of outlaw and moral whiteness of law, these simplifications, and the techniques for pictorializing them, have given us something much more artistically valid.

But more important, *The Birth of a Nation* pointed in the second, and the major, direction of the motion picture art. This direction we can call "symbolic realism"—the apparent imitation of actuality which brings out the symbolic or representational meaning of that apparent reality. This "significant" or "symbolic" realism was demonstrated to be effective in the portrayal of either deep psychological or wide universal meanings. To take a rather titillating example in *The Birth of a Nation* of the first kind of surface realism arranged to illustrate unexpressed psychological truths: Lillian Gish played an innocent love scene with the hero, returned to her room, and seated herself dreamily on the bed; the bed happened to be a four-poster each of whose posts was almost embarrassingly suggestive of masculinity; she dreamily embraced and caressed the bedpost. Some years later, Greta Garbo, as Queen Christina, after three days in bed with John Gilbert, used the bedpost in similar fashion. More significant, perhaps, is the way in which images were juxtaposed in this pioneering picture so as to bring out the universal significance of the concrete instance. The view of the army winding past the mother and child to symbolize the agony and displacements of war; the cart and the carriage as symbols of feudal levels of society; Stoneman's clubfoot representing the maimed wrathful impotence of the mechanical North; little sister adorning her coarse post bellum dress with a bit of cotton rescued from the destroyed plantation fields—these were but a few of the large number of symbolic extensions of the surface, and they pointed the way toward the great documentary symbolic realism of Flaherty, and the imaginative symbolic realism of *The Informer, Sous les Toits de Paris, The River,* and the whole run of wonderful Italian neorealistic films: *Open City, Paisan, The Bicycle Thief,* and *La Strada.*

A preliminary examination of a significant motion picture, then, has yielded some profit as well as some disappointment. The disappointment is largely in the failure of this pioneering picture to measure up to standards of artistic greatness: its failure to achieve that fusion of content and technique which together make up a great work of art. Its failure is doubly disappointing, because it involves an inversion and debasement of epic powers in which those powers pander to popular taste instead of attempting to reach a whole vision, sinewed with moral responsibility. But in this very failure lies some of its profits for us as students of American civilization; better than any other art work, it summarizes every aspect of the Plantation Illusion which is so vigorous a force in the history of American sensibility; for the student of the art form, it will demonstrate the beginnings of techniques which both rescue *The Birth of a Nation* from ugliness, and which, when used to embody more aesthetically malleable content, give us the possibilities of the art of the movie.

NOTES

1. Lewis Jacobs, *The Rise of the American Film* (New York, 1939), p. 175.
2. Seymour Stern, "*The Birth of a Nation* in Retrospect," *International Photographer,* VII (April, 1935), 4.
3. Jacobs, *op. cit.,* p. 175.
4. Stern, *op. cit.,* p. 4.
5. Thomas Dixon, *The Clansman* (New York, 1905), Dedication, n.p.
6. *Ibid.,* Introduction, n.p.
7. *Ibid.,* p. 95.
8. *Ibid.,* p. 90.
9. *Ibid.,* p. 57.
10. Paul M. Angle, *Created Equal?* (Chicago, 1958), p. 235. Dixon, *op. cit.,* p. 46ff.
11. *Ibid.,* p. 93.
12. *Ibid.,* pp. 248-249.
13. *Ibid.,* p. 254.
14. *Ibid.,* p. 171.
15. *Ibid.,* p. 316.
16. *Ibid.,* p. 374.
17. F. P. Gaines, *The Southern Plantation* (New York, 1924), pp. 143-236.
18. Kenneth Stampp, *The Peculiar Institution* (New York, 1956).
19. John Crowe Ransom, "Hearts and Heads," *American Review,* II (March, 1934), 559.
20. Dixon, *op. cit.,* pp. 124-125.
21. Gaines, *op. cit.,* p. 210.
22. Stampp, *op. cit.,* p. 350ff.; W. J. Cash, *The Mind of the South* (New York, 1941), pp. 114-117; Gunnar Myrdal, *An American Dilemma* (New York, 1944), p. 562.
23. Stampp, *op. cit.,* p. 355.
24. Dixon, *op. cit.,* p. 304.
25. Henry MacMahon, "The Art of the Movies," *New York Times,* June 6, 1915, sec. 6, p. 8.

Reaction and Protest

The persistent, often unrecognized, strain of racism in American society has always stimulated a Negro response. The three selections that follow represent responses at different times and places: the pre–Civil War Southwest, post-Reconstruction Georgia, and pre–World War 1 America. The reactions and protests are primarily those of free Negroes. The slave reaction, as already noted, is difficult to assess and has often been cited. The examples used here are less well known, yet they are as significant in their own way in suggesting possibilities for Negro strategy.

In the first article, George Ruble Woolfolk attempts a rehabilitation of the Turner theory of the importance of the frontier in American history, which holds that the frontier acted as a safety valve by drawing off population from Eastern centers, dissipated forces leading to social conflict, and contributed to the formation of a distinctive American character. Dramatic and challenging, the Turner thesis stimulated historians to test it against available data. The oversimplified version has rightly been attacked by historians, although the question is not completely answered. Perhaps a semblance of the frontier thesis may be restored by a kind of marginal analysis of the impact of the limited immigration to the frontier.

In any case, as Staughton Lynd has shown, Turner left the Negro out of his calculations, an omission that Woolfolk corrects. Woolfolk documents the appeal of available land and the prospects of a freer society for the Negro. Unlike Turner who looked at the old Northwest, Woolfolk concentrates his attention mainly upon Texas, and uses the number of migrants into an area as an index of Negro discontent with their pre-

vious condition. Migration within the confines of the United States may be as revealing of attitudes as the less successful but more visible colonization projects. At any rate, one of the avenues open to the Negro is migration, and it would be ironic indeed if Turner's insight were proven partially true by the Negro whom he failed to perceive.

A whole range of possible solutions to increased restrictions on the Negro in post-Reconstruction Georgia appear in Clarence A. Bacote's essay. All the proposals fail in the face of implacable white pressure and poverty of resources, but the extent of the effort shows the Negro did not give way easily. The unsuccessful political means demonstrated the failure of promises given in return for votes, and the failure of migration to the North or to Africa showed how new efforts required more material backing than could be mustered. Bacote outlines the continued resistance and the factors that led some individuals to give up distant alternatives in favor of local solutions. Criticism of the lack of success and the solutions chosen by Georgia Negroes ought to be considered only in terms of the situation in which these persons found themselves.

Thomas R. Cripps's article chronicles Negro reaction to the Birth of a Nation. *He shows the Negro in another role, that of countering the deleterious effect of a new art form. The use of collective pressure to censor the film, the use of public media to gain support, and the political opposition to a Wilsonian endorsement are all increasingly sophisticated defensive efforts. Even the roots of direct action can be seen in these efforts to prevent the stereotyped figure of the Negro from appearing.*

In the Cripps selection, as in the others, two points are obvious. First, the Negro was not a passive observer but actively resisted a discriminatory society. Second, the techniques of Negro resistance are not new. The emphasis may have changed, but historical antecedents can be found. Perhaps the most striking difference between the eras is not the methods but the results.

TURNER'S SAFETY VALVE

AND FREE NEGRO

WESTWARD MIGRATION

George R. Woolfolk

The "safety-valve" theory has been, and continues to be, one of the most controversial aspects of the Turner thesis. It involves a basic problem of the human spirit, viz., the dilemma of the free soul when confronted with the tyranny of orthodoxy and conformity. Frederick Jackson Turner touched a responding chord in the heart of every free spirit when he said:

> Whenever social conditions tended to crystallize in the East, whenever capital tended to press upon labor or political restraints to impede the freedom of the mass, there was this gate of escape to the free conditions of the frontier. These free lands promoted individualism, economic equality, freedom to rise, democracy. Men would not accept inferior wages and a permanent position of social subordination when this promised land of freedom and equality was theirs for the taking. Who would rest content under oppressive legislative conditions when with a slight effort he might reach a land wherein to become a co-worker in the building of free cities and free States on the lines of his own ideal? In a word, then, free lands meant free opportunities.[1]

This brilliant thrust has been pummeled in the scholarly arena and

George Ruble Woolfolk, "Turner's Safety Valve and Free Negro Westward Migration," *Pacific Northwest Quarterly*, LVI, No. 3 (July, 1965), 125-130.

threatened with the junk heap through no fault of its originator's breadth of conception. Devotees of the theory have robbed it of its capacity for creative insights by loading it down with stereotypes in methodology and ideology; critics have challenged it on superficial grounds by holding up to ridicule its economic aspects.

The "safety-valve" theory has suffered from an unfortunate preoccupation with the sterile amoral materialism of institutional economics. Friend and foe alike have sought its validity in an orthodoxy that can be traced to the abstractions of the Italian economist, Achille Loria, and therefore have been forced to restrict their data and assumptions to demography and the business cycle.[2] The theoretical origin also dictated the assumption that the only kind of oppression worth escaping from was of economic origin. There is nothing in the literal reading or in the full implication of Turner's position that justifies this preoccupation.[3] There is certainly nothing in the human spirit that would validate it.

By assuming that the frontier, either as place or as process, must be "culture free," Turner students and their critics reveal a cultural chauvinism and egotism which provide a barrier to seeing successive American "frontiers" in their true cultural aspects. This attitude implies a contempt for the cultural presence not only of the Indians, but of Europeans as well, and has fostered the assumption that the inevitable consequence of the encounter between American frontiersmen and non-Americans must be cultural conquest by the Americans. Undoubtedly this position has been dictated by the "wildlands" assumption in the pattern of acculturation upon which the theory seemed to be predicated. However, few of Turner's students took seriously his admonition that "There was, of course, a contemporaneous Old West on both the French and the Spanish frontiers. The formation, approach and ultimate collision and intermingling of these contrasting types of frontiers are worthy of a special study." [4]

It is the purpose of this paper to probe the following questions. In what respects does the migration of free Negroes westward add to the validity of the "safety-valve" theory? Were conditions in the established areas east of the Mississippi River sufficiently oppressive that free Negroes found flight to the trans-Mississippi Spanish borderlands desirable? Was it commonly understood that the West in general, and the Spanish borderlands in particular, afforded asylum for free Negroes seeking escape from oppression? Is there evidence to show that individuals were so motivated to take advantage of this escape that they would hazard the journey without reference to economic competence or station in life?

This paper will confine itself to the migration of free Negroes to Texas down to the Civil War. With such a limitation, this study cannot be definitive; at best, the data will be sufficient only for arriving at a hypothesis. However, the findings may serve to reverse any "post mortem" defeatism and to reopen the theory to definitive and realistic investigation.

The "safety-valve" theory and the narrow rural-urban labor exchange orientation into which Turner students and their critics have forced the argument were derived from the theoretical generalizations of Italian economists and have been kept alive by the blind following of stereotypes in methodology and ideology. Broader investigation has revealed the error of the assumption of a culture-free frontier and offers evidence that the trans-Mississippi frontier in the Spanish borderlands represented an area of confrontation for two branches of western civilization which were sufficiently different at the core of human relations that an internal conflict was inevitable. These two branches came to this confrontation in an alien world after several centuries of adjustment made necessary by the aboriginal cultures which they had to suppress or accommodate.

The Spanish frontier, from Florida to California, and the Indian subcultures embraced within its bounds had attracted Negro slaves from the beginning. As conditions affecting the existence of free Negroes worsened in the North and in the South, many of them were persuaded that the West in general, and the Spanish West in particular, held the key to their freedom, dignity, and security. Free Negroes fled first to the trans-Mississippi borderlands, where the Latin-Catholic cultural thrust into the wilderness assured freedom for all men; they continued to come after the Anglo-Protestant cultural thrust clashed with the Latin-Catholic in the open cockpit of Texas.

We have raised the question whether conditions imposed upon free Negroes in the established areas east of the Mississippi River were sufficiently oppressive to make flight to the trans-Mississippi Spanish borderlands desirable. Down to the Civil War, the North and the South witnessed a progressive "crystallization" of social rejection for the free Negro.[5] In both regions he felt keenly the economic and political proscription that hardened into a permanent position of social subordination either through law or custom. Even federal land policy barred him from probable escape to the West by denying him the right of pre-emption. James Madison summed up the lot of free persons of color very well when he observed: "They are everywhere regarded as a nuisance, and must really be such as long as they are under the degradation which public sentiment inflicts on them."

Much has been written about the African colonization movement as a solution to the problem of the presence of the free Negro in American society. Coexistent with this solution was the idea that the American West and the Spanish borderlands offered another feasible and, to some, a more acceptable solution to the problem. Important abolitionists, politicians, philanthropists, and some Negro leaders embraced the latter solution as an alternative to permanent banishment implicit in African colonization and saw in it a means of extending American ideology and influence.

Among those opposed to African colonization was Anthony Benezet, a Quaker who was well known for his work in behalf of Negroes. In 1773 he suggested that Negroes be colonized in the territory extending west of the Allegheny Mountains to the Mississippi River "on a breadth of four hundred to five hundred miles." [6] The western solution looked good to another Pennsylvania Quaker, Thomas Branagan. This converted slave trader maintained that the taxes used to support free Negroes could be used to finance their deportation and that a state could be established for them in Louisiana Territory, more than two thousand miles from white settlement.

The western idea found some limited oblique persistence in the Neshoba community on the Wolf River near Memphis, Tennessee. Conceived by the Scottish reformer Frances Wright, and endorsed by Madison, Jefferson, Lafayette, Benjamin Lundy, and Robert Dale Owen, the purpose of the community as a school for freedom, when seen in relationship to its locale and the experience of other such experiments in the Middle West, is significant.[7] The western solution found better expression in Lundy's Texas scheme.[8] Having been interested in both Haiti and Canada, Lundy believed that a colony in the state of Coahuila and Texas would, among other benefits, be salutary because of

> the speedy means it will afford the man of color to become wealthy, and rise above the degradation that slavery and prejudice have imposed on him, thereby further proving to the people of this nation, that here, in America—the land of his birth and his natural home—he may be fitted for freedom and self-government with perfect ease and safety.[9]

Another typical position supporting the West as a solution to the problem of the free Negro was more political than humanitarian. In answer to the southern charge that the Republican party wished to force emancipation and to keep all Negroes in the South as equals of white laborers, Francis P. Blair, Jr., Congressman from a Missouri district, proposed a solution with a *double entendre:* "He would propagate freedom in the American tropics by colonizing free Negroes there. . . ." [10] The federal government's policy of purchasing Indian lands and removing the Indians to western reservations was deemed sufficient precedent for acquiring territory and colonizing free Negroes in Central America. This policy presumably would eliminate the fear induced by the presence of the Negro and at the same time would make him the principal factor in civilizing Central America and developing its commerce with the United States.

Vocal Negro reaction (at least that which has been recorded) was never committed in principle either to African or any other kind of deportation scheme. Rather, it seems to have been directed toward the acceptance of the West or the Spanish borderlands as the lesser of two evils. A convention of free Negroes, meeting in Richmond, Virginia, in 1817, took the position that the idea of colonization was acceptable, but they preferred "being colonized in the most remote corner of the land of our nativity, to being exiled to a foreign country. . . ." The idea persisted in the resolutions of the third annual convention for the Improvement of the Free People of Color held in 1833. The convention opposed any colonization scheme beyond this continent and resolved that

> those who may be obliged to exchange a cultivated region for a howling wilderness, we would recommend, to retire back into the western wilds, and fell the native forests of America, where the plough-share of prejudice has as yet been unable to penetrate the soil. . . .[11]

A minority among those Negro leaders who favored migration continued to wrestle with the problem during the 1850's. The West and the Spanish borderlands loomed larger in the minds of Dr. Martin R. Delany, James T. Holly, and James M. Whitfield. Delany boldly rejected even Canada (which for years had been favored by escapists), because he felt it would soon be absorbed by the United States. He took a firm position for Central and South America, where the Negro could live without fear of annexation or political or economic oppression.[12]

There can be little doubt that abolitionists, politicians, and some Negroes looked upon the West in general, and the Spanish borderlands in particular, as an asylum, a place of retreat from the proscriptions of American life that were the lot of free persons of color. With this tentative validation, an important part of the "safety-valve" theory has turned on the nature of "proof." Demography offers little evidence to adduce individual motivation as a causative factor. Did free Negroes take advantage of "the gate of escape to the free conditions of the frontier?" If so. what were their motivations? Answers to these questions do much to support the "safety-valve" theory in many of its aspects.

The states in which the flight to Texas originated present an interesting pattern.[13] For the period of the Republic and statehood, northern and middle western states and territories contributed a small share.[14] Most of the free Negroes who fled to Texas, however, came from the Old South, with the heaviest concentration from the tidewater region.[15] The greatest number came from Louisiana and Alabama in the Gulf South; and Tennessee sent the largest number of heads of families from the southern border states. It is clear, then, that the findings on the movement of younger sons from neighboring farms or states are not applicable to the movement of free Negroes to Texas. It is also significant that the South in general was tightening legal controls on free persons of color during these years, a fact which undoubtedly gave added incentive to flight.[16]

Personal motivation for flight to the Spanish borderlands arose from several sources. Some free Negroes who found living in organized society difficult followed Sam Houston's ideas and sought escape among the Indians.[17] These mulattoes and blacks (some have a strain of Indian blood) lived in the twilight zone between Indian tribes and white settlements and enjoyed a status based upon their knowledge and skill in dealing with the Indians. Edward Rose and James Beckwourth, Crow chiefs and Rocky Mountain fur traders, Ben Wiggins of Florida, and other colorful figures who were associated with the Seminole chief, Wild Cat, and his military colony, located on the Rio Grande, are typical of this class of escapist.

Many free Negroes whose connections with white parents, husbands, or wives made their position untenable in southern society also sought escape. Among them were such persons as John Bird, Negro son of Dorcas Bird, the daughter of General Bird of Virginia. John and his son, Henry, had "emigrated and settled in Texas under the belief that they would be received as citizens under the colonization laws of Mexican United States and entitled as such to land."[18] In 1827 David Townes (white) and his wife Sophia (Negro) fled with their children to Texas, where they could be married legally under the Mexican regime.[19] Samuel McCullouch came before the Texas Declaration of Independence with Peggy and Rose, two women of color, "desiring that the foresaid two colored persons should be and remain free all the remainder of their lives."[20] This new cultural frontier meant liberation for these people, just as the forest, according to Turner students, offered freedom to men oppressed by legislative and economic conditions.

More poignant still was the plight of the free persons of color whose wives and children were slaves.[21] When the master moved to Texas, ties stronger than a league and labor of (free) land pulled these husbands and fathers after their own. There were single men and women who were either emancipated or bought their freedom in the Old South and fled to the state of Coahuila and Texas just to remain free.[22] Nelson Kavanaugh, a barber freed in Richmond, Kentucky, found sanctuary in Houston, Texas, as did Zylpha Husk and child, one of a number of extraordinary Negro women who found both freedom and opportunity on this frontier.

Land hunger, in the best Turner tradition, was one incentive that encouraged free Negroes to migrate to Texas. Thomas D. Clark's insistence upon the orthodoxy and conformity of the frontier is well taken. Land was not only an item of wealth; it was also a badge of citizenship. Samuel Hardin and his wife came to Texas "under laws that invited their emigration and acquired rights and property to a considerable amount." William Goyens was so successful in acquiring property that the accumulation of holdings became almost an obsession with him.[23] The fabulous Ashworth clan moved from Louisiana into Coahuila and Texas and, by taking advantage of every homestead and headright provision, acquired vast holdings that reached from Jefferson County in the southeast to Angelina County in deep East Texas.

Both mulatto and black free Negroes brought to the Texas frontier the full range of skills which characterized the economy of the Old South. As might be expected, agricultural workers dominated the occupational pattern.[24] Free Negroes added some diversification by engaging in stock raising and serving as herdsmen, occupational endeavors in which they had shown considerable ability even in the Spanish-Mexican period. A goodly representation of domestic servants, artisans, and skilled laborers were to be found in this group; and there were a few professional men. There seems, then, to have been greater diversity in this migration, especially on the lower levels of economic competence, than some of the critics of the Turner students found.

During the 1840's and 1850's, there was a constant movement of free Negroes in the Old South to the urban centers. Few of those who went to Texas chose the towns of the plantation area of East Texas. Urban free Negroes generally preferred the Mexican area below the German barrier, where the towns of Galveston, San Antonio, Brownsville, and Austin were located. Free Negro farmers tended to concentrate in the plantation area of East Texas, running roughly from Nacogdoches County to the Galveston–Jefferson County region. Stock-raising free Negroes naturally tended to concentrate in Jackson County, an old area for cattle. Artisans, servants, and some agricultural laborers also found the German-Mexican areas of central–south Texas more hospitable, and they concentrated there in greater numbers during the late 1850's.

The flight of free Negroes to the West in general, and to the trans-

Mississippi Spanish borderlands in particular, is instructive for those who would examine the "safety-valve" theory with more critical imagination than has hitherto been applied to the discussion of the problem. To be sure, the "culture-free frontier" assumption suffers under this examination; but there is some indication that a "cultural frontier" encourages flight from the tyranny of an oppressive orthodoxy and conformity in established society just as readily as does the forest. The flight of free Negroes also makes clear that it would have been more profitable for investigators of this problem to have examined the full range of possible motivations for flight implicit in Turner's original assertion. This study further indicates that there will have to be a reconsideration of the economic competence of those who came West; for example, little presented here gives any priority to well-to-do farmers.

Surely it is clear by now that, given sufficient provocation, people from all walks of life will seek escape to better situations, and that the distance to the land of Canaan will not deter the will to flight. Freed of the preoccupation with sterile economic abstractions and seen in the rough pragmatism of its social evolutionary aspects, the "safety-valve" theory still has much to say to the student who seeks to understand the meaning of the thrust westward of the civilization or culture that was the legacy of Europe.

NOTES

1. Frederick Jackson Turner, *The Frontier in American History* (New York, 1920), pp. 259-260.

2. Lee Benson, *Turner and Beard* (Glencoe, Ill., 1960), pp. 2, 5-6, 24, 56; Frederic L. Paxson, *History of the American Frontier, 1763-1893* (Boston, 1924), p. 187; Robert Riegel, *America Moves West* (New York, 1930), pp. 639-640; Murray Kane, "Some Considerations on the Safety Valve Doctrine," *Mississippi Valley Historical Review*, XXIII (1936), 186-187; Carter Goodrich and Sol Davison, "The Wage-Earner in the Westward Movement, II," *Political Science Quarterly*, LI (1936), 115; Joseph Schafer, "Was the West a Safety Valve for Labor?"*MVHR*, XXIV (1937), 307; Frederic L. Paxson, *When the West Is Gone* (New York, 1941), pp. 31, 36; Fred A. Shannon, "A Post Mortem on the Labor-Safety-Valve Theory," *Agricultural History*, XIX (1945), 37; George W. Pierson, "Recent Studies of Turner Doctrine," *MVHR*,

XXXIV (1947), 458; Thomas D. Clark, *Frontier America* (New York, 1959), pp. 6, 7, 19-20.

3. Homer C. Hockett, *Western Influences on Political Parties to 1825* (Columbus, Ohio, 1917), p. 42; Merle Curti, *Growth of American Thought* (New York, 1943), p. 569; Carl N. Degler, *Out of Our Past: The Forces That Shaped Modern America* (New York, 1959), pp. 124-130; Ray Allen Billington, *The American Frontier* (Washington, D.C., 1958), pp. 10-12; John Randall, Jr., and George Haines, IV, "Controlling Assumptions in the Practice of American Historians," *Theory and Practice in Historical Study: A Report of the Committee on Historiography* (Social Science Research Council Bulletin No. 54 [1946]), p. 47.

4. Turner, *Frontier in American History*, p. 125 n. 35. Typical of the forest acculturative position is Clark's *Frontier America*, pp. 6, 7, 14. R. A. Billington (*Westward Expansion* [New York, 1949], p. vii, and *The Far Western Frontier, 1830-1860* [New York, 1956], pp. 1, 4) recognizes the existence of other branches of western culture in the westward advance, but he brushes them aside as of little or no consequence before the power of "American Frontier Technique." Paxson, an earlier student (*When the West Is Gone*, p. 31), can be classed with Clark as a part of the culture-free frontier school.

Scholars like Herbert E. Bolton have never underrated the impact and persistence of other European subcultures and values in the American experience. Carlton J. H. Hayes ("The American Frontier—Frontier of What?" *American Historical Review*, LI [1946], 199-216) reminds participants in the Turner discussion of the European continuity. Walter P. Webb shows an interesting development: in *The Great Plains* (New York, 1931), pp. vi, 8, 486, 507, he seems to place emphasis upon technologies and environment; however, in *The Texas Rangers* (New York, 1935), pp. 7, 9, 11, 14, 15, he recognizes more than any student of the West that there are three cultures that will clash in this region, though he shows some egotism by calling the American brand "slow, powerful, and inexorable." Some historians, like Arnold Toynbee (in Chapter 5, "The Psychological Encounter," *The World and the West* [New York, 1953]), are now offering more definitive analyses of cultural confrontations and interchanges. The easy generalizations, dictated either by chauvinism or by cultural egotism, are no longer acceptable.

5. The temptation to overdocument the obvious will be resisted here. Only a few of the representative studies are listed. L. P. Jackson, *Free Negro Labor and Property Holding in Virginia, 1830-1860* (New York, 1942); J. H. Franklin, *The Free Negro in North Carolina, 1790-1860* (Chapel Hill, 1943); O. W. Taylor, *Negro Slavery in Arkansas* (Durham, 1958); D. G. Hill, "The Negro as a Political and Social Issue in the Oregon Country," *Journal of Negro History*, XXXIII (1948), 130-145; Charles S. Sydnor, "The Free Negro in Mississippi before the Civil War," *AHR*, XXXII (1927), 769-788; Richard B. Morris, "The Measure of Bondage in the Slave States," *MVHR*, XLI (1954), 219-240; C. P. Patterson, *The Negro in Tennessee, 1790-1865* (Austin, 1922); C. B. Rousseve, *The Negro in Louisiana* (New Orleans, 1937); Kenneth M.

Stampp, *The Peculiar Institution: Slavery in the Ante-Bellum South* (New York, 1956).

Representative studies of conditions in the North are: Leon F. Litwack, *North of Slavery: The Negro in the Free States, 1790-1860* (Chicago, 1961); L. J. Greene, *The Negro in Colonial New England, 1620-1776* (New York, 1942); N. D. Harris, *The History of Negro Servitude in Illinois, 1719-1864* (Chicago, 1904); E. E. Thorpe, *The Mind of the Negro* (Baton Rouge, 1961); William H. and Jane H. Pease, *Black Utopia: Negro Communal Experiments in America* (Madison, 1963); Charles H. Wesley, "The Negro's Struggle for Freedom in Its Birthplace," *JNH*, XXX (1945), 62-81; J. T. Adams, "Disfranchisement of Negroes in New England," *AHR*, XXX (1925), 543-547. A good study of how the free Negro fared at the hands of the federal government before the Civil War is Leon F. Litwack, "The Federal Government and the Free Negro, 1790-1860," *JNH*, XLIII (1958), 261-278 [and in present study, Part III].

6. H. N. Sherwood, "Early Negro Deportation Projects," *MVHR*, II, (1916), 494-495.

7. W. H. and Jane Pease, *Black Utopia*, pp. 24-30; "Transplanting Free Negroes to Ohio from 1815 to 1858," *JNH*, I (1916), 302-317.

8. Benjamin Lundy, *Life, Travels, and Opinions of Benjamin Lundy* (Philadelphia, 1847), p. 63; Merton L. Dillon, "Benjamin Lundy in Texas," *Southwestern Historical Quarterly*, LXIII (1959), 46-62; Jacob E. Cooke, *Frederic Bancroft, Historian* (Norman, 1957), p. 192.

9. *Genius of Universal Emancipation*, XIII (November, 1832), quoted by Dillon, "Benjamin Lundy," p. 50.

10. Cooke, *Frederic Bancroft*, p. 195; John Hope Franklin, *From Slavery to Freedom* (2nd ed.; New York, 1965), pp. 235-236.

11. W. H. and Jane Pease, *Black Utopia*, p. 16; Franklin, *From Slavery to Freedom*, p. 237; Louis R. Mehlinger, "The Attitude of the Free Negro Toward African Colonization," *JNH*, I (1916), 276-301.

12. Litwack, *North of Slavery*, pp. 258-260; Mehlinger, "The Attitude of the Free Negro," pp. 297-300.

13. Seventh Census of the United States (1850), MSS, Population Schedules (Texas Archives, Texas State Library, Austin); Eighth Census of the United States (1860), MSS, Population Schedules (Texas Archives, Texas State Library). The 1850 and 1860 figures give only the numbers of free persons of color in the organized communities. There were many among the Indians and in Mexican situations who, no doubt, escaped the compilers. What is said herein has direct reference to "heads of families." The wives and children counted in the schedules often indicate that sometimes one or two stops were made by the head of the family before reaching the ultimate destination of Texas.

14. States involved are Maine, Vermont, New York, Pennsylvania, and Illinois. A small number of free Negroes from Africa, England, Cuba, and Jamaica appear on the Texas scene.

15. South Carolina, Virginia, and North Carolina led in 1850 and Virginia, Georgia, and North Carolina in 1860.

16. George Ruble Woolfolk, "Taxes and Slavery in the Ante Bellum South," *Journal of Southern History*, XXVI (1960), 180-200.

17. Kenneth W. Porter, "Negroes and Indians on the Texas Frontier, 1831-1876: A Study in Race and Culture," *JNH*, XLI (1956), 185-214, 285-310; V. O. King, "The Cherokee Nation of Indians," *Southwestern Historical Quarterly*, II (1898), 58-72; James H. Johnston, "Documentary Evidence of the Relations of Negroes and Indians," *JNH*, XIV (1929), 21-43; Wyatt F. Jeltz, "The Relations of Negroes and Choctaw and Chickasaw Indians," *JNH*, XXXIII (1948), 24-37; Ernest Wallace and E. Adamson Hoebel, *The Comanches: Lords of the South Plains* (Norman, 1952), p. 241.

18. Memorial of John and Henry Bird, Sept. 20, 1820 (Texas Archives, Texas State Library). All memorials cited hereafter are in the Texas Archives.

19. Memorial of Louisa, Eliza, Peter, Matilda, Delila, and Colbyer Townes, Oct. 18, 1840.

20. Memorial of Samuel McCullouch, Dec. 29, 1841.

21. Memorial of Louis Edmundson, Nov. 30, 1853; Memorial of Bryant Moses, Dec. 30, 1852; Memorial of Bob, Oct. 22, 1857; Memorial of Pleasant Bious, Nov. 5, 1841.

22. Memorial of Henry Tucker [1840]; Memorial of Nelson Kavanaugh [no date]. A rather remarkable phenomenon is the number of unattached free women of color to be found in Coahuila and in Texas operating on their own. Examples of this are as follows: Memorial of Diana Leonard, Dec. 14, 1840; Memorial of Zylpha Husk, Dec. 16, 1841; Memorial of Harriet Newal Sands, Jan. 5, 1853.

23. Memorial of the Board of Land Commissioners [no date]; Memorial of William Goyens, Sept., 1840; Memorial of Samuel McCullouch, Jr. [no date]; Memorial of Harriet Reynolds, Jan. 22, 1858; Memorial of Henry Lynch, Dec. 15, 1840; Memorial of Samuel Hardin [no date]; Memorial of Andrew Bell, Dec. 4, 1840. The Seventh and Eighth Census MSS sometimes reveal the extent of land ownership in the population schedules. However, the agricultural production stipulations are much more definitive for those free persons of color located in the rural areas and engaged in farming. More reliable still are the Comptroller's Tax Records. Manuscript copies were consulted for this study. A cross-section sample by key counties in five-year periods shows a remarkable pattern of land acquisition over the years. This is true both for town lots and farming lands. The Robert Bruce Blake Research Collection at the Barker Library of the University of Texas has the best account of the extraordinary land operations of William Goyens of Nacogdoches.

24. This analysis is drawn from the Seventh Census of the United States (1850), MSS, Population Schedules, and the Eighth Census of the United States (1860), MSS, Population Schedules (Texas Archives, Texas State Library).

NEGRO PROSCRIPTION, PROTESTS,

AND PROPOSED SOLUTIONS

IN GEORGIA, 1880-1908

Clarence A. Bacote

Following reconstruction in Georgia, the Negro was not only the victim of political disfranchisement and educational discrimination, but also suffered humiliation in the form of "Jim Crow" laws, lynching, and the convict-lease system. These forms of racial proscription brought forth numerous protests from Negroes but to no avail; hence, convinced of the futility of striving for first-class citizenship in such an environment, some Negro leaders proposed three avenues of escape, namely: (1) back to Africa, (2) exodus to the North, and (3) colonization in the frontier West. By these means, they hoped, Negroes might be able to acquire those rights and privileges guaranteed by the United States Constitution.

"It is paradoxical," says Woodward, "that the barriers of racial discrimination mounted in direct ratio to the tide of political democracy among the whites." [1] Antagonism between the poor whites and Negroes dated back to the ante bellum period and continued after the Civil War, but it was intensified as the two groups became competitors in the labor market. Knowing that they were despised by both the upper-class whites and the freedmen, the poor whites struggled to maintain a floor below which no whites would fall and which at the same time would serve as a ceiling to the rise of Negroes. [2]

Clarence A. Bacote, "Negro Proscription, Protests, and Proposed Solutions in Georgia, 1880-1908," *Journal of Southern History*, XXV, No. 4 (November, 1959), 471-498.

Meanwhile, the upper-class whites, who did not wish to see the Southern social and economic structure fractured by a coalition of the poor whites and Negroes, aided and abetted this racial friction by stressing to the poor whites the importance of maintaining white supremacy. Thus white supremacy was the principal theme, and the average white voter was blind to the fact that "Negro domination" was a fantastically false appeal of politicians who had finally succeeded in enslaving the white voter through propaganda. To strengthen the allegiance of the poor whites to the existing social and economic arrangements, the ruling class proceeded in a limited way to establish schools and factories for them. The result was a widening of the educational and economic gap between the poor whites and Negroes.[3]

In 1870, as a result of a bill introduced in the Georgia Legislature by two Negro members, James Porter of Chatham County in the house and George Wallace in the senate,[4] an act was passed which stated that "all common carriers of passengers for hire in the State of Georgia shall furnish like and equal accommodations for all persons, without distinction of race, color, or previous condition." [5] But by 1890, the growing antagonism between the poor whites and Negroes was reflected on the state level when the Alliancemen gained control of the Georgia Legislature by electing 160 of the 219 members.[6] While the Alliancemen advocated a liberal platform,[7] at the same time they enacted several laws which were definitely designed to emphasize the inferior status of the Negro; the most vicious of these was the "Jim Crow" law.

When Representative S. W. Johnson of Appling County introduced a bill in the Georgia House on July 20, 1891, requiring the railroads to furnish separate coaches for whites and Negroes with equal accommodations for both races, Representative Lectured Crawford, a Negro from McIntosh County, told the House that

> The railroads would not give equal accommodations if this act were to become law, and as long as I buy a first class ticket I have a right to such accommodations, whether I am considered below the other race or not. . . . The railroads sell us first class tickets and then put us into cars where white men come in and smoke, use all kinds of indecent language, drink whiskey out of water cups, and they call this first class passage.[8]

While this bill was under discussion in the House, the Georgia Colored Alliancemen were holding their state meeting in Atlanta. A committee to memorialize the legislature was appointed, with J. W. Carter as chairman, to ask for better laws, not race legislation, but "such laws as will better the condition of the colored race, and promote their happiness and advance the cause of education." [9] On July 23, the members of this committee visited the legislature and took seats in the gallery. Representative J. M. Holzendorf, Negro member from Camden County, obtained permission from the house to allow a representative from the Negro Alliance to address them for ten minutes. Just before their spokesman, J. W. Carter, began to speak, the Alliance members were invited to take seats on the floor of the house. In his plea against the bill, Carter said in part:

> The white people . . . have sold themselves to the Negroes. . . . You ask them to vote for you, and when you ask the Negro to vote for you, you are due him a return of the compliment. We Negroes are voting for you now. Some of these days we expect you to vote for us.

After complimenting the Alliance legislature on its successful campaign, Carter turned to the social relationship of the races.

> We don't want social equality. All the Negro wants is protection. You white people attend to your business and let us alone. . . . The politicians and the lawyers say you must keep us Negroes down. But that is not right. . . . If you have a sow that has a lot of pigs, some white ones and some black ones, you don't kill the black ones, do you? No sir. You think just as much of the black pigs as you do the white ones. . . . If this old state of ours should be threatened, these Negroes—your mothers in black—would be the first to offer themselves in her defense.[10]

It was unusual for a Negro visitor to be extended an invitation to address the legislature from the floor, but the speech was well received. Many of the members congratulated Carter for his keen logic. However, despite Crawford's protest and Carter's appeal for justice, the "Jim Crow" bill was passed by both houses and was signed by Governor Northen on October 21, 1891. The law required the railroads to provide equal accommodations in separate cars for whites and Negroes but this did not apply to sleeping cars. In addition, the law authorized streetcar conductors to separate the races as far as possible.[11]

This "Jim Crow" law drew nationwide attention. The Chicago *Appeal* declared that

> A state cursed with such a legislative body almost deserves commiseration. . . . The state of "Wisdom, Justice, and Moderation" is thus set back in this enlightened age by the recent wretched legislation which was a Farmer's Alliance body.[12]

Negroes themselves were disappointed in this group, whose platform seemed to incorporate ideas of justice and fair play. In a lengthy editorial, the Savannah *Tribune* observed:

The past twelve months have been more prolific of legislation in the Southern States directly antagonistic to the Negro than any similar period since the days of Reconstruction.

. . . in the states dominated by the Farmer's Alliance, and in those legislatures where their influence has been strongest and most commanding, has this tendency to reactionary legislation been most active and pronounced. . . . These exhibitions of prejudice . . . are simply an expression of hostility to the Negro injected by the white farmers of the South into the great currents of passing political opinion. They represent the feeling of the agricultural class always more strongly wedded to old ideas and less susceptible to the newer teachings of an enlarged and progressive humanity. They have their origin in an order dominated from its incipiency by a feeling of enmity to the Negro.[13]

Negroes pleaded with Governor Northen to force the railroads to provide equal accommodations for both races, and the Negro Press Association of Georgia drew up resolutions advocating such accommodations.[14] These pleas were ignored; consequently, Negroes were herded into crowded coaches without ice water, towels, or soap, and men and women were forced to use the same lavatory facilities.[15]

Since the railroads refused to provide better facilities for Negroes, the latter were advised to stop patronizing railroad excursions and save their money. In most instances these excursions were frequented by the worst element of Negroes, which did the race much harm.[16] The Reverend J. W. Carter, pastor of the Boulevard A. M. E. Zion Church in Atlanta, said "the colored people keep plenty of money ahead in the railroad treasury from the excursion business to take care of and repair all the Jim Crow cars, where the Negroes and dogs ride together. . . . Enough money is spent in one season by Negro excursions to buy one-fourth of the Indian territory." When Negroes returned home from such excursions, continued the Reverend Mr. Carter, they usually found themselves with insufficient money to pay their rent, to buy food, and to provide for their children.[17]

"Jim Crow" trains were followed by "Jim Crow" streetcars in various cities in Georgia. For years Negroes were privileged to occupy any seat in the streetcars, but beginning with Atlanta in the early part of the 1890's, all Georgia cities gradually enacted ordinances providing for "Jim Crow" seating arrangements on public transportation. This action

by the Atlanta City Council prompted Negroes to initiate a movement
to boycott the streetcars. "The time has come," declared a group of
Negro women in Atlanta, "when such actions are necessary to secure
our rights. What's the use of giving any man or corporation our patron-
age when it is not appreciated." [18] To Negroes, the "Jim Crow" policy
was absurd. "It is no more contaminating . . . for colored persons to
ride in the same car with white persons than for them to cook for them
and do other domestic duties." [19]

Savannah did not establish "Jim Crow" streetcars until 1906, although efforts had been made earlier without success. When such a
proposal was made in 1902, President Baldwin, of the Savannah Electric
Railway, told a reporter for the Savannah *Morning News* that

> It is really not a question of the separation of the races, but of
> the cleanly from the uncleanly. Now, I do not mind sitting by a
> decent clean Negro on a street car, and I believe there are few
> people who do. Uncleanly persons of either race are objectionable,
> however, so that it may be seen that it is really not a question of
> segregation of races.
>
> Whenever the effort to separate the races has been made it has
> resulted unsatisfactorily. . . . People recognize its inconveniences
> and difficulties, and they are soon ready to revert to the old system
> of getting a seat wherever you can.
>
> It is difficult to make the people take the places set apart for
> them by law. A policeman would have to ride on every car to
> enforce a measure for the separation of the races. They had to do
> it in Jacksonville. The white people are worse, too, than the Ne-
> groes. A Negro will sit where he is told, as a rule, but a white
> man will kick. Let a white passenger find all seats in the section
> reserved for his race taken and he will move down to the Negro
> section, if there are vacancies there. He will probably think the
> law all right, but that it wasn't intended for him.[20]

These views of the officials and the better element of Savannah prevented passage of the "Jim Crow" ordinance by the city council at that
time. Shortly after this, a second "Jim Crow" bill was introduced in the
council but was defeated, and the councilman who sponsored the
measure failed to win re-election.[21] However, by 1906 the minds of
white people had been inflamed against the Negro by the race-baiting
tactics of Hoke Smith in the gubernatorial race of that year. Furthermore, many poor whites were moving into the city from the rural areas,
bringing with them their deep-seated prejudices against the Negro.[22]
Thus the time seemed propitious for a "Jim Crow" streetcar law, and

such a measure was proposed a third time in the city council. At first the ordinance was withdrawn, but a resolution was passed suggesting that the city police be authorized to enforce the state segregation law. This was adopted immediately, and the streetcar company complied.[23]

Negroes were incensed and immediately laid plans to boycott the streetcars. Hackmen and street wagons were pressed into service to carry Negroes at a reduced rate. The pastor of the Second Baptist Church, the Reverend J. J. Durham, advised his members to stay off the cars. A group of enterprising Negroes organized the United Transport Company which planned to invest in vehicles to meet the emergency. Negroes were advised to walk because walking was healthy. If they lived a long distance from their destination, they were advised to start earlier, "thereby increasing your health and your wealth." [24] Those who defied the request were castigated as traitors to the race—especially the preachers. "For a few paltry dollars they will sell their manhood rights and endeavor to ruin those who are weak enough to follow them." [25] Despite this defection among the Negroes, the boycott was not a complete failure, for President Baldwin of the Savannah Electric Railway told the city council that the "Jim Crow" law had cost his company fifty thousand dollars in revenue.[26]

Lynching, which added to the social degradation of the Negro, was another weapon used by the Southern whites to keep the Negro in his place. Between 1888 and 1903 there were 241 Negroes lynched in Georgia, which made the state second only to Mississippi with 294 for the same period.[27] Despite the pleas of Negroes to the federal government, urging that legislation be enacted for their protection against this barbarous practice, nothing was done. The Republican party was as lukewarm in this respect as the Democrats.[28] Although there was an anti-lynching law passed during the administration of President Benjamin Harrison, it was inspired by the protests of the Italian government against the lynching of eleven Italians in New Orleans and was designed to protect foreign nationals rather than the Negro. In his last message to Congress, on December 6, 1892, Harrison made the first presidential recommendation to Congress to adopt measures for curbing this evil practice. Since only three months remained in his term, no action was taken. It remained for the only Negro congressman at the time, George White, of North Carolina, to introduce on January 20, 1900, "the first bill to make lynching of American citizens a federal crime," but it died in the Judiciary Committee.[29]

Lynchings were so prevalent in Georgia that Negroes became convinced that few of the victims were actually guilty. In fact, it was proposed that Negroes should set aside Memorial Day, May 30, for the purpose of paying respect to the innocent victims of mob violence, and ministers were urged to enlist the support of their congregations for such a movement.[30] Although rape was the most publicized reason given for lynchings, actually only about one-fourth of them were attributed to that crime. But because Negroes were occasionally guilty of rape, the prejudices of the whites toward them were intensified. On the other hand, while countless Negro women were forced to submit to the lust of white men, Southern "justice" made no provision for this. As the Savannah *Tribune* observed, "The very men who are abridging our rights are the ones who are ruining our daughters." [31]

In the gubernatorial race of 1892, Governor Northen, with the majority of Negro voters supporting him, was re-elected over his Populist opponent, W. L. Peek, and this despite the fact that the bosses of the state Republican organization endorsed the Populist candidate.[32] Most Negroes, like Bishop McNeal Turner of the African Methodist Episcopal Church, felt that Northen deserved the Negro vote because of the courage of his convictions. Furthermore, many Negroes were suspicious of the Populist party, feeling that its members represented the uneducated classes in the state and were responsible for the proscriptive legislation passed by the Alliance legislature of 1890-1891.[33] The governor became very popular among Negroes by recommending in his inaugural address that a more stringent law to prevent lynching should be passed. By his proposal a sheriff who was negligent in protecting a prisoner in his custody would be subject to a fine and imprisonment and suspension or dismissal from office.[34]

This position induced the Negro Press Association of Georgia at its meeting in Atlanta on June 20, 1893, to adopt a resolution endorsing the governor's stand as well as the support given him by the better element of whites. The meeting also expressed its appreciation to the Atlanta *Constitution,* Augusta *Chronicle,* and other papers for the interest they manifested in the general welfare of the Negro.[35] When the legislature passed a law incorporating many of the recommendations of Governor Northen, Bishop Turner issued a call for Negro mass meetings to be held Emancipation Day, January 1, 1894, to give thanks for the new law against lynching. From now on, said Bishop Turner, Georgia would serve as a model for the other states; no state in the Union was blessed with such an honorable body of men to represent them in government. "Prosperity shall enthrone her future." [36]

These were noble words from the acknowledged spiritual leader of the Negroes in Georgia. The lawless element of the white population, however, did not heed them, for lynchings continued unabated. In his message to the legislature on October 23, 1895, Governor W. Y. Atkinson deplored the lynchings and asked the assembly to enact a law which would empower him to remove from office a law officer who permitted a mob to take a man from his custody. In addition, he proposed that the administrator of the victim should have the right to recover from the county the full value of his life. His message was courageous:

> What excuse can be given for this conduct when our race has control of the Legislature and the courts, furnishing both the judges and the jurors? No white man should insist upon the infliction of punishment in a case where he is unwilling to entrust the trial to the most intelligent and upright of his race.[37]

The mounting number of lynchings brought forth impassioned protest from Negro leaders. Bishop Turner was so provoked by the callousness of the Republican party toward lynchings in the South that he announced his intention to support William Jennings Bryan for president in 1900 as opposed to William McKinley. He claimed that he was neither a Democrat nor a Republican but a Prohibitionist who would vote for Bryan

> . . . five times before I would vote for William McKinley . . . because we have tried McKinley for four years and he is of no benefit to the black man, except in giving some of them just a few offices, but the great bulk of my race receive no more recognition at his hands than a man who has been dead twenty years.
> . . . I am willing as a negro to try some other white man. . . . Grover Cleveland turned out to be one of the ablest and best presidents that ever graced the nation. . . . Ohio has given us three presidents, and if any of them was ever any account, so far as the negro is concerned, I have yet to learn about it.

Turner declared that the vital questions concerned discrimination, proscription, disfranchisement, and lynchings, the last having increased almost fourfold since McKinley had been president. Bryan, he thought, would take the necessary measures to curb them.[38]

However, with the disfranchisement movement burgeoning at the turn of the century, many white supremacists attributed lynchings to politics. Mrs. Rebecca Felton, the widow of the leader of the Independent movement in Georgia during the 1880's, declared that "when you take the Negro into your embrace on election day to control his vote . . . so long will lynching prevail." She proudly proclaimed that the white women of the South had to be protected from Negroes, even if it was necessary to lynch one thousand weekly.[39] In explaining a lynching that occurred in Newnan, Governor Candler said that the trouble could be laid to one factor, politics.[40] Ex-governor Northen, who was elected in 1890 and 1892 with the aid of Negro votes, told the Congregational Club at Tremont Temple in Boston on May 23, 1899, that the politics learned by Negroes during Reconstruction were responsible for all the ills that beset the South. Furthermore, he accused the Negro of being ungrateful in that he voted against his best friends in most elections. As long as these conditions prevailed, concluded Northen, lynchings and outrages would continue in Georgia.[41]

Probably the worst lynching outrage occurred when two Negroes convicted of murdering four members of the Hodges family were burned at the stake in Statesboro, Georgia, on August 16, 1904, a crime so heinous that even the Charleston (S.C.) *News and Courier* exclaimed that "The eyes of the country and the civilized world are fixed on Georgia. What will she do?" [42] Referring to this incident in a speech at Spartanburg, South Carolina, Senator John Sharp Williams of Mississippi declared that the Statesboro lynching cost the Democrats the support of a quarter of a million votes throughout the country in the national election of 1904. "The very affair itself," said Williams, "is a confession on the white man's part of his incapacity for self-government under his own laws. . . . I feel it my duty to say to a southern audience that things like the Statesboro affair must stop." [43] This statement, coming from one "who was a little more polished than other demagogues," [44] was a serious indictment against those who advocated Negro disfranchisement but favored preserving the white vote, even though the whites were not educated, because of their "inherited" qualities.

To say that all white citizens in Georgia approved of the open defiance of law and order would be misleading. There was a small minority that voiced its protest, but to an ever diminishing audience. One of these individuals was Superior Court Judge Richard B. Russell of Winder, father of United States Senator Richard B. Russell, Jr. As a judge he proved himself one who desired to see justice prevail regardless of the parties involved. This attitude was demonstrated in 1904 when he ordered the grand jury of Franklin County to bring the lynchers of one John Ware, a Negro, to trial. He denounced lynching as a relic of barbarism, and declared that when mob rule replaced authority "you have created something that is subversive of every principle of good government." [45]

Further degradation of the Negro in Georgia was caused by the peonage-like convict-lease system established by the state to secure cheap labor. This practice was in keeping with the economy program adopted by the Bourbon Democrats, since it relieved the state of supporting the penitentiary and, in theory, was to provide revenue. To provide an abundant supply of convict labor, the criminal code was revised to make petty offenders subject to very little sympathy from the courts. The legislature was generous in granting to vested interests, planters, and politicians, long-term leases extending from ten to thirty years, from which concessions they reaped immense profits.[46]

When the "Prison Reform Bill' was presented to the Georgia House in 1876, Representative James Blue, Negro member from Glynn County, made an impassioned plea for justice to the Negroes. He opened his speech by declaring that he was vitally interested in this question since his people composed three-fourths of the convicts, and that therefore he opposed the practice of farming them out in squads. Citing numerous cases of inhuman treatment, he begged the legislature to make the necessary reforms so that when the prisoners had served their sentences, they "would not go back into the world cripples and invalids in health or outlaws in morals," but come out as reformed men ready to take their places in society once more. The speech was so well received that it had much effect in securing the passage of the reform bill in the house by an overwhelming vote. Later the governor, on April 14, 1876, proclaimed "an act to regulate the leasing of convicts by the Governor, authorizing him to make contracts in relation thereto and for other purposes." [47]

Despite the passage of the bill, abuses continued to be practiced in the convict camps, and a serious debate ensued in the legislature on this issue in 1881. Representative T. W. Milner, a white man, feeling that present safeguards were inadequate, introduced a bill "to provide for the better inspection and control of the convicts of the state." He cited the case of a young white convict in Dougherty County "with a Negro guard on one side, and a Negro guard on the other side, and a Negro guard behind . . . whipping him," and asked that the system be abolished,[48] although his motives seemed to have been based on different grounds than those which were to be expressed by the Negro legislators.

Two of the five Negro members of the house spoke against the convict-lease system. One was Representative Ishmael Lonnon of Dougherty County, who said;

> I am not opposed to leases but to the system. It ought to be abolished, not for awhile, but it ought to be such forever in the indistinguishable ruin of death. Convicts are so terrified that they are afraid to tell how badly they are treated.[49]

The other Negro member to speak against the system was Representative John McIntosh of Liberty County, an 1877 graduate of Atlanta University. He stated that, as a representative of one-half the population of Georgia, he was seeking justice for his people, and referring directly to the convict-lease system, asserted: "I am not afraid of men but when I have seen convicts in charge of guards, these guards looked so ferocious that I felt a horror of them." While he favored the abolishment of the system, he doubted that it would come about and so wished some action would be taken to alleviate the situation created by it. Making a humble plea to the white legislators for justice, he declared:

> Men talk seriously about regulating railroads, and yet smile when we ask them to talk about the system of punishing criminals. . . . The colored people of the South will be as true to you in freedom as they were in slavery. . . . They were true to you then at home and often on the field of battle, and they will be true to you yet if you will protect them. . . . The colored people come to you and in the name of pity ask you to do something to improve the system.[50]

But powerful groups in the state, headed by corporations, influential planters, and politicians, opposed any change. The Atlanta *Constitution,* which was the spokesman for the Bourbon oligarchy, declared that the system was satisfactory, that the issue was raised by scheming politicians to mislead the Negroes.[51] The real fact was, however, that Negroes found themselves the chief victims of this infamous system. The very circumstance that the better element of white people shirked jury duty made the lot of the Negro more precarious, and lacking the power of the ballot, he was subject to the whims of judges and other court officials elected by white voters.[52]

Some state superior court judges used this system to enhance their political fortunes. In order to curry favor with the Democratic bosses of the state, who by and large were the corporations, the planters, and prominent politicians, these judges in meting out punishment to Negroes would sentence them to long terms on the chain gang, which benefited the lessees. The Democratic bosses in turn would show their appreciation by supporting the judges for Congress.[53] Judge John W. Maddox of Rome was alleged to have defeated Congressman Everett from the seventh congressional district in 1892 largely by this method. A Negro, Sam Jackson of Rome, was fined one thousand dollars or a term on the chain gang for gambling, while John M. Vandiver, a white man who later became postmaster of Rome, was fined ten dollars for the same offense.[54] Judge Charles L. Bartlett of Macon was notorious for sending Negroes to the chain gang for trivial offenses. He sentenced one Negro to fifteen years on the chain gang for stealing some milk, and a twelve-year-old Negro boy to twelve years of hard labor on the chain gang for taking a horse to ride a few miles and back.[55]

Such miscarriages of justice resulted in the fact that Negroes constituted about nine-tenths of the prisoners in the convict camps. Since the income from crime rather than the rehabilitation of the criminal was the primary objective, the future of the Negro prisoner was beyond redemption. In 1895, a prison inspector reported to Governor Atkinson that he had visited thirty-four chain gangs in twenty-three counties and found 795 convicts, of whom 19 were Negro women and only 27 white men. No provision was made for separating the sexes either at work or in sleeping quarters, which increased sexual immorality.[56] From 1879 to 1899 the number of Negro convicts in Georgia increased from 1,109 to 1,953 while for the same period the number of whites increased from 121 to 248.[57]

Although it was obvious that the Negro was the victim of various forms of proscription, some Negro leaders were the first to profess that the Negro was not altogether blameless. The Reverend L. B. Maxwell,[58] Atlanta University and Hartford Theological Seminary graduate and pastor of the First Congregational Church (Negro) of Savannah, in a sermon delivered to his congregation in July 1896, declared that

> More than a quarter of a century has passed since the black man first entered the political arena and yet it is true that he holds today a place of influence very little advanced of what he did in the beginning. . . . The common reasons given have been race prejudice and bad leadership, but tonight I beg to take exception to the wholesale acceptance of these reasons. . . . The greatest obstacle has been neither race prejudice nor bad leaders, but something which . . . is far more harmful, it is that curse of narrow, selfish, concentrated individualism which hinders race concentration, race combination and race cooperation.[59]

All of the various proscriptions stimulated Negroes to think seriously of fundamental solutions to the race problem in America. The most crude and reactionary elements of the community appeared to be taking over, and the traditional Southern liberals, always few in number, seemed almost non-existent at the time. When the latter did insist on speaking out in behalf of the Negro, they found themselves subject to threats and abuse from members of their own race. A typical example was that involving the editor of the Hawkinsville (Ga.) *Dispatch*, who received a letter from one of the white citizens of the county dated

July 13, 1891, and threatening him or any other white person who might defend any Negro in his rights. The citizen wrote:

> Mr. Editor if the foling article appears in your Paper Five Dolers will appear in the (PO) addressed to you. But if it don't appear 25 of your subscribers will sure to stop and we will stop all the rest We can Your White Brothers.
>
> Notice, We hereby forewarn any and all Persons from taking up for the nigroes in any shape form or fashion We the undersign will declare any white man that Takes Sides With any nigroes against a white person no matter how lodown he or She is just so they are White We are White men organized For the Perpose of protecting the White Race and we are going to carry out or Plans at the Pearl of our Lives Dark Nights and cool heads Will our work quitly Mr. Editor if this fail to appear in the next issue of Your Paper Will Consider you in favor of civil wrights and We Will deal you properly Many Sitersons.[60]

In view of this growing tension, several suggestions for the improvement of race relations were offered by Negroes. One was for the white press to cease publishing anti-Negro articles. It was pointed out that Southern papers made deliberate efforts to portray Negroes in the most unfavorable light, such as referring to them as "big burly brutes," and branding them as the "aggressors" whenever there was a misunderstanding with the whites.[61]

Some Negroes, however, believed it impossible to reason with the Southern whites, that the Negro had extended the olive branch for twenty-five years and the net result was Southern hate and barbarism. Therefore, rather than remain in an environment offering little hope for the future, the Negro should seek greener pastures if he was to realize the privileges that went along with first-class citizenship.[62]

The first of such plans of escape was the "Back-to-Africa" movement. Foremost advocate of this idea in Georgia, if not in the United States, was Bishop Henry McNeal Turner, of the African Methodist Episcopal Church. The Bishop not only was well acquainted with the Negro and his ills in all parts of the United States, but had actually lived and traveled in Africa. He was convinced that the Negro in America had no future above that of an inferior being. If he had any doubts before 1883, said the Bishop, the United States Supreme Court, when it killed the Civil Rights Act of 1875, completely removed these doubts. He emphasized that this decision was written by a Republican justice and every member of the Court was a Northerner except one, Associate Justice John Marshall Harlan, of Kentucky, who ironically enough, cast the only dissenting vote.[63] Turner was so disappointed in the Republican party that he deserted its banner for that of the Prohibitionists and even supported the Democratic candidates for the presidency in 1900 and 1908. He and others made vigorous attempts to secure appropriations from Congress in support of voluntary colonization of American Negroes in Africa where they could enjoy first-class citizenship. "The Negro . . . is an outlawed inhabitant of the country," said Turner, "for a people divested of their civil rights can hope for nothing but degradation and contempt." [64]

In 1892 the popularity of the "Back to Africa" movement reached its crest among a few of the more credulous Negroes in Georgia. This enthusiasm was partly caused by the "Jim Crow" law that recently had been passed by the state legislature, as well as by the election of Grover Cleveland for his second term as president. On the Sunday following this election a few Negro ministers predicted a dark future for their race. At Big Bethel Church, one of the largest in Atlanta, a minister advised his listeners "to leave Georgia and go to their own country, Africa, where they would have equal rights and help govern and have street cars of their own." At the annual Republican picnic in Blackshear, I. J. White, a Negro, exclaimed "We would rather be eaten by wild Negroes than to be lynched by white men in the South." Some Negroes of Polk County sent a memorial to the Georgia House of Representatives requesting permission to go to Africa or some free country.[65] As late as 1903, a group of Negro women sent a petition to the Georgia House requesting the legislature to appropriate two thousand dollars in order that they might take themselves and their families to Africa. Amid much mirth, the petition was referred to the Committee of Emigration.[66]

These efforts bore no fruit, and few Negroes actually went to Africa. By and large, Negro leaders and the Negro press were opposed to the idea. For example, Representative Lectured Crawford, Negro member of the legislature, declared that the only solution was through education which would reveal to the Negro the folly of such a project.[67] Frederick Douglass, the titular leader of the Negro race at the time, in a speech in Atlanta on May 23, 1892, said "the glory of Africa is in her palm trees and not her men," and that the Negro's home was America.[68] Others thought that it was "dangerous to fly to evils that we know not of." Some suggested that Bishop Turner might demonstrate his sincerity by going to Africa himself instead of remaining in America. It was even hinted that any movement that had as its goal the sending of Negroes to Africa would mean having to take half of the white race, since it was difficult to distinguish almost a third of the Negroes from

Caucasians. The Negro Press Association of Georgia advised Negroes to "remain where they are: go to work industriously with renewed vigor," and "cultivate a friendly feeling with their white neighbors." [69]

The crowning blow to the movement, however, was the testimony of Negroes who actually had been to Africa and reported their experiences on their return home. Such was the case of Green B. Parks, who left Atlanta on May 24, 1891, for Monrovia and returned to Atlanta in September of the same year. He told Negroes that Monrovia was a very undesirable place in which to live and denounced the African movement and those who sponsored it. "The only hunting in Liberia," he said, "is to hunt a way to leave." [70]

Testimony of a more realistic nature was that given by C. H. J. Taylor, a Negro lawyer of Atlanta and prominent Democratic politician who served as United States minister to Liberia during Cleveland's first administration and as recorder of deeds in Washington, D. C., in his second term.[71] While expressing deep admiration for Bishop Turner as a leader of the Negro race, Taylor questioned his glowing accounts of the great possibilities that awaited the Negro in Liberia. Taylor understood, however, that Turner would naturally be inclined to urge African emigration, since the Bishop was Liberian consul in this country, and it was his duty to promote the development of Liberia. He declared that the conditions in Liberia were so degrading that a law should be passed making it a felony for anyone to encourage the Negro to leave the United States for that country. To convey the idea that by going to Liberia Negroes could become officeholders, statesmen, and financiers was absurd. A Negro policeman in Atlanta, he said, would be envied by a cabinet officer in Liberia. Describing the government while he was a resident of Liberia, he stated:

> They have a president . . . cabinet officers in name only . . . a secretary of the treasury, but not a dollar in the treasury . . . a secretary of war with no guns . . . a postmaster general with no postal system. . . . In 1886 the total vote cast for president in the whole republic by all parties was 2,325; of this number of voters, and only Liberians are allowed to vote, 1,333 were officeholders. There were 817 men in the republic's military regiment, 787 of whom were military officers and 30 privates.[72]

While the "Back-to-Africa" movement failed to gain many converts, some Negroes suggested that the salvation of the race lay in a mass exodus to the North. Had not the North been responsible for their emancipation? Did not many Northern orators frequently emphasize human and civil equality? Did not Northern teachers come South after the Civil War to preach social equality to Negroes and urge that they should be protected in their civil and political rights? Thus it was only natural that many Negroes became obsessed with the idea that only by going North could they realize those privileges that were associated with first-class citizenship.

Much to their disappointment, many Negroes who left the South for the North in the 1880's and 1890's to escape Southern proscription found conditions anything but ideal. Although they were not "Jim Crowed" to the extent that they were in the South, they found it extremely difficult to obtain work, since many of the trade unions excluded them from membership. What advantage was there in being able to ride on non-segregated trains, attend non-segregated schools, and enjoy non-segregated amusements if they did not have the money to avail themselves of these opportunities? [73]

Even in New England few jobs were open to Negroes and great pains were taken to prevent Negroes from competing with whites. E. J. Bruce, a Negro of Savannah who went to Providence, Rhode Island, in the 1870's and secured a job with the largest contracting firm in the state, declared that while Negro civil rights were observed more in the North, the economic opportunities were far more limited than in the South. He cited numerous cases in which Negro mechanics were denied work because the whites threatened to strike if they were hired.[74] The Washington (D.C.) *Bee*, a Negro paper, stated that Negroes in the North, even the educated ones, could work only as waiters, caterers, porters, or barbers; and as far as political activity was concerned, they might have their ego inflated by being appointed as doorkeepers at the Republican national conventions.[75] W. R. Davis, a Negro who left the South to live in New York, declared that while Negroes in 1885 had most of the jobs as waiters in hotels and restaurants, by 1895 only a few remained. Even the Negro bootblack was replaced by the Italian. So many opportunities for work had been denied the Negro man that the responsibility for supporting the family fell upon the women, who were forced to take in washing to keep the family from becoming a burden on the community. The situation was becoming so desperate, Davis said, that the Negro was "almost denied the right to breathe." [76]

As a substitute for the "Back-to-Africa" and "Exodus-to-the-North" projects as means of solving the race problem, another distinguished Georgia Negro, Bishop Lucius H. Holsey of the Colored Methodist Episcopal Church, proposed that the federal government set aside out of the public domain a separate state where Negroes might enjoy first-class citizenship. He declared that "two distinct peoples can never live together in the South in peace, when one is Anglo-Saxon and the other

Negro, unless the Negro, as a race or *en masse*, lives in the submerged realm of serfdom and slavery." [77] To justify his stand, he pointed out the refusal of the South to provide adequate educational facilities for the Negro, and the antagonism expressed toward the educated Negro; the denial of political privileges; the "Jim Crow" policy; the lack of protection for Negroes in rural areas; and the prevalence of mob violence.

Under these conditions, said Bishop Holsey, it was not practical to continue to allow the South to settle this problem, since it was national in scope, involving national honor and national law. Therefore, in order that the Negro might enjoy all the privileges that were guaranteed by the United States Constitution, he requested the federal government to establish a Negro state in part of the Indian Territory, New Mexico, or in some other part of the public domain in the West. In this territory white persons would be ineligible for citizenship, except through marriage, and only those white persons who had some official connection with the government would be permitted to reside therein. By having responsibilities of government thrust upon his shoulders, the Negro would become inspired and more willing to help the Anglo-Saxon race to develop a greater civilization in this country. [78]

While the leaders of these movements to provide an escape for the Negroes had good intentions, they failed to convince the Negro masses that their conditions would be improved by leaving the South. A number of Negroes followed "Pop" Singleton to Kansas in 1879 and to several Northern communities, but there was no significant migration northward until World War I. It appears that the Negro masses were resigned to staying in the South, hoping eventually that the tide would turn in their favor. Such a development, they believed, was dependent upon two factors: (1) the ability of the Negro to improve his social, economic, and educational status in order to win the respect of his white neighbors, and (2) the willingness of the whites to cease vilifying the Negro in the white press and at the same time to extend the Negro his constitutional rights.

Not only were Negroes critical of the white press but also of the Northern Negro press for meddling with affairs pertaining to the Negroes in the South. Many of these Northern Negro journals criticized the Southern Negro press for not taking a more militant stand against Southerners who were responsible for repressive measures aimed at the Negroes. This was especially true of the New York *Age*, whose editor, T. Thomas Fortune, became a nationally known figure through his condemnation of the South in his paper. The editor of the Savannah *Tribune* advised Fortune that if he desired to "be so base and outspoken" toward the South, then he should come down to the "seat of battle" and give vent to his feelings.[79]

White people were admonished that the South could not possibly advance unless the Negroes were given the same opportunities as the whites, that it was necessary to encourage Negroes to participate in politics in order that they might have an interest in the community and the community an interest in them. Furthermore, Negroes urged that it was the duty of the parents and teachers of both races to teach their children to respect each other, since the South, unlike the North, had only two races, "both of whom are true American citizens who love themselves, their country and its flag and their neighbors." As the Negro had proven himself to be a faithful worker for over two hundred and fifty years, the whites were advised not to import foreigners as laborers in the South, for such a policy might result in a tragedy similar to the Haymarket riot in Chicago. "Let the Southern Negro and Southern white man ever remain and stick together for they understand each other as no one else understands them." [80]

This sentiment was concurred in by many white people who believed that the Southern whites were the true friends of the Negro. Negroes of Atlanta were reminded of this when an unusual cold spell struck the city in the winter of 1895 and caused considerable hardship for thousands of people. To meet this emergency, the white people formed a relief committee which raised five thousand dollars to care for the victims, and of this amount, forty-five hundred dollars went to the relief of Negroes. The Atlanta *Journal* claimed that while many Negroes owned property and were gainfully employed, they contributed only three dollars and fifty cents to the effort to alleviate the misery among their own people. "If the Negroes will think over this and many similar events," observed the *Journal*, "they will discover who their true friends are and will pay less attention to lying Negro preachers and politicians who preach doctrines of hate and revenge." [81]

Furthermore, the unfortunate experiences of Negroes who had gone North and West to escape Southern proscription convinced the Negro masses that the future of the Negro lay in the South where, even though he received lower wages, he was not denied work on account of his color. Because of the perpetuation of the old slave idea that work was only for "niggers and poor whites," Negroes were able to engage in labor activities which were closed to them in the North. Numerous cases were cited in which Negroes worked alongside of whites without incident, where Southern Negro contractors frequently hired whites and Negroes on jobs.[82] Southern white people were urged to "take away mob violence, court injustices . . . and let us have in full the constitutional rights of this country, and the South, if anywhere, . . . is the best for us. We are more united and progressive there than in any other section of the land." [83]

The Reverend Charles T. Walker, pastor of the Tabernacle Baptist Church in Augusta, and next to Bishop Turner probably the most widely known Negro churchman in the state, declared that it was a mistake for the Negro to leave the South, since prejudice was national and not sectional. He admitted that the North did not disfranchise the Negro nor "Jim Crow" him to the same extent as did the South; but, on the other hand, he noted that the North did not guarantee the same economic security. He advised the Negro to remain in the South, buy land, engage in business, and educate his children, for it was only a matter of time until the best people of the South would come to his aid and defend him in all of his rights. [84]

The Negro editor of the LaGrange (Georgia) *Enterprise*, W. S. Cannon, believed that it was far better to develop friendly relations with the white people of the South, and promised the support of his paper to any movement that would create a spirit of good will between the races, which in the long run would advance the interests of both groups. [85] The point was constantly stressed by many Negroes that the South was the natural home of the Negro and it was his duty to make himself indispensable to the community. "If we cannot vote for president, we can vote five dollar bills in a bank to our credit all day and the cashier will count them. . . . If we cannot govern, we can produce that which the ruling class must have." By doing this, Negro leaders said, the road to political equality, which was the dream of the Negro, would be paved. [86] Furthermore, Negroes were reminded that in certain places in the North Negroes were forced to leave the community in which they lived just because they wanted to earn an honest living. Such was the case in Dent, Ohio. In cities like Boston and Chicago there were signs reading, "No Negro help wanted." In Indiana, upon learning that Negroes were planning to come to the state to work, white men met them at the state line with guns and forced them back. As the Atlanta *Independent* aptly put it: "In the south we make them get a move on them because they won't work, but in the north, they make you move because you want to work." [87]

The economic plight of the Negro in New York by 1908 had become so acute that the Committee for Improving the Industrial Conditions of the Negro in New York, composed of both races and headed by William Jay Schiefflin, addressed a communication to the Negro editors and ministers of the South asking their aid in stemming any further migration of their people to the North. This communication pointed out that due to discrimination against Negroes in the labor field, inferior housing facilities, unfavorable climate, and the increasing crime rate among Negroes as a result of these factors, living conditions in the North were almost intolerable. In their opinion, the solution to the race problem in the South had to be worked out through the cooperation of the better elements of both races, which in the final analysis would prove beneficial to the material and moral growth of the South.[88]

Thus the Negro masses were resigned to staying in the South, hoping eventually that sentiment and conditions would move in their favor. Probably the general attitude of the Negro in Georgia at this time was best expressed by the Reverend C. L. Bonner, pastor of the St. Paul Colored Methodist Episcopal Church of Savannah. At the annual Emancipation Day exercises held in that city on January 1, 1902, the Reverend Mr. Bonner said:

> There are men who are more profound in thought, loftier in ideas . . . than I am . . . who think and express their thoughts differently to me. . . . There is my own Bishop Holsey's doctrine of segregation, Bishop Turner's emigration, ex-Senator Butler's expatriation, John Temple Graves' colonization, T. Thomas Fortune's . . . amalgamation, Ben Tillman's extermination. My doctrine is, if you let me coin a word, *"stayhereation"* and when I say that, I mean stay here as a separate and distinct race, and the God that has brought us thus far can carry us on.[89]

And "stayhereation" it was, as the vast majority of Negroes, either by preference or by circumstances over which they had no control, remained in the South despite segregation, political disfranchisement, mob violence, and other forms of race proscription. As the twentieth century wore on, the Negro would find an increasingly hostile environment. Despite his efforts to improve his economic status, his struggle to educate himself, and his attempts to promote his social betterment, his hopes of attaining first-class citizenship were to be engulfed by the wave of white supremacy which grew in volume and intensity after the turn of the century.

NOTES

1. C. Vann Woodward, *Origins of the New South* (Baton Rouge, 1951), pp. 211-212.

2. Gunnar Myrdal, *An American Dilemma: The Negro Problem and Modern Democracy* (2 vols.; New York, 1944), I, 582.

3. W. J. Cash, *The Mind of the South* (New York. 1957), pp. 178-183.

4. *Journal of the House of Representatives of the State of Georgia, at the Annual Session of the General Assembly Convened at Atlanta, January 10, 1870* (Atlanta, 1870), Part I, p. 309; *Journal of the Senate of the State of Georgia, at the Annual Session of the General Assembly, Atlanta, January 10, 1870* (Atlanta, 1870), Part II, p. 261, Part III, p. 508.

5. *Acts and Resolutions of the General Assembly of the State of Georgia, 1870* (Atlanta, 1871), p. 390.

6. Rebecca Latimer Felton, *My Memoirs of Georgia Politics* (Atlanta, 1911), p. 646.

7. The platform proposed (1) increasing the powers of the railway commission to prevent discrimination, (2) abolishing the convict-lease system, (3) tax revision, (4) public school improvements, and (5) primary and election reforms. Alex M. Arnett, *The Populist Movement in Georgia* (New York, 1922), pp. 105-106.

8. *Journal of the House of Representatives of the State of Georgia at the Adjourned Session of the General Assembly, at Atlanta, Wednesday, July 8, 1891* (Atlanta, 1891), p. 176; *Constitution* (Atlanta), July 21, 1891.

9. *Ibid.*, July 23, 1891.

10. *Ibid.*, July 24, 1891.

11. *Acts and Resolutions of the General Assembly of the State of Georgia, 1890-1891* (Atlanta, 1891), I, 157-158. In order to preserve white supremacy at its lowest level, the Alliance legislature passed an act forbidding white and colored prisoners being chained together while at work. *Ibid.*, pp. 211-212.

12. Quoted in *Tribune* (Savannah), November 28, 1891.

13. *Ibid.*, October 17, 1891.

14. *Ibid.*, November 15, December 31, 1892.

15. *Independent* (Atlanta), September 5, 1908.

16. "A Plea Against Excursions," *Voice of the Negro* (Atlanta), II (August, 1905), 530-531.

17. *Independent* (Atlanta), January 19, 1907.

18. *Tribune* (Savannah), November 5, 1892, August 29, 1906. Albert Thornton, president of the Union Street Railway Company of Atlanta, ad-

mitted that "the Negro is the best patron of the streetcar. If he has a nickel and is going anywhere he will ride; while the white man will walk. . . ." *Constitution* (Atlanta), March 1, 1891.

19. *Tribune* (Savannah), May 22, 1893.

20. *Morning News* (Savannah), quoted in *Tribune* (Savannah), July 12, 1902.

21. *Tribune* (Savannah), September 1, 1906.

22. *Ibid.*

23. *Ibid.*, September 15, 1906.

24. *Ibid.*, September 22, 29, October 6, 1906, and March 9, 1907.

25. *Ibid.*, June 8, 1907.

26. *Ibid.*, March 9, 1907.

27. Ellis P. Oberholtzer, *A History of the United States Since the Civil War* (5 vols.; New York, 1917-1937), V, 716.

28. Rayford W. Logan, *The Negro in American Life and Thought: The Nadir, 1877-1901* (New York, 1954), p. 76.

29. *Ibid.*, pp. 77, 91.

30. W. E. B. Du Bois, *Some Notes on Negro Crime, Particularly in Georgia* ("Atlanta University Publications," No. 9 [1904]), p. 60; *Tribune* (Savannah), May 7, 1892.

31. *Ibid.*, May 21, 1892.

32. *Journal* (Atlanta), September 27, 1892. Northen, who ran on the Alliance platform in 1890, was the Democratic candidate for re-election in 1892.

33. *Ibid.*, September 30, 1892; *Bulletin of Atlanta University*, November, 1892, 4.

34. *Journal* (Atlanta), October 27, 1892.

35. *Tribune* (Savannah), July 1, 1893.

36. *Journal* (Atlanta), December 23, 1893.

37. *Message of the Governor of Georgia to the General Assembly, October 25, 1895* (Atlanta, 1895), pp. 19-20.

38. *Journal* (Atlanta), September 6, 1900. For other protests, see *Tribune* (Savannah), January 7, May 25, 1899.

39. *Journal* (Atlanta), November 15, 1898.

40. *Ibid.*, April 24, 1899. As a rejoinder, the *Tribune* (Savannah), August 5, 1899, stated: "Our governor may be true after all. . . when he says that the placing of the ballot in the hands of the Negro is the cause of so much lynching. The lynching record in this state . . . shows they are trying to get rid of the Negro voters."

41. *Journal* (Atlanta), May 23, 1899.

42. *Ibid.*, August 17, 19, 1904.

43. *Ibid.*, December 3, 1904.

44. Logan, *op. cit.*, p. 90.

45. *Journal* (Atlanta), September 28, 1904.

46. Woodward, *op. cit.*, pp. 212-213. One of the big lessees was Joseph E. Brown who owned the Dade coal mines. He, along with the other lessees

like General John B. Gordon, paid the state twenty dollars annually for each convict, or less than seven cents a day. Arnett, *op. cit.*, pp. 27-28.

47. Quoted in *Telegraph and Messenger* (Macon), March 4, 1876; *ibid.*, April 22, 1876.

48. *Constitution* (Atlanta), August 10, 1881.

49. *Ibid.* Lonnon was dark-complexioned and had a soft tenor voice. He was about five feet three inches tall and weighed about one hundred and sixty pounds. He operated a blacksmith shop in Albany. Although he lacked formal education, he could read and write. Interview with George A. Towns, professor emeritus of Atlanta University, June 2, 1951.

50. *Constitution* (Atlanta), August 10, 1881. Other Negro leaders registered bitter complaints against this iniquitous system, but to no avail. At Negro conventions resolutions were adopted condemning the practice as well as demanding that Negroes be included on jury lists. *Ibid.*, April 1, September 19, 1888; Du Bois, *Some Notes on Negro Crime*, p. 66.

51. *Constitution* (Atlanta), September 7, 1881.

52. Du Bois, *op. cit.*, p. 65.

53. Felton, *op. cit.*, pp. 655, 658-659.

54. Rebecca Latimer Felton, *Country Life in Georgia in the Days of My Youth* (Atlanta, 1919), p. 196.

55. Felton, *Memoirs of Georgia Politics*, pp. 658-659.

56. *Journal* (Atlanta), November 12, 1895. In the Maddox camp in northeast Georgia about twelve children were born of Negro mothers and white fathers (*Tribune* [Savannah], April 28, 1894).

57. *Second Annual Report of the Prison Commission of Georgia from October 1, 1898 to October 1, 1899* (Atlanta, 1899), pp. 5-6. In this number were included three white women and sixty-eight Negro women convicts.

58. The Reverend Mr. Maxwell finished Atlanta University in the class of 1886, and at the commencement exercises he spoke on "A Man Is a Man for That." After he had finished, Senator Colquitt of Georgia walked over and shook his hand and congratulated him on his excellent speech. For a number of years he was the international Sunday School lecturer for Negroes of the Congregational Church. He died in 1902. *Tribune* (Savannah), March 22, 1902.

59. *Ibid.*, August 1, 1896.

60. Quoted *ibid.*, September 12, 1891.

61. *Ibid.*, December 10, 1898.

62. *Ibid.*, February 11, 1893.

63. *Journal* (Atlanta), August 12, 1893. Turner further stated that this decision was even more revolting than the Dred Scott decision since Chief Justice Taney "only voiced the condition of things as they existed in the days of slavery, while Justice Bradley issued a decree on behalf of the supreme court that nullified the plain acts of congress and the expressed provisions of the constitution of the United States."

64. *Constitution* (Atlanta), July 13, 1891; *Journal* (Atlanta), August 12, 1893.

65. *Ibid.*, November 22, 1892, November 30, 1894; *Tribune* (Savannah), May 26, 1894.

66. *Journal* (Atlanta), June 25, 1903.

67. *Constitution* (Atlanta), November 22, 1890.

68. *Ibid.*, May 24, 1892.

69. *Tribune* (Savannah), July 18, 1891, September 3, 30, November 12, 1892.

70. *Constitution* (Atlanta), September 15, 1891.

71. *Tribune* (Savannah), June 3, 1899. At the time of his death in 1899, Taylor was editor of the Atlanta *Appeal* and dean of Morris Brown College. He was born in Alabama in 1856 but spent most of his boyhood in Savannah. He attended the University of Michigan, where he earned the bachelor's and master's degrees. In 1882 he was an assistant prosecuting attorney in Kanas City, Missouri, receiving his appointment from a Democratic mayor and council. After practicing six years there, he was sent to Liberia by President Cleveland. *Constitution* (Atlanta), December 21, 1887.

72. *Journal* (Atlanta), January 29, 1898.

73. Thomas J. Bell, "Does the Colored Man Have a Chance in the North," *Bulletin of Atlanta University*, January, 1894, 2. Bell was a member of the Atlanta University class of 1891 and served as YMCA secretary in New York, Denver, and Brockton, Massachusetts. "Who's Who Among Atlanta University Graduates and Former Students," *Phylon*, III (Second Quarter, 1942), 166.

74. *Tribune*, (Savannah), May 2, 1903.

75. Quoted *ibid.*, January 24, 1903.

76. "Give the Negro Work," *Press* (New York), quoted in *Journal* (Atlanta), April 10, 1895. For a description of the hardships experienced by Negroes who went to Kansas in 1879, see Logan, *op cit.*, pp. 133-134.

77. Lucius H. Holsey, "Race Segregation," in *The Possibilities of the Negro in Symposium*, ed. Willis B. Parks (Atlanta, 1904), pp. 109, 102.

78. *Ibid.*, pp. 104-119.

79. *Tribune* (Savannah), December 2, 1893.

80. *Ibid.*, June 5, 1897, February 4, 1893.

81. *Journal* (Atlanta), March 2, 1895.

82. Bell, *op. cit.*, 3.

83. *Tribune* (Savannah), May 2, 1903. Even Bishop Turner admitted that while Northern whites might be more friendly politically toward the Negro, the South afforded him better economic opportunities. He stated that employment was opened to Negroes in almost every field except that of operating railroad locomotives. *Constitution* (Atlanta), July 14, 1890.

84. *Presbyterian Herald* (New York City), quoted in *Tribune* (Savannah), December 29, 1900.

85. Quoted in *Journal* (Atlanta), January 9, 1901.

86. *Independent* (Atlanta), March 26, 1904, April 8, 1905.

87. *Ibid.*, April 8, 1905.

88. *Tribune* (Savannah), May 9, 1908.

89. *Ibid.*, January 18, 1902 (italics mine).

THE REACTION OF THE NEGRO TO

THE MOTION PICTURE

BIRTH OF A NATION

Thomas R. Cripps

In the decade before Woodrow Wilson's first administration the reforms of urban Progressives were essentially for whites only. Despite the Negro's rising wealth and increasingly successful struggle with illiteracy, the tenuous rapprochement that a few Negro leaders had with Theodore Roosevelt, the formation of active and influential agencies of reform like the National Negro Business League, and (at the behest of several white liberals) the National Association for the Advancement of Colored People and the Urban League, the Wilson years represented the continuation of a decline. Residential segregation was increasing; the ballot box was a distant memory to many Negroes; Jim Crow had become the custom in public accommodations. For the Negro there was a denial of reform even before the resurgent Democratic party brought to Washington a return to southern ideals.[1]

Typical of the ascendency of the ideology of the white South was the circulation of *Birth of a Nation,* a spectacular twelve-reel film, much of which was drawn from *The Clansman,* a romantic, angry novel about the fate of the ideals of the ante bellum South during Reconstruction. Its author was Thomas Dixon of North Carolina, a sometime preacher, a professional Southerner, and a fretful Negrophobe. The novel—which constituted the basis of only the last half of the film—is based on an attempt by a group of defeated Southerners to reassemble the traditional

Thomas R. Cripps, "The Reaction of the Negro to the Motion Picture *Birth of a Nation,*" *Historian,* XXV, No. 3 (May, 1963), 344-362 .

power structure of the South. Hindered and thwarted in their efforts by Stoneman, a thinly disguised Thad Stevens, who with his mulatto mistress rules America after Appomattox, they turn naturally to extralegal means of political expression: the Ku Klux Klan.[2] The director of the film, David Wark Griffith, son of a Confederate soldier, had an affinity for the Lost Cause and a fondness for portraying in melodrama "the pale, helples, slim-bodied heroines of the nineteenth-century poets" being attacked by Negroes. It was Griffith who wrote the first half of the film, a southern view of the Civil War.[3]

The film was significant for other reasons. Artistically, it was the finest work the cinema had ever produced. Socially, it was reflective of the depth of hostility that many white Americans felt toward Negroes and of the degree to which this feeling might be fed by film propaganda and its accompanying mass advertising. It also presented Negro leaders with a dilemma. They could ignore the film and its hateful portrayal, knowing not what damage it might do. They could urge censorship. Or, and least likely, they could finance and make their own films propagandizing favorably the role of Negroes in American life.

Films with an essentially regional tone and even an anti-Negro bias had been made previously. In 1915, the year of *Birth of a Nation*, Paramount was circulating *The Nigger*, another heavy-handed racist film. Griffith himself had made *The Battle*, a Civil War picture of earlier vintage. *The Clansman*, too, had been shot earlier, starring Griffith's wife; in 1906 as a play it had been labeled "as crude a melodrama as has ever slipped its anchor and drifted westward from Third Avenue." [4]

Why was this one film so powerful and so fiercely resented? Aside from the flaws that offended Negroes and some film esthetes, the picture made far greater use of advertising than was normal and consequently drew far larger crowds than earlier films. But the movie created the greatest stir chiefly because it was the nearest to fine art that the cinema had achieved. It reached a technical brilliance, an "art by lightning flash," a kind of visual music with its own rhythm and logic. Its tempo was varied by editing together numerous shots into a montage that could evoke larger-than-life images of past reality. Early critics spoke of this effect as "panoramic drama" or "outdoor drama" rather than private passion so that the "Ku Klux Klan dashes down the road as powerfully as Niagara pours over the cliff . . . [and] the white leader . . . enters not as an individual, but as . . . the whole Anglo-Saxon Niagara." Audiences became mobs "for or against the Reverend Thomas Dixon's poisonous hatred of the Negro." Few viewers could distinguish between art and ax-grinding, technique and content. Only a few critics like Vachel Lindsay could admire the film as "a wonder in its Griffith sec-

tions" with its "mobs splendidly handled, tossing wildly and rhythmi-
cally like the sea," while pointing out the pathological flaws of Dixon's
script.[5]

No earlier American film had been so impressive. Even the producers
referred to their redundant, unimaginative nickelodeon entertainments
as "sausages." And when *Birth of a Nation* was made, the Mutual Company, which had helped finance production, did not take it seriously
enough to back its distribution; Griffith, his cameraman Billy Bitzer, and
a friend and film producer named Harry Aitken had to form the Epoch
Company to circulate the film. Other distributors did not want it for
fear of hurting the receipts of their own films, some of which were also
racist.[6]

Art, technology, advertising, the racism of Dixon—all fell together
into what Negroes took to be a malicious conspiracy. "Every resource of
a magnificent new art has been employed with an undeniable attempt
to picture Negroes in the worst possible light" the NAACP declared in
its *Annual Report.*[7] Lacking funds with which to make propaganda films
of their own, Negroes of the urban North turned to censorship, an acceptable position among liberals of the time who were concerned about
"vice" and its assumed cause—the nickelodeon parlors that dotted
American cities showing corrupting movies.[8] Many cities and some
states had begun to censor films. Negroes turned to these agencies to
stop the showing of *Birth of a Nation.*

In February 1915 the film was shown in Los Angeles and in San
Francisco. A few days later advertising started in the New York newspapers; almost simultaneously the Los Angeles branch of the NAACP
notified the New York office of the west coast opening. The film should
have followed a normal course eastward to the National Board of
Censorship of Motion Pictures, a private agency created by the film
producers who hoped that it would give the movies respectability as
family entertainment and the wider market they thought would accrue to
their product once they were able to squelch the sensational investigations of the nickelodeons.[9] The board, later called the National Board
of Review, was one of many expressions of the intellectual climate of
the time. It was unique in that it was private; yet it was admired by
public censors because 80 per cent of the film exhibitors were said to
abide by its decisions. In Washington the year before, the House committee on the establishment of a motion picture commission had taken
considerable testimony, much of which favored public censorship. But
the committee chose to heed the counsel of Frederic C. Howe, chairman
of the New York board, who recommended that the existing board be

permitted to continue its work without intervention from a superfluous body in Washington.[10]

Two days before the film was to be reviewed by the board, Dixon sidetracked it into Washington and showed it in the East Room of the White House to Woodrow Wilson, members of his cabinet, and their families. The night following this unprecedented event, he showed it in the ball room of the fashionable Raleigh Hotel, with Chief Justice Edward White, the Supreme Court, and members of Congress in attendance. Both showings were granted as favors to Dixon, a former student of Wilson's at Johns Hopkins, with the stipulation that there be no publicity. Dixon stopped in Washington because he hoped to bolster Wilson's known Southern biases, especially his attitude toward the Negro. As he later told Joseph Tumulty, Wilson's secretary,

> I didn't dare allow the President to know the real big purpose back of my film—which was to revolutionize Northern sentiments by a presentation of history that would transform every man in the audience into a good Democrat! And make no mistake about it —we are doing just that thing. . . . Every man who comes out of one of our theatres is a Southern partisan for life—except the members of [Oswald Garrison] Villard's Inter-Marriage Society who go there to knock.[11]

Wilson, according to Dixon, liked the film and congratulated him, saying that it was "history written in lightning." [12] Justice White, before the same showing, in Dixon's words, "leaned toward me and said in low tense tones: 'I was a member of the Klan, sir . . . . Through many a dark night, I walked my sentinels' beat through the ugliest streets of New Orleans with a rifle on my shoulder. . . . I'll be there!'" Thus whenever the NAACP protested the film, Dixon could claim approval in high places. No denials came from Washington until after the New York and Boston runs had begun.[13]

Hence Dixon, even before the New York board saw the movie, had in effect secured the imprimatur of the President of the United States. In New York on February 20 the board allegedly wildly applauded the picture, spurring Dixon to leap to his feet, shouting that it was the "birth of a nation," and the old title, The Clansman, was then and there discarded. The producers, expecting no opposition, advertised the film's opening on March 3 at the Liberty Theater at a top price of two dollars.[14]

The NAACP had eleven days to persuade the board to reject the film. Earlier, the Los Angeles branch had wrung from the local mayor a commitment to cut all scenes suggestive of rape. Soon the *Crisis*, the NAACP organ, working with Fred Moore's New York *Age*, pressed for similar concessions in New York City. It was surprised upon hearing of the board's acceptance of the film in its entirety.[15]

Actually the alleged enthusiasm of the board's approval may have been exaggerated, for even with the cuts that the NAACP was to win, the vote to approve was divided. The Negroes had protested the decision on the basis of the split and had reminded the board that when *The Clansman* had been performed on the stage in Philadelphia, it had caused riots and had been banned. They were also aroused when, after the excisions, they saw that there were still close-ups of leering Negroes (many of whom were crudely made-up whites) pursuing white ingenues. But even with the omission of several shots of a "forced marriage" and a lynching sequence, most of which were poorly contrived anyway, the decision still remained at 15–8 for approval, with the chairman, Howe, among the dissenters. He refused to put his name on the board's seal of approval.[16]

The board felt that its job was not to judge historical accuracy; its job was "moral" and there was never any assumption of jurisdiction over race prejudice. Moreover, the board was a cumbersome barge that steered best in calm waters. Composed of 125 members who were placed in numerous smaller groups in order to view the vast output of films, it acted as a general committee only in case of dispute. A sub-committee had passed on Griffith's work without change; it was because of Howe's insistence that the whole board saw it and decided to pare footage from Part II, the segment drawn from Dixon's novel.[17]

After the producers failed to appeal the first deletions, the NAACP insisted that all of Part II be cut.[18] As the premiere approached, the NAACP demanded that Howe let Negroes preview the film. Howe responded by doling out two tickets, ten fewer than promised, for a March 1 showing with the provision that only whites use them. The Negroes pressed on, having heard that the board had vocally disapproved of the film and might be persuaded to put it in writing. Failing, they sued for an injunction on March 3, the date of the New York opening; they were refused because there had been no breach of peace. The board, in an effort to close the case, stopped answering mail on the subject. But under increasing pressure, the Howe group cracked and admitted that the March 1 action had been unofficial; it decided to allow Jacob Schiff, Jane Addams, Lillian Wald, and other NAACP members to have a private showing. A few Southerners also went along. They all roundly condemned the picture with the vigor of eyewitnesses, which they had become for the first time.[19]

After the viewing the Negro group instituted criminal proceedings against Griffith and Aitken, circularized the movie industry with their case against the Epoch Company, and demanded that the New York Commissioner of Licenses stop the film as a nuisance.[20] Intimidated, the board consented to another viewing and two more cuts were accepted by Epoch. Then Oswald Garrison Villard, one of the founders of the NAACP, refused advertising for the film in his New York *Post.* Three days later he printed a Jane Addams review in which she saw the film as a "gathering [of] the most vicious and grotesque individuals he [Griffith] could find among the colored people, and showing them as representative of the . . . entire race." [21] She, like Wilson, had mistaken verisimilitude for reality.

Although the board gave a final approval on March 15, the NAACP continued its work, nagging the board for the names and addresses of members and urging the mayor to stop the film as detrimental to "public decency." Failing, they sent copies of Francis Hackett's stinging review in the *New Republic* to five hundred newspapers, marking the first time either side used a critic's esthetic standards. Within the week the New York press learned of the board's division and its disclosures brought the NAACP to the mayor's office again. It tried to marshal delegations from many local churches and clubs, but Mayor John P. Mitchell, fearing a riot, refused them a license to parade.[22]

Howe, W. E. B. DuBois of the *Crisis,* Fred Moore, Rabbi Stephen A. Wise, Villard, delegates from the colored and white clergy and the Urban League overflowed into the outer halls of the mayor's office. Mitchell told them that he had no statutory powers over the film; he then droned through his earlier assurances that slashes in the film had already been made, that riot warnings had been issued, and that he could do no more. The announcement that the picture was being shown with excisions surprised the delegates; they meekly acquiesced and departed.[23]

The mayor's conciliatory statement about cuts was achieved at the expense of Negro unity. The meeting in his office revealed the deep fissures that ran through the Negro leadership, an elite that many whites thought was sturdily cemented in common cause. Taking advantage of the strife, the "Tuskegee machine," Booker T. Washington's coterie (a group which it was thought accepted the Negro's low status) had reached the mayor ahead of the NAACP through the efforts of Charles W. Anderson, a friend of Washington and a recently resigned federal office holder. Often antagonistic, but at times cooperative with the NAACP liberals, the Tuskegee group chose this occasion to embarrass the "Vesey Street crowd" (Anderson's name for the liberals) and "take the wind out of their sails" by demonstrating Washington's influence with those in high places. But though the Negro groups were placated, apparently unknown to Anderson, the requested cuts were not made. Thus the New York campaign was lost amid the recriminations that often marked the Negroes' efforts to unify against the bigotry that existed in the United States.[24]

When the film continued to run, the Negro groups moved to friendlier territory in Boston, home of William Monroe Trotter's *Guardian* and the liberal Boston *Post.* Starting early in April, Negro and white pulpit, press, and lectern attacked the film. Nevertheless, on the first Sunday in April Bostonians opened their papers and found a large, sensational, pseudo-religious advertisement for the film which mentioned a forty-piece orchestra, eighteen thousand extras, and three thousand horses. By Tuesday Mayor James Curley, who had banned movies of the Jess Willard–Jack Johnson fight, announced that he was giving public hearings to the numerous Negro societies over *Birth of a Nation.* Just before the hearings a Tremont Theater advertisement reminded the public that Wilson, George Peabody, and others had liked the film.[25] The next day accusations flew: in reply to a statement by Moorfield Storey who had accused the manager of issuing distortions, the theater called DuBois' *Crisis* "incendiary." [26] In turn, Griffith chided Storey for ignoring the historians Wilson, James Ford Rhodes, and Walter Lynwood Fleming—claiming that all would have accepted the film's thesis—and then made brilliant publicity by offering Storey $10,000 if he could prove the film distorted. They parted coolly when Storey complied; later the film interests declared that Storey had not seen the movie.[27]

Curley, perhaps sensing impending violence, promised to get the picture cut by the municipal censor. At the meeting of April 7 tempers were short. The Negroes hissed the mention of Wilson. In demanding censorship they cited the fact that the United States had banned the importation of boxing films and that the Women's Christian Temperance Union favored film censorship. They pointed to the frequent depiction of "sexual excesses" in movies, raised the fear that the film would create race hatred, and read letters from Addams, Wise, Mary W. Ovington, and other liberals. At one point Curley, piqued at the growing mountain of redundant testimony, asked if *Macbeth* tended to incite feeling against whites. Storey bristled and charged Curley with representing the "other side." The meeting broke up amid Curley's denials, Griffith's interjections on his right to film "history" as he saw it, and the mayor offering to cut a scene showing a Negro chasing a white girl.

Curley made good his offer. The chase scene, several leering Negroes, a marriage between a dissolute Negro and a white girl, the

shots of Stoneman alone with his mulatto mistress, and the whole segment showing a corrupt, bacchanalian South Carolina legislature were
removed. Curley made it clear, though, that the cuts were a concession
and not an act of conscience.

During the second week of the film's run in Boston the *Post* began
clearly to take the Negroes' position, though advertising for the film
continued to run in its pages. Its writers reminded Bostonians of the
murderous moods of the New York audiences observed as they left the
Liberty Theater, that Curley's predecessor had stopped the stage production of *The Clansman* in 1906, and they chided the producers for using
clergymen as "authorities" in the advertisements.[28]

Toward the end of the week violence erupted when two hundred
police were summoned because a crowd of Negroes (who were barred
from theaters) attempted to purchase tickets. Eleven people were arrested. Two Negroes managed to worm their way into the theater. When
one hurled an "acid bomb" and the other an egg, they were quickly
arrested. Trotter personally stood bail. On Saturday afternoon rumors
of riots spread through the streets. The next day a wild, hooting crowd
gathered at Faneuil Hall. There, Michael Jordan of the United Irish
League, making common cause with the Negroes, castigated Wilson.
The *Post* later gave the day's events a whole page. Hurriedly, Governor
David Ignatius Walsh and Attorney General Henry Attwill met to
thrash out the limits of their authority to stop the film. As the meeting
progressed both whites and Negroes gathered on the steps outside to
orate. The harried governor promised a delegation that he would ask
the legislature to pass a censorship law covering inflammatory material.
Meanwhile, he ordered the state police to stop Sunday's show. A day
later he managed the excision of another rape scene while the legislature held a hearing on the film.[29]

The publicity caused a few early supporters of the film to have second thoughts. George Peabody labeled the picture "unfair" after an
earlier endorsement. Late in the month Senator Wesley L. Jones of
Washington, several clerics, and others publicly turned on the film. To
conciliate the defectors, the producers introduced a bland prologue ex-
tolling the progress of the Negro, but Negroes were still kept from
the box office.[30]

During the whole Boston affray Booker T. Washington remained
aloof except for his advice and the work of his Negro Business League,
which he was having difficulty controlling. When Griffith, in mid-April,
asked him to make a film about Tuskegee, Washington refused because
he questioned Griffith's sincerity and did not wish to associate with
the makers of the "hurtful, vicious play." Principal Hollis Frissell of

Hampton Institute allowed a similar film to be made of his school for use as the prologue to *Birth of a Nation,* a decision which the *Crisis* attributed to Washington's advice. Although Washington gave no overt support, he was gratified to know that "Negroes are a unit in their determination to drive it out of Boston." At the same time he was very much aware that the campaign was increasing the picture's business, for he remembered when Negroes had been hired in 1906 to oppose *The Clansman* as a promotional "gimmick." In addition to these tactical considerations Washington kept out of the Boston affair because the Boston Negro Business League, in which he exerted considerable influence, was in a factional fight over endorsing the Griffith movie. Two members, it was reported, had already tried to endorse the film in his name. It was said that William Lewis, former United States Assistant Attorney General and a Negro, concurred in the endorsement. Fortunately for Washington the resolution to endorse was blocked in a meeting of the executive council, but even so he had to manipulate the rebel group into remaining in the organization so as to continue the public impression of Negro unity.[31]

Meanwhile the debate went on in Boston. When the Massachusetts lower house passed a censor bill, all the Boston newspapers carried large advertisements attacking it. On April 24 Trotter was arrested and fined twenty dollars when he tried to use tickets he had bought. Negroes still complained that scenes were removed for "moral" rather than racial reasons and insisted that many offensive shots remained. At a meeting at the First Unitarian Church Charles Eliot of Harvard, William Lewis, and others thrashed out the problem of legislation that would distinguish between art and propaganda—in their view *Birth of a Nation* belonged to the latter category. That this distinction was a main issue occurred to few of the antagonists. Most tried to draw a line short of "absolute freedom," to define what should be banned as "mischief," and to decide whether a "travesty of history" was censorable. Only one man at the meeting thought all censorship a "violation of freedom of the press and public expression." The Federation of Churches of Greater Boston condemned the film as "injurious to public morality."[32]

As the situation in Boston worsened, Wilson's southern sympathies—not as deep as Dixon's—wavered; the President and the Chief Justice sought a way out of their endorsement as the adverse press reaction to the film spread. Tumulty suggested "some sort of letter" that would get Wilson out of a corner without appearing to have been bullied by that "unspeakable fellow [Trotter]." Finally, the President permitted Tumulty to write a letter to Representative Thomas Thacher of Massachusetts, asserting that the White House had never sanctioned the film.

Although other correspondents were similarly reassured,[33] the damage had been done, for Dixon had been able to use the President's name for commercial purposes for the better part of three months. The Thacher letter was shown to William Lewis and African Methodist Episcopal Zion Bishop Alexander Walters, who were expected to take the belated news to the Negroes who had despaired at the President's thoughtless endorsement. Thus it took three months for Wilson to approach the position of the urban weeklies that dismissed the film as a spectacle and its audiences as curiosities, that denounced the "censors that passed it and the white race that endures it," that blasted Dixon as a "yellow clergyman," and sometimes noted the paradox of brilliant techniques perverted for specific ends.[34]

After the President's retraction the Boston fight neared the end that Negroes feared. The newly created Massachusetts Board of Censors ignored a petition of six thousand names and permitted the Tremont to continue showing *Birth of a Nation*. The board which had been created partially because of the Negroes' lobbying had turned on its makers. Fitfully, the squabble dragged on through the summer with the *Crisis* impotently recording minor successes with triumphant glee and failures with arch cynicism.[35] As the days grew longer the Negroes of Boston hoped that Booker T. Washington and Bishop Walters would come to town to actively aid DuBois and Trotter in keeping the pot boiling. But New York and Boston had become the scenes of bitter defeats, which were reflected across the land.

By midyear, except in a few cases, the distributors of *Birth of a Nation* could exhibit their film almost anywhere they wished. Mayor William Thompson killed it in Chicago and it was later banned in all of Illinois. In Wilmington, Delaware, the city council approved a fine of fifty dollars for showing it or *The Nigger*. In Cleveland, Harry Smith of the *Gazette* helped to keep *The Nigger* out of the city, but Mayor Newton D. Baker failed to induce the governor to keep *Birth of a Nation* out of Ohio.[36]

The film could be seen in New York, Los Angeles, San Francisco, and Boston. Agitators were at work against the picture in Baltimore, Charleston, West Virginia, Philadelphia, and Atlantic City with scant success.[37] Rarely did the violence and rioting that many Negroes expected occur in these cities. The press at times viewed the film as newsreel reality; often roundly condemned it for the prejudices it presented, argued over authenticity, discussed the social impact; distrusted Dixon; praised Griffith; and except for papers like the New York *Post*, whose editor was accessible to the NAACP, took unequivocal positions one way or the other.[38] The Negro press, too, raged from unconcern to dutiful worry and almost universally failed to see it as art or entertainment. The chief difference between the Negro and white press reactions was that some of the Negro editors were less kind to Griffith.[39]

By the latter half of the year, when the Boston rancor had waned, both the NAACP activists and the more covert Booker T. Washington group reassessed what had happened and gained insights about their functions as pressure groups. The *Crisis* conceded that Griffith was an ill-used but "mighty genius" and that negative opposition was pointless. If the film was a "cruel slander upon a weak and helpless race," DuBois wrote, then the race must learn to use its money for films, poetry, music, and its own history. In October the Negroes in Washington, D. C., began preparations for "The Star of Ethiopia," an all-Negro pageant.[40] At Tuskegee, Washington was badgered by writers who wanted him to make films which would refute the stereotypes of *Birth of a Nation* and "make wonderful propaganda for every kind of social reform." He refused, perhaps fearing the loss of face suffered by Frissell when he let Griffith use Hampton for the locale of a film prologue to *Birth of a Nation*.[41] Consequently, the annual report of the NAACP for 1915 could only record a long, negative battle for censorship. Negroes had demonstrated and had broken into segregated theaters to get a hearing for their censorship pleas—a stand their leaders were coming to reject in principle but tactically were unable to replace with another weapon because of budgets already strained by litigations and demonstrations. And sometimes even censorship backfired, as in Massachusetts, where the board that the Negroes helped create eventually accepted most of the films to which the Negroes objected.[42]

For Negroes, their failure in the fight against *Birth of a Nation* was another reminder that the scant progress made in the Roosevelt years was not necessarily inevitable and that the Wilson era was a time of troubles characterized by a Jim Crow federal government, lynching, and the seed-time of a new Ku Klux Klan. The controversy also demonstrated the seriousness with which films had come to be regarded both as creators and reflectors of opinions and attitudes after only two decades of existence.

NOTES

1. See George C. Osborn, "The Problem of the Negro in Government, 1913," *The Historian,* XXIII (May, 1961), 330-347 for the most recent study of the Negro's plight in the Wilson years.

2. Thomas Dixon, Jr., *The Clansman* (New York, 1907) is one of several editions. A print of *Birth of a Nation* is in the Museum of Modern Art Film Library, New York City (copyright no. LP 6677).

3. Iris Barry, *D. W. Griffith: American Film Master* in the "Museum of Modern Art Film Series No. 1" (New York, 1940), pp. 7-10, 15-21; Arthur Knight, *The Liveliest Art* (New York, 1959), pp. 31, 35; Nicholas Vardac, *Stage to Screen: Theatrical Method from Garrick to Griffith* (Cambridge, Mass., 1949), pp. 64, 199, 208; Seymour Stern, "Griffith: Pioneer of Film Art," in Lewis Jacobs, *Introduction to the Art of the Movies* (New York, 1960), pp. 158-159. For a new scholarly treatment with many fresh insights and sound criticism of earlier students see Edward Wagenknecht, *The Movies in the Age of Innocence* (Norman, Okla., 1962), pp. 99-109.

4. A review in the Harvard Theater Collection, January 8, 1906, cited in Vardac, *Stage to Screen,* p. 64.

5. Nicholas Vachel Lindsay, *The Art of the Motion Picture* (New York, 1915), pp. 41, 46-49.

6. Barry, *op. cit.,* p. 22. In an interview with Rolfe Cobleigh, editor of the *Congregationalist and Christian World,* Dixon claimed to own one-fourth of the picture. See Boston Branch of the NAACP, *Fighting a Vicious Film: Protest Against "Birth of a Nation"* (Boston, 1915), p. 26.

7. NAACP, *Sixth Annual Report* (1915), p. 11.

8. Here, as throughout the paper, the proper noun "Negro" used collectively is shorthand for Negro pressure groups and their white allies. Ideologically, it should not suggest unanimity of opinion or action but only that these people recognized and resented certain social customs and disabilities that whites commonly imposed upon Negroes.

9. Investigations resulted in the creation of censoring boards in Chicago, New York, Kansas, Maryland, and Ohio. The movement entered Congress in the persons of Southern and New England Calvinists and over-zealous progressives who also tended to support prohibition and suffrage for women. Terry Ramsaye, *A Million and One Nights* (New York, 1926), II, 569.

10. U.S. Congress, House of Representatives, *Motion Picture Commission: Hearings before the Committee on Education . . . Bills To Establish a Federal Motion Picture Commission,* 63rd Congress, 2nd session (Nos. 1 and 2, 1914),

Part I, pp. 3-5, 56-62; Part II, p. 79; Ramsaye, op. cit., 11, 482; "Films and Births and Censorship," Survey, XXXIV (April 3, 1915), 4-5. For further comment on the censorship controversy see Donald Ramsay Young, Motion Pictures: A Study in Social Legislation (Philadelphia, 1922), pp. 21, 42, 58, 75, 98; Morris L. Ernst and Pare Lorentz, Censored: The Private Life of the Movies (New York, 1930); and Wagenknecht, op. cit., p. 100.

11. Dixon to Tumulty, May 1, 1915; later Dixon let Wilson know his plans in blander terms, assuring the President that soon "there will never be an issue on your segregation policy," Dixon to Wilson, September 5, 1915, cited in Arthur Link, Wilson: The New Freedom (Princeton, 1956), pp. 253-254. Dixon made a similar reference to the "Negro Intermarriage Society" in an interview with Rolfe Cobleigh (NAACP, Fighting a Vicious Film, p. 26).

12. Mrs. Thomas [Madelyn Donovon] Dixon to Thomas R. Cripps, June 7, 1962; telephone conversation between Mrs. Dixon and Cripps, June 6, 1962. Thomas Dixon, Southern Horizons: An Autobiography, MS in the possession of Mrs. Dixon, Raleigh, North Carolina, cited in Eric Goldman, Rendezvous with Destiny (New York, 1956), pp. 176-177. See also Knight, op. cit., p. 35; and Post (New York), March 4, 1915.

13. Correspondence cited in Link, op. cit., pp. 253-254.

14. New York Times, February 14, 1915. See also Lewis Jacobs, op. cit.; Daniel Talbot, Film: An Anthology (New York, 1959), p. 416, for titling incident. For another version see Wagenknecht, op. cit., p. 99. Dixon in an interview claimed to have hired thirteen Pinkerton men for the New York run (NAACP, Fighting a Vicious Film, p. 16).

15. "Fighting Race Calumny," Crisis, X (June, 1915), 87.

16. Frederic C. Howe to [Joseph P.] Loud in NAACP, Fighting a Vicious Film, p. 33; Survey, XXXIV (April 3, 1915), 4-5.

17. W. D. McGuire, Jr., of the National Board of Review, "Censoring Motion Pictures," New Republic, II (April 10, 1915), 262-263.

18. "Fighting Race Calumny," Crisis, X (May, 1915), 40-42.

19. Ibid.

20. Ibid.

21. Post (New York), March 10, 1915, carried the last advertisement. The review appeared March 13, 1915.

22. Crisis, X (May, 1915), 40-42.

23. Ibid. (June, 1915), p. 87; NAACP, Fighting a Vicious Film, passim; Afro-American Ledger (Baltimore), March 27, 1915.

24. Crisis, X (May, 1915), 40-42; Afro-American Ledger, March 3, 1915; August Meier, "Booker T. Washington and the Rise of the NAACP," Crisis, LXI (February, 1954), 122.

25. Ibid., X (June, 1915), 87; NAACP, Fighting a Vicious Film, passim. See also Sunday Post (Boston), April 4, 1915; Post (Boston), April 6, 7, 8, 1915. The list included Dorothea Dix, Rupert Hughes, Booth Tarkington, Richard Harding Davis, Hugh Johnson, George Peabody, Senators James E. Martine, Duncan U. Fletcher, Henry Lee Myers, Thomas J. Walsh, Wesley L. Jones, Representative Claude Kitchen, the Reverends C. H. Parkhurst and

Thomas Gregory. According to the NAACP, Dixon's method of soliciting approval was to pass out cards between halves of the film; that is, after the predominantly Griffith parts and before his own part.

26. NAACP, *Fighting a Vicious Film*, p. 26.

27. *New Republic*, III (May 5, 1915), 17; see also correspondence in NAACP, *Fighting a Vicious Film, passim; Broad Ax* (Chicago), June 5, 1915; *Post* (Boston), April 24, 1915.

28. *Sunday Post* (Boston), April 4, 11, 1915; *Post* (Boston), April 6, 7, 8, 1915.

29. After the riot the rest of the Boston papers began to cover the movie and its effects. None of them—the *Evening Transcript,* the *Herald,* the *Journal* —adopted a pro-censorship stand or seemed deeply concerned about the struggle over the film. See the issues of April 18, 1915, through April 26, 1915, particularly.

30. *Post* (Boston), April 12, 18, 19, 1915; *Crisis,* X (June, 1915), 87; correspondence in NAACP, *Fighting a Vicious Film,* pp. 30-33.

31. Phil J. Allston to Booker T. Washington, copy, April 12, 1915; Washington to Allston, copy, April 25, 1915; Washington to Allston, copy, April 19, 1915; Charles E. [?]llason to Washington, June 1, 1915; Samuel E. Courtney to Washington, copy, April 19, 1915; Washington to Courtney, copy, April 23, 1915; Rabbi Abram Simon to Washington, confidential telegram, April 14, 1915; Emmett Scott to Simon, telegram, April 14, 1915, Booker T. Washington Papers (Box 75, Library of Congress). Washington wrote one letter of protest to the Atlanta *Independent* (NAACP, *Fighting a Vicious Film,* pp. 35-36). See *Post* (Boston), April 24, 1915, for hints that Allston himself may have expressed approval of the film.

32. *Broad Ax,* June 5, 1915; *Post* (Boston), April 24, 1915; *Evening Transcript* (Boston), April 20, 1915; *Herald* (Boston), April 21, 1915; *Crisis,* X (June, 1915), 87.

33. Link, *op. cit.,* pp. 253-254; Goldman, *op. cit.,* pp. 176-177.

34. "The Civil War in Film," *Literary Digest,* L (March 20, 1915), 608-609; Francis Hackett, "Brotherly Love," *New Republic,* II (March 20, 1915), 185; see also "After the Play," *ibid.,* V (December 4, 1915), 123; *ibid.,* III (June 5, 1915), 125.

35. *Post* (Boston), June 5, 1915, clipping in the Washington Papers; *Crisis,* X (July, 1915), 147-148 insisted there had been no hearing; *ibid.* (August, 1915), pp. 200-201; *ibid* (September, 1915), p. 245; "The Negro Business League," *ibid.* (October), 1915, pp. 280-281; "Social Uplift," *ibid.,* p. 268; "The Birth of a Nation," *ibid.,* pp. 295-296. The *Crisis* claimed to have "wounded the bird" because "the latter half has been so cut, so many portions of scenes have been eliminated, that it is a mere succession of pictures, sometimes ridiculous in their inability to tell a coherent story."

36. See correspondence in note 31. For suggestions of the political motives of Walsh, Curley, and other Massachusetts politicians see *Herald* (Boston), April 18, 26, 1915.

37. *Afro-American Ledger,* May 22, 26, June 5, July 31, August 7, Septem-

ber 25, December 25, 1915; *New Jersey Informer*, August 21, 1915, clipping in the Washington Papers.

38. *Tribune* (Chicago), May 9, 14, 15, 1915; *Sun* (Baltimore), November 1, 1915; *Inquirer* (Philadelphia), March 30, September 5, 23, 26, 27, 1915; *Post* (Boston), March 4, 1915; *American* (New York), March 5, 1915; Vardac, *op. cit.*, p. 224, cites *New York Times*, June 6, 1915; *Sun* (New York), March 4, 1915. See also *Evening Post* (New York), February 20, March 3, 4, 13, 1915; "The Birth of a Nation," *Outlook*, IV (April 14, 1915), 854; "Negro Segregation Adopted by St. Louis," *Survey*, XXXV (March 11, 1915), 694; *ibid.*, XXXVI (April 24, 1915), 96; *ibid.* (July 10, 1915), 344-345; *New York Times*, March 4, 7, 1915. See also Ramsaye, *op. cit.*, II, 638.

39. *Bee* (Washington), February 20, May 1, 27, June 5, 1915; *Appeal* (St. Paul), October 2, 1915; *Afro-American Ledger*, March 3, 13, 20, 1915.

40. *Crisis*, II (November, 1915), 36; "The Slanderous Film," *ibid.* (December, 1915), pp. 76-77. The *Crisis* was probably referring to the fact that Dixon was able to weave his racism into Griffith's art with such finesse that no one could attack ideology and art separately, thus assuring Dixon an audience that he might not have gathered solely on the merits of his own work.

41. Florence Sewell Bond to Washington, June 27, 1915; Washington to Bond, June 30, 1915; Washington to F. P. Hull, personal-confidential copy, April 23, 1915; Emmett Scott to J. H. Beak, St. Paul Association of Commerce, October 27, 1915; Beak to Washington, wire, October 10, 1915; Amy Vorhaus to Washington, July 9, 1915; Laurence Gomme to Scott, June 17, 1915; Scott to Gomme, copy, June 23, 1915, Washington Papers.

42. NAACP, *Sixth Annual Report*, pp. 11-12; Vorhaus to Washington, July 9, 1915; Washington to Vorhaus, July 13, 1915, Washington Papers. For examples of later protest see Francis Grimké, "The Birth of a Nation" (October 15, 1915), in Francis J. Grimké, *Addresses and Pamphlets* (n.p., n.d.); NAACP, *Fighting a Vicious Film;* Reverend W. Bishop Johnson, *The Birth of a Nation; A Monumental Slander of American History; the Negro and the Civil War by Thomas Dixon Analytically and Critically Considered* (n.p., [1916]); Isaac L. Thomas, *The Birth of a Nation: A Hyperbole Versus a Negro's Plea for Fair Play* (Philadelphia, 1916)—all in the Moreland Library, Howard University, Washington, D.C. See also "*Birth of a Nation* Revived, Draws Protest," *Crisis*, XLV (March, 1938), 84.

The Negro Effort

The myth of white beneficence to the Negro has traditionally emphasized three factors. The first is the extent to which abolitionists helped runaway slaves through an underground railroad, the second concerns white military efforts to free the Negro, and the third is the way in which civil rights were given to the Negro by white sympathizers. The three selections here make abundantly clear that the Negro did more than his share in each of these enterprises.

The concluding chapter of Larry Gara's book, The Liberty Line: The Legend of the Underground Railroad, sums up his thesis quite well. The Underground Railroad's chief value was in propaganda designed to credit the abolitionists with more impact upon events than they deserved. Gara's work indicates that the runaway slave freed himself with only casual and incidental help from others. Thus a study of the legend and its inaccuracies shows the real actor behind the scene, the fugitive slave.

Dudley Cornish, who has written the best history of the Negro in the Union Army during the Civil War, judiciously sums up the contribution that Negro troops made in winning the war. His conclusion is that Negroes participated at least as effectively as white soldiers, and under more difficult circumstances. His statistical data prove his point, but beyond this is the effort that cannot be measured. The South owed part of its defeat to Negro troops fighting in a war not originated for their benefit.

Finally, Leslie H. Fishel's article shows how Negro political pressure and action made possible a civil rights law in Wisconsin. In this case study Fishel makes plain that without considerable attention and persistence by Wisconsin Negroes and their representatives, particularly in the Republican party, the bill would have been neither initiated nor passed.

Negro history has continued to emphasize how much the Negro has given of himself to further his own equality. Because these efforts have been underrated in conventional histories, part of the energy of historians of the Negro has been used to uncover and describe those contributions.

THE LIBERTY LINE:

REMINISCENCE AND ROMANCE

Larry Gara

When asked by a writer of local history where his mother had obtained her sources for *Uncle Tom's Cabin*, Charles Edward Stowe replied that he did not know. "You know the recollections of old men consist for the most part of Wahrheit and Dichtung," answered Stowe. "Old men dream dreams and young men see visions, and that gets history in a devil of a mess." His mother had insisted, he recalled, that she had heard Lincoln in 1862 give a speech which had not been delivered until several years later. "That," continued Stowe, "is the reason that the historians have to spend so much time hunting around in dark cellars for black cats that aren't there and never were." [1]

Stowe was perceptive. Seldom do historians accept the reminiscences of aged participants without careful evaluation of such material. Yet in the case of the underground railroad, a dearth of contemporary source materials has led a number of writers to rely heavily upon reminiscent material. The postwar flood of underground railroad literature was primarily, though not exclusively, of abolitionist origin. It was this mass of material, written years after the events, that gave the legend form and substance and an enduring place in the story of America's past.

At best, abolitionist sources presented only one view of a highly controversial period of history, and their characteristic mode of expression was a language rich in invective and hyperbole but lacking in objectivity and precision. William Lloyd Garrison even wished for a "new

Larry Gara, *The Liberty Line: The Legend of the Underground Railroad* (Lexington, Ky., University of Kentucky Press, 1961), chap. viii.

and stronger dialect," he said, for the English language was "inadequate to describe the horrors and impieties of Slavery, and the transcendent wickedness of those who sustained this bloody system." Most abolitionists were sure that the tyrannical South was determined to "subjugate the North for the extension and perpetuation of slavery." When the Civil War came, they viewed it as a "contest pure and simple, between Freedom and Slavery; between the powers of darkness and the powers of light." To them it was, as Frederick Douglass put it, "an Abolition war instead of being a Union war," and when a northern victory brought an end to the conflict and to slavery, they assumed that it was they, the abolitionists, "who had given the American slaves their freedom." One of their most severe critics, Eli Thayer, said they "never exhibited any diffidence or modesty in sounding their own praises." He accused them of "forming a mutual admiration society possessed by an unusual malignity towards those who did not belong to it." Thayer asserted also that their persecution did not stem from their antislavery principles but rather from their "abusive and insulting manner" and from their support of the "unpopular and unpatriotic doctrines of secession and disunion." As ardent fanatics, the abolitionists met with extreme reaction; they saw no value in moderation, and neither did most of their opponents.[2]

The religious motivation of most abolitionists often produced in them a sense of destiny for their cause. Like the men of the Middle Ages, they saw the hand of God in historical events. An Ohio abolitionist revealed in 1874 that he was thankful he had been an abolitionist "from the start" and had never looked upon slavery as anything but "a sin against God and a crime against man. And the hand of God has never been more visible in human history," he said, "than in its signal overthrow in this country."[3] Few of his friends in the antislavery movement would have quarreled with those sentiments.

Once slavery had been abolished, most Americans north and south accepted the decision. In many circles it was popular in the years after the war to have had a record of antislavery activity, and many people whose timidity had been foremost in the prewar years became ardent abolitionists afterward. This, of course, disturbed the bona fide abolitionists. Furthermore, it was not easy to tell who had been an abolitionist before the war because of the many degrees of antislavery and abolitionist sentiment and the many sectarian splits within the antislavery ranks. Lydia Maria Child was amused to find in 1864 that new antislavery friends were "becoming as plenty as roses in June." She wrote Garrison, "Sometimes, when they tell me they have always been antislavery, I smile inwardly, but I do not contradict the assertion; I merely marvel at their power of keeping a secret so long!" The next year an abolitionist wrote that it was "rare to meet one who has ever wished well to slavery, or desired anything but its final abolition." A number of the antislavery workers wrote autobiographical accounts to help set the record straight.[4]

When Professor Wilbur H. Siebert gathered materials in the 1890's for his study of the underground railroad, he wrote letters of inquiry to aged abolitionists and their descendants. Only a few of them denied having recollections of the underground railroad. One informant admitted that he had only a young boy's remembrance and said he could help little, since such information "should be first-hand and accurate." Another said he knew from tradition and personal observation that there was such a road running through Ohio, though he could "recollect but little of the details of its workings." A Granville, Ohio, correspondent revealed that his father and mother had both been antislavery people, always ready "to help in any way in their power to advance that cause," but that the family had had "no immediate or 'official' connection with the 'Underground R.R.'"[5]

An Illinois descendant of abolitionists regretted that he knew so little about the road, since his father had been actively involved in its work. He attributed his ignorance to the prudence of his father. Dr. James C. Jackson of North Adams, Massachusetts, lamented that his extensive collection of abolitionist letters had been destroyed by fire. Thirty years earlier, he said, he could have written a correct history of the underground railroad from memory, but, he admitted, "it exists in my mind now only as a magnificent dream."[6]

If some of the aged abolitionists were reluctant to offer information which they could not verify, others claimed to have excellent memories. Many reacted in the same spirit as the Reverend H. D. Platt, who answered: "There was a peculiar fascination about that 'U.G.R.R.' biz., that fires me up, even now when I recall the scenes of excitement and danger." A ninety-five-year-old Pennsylvania abolitionist was "rather proud of being a son of a Revolutionary soldier, as well as having been both agent and conductor on an Underground Railroad." He claimed that he had helped free nearly a hundred slaves, "taking them at night and on horseback." Another said that he had been an underground railroad agent since 1820 and that he had "enticed slaves away in Louisiana, Missouri and (though they were free) Utah." "The Underground RR was the way we sent fugitives from friend to friend till landed in Canada," said a Michigan veteran of the antislavery movement. Still another aged abolitionist remembered the secrecy and claimed that the underground railroad had had "a regular code of secret signs and passwords by which the members recognized and communicated with each other." Furthermore, he recalled that "each conductor was armed and like the Spartan Soldier never expected to surrender unless mortally wounded." Most of the replies which Siebert received were in general terms, lacking in details. An Illinois correspondent told the eager historian that when he first talked with the aged abolitionists in his neighborhood he thought he would get a great deal of information. But he found "that while they will talk very volubly and at great length what they say, when boiled down so as to get what they know shows but little on paper." [7]

Some veterans of the antislavery movement published reminiscences or histories. As with their prewar efforts, these historians continued to work with a sense of mission. One of them detected a hungering "for a greater knowledge and history of the events of the past," insofar as those events had tended to enlighten mankind and raise it to a higher moral level. William L. Cockrum, who wrote an underground railroad history, "had no apology to make" for his book. He wanted young people to be informed about "how things were carried on during the fifties by the proslavery people who had control of the government." To Cockrum it was clear that "Hot headed southerners had brought on a war hoping to dissolve the Union." Zebina Eastman, a Chicago abolitionist and journalist, was also concerned that the history of the antislavery struggle should be preserved. "It seems to many of us," he told an abolitionists' convention in 1874, "that this nation cannot afford to have this chapter blotted out, and the valuable lessons lost upon our children, who are soon to be followed by other children." The abolitionists who wrote historical accounts were no more capable of objectivity in the postwar years than they had been in the days before the war. For documentation they drew mostly upon their own memories. They repeated the same bitter hatreds, the same oversimplified moralistic interpretations, and even the same loyalty to whatever faction of abolitionism they had happened to join. In 1892 Frederick Douglass confided to a friend that the time had not yet come for a "true and impartial history of the Anti-slavery movement." Differences among abolitionists had "descended from sires to sons and made the task of writing a true history hard if not impossible for the present." He hoped that at a more distant period the scattered material could be "gathered and the chaff of rivalry, sect and passion be winnowed out, and the true wheat" saved. As in war, said Douglass, amid the fire and smoke of battle, "those most engaged see least that is going on over the whole field." [8]

If the abolitionists, as Douglass maintained, were incapable of making a fair evaluation of the various antislavery groups, they were even less objective when viewing their role in history as it related to national events. When writing about what they considered "the supreme era in American history," the abolitionists were looking back upon a time when they had often been hated and scorned. The Reverend Austin Willey wanted to remind the nation of "the odium, the toil, the sacrifice, the mental suffering, the hate," which the great struggle had cost its noble followers.[9]

Vividly remembering the harsh feelings toward them in the prewar years, the abolitionists wrote about their adventures in a great crusade which had achieved its objective, in a cause that had been vindicated. In part, at least, they wrote in order to secure for themselves a proper place in history.

A number of abolitionist reminiscences and histories contained brief descriptions of the underground railroad. Samuel J. May, a Garrisonian from Syracuse, published *Some Recollections of Our Anti-slavery Conflict in 1869*. In it he described the Syracuse branch of the underground railroad and recorded his version of the rescue of Jerry in that city. James Freeman Clarke's *Anti-Slavery Days* appeared in 1883, the same year that Parker Pillsbury's *Acts of the Antislavery Apostles* was published. Austin Willey's *The History of the Antislavery Cause in State and Nation* came out in 1886.

Henry Wilson's three-volume *History of the Rise and Fall of the Slave Power in America* was one of the most popular of abolitionist histories. Wilson, an ardent antislavery politician who served as vice president under Grant, placed the origin of the underground railroad in the period shortly after the War of 1812. He defined it as the "popular designation given to those systematic and co-operative efforts which were made by the friends of the fleeing slave to aid him in eluding the pursuit of the slaveholders, who were generally on his track." Because of its "timely and effective aid thousands were enabled to escape from the prison-house of bondage." There were, according to Wilson, stations at convenient distances always ready to receive fugitives and house them until they could be sent along the way northward. He pictured the whole of the middle and western states east of the Mississippi as "dotted with these 'stations,' and covered with a network of imaginary routes." The cost, risk, and accomplishments were all great, and the epoch of the underground drama, said Wilson, was one of the brightest pages of American history that had yet to be written.[10]

Each of the volumes of memoirs helped establish the legend of the underground railroad firmly in the minds of Americans. Levi Coffin,

Laura S. Haviland, and Robert C. Smedley penned accounts that added substantially to the picture of the underground railroad as a Quaker institution. Others also mentioned the Quakers' contribution. The Reverend Austin Willey emphasized the work of New Englanders in the mysterious institution and the antislavery movement which nurtured it. Marvin Benjamin Butler and William L. Cockrum placed the underground railroad in Indiana, where they had worked. Although the writers did not clearly define the limits of local or regional organization, some of them gave the impression of a nationwide system. According to Eber M. Pettit of Cattaraugus County, New York, the underground railroad was a "spontaneous combination of multitudes of men and women" which extended "from the interior of the slave states to Canada." James Freeman Clarke described a system which "extended from Kentucky and Virginia across Ohio from Maryland through Pennsylvania, and New York to New England and Canada." [11]

Most of the writers of memoirs emphasized the need for secrecy in their dangerous work, although some of the material in their books reveals quite another picture. Marvin B. Butler, for instance, referred to the underground railroad as a "singular secret, and to many, [a] mysterious mode of transportation," though without "formal organization." [12] Levi Coffin, on the other hand, in his description of the underground railroad in an area where it was unusually active, indicates that the abolitionists practiced a minimum of secrecy.

The abolitionist reminiscences seldom included statistics, but almost all of them gave the impression of a thriving underground railroad corporation, never wanting for business. The Reverend Luther Lee of New York and Syracuse maintained that from "about 1840 to the commencement of the War of the Rebellion the road did a large business." By 1844, according to Addison Coffin, "the Wabash line was in good running order and passengers very frequent." "The Underground Railroad did a large business," wrote the Reverend Austin Willey of Maine. [13]

Stories of high adventure characterized abolitionist accounts of the underground railroad. Most of them had at least one encounter with slave hunters to include in their books. One of the aged conductors who penned a sketch for a county history in Iowa assured his readers that the underground history was one to "thrill the heart and quicken the pulse." It involved "hair-breath escapes, perilous journeys by land and water, incredible human sufferings," in addition to "all the various phases of misery incidental to an outraged and downtrodden people fleeing from an unjust bondage." [14] Willliam L. Cockrum recounted thrilling stories of his youthful adventures with the Anti-Slavery League of Indiana, which allegedly sent spies to the South, aided fugitives, used a secret code system, kidnapped slaves, and severely whipped slave hunters. Calvin Fairbank and Dr. Alexander M. Ross also related incidents from their dangerous careers as slave abductors.[15]

Although some of the abolitionists told of fugitives who had escaped alone and unaided, all of them attached great importance to the underground railroad as a device which made most successful escapes possible. It was the heroism and daring of the abolitionists to which they called attention. "Considering the kind of labor performed, the expense incurred and the danger involved," wrote Marvin B. Butler, "one must be impressed with the unselfish devotion to principle, of these men and women thus engaged." Henry Wilson said that those who engaged in underground railroad efforts "were generally Christian men and women, who feared God and regarded man." They undertook such labor because they felt "such service was but obedience to the royal law 'Thou shalt love thy neighbor as thyself.' "[16]

At least four writers included different versions of the origin of the term "underground railroad." Eber M. Pettit recalled an item in a Washington, D.C., newspaper of about 1839 which involved a captured fugitive slave who admitted, after having been tortured, that he was to have been sent north, and that "the railroad went underground all the way to Boston." Pettit added, "thus it will be seen that this famous thoroughfare was first called the 'Underground railroad,' in the city of Washington." Levi Coffin recounted a story of a slaveholder who, after he had abandoned his search for a fugitive, commented that there must be an underground railroad of which Coffin was president. Coffin heard the story at a bank directors' meeting, and it was the first time he had heard the term. Rush Sloane of Sandusky, Ohio, told a story similar to the one reported earlier by William Mitchell. Sloane traced the term to an incident of 1831, when Tice Davids, a fugitive slave, eluded his pursuing master along the Ohio river near Ripley. Davids swam to the Ohio shore and then disappeared. The master eventually gave up and said the "nigger must have gone off on an underground road." Robert C. Smedley told practically the same story, but placed it near Columbia, Pennsylvania.[17]

The Underground railroad reminiscences popularized the jargon of the mysterious institution. "It had, like all other railroads," wrote Eber M. Pettit, "its officers and stations, engineers and conductors, ticket agents and train dispatchers, hotels and eating houses."[18] It also had a full slate of officers. Among those who were listed in the postwar period, either by themselves or others, as president of the underground railroad were Levi Coffin of Cincinnati, Robert Purvis of Philadelphia, Peter Stewart of Wilmington, Illinois, Horace White of Syracuse, and Dr. C. V. Dyer of Chicago.

Reminiscent accounts are bound to be full of inaccuracies. Facts are elusive even to the diligent scholar, but even more so to rambling old folk who are recalling the heroic deeds of their more active days. In 1941, for example, when a local historian in Pennsylvania attempted to get at the facts of the Christiana Riot, he ran into such a confusion of statements that, after weighing the evidence, he concluded that it was "no longer possible to credit any of the local tales" which had been told by participants about the flight of the fugitives from Christiana to Canada.[19]

Two of the most influential underground railroad accounts were those of Levi Coffin and Robert C. Smedley. Coffin published the first edition of his *Reminiscences* in 1876, when he was seventy-eight. He used some letters and other documents to supplement his memory, but the aged reformer admitted that errors would appear and asked his readers to pardon them because of his "advanced age and feebleness." [20] Nevertheless, and despite his evident exaltation of his own role as reputed president, Coffin's description of the underground railroad in Indiana and western Ohio is one of the more reliable firsthand accounts; his knowledge of these activities was apparently more extensive and his taste for melodrama was certainly less pronounced than is the case with most of the memoirists.

Vying with Coffin's book for popularity was the *History of the Underground Railroad in Chester and the Neighboring Counties of Pennsylvania*, by Robert C. Smedley. Although apparently he had not been involved personally in the antislavery crusade, Smedley came to be thoroughly sympathetic to the participants while collecting reminiscent material from aged abolitionists and their families. He tried to be "punctiliously exact and truthful," though his bias colored every page of his manuscript. Smedley had originally planned only a newspaper article, but he decided to write a book instead when his inquiries "revealed such well-established and well-conducted plans, such nobleness of purpose, such an amount of charity and unrecompensated labors freely given, that the idea suggested itself that the true Christian principles and commendable works of those noble philanthropists, should not be allowed to die with the times in which they lived." [21] Smedley's became one of the most frequently consulted books on the mysterious institution. Yet many of the stories he related cannot be substantiated.

The pattern of underground railroad reminiscences and histories was remarkably similar in the various published accounts. There were variations, of course, in the details and emphases of some of the reformers. One book, however, was markedly different from the rest: William Still's *The Underground Rail Road*, which was perhaps the most widely read of them all. Still was a Negro who had been secretary of the Philadelphia Vigilance Committee. His nearly eight-hundred-page volume first appeared in 1872. It contained hundreds of anecdotes, excerpts from newspaper articles, legal documents, and letters from former slaves and abolitionists. Numerous illustrations helped to fix the thrilling underground railroad adventures in the minds of Still's readers.

Most of Still's material was culled from his Philadelphia Vigilance Committee records. The committee had seemed to prefer stories about cruel and libertine masters. When describing their masters, the fugitives often used such terms as "very rough," a "very mean swearing blustering man," a "gambler and spree'r," a "free whiskey drinker," and a "notorious frolicker and a very hard master." Such masters delighted in cruel punishment and in whipping naked slave girls. Some accounts were "too harrowing to detail." A few gave different evidence, but the committee found it difficult to accept it. A twenty-one-year-old woman told the committee that she had "always been used very well" and "had it good" all her life. "This was a remarkable case," wrote Still, "and, at first, somewhat staggered the faith of the Committee, but they could not dispute her testimony, consequently they gave her the benefit of the doubt." Occasionally the committee members also doubted stories of excessive cruelty, like the one about a master who "believed in selling, flogging, cobbing, paddling, and all other kinds of torture."

Still referred to the South as "the prison house" and the "hot-bed of Slavery," though he stated in his Preface that he had taken scrupulous care to furnish "simple facts" and to "resort to no coloring to make the book seem romantic." There is no reason to believe that Still did tamper with evidence, though some of the stories recorded by him for the vigilance committee are obviously exaggerated, probably by the fugitives themselves, who were seeking financial assistance from the committee. Still's Preface revealed his own viewpoint: "Those who come after us seeking for information in regard to the existence, atrocity, struggles and destruction of Slavery, will have no trouble in finding this hydra-headed monster ruling tyrannizing over Church and State, North and South, white and black, without let or hindrance for at least several generations." [22]

But there is a basic difference between Still's work and other abolitionist accounts. The focus of his book is on the brave fugitives rather than on the abolitionists. Although he did not slight the contribution of numerous white abolitionists, Still's hero was clearly the runaway himself. This was no accidental emphasis. Still's avowed aim was to keep green the "heroism and desperate struggles" of the Negroes; he wanted to make the underground railroad "a monument to the heroism of the bondsman under the yoke." Furthermore, he wanted to help prove, by writing a creditable book, the intellectual capacity of Negroes. "We very much need works on various topics from the pens of colored men to represent the race intellectually," Still said. The time had come, he believed, "for colored men to be writing books and selling them too." [23]

Still was a competent businessman who had established a thriving retail coal business in Philadelphia. He used his merchandising skills advantageously in promoting his book. Carefully picked agents were given detailed instructions and obligated to send weekly progress reports to Still. His system proved successful. The agents sold books as fast as they rolled from the press. Still sold books on the installment plan, but he instructed his agents not to deliver the book until the price was paid. Still proudly displayed his volume in the Philadelphia Centennial Exhibition of 1876. A second edition appeared in 1879, and a third in 1883. No other underground railroad book was so well advertised or systematically promoted.[24] But despite his extremely successful sales technique and the popularity of his book, Still's emphasis has made virtually no impact on the popular legend. For it is not the fugitive whose heroism is given the spotlight, but rather the abolitionist who helped him on his way. Still's book was unique in this sense, but its message has been drowned out by the mass of abolitionist-centered literature published in books, popular magazines, and newspapers.

Not all the postwar accounts of the underground railroad were written by participants. Sons and daughters and more distant relatives of abolitionists loved to hear their fathers and grandfathers relate the thrilling incidents of the underground railroad epoch. After the war, when the antislavery cause had become respectable, these descendants doted on the achievements, heroism, and loyalty of their forebears. In articles, in speeches, and in conversation, the relatives of abolitionists repeated the stories they had heard, sometimes with additional material gleaned from the writings of William Still and Levi Coffin. One elderly lady who deposited reminiscences with a local Pennsylvania historical society could claim to be the descendant of three generations of underground railroad operators. She admitted: "In giving reminiscences one thus environed is likely to hark back to years beyond their time and question whether the earliest of them are memories of things seen, heard and remembered or the echoes of former generations." Another proud daughter of a Delaware Quaker abolitionist claimed that her father was known "to be one of those to whom the terrified black man came to be helped into Pennsylvania and farther north, where he would be free." A Maine college professor recalled that his father's house had been "one of the stations on the underground railroad." An Illinois daughter of an underground railroad operator was "proud to be the daughter of a man whose principles of right and justice were so pronounced." [25] Untold numbers of such family stories, repeated again and again, helped to fix the mysterious institution firmly in the legendary history of the United States. Often the tradition was based upon a single incident. Although details became hazy and the stories could seldom be verified, there was no doubt in the minds of the second and third generation tellers of such tales as to their fundamental truth.

Local pride in northern communities also contributed to the growth of the legend. Traditional accounts were published in many city and county histories as well as in journals of local historical societies. Every barn that had ever housed a fugitive, and some that hadn't, were listed as underground railroad depots. One local incident sometimes served to create a legend of widespread underground railroad activity in the area. In a pre–Civil War history of Medford, Massachusetts, published in 1855, it was boasted that "Medford was the first town in the United States that rescued a fugitive slave." The postwar histories were full of similar pronouncements. A local historian claimed that "the name of Newport, Indiana, was made hateful to every slaveholder south of Mason and Dixon's line," and another, writing about Columbia, Pennsylvania, said: "The place soon became known to slave-owners, but early experience taught them to give it a wide berth." A local historian in Ohio claimed that "By courageously saving many Negroes from the torture of slavery the 'agents' of the Underground Railroad aroused public opinion in Ohio and saved it for the Union; Ohio saved Kentucky for the Union cause; and together they aided in the preservation of the United States Government." Another pointed out that "the citizens of Ashtabula County [Ohio] were worthy sons of the New England fathers" and that a fugitive slave at their doors always found shelter and protection. Often local stations were listed in such histories as "main depots," or "principal depots," and a number of historians claimed that their respective states were foremost in the antislavery movement. Local stories reflected pride in past achievement but seldom had any documentary basis. When Wilbur Siebert was collecting information for his book, one of his informants admonished him to "pay no attention to county histories as they abound in mistakes and perversions." Even reminiscences could not be trusted. "It is amusing to me," he wrote Siebert, "to hear men, now there is no odium, tell all about the U.G.R.R. system, knowing nothing at all." [26] Undoubtedly, such was the nature of a great deal of the material used by local historians writing after the war.

Local legends seemed to inspire more such legends, and there are few sections in the North that cannot boast at least one underground railroad depot. Stories are still repeated about underground tunnels, mysterious signal lights in colored windows, peculiarly placed rows of colored bricks in houses or chimneys to identify the station, and secret rooms for hiding fugitives. In 1923 an Ohio newspaper item concerning the destruction of an Indiana underground railroad station by fire alleged that the house had "contained secret closets, secret cellars and in the war period a secret tunnel led to the river." Only a few such stories have been thoroughly investigated, and some of those have been found to lack any real basis in fact. A persistent rumor that tunnels for aiding slaves to escape existed under Cleveland's St. John's Episcopal Church led to two investigations by the Western Reserve Historical Society. Despite repeated word-of-mouth legends, both investigations led to the inescapable conclusion that there had never been tunnels under the church. There was a possibility that the belfry of the church had at one time been used for housing small groups of people, but there was no basis for the wide-spread rumor about tunnels. A New Hampshire librarian found only "vague and wholly untrustworthy traditions in some families concerning the 'Underground Railroad,'" but no documented information. There was often "circumstantial evidence" that a particular house had served as a station, but even secret rooms had many other reasons for existence than the hiding of fugitives. Authentic records were exceedingly scarce. A New York librarian sought information concerning an underground railroad in Westchester County, New York. He found a great many people who claimed that stations had been established at various points, but when these statements were "pinned down to matters of historical fact," the evidence was lacking. Tradition told of numerous stations, but there was no clear proof "to establish the authenticity of such traditions." [27]

Reputations of individuals for service in the underground railroad were frequently exaggerated because of some incident in which the person had been involved. When historian Siebert wrote to the Reverend Joshua Young of Groton, Massachusetts, for any firsthand information that he might have, Young replied that there was very little he could tell. "Perhaps my connection with the U.G.R.R. has been exaggerated," he explained, "owing to the circumstances of my being the only present and officiating clergyman at John Brown's funeral, which gave me some prominence among abolitionists." The underground railroad reputation of Jonathan B. Turner of Jacksonville, Illinois, also rested on shaky ground. Two residents of Jacksonville, who had themselves been referred to Siebert as underground railroad operators, denied having had any connection with its doings but referred the historian to Turner, who was supposedly "a station agent." But the aged professor and journalist pointed out that his reputation rested on nothing more than once having helped in the rescue of three women from their pursuers. He had not even been an abolitionist, though he was antislavery in his views. He told the story of taking the women to a Presbyterian elder who was supposedly proslavery and whose home, therefore, was a safe hiding place, then concluded: "And this is all I ever knew about the Underground Railway, or its stations." Yet Turner's biographer describes the professor as "a member of the Underground Railroad" though "never very zealous in its work," and the historian of Illinois College, where Turner had taught, said he "took a very prominent part in the activities of the Underground Railway in Jacksonville."[28] Unfortunately, it is impossible to determine how many other underground railroad conductors have earned the title with no more justification than Turner, who himself denied it.

For many years after the conflict, Republican politicians capitalized on the memories of the war, waving the bloody shirt from hustings throughout the North. Most of the abolitionists who did not renounce political action eventually joined the Republican ranks, and political references occasionally occur in the postwar underground railroad literature. William Still referred to the "Proclamation of Father Abraham." Chauncey C. Olin's underground railroad reminiscences included a story about his being refused service when traveling with a Negro antislavery speaker. He thereupon made up his mind, he wrote, that the hotel-keeper was a "rock-ribbed Democrat of the first water." Eber M. Pettit's underground railroad book was more explicit. "But for the Republican party," he wrote, "our own free soil would still be hunting ground for the harassed fugitive from slavery. This very ground would be cursed with the tread of hunters for human chattels. Such is what the Democratic party would have made our whole country to this day and forever."[29]

The abolitionists' convention held in Chicago in 1874 was primarily a political rally, occurring as it did at a time when Republicans were frantically calling up memories of the war and the antislavery crusade. Governor John L. Beveridge gave the opening address, reviewing the major events in the abolition crusade with special emphasis on the underground railroad, which he called "an instrument in the hands of a just God for the fulfillment of His grand purposes." He reminded the aged reformers that the train finally stood still, the engine fires went out, "and in a day the proclamation of the immortal Lincoln, backed by the War power, perfected the emancipation. 'Hallelujah! de year of jubilee hab come!'" he exclaimed. Other speakers took the cue. Dr. Jonathan Blanchard also pointed out the contributions of antislavery politicians, claiming that Thaddeus Stevens was "an older abolitionist than Garrison, and carried his principles further than any other man, never allowing a fugitive to be taken back if he could get near enough to defend him in court." The whole convention was so politically oriented that Oliver Johnson, a Garrisonian, complained that the meeting seemed "to have been almost exclusively a 'Liberty party' 'Free Soil' affair." He did not detect in the newspaper accounts of the convention "even an allusion to the origin of the great moral movement" of the Garrisonian abolitionists. Other abolitionist conventions had a similar focus. A speaker at a commemorative meeting in Philadelphia in 1883 reminded the white-haired and battle-scarred abolitionists that "if the history of the thirty years before the war was familiar to our young people, the voting now going on would be somewhat different." [30] Political oratory designed to give young people a correct appreciation of the events of the ante bellum period may well have helped to establish the underground railroad tradition in American folklore.

The postwar popularity of underground railroad stories even led a few people to try to make money from them. An aged Indiana abolitionist offered to sell Siebert a full sketch of his part in the stirring movement at the rate of five dollars per thousand words. Friends of the elderly Harriet Tubman raised money to publish and sell her story as a slave abductor and underground railroad operator when earlier pension plans failed to materialize. In California, James Williams sold his fugitive slave narrative for fifty cents a copy. Besides incidents of his own escape and career as an underground railroad conductor, Williams' pamphlet contained a full description of the underground railroad and comments on various topics ranging from Mormonism and spiritualism to a defense of Chinese immigrants, all equally unintelligible. The literate section of the booklet comprised underground tales which were mostly lifted verbatim from William Still's account. [31]

Newspaper and magazine stories, from the Civil War to the present day, have helped to preserve the tradition. Newspapers carried numerous reminiscences of local underground railroad operators and repeated the traditional accounts when abolitionists died. Dwellings reputed to be underground railroad depots frequently furnish material for feature stories; such local legends are often revived when an old building is being torn down. Commenting on the death of an Indiana abolitionist who, with her husband, had been connected with the underground railroad, a local newspaper said: "This was an organization of those who believed that slavery was wrong and that laws that protected it were made by scheming and corrupt men and that such laws were contrary to the laws of God." A local paper in Pennsylvania included underground railroad material in a series of historical articles. "In the days of slavery in the South," ran the article, "the slaves fleeing from their masters were helped along the way towards Canada and freedom by certain persons of this and other counties who sympathized with the slaves; and this route was called the Underground Railroad." [32] Hundreds of such newspaper stories furnished readers with a picture of the underground railroad as an abolitionist institution, dotting the entire North with stations and giving fearless humanitarians an opportunity to strike a severe blow at the wicked slave system of the South. Many of the stories borrowed material from the published abolitionist accounts, and later from Wilbur Siebert's history of the underground railroad. They ran in a clearly defined pattern with little variation. Probably such newspaper items have done as much as anything to keep the legend alive.

Although the underground railroad has not become a major theme of American fiction, writers from the time of Harriet Beecher Stowe's triumph to the present have occasionally found material in it for novels and short stories. In addition, some of the supposedly factual accounts of the institution were highly fictionalized. One such book was H. U. Johnson's *From Dixie to Canada: Romance and Realities of the Underground Railroad*, which was published in 1894. These stories had been published earlier in Johnson's *Lake Shore and Home Magazine*. Johnson claimed personal familiarity with many of the events he depicted and also said he had gathered information from others. But according to another Ohio editor, Johnson "got things all wrong [that is he filled in the detail]." Wilbur Siebert said that while Johnson's tales were based upon research and included the names of authentic operators and towns, he had used "the license of the story-teller instead of restricting himself to the simple recording of the information he secured." [33]

Johnson's book repeated some of the material from Levi Coffin, Eber M. Pettit, and James Freeman Clarke. He described the underground railroad as a corporation which lasted twenty years, during which time it "extended its great trunk lines across all the northern states from Mason and Dixon's line and the Ohio River to the Queen's Dominion, and its ramifications far into the southern states." It had efficient officers, "side tracks, connections and switches," and its "station agents and conductors" were men "undaunted in danger and unswerving in their adherence to principle." Johnson also pictured a secret code system of "cypher dispatches, tokens and nomenclature." More than thirty-six thousand slaves secured their freedom by riding the secret underground line. Johnson repeated Pettit's story of Washington, D. C., as the place where the underground railroad received its name. Many of his conductors were Quakers, although he told of a proslavery Northerner who helped a near-white fugitive girl who had been sold "to a dealer in the far South for the vilest of purposes." Johnson recounted a story about one Ohio conductor who used "railroad telegraphy" in the form of special songs as signals to his waiting passengers. Johnson's heroes were the abolitionists who organized and maintained the railroad to freedom.[34]

Edmund Fuller's *A Star Pointed North* is a fictionalized account of the life of Frederick Douglass which includes scattered references to the traditional underground railroad. The novel refers to the "mysterious routes of the Underground Railroad" with "scattered way stations" in Pennsylvania and New York. Fuller also included a description of the New York Vigilance Committee and referred to Frederick Douglass' work with fugitive slaves. He drew an indistinct picture of the institution, but implied that it had a high degree of organization. Shirley Graham wrote another very popular book about the life of Douglass, entitled *There Was Once a Slave*. This novel places considerable emphasis on Douglass as an underground railroad operator and as an inspiration to those still in slavery and hoping to run away. The abolitionist conductors in this book are often Quakers, who "planned the connections" and added secret hiding places to their houses. The slaves knew of the train and its numerous facilities, which "might be a skiff," a "peddler's cart, an open wagon filled with hay," or simply a "covered-up path through the woods." [35]

Brion Gysin's *To Master—A Long Goodnight* is a novel about the life of Josiah Henson, the supposed model for Harriet Beecher Stowe's Uncle Tom. The book is mostly an attack on "Uncle Tomism," or the attitude of Negroes who accommodate themselves to notions of white superiority, but Gysin also includes material on the underground railroad. He pictures the road as having been organized in the late 1840's and becoming most significant after the passage of the Fugitive Slave Law of 1850. The novel alludes to secret signs on houses known only to members of the underground, and to underground railroad "shepherds" who enticed slaves from the South. The impression is one of considerable organization, with "directors of the Underground" making definite plans to run off slaves.[36]

A Clouded Star, Anne Parish's novel about Harriet Tubman, centers around one of the heroine's slave-abducting trips. This novel pictures the underground railroad as chiefly Harriet Tubman's organization, but the "stations" as mostly run by Quakers. Another fictionalized biography of Harriet Tubman, a children's novel by Hildegard Hoyt Swift entitled The Railroad to Freedom, presents a picture which conforms more closely to the traditional one. The underground railroad is described with all its legendary trappings—secret doors and rooms, code signals, the grapevine telegraph, and strange and secret tricks. It was a "mysterious organization whose main lines and branches stretched like a great network over the country from the Mississippi to the coast," but the number of passengers is placed at only a thousand a year. Harriet Tubman is clearly the heroine, but assistance from the abolitionist organization was essential to her success.[37]

Another children's book, Stories of the Underground Railroad, by Anna L. Curtis, furnishes younger readers with a picture of a well-organized, secret network of routes "northward to Canada, across all the Northern States, from Kansas to Maine." The impression is one of a very busy road vitally important to escaping slaves. The stories describe many thrilling pursuits by slave catchers, who are always eluded by the cunning Quaker or Negro conductors. There are the usual false partitions and clever hiding places.[38]

The recurrence of underground railroad material in literary works provides further indication of its widespread familiarity. No other work using the theme approaches the significance of Uncle Tom's Cabin either as literature or as propaganda. Yet all the books which contain descriptions of the mysterious institution have helped in some measure to keep the legend alive for numerous American readers.

Historians, too, have tended to accept the traditional accounts as substantially correct, even though most of the source materials were written at least a decade after the events had taken place. These accounts are useless as sources for such specific questions as how many slaves fled to Canada, or even how many were actually aided in their flight. Probably because of a dearth of contemporary evidence, some scholars dealing with the antislavery movement used these abolitionist memoirs much less critically than would ordinarily have been the case.

The abolition of slavery seemed to give new prestige to the abolitionists' pronouncements, and their own view of the crusade was largely accepted.

Some historians close to the events in point of time lowered the numbers of successful slave escapes. Hermann von Holst believed that Senator Andrew Pickens Butler's 1850 estimate of annual loss to the South of $200,000 was "much too high although the traffic on the underground railway was already quite lively." James Ford Rhodes accepted the government census figures of only a thousand slave escapes to the North each year. Writing half a century later, Allan Nevins pointed out that the three major studies of the underground railroad all gave the impression of more organization than actually existed and all exaggerated the amount of active opposition to the Fugitive Slave Act of 1850.[39]

Another scholar who modified the traditional underground railroad history was Edward Channing, who refused to accept abolitionist sources uncritically. He rejected the idea that all the slaves were chafing at their bonds, concluded that most escaping slaves came from the border states, and suggested that the actual number was "very difficult to ascertain." He pointed out that the sight of a fugitive might have aroused humanitarian impulses in people who were not necessarily abolitionists. Though Channing believed there was some "organized system of relief and evasion," his perusal of original sources "convinced him that there was much less system and much more spontaneity than has generally been supposed."[40]

Much more influential than the works of those who modified the traditional story were the writings of Wilbur H. Siebert, whose first book, *The Underground Railroad from Slavery to Freedom*, appeared in 1898 and was followed by several other books and numerous articles on the same subject.[41] Siebert was painstaking in his methods, copying all material pertaining to the underground railroad that he could find in published sources, and sending out a detailed questionnaire to hundreds of former antislavery workers.[42] He accepted the elderly abolitionists' statements at face value and defended the use of such material on the ground that the memories of the aged were more accurate than those of young people.[43] The romantic stories of the abolitionists were apparently difficult for him to reject, and he did not modify his early impressions in any of his later writings. In a 1923 article he defined the underground railroad as "a vast network of secret routes over which fugitive slaves were passed along, chiefly in the night time, from the Southern States to Canada during a prolonged period before the Civil War."[44]

Siebert believed that historians had previously neglected the under-

ground railroad or had overlooked its real importance, and he was determined to set the record straight. On a map he located hundreds of
underground railroad stations and included in an appendix an impressive
list of conductors. The underground railroad, Siebert concluded, was
effective both as an aid to the fleeing bondsmen and as a force for assuring an eventual northern victory in the sectional struggle; it was
"one of the greatest forces which brought on the Civil War, and thus
destroyed slavery." He depicted it as mysterious and secret in its operations. Although he did not include an estimate of the total number of
underground railroad passengers, he completely rejected the ante bellum
census statistics and implied that the number of slave escapes was very
high. He calculated that in a thirty-year period, forty thousand fugitive
slaves rode the underground line in Ohio alone. He tended to accept at
face value the propaganda statements of southern fanatics and the vague
impressions of abolitionists recorded in publications or correspondence
many years after the Civil War. He also identified more than thirty-two
hundred alleged underground railroad conductors and warned that this
was a minimum figure.[45] It would be difficult to exaggerate the influence of Professor Siebert's work. Numerous graduate students have
further documented his thesis, and many writers and historians have
borrowed generously from his monumental labors. Few writers working
since Siebert's book was published have dealt with the underground
railroad without consulting its pages, and in most cases his ideas and
conclusions have been borrowed as well. His is the standard work on the
mysterious institution.

Professor Channing believed that Siebert had earned the "thanks of
all students of Amercian history" for his work of gathering and publishing such a wealth of material, but he also pointed out that the book
was in some places "perhaps a little credulous, and it is partly based on
the recollections of old men." Few others saw shortcomings in Siebert's
writing. One reviewer of Siebert's first publication saw in its pages a
"categorical demonstration that the 'Underground' was in reality a
'system' and a far-reaching and complex one. The 'Road' soon, in fact,
became the most effective and the grandest protest that Abolitionism
ever made." Another reviewer learned from Siebert's book that abolitionists, in aiding the fugitives, were "helping the oppressed, ... eluding
the oppressor," and at the same time "enjoying the most romantic and
exciting amusement open to men who had high moral standards." A
study of Siebert's volume led Benjamin E. Smith to deplore the lack
of an estimate as to the number of underground railroad passengers,
which Smith guessed was not less than a hundred thousand. Quite
unintentionally, Professor Siebert had contributed to the growth of a

legend. His work seemed to establish a basis in fact for the many underground railroad traditions which circulated in the era following the Civil War.[46]

In dealing with history rather than legend, it is necessary to question the validity of local traditions. Hearsay, rumor, and persistent stories handed down orally from generation to generation are not proof of anything. Each local story should be investigated, the basis for the tradition examined, and the sources evaluated; if there is no historical evidence, the story may be considered imaginative rather than factual. The legend and its widespread popularity have made such tales appear plausible. Each local tradition fits into a general pattern which in turn seems to prove the truth of the local legend. The further removed people are from the Civil War, the more willingly they seem to accept such tradition as fact.

The characteristic outlines of the traditional version reveal that it is largely derived from postwar abolitionist reminiscences. The abolitionists' accounts tended to neglect the role of the fugitive slaves themselves in the escape drama, gave the impression that all successful escapees were passengers on the mysterious line, and implied that the "railroad" was a nationwide abolitionist organization which operated in secret. In reality, it is probable that fugitive slaves succeeded, if at all, mostly by their own efforts. Such help as they received came sometimes from abolitionists, sometimes from other groups, and was often casual and temporary. In the period of the slavery controversy the underground railroad was more important as a propaganda device than as an aid to the fleeing slave. Far from being secret, it was copiously and persistently publicized, and there is little valid evidence for the existence of a widespread underground conspiracy.

The legend not only distorts the nature of the activity but exaggerates its impact on national events. An abolitionist writer of memoirs said that the underground railroad "did more to hasten the crisis and final clash of arms that resulted in making this a free nation than any other agency." Wilbur Siebert and other scholars, assuming the existence of a widespread and successful conspiracy to transport slaves from the South, have attributed to that conspiracy almost as profound an effect as did the memoirist. Even in a study which gives detailed attention to the fugitive slave controversy appears the statement that "the underground railroad was one of the greatest forces that brought on the Civil War," suggesting an underlying assumption that the "railroad" was substantially the institution described in popular legend.[47]

There is a great deal that will never be known about the underground railroad and its impact on slavery and on the sectional controversy, but there is no justification for accepting at face value the emotional and biased accounts of either the abolitionists or their southern antagonists. Thirty-three years after the war, when the memoir writers were at the height of their activity, an Ohio abolitionist who had himself been prosecuted under the Fugitive Slave Law of 1850 wrote: "It was said by the poet that 'distance lends enchantment to the view'; and in regard to the escape of fugitive slaves by what was called the 'Underground Road,' I am convinced that the number passing over this line has been greatly magnified in the long period of time since this road ceased to run its always irregular trains." [48] This was only one man's opinion, but coming from a participant and deviating as it does from the usual pattern of abolitionist reminiscence, it is significant. Other evidence tends to substantiate his conclusion. The greater the distance, the more enchantment seems to adhere to all aspects of the underground railroad, the legend that grew up around it, and its role in America's heritage.

NOTES

1. W. D. Waldrip quotes the Charles Edward Stowe letter in "A Station of the Underground Railroad," *Indiana Quarterly Magazine of History*, VII (June 11, 1911), 67-68.

2. William Lloyd Garrison, "Hard Language," in *The Liberty Bell: By Friends of Freedom* (Boston, 1848); Charles Sumner, "The Struggle," in Julia Griffiths (ed.), *Autographs for Freedom* (Boston, 1853), p. 77; Western Anti-Slavery Society Minute Book, entry for August 24–26, 1851 (Library of Congress); Dustin G. Cheever Diary, entry for January 1, 1857, Dustin G. Cheever Papers (State Historical Society of Wisconsin); J. Miller McKim to Richard D. Webb, February 17, 1862, William Lloyd Garrison Papers (Boston Public Library); speech of Frederick Douglass in *Proceedings of the American Anti-Slavery Society, at Its Third Decade, Held in the City of Philadelphia, December 3d and 4th, 1863* (New York, 1864), p. 112; letter from Frederick Douglass, April 3, 1874, in unidentified clipping in scrapbook "Abolitionists' Convention" (State Historical Society of Wisconsin); Eli Thayer, *A History of the Kansas Crusade: Its Friends and Its Foes* (New York, 1889), pp. 95-96.

3. Samuel Wolcott to the Committee on the Abolitionists' Convention, May 27, 1874, Zebina Eastman Papers (Chicago Historical Society).

4. Lydia Maria Child to William Lloyd Garrison, *Liberator*, February 19, 1864; "Early Anti-Slavery," *Liberator*, February 24, 1865. For a pre–Civil War

example of an individual's claiming a more consistent antislavery record than he actually had, see Merton L. Dillon, "John Mason Peck: A Study of Historical Rationalization," *Journal of the Illinois State Historical Society* (Winter, 1957), 385-390.

5. Letters to Wilbur H. Siebert from C. F. Atkinson, May 2, 1896, in scrapbook "The Underground Railroad in Massachusetts, vol. 2," and E. S. Shepardson, October 21, 1896, in scrapbook "The Underground Railroad in Ohio, vol. 7," Wilbur H. Siebert Papers (Houghton Library of Harvard University); William Johnston to Siebert, August 23, 1894, in scrapbook "The Underground Railroad in Ohio, vol. 4," Siebert Papers (Ohio Historical Society).

6. Letters to Siebert from Nathan L. Burton, January 28, 1896, in scrapbook "The Underground Railroad in Illinois, vol. 2," and Dr. James Caleb Jackson, November 20, 1893, in scrapbook "The Underground Railroad in Massachusetts, vol. 1," Siebert Papers (Houghton Library).

7. Letters to Siebert from the Reverend H. D. Platt, March 20, 1896, in scrapbook "The Underground Railroad in Illinois, vol. 1," and John F. Williams, March 21, 1893, in scrapbook "The Underground Railroad in Indiana, vol. 2," Siebert Papers (Houghton Library); letters to Siebert from H. H. Northrop, May 2, 1896, in scrapbook "The Underground Railroad in Michigan," the Reverend James Lawson, April 22, 1896, in scrapbook, "The Underground Railroad in Pennsylvania, vol. 3," and D. J. Murphy, May 7, 1896, in scrapbook "The Underground Railroad in Illinois, vol. 2," Siebert Papers (Ohio Historical Society); E. M. Stevenson to Mr. White, February 24, 1897, in scrapbook "The Underground Railroad in Pennsylvania, vol. 2," Siebert Papers (Ohio Historical Society).

8. Samuel S. Tomlinson to J. J. Janney, June 27, 1892, in scrapbook "The Underground Railroad in Ohio, vol. 7," Siebert Papers (Houghton Library); William L. Cockrum, *History of the Underground Railroad, As It Was Conducted by the Anti-slavery League* (Oakland City, Ind., 1915), p. v; Zebina Eastman's address in unidentified clipping in scrapbook "Abolitionists' Convention" (State Historical Society of Wisconsin); Frederick Douglass to Marshall Pierce, February 18, 1892, Nathaniel P. Rogers Collection (Haverford College Library).

9. Austin Willey, *The History of the Antislavery Cause in State and Nation* (Portland, Me., 1886), p. 403.

10. Henry Wilson, *History of the Rise and Fall of the Slave Power in America* (3 vols.; Boston, 1872-1877), II, 63-69, 85-86.

11. Coffin, *Reminiscences;* Laura S. Haviland, *A Woman's Life-Work: Labors and Experiences* (Chicago, 1887); Robert C. Smedley, *History of the Underground Railroad in Chester and the Neighboring Counties of Pennsylvania* (Lancaster, Pa., 1883); Willey, *Antislavery Cause;* Marvin Benjamin Butler, *My Story of the Civil War and the Under-ground Railroad* (Huntington, Ind., 1914); Cockrum, *Underground Railroad;* Eber M. Pettit, *Sketches in the History of the Underground Railroad Comprising Many Thrilling Incidents of the Escape of Fugitives from Slavery and the Perils of Those Who*

Aided Them (Fredonia, N.Y., 1879), p. xiv; James Freeman Clarke, *Anti-Slavery Days* (New York, 1883), pp. 80-81.

12. Butler, *Story of the Civil War*, p. 179.

13. *Autobiography of the Rev. Luther Lee, D.D.* (Cincinnati, 1882), p. 320; Addison Coffin, *Life and Travels of Addison Coffin* (Cleveland, 1897), pp. 88-89; Willey, *Antislavery Cause*, p. 369.

14. *History of Clinton County, Iowa* (Chicago, 1879), p. 413.

15. Calvin Fairbank, *Rev. Calvin Fairbank During Slavery Times. How He "Fought the Good Fight" To Prepare "The Way"* (Chicago, 1890); Alexander Milton Ross, *Recollections and Experiences of an Abolitionist; from 1855 to 1865* (2d ed., Toronto 1876), and *Memoirs of a Reformer* (Toronto, 1893).

16. Butler, *Story of the Civil War*, p. 180; Wilson, *Rise and Fall of the Slave Power*, II, 85.

17. Pettit, *Sketches*, pp. 35-36; Coffin, *Reminiscences*, p. 190; Rush R. Sloane, "The Underground Railroad of the Firelands," *Firelands Pioneer*, N.S. V (July, 1888), 36; Smedley, *Underground Railroad*, p. 35.

18. Pettit, *Sketches*, p. xv.

19. Joseph Hutchinson Smith, "Some Aspects of the Underground Railway in the Counties of Southeastern Pennsylvania," *Bulletin of the Historical Society of Montgomery County, Pennsylvania*, III (October, 1941), 7.

20. Coffin, *Reminiscences*, p. ii.

21. Smedley, *Underground Railroad*, p. xii.

22. William Still, *The Underground Rail Road* (Philadelphia, 1872), pp. 3-5, 304, 435.

23. William Still to J. W. Jones, November 4, 1873, to Dr. Henry Charles, June 6, 1873, to J. C. Price, June 3, 1873, and to W. F. Teister, June 23, 1873, William Still Papers (Pennsylvania Historical Society).

24. Letters from Still to G. W. Gaines, June 6, 1873, W. H. Jones, June 3, 12, 1873, and E. Sanborn, June 11, 1873, Still Papers; James P. Boyd, "William Still," in Still, *Underground Rail Road*, p. lxiii.

25. Mrs. Sarah Louise Oberholtzer, undated MS, "Reminiscences of the Underground Railroad in Chester County" (Collections of the Chester County, Pa., Historical Society); Mary Corbit Warner, MS address, "An Incident of the Corbit Mansion in the Days of Slavery before the War of 1861-4," Slavery Collection (Delaware Historical Society); "Obituary of Mrs. Frances E. Otwell," *Journal of the Illinois State Historical Society*, XXIII (April 1931), 166; Emma Julia Scott, "The Underground Railroad," prepared for the Woodford County (Ill.) Historical Society and read at the society's annual picnic, August 30, 1934.

26. Charles Brooks, *History of the Town of Medford, Middlesex County, Massachusetts, from Its First Settlement, in 1630, to the Present Time, 1855* (Boston, 1855), p. 440; Waldrip, "A Station of the Underground Railroad," p. 64; Theodore W. Bean (ed.), *History of Montgomery County, Pennsylvania* (Philadelphia, 1884), p. 304; Ralph M. Watts, "History of the Underground Railroad in Mechanicsburg," *Ohio Archeological and Historical Society Quarterly*, XLIII (1934), 254; typewritten excerpts from *History of Ashtabula*

County, Ohio, pp. 33-34; and Benjamin D. Blackstone to Siebert, March 3, 1896, in scrapbook "The Underground Railroad in Ohio, vol. 1," Siebert Papers (Ohio Historical Society).

27. *Evening Dispatch* (Columbus), July 9, 1923; MS no. 2787, regarding attempts to discover evidence of tunnels under St. John's Church (Western Reserve Historical Society); Priscilla Roys to Siebert, April 29, 1935, in scrapbook "The Underground Railroad in New Hampshire," John W. Dow to Siebert, October 28, 1935, in scrapbook "The Underground Railroad in Vermont," Myrtle V. Newton to Siebert, March 19, 1945, in scrapbook "The Underground Railroad in Pennsylvania, vol. 4," and William S. Hadaway to Siebert, January 31, 1933, in scrapbook "The Underground Railroad in New York, vol. 3," all in the Siebert Papers (Ohio Historical Society).

28. Joshua Young to Siebert, April 21, 1893, in scrapbook "The Underground Railroad in Vermont," J. S. True to Siebert, January 27, 1896, Julius F. Pratt to Siebert, January 27, 1896, and Jonathan B. Turner to Siebert, March 6, 1896, in scrapbook "The Underground Railroad in Illinois, vol. 3," Siebert Papers (Ohio Historical Society); Theodore Calvin Pease, *The Frontier State, 1818-1848 (The Centennial History of Illinois,* II; Springfield, 1918), pp. 440-441; May Turner Carriel, *The Life of Jonathan Baldwin Turner* (Jacksonville, Ill., 1909), p. 52; Charles Henry Rammelkamp, *Illinois College: A Centennial History* (New Haven, 1928), p. 106.

29. Still, *Underground Rail Road*, p. 541; Chauncey C. Olin, *A Complete Record of the John Olin Family, the First of That Name Who Came to America in the Year A.D. 1678. Containing an Account of Their Settlement and Genealogy up to the Present Time—1893* (Indianapolis, 1893), p. xliii; Pettit, *Sketches*, pp. 173-174.

30. Newspaper clippings in scrapbook "Abolitionists' Convention, 1874" (State Historical Society of Wisconsin); Oliver Johnson to Zebina Eastman, June 15, 1874, Zebina Eastman Papers; *Commemoration of the Fiftieth Anniversary of the Organization of the American Anti-Slavery Society in Philadelphia* (Philadelphia, 1884).

31. J. H. Mendenhall to Siebert, February 5, 1896, in scrapbook "The Underground Railroad in Indiana, vol. 1," Siebert Papers (Ohio Historical Society); Sarah H. Bradford, *Scenes in the Life of Harriet Tubman* (Auburn, N.Y., 1869); James Williams, *Life and Adventures of James Williams with a full description of the Underground Railroad* (5th ed.; Philadelphia, 1893).

32. *Cleveland Press*, February 20, 1932; "Death of Mrs. Sally Towell Thompson," undated item copied from *Republican Leader* (Salem, Indiana) in scrapbook "The Underground Railroad in Indiana, vol. 2," Siebert Papers (Ohio Historical Society); "The Under-Ground Railroad," February 23, 1925, unidentified newspaper clipping in Friends Historical Library, Swarthmore College. Numerous other examples of newspaper items on the underground railroad are scattered throughout the Siebert Papers.

33. Undated copy of interview with James E. Chambers, editor of *Northern Ohio Journal,* in scrapbook "The Underground Railroad in Ohio, vol. 4,"

Siebert Papers (Ohio Historical Society); Wilbur H. Siebert, *The Underground Railroad from Slavery to Freedom* (New York, 1898), p. 4.

34. H. U. Johnson, *From Dixie to Canada; Romances and Realities of the Underground Railroad* (Orwell, Ohio, 1894), pp. 12-13, 147, 181-182.

35. Edmund Fuller, *A Star Pointed North* (New York, 1946), p. 249 and *passim;* Shirley Graham, *There Was Once a Slave . . . The Heroic Story of Frederick Douglass* (New York, 1947), pp. 85-87.

36. Brion Gysin, *To Master—A Long Goodnight. The Story of Uncle Tom, a Historical Narrative* (New York, 1946), pp. 73-76.

37. Anne Parrish, *A Clouded Star* (New York, 1948), *passim;* Hildegard Hoyt Swift, *The Railroad to Freedom: A Story of the Civil War* (New York, 1932), pp. 94, 211-212.

38. Anna L. Curtis, *Stories of the Underground Railroad* (New York, 1941), p. 7 and *passim.*

39. Hermann von Holst, *Constitutional and Political History of the United States* (8 vols.; Chicago, 1881-1892), III, 552; James Ford Rhodes, *History of the United States from the Compromise of 1850* (5 vols.; New York, 1900-1909), II, 76-77; Allan Nevins, *Ordeal of the Union* (2 vols., New York, 1947), I, 384n.

40. Edward Channing, *A History of the United States* (6 vols.; New York, 1925), VI, 103-104.

41. Siebert's voluminous writings include: *The Underground Railroad from Slavery to Freedom* (New York, 1898); *The Mysteries of Ohio's Underground Railroad* (Columbus, 1951); "Light on the Underground Railroad," *American Historical Review,* I (April, 1896), 455-463; "The Underground Railroad in Massachusetts," American Antiquarian Society *Proceedings,* n.s. XLV (April, 1935), 25-100; "The Underground Railroad in Ohio," *Ohio Archeological and Historical Publications,* IV (1895), 44-63, and *Vermont's Anti-Slavery and Underground Railroad Record* (Columbus, 1937).

42. "Inquiry concerning the 'Underground Railroad' " to postmaster at Lawn Ridge, Illinois, April 13, 1896, in scrapbook "The Underground Railroad in Illinois, vol. 3," Siebert Papers (Houghton Library).

43. Siebert, *The Underground Railroad,* pp. 11-12.

44. Wilbur H. Siebert, "The Underground Railroad in Michigan," *Detroit Historical Monthly,* I (March, 1923), 10.

45. Siebert, *The Underground Railroad,* pp. 346, 351.

46. Channing, *History of the United States,* VI, 116; clippings of reviews of Siebert, *The Underground Railroad,* in *Tribune* (New York), August 5, 1899, *Book News,* February, 1899, *New York Times,* January 21, 1899, in scrapbook "Publication of *The Underground Railroad,*" Siebert Papers (Houghton Library).

47. Pettit, *Sketches,* pp. 72-73; Russel B. Nye, *Fettered Freedom: Civil Liberties and the Slavery Controversy, 1830-1860* (East Lansing, Mich., 1949), p. 213.

48. Sloane, "The Underground Railroad of the Firelands," p. 28.

THE SABLE ARM

". . . Even the Slave Becomes

a Man . . ."

Dudley Cornish

"Gentlemen, the question is settled; negroes will fight."

This is the verdict pronounced by Major General George H. Thomas as he rode over the battlefield of Nashville in December, 1864, and observed "the bodies of colored men side by side with the foremost on the very works of the enemy." [1] Thomas was neither the first nor the last Union commander to reach that verdict.

Rufus Saxton had expressed the same opinion back in 1862. The behavior of Negro troops at Port Hudson, Milliken's Bend, Honey Springs, and Fort Wagner in mid-1863 had proved its validity. But throughout the war, whenever Negro soldiers fought, they had to prove it all over again. As late as April 13, 1865, four days after Lee had surrendered to Grant at Appomattox, Colonel Charles A. Gilchrist, commanding the 50th U.S. Colored Infantry, thought it necessary to conclude his report of the conduct of his troops in the siege and assault on Fort Blakely, guarding Mobile, with this statement: "The conduct of none could be criticized to their discredit, and the behavior of the men when constructing trenches under fire, than which there could scarcely be a more trying position, was a convincing proof that the former slaves of the South cannot be excelled as soldiers." Colonel A. Watson Webber, com-

Dudley Cornish, *The Sable Arm: Negro Troops in the Union Army, 1861-1865* (New York, Longmans, Green, 1956), Chap. xiii.

manding the 51st U.S. Colored in the same operations, concluded his report in almost the same language: "There can be no doubt now, in the minds of their officers at least, but that our colored soldiers are brave and will fight." [2]

It is hard to realize, ninety years after the Civil War, how revolutionary the experiment of permitting Negroes to bear arms was considered, how fraught with imagined dangers to the Union cause, how galling to white pride, how difficult of popular acceptance. And yet today, ninety years after Appomattox, the same questions are still asked when Negro soldiers are mentioned: How did they behave? Did they fight or did they run? Did they dare to face their former masters? Did they require white soldiers with them to sustain their courage—and perhaps to keep them from running? Now, as then, the Negro soldier is a stereotype in the public mind, and the actual performance of actual Negro soldiers, which shows the stereotype for what it really is, is still slow to be accepted. Only through steady repetition of steady soldierly conduct could the Negro soldier break the stereotype. Even with integration officially a fact in the armed forces of the United States, the stereotype lingers, and now as then Negro soldiers, airmen, seamen, and marines, officers and men alike, have always to prove themselves over and over again.

Daniel Ullmann was no social scientist, and yet some of his observations on Negro troops and popular conceptions regarding them are worth noting. The common error in judging them, Ullmann thought, was "to look at them as a unit, as a whole, as being all alike—the inferior specimens are selected as examples of all—" and he asked a searching question: "How would the white races stand such a test?"

Of the quality of colored troops Ullmann had this to say: "Now, I have commanded colored regiments, as good troops as need be, and I have commanded some indifferent, and some very inferior. In their abnormal state, they require good officers more than other soldiers. I have seen colored regiments—weak, disorganized, inefficient—which stripped of their miserable officers, and placed in the hands of men who both knew their duty and discharged it, were raised speedily to a high degree of discipline and effectiveness." Few readers with any military experience will disagree that Ullmann could have been speaking of white troops as well. "The privates of the Colored Troops," he continued, "were pretty uniformly reported to me to be sober, docile, subordinate, obedient, attentive, and as soldiers, enthusiastic. As sentinels, and on general picket duty, they have no superiors. On a march, it was generally necessary to check them. Their powers of endurance none will question. As to their fighting qualities, it is surprising that doubts were so extensively entertained. . . ." [3] Extensively, stubbornly, exasperatingly, and it almost seems, eternally.

Despite their painfully accumulated battle record, there was widespread lack of agreement on the ability of the Negro soldiers throughout and after the Civil War. Although the problem had ceased to exist as far as the promulgation of national policy was concerned, the complex details of the problem continued to plague president, War Department, and Negro soldiers themselves. The insistent and persisting questions of the proper employment of Negro troops—as garrison soldiers, labor battalions, prison guards, infantry and cavalry in the field; of their pay; of their recruitment in the sensitive Border states; of their impressment into service, of their treatment when captured, of their ability to re-form and return to the fight after having once been driven back; of their self-control in the heat of battle—these and others of less importance continued to be asked even after the answers were obvious. The Nashville *Daily Union* came close to the heart of the matter when it asserted on August 1, 1863, that "Copperhead officers would have called [the 54th Massachusetts] cowardly if they had stormed and carried the gates of hell. . . ." There were persons in the United States who simply refused to believe that Negroes could and would make good soldiers, for whom the evidence was never sufficient, the testimony of commanding generals never convincing. Their descendants have stubbornly survived to this day.

From the beginning of 1864 on through the rest of the war Negro soldiers were permitted to do soldiers' work. They had given definite indications during 1863 of what could be expected of them. If doubt still remained in some minds—as it did—their combat performance during 1864 and 1865 should have removed a great deal of it.

The increasing contribution of colored troops to actual fighting is clearly shown in the number of engagements in which they participated in the different years of the war. The *Official Army Register* in 1867 listed the total of "battles" in which colored troops took part as 250: 1 in 1862, 28 in 1863, 170 in 1864, and 51 in 1865.[4] This is patently an incomplete list: for example, it shows only one engagement for 1862, the minor engagement of Island Mound, Missouri, in which the 1st Kansas Colored made its debut as a fighting organization.[5] The Official Records, however, contain reports of a number of other engagements in the fall of 1862 in which Negroes fought: two expeditions by portions of the 1st South Carolina Colored and several operations in which Butler's Louisiana regiments took part. There are omissions in the listings for the other years also. The expeditions against Fort Fisher near Wilmington, North Carolina, in December, 1864, and January, 1865, are the most obvious of these omissions.

The *Army Register* list of "battles" deserves further criticism because it makes no differentiation between minor skirmishes, brushes with Confederate pickets, affairs, and major battles, sieges, and campaigns. The operations around Petersburg, lasting from May, 1864, through April of the next year, are disposed of in this list as one "battle" and, aside from the number of colored regiments involved, there is no indication that this "battle" was of any greater significance than the skirmish at Magnolia, Tennessee, on January 7, 1865, in which the 15th U. S. Colored suffered no casualties at all.[6] One explanation of these errors is that when the *Register* was published in 1867 reports and records were still being collected and many were probably not available to the War Department compilers.

Frederick Dyer's well-known *Compendium*, published in 1908, drew on the relatively complete records published between 1880 and 1901 in the *Official Records*. Dyer listed 449 engagements in which colored troops fought, 200 more than the *Register*.[7] Of these, Dyer rated 39 as major engagements. He also took the trouble to differentiate between battles, campaigns, brushes, and affairs, so that his list is more meaningful and of greater value to any analysis of the combat contribution of the Negro.

For all its obvious faults, the *Army Register* list still has value. It shows clearly, if inaccurately, how the military employment of colored troops increased steadily from an extremely small number of engagements in the first year of their organization to a substantial number in 1863, and to wide use as combat troops in 1864. In 1862 the organization of Negro regiments was merely beginning. The idea was new, tentative, extremely unpopular. Accordingly, Negro soldiers were given few opportunities to show their fighting ability. In 1863 they were still on an experimental basis; they were still expected to make their contribution to the war by providing a labor force for the armies, by garrisoning forts, by relieving white troops for combat. Circumstances forced the issue: colored regiments in a few scattered actions demonstrated that as combat troops Negroes could perform with courage and skill and determination. After serving their apprenticeship in 1863, it was logical and natural that Negro soldiers should have found themselves more and more in action in 1864.

They continued to serve as garrison troops, of course, with and without the company of white soldiers. With the freeing of the Mississippi in 1863, the main theater of war shifted toward the east and the battle of behemoths in Virginia, but Union garrisons from Columbus, Kentucky, to Forts Jackson and St. Philip downstream from New Orleans, continued to be necessary, and Negro troops made up the bulk of them. General E. R. S. Canby's statement of "troops left in garrison on the Mississippi" in March, 1865, showed a total effective strength of 27,876 Union soldiers. Of this total, 18,299—65 per cent—were colored soldiers of 27 different regiments.[8] But this was by no means the end of their participation in the closing rounds of the war.

Instead, Negro soldiers won an enviable reputation by their stubborn fighting with the Army of the Frontier under Blunt and Schofield and Steele. They fought repeatedly against Forrest in Tennessee and Mississippi. They aided materially in the defeat and demolition of Hood's army at Nashville. Nine Negro regiments were in on the difficult assignment of reducing Fort Blakely in the final assault on Mobile, and victory rode their bayonets. Other Negro regiments fought in Florida, South Carolina, Georgia, and North Carolina, but by far the greatest number in any single theater of war were involved in the slow, bloody work of wearing down the Army of Northern Virginia from May, 1864, through April, 1865.

Mere numbers of colored troops engaged in Virginia in the last twelve months of war are impressive. Thirteen Negro regiments fought at Chaffin's Farm at the end of September, and of a total of thirty-seven Congressional Medals of Honor awarded to participants in that two-day struggle, fourteen went to members of colored organizations.[9] Four of those same regiments fought again at Darbytown Road on October 13, six at Fair Oaks, five at Hatcher's Run, and five at Deep Bottom toward the end of the month. Twenty-two regiments were at one time or another engaged in the terrible and costly fighting before Petersburg in 1864 and 1865. Fifteen regiments served in the XVIII Corps of Butler's Army of the James; eight served in the IX Corps of the Army of the Potomac, fifteen in the X Corps. Finally, in December of 1864, the XXV Corps was organized under General Godfrey Weitzel. Unique in American military history, it was an entire army corps made up of Negro regiments, thirty-two in all. When the Confederacy had been defeated and the war was over, more than thirty Negro regiments (substantially the whole XXV Corps) were transferred to the Department of Texas for duty along the Rio Grande, to give force to State Department protests against French interference and the puppet empire of Maximilian in Mexico.[10] In the closing years of the war, and particularly during the last twelve months of conflict, the American Negro soldier proved himself worthy of the uniform he wore and the flag he defended.

Charles Francis Adams, Jr., wrote of the Union fiasco of the Petersburg mine on July 30, 1864: "All who dislike black troops shoulder the blame onto them—not that I can find with any show of cause. They seem to have behaved just as well and as badly as the rest and to have suffered more severely." [11] Adams' observation has value not for Petersburg and the battle of the crater alone but for the performance of Negro soldiers generally. If their battle record in the Civil War proves anything, it is that Negro soldiers measured up to the standard set for American soldiers generally. It is obviously impossible to discuss every engagement in which colored troops fought and to analyze their varying behavior in action. Certainly, however, examination of some of their engagements, major and minor, ought to be of value in discovering what they did and how they did it.

In the battle of Olustee, or Ocean Pond, fifty miles west of Jacksonville, Florida, on February 20, 1864, three Negro and six white regiments (plus smaller artillery and cavalry units) were defeated by Confederate troops after a stubborn fight. Colonel Joseph R. Hawley, commanding a brigade consisting of the 7th Connecticut, 7th New Hampshire, and 8th U.S. Colored Troops, wrote afterward: ". . . Colonel Fribley's black men met the enemy at short range. They had reported to me only two or three days before; I was afterward told that they had never had a day's practice in loading and firing. Old troops, finding themselves so greatly over-matched, would have run a little and re-formed—with or without orders." The 8th U. S. Colored was a new regiment; its men had never been in action before. They "stood to be killed or wounded—losing more than three hundred out of five hundred and fifty." [12] Of the eight infantry regiments involved at Olustee, Fribley's command suffered the highest number of men killed on the field, forty-eight. The regiment was second only to the hard-hit 47th New York Volunteers in total casualties: 310 killed, wounded, or missing in the 8th; 313 in the 47th New York. Total Union casualties at Olustee were 1,861. [13]

The 35th U. S. Colored and the 54th Massachusetts were at Olustee, too, brigaded together under Colonel James Montgomery. While the 35th (the 1st North Carolina Colored Volunteers) lost heavily in action—230 killed, wounded, or missing—the 54th seems at first glance to have come off with relatively light casualties: only eighty-six. One of the 54th's officers described the regiment's part in the action in a letter to a Boston friend. His letter, written three days after the fight and published in the Chicago *Tribune* on March 9, 1864, came directly to the point: "We have had a fight, a licking, and a foot-race," the Massachusetts officer wrote. "We marched 110 miles in 108 hours, and in that time had a three hour's fight. Our regiment lost one man in every five

—going in five hundred strong, and losing one hundred in killed, wounded, and missing. . . . When we returned to Jacksonville we were all crippled from severe marching." The letter rather emphasized the role of the 54th in the battle. "Before going into battle [we] were double-quicked for a mile, and as [we] went in Gen. Seymour said to Colonel Hallowell, 'the day is lost; you must go in and save the corps.' We did go in and did save it, checked the enemy, held the field, and were the last to leave—and covered the retreat."

Colonel Hallowell's report was in general agreement with this officer's letter, although he maintained that the regiment had double-quicked two miles to get into action. He listed the 54th's losses as eighty-seven: thirteen killed, sixty-six wounded, eight missing. He cited Sergeant Stephen A. Swails for "coolness, bravery, and efficiency during the action" despite a severe wound; the sergeant later became the first Negro commissioned in the 54th.[14]

Brigadier General Thomas Seymour, in command of the Union forces, had the difficult task of explaining his defeat. He reported: "The colored troops behaved creditably—the Fifty-fourth Massachusetts and First North Carolina like veterans. It was not in their conduct that can be found the chief cause of failure, but in the unanticipated yielding of a white regiment from which there was every reason to expect noble service, and at a moment when everything depended on its firmness." Seymour was referring to the 7th New Hampshire, Colonel Hawley's brigade, which in the early maneuvering of the action failed to carry out Hawley's orders with the result that "All semblance of organization was lost in a few moments, save with about one company. . . ." This regiment lost 208 in killed, wounded, or missing; the extent of its disorganization is suggested by the fact that it had the highest number of missing of any regiment engaged, 120 men. General Seymour suggested that its "misfortune arose, doubtless, from [its] having lately been filled with conscripts and substitutes, of a very inferior class."[15]

Lieutenant M. B. Grant, a Confederate engineer, had a curious observation in his report of the engagement: "As usual with the enemy, they posted their Negro regiments on their left and in front, where they were slain by hundreds, and upon retiring left their dead and wounded Negroes uncared for, carrying off only their whites, which accounts for the fact that upon the first part of the battlefield nearly all the dead found were Negroes." That this is at least slightly exaggerated is indicated by the federal casualty lists: total Negro soldiers killed, 81; wounded, 365; missing, 157; total Negro casualties, 503.[16] Whatever the truth of the matter, the Negro troops themselves seem to have fought with valor if not with discretion.

The stubborn tenacity of Negro soldiers, motivated in part by their awareness that as prisoners they had no rights which the Confederates were bound to respect, made them of considerable value as holding forces and as rear guards in withdrawals under superior enemy pressure. Lieutenant John Merrilies, serving with a battery of Illinois light artillery in the disastrous rout of the Sturgis expedition from Brice's Cross Roads on June 10, 1864, recorded the part of the colored troops in preventing Forrest's men from making the disaster more complete than it was. "The Cavalry . . . were formed in line on one flank," Merrilies wrote in his diary after he had reached a place safe enough for literary work, "and the Colored Brigade on the other, checking the onward rush of the enemy till the artillery had passed and then covering the rear of that and the ammunition train." As the Union forces retreated in vast disorder, more Negro soldiers won the admiration of the Illinois lieutenant. "The 59th U.S.C.," he wrote on June 13, "was also detailed [with some cavalry] to cover the rear and altho the first fighting they have seen, they behaved, under very trying circumstances, with a coolness and confidence worthy of old troops." Merrilies was particularly astonished at their indifference to wounds. He had seen "numbers shot in the arms, hands, legs, their clothing soaked with blood, marching along with the rest, without a sign of pain." [17]

While Sturgis and his troops fell back in confusion upon their Memphis base, other Union troops under Grant were moving forward in Northern Virginia. Among them were Negro regiments, finally permitted to play the soldier's role they had long desired. The "Record of Events" sections of muster rolls kept by company commanders in these regiments are a fruitful source of information on the activities of some of these Negro troops. The narrative of the operations of Company A, 30th U.S. Colored, covering the period from April 30 to June 30, 1864, shows the work of that unit in great detail. "The Company has been on the march since May 4th," Captain Charles N. Swift wrote on June 30. "Starting from Manassas Junction . . . and arriving at Petersburg . . . or near there, June 28th, 1864, passing through Catlett's and Bristow Station, Warrenton Junction, Rappahannock, Rapidan, Matapony, Pamunky, Chickahominy, and James Rivers. . . ." It was not all marching, either. "The Company being on picket at Old Church . . . June 10th . . . commanded by Lieutenant Bowen, were attacked by a body of Rebel cavalry (who had dispersed a Battalion of the 18th Pennsylvania cavalry). The men held their ground and drove the enemy away from their works." Proudly Captain Swift recorded these lines: "They received the praise of Gen'l Ferrero commanding 4th Division 9th A[rmy]. C[orps]. No loss sustained by the company—the enemy carried away several wounded." At the end of the two-month report period, the company had been "under fire before Petersburg three days and four nights, no loss." Although experts on the geography of Virginia may dispute Captain Swift, he must have penned the last line of the report with solid conviction: "The distance marched by the company is nearly four hundred miles." [18]

What happens to a company of infantry that has marched "nearly four hundred miles," much of it in the presence of the enemy? A comparison of the muster roll of Company A for the period February 29 to April 30 with the roll for May and June shows that this unit underwent a transformation similar to that of most combat outfits. The muster rolls show these remarks by the mustering officer, Colonel Delevan Bates, the regimental commander:

	April 30	June 30
Discipline:	good	good
Instruction:	progressive	progressive
Military appearance:	very good	fair
Arms:	very good	very good
Accoutrements:	good	very good
Clothing:	good	poor

While their appearance had slipped from "very good" to "fair" and their clothing had been worn from "good" to "poor," their arms had been maintained in very good condition, and they had learned in two months of campaigning to look after their equipment and keep it in top condition ready for instant use. In short, Company A no longer presented a crisp parade-ground appearance, but it had become a company of "poor, bloody infantry," seasoned by continued campaign and contact with the enemy. They needed all the seasoning they could get.

The muster rolls of Company E, 30th U.S. Colored, for the last eight months of 1864, throw much light on the kind of work these troops performed before Petersburg. The report for May and June is brief: "This regiment started from Manassas Junction, May 4. . . . We were rear guard until we reached the James River, June 17th. Ordered to the front. Went to rifle pits the morning of the 21st, came out the morning of the 25th." In view of the deadly action in which the 30th fought in the crater before Petersburg on July 30, the report for July and August is disappointingly brief and may reflect the grim humor of the infantry. "Since last muster," the company commander wrote, "have not had much marching to do. Have been in front of Petersburg the most of the time. Have built forts, thrown up breastworks, chopped timber, &c.,&c. We have been on the front line at different times and for shorter or longer periods. The Company was in the charge on the 30th of July, in which we were repulsed for some reason."

While it is not unusual for infantry to spend most of their time digging-in a position only to leave it almost at once and begin to dig-in another position, the Company K was almost invariably ordered to move a few days after making its position safe and substantial. "From 1st September till 8th remained in camp near Curley House," the "Record of Events" section began, but it was only the calm before the storm. "The night of the 4th, received orders at 11 P.M. to build breast work in our front, worked that night and the next two days. The 8th moved a mile to the left and went into camp. Worked on forts and felling timber for several days. The night of the 25th ordered to move and went on line to left of Fort Warren. While there reconnoitered the enemy's line several times." But there was no rest for the infantry.

"About the 1st October," the Company K saga continued, "moved farther to left near the 'Yellow House.' Finally the 7th October were ordered on the newly acquired line west of the Weldon RR. and near the 'Peebles House.' We immediately commenced building breastworks, Forts, and felling timber. We were busy perfecting our line for two weeks. On the 26th were ordered to provide six days rations and sixty rounds cartridges, and be ready to move at 2 P.M. the 27th. Did not start til 6." Despite this unpromising, if typical, beginning, the expedition turned out to be more than the usual digging and felling timber. "Went west about two miles and half, where formed line, advanced, striking the enemy's line very suddenly, ascertaining their position and strength. While doing this, we had one officer mortally wounded and twenty men more or less seriously. We fell back 20 rods in the woods and threw up a temporary line which we held till next morning, when we fell back." [19] Nothing very glorious, just the usual hard, dangerous work of infantry in the Army of the Potomac.

Negro troops fighting before Petersburg had their moments, however. The Leavenworth *Daily Conservative* reported on June 21, 1864, from Virginia: "The hardest fighting has been done by the black troops. The forts they stormed were the worst of all. After the affair was over General [William F.] Smith [commanding the XVIII Corps] went and thanked them; told them he was proud of them, their courage and dash. He says they can't be excelled as soldiers and hereafter he will send them to a difficult place as readily as the best white troops." Smith praised their conduct in his report of the action, and in a proclamation of appreciation he called them to the attention of the entire corps. "They have stormed the works of the enemy and carried them," the proclamation concluded, "taking guns and prisoners, and in the whole affair they have displayed all the qualities of good soldiers." [20] With that sort of recommendation, Negro soldiers were bound to get soldiers' work. In mid-summer a division of them were sent to a "difficult place" —into the crater blown in the Confederate lines early in the morning of July 30.

The original plan for this well-conceived but disastrously executed assault was to have Brigadier General Edward Ferrero's 4th Division of the IX Corps jump off immediately after the huge mine had been blown. Ferrero had two colored brigades: the first, commanded by Colonel Joshua K. Sigfried, included the 27th, 30th, 39th, and 43rd U.S. Colored Troops; Colonel Henry G. Thomas commanded the second, which included the 19th, 23rd, 28th (one battalion of six companies), 29th, and 31st regiments. The division numbered about 4,300 men, 2,000 in Sigfried's brigade, 2,300 in Thomas's. "We were all pleased with the compliment of being chosen to lead the assault," Colonel Thomas recalled afterward. "Both officers and men were eager to show the white troops what the colored divsion could do."

The men had reacted curiously to the news that they would lead. As Colonel Thomas put it, "the news filled them too full for ordinary utterance." They sat silent in little circles in their company streets until a single deep voice began to sing, rather tentatively at first and then over and over with hardening conviction: "We-e looks li-ike me-en a-a-marchin' on, we looks li-ike men-er-war." Then the singer's circle took up the shout and it rapidly spread through the encampment until "a thousand voices were upraised." It must have been a magnificent, barbaric spectacle: the "dark men, with their white eyes and teeth and full red lips crouching over a smouldering campfire, in dusky shadow, with only the feeble rays of the lanterns of the first sergeants and the lights of the candles dimly showing through the tents." And the voices of a thousand Negro soldiers, making their own harmony, lifting the words up into the night sky like some great shapeless battle flag: "We looks like men a-marching on, we looks like men-er-war." "Until we fought the battle of the crater," Colonel Thomas remembered, "they sang this every night to the exclusion of all other songs." [21]

"It is an axiom in military art," Thomas wrote twenty years later, "that there are times when the ardor, hopefulness, and enthusiasm of new troops not yet rendered doubtful by reverses or chilled by defeat, more than compensate, in a dash, for training and experience. General Burnside, for this and other reasons, most strenuously urged his black division for the advance." The officers and men of the division were prepared: they drilled and rehearsed "certain movements to be executed in gaining and occupying the crest" of the enemy's lines. They were ready. But Burnside was overruled, and late in the afternoon of July 29, about twelve hours before the mine was to be detonated, the orders were changed. The golden moment was lost.

It was Ulysses S. Grant who ordered the change. Grant had sound reasons for disrupting the plans, as his testimony before the investigating Committee on the Conduct of the War shows. "General Burnside wanted to put his colored division in front," Grant stated, "and I believe if he had done so it would have been a success. Still," he admitted, "I agreed with General Meade in his objection to that plan. General Meade said that if we put the colored troops in front, (we had only that one division) and if it should prove a failure, it would then be said, and very properly, that we were shoving those people ahead to get killed because we did not care anything about them. But that could not be said if we put white troops in front." [22]

Call it a wrong decision based on right premises. It was a hard decision to make, but it was made. The next thing to be done was to select the white troops to put in front. No one seems to have considered postponing the action until a white division could be prepared for the assault. The three generals commanding the white divisions making up the bulk of the IX Corps drew straws. General James H. Ledlie, commanding the battle-weary and understrength 1st Division, drew the short straw. Time permitted only a brief reconnaissance of the position, and that after dark on the night of the twenty-ninth. Ledlie alerted his division and formed them just behind the Union battle lines at about midnight.

After all three white divisions had been committed, Ferrero's men were ordered into action around six o'clock on the morning of the thirtieth, about two hours after the mine had been "sprung." The white troops, worn down by fairly constant campaigning in the weeks just preceding the assault and unprepared by any special training or even instructions for the task before them, had not moved promptly to the attack with the explosion of the mine. Once in, they had milled about in confusion in the huge crater. The supreme error seems to have been made in delaying the first infantry attack for about half an hour after the explosion, long enough at any rate for the Confederates to recover somewhat from shock and surprise and to bring forces to bear on the breach in their lines.

The Negro brigades went in finally at about seven-thirty in the morning. The press of returning white troops in the covered ways, the only paths for forward movement, held them back, and the painful flood of wounded probably did their morale no good. But, once in, the

Negroes forced their way through the troops in the crater and went some two hundred yards beyond, recovering some captured battle flags and taking prisoners. This success was only temporary. Many of their officers were shot down; "the men were largely without leaders, and their organization was destroyed." A second assault was somehow mounted when Thomas' brigade went in, but this too came reeling back in disorder as more officers went down. Colonel Sigfried, commanding the first brigade, maintained afterward that "Had it not been for the almost impassable crowd of troops of the other divisions in the crater and entrenchments, the hill would have been ours." The 4th Division suffered the heaviest casualties: 1,327, as compared with 654 in the 1st, 832 in the 2nd, and 659 in the 3rd. The total killed in the colored brigades was 195, as compared with 227 killed in the three white divisions combined. Officer casualties were extremely heavy, too: the IX Corps lost 50 officers killed, of whom 14 were in the 4th Division; 124 were wounded, of whom 41 were with the colored troops; and 79 were missing, 20 from the 4th Division.[23]

George L. Kilmer, an officer of the 14th New York Heavy Artillery, 2nd Brigade, Ledlie's 1st Division, went into the crater with the first wave and reported afterward that "The last rally was when the colored division moved out from our works in splendid order, which promised us success. Growlers were now put to shame, and the most of the men fell into line, to go forward. Some few declared that they would never follow 'niggers' or be caught in their company and started back to our own lines but were promptly driven forward again." When the colored assault halted, broke, and streamed back, Kilmer recalled, "pandemonium began. The bravest lost heart, and the men who distrusted the Negroes vented their feeling freely. Some colored men came into the crater, and there they found a worse fate than death in the charge." Long after the war Kilmer recalled the horror of the scene. "It has been positively asserted," he wrote, "that white men bayoneted blacks who fell back into the crater. This was in order to preserve the whites from Confederate vengeance. Men boasted in my presence that blacks had thus been disposed of, particularly when the Confederates came up." [24]

Newspaper comment on the Petersburg fiasco was divided along political lines. The Leavenworth *Conservative* of August 3, 1864, gave credit to the colored troops for bravery in the face of furious Confederate fire. The *Putnam County Courier,* a stridently Democratic weekly published at Carmel, New York, declared on August 6: "Nothing in the details of the battle yet received tends to extenuate the conduct of the Negro troops, or to relieve the officers having immediate direction of the operation, from the accusation of blundering." The *Courier* cited the New York *Tribune's* own account of the assault to prove that the Negroes had fallen back "in confusion through our lines, repulsed and demoralized."

The seventeen-day court of inquiry found that there had been some blundering and cited Generals Burnside, Ledlie, and Ferrero, Colonel Z. R. Bliss, commanding the 1st Brigade, 2nd Division, and General O. B. Wilcox, comamnding the 2nd Division, for particular failures. Ledlie and Ferrero were especially criticized for having retired to a bombproof shelter behind the Union lines to get "stimulants" from Surgeon H. E. Smith while their divisions were engaged in the crater.

The court asked rather pointed questions on the behavior of the colored division. Burnside's testimony seems frank and fair. "It is a fact," he admitted, "that the black troops broke and ran to the rear in considerable of a panic, which indicates misbehavior; but they went in late, found in the enemy's works quite a mass of our own troops unable to advance, and during their formation, and in fact during their advance between the two lines, they were subjected to probably the hottest fire that any troops had been subjected to during the day; and I do not know that it is reasonable to suppose that after the loss of so great a portion of their officers they could have been expected to maintain their position. They certainly moved forward as gallantly under the first fire and until their ranks were broken as any troops I ever saw in action." [25]

Colonel Thomas was as frank in his testimony. "They went up as well as I ever saw troops go up," he said of his colored soldiers, "—well closed, perfectly enthusiastic. They came back very badly. They came back on the run, every man for himself." That was not quite all the story. "It is but justice to the line officers," Thomas continued, "to say that more than two-thirds of them were shot, and to the colored troops that the white troops were running back just ahead of them." General J. F. Hartranft, commanding the 1st Brigade, 3rd Division, offered some explanation of what happened to the Negro soldiers. "They passed to the front just as well as any troops," he asserted, "but they were certainly not in very good condition to resist an attack, because in passing through the crater they got confused; their regimental and company organization was completely gone."

Colonel Thomas' report of the action, written three days after the battle, reflected frustration and bewilderment: "Whether we fought well or not, the scores of our dead lying as if mowed down by the hand of some mighty reaper and the terrible loss of the officers can best attest." How his men felt about their day's work cannot be stated accurately. But Thomas noted that they never sang their marching song again.[26]

Captain James A. Rickard, who was with Thomas' own regiment, the 19th U. S. Colored Troops, argued that their crater performance improved the status of Negro soldiers. "The charge of Ferrero's division . . . through a broken and demoralized division of white troops, then forming line inside the enemy's works, and temporary capture of their interior works, with awful losses in killed, wounded and murdered, is a record," Rickard insisted, "to win back the previously prejudiced judgment of the president, cabinet, generals, and officers of the Army of the Potomac, who up to this time had thought Negroes all right for service in menial capacity, but from henceforth to take responsible places, like the right flank of the army at Deep Bottom, Va., and the storming of strong works like Forts Alexander and Gregg." [27] Rickard was not merely exercising his own obvious prejudice in favor of colored troops. The facts of combat in the remaining months of 1864 bear out his assertions. He might have added New Market Heights and Fort Gilmer while he was about it.

In the actions around Deep Bottom, August 13 through 20, Brigadier General William Birney's colored brigade of Major General David Birney's X Corps did soldiers' work. There, four regiments of colored troops fought; their casualties were relatively light as compared to those of the white brigades participating. But David Birney, the corps commander, reported that they had "behaved handsomely" and were "in fine spirits." "In front of one colored regiment," he wrote with evident satisfaction, "eighty-two dead bodies of the enemy were counted." [28]

The battle of the crater convinced Benjamin F. Butler, but not in the way suggested by Captain Rickard. Butler, commanding the Army of the James, saw the Petersburg action as further evidence that "in the Army of the Potomac Negro troops were thought of no value. . . ." With the qualified exception of Smith's good use of Hinks' colored division in the assaults of June 15, Butler felt that "Negro troops had had no chance to show their valor or staying qualities of action." His fertile mind grappled with the problem and devised a plan of action. "I want to convince myself," he told Grant in discussing this plan, "whether, under my own eye, the Negro troops will fight; and if I can take with the Negroes, a redoubt that turned [Winfield Scott] Hancock's corps on a former occasion, that will settle the question." The redoubt was the strong Confederate position at New Market Heights. On the night of September 28 the Army of the James, consisting of Birney's X Corps and Ord's XVIII Corps, moved to assault positions. [29]

Brigadier General Charles J. Paine's report of the actions of his 3rd Division of Ord's Corps told the story:

September 29.—The entire division, with the exception of the Tenth U. S. Colored Troops, moved from Deep Bottom, and was successfully engaged in the assault on the enemy's works, losing heavily in officers and men.

Birney's report for his colored brigade was only slightly more detailed:

September 28.—Moved across the Appomattox and James Rivers to Deep Bottom, Va.

September 29.—Moved out from Deep Bottom. In the afternoon participated in an assault on Fort Gilmer, a rebel earthwork near Chaffin's farm, which was unsuccessful.

September 30.—Took part in engagement at Fort Harrison, Chaffin's farm, in which the enemy were repulsed, with loss. The loss of the brigade in these two engagements amounted to 434 officers and men.[30]

The casualty reports were more extensive. The X Corps suffered a total of 963 killed, wounded, or missing. The 1st and 2nd divisions lost 433, while Birney's colored brigade of five regiments lost 430. The 7th U.S. Colored was the hardest hit: 20 killed, 76 wounded, and 129 captured or missing, a total of 235 casualties. Ord's XVIII Corps came through with 2,328 casualties, with General Paine's Negro 3rd Division suffering 1,302 of that total. The 5th U.S. Colored even exceeded the terrible losses of the 7th, with 28 killed, 185 wounded, and 23 captured or missing, a total of 236.[31]

What had happened in this two-day engagement or series of engagements, called Chaffin's Farm in the records, was more than the sum of the enormous Union casualties. Butler had his proof.

Under his personal command, the Negro division of the XVIII Corps, nine infantry (and one dismounted cavalry) regiments, stormed the works of New Market Heights in the early dawn of September 29. With the caps removed from the nipples of their guns so that there could be no confused or confusing firing during the advance, the Negro soldiers moved across a stream, up the slope, through two lines of obstructions, and into the fortifications. The garrison fled before the bayonet assault, and the works were in Union hands—at the cost of one thousand casualties. Butler wrote afterward that, as he rode among the victorious, jubilant colored troops at New Market Heights, he "felt in his inmost heart that the capacity of the Negro race for soldiers had then and there been fully settled forever." [32]

William Birney's brigade did not crown its efforts with the same success. His troops were not sent up New Market Heights but thrown against an even stronger position, Fort Gilmer, an important salient in the Confederate line. It was here that the 7th U.S. Colored suffered its heaviest losses. Four companies under Captain Julius A. Weiss were sent forward, after the 9th Maine had been repulsed at the same point. Confederate fire was fierce from Gilmer; what was even more murderous was enfilading fire from another fort on the right. Worst of all, immediately before Fort Gilmer was a ditch, seven to ten feet deep, twice as broad, which turned into a death trap. Although the Negro troops attempted to move forward, standing on each other's shoulders to reach the edge of the parapet, rifle fire at point-blank range and hand grenades rolled down among them soon forced their surrender. Of the men in the four companies, all but three were killed, wounded, or captured.[33]

For the rest of 1864, Negro regiments in the Army of the Potomac and in the Army of the James found full employment. With the first division of the X Corps, Birney's division of five colored regiments fought on the Darbytown Road on October 13, suffering eighty-one casualties. These were disproportionately light, since Birney's men were engaged only as skirmishers; the ten white regiments of the 1st Division were more heavily engaged and had a total of 315 casualties. The entire X Corps was fully engaged in the actions of Fair Oaks and Darbytown Road on October 27-28, and there the six regiments of the 3rd Division suffered 117 casualties, while the 24 white regiments making up the 1st and 2nd divisions lost, among them, 409. Here the Negro troops seem to have borne a fairly equal share of the battle burden and cost. In the same actions, the XVIII Corps also was heavily engaged, but the 3rd Division of six Negro regiments suffered only 196 casualties, as compared with 850 in the 19 white regiments making up the 1st and 2nd divisions. Ferrero's 3rd Division of the IX Corps, veterans of the battle of the crater, were in action on October 27-28 at Boydton Plank Road, or Hatcher's Run, and the Negroes seem to have borne more than a fair share of the cost. Ferrero's nine regiments lost eighty men altogether, while the other two divisions only seventy between them.[34]

On December 3, 1864, the XXV Army Corps was organized by War Department order from the colored troops of the Department of Virginia and North Carolina under Major General Godfrey Weitzel. This corps, the only all-Negro army corps in American military history, had varied duty during its short career. Large elements of it accompanied Weitzel and Butler on the amphibious expedition against Fort Fisher, guarding the approaches to Wilmington, North Carolina. The bulk of the corps "performed the usual fatigue, picket duty, &c." as 1864 ended, holding sections of the Union lines before Richmond.[35]

As the wheel of the year turned inexorably toward spring, it seemed that Negro troops had arrived. General Grant seemed to be impressed with their performance; as William Birney pointed out after the war, he showed his appreciation by "enlarging the line entrusted to us and ordering us out for review eight different times, for the inspection of General Prim, Secretary Stanton, President Lincoln, and other illustrious visitors." Birney and others were "inspired with hope" and "labored, with unflagging zeal," to get their troops ready "to respond to all demands likely to be made" upon them when the blue hosts should be unleashed in the spring. Their hopes were insecurely founded. "Marching orders for the spring," Birney wrote bitterly afterward, "dispelled our illusions and scattered our hopes. We found our corps broken up, our divisions taken from General Weitzel and placed under strangers; our brigades scattered, our regiments ordered into temporary service with white brigades, our fractured command placed in the rear and on the flank. It was clearly not intended," Birney concluded, "that the colored troops should win any glory in the last events of the war."[36]

Certainly Birney had reasons for his personal bitterness. He had demonstrated on numerous occasions that his Negro brigades and divisions could handle themselves creditably in any kind of action, and the conduct of the final campaign of the war must have been frustrating to his ambitions and hopes. But Negro soldiers were not denied all participation in the closing acts of the drama. The first Union troops to enter Charleston after her fall included the 21st U.S. Colored, closely followed by two companies of the 54th Massachusetts. That was appropriate enough. Even more fitting was the entrance of Union forces into Richmond—with Charles Francis Adams, Jr., leading the 5th Massachusetts Cavalry (colored) in the van. A week later, still "confounded at the good fortune" that had brought him there, Colonel Adams wrote his father of his deep satisfaction: "To have led my regiment into Richmond at the moment of its capture is the one event which I should most have desired as the culmination of my life in the Army."[37]

Adams and his Negro cavalrymen were not alone. Close behind came elements of Godfrey Weitzel's XXV Army Corps, and when the news reached Chicago, the *Tribune* of April 6 could hardly contain its joy. "This war," the lead editorial proclaimed, "has been full of marked coincidence, and that by which the representatives of an enslaved race bore the banner of freedom into the birthplace and also the capital of the Rebellion, is not the least of the historical compensations of the war. We can imagine the sable warriors of Weitzel rolling up the whites of their visual orbs, and exhibiting an untarnished display of nature's dentistry, as they passed the offices of our contemporaries of the press—the Richmond *Sentinel, Examiner, Whig,* and *Dispatch.* Perchance Richmond hears from their own lips, for the first time, the 'wild warbling strains' of 'John Brown's Soul Is Marching On,' or sympathizes opportunely in the sentiment so feelingly expressed by the venerable and aged 'Shady'; 'Good-bye, Massa Jeff, good-bye, Massa Steben!' " To the Chicago *Tribune* there was fine poetic justice in the great occasion. "The survivors of those who fell in the disastrous assault of the 'crater' at Petersburg," it recorded approvingly, "have had the post of honor in the final consummation."

There were other posts of honor.

General Birney may have lamented the shabby treatment of Negro troops in Virginia, but elsewhere other regiments of their kind marched along "like men er war." At Nashville in December and at Mobile in April, Negro soldiers had opportunities denied to Birney and his men. Best of all, they used those opportunities well.

Colonel Thomas Morgan of the 14th U.S. Colored Troops led his men into their first action at Dalton, Georgia, on August 15, 1864. This was the beginning of the regiment's combat history. They performed so satisfactorily at Dalton in helping to rout an attack by Confederate Cavalryman Joe Wheeler that the men of a white regiment "swung their hats and gave three rousing cheers" for Morgan's colored troops as they returned from the engagement. In late September the 14th stood face to face with Forrest's cavalry at Pulaski, Tennessee, and "stopped their progress." After varied duty from Chattanooga to Decatur, Alabama, during which the regiment saw real soldiers' work on several occasions, Morgan moved his command to Nashville in early December.[38]

As John Bell Hood's forces, battered by John Schofield at Franklin, approached Nashville, George H. Thomas assembled all available Union troops and prepared a suitable reception. Hood was desperate for food and supplies; Nashville, with its great Union storehouses, was a tempting prize. But Thomas, already "the Rock of Chickamauga," was about to become "the Sledge of Nashville." He concentrated his forces and organized his defenses so that when the weather changed on December 15, all was in readiness. With steady carefulness that had the North on edge with anxiety (and Grant impatient to the point of sending John A. Logan to replace Thomas), the loyal Virginian prepared the best battle plan of the entire war.

General James B. Steedman was in command of Thomas' left, a motley "provisional detachment" of quartermaster troops and two brigades of colored troops, five regiments under Colonel Morgan, three more under Colonel Charles R. Thompson. The grand strategy was to open with a feint against Hood's right, with Steedman's troops delivering the blow. Once his left was engaged, Thomas would deliver succeeding blows with his main forces swinging wide and hard against Hood's left. It worked to perfection.

Steedman gave Morgan's colored brigade a prominent role, and Morgan commanded the assault. Just as Thomas had planned, Hood mistook Morgan's feint for the main Union attack and drew forces from his left. Thomas sent in his major thrusts, and Hood's weakened left began to crumble. The first day ended with the battle running strongly against the Confederacy. The second day settled the fate of Hood's army. This was also the day of glory and high casualties for the colored brigade under Colonel Thompson. His particular objective was the strong Confederate position on Overton Hill. The plan of battle called for a feint by Thompson's troops while the main attack on the hill was begun on his right. But Thompson's Negroes became excited as they moved forward in their first battle and "what was intended merely as a demonstration was unintentionally converted into an actual assault." The white brigade was repulsed, and Confederate fire was concentrated on Thompson's regiments. They lost 468 casualties. Alarmed for his right, even as he had been on the first day, Hood withdrew Patrick Cleburne's division from his left, and the stage was set for a re-enactment of the Union successes of the first day. Overton Hill was taken in the second assault, and the whole of Hood's line was overrun.[39]

General Steedman, a prominent Breckinridge Democrat before the war, was frank in his appreciation of the role of the Negro regiments. In reporting the casualties of his provisional troops, he pointed out that "The larger portion of these losses, amounting in the aggregate to fully 25 per cent of the men under my command who were taken into action . . . fell upon the colored troops. The severe loss of this part of my troops," he explained, "was in their brilliant charge on the enemy's works on Overton Hill . . . I was unable to discover that color made any difference in the fighting of my troops. All, white and black, nobly did their duty as soldiers, and evinced cheerfulness and resolution such as I have never seen excelled in any campaign of the war in which I have borne a part." [40]

In the last major campaign of the war, Negro troops again "did their duty as soldiers." Nine colored regiments made up the three brigades of General John Hawkins' 1st Division of the "column from Pensacola" as the Union strangle-hold on Mobile tightened. On April 9, 1865, six days after Adams' cavalry and Weitzel's XXV Corps had entered Richmond and a few hours after Grant and Lee had met at Appomattox, the bayonets of Hawkins' division swept through the tangled abatis and over the ramparts of Fort Blackely. Of the seven divisions in the Union forces engaged in the siege and capture of Mobile, Hawkins' Negro division had the lightest division in point of number of regiments. "The prisoners captured," he reported, "amounted to 21 officers and 200 men—a small number, owing to the fact that when we entered, many of the enemy, fearing the conduct of my troops, ran over to where the white troops were entering." [41]

To measure the contribution of the Negro soldier to final Union victory in the Civil War involves more than counting casualties and listing engagements. Actual combat takes a relatively small part of a soldier's time and energy. While some organizations seem to have been kept pretty constantly in forward positions, others, although actively engaged in prosecuting the war, found themselves in less harrowing situations, fighting the boredom that is a constant in the soldier's equation, guarding prisoners, preparing fortifications, escorting wagon trains, standing retreat parade for visiting dignitaries, drilling, working, and "wishing for the war to cease." It was like that with all who fought in the Civil War, white or colored, Union or Confederate. By and large, colored soldiers shared every kind of soldier's duty with their white comrades.

Had Negro soldiers been used uniformly throughout the armies of the Union only as garrison troops, or labor battalions, or assault infantry, the task of assessing their contribution would be less difficult. As it was, their uneven employment in all the variety of duties incident to the conduct of total war—civil war at that—makes the task more involved. In the trans-Mississippi West, colored troops were used as an integral part of the Army of the Frontier, working, foraging, fighting, and dying, side by side with white troops in Kansas, Missouri, Oklahoma, and Arkansas, from 1862 on through the war. In the Mississippi Valley, Negro regiments were used as commanding generals saw fit and as the changing tactical situation demanded. They fought against small bands of guerrillas or Forrest's roving columns; they garrisoned forts from Cairo to the Gulf; they dug-in the parallels approaching the Confederate fortifications surrounding Mobile, and they came out of those parallels with a shout in the last assault wave of the war. They protected contrabands chopping cotton on captured plantations. They worked in the swirling waters of the Red River to build Colonel Joseph

Bailey's dams and save Porter's fleet in the ill-starred Banks expedition of the spring of 1864. At the end of the war, Bailey, then a general commanding a brigade of engineers at Mobile, was careful to mention them by name in his final report. "No troops during this war have labored more severely or arduously," he wrote of his engineers, "but those to whom most credit is due are the Ninety-sixth and Ninety-seventh U.S. Colored Engineer Regiments. Night and day without complaint those regiments worked, and it is difficult to comprehend how they endured through it. The regiments manifest very great care and ability in their organization and discipline. The officers of both, with two exceptions, now out of service, labored assiduously. Of none of them can I do other than speak in the highest terms." [42]

Captain J. M. Addeman of the 14th Rhode Island Heavy Artillery (colored) served from the organization of his regiment through to the end of the war. It was the fate of the 14th to have various garrison, picket, and outpost duties in the river parishes of Louisiana, at Plaquemine and Donaldsonville. They never knew the mingled panic and enthusiasm, the pain and the glory of full combat with bugles and colors and three rousing cheers from the white regiment on their left. They lasted out the war near Plaquemine, the officers caught in the routine of reports, courts-martial, inspections, staff work, and the like, the enlisted men painfully learning to read and write in the regimental schools, building forts, standing guard, or doing picket duty. Their greatest enemies were not Confederates but "yellow jack," "breakbone fever," and boredom. But Nathaniel Banks complimented them in orders, and Thomas W. Sherman called them "a noble regiment." They wanted to fight, Addeman maintained: "The call was hopefully expected but disappointingly unheard. Yet," he asked, "may they not fairly claim to share in the glory of the result, and to them may not the words of the poet justly apply—'They also serve who only stand and wait.' " [43]

Along the Atlantic coast Negro soldiers saw more mixed duty as occasion demanded. They sweated in the Union trenches around Charleston. They died in such ill-planned and badly executed battles as Olustee and Honey Hill. In Northern Virginia they fought, dug, entrenched, reconnoitered the enemy's lines, and fought again, as the need arose. They guarded Confederate prisoners at Rock Island, Illinois, at Point Lookout, Maryland, and on the Dry Tortugas. Negro soldiers, in whatever theater of war they found themselves, seem to have done everything that soldiers might conceivably be expected to do.

It is hard to find a fairer estimate than what Charles Francis Adams, Jr., wrote of their part in the crater at Petersburg: "They seem to have behaved just as well and as badly as the rest and to have suffered more severely." Adams, nearly half a century after the war, wrote bitterly of his personal disappointment at the conduct of his Negro troopers in the movement that carried them into the burning Confederate capital; it was "convincing proof," he declared, "that the Negro was wholly unfit for cavalry service, lacking absolutely the essential qualities of alertness, individuality, reliability, and self-reliance." [44] But of the over-all performance of Negro soldiers, his earlier observation seems the fairer judgment.

In numbers alone Negro troops made a measurable contribution to the strength of Union arms. Under the draft call of December, 1864, some ten thousand colored soldiers were added to the force already enrolled. On July 15, 1865, a total of 123,156 Negro soldiers were in the Union Army, organized into 120 infantry regiments, 12 regiments of heavy artillery, 10 batteries of light artillery, and 7 regiments of cavalry. They made up, at war's end, a good 12 per cent of the estimated one million men then in the armies of the Union. The whole number of colored troops recruited and organized during the war is usually given as 186,017, but since that figure includes 7,122 officers, a more nearly correct total is 178,895. The exact total will never be known, since records in some regiments were incorrectly kept or lost and since some organizations may have had their own rather irregular methods of securing replacements without either entering the casualties on the muster roll or changing the names on the roll. Joseph T. Wilson insisted that sometimes "if a company on picket or scouting lost ten men, the officers would immediately put ten new men in their places and have them answer to dead men's names." Wilson asserted that this practice was followed in Missouri, Tennessee, and Virginia. As a consequence, Wilson suggested, the total number of colored troops who served in the Union Army may run as high as 200,000.[45] But accepting the figure of 180,000 as probable, Negro troops made up between 9 and 10 per cent of the total number of Union soldiers. Losses among Negro troops were high: 68,178 from all causes were reported, or over one-third of the total enrolled. Of these, 2,751 were killed in action; the balance died of wounds or disease or were missing. Disease took far more lives than bullets; this was true of the entire Union Army, and of the Negro troops serving in it, too. To cite an extreme case: the 56th Colored saw over two years of service, chiefly post and garrison duty at Helena, Arkansas, and participated in three minor engagements, with a battle loss of 4 officers and 21 enlisted men killed or mortally wounded. But this regiment lost 6 officers and 647 men from disease.[46]

Whatever duties they performed, Negro soldiers responded to the Union call when war weariness and anti-Negro feeling were at high tide in the North. Despite impressment, discrimination in pay and duty, and the constant threat of death or return to slavery if captured, Negro soldiers did not desert in abnormally large numbers. Some 14,887 went "over the hill" permanently, or roughly 7 per cent of the total desertion, over 200,000 from the Union Army.[47] Negro soldiers worked hard and they fought hard; they improved themselves by study when more pressing demands of a military nature permitted; they were generally a challenge to their officers. It is not in the province of the historian to speculate on what might have been, but it is tempting to wonder how many Negro regiments might have been raised if the pay scale for colored troops had been the same as that for the rest of the Union Army from August, 1862—or even from January, 1863—through the war. It is tempting, too, to wonder how a hundred colored regiments, adequately armed and trained in the use of those arms, might have performed as an independent army corps under sympathetic and intelligent officers who appreciated their worth and their potential.

Hindsight and speculation on the basis of hindsight seldom win battles or campaigns. Soldiers are seldom adequately trained until a war is over. Conditions are never ideal. It is enough that they served as soldiers, that they were admitted finally into the ranks of armies organized to preserve the Union and to win freedom for the Negro. In summing up the part his colored troops had played in the battle of Nashville, Colonel Thomas Morgan used words appropriate to their role in the war: "Colored soldiers had fought side by side with white troops. They had mingled together in the charge. They had supported each other. They had assisted each other from the field when wounded, and they lay side by side in death. The survivors rejoiced together over a hard-fought field, won by common valor. All who witnessed their conduct gave them equal praise. The day we longed to see had come and gone, and the sun went down upon a record of coolness, bravery, manliness, never to be unmade. A new chapter in the history of liberty had been written. It had been shown that marching under the flag of freedom, animated by a love of liberty, even the slave becomes a man and a hero." [48]

The new chapter had been written. Negro soldiers had helped write it. And, as Frederick Douglass had foreseen in the opening weeks of war, they had helped themselves enormously by their soldierly participation. As occasion provided, they had learned their first lessons in reading and writing at company and regimental schools. Of more significance, Negro soldiers learned their first lessons in self-reliance and in the exercise of authority, choice, and discretion. They bore arms like white men, and as officers and noncommissioned officers they gave orders, kept records, and shouldered new responsibilities. They learned important lessons in loyalty to the Union, and after the war they found respectful treatment and honor when, as veterans of the Union Army, they joined the Grand Army of the Republic. In the GAR, Negro veterans rose to positions of trust and distinction: George Washington Williams in 1888 signed himself "Colonel and Late Judge Advocate in the Grand Army of the Republic." Joseph Wilson became aide-de-camp to the commander in chief of the G.A.R.[49]

In the period between the close of the Civil War and the end of the century, the Negro veteran enjoyed wide respect and some equality of treatment and consideration throughout the North. In the rather florid language of Ben Butler, the Negro soldier had "with the bayonet . . . unlocked the iron-barred gates of prejudice, and opened new fields of freedom, liberty and equality of right." [50] Opportunity was his after the war: he served in state and local elective offices; he went to constitutional conventions in Southern states; he went to the Congress of the United States. He was permitted to become an integral part of the regular army. As part of that army he helped to garrison the conquered South and to guard the westward marches. As infantryman and especially as cavalryman on the western plains, he added new laurels to those won at Petersburg, New Market Heights, and Nashville.

If there had been a better integrated and more widely accepted Negro soldier policy in the Lincoln administration and in the Union Army earlier, very probably Negro soldiers might have been allowed a larger share of what William Birney called the "glory" of the closing campaigns. But the Negro soldier had won glory enough. He had fought his way into the Union Army by his courage and tenacity and sacrifice. Once he had been officially recognized as a soldier, he had fought to maintain his position as a soldier and to broaden the scope of his military usefulness. As a soldier, he had gradually subdued much of the Negro's worst enemy, white prejudice. As a soldier in the Union Army, the American Negro proved his manhood and established a strong claim to equality of treatment and opportunity. In the Fourteenth and Fifteenth Amendments to the Constitution of the United States, his manhood and his claim were recognized by the nation.

Had the Negro played a merely passive role as spectator during the Civil War, had he served only in his traditional menial capacity as cook and teamster and laborer, that national recognition of him as man and as citizen must have been postponed indefinitely. The Southern position that slaves could not bear arms was essentially correct: a slave was not a man. The war ended slavery. The Negro soldier proved that the slave could become a man.

NOTES

1. Thomas J. Morgan, *Reminiscences of Two Years with the Colored Troops*, Soldiers and Sailors Historical Society of Rhode Island series, *Personal Narratives of Events in the War of the Rebellion*, No. 7, Second Series (Providence, 1880), p. 48.

2. *The War of the Rebellion: A Compilation of Official Records of the Union and Confederate Armies*, 128 vols. (Washington, D.C., 1880-1901), ser. 1, XLIX, Pt. I, 294, 295.

3. Daniel Ullmann, *Address by Daniel Ullmann, LL.D., Major General U.S.V., before the Soldiers and Sailors' Union of the State of New York, on the Organization of Colored Troops and the Regeneration of the South, delivered at Albany, February 5, 1868* (Washington, D.C., 1868), in Ullmann File, Generals' Reports, National Archives, pp. 5, 6.

4. *Official Army Register of the Volunteer Forces of the Army for the Years 1861, '62, '63, '64, '65, in 8 Parts* (Washington, D.C., 1867), Part VIII, pp. 321-342.

5. *Official Records*, ser. 1, LIII, 455-458.

6. *Official Army Register*, Part VIII, p. 339, Petersburg; p. 337, Magnolia.

7. Frederick Henry Dyer, *A Compendium of the War of the Rebellion* . . . (Des Moines, 1908), p. 1720. Cited hereafter as Dyer, *Compendium*.

8. *Official Records*, ser. 1, XLVIII, Pt. I, 1107-10.

9. *Official Records*, ser. 1, XLII, Pt. I, 848-850.

10. Dyer, *Compendium*, pp. 1720-40.

11. Worthington Chauncey Ford (ed.), *A Cycle of Adams Letters, 1861-1865*, 2 vols. (Boston, 1920), II, 172.

12. Robert U. Johnson and Clarence C. Buel (eds.), *Battle and Leaders of the Civil War* (4 vols.; New York, 1888), IV, 80.

13. *Official Records*, ser. 1, XXXV, Pt. I, 298.

14. *Ibid.*, pp. 298, 315.

15. *Ibid.*, pp. 290, 304, 298.

16. *Ibid.*, pp. 341, 298.

17. *Merrilies Diary* (3 vols.; Chicago Historical Society, Manuscript Division), III, 17, 20.

18. Muster Rolls, Company A, 30th Regiment United States Colored Troops, from April 30 to June 30, 1864, *Regimental Records* (War Records Division, National Archives).

19. Muster Rolls, Company A. March–April, May–June, 1864; Company E, May–June, July–August, 1864; Company K, September–October, 1864; all companies of 30th U.S. Colored Troops, *Regimental Records* (War Records Division, National Archives).

20. *Official Records,* ser. 1, XL, Pt. I, 705, 706.

21. Henry Goddard Thomas, "The Colored Troops at Petersburg," *Century Magazine,* XII (September, 1887), 777, 778.

22. *Ibid.,* p. 777; *Report of the Committee on the Conduct of the War on the Attack on Petersburg, on the 30th Day of July, 1864* (Washington, 1865), p. 5.

23. Thomas, *op. cit.,* pp. 778-781; *Official Records,* ser. 1, XL, Pt. I, 246-248.

24. George L. Kilmer, "The Dash into the Crater," *Century Magazine,* XII (September, 1887), 775, 776.

25. *Official Records,* ser. 1, XL, Pt. I, 118-119, Surgeon Smith's testimony; p. 73, Burnside's testimony.

26. *Ibid.,* p. 106, Thomas; p. 102, Hartranft; p. 599, Thomas' report; Thomas, *op. cit.,* p. 778.

27. James A. Rickard, *Services with Colored Troops in Burnside's Corps,* Soldiers and Sailors Historical Society of Rhode Island series, *Personal Narratives of Events in the War of the Rebellion,* Ser. 5, I (Providence, 1894), pp. 31-32.

28. *Official Records,* ser. 1, XLIII, Pt. I, 106, 108.

29. Benjamin Franklin Butler, *Autobiography and Personal Reminiscences of Major-General Benjamin F. Butler—BUTLER'S BOOK. A Review of His Legal, Political and Military Career* (Boston, 1892), pp. 721-722, 730.

30. *Official Records,* ser. 1, XLII, Pt. I, pp. 106, 108.

31. *Ibid.,* pp. 133-134, 134-136, 137.

32. *Butler's Book,* pp. 731-733.

33. George R. Sherman, *The Negro as a Soldier,* in *Personal Narratives of Events in the War of the Rebellion . . .* (Ser. 7, No. 7; Providence, 1913), pp. 21-22; *Official Records,* ser. 1, XLIII, Pt. I, 134.

34. *Official Records,* ser. 1, XLII, Pt. I, 147, 148-150, 151, 157-159.

35. *Ibid.,* pp. 113-114.

36. William Birney, *General William Birney's Answer to Libels Clandestinely Circulated by James Shaw, Jr. . . .* (Washington, 1878), p. 8.

37. Luis F. Emilio, *History of the Fifty-Fourth Regiment of Massachusetts Volunteer Infantry, 1863-1865* (Boston, 1891), pp. 282-283; *Adams Letters,* II, 261-262. General Weitzel's report (*Official Records,* ser. 1, XLVI, Pt. I, 1227-1228) gives the palm for being first into Richmond to the 4th Massachusetts Cavalry, a white regiment, but Adams was there among the first.

38. Morgan, *Reminiscences,* pp. 28-38.

39. *Ibid.,* pp. 38-47; Henry Stone, "Hood's Invasion of Tennessee," *Century Magazine,* XII (August, 1887), 612, 615.

40. *Official Records,* ser. 1, XLV, Pt. I, 508.

41. *Official Records,* ser. 1, XLIX, Pt. I, 110-115, 287.

42. *Ibid.*, p. 140.

43. J. M. Addeman, *Reminiscences of Two Years with the Colored Troops*, in *Personal Narratives of Events in the War of the Rebellion* . . . (Ser. 2, No. 7; Providence, 1880), pp. 15, 25, 27, 30, 36-40.

44. *Adams Letters*, II, 172; *Charles Francis Adams, 1835-1915, An Autobiography* (Boston, 1916), p. 166. His men, contrary to the general performance of Negro soldiers in the Civil War, straggled badly on the advance and, what was worse, stole some horses, with the result that Colonel Adams was put in arrest for about two weeks. Adams seems not to have considered that he was assuming the extraordinary in expecting his troops to be transformed from prisoner of war guards to well-behaved cavalry on their first road march. March discipline is extremely difficult to attain and usually requires time and patience; Adams seems to have had neither. To complicate matters the more, he was worn out physically and at the point of collapse, in no mood for nonsense. His last weeks with his regiment were his worst, and his judgment of Negro troops was permanently warped by that unhappy time. See *Adams Letters*, II, 267-270, for full particulars.

45. *Official Records*, ser. 3, V, 661-662; Joseph T. Wilson, *The Black Phalanx: A History of the Negro Soldiers of the United States in the Wars of 1775-1812, 1861-'65* (Hartford, 1888), p. 143. Major Foster of the Bureau for Colored Troops reported the aggregate as 186,097 officers and men, but an error in addition accounts for the increase. See *Official Records*, ser. 3, V, 138.

46. *Official Records*, ser. 3, V, 138; William F. Fox, "The Chances of Being Hit in Battle," *Century Magazine*, XIV (May, 1888), 104-105; *Official Army Register*, VIII, 229; Dyer, *Compendium*, p. 1753.

47. *Official Records*, ser. 3, V, 1030.

48. Morgan, *Reminiscences*, pp. 44-45.

49. George Washington Williams, *A History of the Negro Troops in the War of the Rebellion, 1861-1865* . . . (New York, 1888), title page; Wilson, *Black Phalanx*, title page.

50. L. D. Reddick, "The Negro Policy of the United States Army, 1775-1945," *Journal of Negro History*, XXXIV (January, 1949), 18; *Official Records*, ser. 1, XLVI, Pt. II, 71.

THE GENESIS OF THE FIRST
WISCONSIN CIVIL RIGHTS ACT

Leslie H. Fishel, Jr.

Early in 1950 an irate owner of a Wisconsin summer resort accosted the executive secretary of the Governor's Commission on Human Rights, shook his finger in her face, and demanded to know the names of the legislators who were responsible for the state's civil rights act. "I wouldn't know," she told him. "It was passed in 1895 and that was before my time." [1]

The businessman's angry reaction to the law which penalized discrimination in places of public accommodation on grounds of race, creed, or color was not without precedent. In the North generally, whites had tried for over a century to segregate the Negro in schools, housing, employment, cemeteries, and in places generally open to the public: theaters, hotels, restaurants, railroad cars, and roller rinks.

In early Wisconsin, this white posture is best seen in the seventeen-year effort to keep colored men from voting, an effort which the state supreme court terminated in 1866 with a decision admitting them to the polls. Outside of suffrage, the evidence is slim, largely because Wisconsin's Negro population in the last century was only a fraction of the total population of the state. There were only 2,444 Negroes in Wisconsin out of a total of more than 1,680,000 people in 1890. Milwaukee had a population of over 204,000, of which fewer than 500 were colored. Five years later, Milwaukee's Negro population had climbed to 550 and there was a sprinkling of colored people in other cities. Superior

Leslie H. Fishel, Jr., "The Genesis of the First Wisconsin Civil Rights Act," *Wisconsin Magazine of History*, XLIX, No. 4 (Summer, 1966), 324-333.

and Fond du Lac had 181 and 129 respectively, while Sheboygan had only two Negroes and Neenah and Menasha had none at all.[2] Yet even so small a fraction of the population felt strongly enough about the white posture to want to rectify it.

What happened in Wisconsin was strongly influenced by national events. After several unsuccessful attempts Congress finally passed a civil rights act in 1875, excluding all reference to education but penalizing discrimination in places of public accommodation. Aimed at the South—a last arrow before the final collapse of Reconstructon—the act was important for the North. Its significance, however, was not really manifest until 1883, when the United States Supreme Court struck down the law as unconstitutional.

The law had given Negroes the right to equal accommodation at hotels and theaters, on railroads, and in other places of public use. For the Court the issue was its constitutionality; for America's Negroes the issue was more complex. The removal from the statute books of a federal statement supporting the right of a colored person to equal treatment in public places left a clear implication of second-class citizenship. It also left the question to the individual states.

In the Civil Rights Cases decision, Justice Joseph P. Bradley spoke for the Supreme Court. He pointed out that the statute could rest only on the first section of the Fourteenth Amendment, and that it was unconstitutional because it was an affirmative assignment of rights, not a prohibition against state action. The Fourteenth Amendment, he asserted, "does not invest Congress with power to legislate upon subjects which are within the domain of state legislation. . . . It does not authorize Congress to create a code of municipal law for the regulation of private rights. . . ." Using a literal definition of slavery, he dismissed as irrelevant the plaintiffs' argument that congressional power rested also in the Thirteenth Amendment, which abolished slavery and involuntary servitude.[3]

Justice John Marshall Harlan stood alone in dissent. He argued that the Thirteenth Amendment was "a change in the fundamental law," invalidating the institution of slavery and creating "universal freedom." Slavery rested on the assumed inferiority and real proscription of the colored people. Under the Thirteenth Amendment Congress "may enact laws to protect that people against the deprivation, because of their race, of any civil rights granted to other free men in the same state. . . ." With its grant to Congress to enforce it by appropriate legislation, it was clear authority for "direct and primary" congressional action. Justice Harlan pointed out that even the majority admitted that the

Civil Rights Act of 1866, securing to all citizens the right to make and enforce contracts, to sue and be sued, and to handle property, was grounded in this statement.

He went on to argue that public conveyances, inns, and places of public amusement were in reality instruments of the state and that "discrimination practised by corporations and individuals in the exercise of their public or quasi-public functions is a badge of servitude" subject to congressional prohibition under the Thirteenth Amendment. He returned to this point in rebuttal to the majority argument that the Fourteenth Amendment merely prohibited state sanction of discrimination, asserting that "a denial, by these instrumentalities of the State, to the citizen, because of his race, of that equality of civil rights secured to him by law, is a denial by the State, within the meaning of the Fourteenth Amendment."

Justice Harlan was even more concerned with enlarging the interpretation of the Fourteenth Amendment itself to permit direct federal legislation. The first clause of the first section, he pointed out, is an affirmative statement creating U.S. citizens of "all persons born or naturalized in the United States" and making them citizens of the state in which they resided. This clause brought Negroes under the umbrella of the Fourth Amendment, which guarantees to citizens of each state the privileges and immunities of citizens of the several states. The Fourteenth Amendment also has an empowering clause, granting Congress the authority to enforce it by appropriate legislation. "If, then, exemption from discrimination, in respect of civil rights, is a new constitutional right, secured by the grant of State citizenship to colored citizens of the United States . . . why may not the nation, by means of its own legislation of a primary direct character, guard, protect and enforce that right? It is a right and privilege which the nation conferred. It did not come from the States in which those colored citizens reside."

In a final lament, the Supreme Court justice displayed some of the frustration already characteristic of the Negro's struggle for equality. The major purpose of congressional legislation since the Civil War had been to permit the Negroes to "take the rank of mere citizens. The difficulty has been to compel a recognition of the legal right of the black race to take the rank of citizens, and to secure the enjoyment of privileges belonging, under the law, to them as a component part of the people for whose welfare and happiness government is ordained." [4]

The importance of the now-defunct federal law became immediately apparent, and Negroes across the North reacted vigorously. "That decision will close hundreds of hotels, places of amusement and other public places here in the North to our people," wrote a Negro editor in

Cleveland. Negroes protested the Court's decree at conventions in Washington, Pittsburgh, Cleveland, Youngstown, and at a statewide meeting in Connecticut before the close of 1883. The *Nation's* comment that Negroes would concentrate on state legislatures for redress was correct. In spite of a number of bills introduced into Congress, the next moves were staged at state capitals, where the Negro demonstrated surprising political strength.[5]

Only three states had had civil rights acts before 1883: Massachusetts (1865) and New York and Kansas (1874). After the Supreme Court decision, some states acted with haste. The Ohio Legislature passed a law as early as February, 1884, in a flurry of partisan activity which took Negroes by surprise and left them angered by the apparent impotence of the law. "The act as passed is of no practical benefit to the colored people," the Ohio Equal Rights League resolved in early March. Connecticut was next with a law in April, four months after the statewide convention of Negroes had drawn up a petition urging "the same privileges for the colored people [as] enjoyed by others. . . ." Connecticut's Negroes were active in drafting and lobbying for this bill. Iowa and New Jersey also enacted civil rights statutes in 1884.[6] Seven Northern states passed civil rights acts in 1885 and two more were added for a total of sixteen before 1895. Yet the problem of access to public places was of continuing concern to Northern Negroes, and there were complaints from Ohio, Illinois, and Iowa that some state laws were too weak or that courts were hesitant in enforcing them.

The Michigan Supreme Court overturned one such lower-court decision, asserting that although "the prejudice against association in public places with the Negro" had lessened somewhat, it was still "unworthy." Courts should not "cater to or temporize with a prejudice which is not only not humane but unreasonable." In New York, efforts by whites and Negroes to strengthen the existing law began in the late 1880's and were not successful until the Malby Act of 1895. Minnesota enacted a civil rights act in 1885, but two years later St. Paul Negroes organized a Civil Rights League which, after congratulating the state on its "just and liberal laws" and "kindly feelings," pointedly announced their unity in the face of those people who were disposed to "abridge" their guaranteed rights.[7]

Wisconsin's Negroes, too, were caught up in the growing irritation brought about by the Civil Rights Cases decision and its consequences. In the early summer of 1886, two young colored men were refused a drink "in one of the best saloons" in Milwaukee, and an observer who reported the incident commented that "Wisconsin needs a Civil Rights bill. . . ." This was a straw in the wind. Three years later, when a

Negro was refused a seat in a theater, memories of other irritating incidents came bubbling to the surface. Frederick Douglass had been refused hotel accommodations in Janesville. Colored members of the GAR were "wilfully insulted in some of our leading hostelries" at a recent encampment in Milwaukee. At a state teachers' convention in Madison, some Negro teachers were not permitted to register at the hotels. Wisconsin's Negroes were ripe for an organized effort to obtain a civil rights law.[8]

In early September, 1889, a Milwaukee Negro, Owen Howell, purchased a ticket by messenger at the Bijou Opera House for a play, *The Runaway Wife*. When he appeared to take his seat in the parquette, the head usher refused him admission and tried to send him to the gallery. Within weeks, Howell had hired an attorney and filed suit.

The Milwaukee community was immediately made aware of the case. The rector of fashionable St. Paul's Episcopal Church preached a sermon on the incident and accused the theater of "contemptible barbarism," contrasting the manager's exclusion of a colored person with his admission of a "drunkard, a gambler, a thief or a prostitute, provided the skin was white." Milwaukee's Negroes gathered together and issued a call for a state convention to organize a state Civil Rights League. Prominent among the signers of the call were the Reverend Daniel P. Brown of St. Mark's African Methodist Episcopal Church, and William T. Green, the man who was to emerge as the leading figure in Wisconsin's civil rights struggle.[9]

The convention call cited instances of recent discrimination against Negroes in "public places," and emphasized that there was no law in Wisconsin to protect the race from insults and humiliation. The convention, meeting in Milwaukee in late November, took the same tack, encouraged by the "earnest wishes" of Governor William D. Hoard, who wrote that "Wisconsin should not be behind any of the states in guaranteeing to the colored people all of those rights given them by the constitution of the United States." The convention's resolutions listed the usual grievances: discrimination in "certain hotels, restaurants, barber shops, public inns and places of amusement" and by "certain" life insurance companies, and the absence of Negroes in "permanent" state jobs "of any consequence." The convention asked the governor to recommend a civil rights law in his next message to the legislature.

The convention was primarily an attempt to demonstrate the political potential of the Negro group. The delegates resolved in favor of a national convention of Negroes, following the appeal of T. Thomas Fortune, editor of the New York *Age* and prime mover of the infant Afro-American League, the first national Negro protest organization.

They endorsed Wisconsin's Senator John C. Spooner and urged that Negro votes and political support be given only to "true friends of the American Negro," regardless of party. In taking these stands, Wisconsin's Negroes followed the lead of colored men in other states who were, with limited success, striving for political recognition on a state and national basis.[10]

The threat of an organized Negro vote caused no discernible ripple in 1889, though the public declaration in favor of a civil rights law was disturbing to some newspapers. In the Fox River Valley one editor took the position that there should be no prejudice "either for or against the colored race." A man should be neither ignored nor honored for the color of his skin. The editor retreated to the pious hope that "some time in the future" the color line and race problems would disappear. The Milwaukee *Sentinel* was less circumspect, asserting that common law protected black and white alike and that a special law for Negroes would be ineffective. "We are in no way opposed to its enactment, except in the general sense of objecting to useless legislation." The *Sentinel* vehemently opposed "senseless prejudice" and just as vehemently supported "every effort to banish" it, but added that "we do not hope for anything through legislation." [11]

This not unexpected ambivalence was related to another thread which ran through many reactions. The Episcopal rector of St. Paul's in Milwaukee suggested that the best whites did not discriminate, and the paper which quoted from his sermon commented that "the first-class theaters" in the city had never had any trouble. The Negro convention resolutions were even more explicit, charging that "malefactors" came chiefly from "the lower classes of ill-bred and poorly-educated people," and cited an example to prove it. Whether, as the judge was to say in his charge to the jury in the Howell case, the relative absence of prejudice stemmed from the strong admixture of foreigners in Milwaukee or whether the Negroes believed they could win more friends by identifying a class scapegoat as the "malefactor" is a moot point. But, without question, the Negro believed himself to be circumscribed at the beginning of the last decade of the nineteenth century, and he had the evidence to support it. What he needed, and was working to get, was political assistance and moral support.[12]

Judge Daniel H. Johnson provided Negroes with a boost in morale in the case of *Howell* v. *Litt*. Reared in Canada and seasoned on Wisconsin's mining frontier, Judge Johnson had read law in Prairie du Chien before moving to Milwaukee, where he practiced law and played with politics. He wrote short stories and had a few published by *Atlantic Monthly*. He helped to frame the Milwaukee city charter and served on the school board. After supporting the Liberal Republicans in 1872, he became a Democrat and was elected to the bench in 1887 at the age of sixty-two. Three years later, he presided over Wisconsin's first civil rights case.[13]

When *Howell* v. *Litt* came to trial in the early summer of 1890, the court was crowded with Negroes. They followed the proceedings carefully, filling the room with laughter when Howell's attorney, G. W. Hazleton, twitted a theater employee. Yet they must have been solemnly quiet when the judge began to read his charge: "Gentleman of the Jury—In this case you must find for the plaintiff. . . ." The all-white jury awarded Howell $100 damages and $51.85 costs, but the lasting value lay in the judge's words.[14]

A place of public resort, Judge Johnson declared, was one "to which the whole public are invited." This included any man who was "decently dressed" and behaved with decorum. As a race stigmatized by slavery, Negroes "in these Northwestern states" were "treated as a servile and inferior people" before the Civil War. The Thirteenth and Fourteenth Amendments were passed to rectify this situation.

Ignoring the majority decision in the Civil Rights Cases, Judge Johnson accepted Justice Harlan's interpretation. "The effect of these amendments, in my judgment, was to render unlawful every discrimination on account of color or race, which existed, either by statute or by common law, or by ordinance, or by any other means, in any of the states of the Union." No public place was closed to any person on grounds of color. Those who claim that it was "proper to provide a separate place, an inferior place of some sort" for colored people were abridging the constitutional rights of Negroes, for segregation placed a greater stigma on the restricted than complete denial: "To say a man shall not enter a theater is not so great a stigma upon him, it does not mark him as a servile and inferior being as distinctly as an arrangement which says you may go up there into the gallery, over there among those free seats, yonder in that car set apart for your kind of people, but you must not go anywhere else."

The law of the land, the judge asserted, opened all places of public resort to all who paid the price and behaved acceptably, without restriction as to parts of a public place and without exclusion on grounds of race, creed, or previous condition of servitude. In Ohio and Kansas, he noted, colored children were excluded from the public schools because of race prejudice. This situation did not prevail in Milwaukee where "there are no separate schools provided for them and I trust there never will be." In fact, he added, he knew only of this one theater, of all public places including churches, which discriminated against Negroes.

The judge could have rested at this point, but he chose instead to probe even more deeply. Prejudice, he observed, should have no basis in any court of law, "based as it is upon apprehension of social equality or social intimacy." Social relations were personal, a matter of choice, and were not affected by "the free intermixture of all people in purely public places. . . ." Two men sitting together in a theater would not bring about a social relationship if either or both wished to avoid it.[15]

"Take this case," he charged the jury, "and consider it the same as you would consider a case between two white men or two black men. . . . Wherever the distinction between white and black men may be permitted to survive, it must not be in a jurybox or court of justice. There all men are equal in law . . ." [16]

Six months before Judge Johnson charged the jury, in December of 1889, a bill had been drawn up to protect Wisconsin's Negroes in their civil rights, but it was not until January, 1891, that the legislature convened and the bill was introduced. The bill was comprehensive, listing "inns, restaurants, saloons, barber shops, eating houses, public conveyances on land and water, theaters and all other places of public accommodation or amusement" as open to all persons alike, even specifying that no person could be required to pay more than the regular rate for these services. Violators would be charged with a misdemeanor and fined no less than twenty-five dollars nor more than five hundred dollars and/or imprisoned for up to one year for each offense.[17]

The bill was undoubtedly drafted by Milwaukee Negroes or their friends immediately after their 1889 civil rights convention. It was introduced by a Milwaukee assemblyman, Orren T. Williams, who was serving his first and only term in the legislature and represented the fourth ward, where William T. Green resided. A Republican, Williams was in the minority as a result of the Democratic landslide the previous November. He was a minority member of the Judiciary Committee, to which the bill was referred. At the committee hearing at least one Negro testified; he was probably William Green, who was then attending law school in Madison. His appearance was effective enough to make a favorable impression on a legislative leader who was opposed to the bill, but it did not change his vote. The committee emasculated the bill by striking out the entire list of public places, except inns, and reported back. On Wednesday, March 11, the lower house devoted most of the morning to a spirited debate on the bill, the partisan nature of which was revealed in the headlines of the Madison Democrat: "Republicans seek to make capital out of the Civil Rights Bill, but their game is blocked and they themselves placed on record."

Williams opened the debate by citing the examples of Michigan and Minnesota, which had already passed civil rights acts, and by using the case of *Howell* v. *Litt* as proof of the need in Wisconsin. He read portions of Judge Johnson's charge to the assembly. The opposition called the original bill "too broad" imposing "extreme exactions" on businessmen. Prejudice is here to stay, one assemblyman stated. "There is no member of the house who desires to be placed upon an equality with the Negro. . . . The Negro in Wisconsin had . . . all the rights he can reasonably expect." Other assemblymen argued that there was no need for a law of this type and that this bill was a Republican trick to embarrass the Democratic majority. The Republicans, one Democrat taunted, had had more than two decades of legislative control in which to enact a civil rights statute. Assemblyman John Winans, a member of the Judiciary Committee, asked, "Where is the man on this floor who will say the colored man is the equal of the white man? God did not create them equal," he added, and legislation to make them equal would do them harm. Occasional colored men deserved "that highest consideration," but not the rank and file. It was too much to ask "that the wives and daughters of the members of this legislature shall mingle with the black men. . . ." Orren Williams made a final unsuccessful effort to enlarge the bill to approximate its original meaning; then the assembly, with Winans absent, approved the emasculated version.[18]

The Winans speech had "a deal of moss on it," the *Wisconsin State Journal* snorted the next day and ridiculed the assemblyman for raising the intermarriage bogey. But the senate would not even have the watered-down version, and the bill failed.[19] Wisconsin's Negroes needed a good deal more political leverage, and they now set about acquiring it within the Republican party.

The Republican state convention of August, 1892, was held in Milwaukee. It was a smooth affair, well controlled by professional politicians. "A business convention," the Milwaukee *Sentinel* called it. "There were no spangles or bunting about it." Before the convention, Senator John Coit Spooner, who was soon to be nominated for governor by acclamation, was asked if the party would pass a civil rights bill. He replied expansively that "the Republican Party will do any and everything that they think is right." [20]

Among the delegates from the fourth ward of Milwaukee was William T. Green. His nomination had been urged upon the party by a meeting of Negro voters in Milwaukee whose resolutions, properly dressed in *Whereases*, recited the "outrages" suffered by the race, the "proscription" in Wisconsin which blocked "progressive and capable citizens" from "other than menial positions," and denounced the outrages and the prejudices abroad in the "north and northwest." The meeting endorsed United States Senators Spooner and Philetus Sawyer and Wisconsin congressmen generally "for their noble defense of the rights of Afro-Americans" and, speaking for Wisconsin's Negroes "unanimously," backed Green's election as a delegate to the convention.[21]

The convention droned through its uncontested nominations and its unexciting platform committee report. Just before the delegates acted on the motion to adopt the report, Green jumped to his feet and the chair recognized him. He asked if he could present an amendment to the report before the convention, and, after receiving the floor, proceeded to read a denunciation of "the cruel and barbarous treatment of American citizens in some of the Southern states. . . ." He sat down and, according to a reporter, "The cheers told Mr. Green that he had made a hit. The amendment and the platform were both unanimously adopted. . . ."[22]

There was a touch of pathos in this vignette. Green's "unanimous election" as a delegate was cause for self-congratulation by the Negro group; their newspaper declared that it was a triumph which demonstrated what Negroes could accomplish "as a people," with the help of white friends. But the real problem was the failure of the 1891 civil rights bill and the "damnable prejudice . . . on the part of some foolish, ill-bred people in our city. . . ." Almost as the editor was writing copy which would exhort Milwaukee's Negroes to "continue the fight for recognition" and "learn how to have nerve and 'kick,'" William T. Green was on his feet before the convention, denouncing the mistreatment of Negroes who were hundreds of miles beyond Wisconsin's borders. Ignoring the proscription and "damnable prejudice" at home, the colored delegate showed his "nerve" by aiming his "kick" at Southern whites.[23]

While vilification of Southern practices had little practical effect, Green's move made political sense. Green was still young, only twenty-nine, and had been admitted to the bar but three months earlier. He had just entered or was about to enter into a partnership with a white lawyer.[24] His emergence as a leader of the Negro group was too recent for a direct challenge to the state Republican party. The party itself, struggling to return to power, had made an unsuccessful effort to enact a civil rights law in 1891 and was undoubtedly not anxious to give the Democrats a wider opportunity to exploit the civil rights issue on the stump. The Green amendment attacking Southern barbarism was a safe compromise, and the fact that the colored delegate was allowed to introduce it from the floor at least gave encouragement to Wisconsin's Negroes.

The Republicans lost again in the 1892 elections, but the Negroes' public activity increased. Milwaukee's Negro newspaper, the *Wisconsin Afro-American,* soon to change its name to the *Northwestern Recorder* and become a monthly, was sprinkled with reports of race progress in employment and immigration. "We need more colored people, but for God's sake, let them be a class who are willing to work and help build up a race." Mixed with demands for justice were assurances by the editors, George A. Brown and Thomas H. Jones, that the whites would help those who helped themselves, since "no white man respects a 'dog' that will bring a bone." [25]

The name of William Green cropped up with greater frequency, as a successful lawyer and a politician. In November, 1894, he and Theobold Otjen, a prominent white politician, addressed a crowded meeting of colored Republicans. So tempting had the Negro vote become that even a Democratic candidate for Congress stumped for it, probably "the first time a Democratic candidate has ever addressed a colored audience in a political campaign." As Negroes made themselves known in Milwaukee, the press began to regard them as newsworthy.[26]

The Democrats maintained their control over the 1893 legislature and no effort was made to introduce a civil rights bill. The elections of 1894 brought the Republicans back to power, and a former Milwaukee assemblyman, William H. Austin, returned as a freshman senator. A young man with a distinguished legal and civic career still before him, Senator Austin introduced in February of 1895 the original 1891 civil rights bill, by request, on the last permissible day. On the same day, Assemblyman Reinhardt Klabunde, a liquor dealer from Milwaukee, did the same in the lower house. It was February 12, Lincoln's Birthday.[27]

Unlike the bill of four years earlier, this civil rights bill moved through both committee and legislature without public notice of any kind. The senate committe amended the bill by reducing the penalties. The assembly passed its bill without amendment, but finally concurred in the senate bill. On April 20, 1895, Governor W. H. Upham signed the bill and Wisconsin had its first civil rights act, prohibiting racial discrimination at inns, restaurants, and a long list of other public places under penalty of a fine from five to one hundred dollars or six months' imprisonment. For Wisconsin, and for the period, it was a good law.[28]

Whatever pressure had been mounted behind the quick and quiet passage, it was largely unseen. The bill came into both houses by request, introduced by Milwaukee legislators with no known interest in this kind of reform. Newspapers ignored it, mass meetings passed it by, speakers, pamphleteers, letter-writers, and diarists on the subject have not been found. Nationally, race relations seemed to be moving in the opposite direction, with the Southern states pushing for disfranchise-

ment and segregation. The year of the act, 1895, was the year of the
Atlanta Compromise, advanced by Booker T. Washington in his Atlanta
exposition address, which endorsed segregation and catapulted him into
the national limelight. The following year, the Southern point of view
was to be declared constitutional by the Supreme Court in the *Plessy* v.
Ferguson decision. The time did not seem ripe for a civil rights act just
to happen in Wisconsin.

Indeed, it did not just happen. There was a ferment abroad in the
North, obscured perhaps by events of greater moment. Between 1890
and 1895 two Northern states (Washington and Wisconsin) passed civil
rights acts. Six other states (Iowa, Ohio, Colorado, Massachusetts, Nebraska, and New York) acted twice in this five-year period. And between 1895 and 1900, Minnesota revised its civil rights law twice and
California passed an original statute. Activity of this type and quantity
was not mere coincidence.[29]

The key to the puzzle in Wisconsin, as elsewhere, was the Negro
group. It had come alive, especially in Milwaukee. The Negro had
become increasingly aware of—and dissatisfied with—his disadvantaged
position. The Republican party was becoming more sensitive to the
Negro vote. The man who undoubtedly engineered the bill was en-
grossed in politics and in touch with political leaders, even though he
was not credited with the accomplishment until after the fact. William
T. Green was "the author of our civil rights bill," Milwaukee's Negro
paper twice testified in 1899, and "secured its passage" with the assistance of "our" representatives in the legislature. And two years later,
Green was again identified as the author of the act, "the passage of
which he secured by appearing before the legislature committee in its
behalf." Given Green's position as a leading Negro in the Republican
party before the act, and his prominence in Negro life and politics
after its passage, it would appear that he deserved the credit.[30]

Within months the 1895 statute was challenged, right up to the
state supreme court. A Negro sleeping-car porter from Milwaukee and
a white sheriff from Michigan were refused service in a Milwaukee
restaurant. The porter, Isaac T. Bryan, was helping Sheriff Silas H.
Corbett locate witnesses for a Michigan court case. The two men had
begun their day without incident with breakfast at Henry Adler's restaurant and, late the same afternoon, went back for supper. They were
not served and ate elsewhere, but returned in the evening to ask
Adler for an explanation. Bryan even suggested to Adler that he dismiss
the errant waiter.

Bryan later testified that it was his own idea to bring suit because
"[I] didn't think I was treated right."

His attorney was G. W. Hazelton, who had appeared before Judge

Johnson in *Howell* v. *Litt.* The attorney for Adler, the restaurant owner, was Senator William H. Austin, who had introduced the civil rights bill in the legislature. The superior court judge, R. N. Austin (a close friend but not a relative of the defense attorney), held that since the waiter who had refused service had been dismissed for his action, the restaurant was not liable. The state supreme court reversed this decision, holding that the act of the servant "within the scope of his employment" was identical with the act of the master. By closing this loophole in the civil rights act—pointed out, ironically, by the bill's legislative sponsor—the supreme court strengthened both the statute and the state's resolve to do justice under the law.[31]

By the turn of the century, the Wisconsin Civil Rights Act was firmly and substantially the law of the state. Its passage had depended upon the initiative and persistence of Negroes, a pattern which had developed in other Northern states which enacted civil rights legislation after the 1883 Supreme Court decision. At a time when Southern whites were cresting their campaign for stringent segregation and Northern whites busied themselves with other concerns, this form of Negro resistance to discrimination and subordination suggested both the restlessness and the power of Northern Negroes. While their restlessness was largely unharnessed and their power limited and still bound to and channeled through the Republican party, Northern Negroes actively worked to erode their second-class citizenship and to achieve parity with whites. The Atlanta Compromise of Booker T. Washington has tended to obscure their dissatisfaction with their status and has minimized their successes. Wisconsin's civil rights achievement, in the year of the Atlanta Compromise, testified to the conviction and the capabilities of the Negro group in the North.

NOTES

1. *Journal* (Milwaukee), May 21, 1950.
2. On the suffrage issue, see L. H. Fishel, Jr., "Wisconsin and Negro Suffrage," in the *Wisconsin Magazine of History*, XLVI (Spring, 1963), 180-196; U.S. Bureau of the Census, *Twelfth Census of the United States* (Washington, 1901-02), I, 563-564; Bayrd Still, *Milwaukee, The History of a City* (Madison, 1948), p. 571; *Tabular Statement of the Census Enumeration . . . of the State of Wisconsin* (Madison, 1895), pp. 60-108.

3. 109 U.S. 8-26 (1883), especially pp. 11, 17-18, 20-23. See also Milton R. Konvitz and Theodore Leskes, *A Century of Civil Rights* (New York, 1961), pp. 102-107.

4. 109 U.S. 26-62. See also Konvitz and Leskes, *op. cit.*, pp. 108-119, 121.

5. *Gazette* (Cleveland), October 20, 27, November 3, 17, 24, December 1, 15, 1883; *Globe* (New York), October 20, November 3, December 22, 1883, January 5, 1884; *Nation*, XXXVII (November 1, 1883), 361. Cf. William W. Patton, "The U.S. Supreme Court and the Civil Rights Act," in *The New Englander*, XLIII (January, 1884), 13-15.

6. Konvitz and Leskes, *op. cit.*, p. 157; *Gazette* (Cleveland), January 12, February 9, 16, March 8, 1884; *Globe* (New York), April 5, 26, 1884.

7. Konvitz and Leskes, *op. cit.*, p. 157; *Gazette* (Cleveland), March 15, 1884, April 11, 1885, June 6, August 29, September 19, November 7, 1885, January 16, 1886, June 20, 1891, April 1, 8, 15, May 6, 1893; *Age* (New York), November 1, 1890; *Gazette* (Cleveland), June 23, 1888; *Age* (New York), February 23, 1889, May 12, July 5, 12, 19, 1890, October 17, 1891; *Gazette* (Cleveland), October 19, 1895; John C. Dancy *et al.*, "The Report on the State of the Country, Unanimously Adopted by the New York Conference of the A.M.E. Zion Church," *AMEZion Quarterly Review*, V (July, 1895), 135-136; *Age* (New York), November 26, 1887.

8. *Gazette* (Cleveland), June 12, 1886, November 9, 1889; *Sentinel* (Milwaukee), November 28, 1889.

9. *Howell* v. *Litt*, Circuit Court Case #11193, Law Book, Vol. 52, p. 305; *Journal* (Milwaukee), September 30, 1889; *Gazette* (Cleveland), November 9, 1889.

10. *Sentinel* (Milwaukee), November 28, 1889.

11. *Neenah Daily Times*, October 30, 1889; *Sentinel* (Milwaukee), November 29, 1889. For a Negro newspaper's reaction to the *Sentinel's* editorial, see *Age* (New York), December 14, 1889.

12. *Journal* (Milwaukee), September 30, 1889; *Sentinel* (Milwaukee), November 28, 1889; *Wisconsin Weekly Advocate* (Milwaukee), March 30, 1899.

13. *Report of the Annual Meeting of the Wisconsin State Bar Association* (Madison, 1902), IV, 263-240; John R. Berryman, *A History of the Bench and Bar of Wisconsin* (Chicago, 1898), I, 389-392; *Dictionary of Wisconsin Biography* (Madison, 1960), p. 192.

14. *Sentinel* (Milwaukee), July 1, 1890; *Howell* v. *Litt*, Circuit Court Case #11193, Law Book, Vol. 52, pp. 305-306; *Wisconsin Weekly Advocate*, March 30, 1899.

15. These observations on the evils of segregation and the law of the land are one court's expression of a doctrine which was to be explicitly rejected six years later by the United States Supreme Court in *Plessy* v. *Ferguson*. Judge Johnson's statement from the bench was unique for its time and was not to find acceptance from the highest court, until the school desegregation cases of 1954.

16. *Wisconsin Weekly Advocate*, March 30, 1899.

17. Wisconsin Legislative Bills, 2/2/1, Box 279, State Archives (State Historical Society of Wisconsin); *Assembly Journal* (1891), pp. 476-479.

18. *Wisconsin State Journal*, March 11, 1891; *Democrat* (Madison), March 12, 1891; on Williams, see *Wisconsin Blue Book* (1891), p. 596.

19. *Wisconsin State Journal*, March 12, 1891.

20. *Sentinel* (Milwaukee), August 18, 1892; *Wisconsin Afro-American*, August 20, 1892.

21. *Ibid.*, August 20, 1892.

22. *Sentinel* (Milwaukee), August 18, 1892.

23. *Wisconsin Afro-American*, August 20, 1892.

24. *Wisconsin Weekly Advocate*, May 11, 1899; *Indianapolis Freeman*, April 2, 1892.

25. *Wisconsin Afro-American*, October 8, 22, 1892; *Northwestern Recorder*, November 19, December 3, 10, 17, 1892, January 7, 1893; *ibid.* (monthly), February, 1893, p. 4.

26. *Northwestern Reporter*, February 4, 1893; *Sentinel* (Milwaukee), November 3, 6, October 26, 1894, January 8, and February 9, 15, 27, 1895; *Wisconsin State Journal*, February 18, 1895.

27. *Senate Journal* (1895), p. 178; *Assembly Journal* (1895), p. 251. On Austin see *Sentinel* (Milwaukee), October 7, 1895, October 16, 1922; Berryman, *op. cit.*, I, 525-528; on Klabunde, see *Sentinel* (Milwaukee), October 7 1895, November 8, 1894; *Wisconsin Blue Book* (1895), p. 685.

28. *Senate Journal* (1895), pp. 178, 326, 351, 387, 412, 433, 449, 465, 689-690, 717, 859; *Assembly Journal* (1895), pp. 251, 590, 602, 713, 773, 875, 966; *Laws of Wisconsin* (1895), pp. 428-429.

29. Gilbert T. Stephenson, *Race Distinctions in American Law* (New York, 1911), p. 121.

30. *Wisconsin Weekly Advocate*, March 16, May 11, 1899, May 23, 1901. The extant issues of this paper are particularly full of Green material, 1898-1902, and his obituaries make clear his prominence. See *Sentinel* (Milwaukee), December 4, 1911; *Defender* (Chicago), December 9, 1911.

31. Case #12786, Superior Court, Milwaukee (1895), Milwaukee County Courthouse; *Bryan* v. *Adler*, 97 Wisconsin Reports 124. Just before the turn of the century, a young Negro girl was refused admittance to a roller-skating rink in Oshkosh. She sued under the civil rights law and was awarded the verdict with minimum damages and costs. *Minute and Record Book*, II (February 10, March 4, 11, 1899), Municipal Court of Oshkosh, Winnebago County, Wisconsin; *Wisconsin Weekly Advocate*, March 16, 23, 1899.

The Unbalanced Scales

Another of the continuing myths in American history has been the belief that the federal government, outside of protecting slavery, was neutral in its treatment of citizens, black and white, before the Civil War. Further, after the Civil War, the assumption prevails that the agencies of the United States government strove hard to achieve equality for all. Both conceptions are erroneous. Reflecting the implicit racial views of its citizens, the federal government intervened more often in support of inequality over the long run, and in particular instances its support of equality has been hedged and limited. A commitment to full civil rights backed by a willingness to enforce such rights is difficult to find in past history.

Leon F. Litwack's essay documents quite clearly the ways in which the federal government discriminated against the free Negro before the Civil War. Some of the measures were petty, others denied the free Negro the means to compete equally for economic advantage with whites. The restrictions did not originate in the middle of the nineteenth century; they are almost contemporaneous with the founding of the republic. Nor does the treatment of the free Negro seem directly connected with the slavery controversy—save to bring the Negro into public notice. Rather, it reflects a uniform belief in a social structure where the Negro occupied a permanently inferior slot. Chief Justice Taney's delineation of the status of the Negro in American society in the Dred Scott case and his denial that the Negro could be a citizen of the United States may have been more consistent with practice than has been supposed.

Kenneth W. Porter examines the causes and conduct of a forgotten war in the next selection. The Mexican War involved primarily a question of slavery extension in the eyes of its opponents, and is so reported in today's textbooks, but the Seminole War receives little attention. No doubt part of the reason for this slighting is a lack of emphasis upon Indian wars in general in the study of the American past. Whatever the reason for the neglect of the war, Porter presents a convincing case that slaveowner pressure upon the government was a factor both in the beginning of hostilities and in the ultimate conditions of settlement. More than this, he shows how a conflicting model of slave society, one in which the person of the slave was less important, threatened the severe slavery of the American South. Indian slavery was more humane and demanded only tribute. The war itself also shows how much involved Negroes were in fighting with the Indians against the Army. The neglected war against the Seminoles provides insights into both the anxieties of the South and the policies of the federal government.

Whenever the question of federal intervention on behalf of the Negro is broached, the supposedly pernicious example of Reconstruction always is the buttress of a negative response. The commonly held idea is that Reconstruction was long, hard, punitive, and unfair. Recent revisionist historians have attacked this conception, which usually reflects a Southern view of Reconstruction, and have denied many of the allegations. Everette Swinney's study of the Enforcement Acts of 1870-1871 is one example of current scholarship. The Enforcement Acts, designed to put teeth into the Fifteenth Amendment, were not radical departures from past practices, according to Swinney. Seen from the present, the acts seem reasonable and constitutional. Swinney also shows how original vigor did win early enforcement cases, while after 1874 a combination of an unfavorable Supreme Court ruling, Southern intractability and solidity, and Northern apathy spelled inevitable retraction. The failure of this first attempt to gain Negro political rights can be summed up as too little effort over too short a time.

Shifting from the nineteenth to the twentieth century, the next two articles concern Woodrow Wilson and Franklin Roosevelt, two of the most influential presidents of this century. Kathleen Wolgemuth considers the key role of Wilson in fixing official segregation policies in the federal service. With a Southern background and Southern advisers, Wilson saw nothing wrong in reinforcing the tacit segregation of the larger society, throwing the weight of government sanction on the unbalanced side of the scales. Once again, Negro protest availed little; the government made a small retreat. Miss Wolgemuth makes two important points: one, official segregation in federal service came later than has been acknowledged; two, the Southern liberal—if Wilson can be called a liberal—was in this period a racist.

The last article in this section recounts the problems of President Roosevelt in enforcing equal treatment of Negroes in the Civilian Conservation Corps. John S. Salmond shows how impotent the President was in the face of determined opposition, within and without the administration. Roosevelt, who did much for Negro rights, appears here as more conscious of political realities than of racial justice. It is unfair to cast Roosevelt as a contemporary civil libertarian, but the memories of his opponents as well as his friends have distorted the record. In retrospect his policy seems timid.

The total thrust of the five selections is that the federal government, until the Civil War, contributed to the distinction between white and black; that immediately after the war the same government did not pursue Negro equality long and vigorously; that in the twentieth century, under two strong presidents, one administration contributed to a separate society while the other moved at a snail's pace to achieve an integrated one. While one should not make the ahistorical error of equating Roosevelt with Wilson or the Enforcement Acts with the Pre-emption Act, still the common thread linking all is the lack of an effective effort for equality for all.

THE FEDERAL GOVERNMENT AND
THE FREE NEGRO, 1790-1860

Leon F. Litwack

In the absence of any clear constitutional or judicial directive, the federal government and the individual states separately defined the legal status of ante bellum free Negroes. Prior to the Fourteenth and Fifteenth Amendments, each state determined their political and educational rights. In many cases, this resulted in disfranchisement, immigration restrictions and public segregation. Various branches of the federal government also confronted problems involving the constitutional rights of free Negroes, an aspect of federal policy that historians have generally neglected.

During the Missouri controversy of 1819-1821, Congress exhaustively debated the Negro's legal status but failed to clarify it. Not until 1857, when the Supreme Court settled the Dred Scott case, did the federal government finally resolve the question. By then, Chief Justice Roger B. Taney could turn to federal legislation and "the conduct of the Executive Department" for precedents.

II

Reflecting the popular conception of the United States as a white man's country, early congressional legislation frequently excluded Negroes from

Leon F. Litwack, "The Federal Government and the Free Negro, 1790-1860," *Journal of Negro History*, XLIII, No. 4 (October, 1958), 261-278.

federal rights and privileges. In 1790, Congress limited naturalization to "any alien, being a white person"; in 1792, it organized the militia and restricted enrollment to "each and every free, able-bodied white male citizen"; in 1810, it excluded Negroes from carrying the United States mails; in 1820, it authorized the citizens of Washington, D.C., to elect "white" city officials and to adopt a code governing free Negroes and slaves.[1] It repeatedly approved the admission of states whose constitutions severely limited the legal rights of Negroes.[2] On one occasion, however, the House of Representatives momentarily recognized Negro citizenship when it resolved in 1803 "to enquire into the expediency of granting protection to such American seamen citizens of the United States, as are free persons of color."[3]

These measures elicited only minor discussion. But after 1821 legislation affecting the legal position of Negroes frequently involved Congress in lengthy and bitter debates. As abolition sentiment and agitation increased, southern and "Doughface" congressmen seized upon opportunities to show the inconsistency of pronouncements on equality and freedom with the treatment accorded free Negroes in the North. In the famous exchange between Daniel Webster and Robert Hayne, for example, the South Carolina Senator defended Negro bondage and charged that slaves were induced to leave their masters and go North where they were treated as outcasts and assigned to "the dark and narrow lanes, and obscure recesses" of the cities. "Sir," he cried, "there does not exist on the face of the earth, a population so poor, so wretched, so vile, so loathsome, so utterly destitute of all the comforts, conveniences, and decencies of life, as the unfortunate blacks of Philadelphia and Boston."[4] Senator Felix Grundy of Tennessee observed in 1830 that the treatment of Negroes in the free western states proved that "general notions about the liberation of slaves are idle and visionary."[5] On denouncing northern interference with slavery, a Virginia representative asked, "Do you permit the black man to sit on juries, to enter the learned professions, and to associate with you upon an equal footing, or, indeed, to worship by your side in the house of God? It is notorious you permit none of these things. . . . Go home, and emancipate your free Negroes. When you do that, we will listen to you with more patience."[6]

III

After 1840, southern congressmen could assert that the federal government itself offered authoritative proof of the benign influence of slavery on Negroes. The Sixth Census of the United States, released in 1841, enumerated for the first time the mentally diseased and defective—or "insane and idiots" as they were then officially described—and contained the startling revelation that their prevalence among free Negroes was about eleven times higher than among slaves. In the southern states, the ratio of insane or idiotic among the Negro population stood at one to every 1,558; in the northern states, it was one to every 144.5.[7] In fact, the frequency of these afflictions among Negroes decreased from Maine to Louisiana with virtual mathematical precision. For example, it was found that in Maine every 14th Negro was either a lunatic or an idiot; in New Hampshire every 28th; in Massachusetts every 43rd; in Connecticut every 184th; in New York every 257th; and in New Jersey every 297th. This was in sharp contrast with the South where the proportion ranged from one in 1,299 in Virginia and one in 2,477 in South Carolina to one in 4,310 in Louisiana.[8]

Such statistics not only offered obvious moral lessons but gave official credence to popular "scientific" ideas about the peculiar suitability of Negroes for slavery. One northern observer, in a letter to a New York business journal, explained that the prevalence of insanity among local Negroes resulted from "the rigors of a northern winter, which have no influence on the temperament of the whites" but "which affect the cerebral organs of the African race." He admitted, however, that slavery undoubtedly lessened such occurrences.[9] The *Southern Literary Messenger* printed the insanity returns, declared that the sectional disparity resulted from "moral causes, arising from their situation, and in no degree the effect of climate," and concluded "that where slavery has been longest extinguished, the condition of the colored race is worse." It painted a dark picture of what would happen in the event of emancipation. "Let us then suppose," it remarked, "a half a million of free Negroes suddenly turned loose in Virginia, whose propensity it is, constantly to grow more vicious in a state of freedom. . . . Where should we find Penitentiaries for the thousands of felons? Where, lunatic asylums for the tens of thousands of maniacs? Would it be possible to live in a country where maniacs and felons met the traveller at every cross-road?"[10] In Congress, a Mississippian used the census tables to contrast "the happy, well-fed, healthy, and moral condition of the southern slaves, with the condition of the miserable victims and degraded free blacks of the North." Such must be the case, he declared, for "idiocy and lunacy . . . in the lower classes, had been shown by medical men to be invariably caused by vice and misery."[11]

These remarkable statistics eventually found their way into the diplomatic crisis over Texas. The British government, in a communication to Secretary of State Abel Upshur in 1844, had expressed a desire to see slavery abolished in Texas and throughout the world. John C. Calhoun, Upshur's successor, replied that slavery in Texas was the concern of neither the British nor the federal government, but was a local matter. Calhoun nevertheless lectured the English foreign secretary on the relative merits of slavery and freedom for the Negro population, and he used the latest statistics to support his argument. "The census and other authentic documents," he declared, "show that, in all instances in which the States have changed the former relation between the two races, the condition of the African, instead of being improved, has become worse. They have been invariably sunk into vice and pauperism, accompanied by the bodily and mental inflictions incident thereto—deafness, blindness, insanity, and idiocy—to a degree without example." [12]

But Calhoun's "unquestionable sources" were already seriously challenged by Dr. Edward Jarvis, a Massachusetts-born physician and specialist in mental disorders, and a founder of the American Statistical Association.[13] In his first reaction to the returns on insanity and idiocy, Jarvis remarked that slavery must have "a wonderful influence upon the development of moral faculties and the intellectual powers." [14] Upon more careful investigation, however, he found that the errors in these returns were nearly as startling as the statistics themselves, and in January, 1844—four months prior to Calhoun's first letter—he thoroughly refuted the census findings. Contrasting the population returns with the insanity figures, Jarvis found that in numerous northern towns insane Negroes were enumerated where no Negro population existed, and that in others they exceeded the reported number of Negro residents. He concluded that "the sixth census has contributed nothing to the statistical nosology of the free blacks" and was, "in respect to human ailment, a bearer of falsehood to confuse and mislead." [15]

Similar objections were raised throughout the North. A Boston newspaper examined the returns and concluded that "the remarkable prevalence of insanity among the colored people of the free States . . . exists only in the errors of the census." [16] The *North American Review* regretted that the census was "vitiated by carelessness in regard to the statistics of insanity." [17] In a letter to the New York *Tribune*, a Negro leader declared, "Freedom has not made us mad; it has strengthened our minds by throwing us upon our own resources, and has bound us to American institutions with a tenacity which nothing but death can overcome." [18]

Demands arose for a correction of the census. Jarvis declared that it was "due to the honour of our country, to medical science, and to truth." The American Statistical Association sent a memorial to Congress enumerating the errors.[19] A group of New York Negroes met "to consider the calumnies recently uttered against the free people of color by John C. Calhoun," and memorialized Congress to re-examine the returns in view of the many glaring inaccuracies.[20]

In Congress, Representative John Quincy Adams of Massachusetts demanded a correction. On February 26, 1844, the House directed the secretary of state, who was responsible for the conduct of the census, to inform them "whether any gross errors" were discovered, but Calhoun evaded the inquiry by finding a technical error in the resolution.[21] Adams then called on Calhoun and was told "that where there were so many errors they balanced one another, and led to the same conclusion as if they were all correct." [22] In June the House committee, to which the memorial of the American Statistical Association had been referred, reported that they "have no reason to doubt the correctness of the statements in the memorial, and feel that they destroy the utility of the printed census, so far as the subjects referred to are concerned and render completely nugatory any conclusions which may be based upon them." The committee hoped that no such errors would appear in the next census.[23]

But Calhoun remained adamant. In response to a new House resolution, he stated that the "gross and glaring errors" imputed by the memorialists had been given a "full and thorough examination," and "the result would seem fully to sustain the correctness of the census." While errors could be expected in any such undertaking, they did not, he declared, alter the conclusion that a far greater prevalence of the diseases of insanity, blindness, deafness, and dumbness existed among northern Negroes. This fact, Calhoun asserted, "stands unimpeachable." [24]

In the absence of any revision, the census of 1840 continued to serve the purposes of anti-abolition orators and editors. In fact, a Georgia congressman reportedly admitted to Jarvis that the census contained numerous errors but he added, "It is too good a thing for our politicians to give up. They had prepared speeches based on it, which they could not afford to lose." [25]

IV

The congressional debates on slavery expansion in the 1840's and 1850's had little significance for the political or economic progress of northern Negroes. Most proponents of slavery restriction tried to make it clear that their concern was not for the plight of the Negro but for the welfare of the white race. When Representative David Wilmot of Pennsylvania introduced his proviso to exclude slavery from the territories acquired from Mexico, he carefully explained that he did not propose to interfere with southern institutions, and that he possessed "no squeamish sensitiveness upon the subject of slavery, no morbid sympathy for the slave." What he wanted were free states for free white men. "I plead the cause and the rights of white freemen," he declared in 1847. "I would preserve to free white labor a fair country, a rich inheritance, where the sons of toil, of my own race and own color, can live without the disgrace which association with Negro slavery brings upon free labor." [26] The following year, a New York representative proposed that Congress "inquire into the expediency of setting apart a portion of the public lands for the exclusive use and possessions of free black persons." [27]

In order to reserve the new territories for whites, Negroes would have to be barred from the benefits of federal land policy. The Senate attempted this in 1841 when it voted to confine the privileges of the new pre-emption law to whites. Augustus Porter of Michigan, the lone dissenter, observed that no previous act had embodied such a clause and that it conflicted with the right to buy and dispose of property. While Negroes enjoyed no political rights in his state, they were entitled, he declared, to all the civil rights conferred by the Constitution, including that of holding property. By "general consent," the Senate deleted the restriction from the bill before its final passage.[28] But it still required an opinion from the attorney general's office to qualify Negroes for the benefits of the act. In the 1850's Congress frequently tacked amendments onto land and homestead bills excluding Negroes from their provisions, because granting them land would encourage and prolong "their common residence in this Confederacy" with white people.[29]

The Dred Scott decision dealt a severe blow to the Negro's pre-emption rights. The secretary of the interior had previously written a New York Negro that "there is nothing in the laws of the United States which would prevent you, as a Freeman of African descent, from settling upon land in the Territory of Minnesota, and acquiring a right of pre-emption." Soon after the Supreme Court ruling, however, the commissioner of the General Land Office announced that since Negroes were not citizens, they could not qualify for pre-emption benefits.[30]

V

As early as 1810 the federal government excluded Negroes from the postal service. Postmaster General Gideon Granger, in "a private representation" to Senator James Jackson of Georgia, declared in 1802 that objections existed to Negroes handling the mail, "of a nature too delicate to engraft into a report which may become public, yet too important to be omitted or passed over without full consideration." Granger feared that they would use the postal service to coordinate insurrectionary activities, particularly in the southern states. "Every thing which tends to increase their knowledge of natural rights," he warned, "of men and things, or that affords them an opportunity of associating, acquiring, and communicating sentiments, and of establishing a chain or line of intelligence" must excite alarm. As post riders, Negroes would mix with other people, acquire information, and "learn that a man's rights do not depend on his color." [31] Congress responded in 1810 by providing "that no other than a free white person shall be employed in conveying the mail." [32] Postmaster General John McLean instructed his deputies in 1828 to adhere strictly to this regulation. If Negro labor was required "to lift the mail from the stage into the post office," it must be "performed in the presence and under the immediate direction of the white person who has it in custody." [33]

Not until 1862 did Congress attempt to abrogate the restriction. In that year the Senate passed Charles Sumner's bill to revoke the clause, and thereby caused the Boston *Journal* to remark that it was the first time, within their recollection, "that any bill having the Negro in it, directly or indirectly, has been passed by the Senate without debate." But the House tabled the bill after Schuyler Colfax, Republican chairman of the post office committee, objected to it on the grounds that no public demand existed for its repeal, that it would qualify Negroes and Indians as mail contractors and even officers in the department, and that the postmaster general had not recommended passage and did not regard it in "the best interests of the Department." [34]

VI

In citing "the conduct of the Executive Department" as a precedent for his opinion, Chief Justice Taney referred specifically to the refusal of the state department to grant passports to Negroes. Actually, Negroes secured passports in several cases as late as 1854.[35] However, the secretary of state rejected the application of a Philadelphia Negro in 1839 on the grounds that the newly revised Pennsylvania Constitution did not recognize Negroes as citizens.[36] In 1847 Secretary of State James Buchanan clarified this policy when he declared that it was customary to grant free Negroes "not a pass port, in the ordinary form, recognizing them as citizens, but a certificate suited to the nature of the case."[37] His successor, John M. Clayton, stated two years later that passports "are not granted by this department to persons of colore, and that protections are only given to them when they are in the service of diplomatic agents, &c., of the United States going abroad."[38] This prompted one observer to write that "the colored man is not only insulted and wronged at home, and in half the Union is utterly defenceless, but if he would leave this cruel country he must go abroad as an outlaw."[39] Severely censured by several newspapers, Clayton justified his action with the assertion that this had been the "settled regulation of the Department."[40]

In the late 1840's and in the 1850's, numerous Negro leaders sought passports for England where they planned to lecture and raise money for the abolitionist cause, but in most cases their applications were rejected. The hardening of state department policy was evident in an official letter accompanying the refusal of passports to eleven northern Negroes in 1856. It declared that the question of Negro citizenship "has repeatedly arisen in the administration of both the national and State governments," and it cited the opinion of Attorney General William Wirt in 1821 that free Negroes were not citizens under the Constitution. According to this interpretation, the letter continued, free Negroes "cannot be regarded, when beyond the jurisdiction of the Government, as entitled to the full rights of citizens." The department was willing, however, to grant certificates "that they were born in the United States, are free, and that the government thereof would regard it to be its duty to protect them if wronged by a foreign government, while within its jurisdiction for a legal and proper purpose." [41]

Following the Dred Scott decision, the state department relied on Taney's ruling as proper and sufficient grounds for rejecting Negro applicants. But Secretary of State Lewis Cass went so far as to assert that "a passport being a certificate of citizenship, has never since the foundation of the Government, been granted to persons of color." [42] Several newspapers thereupon enumerated for Cass's edification those passports that had been granted to free Negroes.[43] "If the statement is a blunder on the part of General Cass, it betrays reprehensible ignorance," a Cleveland newspaper declared; "if a deliberate falsification, it is deserving of the severest censure." [44] One rejected Negro applicant remarked that his only hope now was "to go to some foreign country, and through the assistance of friends, claim its protection, or else, through their assistance, get permission to travel as an American outlaw!" [45] The Massachusetts Legislature decided that since the Dred Scott decision "virtually denationalized" the state's Negro citizens, it would authorize its own secretary of state to grant passports to any citizens of the Commonwealth "whatever his color may be." [46] In 1861, the new secretary, William H. Seward, reversed state department policy.

VII

The opinions of the attorneys general demonstrated that differences did exist in the federal interpretation of Negro citizenship. In 1821, William Wirt ruled that free Negroes in Virginia were not citizens of the United States and, therefore, could not command vessels according to the acts regulating the foreign and coasting trade. However, since Wirt defined "citizens of the United States" as "those only who enjoyed the full and equal privileges of white citizens in the States of their residence," he implied that Negroes could be so considered.[47] Two years later, Wirt ruled that Negro soldiers were entitled to the bounty lands promised them for service in the War of 1812, although he felt "that it was not the intention of Congress to incorporate Negroes and people of color with the army any more than with the militia of the United States." [48]

In 1822, the South Carolina legislature passed the first in a series of southern acts which provided for the imprisonment of free Negro seamen while their vessels remained in port. After formal protests by the British government, Wirt advised that the acts violated "the Constitution, treaties, and laws of the United States" and were "incompatible with the rights of all nations in amity with the United States." [49] Seven years later, however, Attorney General John Berrien found the acts to be a lawful exercise of state police powers.[50] Upon the receipt of another British protest in 1831, Secretary of State Edward Livingston asked the new attorney general, Roger Taney, for his opinion. Taney's reply, although never completed for publication, clearly anticipated his decision twenty-five years later as Chief Justice. "The African race in the United States even when free," he wrote, "are everywhere a degraded class, and exercise no political influence. The privileges they are allowed to enjoy, are accorded to them as a matter of kindness and benevolence rather than of right. . . . And where they are nominally admitted by the law to the privileges of citizenship, they have no effectual power to defend them, and are permitted to be citizens by the sufferance of the white population and hold whatever rights they enjoy at their mercy." Negroes were "a separate and degraded people to whom the sovereignty of each state might accord or withhold such privileges as they deemed proper." Consequently, the framers of the Constitution had not regarded them as citizens and they "were evidently not supposed to be included by the term citizens." [51]

Attorney General Hugh Legaré decided in 1843 that free Negroes were neither aliens nor citizens but occupied an intermediate position. When asked whether they were entitled to the benefits of the new pre-emption act, Legaré replied that they had previously been admitted to the benefits of these laws and he saw nothing in the new act "that necessarily excludes them." The "plain meaning" of the act was to exclude aliens and to grant pre-emption rights "to all denizens"; any foreigner who filed his intention of citizenship could thus qualify for its benefits. "Now, free people of color are not aliens," Legaré advised, "they enjoy universally . . . the rights of denizens. . . . How far a political status may be acquired is a different question, but his civil status is that of a complete denizenship." [52] However, this newly discovered legal position for the free Negro did not meet the approval of a later attorney general, Caleb Cushing. He charged in 1856 that Legaré "had . . . been carried away in argument by a generous disposition to protect in the given case the claim of a free African, without admitting him to be a citizen of the United States." A free Negro could be entitled to pre-emption rights, Cushing asserted, only if Wirt's opinion was first over-ruled and he had no intention of doing this.[53]

The constitutional rights of free Negroes were finally recognized during the Civil War. Attorney-General Edward Bates advised in 1862 that citizenship was "not dependent nor coexistent" with color, race, "the degradation of a people," or the legal right to vote and hold office. "Free men of color, if born in the United States, are citizens of the United States." [54] Six years later, the Fourteenth Amendment confirmed this opinion.

VIII

If any confusion existed in the federal government prior to 1857 on the constitutional rights of Negroes, it was finally dispelled by the decision of the Supreme Court in *Dred Scott* v. *Sanford.* The Missouri Compromise and Negro citizenship were both found to be unconstitutional.

Chief Justice Taney constructed his opinion on a review of the historical status of the Negro population, and he placed particular emphasis on their legal position at the time of the Constitutional Convention of 1787. For more than a century prior to that convention, Taney declared, Negroes had "been regarded as beings of an inferior order, and altogether unfit to associate with the white race, either in social or political relations; and so far inferior, that they had no rights which the white man was bound to respect." Colonial legislation demonstrated the extent of public antipathy toward Negroes. Although the northern states abolished slavery, this resulted not from "any change of opinion in relation to this race" but from its unprofitability in the northern climate and economy. That no moral revolution had occurred, Taney continued, was nowhere more clearly demonstrated than in the laws passed by several states to control free Negroes.[55] "It cannot be supposed," he stated, that the framers of the Constitution intended to grant Negroes "rights and privileges, and rank, in the new political body throughout the Union, which every one of them denied within the limits of its own dominion." Consequently, Negroes were "not intended to be included, and formed no part of the people who framed and adopted" the Declaration of Independence and the Constitution.[56]

State and federal citizenship must not be confused, Taney asserted, for while a state can legally naturalize its own inhabitants, it has no power to secure to them the rights and privileges of citizens in other states or in the United States. Since Congress alone possesses the right to establish a uniform rule of naturalization, states are prohibited from introducing any new members "into the political community created by the Constitution," and "for the same reason" they "cannot introduce any person, or description of persons, who were not intended to be embraced in this new political family." That this applied to Negroes was abundantly clear to the chief justice. Had not Congress restricted naturalization to "free white persons"? Subsequent legislation and the practices of the executive department, Taney believed, confirmed his conclusion that Negroes "are not included, and were not intended to be included, under the word 'citizens' in the Constitution, and can therefore claim none of the rights and privileges which that instrument provides for and secures to citizens of the United States." [57]

Two justices joined Taney in his opinion on Negro citizenship, four avoided the issue, and two others—John McLean and Benjamin R. Curtis—wrote vigorous dissents. Curtis contended that the right to confer citizenship rested with the states and that the federal government could only specify the manner in which an alien's disabilities might be removed. Free native-born citizens of each state were thus citizens of the United States. Curtis denied that the Constitution was a white man's document. At the time of the ratification of the Articles of Confederation, he pointed out, free Negroes were not only citizens in five states—New Hampshire, Massachusetts, New York, New Jersey, and North Carolina—but actually exercised the right of suffrage on equal terms with whites. The framers of the Articles must have known this, Curtis declared, for they rejected a move by South Carolina to restrict the privileges and immunities clause to white persons. Negroes, he concluded, "were not only included in the body of 'the people of the United States,' by whom the Constitution was ordained and established, but in at least five of the states they had the power to act, and doubtless did act, by their suffrages, upon the question of its adoption." They were thus clearly entitled to its privileges and immunities.[58]

While many northern political leaders and newspaper editors assailed Taney's decision, they indicated more concern over its repudiation of that sacred sectional compact, the Missouri Compromise, than over the constitutional rights of Negroes. However, the Negro community bitterly condemned the ruling. One protest meeting called it "a palpably vain, arrogant assumption, unsustained by history, justice, reason or common sense." [59] Frederick Douglass declared that "the National Conscience" would not be silenced "by such an open, glaring, and scandalous tissue of lies as that decision is, and has been, over and over, shown to be." [60] But Robert Purvis, a colored abolitionist, warned his people not to comfort themselves with the thought that this decision was unconstitutional. It was, he declared, "in perfect keeping with the treatment of the colored people by the American Government from the beginning to this day." [61] This sentiment was shared by other Negro leaders who, while condemning the decision, expressed no great surprise. After all, one

Negro protest declared, it was but "final confirmation of the already well known fact that under the Constitution and Government of the United States, the colored people are nothing, and can be nothing but an alien, disfranchised and degraded class." [62]

NOTES

1. *Appendix to the Annals of Congress,* 1st Congress, 2nd Session, 2nd Congress, 1st Session, p. 1392; 11th Congress, 1st and 2nd Session, p. 2569; 16th Congress, 1st Session, pp. 2600-2610; 18th Congress, 2nd Session, p. 91.

2. Charles H. Wesley, "Negro Suffrage in the Period of Constitution Making 1787-1865," *Journal of Negro History,* XXXII (1947), 154. Vermont (1790), Kentucky (1792), and Tennessee (1796) made no provision in their constitutions excluding Negroes from the suffrage. With Maine (1819), they were the only states which entered the Union, prior to the admission of Nebraska in 1867, which did not restrict the suffrage to whites. Kentucky and Tennessee subsequently enacted such a restriction.

3. *Journal of the House of Representatives,* 8th Congress, 1st Session, p. 224.

4. *Register of Debates,* 21st Congress, 1st Session, p. 47.

5. *Ibid.,* p. 215.

6. *Congressional Globe,* 30th Congress, 1st Session, p. 602; 29th Congress, 2nd Session, p. 349.

7. Albert Deutsch, "The First U.S. Census of the Insane (1840) and Its Use as Pro-Slavery Propaganda," *Bulletin of the History of Medicine,* XV (1944), 469-482. Aside from the Deutsch article, I am indebted for suggested references to William R. Stanton, "The Leopard's Spots: Science and the American Idea of Equality, 1815-1860" (Ph.D. dissertation, Brown University, 1955), pp. 87-100. For the original returns, see *Compilation of the Enumeration of the Inhabitants and Statistics of the United States, as Obtained at the Department of State, from the Returns of the Sixth Census* (Washington, D.C., 1841), pp. 4-104.

8. "Reflections on the Census of 1840," *Southern Literary Messenger,* IX (1843), 341; Edward Jarvis, "Insanity among the Coloured Population of the Free States," *American Journal of the Medical Sciences,* VII (1844), 71-83.

9. "Table of Lunacy in the United States," *Hunt's Merchants' Magazine and Commercial Review,* VIII (1843), 460-461.

10. "Reflections on the Census of 1840," pp. 342, 344, 346-347.

11. *Congressional Globe,* 28th Congress, 1st Session, p. 239.

12. John C. Calhoun to Lord Richard Pakenham, April 18, 1844, "Proceedings of the Senate and Documents Relative to Texas," *Senate Document,*

28th Congress, 1st Session, no. 341 (1844)), pp. 50-53. This letter also appears in Richard K. Cralle (ed.), *The Works of John C. Calhoun* (6 vols.; New York, 1853-1855), V, 333-339. In a subsequent communication, Calhoun denied that he had defended slavery in his previous letter. His intention had simply been to demonstrate "from unquestionable sources" the depraved condition of Negroes in those states which had abolished the institution. Calhoun to Pakenham, April 27, 1844, "Proceedings of the Senate and Documents Relative to Texas," pp. 65-67, and Cralle, *op. cit.*, V, 343-347.

13. Jarvis went to Louisville, Kentucky, to practice in 1837 but his antipathy to slavery prompted his return to Massachusetts six years later. He became a leading statistician, served for thirty-one years as president of the American Statistical Association, and helped to prepare the census of 1850, 1860, and 1870. For further biographical information, see William R. Leonard, "Edward Jarvis," in Allen Johnson and Dumas Malone (eds.), *Dictionary of American Biography* (22 vols.; New York, 1928-1944), IX, 621-622, and Robert W. Wood, *Memorial of Edward Jarvis, M.D.* (Boston, 1885).

14. Edward Jarvis, "Statistics of Insanity in the United States," *Boston Medical and Surgical Journal*, XXVII (1842), 116-121, as quoted in Stanton, *op. cit.*, pp. 87-88. Neither Deutsch nor Wood, in their studies of Jarvis' efforts to correct the census, mention his first reaction.

15. For example, in Maine, where every 14th Negro was supposedly insane, the census listed six such Negroes in Scarsboro but no Negro population, and credited Dresden with twice as many insane Negroes as Negro residents. In Worcester, Massachusetts, the census found 133 insane out of a Negro population of 161. Actually, this former number represented the white patients in the state hospital for the insane at Worcester. *Compilation of the Enumeration of the Inhabitants and Statisics of the United States*, pp. 5, 7, 9, 11; Deutsch, *op. cit.*, pp. 475-476.

16. *Daily Advertiser and Patriot* (Boston), as reprinted in *The Liberator*, August 18, 1843.

17. "Review of Edward Jarvis, 'What Shall We Do with the Insane,'" *North American Review*, LVI (1843), 172-173n.

18. James McCune Smith to the Editor of the *Tribune* (New York), January 29, 1844, as reprinted in *The Liberator*, February 23, 1844.

19. "Errors in Sixth Census," *House Report*, 28th Congress, 1st Session, no. 580 (1844), pp. 1-9.

20. *The Liberator*, May 10, 31, 1844. See also Herbert Aptheker (ed.), *A Documentary History of the Negro People in the United States* (New York, 1951), pp. 238-243.

21. Charles F. Adams (ed.), *Memoirs of John Quincy Adams, Comprising Portions of His Diary from 1795-1848* (12 vols.; Philadelphia, 1875), XII, 22-23.

22. *Ibid.*, p. 29.

23. "Errors in Sixth Census," p. 1. A Senate committee reached identical conclusions. See *Senate Document*, 28th Congress, 1st Session, no. 146 (1845), pp. 1-2.

24. *Niles' National Register*, June 7, 1845.

25. Wood, *Memorial of Edward Jarvis,* quoted in Deutsch, *op. cit.,* p. 478.

26. *Appendix to the Congressional Globe,* 29th Congress, 2nd Session, p. 317.

27. *Congressional Globe,* 30th Congress, 1st Session, p. 778.

28. *Ibid.,* 26th Congress, 2nd Session, pp. 77, 114; *Appendix,* p. 27.

29. For example, see *Congressional Globe,* 31st Congress, 1st Session, 33rd Congress, 1st Session, pp. 1057-1058, 1071-1073. Frederick Douglass and Rep. Gerrit Smith strongly condemned the "white" restriction in the Homestead Bill of 1854. *Frederick Douglass' Paper,* March 17, 1854.

30. *Daily Times* (New York), August 21, 1857; *Annual Reports of the American Anti-Slavery Society . . . for the years ending May 1, 1857, and May 1, 1858* (New York, 1859), p. 130.

31. *American State Papers. Documents, Legislative and Executive, of the Congresses of the United States . . .* (38 vols.; Washington, D.C., 1832-1861), Class VII: Post Office, p. 27.

32. The restriction was enacted without change in 1825. *Appendix to the Annals of Congress,* 11th Congress, 1st and 2nd Session, p. 2569; 18th Congress, 2nd Session, p. 91.

33. William Jay, "A View of the Action of the Federal Government in Behalf of Slavery," in *Miscellaneous Writings on Slavery* (Boston, 1853), p. 233; William C. Nell, *The Colored Patriots of the American Revolution, with Sketches of Several Distinguished Colored Persons: To which is added a Brief Survey of the Condition and Prospects of Colored Americans* (Boston, 1855), p. 312.

34. *Congressional Globe,* 37th Congress, 2nd Session, pp. 1260, 1390, 1626, 2231-2232, 2262-2263; Charles Sumner, *The Works of Charles Sumner* (15 vols.; Boston, 1870-1883), VI, 385-388.

35. For example, the State Department issued passports to Robert Purvis in 1834, Peter Williams in 1836, William Wells Brown in 1849, and John Remond in 1854. Arnold Buffum to Roberts Vaux, May 16, 1834, Historical Society of Pennsylvania, Philadelphia; *The Liberator,* April 16, 1858.

36. Sarah M. Grimké to Elizabeth Pease, August 25, 1839, in Gilbert H. Barnes and Dwight L. Dumond (eds.), *Letters of Theodore Dwight Weld, Angelina Grimké Weld and Sarah Grimké, 1822-1844* (2 vols.; New York, 1934), II, 792-793. The Pennsylvania Constitutional Convention of 1837-1838 restricted the suffrage to white males.

37. James Buchanan to N. H. Davis, March 8, 1847, in John Bassett Moore (ed.), *The Works of James Buchanan* (12 vols.; Philadelphia, 1908-1911), VII, 236.

38. *The North Star,* July 20, August 24, 1849. See also *The Non-Slaveholder,* IV (1849), 191, and *Eighteenth Annual Report, presented to the Massachusetts Anti-Slavery Society . . . January 23, 1850* (Boston, 1850), pp. 44-45.

39. *The Non-Slaveholder,* IV (1849), 191.

40. John M. Clayton to the Editor of the Salem *Register,* in *The* [10th] *Annual Report of the American and Foreign Anti-Slavery Society, presented at New York, May 7, 1850, . . .* (New York, 1850), pp. 128-129.

41. *The Liberator*, November 28, 1856; Edward Bates to Salmon P. Chase, November 29, 1862, in *Official Opinions of the Attorneys General of the United States*, . . . (40 vols., Washington, D.C., 1791-1948), X, 404. The letter, writen by Assistant Secretary J. A. Thomas, conveyed the opinion of Secretary of State William L. Marcy.

42. *New York Times*, April 12, 1858.

43. "The Oppression of the Buchanan Administration Towards Colored Citizens," *Daily Bee* (Boston), reprinted in *The Liberator*, April 16, 1858.

44. *Leader* (Cleveland), April 20, 1858.

45. *Ibid.*, May 4, 1858.

46. *The Liberator*, April 24, 1857.

47. *Official Opinions*, I, 506-509.

48. *Ibid.*, I, 602-603. The acts of Congress under which these Negro troops were raised called for "able-bodied, effective" men (1811) and "free, effective, able-bodied men" (1814). Wirt decided that Negroes could satisfy either of these requirements and therefore must receive the promised bounties.

49. *Ibid.*, I, 659-661.

50. *Ibid.*, II, 426-442.

51. Carl Brent Swisher, *Roger B. Taney* (New York, 1936), p. 154.

52. *Official Opinions*, IV, 147-148.

53. *Ibid.*, VII, 751-773.

54. *Ibid.*, X, 382-413.

55. Taney cited as examples the Massachusetts and Rhode Island laws forbidding interracial marriages (1786 and 1822); the Connecticut law prohibiting the establishment of any school for the instruction of Negroes not inhabitants of the state (1833), and the decision of a Connecticut court upholding that law (1834); and the New Hampshire act barring Negroes from the militia (1815).

56. *Dred Scott* v. *Sanford*, 19 Howard, pp. 407-410, 412-416.

57. *Ibid.*, pp. 404-406. Federal practices and legislation cited by Taney included the militia law of 1792; an act of 1813 prohibiting employment on vessels to "any person or persons except citizens of the United States, or persons of color, natives of the United States"; the Washington, D.C., administrative act of 1820; the opinions of Attorneys General Wirt and Cushing; and the passport policy of the State Department.

58. *Ibid.*, pp. 572-582.

59. *The Liberator*, July 9, 1858. Meeting of New Bedford Negroes on June 16, 1858.

60. "The Dred Scott Decision, Speech delivered before the American Anti-Slavery Society, New York, May 11, 1857," reprinted in Philip S. Foner (ed.), *The Life and Writings of Frederick Douglass* (4 vols.; New York, 1950-1955), II, 411.

61. *The Liberator*, April 10, 1857.

62. *Ibid.*

NEGROES AND THE SEMINOLE

WAR, 1835-1842

Kenneth Wiggins Porter

The second Seminole War lasted from December 1835 to August 1842 and cost over forty million dollars and the lives of approximately fifteen hundred members of the armed forces of the United States, [1] in addition to those of white settlers and militiamen. It is usually referred to as the country's most protracted and expensive Indian war,[2] but Major General Thomas Sidney Jesup, who was in command in Florida during its most crucial period, announced emphatically late in 1836, "This . . . is a negro, not an Indian war." The general, of course, was employing hyperbole to emphasize his belief that if the war were "not speedily put down, the south will feel the effects of it on their slave population before the end of the next season" [3]—in other words, that a general slave insurrection might ensue. Actually the war, which was undoubtedly an Indian war, was just as certainly a Negro war during its most critical years. There is abundant evidence that Negroes were more important than Indians in bringing it about and keeping it up, as well as largely influential in bringing it to a conclusion.

Of the Negroes in the Florida Indian country the most important group were those with a recognized position in the Seminole tribe. A few of these were admittedly the lawful slaves of the Indians and an even smaller number were legally free; the great majority, perhaps four-fifths, were runaway or "captured" Negroes and their descendants, all of whom were thus legally the property of white citizens.[4] White ob-

Kenneth W. Porter, "Negroes and the Seminole War, 1835-1842," *Journal of Southern History*, XXX, No. 4 (November, 1964), 427-450.

servers, however, were inclined to regard all these Negroes—except for very recent runaways or captives—as in some sense the Indians' slaves. Nearly all, regardless of legal status, received almost identical treatment from the Indians, which differed so much from the treatment of slaves by whites that it was a difference of kind rather than of degree. Indian agent Gad Humphreys in 1827 declared, "The negroes of the Seminole Indians are wholly independent . . . and are Slaves but in name; they work only when it suits their inclination"; while brevet Major General Edmund P. Gaines, a decade or so later, referred to them not as the Indians' slaves but as "their black vassals and allies." [5]

Although the Seminole Indians were of all the so-called civilized tribes the least influenced by European-American civilization, some of their chiefs, for reasons of prestige, had purchased Negro slaves; and as traditional allies of the British the Seminole also had no scruples about capturing slaves or receiving fugitive Negroes from the rebellious Americans or the Spaniards. The Indians, however, had no intention of spending their lives in supervising Negroes; so, save for a very few employed in personal service, the Negroes were furnished with axes, hoes, and seed corn and left to take care of themselves.

A system of relationships between the Seminole Indians and their Negroes developed which was the admiration or horror of all beholders. The Negroes lived in separate villages of well-built houses, raised crops of corn, sweet potatoes, other vegetables, and even cotton, and possessed herds of livestock; their masters, or rather protectors, never presumed to meddle with any of this property so long as they received a reasonable "tribute" at harvest and butchering time.[6] The Negroes also had plenty of time for hunting and fishing, and under this almost idyllic regime they throve amazingly. Dressed in the easy Indian costume, they were, according to one observer, "stout and even gigantic in their persons . . . the finest looking people I have ever seen." They were known, moreover, as well-armed and brave warriors; a major of Georgia militia in 1812 declared of the Seminole that the Negroes were "their best soldiers." [7]

The Seminole Negroes' prestige and influence among the Indians were what impressed observers most forcibly. The Negroes speedily acquired the Muskogee or Hitchiti tongue of their protectors without forgetting the English or Spanish they had learned among the whites, which made them valuable interpreters. From interpreting it was an easy step to advising and counseling. Some observers believed they governed the Indians, and one with a taste for classical comparisons said that the Seminole nation approached a doulocracy.[8] A few groups of fugitive Negroes established villages which were not under Seminole control, and the Indians sometimes found it convenient to assert that all Negro settlements in their country were of this character.[9]

For obvious reasons it is impossible to determine how many Seminole Negroes there were on the eve of the Seminole War. Estimates ranged from three hundred or four hundred to as many as eleven hundred; the estimate of "more than five hundred" made in 1834 is perhaps the best.[10] The Negro population in Florida, however, consisted mostly of plantation slaves. In East Florida, the principal arena of the Seminole War, about half the population was colored; there were 4,095 slaves, 343 free colored, and 4,515 whites. In the counties bordering on the Indian country the Negroes considerably outnumbered the whites.[11] The slaves in East Florida were looked upon as potentially more dangerous than those in other slaveholding regions. According to an old settler, most of the male slaves in the Mosquito region near the St. Johns River owned guns for hunting to save their masters the expense of supplying them with the usual salt-pork ration. Both slaves and free Negroes were well acquainted with the Seminole Indians and Negroes, their way of life, and their language. Many of the slaves had "wives among the Indian negroes, and the Indian negroes had wives among them." [12] Ownership of firearms and acquaintance with the Indians were doubtless most extensive among those Negroes owned by whites whose traditions went back to "Spanish days"; but Governor William P. DuVal is quoted as saying in 1828 that "many of the slaves taken to Florida are the very worst in the Union," [13] and the need for labor on a newly opened frontier may indeed have resulted in an unusually large proportion of slaves who had been "sold down the river" for bad conduct.

Although the attempt to remove the Seminole from Florida—the spark which set off the seven-year war—was ostensibly part of the general program for Indian removal, the presence and peculiar position of the Negroes among them was a decisive factor. The Seminole, who did not lie directly in the path of white settlement, might have been permitted to remain on the peninsula had it not been for the Negroes; in fact, the hardier and more obdurate of the Florida Seminole were in the end allowed to stay.

Sentiment for the removal of the Seminole Negroes preceded that for Indian removal. As early as 1821 the Florida Indian agent said of "the maroon negroes, who live among the Indians" that it would "be necessary to remove from the Floridas this group of lawless freebooters, among whom runaway negroes will always find a refuge," although he admitted that if force were employed the Indians would probably take the Negroes' part.[14] It was soon recognized that it was impossible to persuade the Indians to rid Florida of a "Serious nusance [sic]" by selling their Negroes, because of the Indians' attachment to them. The bodily removal of the Indians themselves was increasingly regarded as the only solution to the Negro problem.[15]

The citizens of Florida, however, would not have been content with the removal of the Seminole Indians if it meant that the Indians would take their Negroes west with them. Planters who had lost slaves through flight to the Indian country were determined to repossess them. Official circles in Florida argued strongly that the baneful influence which the alleged indolence of the Negroes exerted on the Indians made their separation necessary,[16] but earlier attempts through pressure and fraud to gain possession of the Indians' Negroes [17] suggest that the desire of white men for cheap slaves was a more important motive for the proposed separation of the Negroes from the Indians.

The program for Seminole removal reached a climax on March 28, 1833, when a Seminole delegation inspecting the Indian Territory was wheedled and bullied into expressing satisfaction with the region of Creek country set aside for the Seminole and with the plan of uniting them with the powerful Creeks as one people. The government then asserted that this so-called treaty of Fort Gibson committed the entire tribe to move west within three years. The Seminole, insisting that the delegation was without power to bind the Nation, strongly objected to removal in general and in particular to the prospect that they would become a despised minority in the powerful half-breed-dominated Creek confederacy. One of their objections was that the Creeks claimed the Negro "property" of the Seminole because of slaves who had escaped to the Seminole when the latter were still considered Lower Creeks and for whom the Creek Nation had been forced to pay; they feared that the Creeks would attempt to seize their Negroes, either in satisfaction of the claim or merely by *force majeure*. For the Seminole Negroes, seizure by the Creeks would mean at best substitution of a stricter control in place of slavery in name only; at worst, sale into real servitude among the whites.

The Seminole Negroes' greatest dread was that they would never reach the Creek country. All, regardless of legal status, belonged to a race the members of which normally occupied the position of chattels; the Negro without a recognized owner or without the clearest evidence of freedom was liable to seizure, no matter how long he had been in effect his own master or how dubious the claimant's title might be. Since the Seminole were to be assembled at a central point for transportation west under military supervision, this would give opportunity both for the white owners of fugitive Seminole Negroes to present their legal claims and for the unscrupulous to urge illegitimate claims or even simply to kidnap likely Negroes. Whites, indeed, had already seized or fraudulently acquired numerous Negroes claimed by Indians. John Hicks, onetime principal Seminole chief who was friendly to the whites, complained in 1829, "A white man sells us a Negro, and then turns around and claims him again, and our big father orders us to give him up." [18] If this could happen when the Seminole were more or less secure in their own country, what would be their fate when surrounded by white men and in their power? An outrage committed shortly after the outbreak of the Seminole War demonstrates that their fears were not groundless. A band of whites raided the village of the friendly old chief Econchattemicco, rounded up the Negroes, including the chief's half-Negro granddaughter, and carried them off to slavery in Georgia. [19]

The Negroes, described in April, 1835, by the officer commanding in East Florida as "bold, active, and armed," were determined not to submit to removal and to do all in their power to persuade their Indian protectors not to remove. [20] They possessed able leaders in Abraham, head chief Micanopy's principal Negro, a middle-aged runaway slave of fluent speech and polished manners from Pensacola, and John Caesar, a shrewd, fierce old man who had been brought up among the Indians and was the "chief Negro" of King Philip (Emathla) of the St. Johns Indians, the second chief in the Nation. [21] During the three years of grace Abraham and Caesar, Osceola and Yaha Hajo, and other Negro and Indian militants were busy preparing for resistance. The plantation slaves, well aware of the idyllic existence of even the "slaves" of the Seminole, were in many cases receptive to urgings that, when war broke out, they should rise with axe and torch, wreak havoc on the plantations, and then, laden with plunder, escape into the swamps and hammocks to a life of freedom and plenty. [22]

Abraham, Caesar, and their associates did not neglect the three or four hundred free colored people of East Florida, nearly half of whom were residents of St. Augustine and vicinity. These free blacks had much more to lose and less to gain by supporting Seminole resistance than did the plantation slaves, but they were disgruntled at having recently been deprived of the privileges they had enjoyed under Spanish law and at being put under a territorial code so severe that it had inspired protests even from prominent white citizens. [23] Abraham and the others did not call on those comparatively few free Negroes to rise in arms but rather to furnish supplies and information. With their help, and with that of the Spanish, Indian, and Negro fishermen, lumbermen, and smugglers of the southern coast, Abraham proceeded to build up a reserve of ammunition. After the war had been going on for a year he reportedly was still receiving consignments of powder, disguised as barrels of flour, from a free St. Augustine Negro.[24]

Near the end of December, 1835 the long-smoldering conflict broke out. The Seminole did not wait for brevet Brigadier General Duncan L. Clinch to attempt to carry out his threat that if they were not at Tampa Bay by January 8, 1836, he would remove them forcibly. Instead they took the initiative. On December 26-27 King Philip's Indians and Indian Negroes, with the assistance of many cane-field slaves, fell on the sugar plantations of the St. Johns valley. On December 28 Micanopy's Indian and Negro warriors ambushed and annihilated brevet Major Francis L. Dade's command of over a hundred men near the Wahoo Swamp; an intelligent and literate slave named Luis Pacheco, who had been hired as guide and interpreter to Dade's command, is said to have assisted the hostiles in laying their fatal ambush.[25] Two days later Micanopy's band—numbering from 200 to 250 warriors, of whom from 30 to 50 were Negroes—repulsed 600 regulars and militiamen from the Withla-coochee. Of the three Seminole killed and five wounded in this action, two of the slain and three of the wounded were Negroes.[26]

For many of the whites on the St. Johns, the destruction of Dade's command was less horrifying than the enthusiasm with which plantation slaves rallied to the hostiles. Although the young South Carolina volunteer and writer W. W. Smith insisted that with very few exceptions the slaves preferred to remain in their "happy and secure state of servitude," Florida planters and militia officers in closer contact with the situation were under no such illusions. Nearly four hundred Negroes, it was reported, "have joined the Indians and are more desperate than the Indians." That most of them were not captives but volunteers was evidenced by the numbers seen under arms and in war paint. With their support the Seminole swept through the region east of the St. Johns and south of St. Augustine with torch and tomahawk, driving the population to take refuge in St. Augustine and other places of comparative safety.[27] Slave recruitment did not end with the early weeks of the uprising but continued into the spring and summer.

The slave uprising on the St. Johns spread alarm, indeed almost hysteria, throughout Florida and even into adjacent states.[28] The situation in St. Augustine, where displaced planters had taken refuge with such of their Negroes as had not "moved off" with the Seminole, was particularly critical. With several hundred Negroes who were well acquainted with the Indians and their language concentrated within the city walls, "strong apprehensions were felt . . . that they would fire the town, and that, during the confusion," the Indians, "influenced by revenge, cupidity, and the advice of their black counsellors," might attempt to rush the city itself. St. Augustine whites also had to guard against attempts by Seminole emissaries to enter the town in order to stir up the Negroes and to obtain information, and at the same time forestall attempts by local Negroes to escape to the hostiles with information and supplies. Despite the vigilance of all the available dismounted force, Negroes did escape, meet with the hostiles, and return. Florida passed a bill providing that free Negroes aiding the Seminole should be sold into slavery, and Major Benjamin A. Putnam of the Florida militia urged Governor Richard K. Call on July 26, 1836, to see to the strict enforcement of this law, suggesting a standing court-martial to deal summarily with captured Negroes. A few days later the major wrote to Secretary of War Lewis Cass that "if strong measures were not taken to restrain our slaves, there is but little doubt that we should soon be assailed with a servile as well as Indian war." [29] The major was still unwilling to admit that the war was already what he said he feared it would become.

Sporadic but frequently heavy fighting meanwhile continued in the Withlacoochee region. The Negroes, their ranks swelled by recent runaways, bore at least their full share of the "burden and heat of the day." Two authorities agreed on an estimated total of 250 Negro fighting men (a figure which one divided into 100 "Indian slaves" and 150 runaways) as compared to 1,450–1,650 Indian warriors; but when General Edmund P. Gaines was besieged on the Withlacoochee early in March by a force estimated at about 1,500 warriors, one observer said "there might have been four or five hundred Negroes among them." Of three Seminole killed during the siege one was a Negro.[30] The principal action of an October expedition was an attack on a Negro town protected by a stream, but the Negro warriors, posted in and behind trees and assisted by Indian comrades, gave the troops such a warm reception that they were unable to cross.[31] An expedition of the following month drove a body of hostiles into the Wahoo Swamp, where—outnumbered more than three to one—they turned at bay. The force consisted of an estimated 420 Indian warriors and 200 Negro fighting men, "one of the most distinguished leaders" of whom was "a Negro, the property of a Florida planter." The whites claimed a victory but on November 21 withdrew.[32]

The first year of the war had ended in complete failure to repress Seminole resistance. Early in December 1836, however, Major General Thomas Sidney Jesup assumed command in Florida. Jesup, recognizing the importance of the Negroes, immediately set about ascertaining their number and location. "Micanopy, Philip, and Cooper [Osoochee] . . .

each with from one hundred and twenty to two hundred Indian and Negro warriors—the latter, perhaps, the more numerous"—were reported not far from Jesup's encampment. Osceola, Jumper, and Little Alligator also had numerous Negro followers. It was at this point that the general delivered his famous judgment that this was a Negro and not an Indian war.[33]

Shifting from the attempt to crush Seminole resistance in the field, Jesup instituted a policy of hunting down and capturing the Seminole in their camps, particularly the women and children, who could be used to exert powerful pressure for surrender upon the hostiles. He put special emphasis on raiding Negro villages, a device not original with him [34] but which under his command was made effective for the first time. Jesup was greatly assisted in his program by a regiment of Creek scouts who had been promised "such plunder as they may take from the Seminoles"—"plunder" being understood to mean primarily captured Negroes. From early December 1836 to late January 1837 Jesup's troops were engaged in combing the swamps, destroying villages, and driving to the east such Indians and Negroes as they failed to kill or capture. Their captives numbered 131, nearly all Negroes and mostly women and children. Their greatest triumph was breaking up Osceola's headquarters, a Negro village in the Panosufkee swamp, and capturing fifty-two of his Negro followers and three Indians.[35]

The "principal Indian and negro force . . . retired from the Ocklawaha . . . towards the head of the Caloosahatchee," and on January 27 the army was close on its heels. A captured Negro said "a large number of negroes were in advance, and from forty to fifty Indians, with Abraham . . . in our rear." A sudden dash resulted in the seizure of the Negro baggage train of over one hundred ponies and in the capture of something over twenty prisoners, mostly Negro women and children. The main body of the Seminole plunged into the Great Cypress Swamp and in a running fight killed two Marines and wounded four others. The bodies of two Negroes and an Indian were found on the field, and several more Negroes were captured.[36]

Jesup then conceived the idea of using a Negro captive named Ben, one of Micanopy's principal "slaves," to negotiate with Abraham and through him with the head chief and his circle. The Seminole had been roughly handled and might therefore be in a receptive mood, but no important warrior had surrendered or been captured. "The warriors," Jesup commented, "have fought as long as they had life, and such seems to me to be the determination of those who influence their councils—I mean the leading negroes." [37] Conciliation of the Negroes was seen as essential to successful negotiations.

Recent developments near St. Augustine had made Jesup particularly anxious to terminate the war. His campaign had driven Osceola's and Micanopy's people toward King Philip's territory. Philip himself, old and weary, hesitated to act, but his chief Negro, John Caesar, recognized the necessity of a diversion and organized a guerrilla campaign, employing principally runaway slaves. His campaign, however, was brief. Interrupted on January 17, 1837, in a horse-stealing raid on a plantation only two miles west of St. Augustine, his band was trailed to their camp; Caesar and two others, including a young free Negro named Joe Merritt, were killed and the rest fled in confusion. One would have expected such a coup to produce general satisfaction among the white population of St. Augustine, but actually it caused more alarm than relief. That a band composed almost entirely of Negroes—and plantation slaves at that—should have dared a raid so close to the city, and that their abandoned packs should have contained articles recently purchased in local shops, revived something of the panic of a year before. The county council, declaring that "we know not how soon fire-brands may be thrown amongst us," demanded that the militia company responsible for the disruption of Caesar's band be kept near home and "employed to scour the country in the neighborhood." [38]

The most important and far-reaching effect of Caesar's abortive raid, however, was on Jesup. This raid was doubtless in his mind when on January 21 he wrote to General J. M. Hernandez of the Florida militia —one of whose slaves had been in Caesar's band—denouncing the father of the slain Joe Merritt as an agent of Abraham and reiterating, "This war . . . is a negro, not an Indian war." [39] Doubtless, too, it was in his mind a few days later when he sent out the Indian Negro Ben to arrange for a meeting with Abraham.

On January 31 the Seminole Negroes, and Abraham in particular, undertook a new and important role. An army officer has described them as "a most cruel and malignant enemy . . . active . . . blood-thirsty and cruel"; but the Seminole Negro leaders, even fierce old John Caesar, although opposed to a surrender which would expose them to servitude, had never been averse to negotiations.[40] Abraham now had the responsibility both of interpreting the talks between the general and the chiefs and of seeing to it that any peace terms should be acceptable to the Negroes.

Jesup's *sine qua non* for peace was immediate emigration. "There would be no difficulty in making peace . . . were it not for that condition. . . . The negroes . . . who rule the Indians, are all averse to removing to so cold a climate." [41] The Negro Abraham, however, an intelligent and widely traveled man who had been on a mission to Washington, D C., and another to the Indian Territory, recognized the impossibility of achieving a decent life in Florida in the face of the government's determined attitude. His objective had been to put up a strong resistance until the Negroes were given satisfactory assurances. Now he felt that the time was ripe for negotiations.

The negotiations went on for over a month. On March 6, 1837, representatives of Micanopy and of Alligator—among the latter the subsequently famous Indian-Negro subchief John Ca-Wy-Ya (Cavallo)—signed an agreement to suspend hostilities and for the entire Nation to move to the west, for the performance of which the Indians gave hostages. The provisions affecting the Negroes were necessarily in cryptic language: "Major General Jesup, in behalf of the United States, agrees that the Seminoles and their allies who come in, and emigrate to the West, shall be secure in their lives and property; that their Negroes, their bona fide property, shall accompany them to the West. . . ." By "their allies" the Seminole understood the Negroes living among them, and since before the war an estimated four-fifths of the Seminole Negroes, including Abraham, were runaway slaves—and during the war the Seminole had been joined by several hundred more runaways—the Seminole "allies" numbered far more Negroes than the Seminole "slaves." But at this point no United States army officer could explicitly provide for the transportation west of Negroes on whom United States citizens might have a claim; brevet Major General Winfield Scott, one of Jesup's predecessors, had been specifically directed to "allow no pacification with the Indians while a living slave, belonging to a white man, remained in their possession." [42]

Jesup, nevertheless, at first intended to carry out his agreement in good faith. "The negroes," he wrote on March 26, "rule the Indians, and it is important that they should feel themselves secure; if they should become alarmed and hold out, the war will be renewed." But by the end of the month so many Seminole had assembled at Tampa Bay that the general become overconfident and, under pressure from Florida planters, decided to change his interpretation of the agreement. On April 8 he entered into a clandestine arrangement with Coi Hajo and other chiefs "to surrender the Negroes taken during the war." It was easier, however, to make such an agreement than carry it out. Some of the "captured Negroes," to be sure, had been taken against their will and were glad to be returned to their masters, but others, when they heard of the new arrangement, banded together for defense whether against white men or Indians. They were supported by more militant Indians like Osceola, who, when Coi Hajo announced in council that the runaways were to be returned, rose in a rage, declaring that so long as he was in the Nation it should never be done.[43]

Apparently Jesup had not sufficiently considered that legally most of the influential Seminole Negroes were as much the slaves of white men as were the recent runaways. When several Floridians arrived in the emigration camp to search for slaves the Negroes and many Indians fled.[44] On June 2 the young militants, Osceola, Philip's son Wild Cat, and John Cavallo, seized and carried away the Seminole hostages given under the terms of the truce. "All is lost," Jesup despairingly announced, "and principally . . . by the influence of the Negroes."[45] The Seminole force was still largely intact, although an estimate that the warriors in East Florida numbered 2,500, not including Negroes, "who fight as well as the best of them,"[46] was probably an exaggeration.

Jesup was reduced to drafting plans for the future—the confusion of which indicated his own confused state of mind—and putting the best face possible on an admittedly bad situation. He was principally concerned with preventing the war from developing any further slave unrest. "The two races, the negro and the Indian," he declared, "are rapidly approximating; they are identified in interests and feelings." Plantation slaves had been prominent in depredations and one had occupied a position of leadership. "Should the Indians remain in this territory," Jesup continued, "the negroes among them will form a rallying point for runaway negroes from the adjacent states; and if they remove, the fastnesses of the country will be immediately occupied by negroes." But, somewhat inconsistently, he believed that the Indians would agree to "surrender all runaway slaves" if permitted to remain in "a small district near Florida Point."[47]

He also pointed out that he had been able to turn over about ninety captured Negroes to their legal owners and, much more important, had seized over a hundred Indian Negroes, among them a score of warriors including Abraham and three other chiefs. "The Negro portion of the hostile force of the Seminole nation not taken," the General optimistically declared, "is entirely without a head."[48] More significantly, the capitulation had committed to emigration, on conditions, the most powerful East Florida group, the Alachua, or "original" Seminole, under Micanopy. And with Micanopy's chief Negro, Abraham, still in his hands, Jesup was well equipped to reopen negotiations with the Micanopy group and, through them, with other groups.[49]

The 1837 summer season was, as usual, uneventful, but early in September a serious break appeared within the Seminole ranks. It involved the Seminole Negroes, previously regarded as the strongest element of the hostiles. It came at a point where the Negroes in the Indian country had been quantitatively strengthened but qualitatively weakened by the mass recruitment of plantation slaves. Twenty months of fighting and hardship since the revolt of the St. Johns plantation slaves had operated to separate the strong, determined, freedom-loving Negroes from those who had been merely caught up in the enthusiasm of the December days and were now ready to exchange freedom to go hungry in the swamps for the regular rations of servitude. Early in September plantation Negroes, half-naked, "haggard and emaciated," began to straggle into forts and camps with pitiable tales of ill-treatment by the Indians. By mid-November over fifty had surrendered. Far more important, John Philip, a "slave" of King Philip and a former member of Caesar's daring guerrilla band, was persuaded by his wife, a plantation Negro, to "come in" and surrender.

The surrender on September 8 of John Philip, whom Jesup now enthusiastically identified as "the only negro chief who had not been previously seized," was comparable to pushing over the first of a line of upright dominoes. The Indian Negro volunteered to guide a detachment to the camp of King Philip, who was captured with his entire party.[50] When King Philip's son Wild Cat learned of this, he rode to St. Augustine and offered, in exchange for his father's release, to bring in Philip's subordinate chiefs for a "talk" and to return all captured Negroes. Seventy-nine Negroes were shortly on their way, although probably under no compulsion since they were unescorted and said to be "in a starving condition." Later, however, the theory was advanced that Wild Cat and his followers had intended to rescue King Philip and that the Negroes had been sent to be on hand for the attack.[51]

Micanopy and his associates in the meantime had sent the young Negro-Indian subchief John Cavallo to confer with King Philip, Wild Cat, Osceola, and their associates and, if necessary, to interpret between them and white officers. A conference at the Indians' camp near St. Augustine between these chiefs and Hernandez, who represented Jesup, was arranged, but Cavallo's part in carrying away the hostages in June caused Jesup, who had come to expect "foul play" wherever Cavallo was involved, to order Hernandez to have him and the other Seminole seized at once if they did not reply satisfactorily to a specified set of questions in regard to surrendering "captured Negroes." While the chiefs were discussing these and other questions they were surrounded and captured.[52]

Wild Cat and Cavallo remained prisoners less than six weeks. On the night of November 29-30 they with eighteen others escaped from Fort Marion—with the help, Jesup was convinced, of local Negroes.[53]

Their escape, however, had come too late to prevent a series of important surrenders. On November 30, Osceola's family and about forty plantation slaves surrendered,[54] and a few days later all chiefs belonging to Micanopy's group except Alligator agreed to give themselves up.

By December 1837 two opposing movements had set in among the Seminole Indians and Negroes still at large. One was toward the emigration camp. About fifty Indian Negroes proceeded to Tampa Bay, in response either to the orders of Micanopy and his group or to new appeals from Jesup promising them "something . . . GOOD" if they would "get away from the Indians." [55] The other current was toward the lower Kissimmee and Lake Okeechobee where Wild Cat, Sam Jones, Alligator, and Cavallo were mustering die-hard Indians and Negroes for a last-ditch stand. Most of the Seminole Negroes still at large moved toward the camps of these stalwarts. In fact, some Negroes who had started out toward Tampa Bay turned back to join the resistance forces.[56]

During a period of about a month these die-hards fought three of the most savage battles of the seven-year war. On Christmas 1837, 380 Indians and Negroes, with Lake Okeechobee behind them and a swamp in front, met an attack by Colonel Zachary Taylor's thousand regulars and militia. Before the Indian-Negro force retreated they had killed twenty-six men and wounded over a hundred others. The bodies of eleven Indians and only one or two Negroes were found on the field, which suggests that Okeechobee was principally an Indian battle; probably most of the Negroes who had separated from Tampa-bound masters had not yet reached the camp of the holdouts. On January 15, 1838, however, a landing party of sailors and regulars near Jupiter Inlet was furiously attacked and badly routed, and nine days later Jesup himself encountered at the Locha Hatchee a force estimated at from two to three hundred Indian warriors and "probably as many negroes." This was believed to be the same force which had defeated the whites at Jupiter Inlet. In both encounters the whites suffered heavy losses.[57]

After these costly engagements Jesup built a stockade called Fort Jupiter and considered his next move. His officers urged ending the war by a treaty which would permit the Seminole to remain in the southern part of the peninsula, a plan in accord with the General's own views and one which, when finally carried out over four years later, terminated the war. Negroes who had surrendered reported that if permitted to remain in Florida the Indians "would . . . sell and deliver up the plantation negroes." Jesup communicated his plan to Washington and sent out a Seminole Negro to invite the chiefs to a conference. By the end of February about 400 Indians and perhaps 150 Indian Negroes were encamped near the fort. The Negroes, according to a fascinated and re-

pelled Southern officer, were "the most diabolical wretches I ever saw.
. . . They had none of the servility of our northern blacks, but were
constantly offering their dirty paws with as much hauteur and non-
chalance as if they were conferring a vast deal of honor."

Jesup, however, was even more pleased with the presence of these
Negroes, whatever their appearance, than he was with that of the
larger number of Indians. Convinced that the Negroes would be a
source of difficulty so long as they remained in Florida, that the Indians would not surrender so long as the Negroes held out, and that the
Negroes would not give in until assured of their freedom, he appealed
through Seminole Negro emissaries to "the negro chiefs August & John
Cavallo" and to another named July, "to whom, and to their people, I
promised freedom and protection on their separating from the Indians
and surrendering." This was the vague "something . . . GOOD" hinted at
the previous December.

The attraction of the offer was not, of course, "freedom" from
Seminole "masters" but rather the "protection" of a United States general and United States troops against claims or kidnapping by whites. As
Indian Negroes in Florida would be a constant encouragement to runaways, "it was stipulated that they should be sent to the west, as a part
of the Seminole nation" which had already migrated; Abraham, however,
assured them that it was a fine country, though a bit chilly, and certainly preferable to the Everglades. During February and March the
Negro chiefs August and July, reassured by these promises, voluntarily
came in with about 150 Indian Negroes and five slaves of white citizens.
Most of the Indian Negroes were promptly sent off "to join their
masters," as an officer put it, "in their new homes west of the
Mississippi." [58]

But how could Jesup justify granting freedom to Negroes four-fifths
of whom were either runaways or their descendants and thus legally
slaves? The answer is, of course, wartime necessity. In the first place,
the Negroes were regarded as more dangerous than the Indians; persuading the Negroes to surrender would weaken the Indians "more than
they would be weakened by the loss of the same number of their own
people." [59] In the second place, it was imperative to remove from the
slaveholding south all Negroes who had tasted freedom and knew the
fortress of Florida. A well-informed officer commented,

> The negroes, from the commencement of the Florida war,
> have, for their numbers, been the most formidable foe, more
> bloodthirsty, active, and revengeful, than the Indians. . . . The
> negro, returned to his original owner, might have remained a few

days, when he again would have fled to the swamps, more vindictive than ever. . . . Ten resolute negroes, with a knowledge of the country, are sufficient to desolate the frontier, from one extent to the other.[60]

The sort of thing Jesup feared was illustrated by a communication of February 10, 1839, from an officer at Fort Heileman, stating that the recalcitrant Creek Indians had "all left the Okefenokee & gone South," presumably to join the hostile Seminole. "There were seven runaway negroes from Georgia among them," the officer continued, "well armed & plenty of ammunition . . . the negroes have done most of the mischief in that quarter; the negroes also have left and on their way south burned the houses in the vicinity." [61]

Jesup had adopted the policy of shipping all Indian Negroes west as early as the preceding September, when he had revoked his promise to his Creek allies that they should have all the enemy property they could capture and offered instead to purchase their claims to ninety captured Negroes for $8,000, since, as he wrote, "it is highly important to the slave-holding States that these negroes be sent out of the country." The Creeks declined this less than generous offer, but the army hung on to the Negroes claimed by the Creeks and succeeded in delivering them in the Indian Territory.[62]

To give his policy legal justification Jesup resorted to the fiction that all Indian Negroes, instead of a small minority, were legitimate Indian property. One statement of his order was that "all the property [sic] of the Seminole Indians . . . who separated themselves [sic] from the Indians, and delivered themselves up to the Commanding officer of the troops, should be free." [63] Technically, this order would apply only to that small minority to whom Indians had valid title and to only those in that small group who actually "separated themselves" from the Indians. As a practical matter, however, all Indian Negroes who came in were promptly marched to the emigration camp and embarked for the west.

Later, in 1841, the War Department decided that the 1832 treaty of Payne's Landing had canceled all claims against the Indians for any Negroes run away or captured prior to that treaty. "No demand can therefore be recognized for any negroes except those lost since the date of the treaty, unless the Indians are willing to give them up voluntarily. All except these must positively be removed with the Indians to the West. . . ." Still another legal fiction was developed in regard to those Negroes whose status as "Indian slaves" was most doubtful—who were, indeed, with little question the legal slaves of white citizens, captured or run away since the Payne's Landing treaty. The War Department order that these Negroes "should be surrendered" contained the all-important proviso, "unless the effect of this would be to prevent the Indians from coming in and removing." If so, "it will be better, rather than incur this danger that even the negroes to which the whites have valid claim should also be removed." [64] On August 19, 1841, accordingly, Lieutenant Colonel W. J. Worth announced, "Indians have been solemnly guaranteed retention of slaves indifferently . . . to the mode or time . . . they obtained possession. . . ." That is, if an Indian claimed a Negro, his claim would be recognized without necessity of legal proof, while the citizen claiming such a Negro was, "upon identifying and proving property, paid a fair equivalent, determined upon by a board of officers." In defense of his policy Worth pointed out that "if . . . the swamps of Florida become . . . the resort of runaways, their intelligence, so superior to the Indian, might impose upon the general government a contest quadruplicate in time and treasure than that now being waged." [65]

Although the policy of ignoring the legal status of even recent runaways was not publicly and explicitly announced until 1841, it had been applied several times by 1838. The classic example was that of the famous Luis Pacheco, who, despite his well-known status as slave to Mrs. Antonio Pacheco, had been shipped out of the county as a slave of Chief Jumper, because Jesup thought he was too dangerous to be left in Florida.[66]

Most of the slaves who during the war escaped from plantations or were captured by the Seminole probably were recovered by their owners, principally by voluntary surrender, but those recent runaways who were unwilling to return to plantation slavery and could induce Indians to claim them—no difficult task—could go west with the more legitimate "Indian slaves."

So far as the formidable Seminole Negroes were concerned, the war was practically over by the end of March, 1838. During the campaign of September 1837–March 1838, about 250 Seminole Negroes had surrendered or been captured; Operation Fort Jupiter alone had accounted for the taking of 167 Negroes (including 15 slaves of whites), over 40 of whom were warriors, "nearly all armed with rifles." Over 500 Indians, too, had been made prisoners, for when the Secretary of War refused to approve Jesup's peace terms, the general on March 21 simply surrounded their camps near Fort Jupiter and scouring the country that night and the next two days succeeded in rounding up that number.[67]

Jesup was still confronted with the problem of the Negroes and Indians who, justifiably suspicious of all promises, had stayed away from Fort Jupiter. A large part of the Negroes still out were with Alligator and Cavallo, the last Negro chief still in the field. To them the general dispatched the Negro counselors Abraham and Holatoochee, said to have been Cavallo's brother-in-law. Their mission resulted in the surrender of Alligator, "with 88 of his people, among whom was John Cowaya and 27 blacks," and Alligator's capitulation led to the surrender during April of about 360 more Indians and Negroes, including 100 warriors.[68]

These captures and surrenders reduced any future actions to mere raids and skirmishes. They also marked the disappearance of Negroes as a major element in Seminole resistance. A few hostile Negroes, both "Indian Negroes" and recent runaways, continued as interpreters, counselors, and fighting men, and their influence with the hostile Indians was recogized in the government's decision of 1841 to abandon the idea of restoring "to their rightful owners" any slaves still among the Indians and instead remove them all to the west.[69] But we usually glimpse these Negroes fleetingly and singly [70]—in sharp contrast to the days when Negro warriors were numbered in the hundreds and on some occasions were reportedly as numerous as the Indians. Wild Cat's sadly shrunken band probably included the greatest number of remaining Negroes, some of whom he skillfully employed as spies, but when he was seized in May, 1841, his immediate following consisted of fifteen Indians and three Negroes. The company of 229 in which he was shipped west the following October included eighteen Negroes.[71]

The Seminole Negroes, having lost their importance as a factor in resistance, assumed the comparatively new role of government agents whose task it was to induce hostile Indians to surrender. Negro guides, interpreters, and negotiators—often in co-operation with Indian chiefs who had surrendered—were indispensable in establishing contact and communicating with the remaining hostile Indian leaders and, if they remained obdurate, in assisting the troops to locate their camps.

Several Negro guides and interpreters performed outstanding service. Sandy Perryman distinguished himself by locating and bringing in a number of chiefs to Fort King on May 15, 1839, for negotiations which resulted in an agreement that, in return for peace, the Indians should be permitted at least temporarily to remain in southern Florida. Two months later, however, a band of Indians not party to this agreement massacred on the Caloosahatchee a party for which Sandy was serving as interpreter and put him to death by torture.[72] Negro John, a "captured" slave of Dr. H. B. Crews, served as guide to the aggressive Lieutenant Colonel W. S. Harney on an expedition of December, 1840, which resulted in the killing of the Spanish Indian chief Chekika, a leader in the Caloosahatchee and Indian Key Massacres, and eight of his warriors. John himself was wounded in the encounter.[73] Sampson, who had been wounded and taken prisoner in the Caloosahatchee massacre, escaped after two years and in December, 1841, served with distinction as guide on an expedition into the Big Cypress which drove the hostiles out of their fastnesses and so softened them up that in the following summer the chiefs in southern Florida accepted the peace agreement which they had flouted three years earlier, thus bringing the long war to an end.[74]

Most important of these Negro agents was John Cavallo, or Gopher John as he was called by the officers. He had been the last Negro chief to surrender, and it was he who was responsible for the suggestion that delegations of prominent chiefs should be brought from the Indian Territory as proof positive to the hostiles that those who had surrendered had not been put to death but had been both spared and well treated. This move, which utilized Cavallo's old commander Alligator and his brother-in-law Holatoochee, proved highly effective. Cavallo was declared to have personally participated in bringing in 535 Indians and during the last two years of the war was very nearly the "indispensable man" in the army's relations both with the Indians who were still "out" and those who had finally consented to "come in." [75]

The decision to remove the Seminole from Florida was strongly influenced by the presence and position of the Negroes, and the Seminole Negroes also strongly influenced the general decision to resist removal. These Negroes were shrewd and farsighted in their plans for resistance and active and aggressive in carrying them out. Once convinced, however, that the government was inflexibly determined on Seminole removal, and persuaded, too, that if they and the Indians surrendered, their own freedom and the lives of both would be respected, they were almost as influential in persuading the more recalcitrant Indians to surrender as they had previously been in rallying Seminole resistance. Prolonged as the war was, the promise of freedom to the Negroes "tended very materially towards affecting the main object": the emigration of the great majority of the tribe.[76] It also made possible the termination in August 1842 of a struggle which, having already lasted seven years, might otherwise have dragged on for another decade or more with the loss of millions of dollars to the government and hundreds of lives to both whites and Seminole.

NOTES

1. George Catlin, *Letters and Notes on the Manners, Customs, and Condition of the North American Indians* (2 vols.; New York, 1841), II, 219n; John T. Sprague, *The Origin, Progress, and Conclusion of the Florida War . . .* (New York, 1848), pp. 526-550; Joshua R. Giddings, *The Exiles of Florida* (Columbus, Ohio, 1858), p. 315.

2. See, for example, Ethan Allen Hitchcock, *Fifty Years in Camp and Field* (New York, 1909), p. 81.

3. *Court of Inquiry—Operations in Florida . . . : Letter from the Secretary of War . . .* , *House Documents,* 25th Congress, 2nd Session, No. 78 (Serial 323), p. 52; *American State Papers, Military Affairs* (7 vols.; Washington, 1832-1861), VII, 820-821.

4. *Negroes, . . . Captured from Indians in Florida . . . : Letter from the Secretary of War . . .* , *House Documents,* 25th Congress, 3rd Session, No. 225 (Serial 348), pp. 119-120, 57-65; *American State Papers, Military Affairs,* VI, 461, 465.

5. Clarence Edwin Carter (ed.), *The Territorial Papers of the United States* (Washington, 1934-   ), XXIII, 911, XXIV, 669; *American State Papers, Military Affairs,* VI, 470-471, 533-534, VII, 427.

6. Sources cited in note 5, and [Woodburne Potter] *The War in Florida* (Baltimore, 1836), pp. 45-46; John Lee Williams, *The Territory of Florida . . .* (New York, 1837), p. 240; William Kennedy, *Texas: The Rise, Progress, and Prospects of the Republic of Texas* (2 vols.; London, 1841), I, 350. See also, however, George A. McCall, *Letters from the Frontiers . . .* (Philadelphia, 1868), p. 160; and Jedidiah Morse, *A Report to the Secretary of War of the United States on Indian Affairs . . .* (New Haven, 1822), pp. 309-311.

7. See the author's "Negroes and the East Florida Annexation Plot, 1811-1813," *Journal of Negro History,* XXX (January, 1945), esp. 22-23, and "Negroes and the Seminole War, 1817-1818," *ibid.,* XXXVI (July, 1951), esp. 255-256, 273-275.

8. For additional sources on the generally idyllic situation of the Seminole Negroes see: [William Hayne Simmons] *Notices of East Florida* (Charleston, S.C., 1822), pp. 44-45, 50, 76; Mark F. Boyd, "Horatio S. Dexter and Events Leading to the Treaty of Moultrie Creek with the Seminole Indians," *Florida Anthropologist,* XI (September, 1958), 84; [W. W. Smith] *Sketch of the Seminole War and Sketches During a Campaign* (Charleston, S.C., 1836), pp. 21-22.

9. Boyd, *op. cit.,* pp. 91-92; David Y. Thomas, "Report on the Public

Archives of Florida," American Historical Association, *Annual Report, 1906* (2 vols.; Washington, 1908), II, 152.

10. Carter, *op. cit.*, XXIV, 668, 643-645; *American State Papers, Military Affairs*, VI, 465.

11. *Memorial of the People of the Territory of Florida for Admission into the Union, House Documents*, 25th Congress, 3rd Session, No. 208 (Serial 347), p. 25; Carter, *op. cit.*, XXIV, 505-506, 643-645.

12. *Reminiscences of James Ormond Concerning the Early Days of the Halifax Country* (n.p., Ormond Village Improvement Association, 1941), pp. 5-6; Thomas Douglas, *Autobiography of Thomas Douglas, Late Judge of the Supreme Court of Florida* (New York, 1856), pp. 120-123.

13. Carter, *op. cit.*, XXIII, 1059.

14. Morse, *op. cit.*, pp. 149-150.

15. Carter, *op. cit.*, XXIII, 434, 454, XXIV, 668, 679.

16. *Ibid.*, XXIII, 414, 1003, XXIV, 668.

17. *Ibid.*, XXIII, 472-475, 483-484; Sprague, *op. cit.*, pp. 34, 65-67.

18. Carter, *op. cit.*, XXIII, 472-475, 483-484, 549-550; Potter, *op. cit.*, pp. 24-26; Sprague, *op. cit.*, pp. 51, 57, 66.

19. R. H. Stewart to Richard K. Call, May 25, 1836, in Caroline M. Brevard, *A History of Florida from the Treaty of 1763 to Our Own Times* (2 vols.; Deland, Fla., 1924), I, 278-279; Potter, *op. cit.*, pp. 15-16.

20. Carter, *op. cit.*, XXV, 133; Sprague, *op. cit.*, pp. 100, 81; *American State Papers, Military Affairs*, VI, 454, 458.

21. See the author's "The Negro Abraham," *Florida Historical Quarterly*, XXV (July, 1946), 1-43, and "John Caesar: Seminole Negro Partisan," *Journal of Negro History*, XXXI (April, 1946), 190-207.

22. *Courier* (Charleston, S.C.), April 30, 1836; Douglas, *op. cit.*, pp. 120-123; Myer M. Cohen, *Notices of Florida and the Campaigns* (Charleston, S.C., 1836), pp. 81, 86-89; John C. Casey to Lt. F. Searle, August 25, 1837, in Thomas Sidney Jesup Papers (War Department Files, National Archives), No. 2; and the author's "Florida Slaves and Free Negroes in the Seminole War, 1835-1842," *Journal of Negro History*, XXVIII (October, 1943), 393.

23. Carter, *op. cit.*, XXIV, 800-802.

24. Thomas Sidney Jesup to Brig. Gen. J. M. Hernandez, January 21, 1837, in Jesup Papers, box 14.

25. *Niles' Weekly Register*, XLIX (January 30, 1836), 365-370; Smith, *op. cit.*, pp. 36-37; Cohen, *op. cit.*, p. 72; Sprague, *op. cit.*, p. 91. See also the author's "Louis Pacheco: The Man and the Myth," *Journal of Negro History*, XXVIII (January, 1943), 65-72, and "The Early Life of Luis Pacheco ne Fatio," *Negro History Bulletin*, VII (December, 1943), 52, 54, 62, 64.

26. Sprague, *op. cit.*, pp. 92-93.

27. For the participation of plantation slaves in depredations during the early days of the war, see Porter, "Florida Slaves and Free Negroes," pp. 393-395. See also Mrs. Jane Murray Sheldon, "Seminole Attacks near New Smyrna, 1835-56 [sic]," *Florida Historical Quarterly*, VIII (April, 1930), 188-196; Earl C. Tanner (ed.), "The Early Career of Edwin T. Jenckes: A Florida Pioneer

of the 1830's," *Florida Historical Quarterly*, XXX (January, 1952), 270-275; *American State Papers, Military Affairs*, VII, 259; Sprague, *op. cit.*, p. 106; Smith, *op. cit.*, pp. 20-23.

28. Porter, "Florida Slaves and Free Negroes," pp. 395-398; Carter, *op. cit.*, XXV, 283.

29. Porter, "Florida Slaves and Free Negroes," pp. 396-398; Carter, *op. cit.*, XXV, 265, 327-328.

30. Sprague, *op. cit.*, pp. 97, 112-113; *Army and Navy Chronicle*, VIII (March 7, 1839), 154; II (1836), 151; *American State Papers, Military Affairs*, VII, 369.

31. *American State Papers, Military Affairs*, VI, 998; *Niles' Weekly Register*, LI (November 5, 1836), 148-149.

32. Sprague, *op. cit.*, pp. 162-166; *Court of Inquiry—Operations in Florida*, p. 52.

33. Porter, "Florida Slaves and Free Negroes," p. 400.

34. *Niles' Weekly Register*, L (May 14, 1836), 188, and LII (April 1, 1837), 71; *American State Papers, Military Affairs*, VII, 277.

35. *American State Papers, Military Affairs*, VII, 820, 825-828; *Army and Navy Chronicle*, IV (January 5, 1837), 12, and IV (February 2, 1837), 79, 111; "Major Childs, U.S.A.: Extracts from His Correspondence with His Family," *Historical Magazine*, Ser. 3, II (December, 1873), 371-372; Sprague, *op. cit.*, pp. 167, 170-171.

36. "Major Childs," pp. 372-373; *American State Papers, Military Affairs*, VII, 828-830; *Court of Inquiry—Operations in Florida*, pp. 69-70; *Niles' Weekly Register*, LII (March 11, 1837), 30-31; Sprague, *op. cit.*, pp. 170-172.

37. *American State Papers, Military Affairs*, VII, 828-830, 832; "Major Childs," p. 373; *Army and Navy Chronicle*, IV (February 2, 1837), 80, and VIII (March 7, 1839), 154-155.

38. Porter, "John Caesar," pp. 197-201, and "Florida Slaves and Free Negroes," pp. 401-404.

39. Jesup Papers, box 14.

40. Sprague, *op. cit.*, 100, 81; Porter, "John Caesar," pp. 194-196.

41. *American State Papers, Military Affairs*, VII, 827.

42. Porter, "Florida Slaves and Free Negroes," pp. 404-405; *American State Papers, Military Affairs*, VII, 834; *Message from the President . . . Relative to Indian Hostilities in Florida*, Senate Documents, 24th Congress, 1st Session, No. 152 (Serial 281), p. 5.

43. Porter, "Florida Slaves and Free Negroes," pp. 404-407.

44. *Ibid.*, pp. 408-409.

45. Jesup to Brig. Gen. R. Jones, October 21, 1837, in War Department, AGO Files (*National Archives*), p. 207; *Seminole Indians—Prisoners of War: Letter from the Secretary of War . . .*, House Documents, 25th Congress, 2nd Session, No. 327 (Serial 329), pp. 10-11; *Negroes, ... Captured from Indians*, p. 18; *Niles' Weekly Register*, LIII (December 23, 1837), 263.

46. Lt. Col. W. S. Harney to Jesup, May 4, 1837 (photostat, Florida His-

torical Society); *American State Papers, Military Affairs*, VII, 871; *Army and Navy Chronicle*, IV (1837), 5329.

47. Porter, "Florida Slaves and Free Negroes," pp. 409-411.

48. *American State Papers, Military Affairs*, VII, 842, 851-852; *Negroes, . . . Captured from Indians*, pp. 18, 65-69.

49. Grant Foreman, *Indian Removal: The Emigration of the Five Civilized Tribes of Indians* (Norman, Okla., 1932), p. 349; "Letters of Samuel Forry, Surgeon, U.S. Army, 1837-1838," *Florida Historical Quarterly*, VI (January, 1928), 214.

50. Jacob Rhett Motte, *Journey into Wilderness: An Army Surgeon's Account of Life in Camp and Field During the Creek and Seminole Wars, 1836-1838*, ed. James F. Sunderman (Gainesville, Fla., 1953), pp. 116-123, 132-133; *American State Papers, Military Affairs*, VII, 849-850, 882; *Army and Navy Chronicle*, V (September 28, 1837), 200, 203; Capt. Harvey Brown to Lt. J. A. Chambers, October 8, 1837, in Interior Department, Indian Office (Emigration) Files (1837, National Archives), pp. 196-447; *Court of Inquiry —Operations in Florida*, pp. 181, 109-112; Capt. Nathan S. Jarvis, "An Army Surgeon's Notes of Frontier Service, 1833-1848," *Journal of the Military Service Institution of the United States*, XL (January-February, 1908), 277-278; *Niles' Weekly Register*, LIII (September 30, 1837), 66.

51. Motte, *op. cit.*, pp. 136-138; *Army and Navy Chronicle*, V (October 12, 1837), 236, and V (October 26, 1837), 269-70; *Niles' Weekly Register*, LIII (October 14, 1837), 98, and LIII (November 18, 1837), 178; "Letters of Samuel Forry," pp. 88-105 *passim*.

52. Motte, *op. cit.*, p. 138; Jarvis, *op. cit.*, p. 278; *Army and Navy Chronicle*, V (November 2, 1837), 284-285, and V (December 14, 1837), 377-378, and VII (July 26, 1838), 50; *Niles' Weekly Register*, LIII (November 4, 1837), 146, LIII (November 11, 1837), 165-166, and LIII (December 23, 1837), 262-263; *Seminole Indians—Prisoners of War*, 2-8, 11; Hernandez to Jesup, October 22, 1837, and Jesup to Jones, October 21, 1837, both in War Department, AGO Files.

53. See the author's "Seminole Flight from Fort Marion," *Florida Historical Quarterly*, XXII (January, 1944), 112-133, esp. 121.

54. Jarvis, *op. cit.*, p. 285; Frank L. White (ed.), "The Journals of Lieutenant John Pickell, 1836-1837," *Florida Historical Quarterly*, XXXVIII (October, 1959), 159-160.

55. Brig. Gen. W. K. Armistead to Lt. J. A. Chambers, December 20, 25, 1837, in Jesup Papers, box 5; Lt. R. W Kirkham to Jesup, August 1, 1846, with statement by Tony Barnett, May 14, 1846, in War Department, QMGO Consolidated Files (National Archives).

56. See, for example, White, *op. cit.*, p. 167.

57. Sprague, *op. cit.*, pp. 203-214, esp. 214; "The Battle of Okee Chobee," *United States Magazine* (February, 1857); *Niles' Weekly Register*, LIII (February 17, 1838), 388, and LIII (February 10, 1838), 369-371; *Army and Navy Chronicle*, VII (July 26, 1838), 49-54; Motte, *op. cit.*, p. 195.

58. Jesup to Wm. L. Marcy, April 5, 1848, in Jesup Papers, box 15; Kirkham to Jesup, August 1, 1846, with statement by Barnett, May 14, 1846, in War Department, QMGO Consolidated Files; Jesup to Wm. L. Marcy, July 1, 1848, in Interior Department, Indian Office, Seminole Files (National Archives), W-244, and M. Arbuckle to Brig. Gen. R. Jones, January 8, 1849, *ibid.*, J-143; *American State Papers, Military Affairs*, VII, 825-826; *Official Opinions of the Attorneys General of the United States* . . . (Washington, 1852-   ), IV, 720-729; *Army and Navy Chronicle*, VI (March 22, 1838), 177, 190; Motte, *op. cit.*, pp. 207, 210-211; Sprague, *op. cit.*, pp. 193-195.

59. Jesup to Brig. Gen. R. Jones, February 28, 1838, in Seminole Files, W-244.

60. Sprague, *op. cit.*, p. 309.

61. Col. D. E. Twiggs to Gen. A. Macomb, February 10, 1839, in War Department, AGO Files, p. 66.

62. *American State Papers, Military Affairs*, VII, 882; *Negroes, . . . Captured from Indians*, pp. 20-22, 70-71; Foreman, *op. cit.*, pp. 347, 349, 365-366.

63. Certificate from Bvt. Brig. Gen. Z. Taylor, April 30, 1840, in Interior Department, Indian Office Files.

64. Carter, *op. cit.*, XXVI, 282-283.

65. Sprague, *op. cit.*, pp. 309-310; Porter, "Florida Slaves and Free Negroes," p. 419.

66. *Negroes, . . . Captured from Indians*, pp. 93-94; *Report . . . [on] the Petition of Joseph Elzaudi, House Reports*, 30th Congress, 1st Session, No. 187 (Serial 524), pp. 1-6; Edwin C. McReynolds, *The Seminoles* (Norman, Okla., 1957), p. 240.

67. *Negroes, . . . Captured from Indians*, pp. 25, 81-89; *Army and Navy Chronicle*, VI (April 19, 1838), 248, and VI (April 26, 1838), 269; Jarvis, *op. cit.*, pp. 453-454.

68. Sprague, *op. cit.*, p. 195; *Niles' Weekly Register*, LIV (May 5, 1838), 145; Abraham to Jesup, April 25, 1838, in *Florida Historical Quarterly*, XXV (July, 1946), 38-39.

69. Carter, *op. cit.*, XXVI, 276-277, 374-375.

70. *Army and Navy Chronicle*, IX (August 8, 1839), 93, and XI (October 22, 1840), 268-269; *Niles' Weekly Register*, LIV (August 18, 1838), 386, LVIII (May 23, 1840), 179-180, LVIII (June 27, 1840), 260, and LX (April 10, 1841), 90; Hester Perrine Walker, "Massacre at Indian Key, Aug. 7, 1840, and the Death of Dr. Henry Perrine," *Florida Historical Quarterly*, V (July, 1926), 26-27.

71. Sprague, *op. cit.*, pp. 277, 380, 322.

72. *Army and Navy Chronicle*, VIII (June 13, 1839), 379, and X (January 16, 1840), 39-40; *Niles' Weekly Register*, LVI (July 20, 1839), 321, and LVII (September 14, 1839), 44; Sprague, *op. cit.*, pp. 233, 316.

73. Logan Uriah Reavis, *The Life and Military Services of General William Selby Harney* (St. Louis, 1878), pp. 144-145; *Niles' Weekly Register*, LX (April 3, 1841), 71-72; Lt. Col. W. S. Harney to Capt. W. W. Bliss, December 24, 1840, in War Department, AGO Files, A354, and "Old Book 3, Dept.

of Florida, Bound as 1, Dept. of New Mexico, Feb. 1, 1842—Aug. 17, 1842";
ibid., p. 30.

74. Sprague, *op. cit.*, pp. 315-316, 357, 362, 364, 368, 370; White, *op. cit.*,
p. 160.

75. Kenneth W. Porter, "Davy Crockett and John Horse: A Possible Origin
of the Coonskin Story," *American Literature*, XV (March, 1943), 10-15; Brig.
Gen. W. K. Armistead to the Adjutant General, June 15, 1840, in War Department, AGO Files (1840), p. 146. See also Letter Book of Officer Commanding 8th Infantry (1840-1842), pp. 95, 100-101, 103, 113-114, and
"Head Quarters 9th M Department: Letters, from June 2d. 1841 to February
1st. 1842" I, 95-96, 223, both in War Department, AGO Files.

76. Capt. J. T. Sprague to Jesup, July 25, 184[?], in War Department,
QMGO Consolidated Files, "Seminoles."

ENFORCING THE FIFTEENTH
AMENDMENT, 1870-1877

Everette Swinney

Since 1940 when Howard K. Beale called for a re-evaluation of the Reconstruction period in American history, revisionist monographs and articles have been appearing in ever increasing numbers.[1] Much work, however, remains to be done. For instance, no one has attempted any fundamental research on the federal Enforcement Acts since the days of William A. Dunning and James Ford Rhodes. These acts, which lay at the heart of the Grant administration's Southern policy, were its response to the South's challenge to the Reconstruction program of the radicals.

Begun in March 1867 and completed by the summer of 1870, the Reconstruction settlement showed signs of crumbling at its foundation even before the edifice was completed. The election of 1868 amply demonstrated the tenuous nature of Republican supremacy upon which the success of the radical program rested. President Andrew Johnson's amnesty proclamations of September 7 and December 25, 1868, restoring the suffrage to most former Confederates did not help matters, and the victory of the Democratic party in 1869 and 1870 at the polls in Virginia, North Carolina, and Georgia was discouraging. But most alarming of all was the way in which the Ku Klux Klan and other similar extralegal bodies were, by violence and intimidation, preventing Negroes from voting.[2]

In the face of these cumulative threats to Republican ascendancy Congress moved expeditiously, passing within a twelve-month period in

Everette Swinney, "Enforcing the Fifteenth Amendment, 1870-1877," *Journal of Southern History*, XXVIII, No. 2 (May, 1962), 202-218.

1870-1871 three laws designed to protect the Negro in the enjoyment of his newly-won political and civil rights. The First Enforcement Act, which became law on May 30, 1870, was long and complex. It forbade state officials to discriminate among voters on the basis of race or color in the application of local election laws, outlawed "force, bribery, threats, and intimidation" of voters, and made it a misdemeanor to deprive a citizen of "employment or occupation" in order to control his vote. Most important, the law prohibited disguised groups from going "upon the public highways or upon the premises of another" with intent to interfere with constitutional liberties.[3] The Second Enforcement Act, passed following the disheartening midterm elections of 1870, extended further the federal control of the voting process. Supervisors of election, to be stationed in cities where election irregularities were considered likely, were to stand guard over and scrutinize registration and voting procedures and to certify returns.[4] The third law, popularly known as the Ku Klux Act, made it a federal offense to conspire to "overthrow . . . or destroy by force the government of the United States" or to conspire to prevent persons from holding offices, serving on juries, enjoying equal protection of the laws, or voting.[5] The three laws provided for extensive enforcement machinery. The President was given authority to call out the army and navy and to suspend the writ of habeas corpus; United States marshals were authorized to use the *posse comitatus;* and federal troops were empowered to implement court orders. In the hope of reducing the effect of local pressures against enforcement, exclusive original jurisdiction in all suffrage cases was reserved to the federal courts.

Historians have been far from favorable in their evaluation of this legislation. William W. Davis, whose study published in 1914 has been somewhat of a standard account of the enforcement program, wrote, "The enactment of the law and its enforcement meant the desertion, for the time being, by the national government of certain principles in political procedure which make working democracy in America a practical possibility." He found "considerable similarity between the arbitrary order and mailed fist in the South during the seventies and the past oppression of Ireland by England, of Bohemia and Italy by Austria, of Finland and Poland by Russia, of Alsace and Lorraine by Germany."[6] His interpretation has been perpetuated in textbooks where terms "harsh," "drastic," or "iniquitous" are commonly used to describe the laws.

The acts were comprehensive it is true; but the fact is that they did not go beyond the intent of the Fifteenth Amendment, which took a moderate and statesmanlike position on voting. The Fifteenth Amendment, unlike the Reconstruction Act of 1867, did not grant the Negro the right to vote; it merely outlawed the use of race as a test for voting. The Enforcement Acts of 1870-71 accorded with the Fifteenth Amendment in leaving to the state full freedom to restrict suffrage on any basis except race or color. As a matter of fact, the constitutionality of the Enforcement Acts was challenged at the time not for any federal invasion of the states' reserved power to establish suffrage requirements but for alleged encroachment upon the states' police power. The opponents of the acts denied that the Fifteenth Amendment authorized the federal government to punish private citizens who prevented persons from voting for reasons of race, holding that the amendment limited only state and federal action and could not be construed as extending "one hair's breadth further." [7]

Recent developments have gone far to destroy the force of Davis' argument that the Enforcement Acts "belonged to a more arbitrary period," suggesting "an autocracy rather than a democracy." [8] The Civil Rights Acts of 1957 and 1960, which were hailed by libertarians, demonstrate that the United States Congress has returned to the principles of 1870 in its approach to voting, and by its 1961 report the Civil Rights Commission shows that it has gone far beyond such principles in its demand for federal supervision of elections.[9] Finally, the provisions for enforcement of the acts of 1870–71—with the exception of the authorization to suspend the writ of habeas corpus, which was done only once—were not innovations but were consistent with traditional usage. Whatever the motives of those who promoted the legislation, the laws as enacted were essentially in accord with the democratic credo.

Under these laws the Department of Justice made a determined effort to enforce the Fifteenth Amendment. Between 1870 and 1896, when the bulk of the legislation was repealed, 7,372 cases were tried, and hundreds of offenders who were never brought to trial were arrested.[10] Despite this widespread activity, the disfranchisement of the Negro proceeded apace. By 1877 the Negro vote had been largely neutralized and a solid Democratic South assured. Complete disfranchisement of the Negro was to follow. The few historians who have attempted to evaluate the operation of the Enforcement Acts have emphasized the fact that there were relatively few convictions. William A. Dunning, who laid down the general lines of interpretation which have since prevailed, wrote,

> The proportion of convictions to indictments was ridiculously small and sufficiently illustrated the iniquity of the laws. In the year ending June 20, 1874, for example, there were 102 convictions out of 966 cases, or 10.5 percent, while for all other classes

of cases in the same courts . . . the percentage of convictions was 49.9.[11]

E. Merton Coulter, generalizing upon Dunning's calculations, observed that "in all the trials throughout the South for the next few years, only about 10 per cent of the defendants were convicted." He concluded that "arrests were made more to terrorize the people and to promote the Radical party than to secure actual justice." [12]

These assertions give a distorted picture. The percentages hold true only for the years after 1874. In 1870 the government won 74 per cent of its enforcement cases; in 1871, 41 per cent; in 1872, 49 per cent; and in 1873, 36 per cent. After 1874, it is true, convictions seldom passed the 10 per cent mark and were often considerably below it.[13] If, as Dunning and Coulter aver, the low percentage of convictions proved the iniquity of the laws, one would have to conclude that the laws became iniquitous only after 1874.

The proper explanation is somewhat less absurd and more complex. In the first place, by 1874 the government was ready to pursue a more moderate policy. Attorney General George Williams justified this change in strategy by two arguments, both of which were probably fallacious. He took the position that the worst of the Ku Klux activity had been brought under control and that it was safe for the government to relax its vigilance. The attorney general wrote in 1874 that "the Government has reason to believe that its general intentions in prosecuting these offenses . . . have been accomplished . . . and that there are good grounds for hoping that it will not return." [14] Most scholars have accepted the view that the backbone of the Klan proper was broken by the initial impact of the prosecutions; it is certain, however, that violence continued and that the Negro's position in Southern society was anything but secure. Williams also sought to justify the change in policy on the grounds that the government's enforcement program had proved to be an irritant which provoked disrespect for authority and incited lawlessness. "My intention," Williams announced, "is to suspend these prosecutions except in some of the worst cases, in the hope that the effect will be to produce obedience to the law and quiet among the people." [15] Republican control and Negro equality, not the enforcement program, were the real irritants; and it was unlikely that token concessions on procedure would soothe where major concessions on principle were demanded. The South was determined to have a free hand in settling the Negro question, and nothing approaching real peace would come to that section until this was realized.

The attorney general's arguments disguised rather than revealed the government's real motivation for instituting a more lenient program.

Expediency was the primary consideration. The South had remained obdurate in its opposition to enforcement; and the North, preoccupied with the depression, was beginning to lose interest. Erstwhile friends of coercion like Carl Schurz and E. L. Godkin had become critical before the time of the Liberal Republican revolt. Williams himself, a fairly influential radical at the time of his appointment, was now in 1874 one of the most unpopular men in the country. A congressional committee questioned him about alleged excesses in the use of troops, and he was ridiculed in the press as "Grant's Secretary of State for Southern Affairs"; the year before, in 1873, the Senate had rejected his appointment to the Supreme Court. The point is that the Republicans controlled Congress by a scant thirty-five votes with the midterm elections approaching. Under the circumstances, it is not surprising that in the spring and summer of 1874 Williams instructed district attorneys to dismiss all indictments "excepting such as involve charges of high crime committed in furtherance of the object of the conspiracy." They were told to "enter a *nolle prosequi*" in all cases in which the charge was "merely that of belonging to the Ku Klux Klan . . . of co-operating in its general purposes, or of committing some minor misdemeanor." [16] Many of the indictments which never came to trial were dismissed as a direct result of changing policy.

A second and perhaps more important reason for the abrupt decline in the number of convictions was that adverse court rulings made successful prosecutions after 1874 almost impossible. The constitutionality of certain portions of the Enforcement Acts had been questioned at the very outset. In the famous Ku Klux trials at Columbia, South Carolina, in 1871 defense attorneys Reverdy Johnson and Henry Stanbery developed a powerful case against the constitutionality of the laws, and several federal judges, notable among whom was Bland Ballard of Kentucky, were known as early as 1872 to view the legislation with suspicion.[17] In 1873 three election judges of Louisville, Kentucky, were brought before Ballard and Circuit Judge Halmor H. Edmunds, in the case of *United States* v. *Reese et al.*, on four counts of violation of sections three and four of the First Enforcement Act. The indictments were found defective, and Ballard in an *obiter dictum* declared the law invalid; the government appealed to the Supreme Court.[18] Meanwhile, another case (*United States* v. *Cruikshank et al.*) was taking shape in Louisiana. The bloody Colfax massacre of April, 1873—a by-product of the struggle between the McEnery and Kellogg governments for control of the state—had resulted in the slaughter of about sixty Negroes. At the April, 1874 term of the circuit court for the district of Louisiana more than one hundred persons were indicted under sections five and six of the First Enforcement Act.[19] Supreme Court Justice Joseph P.

Bradley, who was reputed to believe the law unconstitutional, sat in on the trial. "It was an ill-starred hour for this state when he put in his appearance in this Circuit in time to meddle with the trial," District Attorney James Beckwith complained to Washington. "His presence in the district was to me a nightmare while he remained." [20] In a closely reasoned opinion Bradley questioned the scope of the Fifteenth Amendment. It was clear, he said, that Congress has the power to enforce "every right and privilege given or guaranteed by the Constitution" but that the mode of enforcement depends upon the character of the right. Where the right is guaranteed by the Constitution "only by a declaration that the State or the United States shall not violate it," as in the Fifteenth Amendment, the power of affirmative enforcement is retained by the state "as part of its residuary sovereignty." Hence, "the power of Congress . . . to legislate for the enforcement of such a guarantee, does not extend to the passage of laws for the suppression of ordinary crime within the States." The other trial justice, Circuit Judge William B. Woods, did not agree, and the case went to the Supreme Court on a division of opinion.[21]

While the Reese and Cruikshank cases were pending before the Supreme Court (1874–1876), the enforcement program was arrested. "As I do not believe any convictions can be obtained under existing circumstances," Williams informed district attorneys, ". . . I am of the opinion that criminal prosecution under these acts ought to be suspended until it is known whether the Supreme Court will hold them constitutional or otherwise." [22] The Supreme Court decisions, rendered in the spring of 1876, constituted a major reversal for the radicals. Chief Justice Morrison R. Waite, speaking for the court in both cases, adopted the narrow interpretation of the Fifteenth Amendment adumbrated in Bradley's opinion in the Louisiana case two years before. "The Fifteenth Amendment," he argued, "does not confer the right of suffrage upon any one." The right to vote comes from the states; only "the right of exemption from the prohibited discrimination comes from the United States." Congress can legislate only to prevent official discrimination by the states or the United States but not to prevent obstructions and discriminations generally, as it had done in the First Enforcement Act.[23] Technically, just two sections of the act were declared unconstitutional, but the whole law had been brought under a shadow. The effect of the decisions was to bring to a close the active policy of the government to enforce the Fifteenth Amendment.

By going behind the statistics one discovers that there were other factors which made successful prosecutions difficult. White Southern Democrats insisted from the outset that the enforcement laws were unconstitutional, oppressive, and not worthy of respect. Linton Stephens of

Georgia well expressed this view when brought before a United States commissioner for a preliminary hearing on an alleged violation.

> I am accused under the Enforcement Act of Congress [Stephens said]. My first position is that this whole act is not a law, but a mere legal nullity. It was passed with the professed object of carrying into effect what are called the 14th and 15th Amendments to the Constitution . . . and depends on their validity for its own. These so-called amendments are . . . not true amendments of that sacred instrument. They are nothing but usurpations and nullities, having no validity themselves and therefore incapable of imparting any to the Enforcement Act or to any other act whatsoever.[24]

With such a view widely held it was extremely difficult to gather evidence. Native whites were usually unco-operative, and Negroes were often reluctant to testify in the face of white hostility. Those witnesses who were persuaded to testify might find their property and lives in danger. In 1872 G. Wiley Wells, district attorney of the northern district of Mississippi, saw his case fall apart when five key witnesses were murdered. "I cannot get witnesses," he reported to Washington, "as all feel it is sure death to testify before the Grand Jury." [25] Frightened witnesses appealed to the President and Department of Justice for protection, but they received little comfort. The best the attorney general could do was to exhort Negro witnesses to have courage, to "take the position that the country is as much yours as it is theirs—that you have as good a right to live in it as they—and that you are determined to live in it, and enjoy all your rights; or to die in it, bravely asserting your rights." [26]

State and local authorities often failed to co-operate with federal officials; indeed, on numerous occasions they impeded the operation of the federal program. In virtually every Southern state, at one time or another during the decade of the 1870's, federal deputy marshals, supervisors of election, or soldiers were arrested by local law enforcement officers on charges ranging from false arrest or assault and battery to murder. In South Carolina no less a figure than Major Lewis Merrill, commander of the troops stationed in York County during the period of martial law, was taken into custody for false arrest.[27] A favorite stratagem was to prosecute for perjury Negroes who had testified against Klan members before United States commissioners.[28] The government never worked out a reliable device for combating these practices. Sometimes district attorneys were instructed to sue for a writ of habeas corpus in United States courts, but usually they were directed merely to defend the accused before the state tribunal.[29] The most effective way to protect the federal officer was to get the case removed to a federal court for trial, which could sometimes be done under section eighteen of the First Enforcement Act, but only with "exceeding difficulty."[30]

Securing juries that would convict was a perennial problem. In the words of Judge Amos Morrill of Texas, "Jurors drawn at random from the list of voters . . . would not be convinced that any man had violated the revenue acts or the enforcement acts by any testimony."[31] Consequently, in many districts the marshal was given full authority to select jurors and was advised by the Department of Justice to avoid jurors "unfriendly to the laws and the government."[32] Even ostensibly friendly juries were anything but reliable. In 1876 a grand jury in Mississippi refused to indict several persons for violations of the Enforcement Acts even though, as the foreman admitted, the evidence was overwhelming. The reason given was that key witnesses, fearful of reprisals, would not agree to testify in open court, and the jury saw little use in involving the government in the expense of an abortive trial.[33] In many districts there was experimentation with part Negro juries, but the effect fell short of expectations. District Attorney Henry P. Farrow of Georgia placed six Negroes on a petit jury in 1873, only to see the term frittered away in an endless debate as to their qualifications.[34] Only in those districts where officials were willing to impanel all Negro juries, fully protected by federal troops in the courthouses, could convictions be relied upon. The price paid at the bar of Southern public opinion for such success was, of course, high.

Intimidation of witnesses and juries might have been prevented had marshals enjoyed sufficient power to guarantee protection. Indeed, in theory the marshal had ample resources, but in practice he was often impotent. He could call upon the *posse comitatus*, but social pressure made the bystanders reluctant and undependable. Federal troops were stationed throughout the South, but they were seldom available for routine police duty. Securing troops involved much red tape, and requests for them were turned down as often as they were granted; unless actual riot impended, there was little chance of military aid. District Attorney Gabriel C. Wharton of Kentucky made an urgent request for troops in 1875 and received the terse reply, "not a case yet for United States soldiers . . . send written report." Wharton, by return mail, expressed what must have been the unspoken thoughts of many a federal officer, "When there is a case for United States troops in this state there is not time for a written report." As an afterthought, he added, "The Ku-Klux never fire on United States soldiers, but they do not hesitate to shoot . . . Marshals whenever an opportunity is presented."[35]

Perhaps more basic in the failure of enforcement than the unavailability of troops to protect witnesses and juries was the lack of money. The enforcement program was expensive, as a sampling of court costs in the South reveals. Between fiscal 1870 and 1873 the cost of maintaining the courts in the western district of North Carolina rose from $35,000 to $125,000, in South Carolina from $41,000 to $128,000, and in northern Mississippi from $9,000 to $84,000. Congress, harried by demands for lower taxes, was reluctant to provide adequate funds. About a million dollars a year, far less than was necessary, was allocated for court expenses under the new program.[36] Consequently, the attorney general was forced to urge economy from the beginning, and starting in 1873 instructed district attorneys that "no case be prosecuted under the Enforcement Acts . . . unless the public interest imperatively requires it." [37] Emergency requests for money made by marshals and attorneys were halved and sometimes quartered before being approved. After the Democrats gained control of the House in the elections of 1874, a congressional committee was set up to investigate the expenses of the Department of Justice, and the judicial appropriation for 1876-1877 was cut by a half million dollars. Attorney General Alphonso Taft saw little alternative but to put each district on a strict budget, allowing only a little more money than had been available prior to 1870.[38] By the end of the Reconstruction period the vigor of the enforcement program was clearly circumscribed by financial considerations.

The enforcement program was further handicapped by the inadequacies of the federal court system. The Enforcement Acts imposed an unmanageable extra burden on an antiquated judicial structure. The attorneys general frequently complained of the inability of courts to clear their dockets. By October, 1870, some 472 persons had been arrested in South Carolina for alleged violation of the Enforcement Act. At the November term of the circuit court, 420 were indicted, but at the end of the one-month session only five had been brought to trial.

> With the caution and deliberation which the law wisely observes in criminal proceedings [Attorney General Akerman wrote], it is obvious that the attempt to bring to justice . . . even a small portion of the guilty in that state must fail. . . . If it takes a court over one month to try five offenders, how long will it take to try four hundred, already indicted, and many hundreds more who deserve to be indicted? [39]

Similar problems arose in North Carolina and Mississippi. Faced by this dilemma, the attorney general had little choice but to compromise. District attorneys were instructed in 1871 to prosecute vigorously only such

persons "as appear to have been leaders in the conspiracies." Others
were ordered to be "released on light bail" and their cases pushed to
trial only if time allowed. "Those whose connection with the conspiracies was compulsory and reluctant" were not even to be indicted.[40]

Assuming that Congress had provided adequate machinery for enforcement, the vitality of the program would still have rested, in the
last analysis, upon federal officials in the field, i.e., with the United
States judges, district attorneys, marshals, and commissioners. It is impossible to generalize about the quality of the Department of Justice
bureaucracy except to say that it was uneven. Evaluation of the quality
of the work done by individual officeholders is likewise difficult, even
when biographical information is available, because of the biased nature of the sources and the conflicting criteria of judgment. Corruption,
irresponsibility, and rank political partisanship were to be found, of
course, but it is safe to say that the caliber of federal officialdom, with
some notable exceptions, was somewhat higher than has usually been
acknowledged. Nor were federal appointments in the South the special
preserve of the carpetbagger; a perusal of the roster of Department of
Justice officers reveals that a majority were Southern born.[41]

Neither is it true that all officials shared the same sociopolitical views.
Many, of course, were radicals in the tradition of Charles Sumner and
Thaddeus Stevens. Hugh Lennox Bond from Maryland, judge of the
fourth judicial circuit, had been a staunch Unionist during the war,
supported the politics of Henry Winter Davis, and was one of the
founders of the Association for the Improvement of Colored People. As
presiding judge at the famous Ku Klux trials at Columbia, South Carolina, in 1870, he showed little leniency toward lawbreakers, and in two
notable cases he upheld the constitutionality of the enforcement legislation.[42] Richard Busteed, district judge for Alabama, was considered one
of the most obnoxious men in the state because of his equalitarian ideas
and his political harangues from the bench. "He taught that the boy
who could read and write was worth twice as much to himself and to
the community as he that could not, and that the public school should
know the public weal only . . . with open door to all creeds and all
races alike." [43] D. H. Starbuck, district attorney for eastern North Carolina, who won forty-nine convictions in 1871, saw the Enforcement Acts
as a partisan weapon.

> We who were born and raised [in the South, he wrote], know too
> well the terrible outrages committed by these bands of conspira-
> tors whose purposes were to destroy the freedom of elections and
> stab the government at its vitals. . . . We are entitled to the
> gratitude and thanks of the Republican or Union Party of this

nation which it was the purpose of this daring conspiracy to destroy.[44]

The administration was sensitive to charges of partisanship and consistently sought to control overzealous authorities. In November 1871, Attorney General Akerman tactfully cautioned District Attorney John A. Minnis of Alabama, "I am glad to observe your zeal, and this I trust will never flag as long as the crime exists, though of course it should be guided by discretion. The government in these matters is not vindictive, and wishes to worry no citizen unnecessarily. . . ." Later the attorney general spelled out his meaning:

> I suggest the expediency of taking great care to keep the administration of the law unconnected with mere party feuds. As a matter of fact, I suppose that the crimes at which the law aims have principally been perpetrated by one party; but if the members of the other party commit the same offenses . . . they must receive the same treatment. In each instance it seems to one that the case should be clear, both for the moral and legal effect of the prosecution.[45]

As the election of 1874 approached, Attorney General Williams urged district attorneys and marshals in Alabama, South Carolina, Louisiana, Kentucky, and Tennessee "to proceed with all possible energy and dispatch to detect, expose, arrest, and punish" Ku Klux marauders, but he added, "You understand, of course, that no interference whatever with any political or party action not in violation of the law" should be undertaken.[46]

Moderates, conservatives, and even a few Democrats were to be found among the federal authorities in the South. The judiciary in particular was dominated by conservative ideas, and several judges endeared themselves to the Southern population by their refusal to embrace doctrines of social equality and constitutional change. William B. Woods, of the fifth judicial circuit, was a former Ohio Democrat who had come to the support of "Lincoln's war" only reluctantly. Ultimately he joined the Union Army and served with Sherman; when the war was over he settled in Alabama and became a conservative on civil rights questions.[47] George W. Brooks, judge of the district of North Carolina, was a Johnson appointee with a reputation for industry and sound judgment. In 1870 Governor W. W. Holden declared two counties under martial law and sent in troops; Brooks released the prisoners under writ of habeas corpus basing his action on the Fourteenth Amendment and thereby becoming the first judge to use the Fourteenth Amendment to protect the personal liberties of white men.[48] Of Henry Clay Caldwell, judge of the eastern district of Arkansas, it was said that "during the six years that the carpetbag regime lasted he was the greatest protection that the people of the state had. . . ."[49] Other judges like John Erskine of Georgia, who never took an enforcement case when he could avoid it, and Robert A. Hill of Mississippi, who enforced United States laws with as much leniency as possible, won the confidence, respect, and gratitude of the Southern people.

Some marshals and district attorneys were either sensitive to Southern public opinion or in substantial agreement with it. James H. Pierce, Mississippi marshal, was very concerned about Democratic charges early in his term. The attorney general sought, in instances like this, to bolster morale:

> You give greater consideration than I think is due to the censures of a party press. While of course you should give no occasion for well grounded censures, yet on the other hand, you should not be deterred by unfounded censures for doing your full duty.[50]

Another Mississippi marshal supported the Democratic ticket in the election of 1872, and the marshal and district attorney of the eastern district of Texas packed juries with Democrats in order to prevent convictions.[51] When such defections became known to the attorney general, investigations were undertaken, and removal from office usually resulted. Georgia District Attorney John D. Pope, a Johnson appointee, is a case in point. Georgia Republicans early complained that Negroes were receiving no protection from the district attorney's office, and the secret service, investigating Ku Klux disturbances in Georgia in 1871 and 1872, found that Pope would not allow Klan "victims" to testify in court. "If there is not a United States attorney sent here to prosecute these fellows in earnest," one operative observed, "I can see but little use for us to work them up, run the risk of our lives and bring them to Atlanta, there to see them discharged."[52] Pope was shortly replaced by Henry P. Farrow and prosecutions of Klansmen began.

Although the Department of Justice was involved in none of the great scandals of the Grant administration, there was to be found among department personnel some of the low morality characteristic of the age. Extravagance was perhaps the most common failing. Virgil S. Lusk, district attorney of the western district of North Carolina, was repeatedly warned about laxity in financial matters.

> So conduct the business of your office [Williams cautioned], that hereafter it will be unnecessary for me to complain of extravagance in its administration. As the Comptroller [of the Treasury] well says, referring to your district, the number of warrants issued ap-

pears to be limited only by inability to serve them all. . . . There is ground for suspicion that persons concerned in criminal prosecutions in your district are sacrificing the interests of the government . . . to the accumulation of their fees.[53]

Misconduct was most usually found among minor officials such as commissioners, supervisors of election, and deputy marshals. Drunkenness, arbitrary use of power, and blackmail were the most common complaints lodged against them. Reports of such misconduct were a source of much discomfort to the attorney general, and marshals were encouraged to select only "prudent and fearless" subordinates. "It is important," Williams emphasized, "that you delegate . . . power to none but careful and responsible persons." [54] The most notorious scandal involving the Department of Justice occurred in the western district of Arkansas. This district, with headquarters at Fort Smith, embraced the "Indian Territory," a lawless area inhabited by cutthroats and renegades. Successive United States attorneys and marshals and Judge William Story were all implicated in fraud, bribery, and other misconduct; not until Isaac C. Parker, the "hanging judge," took office in 1875 was the mess cleaned up.[55]

In attempting to reach a fairer evaluation of the enforcement program, one additional factor must be considered. As in other phases of Southern history it is dangerous to overwork the concept of the "Solid South." Although the South ultimately presented a united front on the race question, there was initially considerable difference of opinion on this matter between the Black Belt planter and the upcountry farmer. The Ku Klux movement was strongest in the former non-slaveholding regions, such as western North Carolina, eastern Kentucky and Tennessee, and northern South Carolina, Georgia, and Alabama. The congressional committee which investigated the Klan tacitly recognized this fact when it limited its investigations to six states, and reports from federal officials in the field show conclusively that life and property were a good deal less secure in some districts than in others.[56] Since the Enforcement Acts were essentially, although not exclusively, designed to combat the Klan, it is not surprising to find that outside of the former non-slaveholding areas there was relatively little activity under the legislation. The following table shows the number of cases instituted in each of the Southern states during 1870-1877.[57]

South Carolina	1,387	Kentucky	116
Mississippi	1,175	Georgia	73
North Carolina	559	Maryland	56
Tennessee	214	Florida	41
Alabama	134	Texas	29

West Virginia	27	Arkansas	3
Virginia	16	Missouri	3
Louisiana	4		

These statistics reveal a correlation between Klan concentration and enforcement activity and suggest that prosecutions were more justified than Coulter, Dunning, and others have admitted.

In conclusion, it may be pointed out that most existing studies of the federal government policy in the 1870's were written at a time when disfranchisement and Jim Crowism were accepted as the normal state of affairs in both North and South; political and social inequality, it was assumed, was the logical result of racial inferiority. Such attitudes affected the validity of scholarly findings. Today, we may agree with Dunning and Rhodes that unlimited Negro suffrage was a mistake. But we cannot accept the corollary of this, that universal Negro disfranchisement was a valid alternative.

In 1870, measures to preserve the Negro's constitutional rights were desperately needed, and Congress responded with the passage of the Enforcement Acts of 1870 and 1871. These laws, essentially sound, worked fairly well for three or four years. Implementation, however, was difficult. The Grant administration, whose radicalism has perhaps been overemphasized, used federal power conspicuously on a few well-known occasions, but shortages of troops, money, and courts plagued law enforcement officers from the beginning. After 1874, the acts were virtually dead letters. In the final analysis, Southern intransigence and Northern apathy together brought about the collapse of the enforcement program; white supremacy proved to be a more vital principle than Republican supremacy. The South, in its determination to win home rule, was willing to face the prospect of race war; the North was not. In the end, the policy of enforcement failed; but this does not mean that the policy was iniquitous nor that its failure was a blessing. A complete re-examination of the subject should tell us much about the later Reconstruction period and might well provide useful object lessons for the present.

NOTES

1. See Howard K. Beale, "On Rewriting Reconstruction History," *American Historical Review*, XLV (July, 1940), 807-827; and Bernard A. Weisberger, "The Dark and Bloody Ground of Reconstruction Historiography," *Journal of Southern History*, XXV (November, 1959), 427-447.

2. See Charles H. Coleman, *The Election of 1868; the Democratic Effort to Regain Control* (New York, 1933); Jonathan Truman Dorris, *Pardon and Amnesty Under Lincoln and Johnson: The Restoration of the Confederates in Their Rights and Privileges, 1861-1898* (Chapel Hill, 1953), 339-361; and James A. Rawley, "The General Amnesty Act of 1872: A Note," *Mississippi Valley Historical Review*, XLVII (December, 1960), 480-484.

3. *Statutes at Large of the United States*, XVI (1871), 140-146.

4. *Ibid.*, pp. 433-440.

5. *Ibid.*, XVII (1873), 13-15.

6. William W. Davis, "The Federal Enforcement Acts," *Studies in Southern History and Politics; Inscribed to William A. Dunning* (New York, 1914), p. 205.

7. *Congressional Globe*, 41st Congress, 2nd Session, Pt. IV, p. 3662.

8. Davis, *op. cit.*, p. 228.

9. *Statutes at Large of the United States*, LXXI (1958), 637; LXXIV (1961), 88-92; U.S. Commission on Civil Rights, *Report, 1961* (5 vols.; Washington, 1961), I (*Voting*), 139-142.

10. Davis, *op. cit.*, p. 224.

11. William A. Dunning, *Reconstruction, Political and Economic, 1865-1877* (New York, 1907), p. 271.

12. E. Merton Coulter, *The South During Reconstruction, 1865-1877* (Baton Rouge, 1947), p. 171.

13. *Annual Report of the Attorney General*, 1870, *House Executive Documents*, 41st Congress, 3rd Session, No. 90 (Serial 1454); 1871, *ibid.*, 42nd Congress, 2nd Session, No. 55 (Serial 1510); 1872, *Senate Executive Documents*, 42nd Congress, 3rd Session, No. 32 (Serial 1545); 1873, *House Executive Documents*, 43rd Congress, 1st Session, No. 6 (Serial 1606); 1874, *ibid.*, 43rd Congress, 2nd Session, No. 7 (Serial 1638); 1875, *ibid.*, 44th Congress, 1st Session, No. 14 (Serial 1686); 1876, *ibid.*, 44th Congress, 2nd Session, No. 20 (Serial 1751); 1877, *ibid.*, 45th Congress, 2nd Session, No. 7 (Serial 1802); 1878, *ibid.*, 45th Congress, 3rd Session, No. 7 (Serial 1852), *passim*.

14. Attorney General George Williams to Virgil S. Lusk, April 25, 1874, in Record Group 60 (National Archives), *Instructions to United States Attorneys and Marshals*, D., p. 511.

15. Quoted in Homer Stille Cummings and Carl McFarland, *Federal Justice: Chapters in the History of Justice and the Federal Executive* (New York, 1937), p. 238.

16. Williams to Lusk, April 25, 1874, in *Instructions*, D, p. 511.

17. For the Johnson and Stanbery arguments, see U.S. Congress, Joint Select Committee on Condition of Affairs in the Late Insurrectionary States, *Report, House Reports*, 42nd Congress, 2nd Session, No. 22 (13 vols.; Serials 1529-41), also *Senate Reports*, 42nd Congress, 2nd Session, No. 41 (13 vols.; Serials 1484-96), V, 1615-72. See also Gabriel C. Wharton to Williams, March 27, 1872, in Record Group 60, *Selected Records Relating to Reconstruction*, Source-Chronological for Kentucky.

18. Wharton to Williams, November 10, 1873, and Benjamin H. Bristow to Williams, October 24, 1873, *ibid.*

19. Robert Selph Henry, *The Story of Reconstruction* (Indianapolis, 1938), pp. 484-492.

20. James R. Beckwith to Williams, June 24, 1874, in *Selected Records . . . ,* Source-Chronological for Louisiana.

21. *United States* v. *Cruikshank et al.,* 25 Fed. Cas. 707 (1874), quotation on p. 710.

22. Williams to W. W. Murray, May 5, 1875, in *Instructions,* E, pp. 443-444.

23. *United States* v. *Reese et al.,* 92 U.S. 214 (1875), and *United States* v. *Cruikshank et al.,* 92 U. S. 542 (1875).

24. John D. Pope to Williams, February 7, 1871, in *Selected Records . . . ,* Source-Chronological for Georgia.

25. G. Wiley Wells to Williams, January 17, 1872, in *Selected Records . . . ,* Source-Chronological for Mississippi.

26. Cummings and McFarland, *op. cit.,* p. 238.

27. Bristow to Wells, September 19, 1871, in *Instructions,* C, p. 370.

28. Williams to Henry P. Farrow, January 4, 1875, *ibid.,* E., p. 214.

29. Habeas corpus proceedings in the federal courts to release citizens from state custody were authorized by statutes passed in 1833 and 1867, but not until late in the century was the constitutionality of this procedure fully established. *Statutes at Large of the United States,* IV (1850), 634; XIV (1868), 385; *In re Neagle,* 135 U. S. 1 (1890); *In re Loney,* 134 U. S. 372 (1890).

30. Williams to George M. Duskin, February 11, 1875, in *Instructions,* E, p. 266, and Attorney General Edwards Pierrepont to N. S. McAfee, September 11, 1875, *ibid.,* F, p. 157.

31. Amos Morrill to Williams, April 3, 1873, in *Selected Records . . . ,* Source-Chronological for Texas.

32. Attorney General Amos T. Akerman to James H. Pierce, August 28, 1871, in *Instructions,* B, p. 336.

33. James R. Cavett to Alphonso Taft, August 28, 1876, in *Selected Records . . . ,* Source-Chronological for Mississippi.

34. Farrow to Williams, March 15, and May 1, 1873, in *Selected Records . . . ,* Source-Chronological for Georgia.

35. Wharton to Pierrepont, July 7, 1875, in *Selected Records . . . ,* Source-Chronological for Kentucky.

36. Treasury Department, *An Account of the Receipts and Expenditures of the United States, 1870-1873, passim.* See also *Statutes at Large of the United States,* XVII, 134, and *Annual Report of the Secretary of the Treasury on the State of the Finances, 1870, House Executive Documents,* 41st Congress, 3rd Session, No. 2 (Serial 1451); 1873, *ibid.,* 43rd Congress, 1st Session, No. 2 (Serial 1603).

37. Williams to All Marshals, March 8, 1873, and Williams to William H. Smyth, February 5, 1873, in *Instructions,* C, pp. 645, 608.

38. Taft to Robert P. Baker, August 1, 1876, *ibid.,* F, pp. 571-574.

39. *Annual Report of the Attorney General,* 1871, pp. 4-5.

40. Akerman to D. T. Corbin, November 10, 1871, in *Instructions,* C, pp. 33-34.

41. *Register of the Department of Justice and the Judicial Officers of the United States* (eds. 1-5; 1871-1876), *passim.*

42. *United States* v. *Crosby et al.,* 25 Fed. Cas. 701 (1871), and *United States* v. *Petersburg Judges of Election, same* v. *Petersburg Registrars of Election,* 27 Fed. Cas. 506 (1874).

43. John Witherspoon DuBose, *Alabama's Tragic Decade: Ten Years of Alabama, 1865-1874,* ed. James K. Greer (Birmingham, 1940), p. 255; *National Cyclopaedia of American Biography,* IV, 531; Walter L. Fleming, *Civil War and Reconstruction in Alabama* (New York, 1905), pp. 394, 744.

44. Cummings and McFarland, *op. cit.,* p. 237.

45. Akerman to John A. Minnis, November 11 and 24, 1871, in *Instructions,* C, pp. 22, 64-65.

46. Williams to District Attorneys and Marshals, September 3, 1874, *ibid.,* E, pp. 13-14.

47. Alonzo H. Tuttle, "William Burnham Woods," *Dictionary of American Biography,* XX, 505-506. For Woods's opinions see *United States* v. *Harris,* 106 U. S. 629 (1882), *Presser* v. *Illinois,* 116 U. S. 252 (1886).

48. J. G. de Roulhac Hamilton, *Reconstruction in North Carolina* (New York, 1914), pp. 525-530.

49. H. W. Howard Knott, "Henry Clay Caldwell," *Dictionary of American Biography,* III, 408.

50. Akerman to James H. Pierce, August 28, 1871, in *Instructions,* B, p. 336.

51. Williams to Marshal Robert J. Alcorn, July 8, 1873, *ibid.,* D, p. 115; and Governor E. J. Davis to Williams, February 2, 1872, in *Selected Records . . . ,* Source-Chronological for Texas.

52. J. R. W. Johnston to Williams, February 15, 1872, in *Selected Records . . . ,* Source-Chronological for Georgia, and Record Group 60, Hiram G. Whitley, *Reports Regarding the Ku Klux Klan,* Report No. 2, pp. 9-10.

53. Williams to Lusk, February 3, 1874, in *Instructions,* D, pp. 386-387.

54. Williams to All Marshals, September 30, 1874, *ibid.,* E, p. 63.

55. David Y. Thomas, "Isaac Charles Parker," *Dictionary of American Biography,* XIV, 225-226. See also *Selected Records . . . ,* Source-Chronological for Arkansas, *passim.*

56. See, for example, *Message on Political Affairs in the Southern States, House Executive Documents,* 42nd Congress, 2nd Session, No. 268 (Serial 1515).

57. *Annual Report of the Attorney General,* 1870-1877, *passim.*

WOODROW WILSON

AND FEDERAL SEGREGATION

Kathleen Wolgemuth

When Woodrow Wilson assumed the presidency in 1913 many Negroes believed that he would champion their cause for advancement. An unprecedented number of Negroes had cast their vote for Wilson, risking ostracism or ridicule from others of their race for so departing from the ranks of the Republican party.[1] This deviation from the traditional line of Negro support was nurtured by discontent with the Republican and Progressive candidates, Taft and Roosevelt, and their platforms. It was spurred by the stirring assurances of wholehearted support to the Negro race by Woodrow Wilson.

Yet it was in Woodrow Wilson's administration that the most bitter blow to Negro hopes of advancement fell: the introduction of segregation into several of the federal departments.[2] This action raised questions of vital concern to government-race relations, and created a sensation among nearly all elements of the colored world as well as among some of the white.

The subject of Negro-white relationships in government was raised in a cabinet meeting, April 11, 1913, soon after the new administration had come into power. Albert Burleson, the southern-bred postmaster general, expressed his concern to that small, closed meeting regarding certain "intolerable" conditions in the Railway Mail Service where, he said, whites not only had to work with blacks, but were forced to use the same drinking glasses, towels, and washrooms. Burleson contended that it was to the advantage of both races to be separated in their work.

Kathleen Wolgemuth, "Woodrow Wilson and Federal Segregation," *Journal of Negro History*, XLIV, No. 2 (April, 1959), 158-173.

He announced plans to implement this philosophy of segregation in the Railway Mail Service, in a gradual way, and continuing the employment of Negroes where such "would not be objectionable." The project was aimed at only one section of the federal service, but Burleson voiced a hope that segregation could be promoted in all departments of government.[3]

If there was any dissension to Burleson's plans, it was not recorded. President Wilson was noted as saying that he desired, above all, to avoid friction in federal service posts. Later events were to show that a large measure of support for governmental segregation was given by other cabinet members, particularly William McAdoo, secretary of the treasury, Josephus Daniels, secretary of the navy, and Burleson.

Coincident with the secret cabinet talks on segregation was the formation of a non-governmental group in Washington, D. C., the National Democratic Fair Play Association, whose purpose was the same as Burleson's. In fact, Burleson's attention had perhaps been drawn in the first instance to the Railway Mail Service's integrated organization by a letter from the Fair Play Association condemning the "low and criminal elements" employed in the Railway Mail Service, a copy of which was sent to the postmaster general. The writer, an unidentified postal clerk working in St. Louis, Missouri, called for abolition of a mixed service because, he said, the existing setup was driving away all worthy whites.[4] The Fair Play Association was concerned not only with the Railway Mail Service. At its first mass meeting, May 1, 1913, the group pledged itself to fight for segregation in all government offices, and, citing figures that 24,500 of the 490,000 workers were Negro, anticipated an arduous campaign. The climate of opinion is seen in a letter, said to be written by a white woman working in the General Land Office of the Department of the Interior, which the president of the group read to the assembly. The writer complained that she had to take dictation from drunken Negroes. "I also worked for a dark-skinned, woolly-headed Negro. I then felt if a human would ever be justified in ever ending his existence I would then, for I was a Southern woman, my father a distinguished officer during the Civil War. . . ."[5] In the following weeks and months, the Fair Play Association employed effective Negro-baiting techniques to acquaint all who might not know of the "invidious situation" in the government. Mass meetings, petitions, circulars, and personal letters to high-ranking officials spread the news of white women who had to work alongside some "greasy, ill-smelling Negro man or woman." These conditions, it asserted, were "UnDemocratic, UnAmerican, and UnChristian."[6] President Wilson was sent copies of these letters.

Soon the fondest hopes of the Fair Play Association were being realized in several new governmental departments. Although that group did not know definitely of the April 11 cabinet discussion, news of segregationist activities began to leak out. Presently a whole new pattern was apparent for all to see.

The departments involved at first were those of the post office, under Burleson, and the treasury, under McAdoo. No executive orders were issued, and changes were discreet and gradual. Such respectable papers as the *New York Times* carried only a few indirect references to those activities, and the various, apparently disconnected, segregation actions found publicity largely in the Negro press alone. In June, articles began to appear asking questions about the reported screening off of Negroes in a certain office, or directing attention to separate lavatory facilities for Negroes in another area. The trickle of news regarding federal segregation soon became a flood. It was becoming apparent to white and black alike that the government's segregation policy was no accident, nor confined to a few separate offices, but was an official and widespread program, albeit enacted with no executive orders.[7]

By the end of 1913, segregation had been realized in the Bureau of Engraving and Printing, the Post Office Department, the Office of the Auditor for the Post Office, and had even begun in the City Post Office in Washington, D. C. This involved not only separated or screened-off working positions, but segregated lavatories and lunchrooms.[8] Segregation appeared to a lesser extent in the office of the Auditor of the Navy. In the navy itself, Negroes traditionally held menial posts, but segregation in the auditor's office was new. Screens set off Negroes from whites, and a separate lavatory in the cellar was provided for the colored clerks.[9]

While Federal segregation was being enacted to keep Negroes and whites apart, other steps were taken to appoint Negroes only to menial posts or to prevent them from obtaining Civil Service jobs. Photographs were required of all candidates for Civil Service positions from 1914 on. This was explained as a necessary device to prevent impersonation and to enable appointing officers "to form some opinion in regard to eligibles certified." [10] But many Negroes charged that officials used the photographs for one purpose alone, that of weeding out colored applicants. Equally useful for such officials was the rule whereby appointing officers were given three names of candidates from which to choose their staff replacements. This was a Civil Service practice of long standing, but now Negroes asserted that such department heads as Burleson continually by-passed any Negro in the eligible group. Whatever the techniques, it is apparent that there were ample means to avoid the appointment or advancement of Negroes in the Civil Service. That discrimination did result is evidenced in the many accusations by Negroes against the practices.[11]

The question inevitably arose: how much did President Wilson know of the segregation policy of Burleson, McAdoo, and Daniels? When the first minor changes were performed in spring and summer, 1913, many of the persons concerned blamed only Wilson's cabinet members, particularly the three named above. Wilson, they said, perhaps was not aware of their actions.[12] There was, after all, no executive order.

But Wilson did know about the plans for racial separation in the government. He approved of them. He vigorously defended the official policy of segregation in a series of personal letters to one of his closest friends and most loyal supporters, Oswald Garrison Villard. Villard was editor of a leading liberal newspaper, the New York *Evening Post,* and had been an active worker for Wilson in the presidential campaign. Villard, the grandson of William Lloyd Garrison, was involved as well in the activities of the young National Association for the Advancement of Colored People (NAACP), the "radical" group which was challenging the more conservative group of Booker T. Washington. As a co-worker with W. E. B. DuBois and as a correspondent with DuBois' rival, Booker T. Washington, Villard was the natural person to question the President on the federal segregation.

Villard asked Wilson bluntly if he were aware of the actions which had been taken in several departmental offices. Did Wilson realize, he wondered, the extent to which these actions had gone, and the dangers involved? Did he know that they would lead to a return of Negroes to the Republican party? He received an answer to this letter of July 21, 1913, two days later. Wilson, in reply to the "distressing letter," affirmed the presence of federal segregation, begun upon "the initiative and suggestion of the heads of departments." He knew about it, and believed it was in the interests of both races. It had been introduced, Wilson continued, "with the idea that the friction, or rather the discontent and uneasiness which had prevailed in many of the departments would thereby be removed." He expressed sorrow that Villard should so misjudge his action which, he said, was intended to render Negro federal workers "more safe in their possession of office and less likely to be discriminated against." [13]

Now that Wilson's position was clear, Villard went on to try and convince the President that it was an erroneous stand to take. He urged Wilson to accept the plans put forth earlier by the NAACP for a race commission to study scientifically the entire Negro-white situation in the United States. Wilson had indicated great interest in the idea to

Villard in 1912, promising to consider it when he reached the White House, and in May, 1913 Villard had submitted the tentative plan. But in August, Wilson wrote Villard that he could not accept it in view of the sentiment of certain senators. This was a bitter setback to Villard and the NAACP which sponsored the commission plan. But more urgent was the fight against federal segregation, and Villard quickly renewed his efforts to influence Wilson against it.

Villard added strength to his arguments that Negroes were bitterly resentful of the new policy by forwarding a letter to the President from the outstanding Negro leader in the country, Booker T. Washington. Opposition was not only from the militant Negro wing. Washington wrote, in part, "I have recently spent several days in Washington, and I have never seen the colored people so discouraged and so bitter as they are at the present time." Washington asked Villard to seek a change from the "hurtful" policy before it went further.[14] Wilson was not encountering a divided Negro opinion on the segregation issue. Negroes were divided on other questions of race philosophy, but they were united in their condemnation of federal segregation.

Wilson was deeply troubled by the unexpected and violent attacks on a policy which he felt to be moderate, conciliatory and just. But he believed that segregation was essential to the avoidance of friction. He urged Villard "to see the real situation down here," to understand that what he, as President, was trying to do "must be done, if at all, through the cooperation of those with whom I am to sit in the government." Nothing could be accomplished, he warned, if a "bitter agitation" were inaugurated. "I appeal to you most earnestly to aid in holding things at a just and cool equipoise until I can discover whether it is possible to work things out or not." [15]

In September, 1913, Wilson wrote similar sentiments to a prominent Negro minister, Reverend H. A. Bridgeman, editor of the *Congregation and Christian World*. This was the President's first public statement on federal segregation. "I would say that I do approve of the segregation that is being attempted in several of the departments," he wrote.[16] Later on in the year he promised a Negro delegation, led by the fiery young editor of the Boston *Guardian*, William Monroe Trotter, to investigate the segregation. One year later the group returned to demand the reason for continued segregation. Wilson reported to them that investigations by him and his cabinet revealed that federal segregation was necessitated by friction betwen Negro and white workers, and was not instituted to embarrass or harm colored workers. He admired the progress the Negro race had made and wanted to see it "continue along independent lines," but inasmuch as prejudice still remained and it would take "one hundred years to eradicate this prejudice," he said, "we must deal with it as practical men." Wilson stressed his contention that harm was interjected when Negroes were told that federal segregation was a humiliation.[17]

Segregation would be continued, but Wilson told the group he would gladly investigate any specific cases of discrimination which were presented to him from time to time. He maintained that the whole question had no place in politics; it was a "human problem" not a political one.[18] The *New York Times*, which carried the story of the delegation's visit on page one under the headline, "President Resents Negro's Criticism," wrote this description of Wilson's answer to Trotter's warning that he would never again gain Negro support unless his policies were altered: [19]

> With some emotion he asserted that he was not seeking office, and that a man who sought the office of the Presidency was a fool for his pains. He spoke of the intolerable burden of the office and the things he had to do which were more than the human spirit could carry.

After labeling Trotter's words on the Negro vote as blackmail, Wilson dismissed the delegation.

From Autumn 1913 on, after Wilson's approval of federal segregation had been made public and evidence on the size and extent of the official policy mounted, Negro opposition was united, hitting hard at what was felt to be the most serious blow at Negro rights since the days of slavery. Important and little-known Negroes, important and little-known groups found common ground in demanding its abolition.

Wilson himself received letters of protest from every state in the Union, from blacks and whites. DuBois, Villard, and other officers of the NAACP sent both public appeals which were published in the NAACP news organ, *Crisis*, and private letters. Booker T. Washington expressed the concern of his group in the letter forwarded by Villard. Prominent members of the scholarly world, of which Wilson had been so recently a part, joined in the protest along with such political personages as the governors of Massachusetts and Michigan. The Wilson Papers are full of letters from Negroes and whites in every walk of life.[20]

Petitions were another method of protest. Circulated in cities throughout the country and sent to the President, they varied in size from a few hundred signatures to one brought by William Monroe Trotter which was purported to contain over 21,000 names. The NAACP led the drive, collecting signatures of both Negroes and whites. Several church organizations joined the crusade. The National Council of Congregational Churches of the United States registered its official resolution against federal segregation at the October, 1913 convention. The International Council of Churches added a more universal censure in a letter to Wilson, August 21, 1913.[21] Many other church groups and individual ministers of all faiths protested. No religious group appears to have written Wilson in favor of the federal segregation policy.

Another method of attack was that of mass meetings. NAACP branches held open hearings on the mounting evidence of segregation, and NAACP national officers toured through such eastern cities as Boston, New York, and Washington to arouse and inform the public. Trotter, representing the National Independent Political League, a Negro group which had been recognized by the Democratic party and had supported Wilson in the election, stood before enormous audiences in Boston and called for a united Negro front to stop the advance of "Jim Crowism" in Washington, D. C.

Villard turned to the public in October 1913 through the medium of mass meetings after his letters and talks to Wilson convinced him that the President would not change his policies. Prior to a meeting scheduled for late October, Villard advised McAdoo what he intended to say there, and alluded to the deep sorrow he felt in opposing Wilson. "I told the President the other day that I should have to do this, but that I should do it with complete respect both for your sincerity and for his, and I have tried to put that note into this address. It is harder for me to make this speech than you could have any idea of." [22] McAdoo's reply was intended to correct "certain erroneous statements" in Villard's speech. There was no segregation issue in the Treasury Department, he wrote. They had planned to make the registry section an all-colored division under a Negro supervisor, he explained, and when the Negro candidate for Registrar of the Treasury withdrew from candidacy, the experiment was abandoned. Now there were 60 per cent white and 40 per cent black workers in that area. Of the alleged discrimination, McAdoo stated, "There has been an effort in the departments to remove the causes of complaint and irritation where white women have been forced unnecessarily to sit at desks with colored men. Compulsion of this sort creates friction and race prejudice. Elimination of such friction promotes good feeling and friendship." He chastised Villard's "unjust" speech as reflecting wrong on Wilson "than whom no truer, nobler and braver soldier in the cause of humanity has appeared since the death of Lincoln." [23]

This letter from McAdoo was read to the mass meeting in Washington on October 27, 1913. It was a packed hall, and over four thousand, chiefly Negroes, had been turned away for lack of room. Villard related the outcome to McAdoo.[24] McAdoo's letter had not been received well, he said, because a great number in the audience were segregated clerks. When the sentence "There is no segregation issue in the Treasury Department" was read, a great derisive laugh had risen from the throng. Villard insisted that all the facts he had presented were true, based on painstaking research conducted both by the NAACP and by himself. He would continue to spread these facts.

If mass meetings, petitions, and letters were the major weapons of the antisegregationists, the press was equally important in publicizing conditions within the departments and in covering those methods of protest which were being employed to put an end to federal segregation. The major burden was assumed by the Negro newspapers and magazines. White progressive papers such as Villard's *Evening Post* added their strength, and from time to time a number of white papers of Republican or Independent leanings remarked on the changing conditions among colored government workers and questioned the merit of the change.[25]

The breadth of Negro opposition to federal segregation was suggested in the fact that colored newspapers and magazines whose policies were ordinarily opposed to each other united on this one cause. The National Negro Press Association, representing 126 newspapers at its national convention in August, 1913, sent a petition to Wilson to end the separationist policy. This group was reputed to support the policies of Booker T. Washington.[26] The *Crisis,* edited by Washington's adversary, W. E. B. DuBois, was another potent journalistic voice raised in opposition to Wilson's policies. Not the least of the services of the Negro press was to editorialize on the effects of segregation, to present the united voice of Negro opposition and its reasons for opposition.

That the protest was a large one was clear. Moreover its weapons were sharp. Its arguments were serious, thoughtful analyses of the present and potential threat federal segregation presented.

The major Negro arguments against federal segregation were repeated in petitions, mass meetings, letters, and editorials. They began on the general theme that the present situation was unfair and unwarranted, for "never before has the federal government discriminated against the civilian employees on the ground of color." [27] The government was presenting segregation in violation of accepted policy. Conditions had not changed to justify this abandonment of a non-segregated federal service. Negro employees had worked alongside white employees for many years, under Republican and Democratic administrations, with no apparent dissatisfaction on either side. The President wished to remove friction where friction did not even exist.

The arguments became more specific. The separate departmental facilities were said to be equal, but in reality they were not. Negroes were separated *from* whites, not the reverse. Negroes invariably were allocated the less desirable rooms, the inconveniently located lavatories, the poorly-lit alcoves. Instead of lessening insults, it created an opportunity for them by presenting the Negro in an inferior position. Already Negroes were being treated as social "lepers." [28]

Furthermore, it was charged, the faith Wilson had made with Negroes before the election had been violated. The Negro policy he supported now was inconsistent with his campaign promises of "fair play" and at variance as well with his entire Christian and Democratic philosophy. [29] Despair was rising in the Negro race. Never again would it support either Wilson or the Democratic party for political office. The great gain won in splitting the solid Negro vote was lost.

But even more important harm would follow, the protest continued. Federal segregation was by far the worst blow dealt the Negro race in its years of freedom, for it signified official approval of a practice against which Negroes were fighting by gradual or active means. It was an "establishment of caste in this free Republic." Segregation invariably led to excesses and abuses, for "injustice once started is bound to spread apace." [30] Now that the government was entering the arena of segregationist activities, such tendencies would increase and would operate with official sanction. The arguments Wilson gave to explain the government's conduct were similar to those defenses of segregation which were so familiar in the South. Perhaps Wilson was sincere when he said segregation in the government was in the best interests of the Negro. But regardless of his sincerity, segregation could be and was being used by whites to subjugate the Negro. The President said he favored segregation so that the Negro could have freedom in his own circle to advance independently, but in practice segregation actually was used to curtail the Negro's advancement. It did not matter what reasons were given to support segregation. In the end, the results were the same.[31]

Furthermore, the protesters continued, departmental segregation was inconsistent with the tenets of the New Freedom which promised equal rights for all in every area of activity, as well as with that philosophy upon which the United States had been established. The President had neither moral nor legal right to declare a political division on the ground of racial difference, no matter what his personal beliefs. The federal government had always refrained from defining social customs, yet Wilson's administration was in essence doing that very thing. The government did not exist "for the purpose of formulating rules of social etiquette." Departmental segregation was undemocratic in its recognition of the aristocracy of birth. A government which was unfaithful to its own principles was, in reality, hurting itself. Constitutional validity was also involved. Perhaps the Constitution was wrong in giving equal political rights to all, "but at least it is the law of the land and as such is not to be nullified by any individual who happens to believe that in this respect the Constitution is inversely drawn." [32]

Segregation in the nation's capital had special significance. Washington, D.C., although a southern city, was the center of Negro society, and the social status of the Negro there had been unequalled anywhere else in the country.[33] It had the largest Negro population of any city in the United States, 94,446 in 1910 according to the official census. Federal segregation, with its concomitants of residential and transportation segregation, was therefore a heavy burden for these Negroes who had enjoyed a measure of equality with whites for so long.

The importance of the Negro protest may be assessed in several ways. Most immediate was the impact it had upon the system it was attacking. Villard reported late in 1913 that federal segregationists had been ordered to take a back seat because of the rain of complaints.[34] A newspaper in Boston reported in December that segregation in the Post Office Department was being abandoned. The trend to remove segregation continued, and January 6, 1914 the officers of the NAACP wrote President Wilson of their joy at the reported checking of federal segregation. Two months later, a news source stated that the last vestiges of federal segregation were being destroyed under order of Assistant Secretary of the Treasury C. S. Hamlin.[35] It is improbable that integration was restored in full, but segregation as a recognized system was banished. Negro opposition had been strong, and was victorious.

It was upon Negroes themselves that the protest left a deeper mark. Federal segregation had been an issue upon which the colored population had leveled a full-scale attack, and out of this attack emerged new spokesmen and new ideas. The first decade of the twentieth century had seen the stirrings of a group of young Negroes who were dissatisfied with the moderate teachings of the accepted leader, Booker T. Washington. Of the rebels, the most outstanding was W. E. B. DuBois, the northern-born, Harvard Ph.D. who was active in the founding of the NAACP in 1910. His criticisms of Booker T. Washington had been strong, but as a member of the national board of the NAACP and as editor of its magazine, the *Crisis*, his philosophy reached a far wider audience.

The segregationist activities of the Wilson administration provided an explosive issue against which the contrasting philosophies of Washington and DuBois could be tested. Both of the men condemned the federal segregation, but their methods of protest were far different. Washington, a supporter of Taft and Roosevelt in the past, had little connection with the Democratic administration, was no longer the adviser to the President on matters which affected his race. Nor did he consult Wilson, with the exception of that letter sent through Villard. If he worked in secret against federal segregation, it was not recorded, and his public utterances were the same optimistic statements on the growth of Negro economy or the alleged decrease of lynching.[36]

In contrast, DuBois was outspoken in demanding the repeal of federal segregation. He gave voice to the growing feelings of racial solidarity. Federal segregation had intensified the Negro's sense of racial entity and convinced an increasing number of Negroes that Booker T. Washington's gradualism, while advancing the race's position in some areas of endeavor, would never answer the problems raised by white resentment and fear.

In effect, federal segregation had turned the spotlight upon the NAACP and DuBois. The *Crisis* stressed tangible and aggressive steps which must be taken to win political, economic, and social equality for the Negro race. Negroes should fight obstructions by making courts fair, seeking remedial legislation, winning national aid to education, gaining the removal of all legal discrimination based on race and color. The circle of human contact between the races should be increased, and the publication of truth about the Negro extended. Economic cooperation between the races should be increased, and the publication of truth should be promoted. The *Crisis* encouraged pride in race as well, with its emphasis upon the revival of Negro art and literature, and its attempts to enlighten the Negro voter by publishing the answers of all presidential and congressional candidates to NAACP questionnaires which called for the candidates' stands on such issues as segregation and lynching-laws. The Negro should continue to organize, and the NAACP was ready to extend its ranks.[37]

How successfully the NAACP appealed to the Negro may be seen in the rapid growth in membership and branches. In 1912, there were 329 members and 3 NAACP branches; by 1914, 3,000 members and 24 branches; by 1916, 8,785 members and 50 branches. From 1917 to 1920 the number jumped from 9,282 to 88,377, the branches from 80 to 356.[38] The early years of its growth, those years of activity against Wilson's program, and conditions in the country at large, were important ones for the association. They provided vital issues upon which the NAACP centered its program. The intense vigor and spirit with which this program was pursued attracted the attention of the discouraged Negro race. Although the board of directors was composed of twenty-seven whites to seven Negroes in 1910, the NAACP was essentially a Negro group, for as DuBois has recently pointed out, the life-blood of the association was the Negro in branch membership and in financial contributions.[39] The phenomenal jump in membership is evidence of the mounting faith of Negroes in the NAACP.

Thus the Negroes weathered the first administration of Woodrow Wilson. Loss of federal offices, anti-Negro bills in Congress by the score, increases in lynching of Negroes, the introduction of segregation into federal departments—these and other actions pointed to a marked decrease in Negro status. They contrasted sharply with the idealistic phrases of Wilson's New Freedom.

NOTES

1. Statistics on Negro votes in the 1913 presidential election are non-existent. Of those ten northern cities with the largest colored population according to the 1910 Census, none has kept such records. However, numerous accounts in Negro newspapers (Democrat, Republican, Independent) as well as accounts by leading Negro figures have convinced this writer that the shift in votes was indeed large. See *Bee* (Washington, D.C.); *Planet* (Richmond, Va.); *Kelly Miller's Monographic Magazine* (May, 1913), copy in Woodrow Wilson Papers; William P. Morton, "The Future of the Negro in Politics," pamphlet and letter to Wilson, March 14, 1913, and Morton to Wilson, November 9, 1912; Oswald Garrison Villard Papers; Alexander Walters, *My Life and Work* (New York, 1917); W. E. B. DuBois, *Dusk of Dawn* (New York, 1940), and Interview, November 29, 1955. For a leading secondary source, see Arthur S. Link, "The Negro as a Factor in the Election of 1912," *Journal of Negro History*, XXXII (Jan., 1947).

2. This subject is touched upon in Arthur S. Link, *The New Freedom* (Princeton, N.J., 1956), II. See also the author's article "Woodrow Wilson's Appointment Policy and the Negro," *Journal of Southern History*, XXIV (November, 1958), 457-471.

3. Josephus Daniels' *Desk Diary*, April 11, 1913 entry, Daniels Papers.

4. *Ibid.*

5. *New York Times*, May 4, 1913.

6. Fair Play Association Circular, May 9, 1913, copy in Wilson Papers.

7. "The President and the Negro," *Nation*, XCVII (August 17, 1913), 114; *Crisis*, VI (June, 1913), 60-61, 79; *Crisis*, VII (November, 1913), 332, for

summary of newspaper comment on segregation; "Segregation in Government Departments," *Ibid.*, pp. 343-344; "Race Discrimination at Washington," *Independent*, LXXVI (November 20, 1913), 330; O. G. Villard, "The President and Segregation at Washington," *North American*, CXCVIII (December, 1913), 800-807; McGregor, "Segregation in the Departments," *Harper's Weekly*, LIX (December 26, 1914), 620-621. The National Negro Press Association, representing 126 publications, protested to Wilson on federal segregation October 13, 1913, copy in Wilson Papers; the NAACP sent an open letter of protest to Wilson August 15, 1913, Wilson Papers, and reprinted in *New York Times*, August 18, 1913.

8. Villard, *loc. cit.*

9. L. J. Hayes, *Negro Federal Government Worker, 1883-1938* (Washington, 1941), p. 37.

10. U.S. Civil Service Commission, "Minutes of Proceedings," May 27, 1914, p. 228, cited in Hayes, *op. cit.*, p. 55.

11. See *Crisis*, XV (March, 1918), 218; *Republican Campaign Text Book, 1916;* Kelly Miller to Woodrow Wilson, July 6, 1918, Wilson Papers; *Crisis*, XXXV (1928), 287-288; *Congressional Record* 70th Congress (1928) 1st Session No. 79, pp. 10657, 6486, 7593.

12. Villard to McAdoo, November 9, 1913; "Another Open Letter to Woodrow Wilson," *Crisis*, VI (September, 1913), 233-236; "The President and the Negro," *Nation*, XCVII (August 7, 1913), 114.

13. Villard to Wilson, July 21, 1913, Villard Papers; Wilson to Villard, July 23, 1913, Wilson Papers.

14. Villard to Wilson, August 24, 1913, Villard Papers.

15. Wilson to Villard, August 29, 1913, Villard Papers.

16. Wilson to Bridgeman, September 4, 1914, Wilson Papers.

17. *Crisis*, IX (January, 1915), 119-127.

18. *Ibid.; New York Times*, November 13, 1914.

19. *Ibid.*

20. E.g., Governor Woodbridge N. Ferris, Michigan, to Wilson, August 1, 1913; Governor Eugene N. Foss, Massachusetts, to Wilson, October 20, 1913; Alfred Hayes, professor of law at Cornell University, to Wilson, September, 1913; George Cook, secretary and business manager of Howard University, September 19, 1913. The latter are but two of many strongly worded entreaties from educators. Private letters of protest appear in the Wilson Papers from over thirty-four states.

21. Congregational Churches of the United States to Wilson, November 14, 1913; International Council of Churches to Wilson, August 21, 1913; Unitarian Conference of Middle States and Canada to Wilson, November, 1913, Wilson Papers.

22. Villard to McAdoo, October 25, 1913, Villard Papers.

23. McAdoo to Villard, October 27, 1913, Villard Papers.

24. Villard to McAdoo, October 28, 1913, Villard Papers.

25. See footnote 7. The *New York Times* was not of this group. Its stories relating to Negroes, few in the first place, applied largely to the more opti-

mistic pronouncements of Booker T. Washington, to aggressive, belligerent Negro meetings, or to charges made by the Fair Play Association. One *Times* editorial advocated repeal of the Fifteenth Amendment.

26. Meier, "Booker T. Washington and the Negro Press," *Journal of Negro History*, XXXVIII (January, 1953), 57; B. F. Lee, "Negro Organization," *Annals*, CIL (September, 1913), 135.

27. DuBois, Villard, Storey to Wilson, August 15, 1913, Wilson Papers.

28. NAACP Report of Segregation, August 13, 1913, Wilson Papers.

29. Petition to Wilson from Seattle, Washington, September 8, 1913, Wilson Papers.

30. Calvin Chase to Wilson, August 2, 1913, Wilson Papers; *Congregational and Christian World*, October, 1913, Wilson Papers.

31. *Crisis*, VI (November, 1913).

32. *Courier-Citizen* (Lowell, Mass.), as cited in *Crisis*, IX (January, 1915).

33. Interview with W. E. B. DuBois, November 21, 1955.

34. Villard, *Fighting Years, Memoirs of a Fighting Editor* (New York, 1939), p. 241.

35. *Boston Advertiser*, December 10, 1913; NAACP to Wilson, January 6, 1914, Wilson Papers; *Boston Advertiser*, March 7, 1914, drawn to the author's attention by Arthur S. Link in letter, September 10, 1957.

36. E.g., *New York Times*, January 12, 1913. An exception to his usual optimistic public statements is an article on segregation published after his death: Washington, "Segregation," *New Republic*, cited in *Crisis*, XI (February, 1916), 176.

37. E.g., DuBois, "The Immediate Progress of the American Negro," *Crisis*, IX, 311-312.

38. *Crisis*, XIX (March, 1920), 241.

39. Interview with DuBois, November 21, 1955; Letter from DuBois, September 19, 1957.

THE CIVILIAN CONSERVATION

CORPS AND THE NEGRO

John A. Salmond

On March 31, 1933 President Franklin D. Roosevelt signed a bill authorizing the creation of the Civilian Conservation Corps, an agency designed to help relieve poverty and provide training for young men by employing them in conservation work on the nation's forests, parks, and farms.[1] The new President had experience and a personal interest in conservation of land and resource programs. His own Hyde Park estate was a laboratory in forestry techniques and as governor of New York he had fostered a scheme to put ten thousand unemployed men to work in the state forest and parks.[2] Now, the social chaos of the Depression gave him the opportunity to institute a national plan.

The CCC became one of the most popular and successful of all New Deal experiments. Before it was abolished in 1942 more than two and one half million young men passed through its ranks,[3] a major battle was fought against the ravages of a century of waste and depredation upon the land, and in regenerating the land the enrollees improved their own condition. Life in the CCC brought corpsmen better health and a second chance to get the education and training necessary for better employment. It also made better Americans. City and farm youth worked side by side. New Yorkers spent time in Iowa and South Carolinians in Vermont.[4] The result was a more national outlook and a greater understanding of the American people. The present purpose, however, is not to enumerate the CCC's successes, but rather to examine one of its few areas of failure—the official policy which prevented full participation by Negroes.

John A. Salmond, "The C.C.C. and the Negro," *Journal of American History*, LII, No. 1 (June, 1965), 75-88.

Operation of the CCC involved four federal departments and a national director. The Department of Labor, working through state and local relief agencies, selected the members. The Department of War administered the work camps or companies and placed army officers in command. The departments of Agriculture and Interior were responsible for organizing and supervising the work projects. And at the center of the entire endeavor the director of the CCC formed policy and coordinated all operations.[5] For this important post Roosevelt selected a prominent labor official, Robert Fechner. Some organized labor leaders had expressed fear that the CCC was the forerunner of an attempt to regiment the labor force, and Fechner owed his appointment as much to the need to pacify organized labor as to his administrative ability. The tall, slow-spoken, high-booted Tennesseean, who once quipped that his clerks were better educated than he, was not the arch-typical New Deal administrator.[6]

The act of March 31, 1933, which gave the CCC legal existence, contained the clause: "That in employing citizens for the purposes of this Act, no discrimination shall be made on account of race, color, or creed." [7] The intention was clearly to protect the rights of Negro citizens in the matter of selection for the CCC organization, but these mere words did not ensure them full equality.

Certainly no group needed help more. The Depression had added further misery to the Negro's normal condition of chronic poverty. In 1933 Negro unemployment rates were double the national average, and more than two million were on relief. In northern states Negro laborers found that the adage "first fired, last hired" rang bitterly true, while in the South the Depression had erased even the structure of traditionally "Negro" jobs. White men now cleaned the streets in Atlanta, or collected garbage in Memphis, and Negro deprivation increased. Federal relief schemes were almost all that was left for the Negro.[8]

Scarcely had selection begun for the CCC camps when reports from the South indicated that in that desperately poor region local selection agents often sought to exclude Negroes from participation in CCC activities. Particularly deplorable were events in Georgia where the Negro population in 1930 was 1,071,125 or 36.8 per cent of the total.[9] On May 2, 1933 an Atlanta resident, W. H. Harris, protested to Secretary of Labor Frances Perkins that no non-whites from Clarke County had been selected for CCC work even though the population was 60 per cent Negro.[10] W. Frank Persons, the Department of Labor's director of CCC selection, immediately demanded an explanation from the Georgia state director of selection, John de la Perriere. The Georgia director replied that all applications for CCC enrollment in Clarke County were "classed A, B and C. All colored applications fell into the classes B and C. The A class being the most needy, the selections were made from same." [11] Persons reiterated his insistence that selection be made regardless of race, but reports trickling in from other Georgia counties indicated that de la Perriere was making little effort to comply. Jessie O. Thomas, secretary of the Atlanta branch of the National Urban League, complained on May 9 that no Negroes were included in the first fifty men selected from Washington County although in that county too the population was more than 60 per cent colored.[12] Persons was reluctant to take stronger action at that time. He stressed to Fechner the importance to the success of the CCC in the South of adjusting the matter locally "without any apparent intervention from Washington." The extent of his action, then, was to write to de la Perriere and Georgia officials asking firmly that they treat Negro applicants fairly.[13]

On May 19 a long telegram from Will Alexander, widely respected southern liberal and director of the Committee on Interracial Co-operation in Atlanta, spurred Persons to more positive action. In his plea for more decisive federal action Alexander claimed that local committees in Georgia were not registering Negroes, nor did they believe that the federal government was serious in directing them to do so. "Rural politicians," devout adherents to the dogma of white supremacy, administered Georgia's relief programs, he contended, and as a result of their discrimination the Communists had been given a strong opportunity "for further agitation" in their drive for Negro support.[14]

Upon receipt of the telegram Persons immediately telephoned de la Perriere, who admitted that Negroes were not being selected but denied that this was due to racial discrimination. Rather, he insisted that "at this time of the farming period in the State, it is vitally important that Negroes remain in the counties for chopping cotton and for planting other produce. The Negroes in this way are able to obtain work on the farms throughout the state." [15] Since this optimistic picture of full Negro employment did not coincide with figures on the state of Negro joblessness in Georgia, Persons asked de la Perriere for a definite commitment to increase Negro enrollment. When this was not forthcoming he called Governor Eugene Talmadge. At first Talmadge showed few signs of cooperating, but when Persons threatened to withhold Georgia quotas entirely unless Negroes were selected the governor reluctantly agreed to "instruct Mr. de la Perriere" to proceed with their enrollment.[16]

The Selection Division had won its first battle, but executing the agreement was not without further tribulations. Indeed, de la Perriere protested to Persons on June 1 that county committees believed that "there are few Negro families who . . . need an income as great as $25 a month in cash." [17] Hence their reluctance to enroll them. Nevertheless, Fechner was able to report to the President that Negroes were at last being enrolled in Georgia though "not as many as the Department of Labor would like." [18] Persons, however, realized the basic weakness of his position and was satisfied with what small gains he had made. He knew that the attitudes of local communities in Georgia could not be revolutionized "by means of our transitory contacts with the race problem in that state." [19]

Georgia was not the only southern state to balk at the selection of Negroes on the same basis as white enrollees. The relief director of Florida, John C. Huskisson, reported that "on the basis of merit, no Negroes have yet been selected for the CCC." After Persons applied pressure, he agreed to "lower his standards" enough to accommodate two hundred Negroes, though he refused to select them at the same depots as whites.[20] Similarly, after investigating an NAACP complaint of discrimination in Arkansas Persons again threatened to withhold quotas. The state's indignant relief director, William A. Rooksbery, unequivocally denied the charge that no Negroes had been selected. No less than three had in fact been enrolled, he protested, but Persons was unimpressed. The chastened state official promised to induct more within the following few weeks.[21] In Alabama Persons won the cooperation of the state director of relief, Thaddeus Holt, who was willing to select Negroes, but found that some local councils were "trying to force" them not to enroll. Persons once more threatened to withhold quotas pending compliance with the law.[22]

Gradually, by combining pressure and persuasion, Persons was able to insist that southern state directors enroll at least a token number of Negroes in their CCC quotas. By June 12 Georgia had selected 178 and Alabama 776. Mississippi, with a Negro population of over 50 per cent, had the poorest record with 46, or only 1.7 per cent of the total enrollment, and South Carolina, also with a Negro population of over 50 per cent, established the best record with Negro enrollment accounting for 36 per cent of the state's total.[23] The unusual exertion required to effect this meager enrollment portended what was to follow as the CCC tried to place its Negro enrollees in work camps throughout the country.

It was never the policy of CCC officials to attempt to create a nationwide system of integrated camps. Given the customs of the era, to do so would have invited trouble. From the first the mixing of the races was permitted only in those regions where Negro enrollment was so slight that no colored company could be formed. Elsewhere Negroes were assigned to all-Negro camps. Scarcely had Negro camps been established when angry complaints began to flood Fechner's office insisting that they be filled with white enrollees or be removed.[24] Not all the agitation came from the South. In fact, Fechner attested that "there was far less protest" from southern communities than from other regions.[25] He complained that "there is hardly a locality in this country that looks favorably, or even with indifference, on the location of a Negro CCC camp in their vicinity."[26] Recognizing that the success of Negro camps was conditional on winning the acquiescence of the local communities in their establishment, the director moved to relieve local tensions by ruling that no Negro was to be transported outside his own state and that all-Negro campsites were to be selected by the state's governor. But despite these changes local apprehension persisted.[27]

The reasons for the disinclination to accept Negro camps varied in detail from locality to locality but were similar in general trend. Residents feared the effect of a large body of Negroes on the social values of their community. They anticipated great increases in drunkenness and other social vices and, in particular, they feared for the safety of white women and children. The citizens of Thornhurst, Pennsylvania, for example, hearing a rumor that a Negro CCC camp would be established in their area, petitioned Fechner "righteously and vigorously" for its removal. While "truly disavowing any prejudice against those people on account of race and color," the petition pointed out the social danger of "isolating so great a number of unattached Negro males" in an area occupied "permanently and exclusively by white people."

> Many of these, especially unescorted women of various ages, are obliged . . . to travel by the site of these camps and along the highways thereabouts at all hours of the day and night. Among the families who live . . . at Thornhurst . . . are to be found scores of boys and girls just attaining youth and early womanhood who should not be exposed to dangers that are possible, if not indeed, probable.[28]

Similar protests came from most parts of the country. Residents of Washington, D. C., protested the establishment of a Negro camp near a residential area where "women are left alone."[29] Citizens of Contra Costa County, California, noted that members of a Negro company there were frequently "in an intoxicated condition," and that the camp was "a menace to the peace and quiet of the community."[30] In vain Fechner countered that there had not been "one single case where the conduct of Negro enrollees in the CCC camps had disturbed the peace and quiet of any community."[31] Most of the examples of moderation on the issue came, somewhat paradoxically, from southern communities, particularly in Alabama where a well-rounded Negro CCC program developed by Governor Bibb Graves performed much useful work.[32] Arkansas citizens, too, accepted with equanimity many Negro camps. Residents of Laurens County, Georgia, considering themselves "above prejudice" in racial matters, successfully petitioned Fechner for the establishment of a Negro camp to combat soil erosion in their vicinity. White citizens of Morton, Mississippi, declared that they had had no trouble with the two colored camps in their district and predicted that if other communities could see the high standard of the work accomplished they "would be glad to get them instead of some white camps."[33] But such isolated gestures could not balance the widespread hostility toward Negro camps. Fechner himself never attempted to force communities to accept them. He frequently said that he was "a Southerner by birth and raising" and "clearly understood the Negro problem."[34] If protests showed no signs of abating he usually removed the camps either by cancelation or by transfer to an army reservation.

At the same time Fechner was being petitioned to remove Negro camps, other sources pressured for expanded Negro participation. The NAACP and other Negro action groups complained about discrimination in CCC selection, and although not all their assertions were well founded, they clearly demonstrated that Persons had not convinced most selection agents that Negroes should be given an equal chance to enroll.[35] Some malcontents sought to effect reform by appealing to the President. Alton Wright, superintendent of the Colored Rescue Mission Incorporated in Kansas City, complained to Roosevelt that "Negroes can't get into the CCC," and "no-one seems to care."[36] "Just a Colored Mother" asked the President: "if war was declared, would they pick all the white boys first and leave the Negro boys as the last called for service? This is what they do in the CCC."[37] In at least one state the relief director sought a change in discriminatory practices. Delaware's potential Negro enrollment was insufficient to justify a separate Negro company, yet racial feeling did not permit integrated camps. Therefore no Negroes at all could be enrolled. Fechner told the protesting relief director that the non-existence of CCC opportunity for Delaware's Negroes was a fact "she would have to accept."[38]

An investigation by the Julius Rosenwald Fund confirmed what was only too well known by that time. The fund found that "Negroes have not been placed in CCC jobs at anything like their proportion of the population, to say nothing of their greater need of employment as indicated by relief statistics." The fund's report asked Persons if he "could select 863 white juniors in the State of Florida, and only 18 Negro juniors without discrimination against Negroes. . . ." [39]

Negro complaints were not confined solely to matters of enrollment policy. The corps administration had decided that Negroes would not be widely employed in colored camps in any position of authority other than that of educational adviser, a ruling predictably opposed by the leading Negro spokesmen.[40] Fechner justified the policy on the grounds that the only way to get communities to accept Negro companies "was on the assurance that white supervisors would be in charge of the camps. Because of the practical difficulties of the situation it has not been felt desirable to extend the appointment of Negroes to include any large responsibilities." [41] These protests were laid before the President, who decided in 1936 that colored officers and supervisory personnel should be used in the camps "wherever possible," a statement vague enough to permit wide interpretation yet representing at least a partial victory for Negro interests.[42] Some white groups, of course, bitterly opposed the extension of any responsibility in the camps to Negroes as "detrimental to the best interests" of corps and country.[43]

In 1934 Fechner, in an attempt to draw together the tangled skeins of the Negro problem, ordered a full investigation of Negro enrollment and placement by the war department. The army reported varying practices in each corps area. In the New England states, for example, there were about 250 Negroes assigned to 68 white companies, and similar conditions prevailed in most other areas. Strict segregation was maintained in the South, but in all other regions, though segregated camps predominated, Negroes were attached to many white companies. Some had even been sent out of their home states, strictly contrary to Fechner's ruling. The army report recognized the situation as unsatisfactory but recommended against change. The maintenance of segregated camps in all corps areas would only increase the number of Negro units and compound the problem of placement.[44]

Fechner's response, however, was unequivocal. On September 10 he ordered that all Negroes in camps outside their home states be repatriated as soon as possible, that they be replaced by white enrollees, and that strict segregation be maintained in all Corps areas.[45] There was to be absolutely no latitude allowed. He claimed that by maintaining rigid segregation he would check racial violence within the camps. Such violence, however, had been a negligible factor in the context of the whole Negro problem.[46] What Fechner had done, in fact, was to increase greatly his own difficulties by increasing the need for colored campsites without doing anything to lessen the prejudice in local areas against their establishment. His policy on placement would therefore have to be firmer, or else Negro enrollment would surely have to be curtailed. It is difficult to understand why he made this decision contrary to army advice unless he was strongly influenced by personal beliefs and prejudices. His absorption of southern social mores may have been so complete that he preferred not to act as head of an organization which permitted even the smallest amount of racial intermingling.

The army report also confirmed what reports from the field had long indicated: specifically, that in defiance of the provisions of the CCC act and Persons' repeated instructions local authorities were using a definite quota system in selection of Negro CCC enrollees. Negroes were chosen in most areas only as vacancies occurred in Negro camps. Furthermore this quota system had been established with the direct cognizance and encouragement of area and district military authorities. Several state selection agents reported to Persons that army authorities had refused to accept colored selectees because they had "no vacancies for colored men," [47] and actually had notified selection agents how many, if any, colored enrollees were required from each particular district.[48]

To Persons such policies clearly contravened both the spirit and letter of the CCC legislation. He strongly emphasized to the advisory council that "the Department of Labor is responsible for the enforcement and observance of the law. The law definitely states that there must be no discrimination, and it [the department] cannot be put in the position of discriminating against the Negro race. We have been placed in an intolerable position." [49] In his dealings with state directors, Persons insisted that the labor department's position on the matter be observed. To the Missouri state director, Wallace Crossley, he wrote, "Arbitrary colored quotas are not to be established by the selecting agencies, nor are limitations amounting to discrimination to be placed in the way of qualified applicants voluntarily desiring the privilege of enrollment." [50] To a New Jersey official he stressed that all colored eligibles were to be accommodated even if it meant camp reorganization.[51]

But for all Persons' blustering, Fechner's ruling of September 10, 1934 still held, and state directors could only promise to enroll more Negroes when more Negro camps were established in their states.[52] By insisting on the dual policy of rigid segregation and confinement to the home state Fechner had closed the two safety valves selection agents could use, while his reluctance to override local protests in placing colored camps put definite limits on their expansion. These restrictions forced state directors to use a quota system, in spite of Persons' strong protests. Fechner himself was leaning more and more to authorizing a definite restriction of Negro enrollment as the easiest solution to the problem. He told the CCC Advisory Council: "I think we can easily defend and justify a policy of making replacements in accordance with the color of the vacancy existing. The practical thing is to maintain the organization we've got. Every time we make a change, it constantly brings up more friction." [53] Against such a tendency Fechner's tacit commitment to uphold the intent of the original act was of little consequence. He now needed only an incident of sufficient import to enable him to establish his policy of curtailing Negro enrollment on a national basis.

The chance came in July 1935 when there was serious unrest among white communities in California, Arkansas, and Texas over the proposed establishment of new Negro camps as part of a general plan of CCC expansion. To Senator Joseph T. Robinson, Fechner wrote that he was "completely at a loss to know what I can do in handling these protests. The local welfare boards select the Negroes, and under the law we are compelled to take them. Something should be done to regulate the number of Negroes who are selected. . . ." [54]

"Something should be done," he had written and immediately he resolved to do it. He accordingly instructed Persons to stop all colored enrollment in Texas on the grounds that there were no more camps planned for Negroes there. Negroes were to be accepted only as vacancies occurred in existing camps. Incensed, Persons refused to comply. He considered the director's request to be "a direct violation of the law," especially since "the CCC has never adequately fulfilled its opportunities for the selection of colored enrollees. For us now to expressly deny the right of selection to such men when there are eligible and qualified applications available and when state quotas cannot be filled would be an indefensible procedure." [55] But Fechner was not to be stopped. After Persons' refusal to order the curtailment of Negro enrollment he put the whole position before the President. Roosevelt termed the situation "political dynamite" and decided to approve Fechner's policy though he asked that his name "not be drawn into the discussion." [56] Since Person still refused to issue the required instructions Fechner was forced to do so himself. [57] In his announcement that henceforth Negroes would be selected only as vacancies became available in already established Negro companies, he indicated that the policy had the President's approval. The order applied not only to Texas but to the entire country. [58]

The Selection Division, though objecting bitterly, was forced to acquiesce in the new policy. Dean Snyder, Persons' assistant, angrily told the advisory council that the decision was clearly "a violation of the basic act," but the council, unmoved, upheld the director. [59] Persons made no further attempt to investigate alleged instances of racial discrimination. He had lost his fight and now turned all such matters over to Fechner rather than deal with them himself according to a policy personally repugnant to him. Fechner, courteous but definite, had no interest in reopening the question. He expressed regret that he could not "accept every person who wanted to enroll in a CCC camp" but, he added, this was not possible.[60] That the "degree of impossibility" varied according to the color of the applicant's skin was conveniently overlooked.

Fechner's decision to restrict Negro enrollment did not end agitation for fairer treatment of colored youths, but it rendered it more fruitless. When the slowly improving economy permitted some curtailment of CCC activity Fechner ordered that white and Negro camps be cut in strict proportion.[61] Walter White, Executive Secretary of the NAACP, protested without effect that the new jobs went almost exclusively to white youths and that Negroes needed the CCC as much as ever.[62]

Nor did Fechner permit any compromise on camp segregation, despite the fact that he was forced to break another of his own injunctions in the process and send Negroes outside their home states. Philip La Follette, governor of Wisconsin, requested in 1938 that some Wisconsin Negroes be enrolled in integrated camps within the state rather than be sent to segregated camps in Illinois.[63] The director's office refused, claiming it would be "contrary to official policy," [64] a reply which the executive secretary of the Milwaukee Urban League characterized as "a decided disappointment, coming as it did from a Federal agency." "To my knowledge," he wrote, "there are no units in Wisconsin designated as Italian, Polish, German, or Jewish. Therefore we feel it well within the fitness of things to raise the question as to why Negroes are being set aside into so-called Negro units." [65]

Only in the employment of colored supervisory personnel were significant gains made. Building on an agreement of 1936 to use some Negroes as supervisors in colored camps, it was decided in 1938 that all white supervisors were to be replaced.[66] In spite of the vigorous objections of some white selection agents and army officers the policy was immediately implemented and sustained.[67]

It was not until late 1941 that a substantial increase in the number of Negroes selected was ordered. In that year, white youths, attracted by jobs in the booming war industries or needed at home because of a shortage of farm labor, could not be persuaded to join the CCC. Enrollment dropped from 300,000 in January to 160,000 in October,[68] and the need to continue the corps was called into question. In an at-

tempt to boost sagging enrollment figures the director, now James Mc-
Entee, Fechner's former assistant, authorized increased Negro selection,[69] a move which Persons had insisted on from the beginning.[70]
Thus considerations of expediency and survival, not moral pressure, induced the CCC belatedly to provide some measure of equality for colored enrollees. The move, however, came too late to be of much use.
The CCC was ended in July, 1942.

The outcome of the controversy over Negro enrollment is a blot on
the record of the CCC. The Negro never gained the measure of relief
from the agency's activities to which his economic privation entitled
him. The clause in the basic act prohibiting discrimination was honored far more in the breach than in the observance. Much of the blame
for the curtailment of Negro enrollment must, of course, lie firmly with
the director. His southern attitudes influenced his approach to Negro
policy. Unwilling to permit integrated camps or allow the Negro the
latitude of interstate travel permitted to white enrollees, and only too
ready to heed the demands for removing Negro camps, he made little
enough attempt to extend to Negroes the fullest benefits of CCC life.

Fechner, however, can by no means be held solely culpable. President Roosevelt himself made no attempt to ensure fairer treatment for
Negroes and acquiesced in the restriction of their enrollment. And
much of the responsibility must lie with the local communities, northern and southern, which refused to accept Negro CCC camps. Without
community good will some curtailment of Negro selection was probably
inevitable, even if Fechner had adopted a stronger line. Negroes could
be enrolled only to the extent that there were camps in which to place
them; therefore, in a sense, by restricting their selection Fechner was
merely reflecting a strong section of prevailing white opinion. Moreover,
the director's main purpose was to reduce unemployment and accomplish useful conservation work, not to further the cause of American
race relations. However desirable, the fullest employment of Negroes
was only a matter of subsidiary concern. It should also be remembered
that only 10 per cent of the population was colored and although their
economic state was indeed parlous, Fechner owed an obligation to
numerous white youths whose position was little better. A public outcry
every time he tried to place a Negro camp was hardly good for public
relations, nor did constant bickering with selection agents make for
efficient selection policies. Viewed in this light Fechner's decision appears perhaps more understandable.

In its nine-year life span the CCC enrolled about two and a half
million men. Almost two hundred thousand of these were Negroes.[71]
Though their economic state certainly warranted better treatment, the

corps did provide relief for a considerable number. In so doing it fed many of them better than ever before, provided them with living conditions far superior to their home environments, and gave them valuable academic and vocational training. About 87 per cent of all Negro enrollees participated in the CCC education program which developed a variety of skills particularly apposite to their own job opportunities. Some left the corps to become gardeners, poultry farmers, or cooks; more were placed by corps officials as janitors, table waiters, or chauffeurs. "Negro jobs" they may have been, but in an era when any employment was prized, training for such fields represented the best practical approach to the problem.[72]

To look at the place of the Negro in the CCC purely from the viewpoint of opportunities missed or ideals compromised is to neglect much of the positive achievement. The CCC opened up new vistas for most Negro enrollees. Certainly they remained in the corps far longer than white youths.[73] As one wrote, "as a job and an experience for a man who has no work, I can heartily recommend it." [74] In short, the CCC, despite its obvious failures, did fulfill at least some of its obligations toward unemployed American Negro youth. The failure was not so much one of performance as of potential. Much had been accomplished, but much more could conceivably have been done.

NOTES

1. *Statutes at Large*, XLVIII, Pt. I, 22-23.

2. Nelson C. Brown, "The President Has Long Practiced Forestry," *New York Times*, April 30, 1933, Sec. 8, p. 1; Bernard E. Bellush, *Franklin D. Roosevelt as Governor of New York* (New York, 1955), pp. 94-98.

3. Arthur M. Schlesinger, Jr., *The Age of Roosevelt: The Coming of the New Deal* (Boston, 1958), p. 339.

4. *Ibid.*, pp. 338-340. See also Kenneth Holland and Frank Ernest Hill, *Youth in the C.C.C.* (Washington, 1942).

5. Schlesinger, *op. cit.*, p. 337. For a detailed account see Charles P. Harper, *The Administration of the Civilian Conservation Corps* (Clarksburg, W. Va., 1939).

6. Labor leaders opposed to the CCC included William Green, president of the AFL, Alex F. Whitney, president of the Brotherhood of Trainmen, and Michael J. McDonough, president of the Building Trade Department of the AFL. *New York Times*, March 24-26, 1933; *Time*, Feb. 6, 1939, p. 10.

7. *Statutes at Large,* XLVIII, Pt. I, pp. 22-23.

8. Dixon Wecter, *The Age of the Great Depression, 1929-1941* (New York, 1948), p. 162; Arthur M. Schlesinger, Jr., *The Age of Roosevelt: The Politics of Upheaval* (Boston, 1960), pp. 425-438; Searle F. Charles, *Minister of Relief, Harry Hopkins and the Depression* (Syracuse, 1963), pp. 26-27.

9. Will Alexander to Persons, June 12, 1933, *Records of the Civilian Conservation Corps,* Selection Division, Correspondence: Negro Selection (National Archives); cited hereafter as SDC, NS); U.S. Bureau of the Census, *Fifteenth Census of the United States: 1930,* Vol. III: *Population,* Pt. I, 455.

10. Harris to Perkins, May 2, 1933, SDC, NS.

11. De la Perriere to Persons, May 5, 1933, *ibid.*

12. Thomas to Perkins, May 9, 1933, *ibid.*

13. Persons to Fechner, May 5, 1933, *ibid.*

14. Alexander to Persons, May 19, 1933, *ibid.* Alexander meant, no doubt, "selection" when he wrote "registration." Registration or enrollment was the final state in the selection process. Youths registered with local relief agencies acting in their capacity as CCC selection agents. Then applicants were processed, and some weeks later the prospective enrollees, if successful, were taken to a military post, formally "enrolled" as CCC members and sent to camp. This registration or enrollment was a part of the selection process, though all terms were used very loosely. See U.S. Department of Labor, *Handbook for Agencies Selecting Men for Emergency Conservation Work* (Washington, 1933), pp. 2-5.

15. Persons to de la Perriere (telephone conversation report), May 19, 1933, SDC, NS.

16. Persons to Talmadge (telephone conversation report), May 19, 1933, *ibid.* Talmadge later became a violent critic of CCC work.

17. Persons to Perkins, June 1, 1933, *ibid.*

18. Fechner to Roosevelt, June 1, 1933, *ibid.*

19. Persons to Perkins, June 1, 1933, *ibid.*

20. Persons memo for files, May 19, 1933, *ibid.*

21. Rooksbery to Persons, June 2, 1933, *ibid.*

22. Holt to Persons (telephone conversation report), May 20, 1933, *ibid.*

23. Alexander to Persons, June 12, 1933, *ibid.*

24. Records of CCC: Minutes of the Advisory Council, 1933-42, June 26, 1933 (cited hereafter as Advisory Council Minutes). The Advisory Council was a body which met regularly with the director to discuss matters of policy and operations.

25. Fechner to W. G. Steel, Sept. 16, 1935, Records of the CCC, Correspondence of the Director (cited hereafter as Director Correspondence).

26. Fechner to James G. Polk, Oct. 30, 1934, *ibid.*

27. Fechner to Polk, Oct. 20, 1934; to Herbert H. Lehman, April 3, 1937, *ibid.* In addition to Fechner's desire to relieve local tension one suspects him of "buck passing" here.

28. H. S. Sage to Fechner, Aug. 1, 1935, *ibid.*

29. Petition to Fechner, Oct. 26, 1934, *ibid.*

30. William G. McAdoo to Fechner, Aug. 30, 1935, *ibid.*

31. Fechner to H. S. Sage, Aug. 5, 1935, *ibid.*

32. Fechner to Persons, April 18, 1935, SDC, NS.

33. Joseph T. Robinson to Fechner, June 6, 1935; Laurens County Chamber of Commerce to Fechner, Aug. 14, 1935; W. G. Still to Fechner, Sept. 14, 1935, Director Correspondence.

34. Fechner to Robinson, April 22, 1935, *ibid.*

35. Roy Wilkins to Fechner, Nov. 8, 1933; June 7, 1934; July 31, 1934, *ibid.*

36. Alton Wright to Roosevelt, Nov. 2, 1935, *ibid.*

37. "Just a Colored Mother" to Roosevelt, June 16, 1935, SDC, NS.

38. Fechner to Miss Ethelda Mullen, director, Delaware Emergency Relief Association, Oct. 13, 1934, *ibid.*

39. Garth H. Akridge to Persons, March 10, 1935, *ibid.* "Junior" was the term used to describe enrollees between 18 and 25 years of age, as distinct from veterans, Indians, or other special groups.

40. Fechner to Louis Howe, April 4, 1934, Director Correspondence.

41. Fechner to Thomas C. Hennings, Sept. 3, 1935, Franklin D. Roosevelt Papers, Official File 268, Box 6 (Franklin D. Roosevelt Library, Hyde Park, New York). Cited hereafter as FDRL.

42. Stephen Early to Fechner, Nov. 13, 1936, FDRL, O.F. 268—Misc., Box 18.

43. R. T. Sessions to Robinson, Sept. 23, 1935; John H. Overton to Fechner, Dec. 7, 1936, Director Correspondence.

44. C. P. Gross to Fechner, Aug. 27, 1934, *ibid.* For administration purposes the country was divided into nine CCC "Corps areas."

45. Fechner to Gross, Sept. 10, 1934, *ibid.*

46. Often those Negroes who were placed in predominantly white camps were among the most popular enrollees there. See Holland and Hill, *op. cit.,* p. 112.

47. J. Fred Kurtz to Persons, March 19, 1935, SDC, NS.

48. Persons to Col. Duncan Major, Nov. 2, 1933, *ibid.*

49. Advisory Council Minutes, Nov. 1, 1934.

50. Persons to Crossley, Aug. 10, 1935, SDC, NS.

51. Persons to Chester Barnard, June 28, 1935, *ibid.*

52. Crossley to Persons, July 26, 1935, *ibid.*

53. Advisory Council Minutes, Nov. 1, 1934.

54. Fechner to Robinson, July 19, 1935; to Adjutant General, July 16, 1935; to Dayton Jones, July 16, 1935, Director Correspondence.

55. Persons to Perkins, July 19, 1935, SDC, NS.

56. Fechner to Persons, July 24, Aug. 1, 1935; Hopkins to Persons, Aug. 6, 1935; *ibid.*

57. Persons to Fechner, July 25, 1935, *ibid.*

58. Fechner to Major, July 24, 1935, Director Correspondence.

59. Advisory Council Minutes, Sept. 24, 1935.

60. Fechner to Persons, May 15, 1936, SDC, NS.

61. Fechner to Persons, March 23, 1938, Director Correspondence.

62. Walter White to Fechner, Dec. 28, 1938, *ibid.*

63. La Follette to Fechner, Dec. 19, 1938, *ibid.* At that time there were no Negro camps in Wisconsin.

64. C. Taylor to La Follette, Feb. 21, 1939, *ibid.*

65. William Kelly to Taylor, Feb. 23, 1939, *ibid.*

66. James J. McEntee to Fred Morrell, March 16, 1938, Records of the CCC, Chronological Reference Material by Subjects, No. 784, Project Assistants.

67. Persons to C. C. Graham, March 16, 1940, Director Correspondence.

68. *New York Times,* March 29, Oct. 5, 1941.

69. Advisory Council Minutes, Sept. 23, 1941. Most of the new Negro companies were put to work on military reservations.

70. *Ibid.,* April 22, 1941.

71. Schlesinger, *Politics of Upheaval,* p. 434.

72. Howard Oxley to Fechner, June 30, 1938, Director Correspondence.

73. Fechner to Joseph F. Guffey, March 17, 1939, *ibid.* White enrollees remained in camp for about a year. Negroes stayed an average of six months longer.

74. Luther C. Wandall, "A Negro in the C.C.C.," *Crisis,* XLII (August, 1935), 244-253.

Undiscovered Possibilities

Ｏne of the purposes of any history is to present suitable models of behavior for individuals sharing that history to emulate. Negro history is no exception, but a dearth of such models exists. Too often the categories of distinction are those of the larger society and by definition exclude Negro participation. The Negro then has had to find his own heroes on his own terms. This section contains two articles which show possibilities not usually considered.

John Hebron Moore's article on Simon Gray shows how a slave could become a man of authority directing free white workers. Simon Gray, the flatboat captain, does not fit any of the stereotypes about slavery. He was independent, responsible, and had considerable management ability. The belief that all slaves were servile and unable to change their conditions is as erroneous as the belief that all were happy. The great difficulty in trying to find heroic roles in slavery is revulsion against the institution itself and the inherent expectation that all slaves should be using the same instrument of resistance: revolt. As much credit ought to go to the individual who achieved freedom in other ways, stretching the skin of slavery as far as it would go, achieving a kind of freedom by becoming indispensable. Wade's Slavery in the Cities does indicate that a number of slaves made slavery a paper institution as did Gray.

The second selection concerns the omission of the Negro from the role of the cowboy. Philip Durham recounts reasons why the Negro cowboy was invisible. Authors of Westerns wrote in the romantic tradition, basing their characters and plots on stereotypes. They described the Western myth instead of the real West. Durham sees that the Negro cowboy can be recognized only in "the novel of the West—not the Western story." Durham's thesis is expanded in a book, The Negro Cowboy (1965), with Everett L. Jones, and in another article, "Slaves on Horseback," Pacific Historical Review, November 1964.

Both essays point to new areas of exploration for examples of Negro achievement. The first is unlikely to receive much recognition until slavery becomes a neutral word; the second is more value-free and open for development. The search for genuine heroes continues, and more will be found in regions hitherto not surveyed.

SIMON GRAY, RIVERMAN:

A SLAVE WHO WAS ALMOST FREE

John Hebron Moore

In the lower Mississippi Valley numerous slaves were employed by the cypress lumber industry during the ante bellum period.[1] They worked in the sawmills, participated in logging operations, served as crewmen on log rafts and lumber flatboats. While engaged in these various activities, Negroes often labored beside white employees of the lumber companies, performing the same duties as the whites. Furthermore, the character of the lumber industry prevented these slaves from being supervised as closely as field hands on cotton plantations, and many of them spent much of their time out from under the eyes of their employers. Under such conditions lumbermen tended to allow wide latitude to skilled slaves who had proved themselves trustworthy. This trend was especially apparent in the transportation phases of the business. By 1850 Negro slaves could be found on the Mississippi River and its tributaries in sole charge of rafts and flatboats. Slaves in such positions of authority could scarcely be distinguished in their daily lives from free men.

Simon Gray of Natchez was an outstanding example of the cypress lumber industry's quasi-free Negroes. This slave belonged to Andrew Donnan, a merchant and blacksmith, who hired him out to Andrew Brown, the senior partner of the firm of Andrew Brown and Company.[2] Gray's name first appeared in the records of the company in 1835.[3] At this time he was merely one of several slaves employed by Brown in his construction and sawmilling enterprises. He did not remain in the common labor category for long, however, for by 1838 he was directing

John Hebron Moore, "Simon Gray, Riverman: A Slave Who Was Almost Free," *Mississippi Valley Historical Review*, XLIX, No. 3 (December, 1962), 472-484.

a rafting crew engaged in bringing logs down from the Yazoo River basin to the Brown sawmill at Natchez.[4] As head of a crew Gray was equipped with a pass signed by Brown which authorized him to travel free from interference by the legal authorities anywhere he wished on the "Yazoo or any other river, under good conduct." [5] Brown at this time was also intrusting him with small sums of money for expenses of his crew, and was even permitting him to purchase timber from Yazoo River logmen for use of the mill.[6] When Gray demonstrated his reliability and good judgment in these minor transactions, Brown allowed him to handle cash in large amounts. In one typical instance, the slave was given $800 to deliver to one of Brown's creditors, a task he carried out in routine fashion.[7]

During 1844 the Brown lumber company enlarged the scope of its operations, and the resulting reorganization brought increased responsibility to Simon Gray. In that year, Andrew Brown, Jr., moved from Natchez to New Orleans, and there established a wholesale and retail outlet for the lumber his father was manufacturing at Natchez.[8] Before making this move, young Brown, the sales manager of the company, had been disposing of the cypress lumber which the Natchez market could not absorb by peddling it from flatboats at towns and plantations between Natchez and New Orleans.[9] Gray, when not rafting logs to the mill, had often accompanied Andrew Brown, Jr., on some of these "coasting" trips as his assistant. In this way, the slave learned both the art of flatboating and the business of retailing lumber. In due course he became quite proficient in these dual aspects of marketing cypress lumber. Consequently, when Andrew Brown, Jr., found that he must devote his full time to the New Orleans branch of the firm, he recommended to his father that Gray be allowed to handle the job of transporting the lumber to market.[10] Andrew Brown soon afterward promoted the hired slave to the rank of flatboat captain, a position he retained until the Civil War.

The Negro captain quickly demonstrated that his employer's confidence in his seamanship was not misplaced. On his first voyage in command of a flatboat he brought his lumber-laden craft safely to its destination although it was leaking so badly that only the buoyancy of its cargo kept it afloat.[11] After a second trip in which Gray navigated two flatboats to New Orleans without mishap, the younger Brown wrote from New Orleans that "Simon managed the boats very well last time. He is a first-rate fellow & can be as careful as anyone when he likes." [12]

From 1845 until 1862 Simon Gray served as the Natchez lumber company's chief boatman. When the press of business required that two crews be used to supply the needs of the lumberyard in New Orleans, white men were employed temporarily as flatboat captains, but none of them ever succeeded in replacing the Negro. Andrew Brown, the founder and principal partner of the firm, continued to hold Gray in high regard despite occasional criticism of him by customers and New Orleans business associates.

As captain, Simon Gray exercised a degree of authority that is surprising to the modern student of slavery. His crews, usually numbering between ten and twenty men, were made up of both Negro slaves and white rivermen.[13] Some of the slaves were the property of the company, while others, like Gray himself, were hired from their owners by the firm. The white crewmen, on the other hand, were employed by the Negro, who kept their records, paid their expenses, lent them money, and sometimes paid their wages.[14] Consequently, they looked upon Gray as their employer. Curiously enough, the flatboat captain appears to have been more popular with his white crewmen than with the slaves. The latter sometimes complained to Andrew Brown, Jr., that Gray's manner was unduly overbearing, but the whites did not.[15] Indeed, several of the white rivermen served under the Negro for a period of years. His unusual relations with white crewmen were a subject of comment among the members of the firm. On one occasion, William I. Key, a partner, reported from New Orleans that Gray had insisted on paying the steamboat passage of some white rivermen from New Orleans to Natchez so that they could accompany him on his next trip. These crewmen Key described as the "meanest lot of white men . . . I ever saw." [16]

Gray's flatboat voyages were of two general kinds. The one he undertook most frequently was a simple delivery of lumber from the Natchez mill to the New Orleans lumberyard. The other was the "coasting" trip, which received its name from the "German Coast" district above the Crescent City. On the New Orleans hauls, Gray's duties as captain were comparatively uncomplicated. At Natchez he supervised the loading of the cargoes into the flatboats, at the same time making a count of the number of linear feet of lumber of each variety placed on board. Small flatboats of the type used on the Mississippi approximated 70 by 18 feet, and could carry about 50,000 feet of plank, while very large ones of 170 by 20 feet could hold 200,000 feet. Brown usually furnished Gray with moderate-sized vessels of 100 by 18 feet which delivered 100,000 feet of lumber. On most of his trips, Gray handled two of these boats lashed together, employing a crew of twelve when weather and river conditions were favorable. Upon arriving in New Orleans, he moored his boats at the wharf, and turned them and their cargo over to representatives of the lumber yard there. The empty flatboats were not taken back to Natchez, but were sold to "breakers" who dismantled them in order to reclaim the planks. After delivering a cargo Gray returned to Natchez with his crew by steamboat to await the loading of another pair of flatboats. Ordinarily the trip from Natchez to New Orleans took him a week, but adverse weather and river currents could greatly prolong the voyage.[17]

While on "coasting" trips, which often lasted from two to three weeks, Gray was compelled to exercise considerable initiative and independent judgment. The main object of these ventures was to deliver orders of lumber to customers at riverside plantations. When space was available, however, extra lumber was placed on the flatboat for Gray to sell at retail along the way. In addition to making deliveries he also solicited orders for the mill, quoted prices, extended credit to customers, and collected money owed to the lumber company.[18] As a rule the Negro kept the necessary records himself, but he occasionally hired a clerk when the bookkeeping became burdensome. His memoranda and reports submitted to the company officials in New Orleans reveal that the Negro captain was as literate as most white men of the laboring class and that he was well versed in simple mathematics.[19]

On lengthy retailing expeditions Gray was accustomed to submit reports about his progress by mail to the offices in New Orleans and Natchez. The following letter written from Plaquemine, Louisiana, on June 21, 1850, to Andrew Dott, a company clerk, is typical:

> I now write you these few lines to let you know that I am a little better than I was when I left. I have got along quite well with the boat so far and have delivered Mr. Moss bill [of lumber] according to order and taken a draft for the same. I stoped the boat from leaking in the evening [afternoon] of the 19th of this month. This bill order of Mr. Allens, it is to come with H. K. Moss next bill. I have not made any collections as yet but have the promis of some this morning. This letter that I send in your care I want to send to my wife, if you please.
>
> Nothing more at present. I remain your umble servent &c.[20]

The increasing number of privileges which Brown was according his Negro captain was not approved by William I. Key, Brown's partner, who had taken charge of the New Orleans lumberyard after the death of Andrew Brown, Jr., in 1848. Key objected particularly to Simon's being permitted to undertake retailing trips. As he was having continual difficulty in keeping his yards stocked with lumber, he wanted to abandon the German Coast trade altogether, so that all of the Natchez lumber could be sold in New Orleans. He maintained that he could obtain better prices for the cypress than Gray was obtaining from the planters, and that he could collect accounts in the city more easily.[21] Furthermore, Key had grave doubts about Gray's honesty, which, however, were not shared by Andrew Brown. Although the Negro frequently brought the New Orleans office large amounts of cash which he had collected from his customers, Key nevertheless suspected him of grafting in small matters. These suspicions Key expressed to Dott in 1850: "That fellow Simon, there is no confidence can be placed in him. The very fact of his not wishing anyone with him that will act honestly is the very reason that we ought to have someone on every Boat that can keep a proper account of everything that occurs during the trip." [22] He also complained that Simon was ignoring his orders. Despite repeated instructions to the contrary, the Negro persisted in advancing part of their pay to his white crewmen before reaching New Orleans. He also was inclined to delay reporting to the office after arriving in town, and he sometimes would deliberately, Key thought, miss the steamboat which was supposed to return him and his crew to Natchez.[23]

In July, 1850, Key detected Gray in an act he considered to be highly dishonest. Someone had warned him that the boatman was planning to bring a lumber flatboat belonging to a competitor from Natchez to New Orleans without obtaining authorization from the company.[24] Alerted by this information, Key arranged to intercept the party on the river above the city. When they met he discovered that Gray was indeed transporting the load of lumber in question, using crews belonging to Brown's firm. The manager of the lumberyard was convinced that Gray intended to keep the matter a secret, and that the boatman had been bribed. Key then complained bitterly to Brown—without effect—that "this thing of leaving Simon his own master has been going on too long and must be put an end to." [25]

Instead of restricting Gray's movements because of Key's accusations, Brown accorded increased freedom to the Negro. In August, 1850, he purchased "Simon's family" from Joseph W. Allen for the sum of five hundred dollars.[26] This Brown did only as an act of kindness for the Negro captain, for he made no subsequent use of the woman or her children. The Gray family thus united was domiciled by Brown in a rented house in Natchez, and the monthly rent was charged against the operating expenses of the firm. Further demonstrating his reliance upon the boatman, Brown sent Gray to Plaquemine, Louisiana, in 1852 to bring Dan Tucker, a slave whom Brown had purchased there, to Natchez.[27] This, of course, was a task ordinarily reserved for responsible white men.

In 1853 Simon Gray became free in all but the legal sense of the word. Until this time Brown's company had been paying Andrew Donnan seventy-five cents per day for his services.[28] In addition, Simon himself received a bonus of five dollars for each trip to New Orleans, plus a salary of eight dollars per month.[29] Although the records are obscure on this point, it appears likely that Donnan gave Simon his freedom without going to the trouble to have a special act of emancipation passed by the state legislature. Whether this be true or not, Donnan ceased to receive payment for Simon's hire, and the Negro's monthly wages were increased from eight to twenty dollars.[30] This latter sum was the wage which the lumber company was paying free white boatmen. In December, 1854, Key's assistant in New Orleans wrote that Simon was leaving the city without "I am afraid, having made much progress in emancipation." [31]

Even though Simon Gray continued to remain a slave in the eyes of the law, Andrew Brown nevertheless permitted the Negro to take part in private business enterprises when his services were not required by the company. The first of these ventures occurred in August, 1855. At that time Gray purchased a flatboat in Natchez, filled it with a cargo of 1,700 barrels of sand, and floated it to New Orleans.[32] To help with the navigation of the flatboat, he hired Alfred, one of the slaves belonging to the sawmill.[33] In New Orleans, Key disposed of the load for Gray by selling the sand to builders. A second cargo delivered in October brought twenty-five cents per barrel. As was usual in such cases, the sale was made on credit with 6 per cent interest being charged against the purchasers. Gray eventually grossed $487.44 from his second sand speculation, and in addition was able to dispose of his flatboat for sixty dollars. Out of his profits he had to pay the company for his and Alfred's time at the rate of one dollar per day each, and also had to settle with the owner of the sand bank from which he had obtained his commodity.[34]

These sand trips were followed by many others over the next few years. On one of these completed in March, 1856, Simon grossed $440.00 and netted $225.57. Another trip undertaken the next month was less profitable, for it netted him only $144.50.[35] He continued in the business in spite of price fluctuations, and by June, 1856, had succeeded in accumulating more than five hundred dollars to his credit with the lumber company over and above the small sums he had withdrawn from time to time.[36]

Gray apparently used this money to buy a son, Washington Gray, who had not been included in the purchase of "Simon's family" mentioned earlier. In any case, Andrew Brown acquired "Simon's boy Washington" for five hundred dollars.[37] Subsequently, the mill paid Brown for the boy's services, but whether this money was then retained by him or given to Simon is not clear.[38] In all probability, however, Brown was again accommodating his flatboat captain by acting in his behalf to accomplish an end forbidden by the slave code.

During the years in which Simon Gray was transporting sand to

New Orleans, he also handled lumber flatboats and log rafts for the company as usual. He also took part in an unusual episode in March, 1856, when a log raft moored at the Natchez mill broke loose and drifted downstream. In such cases it was the custom to sell the logs to mills situated down-river; and Gray and a white employee were dispatched to overtake the raft and assume charge of it, but they failed to make contact. The runaway raft drifted past Baton Rouge and finally entered a small tributary of the Mississippi River, the Bayou Lafourche.[39]

Meanwhile, William Key, in New Orleans, received word of the accident by telegraph. He hastened upriver on a steamboat in hopes of intercepting the raft, taking Jim Matthews, a slave who was Simon's counterpart in the rafting division of the company, with him. Failing to sight the raft below Baton Rouge, they returned to New Orleans, where they found Gray and the white workman waiting for them. The two men reported that they had traced the raft into the Bayou Lafourche and had found it tied up at Jacobs' wood yard. The owner of this establishment told them that a white man had sold the timber to him for $500 and then had departed for New Orleans. When Gray convinced Jacobs that the timber was the property of Andrew Brown, he offered the Negro and his white companion a reward of $250 if they would recover his money for him. They promptly left in pursuit of the swindler and overtook him on the wharf in New Orleans. When Brown's men accused the culprit of swindling Jacobs, he readily admitted his guilt, and gave them four hundred dollars on condition that they let him go free. When Gray returned the money to its rightful owner, Jacobs gave him fifty dollars as his share of the reward. To close the matter, Jacobs bought the raft again, this time from the proper owner.[40]

Andrew Brown's various enterprises prospered greatly during the 1850's, reflecting a period of active building in New Orleans. Early in the decade, his firm erected a large steam-powered woodworking plant near the New Orleans lumber-yard, and, under Key's shrewd direction, it soon was doing a rushing business in doors, windows, shutters, and woodwork for stairs and balusters. At the lumber-yard, Key's chief problem became the maintenance of a stock of dry lumber sufficient to supply his customers. By 1856 it became apparent that the capacity of the Natchez mill was inadequate to meet the needs of the woodworking plant and lumber-yard. Key was compelled to buy as many cargoes of pine and cypress at the wharf as he could contract for, as well as importing mahogany from Central America.

In Natchez, Andrew Brown also worked energetically to meet the increasingly pressing shortage of lumber. He rebuilt the sawmill on a larger scale and installed the most modern machinery obtainable in the North. When the renovation was completed he imported skilled sawyers from the Great Lakes region to operate his new machinery. In order to insure a better supply of logs, Brown entered into partnerships with numerous Yazoo Valley logmen, and bought large tracts of standing cypress timber. As these measures still did not correct the situation, he subsidized the erection of several small circular-saw mills along the Yazoo River and contracted for their entire output of cypress plank.

After 1856 Simon Gray became increasingly involved in the Yazoo Valley operations of the company. In January, 1857, Brown intrusted the Negro with an urgent and delicate mission. He was to buy as much plank as he could from a sawmill in Yazoo City operated by Mayfield, Fuget, and Company. The results of the subsequent negotiations he reported to Brown as follows:

> I have closed the trade for the lumber at $16 per M [thousand]. There is about 3000 feet 1 inch plank; the balance [is] 1¼, 1½ & 2 inch. I was just in time to get it. Mr. Klein had sent a man up and he arrived there in one hour after I had closed the bargain. He offered $18 for the lot. I have thought it best to go to Greenwood and see about [buying] the boat [to transport the lumber] and drop it down [to Yazoo City], and then will either come or send to you for hands [to serve as crew].[41]

Gray's purchase consisted of 155,000 feet of cypress lumber, costing $2,473.98. At New Orleans, Key's assistant noted that it was "rather shabby stuff" but welcome in the emergency nonetheless.[42]

From this time until 1863, Simon Gray was largely employed in the Yazoo swamps. When there was sufficient water in the Yazoo River he transported cargoes of cypress lumber manufactured by the small sawmills under contract with Andrew Brown. At times when the stream was not navigable, he directed the activities of a crew working in the cypress brakes, "deadening" timber, rolling logs, building levees and dams, constructing "cribs" of logs, and in general performing all the host of tasks preparatory to rafting the logs to the sawmill at Natchez.[43]

During much of 1858 and 1859 Gray was afflicted with ill health. He visited Hot Springs, Arkansas, to take the baths on numerous occasions, and in the course of these treatments spent nearly a thousand dollars. Apparently he had fallen victim to the occupational diseases of the riverman, malaria and rheumatism. In addition, he was wearing an "elastic stocking" to relieve varicose veins.[44]

Despite these ailments and his advancing age, Simon was able gradually to resume his regular duties. During the summer and fall of 1860 he delivered numerous loads of lumber to New Orleans.[45] By then he was also able to devote some attention to his own business interests. In January, 1861, for example, Gray stopped his lumber flatboat at Baton

Rouge and loaded on a sizable quantity of cordwood which he purchased there for $3.00 a cord. Upon reaching New Orleans the boatman disposed of his firewood at a profit of $1.30 per cord. Key, as usual, was displeased with Gray's business methods, and commented sourly that "Simon should bear a portion of the expenses" of the flatboat which carried his cordwood to New Orleans.[46]

After the capture of New Orleans by the federals cut the Natchez sawmill off from its market in the Crescent City, Andrew Brown moved almost all of his slaves from Natchez to his timber lands in the Yazoo basin for safekeeping. Gray, who had been working in the swamps for more than a year, was now joined by his wife and children, and they continued to live there until after the fall of Vicksburg.[47]

This Union victory in July, 1863, evidently brought the Negro flatboat captain the freedom he desired, for his name disappears from the records of the lumber company after this date. In 1865, Andrew Brown included a debt owed him by Simon among a list of uncollectable accounts.[48]

Almost every aspect of Simon Gray's career violates our modern conception of the lot of the slave in the lower South. Contrary to law and custom the Negro riverman was educated beyond the point reached by the ordinary white workingman. He was permitted to travel about almost as freely as if he had not been a slave. He was paid a regular wage throughout most of his career, and he was able to live in privacy with his family apart from his fellows. More surprisingly, he frequently bought and sold as an agent of his employer and was able to exercise authority effectively over the other employees of the company, both black and white. Gray even owned and made use of firearms with full consent of his employer.[49] In short, the restrictions of slavery rested lightly upon this Natchez Negro.

Gray's status differed from other slaves in the employ of Andrew Brown only in degree. For example, Jim Matthews, a slave who belonged to the firm, pursued a career quite similar to that of Simon Gray. Beginning as a common laborer in the sawmill, he gradually worked his way upward to a position of authority and comparative independence. As early as the 1840's Matthews was commanding rafting crews, paying their expenses, and keeping simple records of their time. Although the raftsman never received a regular wage like the flatboat captain, he did receive pay for extra work performed at night or on holidays, and he often sold to the company logs which he had salvaged from the river. Like Simon, Jim did not take advantage of his liberties to flee to the North. Not until July, 1863, did he leave his duties with the lumber company.[50]

Other slaves employed by Brown in less responsible positions also enjoyed an unusual status. Not a few of them were literate, and one of this group, William Thompson, made use of his ability to read and write to escape from slavery. Forging a travel permit, he journeyed upriver to freedom and eventually made his way to Canada. After finding employment as fireman on a railway locomotive there, Thompson wrote a letter to his old friend Jim Matthews in care of his former master— a letter, by the way, which was delivered. In this communication he described living conditions in Canada, and inquired about his mother's health. Most significantly, he asked in most affectionate terms for news about Andrew Brown and his family.[51] All of Brown's slaves were provided with excellent food, clothing, and medical attention. As in the case of Gray and Matthews they received pay for extra work at the rate of a dollar a day in addition to a cash bonus at Christmas, and they were seldom punished. Indeed, in most respects their lot was quite different from that of the ordinary cotton plantation field hand.

Whether the treatment accorded the slaves employed by Andrew Brown's lumbering firm was typical of non-agricultural enterprises in the lower Mississippi Valley is not yet determined. The testimony of another resident of the area, Horace S. Fulkerson, implies, however, that the privileges these industrial workers enjoyed were not unusual. In his *Random Recollections of Early Days in Mississippi*, written soon after the Civil War, Fulkerson discussed the construction business carried on by George, William, and Thomas Weldon.[52] These Irish brothers specialized in building bridges, jails, courthouses, factories, and other large structures. Their working force consisted of nearly a hundred slaves, some of whom were skilled craftsmen. In fact, John Jackson, their architect, was a Negro, and it was he who designed the Warren County courthouse which still stands in Vicksburg. According to Fulkerson, the Weldons were extremely lenient with their slaves. The Weldon brothers were long-time friends, customers, and business associates of Andrew Brown, and it is entirely possible that the methods of both firms in handling Negro labor conformed to the rule of industry in the lower South. Though these examples are isolated instances, they nevertheless suggest that historians should examine more closely the role of slaves in industry.

NOTES

1. This article is based upon the Learned Collection in the Lumber Archives of the University of Mississippi, a collection which consists of several

hundred cubic feet of correspondence and business records relating to the firm of R. F. Learned and Son, Inc., of Natchez. Although most of the records are concerned with the 1865-1945 period, the quantity of material pertaining to the prewar era is quite extensive. Unless otherwise indicated, the sources cited are located in this portion of the Learned Collection.

2. The business, which still operates under the name R. F. Learned and Son, was founded in 1828 by Andrew Brown, a Scot who settled in Mississippi around 1820. Brown, an architect by profession, entered the construction business in Natchez, and prospered during the booming 1820's and 1830's. In 1828, the Scottish builder bought a small steam-powered sawmill from Peter Little in order to supply his own demand for lumber, but the growing local market for plank eventually caused him to concentrate on sawmilling. His son, Andrew Brown, Jr., joined him in 1840, and became a partner three years later when he bought an interest in the company from Stephen Duncan. At this time the name of the firm was changed to Andrew Brown and Son. After the death of the younger Brown in 1848, William I. Key became a partner in what was then called Andrew Brown and Company. This partnership continued in existence until after the Civil War. A brief history of the company based upon an interview with Rufus Learned, Brown's successor and son-in-law, is contained in Boling Arthur Johnson, "Story of the Learned Mill—Longest Continuous Operation in the United States," *Lumber World Review* (Chicago), XXXVIII (January 10, 1920), 28-30.

3. Andrew Brown Journal (1835).

4. *Ibid.* (1836-1840), p. 268, and Andrew Brown Time Book (1838-1840).

5. Simon Gray Memorandum Book (1841).

6. Andrew Brown Hands Ledger (1840-1841), pp. 13-14; Andrew Brown Journal (1840-1843), pp. 63, 73, and 88.

7. Andrew Brown Journal (1843-1848), p. 69.

8. Andrew Brown, Jr., to Andrew Brown, July 23, 1844, and June 21, 1845, Andrew Brown Correspondence. All letters cited are from the Andrew Brown Correspondence file.

9. *Ibid.*, December 12, 1841.

10. *Ibid.*, May 24, 1845.

11. *Ibid.*, April 11, 1845.

12. *Ibid.*, August 5, 1845.

13. *Ibid.*, September 5, 1845, and December 11, 1847; H. S. Solomon to Brown, January 6, 1849.

14. William I. Key to Brown, February 18, 1850; Simon Gray Memorandum Book (1854).

15. Andrew Brown, Jr., to Brown, September 19, 1846.

16. Key to Brown, February 18, 1850.

17. Gray's operations are revealed by the journals of Andrew Brown and Son and Andrew Brown and Company for the 1845-1860 period.

18. For examples of these activities, see J. C. Daugherty to Brown, January 19, 1849, and Gourier and Auger to Brown, May 20, 1850.

19. Simon Gray Memorandum Book (1849-1850).

20. Simon Gray to Andrew Dott, June 21, 1850. For another example of Gray's correspondence, see Gray to Brown, July 31, 1850.

21. Key to Dott, May 9, 1850.

22. *Ibid.*, May 13, 1850.

23. Key to Brown, February 18, 1850.

24. Key to Dott, July 13, 1850.

25. *Ibid.*, July 18, 1850.

26. Key to Brown, August 17, 1850.

27. Entry dated April 8, 1852, in Andrew Brown Cash Book (1848-1855).

28. Andrew Brown Journal (1848-1853), p. 403; and an entry dated March 23, 1853, in Andrew Brown Receipt Book (1848-1853).

29. Andrew Brown Journal (1848-1853), p. 373.

30. *Ibid.* (1853-1860), p. 63.

31. John F. Paul to Brown, December 6, 1854.

32. Key to H. Solomon, August 21, 1855, and Paul to Brown, August 22, 1855. See also Simon Gray in Account with A. Brown, 1855, Andrew Brown Miscellaneous Financial Papers.

33. Andrew Brown Journal (1853-1860), p. 214.

34. Key to Solomon, October 20, 1855.

35. Simon Gray's Account of His Sand Trips to N. Orleans, 1856, Andrew Brown Miscellaneous Financial Papers.

36. Andrew Brown Journal (1853-1860), p. 266.

37. Paul to Solomon, June 14, 1856; Andrew Brown Journal (1853-1860), p. 273.

38. Andrew Brown Cash Book (1855-1864), p. 47.

39. Paul to Solomon, March 11, 1856.

40. *Ibid.;* also, Key to Solomon, March 15, 1856.

41. Gray to Brown, January 25, 1857.

42. Paul to Key, February 3, 1857.

43. Simon Gray's activities are recorded in Andrew Brown Journal (1853-1860) and Andrew Brown Day Book (1858-1862).

44. Andrew Brown Journal (1853-1860), pp. 399, 408, and 553; Andrew Brown Cash Book (1855-1864), pp. 136, 140, 150, 172, and 184.

45. *Ibid.*, p. 244; Andrew Brown Journal (1853-1860), p. 623; Key to John Shanks, September 15, 1860; and Paul to Shanks, November 20, 1860.

46. Key to Shanks, January 5, 1861.

47. Andrew Brown Journal (1861-1870), pp. 82-83, 167, 393; Manuel Sparling to Brown, March 30 and May 11, 1862.

48. Andrew Brown Journal (1861-1870) p. 269.

49. Bill submitted to Andrew Brown for Simon Gray by L. Odell, January 12, 1858, Andrew Brown Miscellaneous Financial Papers.

50. Jim Matthews' record is to be found in the various journals and day books of the Natchez sawmill for the period 1835-1863.

51. William Thompson to James Matthews, May 14, 1855. See also Key to Solomon, March 18 and June 10, 1856.

52. Horace S. Fulkerson, *Random Recollections of Early Days in Mississippi*, ed. Percy L. Rainwater (Baton Rouge, 1937), pp. 130-131.

THE NEGRO COWBOY

Philip Durham

Who knows, today, about the Negro cowboy and his contribution to the making of the West?[1] Ask anyone. Or read some of the thousands of "Western Stories" which have appeared during the last fifty years; if the Negro cowboy is in one, he is very well hidden. Apparently, then, the existence of the Negro cowboy is currently unknown because the writers of Western stories did not include him: his non-existence is due to the vagaries of fiction. One important reason for his exclusion may have been discovered by Professor Walter P. Webb, who asked several Western story magazine editors to give their reasons for the popularity of the type, and here is an answer:

> The Western story is the most popular type of action story. In order to give reasons for this, one thing must be recognized immediately: it is understood by us, and should be understood by everyone, that we are dealing with the popularity of Western stories as concerns [sic] readers who are white, who may be called Nordics, using this term advisedly. The white race has always been noted for being hard-drinking, hard-fighting, fearless, fair and square.[2]

Quite obviously, the Negro cowboy, in fiction, was confronted with a color line over which he could not ride.

The American cowboy has been described, by men who actually knew him, in these terms: he was independent, loyal, impulsive, generous; he had a hot and hasty temper, a strong sense of right and wrong; and he took his liquor straight. This description is not, however, peculiar to the Anglo-Saxon cowboy; it applies equally to the Negro cowboy, who after the Civil War, moved out across the plains to play a

Philip Durham, "The Negro Cowboy," *American Quarterly*, VII, No. 3, (Fall, 1955), 291-302.

significant role in the development of the cattle industry and became a part of the spirit of the West—a spirit which demanded a conscience but cared little for color.

Western autobiography, which unfortunately has a limited audience, includes the Negro cowboy, and in sufficient numbers to establish his active presence and contributions. Of the three non-fiction books published during the nineteenth century which dealt with the cowboy, two of them included the Negro. The first, Joseph McCoy's *Historic Sketches of the Cattle Trade of the West and Southwest,* published in Kansas City, Missouri, in 1874, describes the cowboys generally, as a type, and does not differentiate among them. The second, however, an autobiographical account, *A Texas Cowboy,* by Charles A. Siringo, refers to the Negro cowboy. This story of range life is accurate, and one senses the authenticity, the realistic approach, without literary affectation. In recording his day-to-day activities, Siringo makes no attempt to set apart the Negro cowboy; rather he is mentioned casually as is everyone else. He writes for example, "At another time, on the same day, I roped a large animal and got my horse jerked over backwards on top of me and in the horse getting up he got me all wound up in the rope, so that I couldn't free myself until relieved by 'Jack' a Negro man who was near at hand." [3] Or, on another occasion, "Henry Coats was in the lead of the herd. Asa Dawdy and Otto Draub on the left point, while Negro 'Gabe' and I kept them from turning to the right." [4]

The third non-fiction cowboy book of the nineteenth century was *The Story of the Cowboy* by Emerson Hough. This book describes a symbolic cowboy which would include them all:

> Rude and unlettered though he be, and treating his companions with a rough and ready familiarity, the cowpuncher yet accords to his neighbour the right to live the life and go the gait which seems most pleasing to himself. One does not intrude upon the rights of others in the cow country, and he looks to it very promptly that no one shall intrude upon his. In the cow towns or at the cow camps one never hears the abusiveness or rude speech common in the older settlements.[5]

With this attitude Hough did not need to identify the Negro cowboy more than to say, when speaking of breaking horses, "Some of the early Southern busters were Negroes, and very good breakers they made." [6]

Although there is, in twentieth-century publications, ample evidence of the Negro cowboy in the biographical, autobiographical, and historical accounts of the West, there has been no attempt on my part, of course, to search these books merely to find his presence. But a few examples are necessary to indicate the manner in which the Negro was treated or referred to in these accounts. Also, it is not only possible but, of course, probable that the Negro was often included in a group of cowboys without being specifically identified. There was no particular reason why he should have been. In *The Cowboy,* Philip Rollins comments on the nationality of the cowboy.

While the men of the Range were mainly English or Irish descent or birth, and had, in frequent instances, claim to early American ancestors of Scottish origin, the Southwest added to its quota of such bloods numerous men of Mexican extraction, and a more than occasional Negro, with here and there men of strain partly Indian. The majority of all the men were American born.[7]

Although Rollins lists national and color types, his interest is in what makes up an American cowboy.

Charles Siringo's twentieth-century autobiography, *Riata and Spurs,* is a rewrite of his earlier work with more literary pretensions. Yet he continues to write casually of the Negro cowboy and reports incidents not recorded in the first book. In referring to a time when he was riding herd with Negro cowboys, he tells how he was being dragged by a horse and Liege saved his life.[8] Again, he wrote, "I hunted up Babe Fisher, a yellow Negro whom I knew could be trusted, and who afterward became a noted outlaw. . . ."[9] One of the episodes concerns a Negro cowboy in the role of a peace officer, losing his life in an attempt to bring in the notorious outlaw, John Wesley Hardin.[10]

The Negro cowboy serving as a peace officer was not unusual. Frank Eaton, more colorfully known on the range as Pistol Pete, includes in his autobiography an incident in which a Negro marshal was successful.

We were just leaving the livery barn when I saw Charlie Pettit walking up to me. Charlie was a big Negro Deputy United States Marshal, from the Wichita Court.

"Frank," he said, "Ernest Lewis is up at the hotel and I have a warrant for him. He may have a gang up there. Come up and help me get him."

We started up to the hotel together. Lewis was sitting on the porch. He started like he was going to make a gunplay, but I put my hand on my gun and shook my head at him and he stopped. He and I had played with guns and he knew I was the best shot.

"Sorry, Mr. Lewis," Pettit said, "but I have a warrant for you and it's a fugitive warrant."

By that he meant that Lewis was paid for if anything went wrong. He had committed a crime that was punishable by death. Pettit's orders were to bring him in dead or alive.[11]

Eaton was, of course, glorifying himself, but it was the Negro ex-cowboy who completed the assignment of taking in a white outlaw.

A book in which the Negro cowboy figures quite prominently is J. Frank Dobie's *A Vaquero of the Brush Country, Partly from the Reminiscences of John Young*. At the outset the word "cowboy" is defined, and the author seeks out its derivation. In Southwest Texas the cowboys were generally referred to as "vaqueros," a term originally applied only to Spanish or Mexican cowboys. "But from an early day," writes the author, "Texans, especially those near the border have used the word without reference to race." Thus in one outfit would be found Mexican, Negro, and white "vaqueros." [12] The Negroes in this book range from comic to heroic. When a Negro cowpuncher went on guard he was told to call the next watch by the stars. Not being able to read the stars properly, he did not know when to call his successor, so he rode herd all night.[13]

Living up to the requirements of the Western Code was naturally expected of the Negro cowboy, and this story illustrates that he did not shirk his duty.

Not alone was it his breed that made the American cowboy stick to herd and horse until only death could drag him loose; it was his occupation.

"We had a Negro cowboy named George," says an old time Plains cowman, "who was not very well clad because he liked to pike at monte too well to buy clothes. We all had colds and coughs till it was like a bunch of Texas pot hounds baying a 'possum! when we tried to sleep. One bitter night I was near George on herd and tried to get him to go to the chuck wagon and turn his horse loose, but he was too game for that. His teeth were chattering as he said to me 'I can stand it if the rest of you all can.' Presently I saw him lean over his saddle horn, coughing, and he looked like he was losing his breath. By the time I got to him he was off his horse, as dead as a mackerel and stiff as a poker. He had simply frozen to death sitting on that horse. We placed his body in the chuck wagon on his bed and drove to the Palo Duro and on the hghest hill we could find we planted the black boy, rolled in his blankets. The ground was sandy; so we could dig a grave deep enough that the coyotes would not claw into it." [14]

Perhaps it is not unusual that an old time cowboy should recall, for the purpose of illustrating the loyalty of the cowboy, an example which just happened to be a Negro.

The inevitable cook must always figure in cowboy yarns. However, for the moment, we are interested in the real kind, not the storybook kind. The cooks were either white or colored, it did not matter which, and they were ex-cowboys. When a cowboy was no longer able to do his share in riding herd, for "physical injury, ordinarily the gift of bucking, and in the form of hernia, allowed to the average men but seven years of active riding," [15] he often preferred to become a cook rather than to leave the range. He was occasionally unhappy because his life became less active, but his position as a cook was not necessarily a degraded one, nor was he helpless. One of the tales in *The Trail Drivers of Texas* is the story of a shooting match between a white cowboy and the Negro cook—a two-year-old heifer against five dollars. The cook was hard to beat and the cowboy won only on a fluke.[16] Reminiscing with John Young provides another sketch:

> The one man in our outfit that I recall most often and most vividly was Sam, the Negro cook. He always had a cheerful word or cheerful song, and he seemed to have an affection for every one of us. When we camped in the vicinity of brush every cowboy before coming in would rope a chunk of wood and snake it up to the chuck wagon. That wood always made Sam grinning happy whether he needed it or not. He was about thirty-five years old, as black as a crow, and weighed around 225 pounds. As he had been raised on a ranch, he was a good rider, and frequently one of the boys would get him to "top off" (ride first) a bad horse.[17]

In those days Sam could hold his own among the men of the West.

It would be unforgivable to discuss the cattle range and the cowboy without including at least one stampede. The following, from the "Recollections" of Charles Goodnight, one of the most famous of the rangemen of the Southwest, has a Negro cowboy and also a touch of frontier humor. Charlie Goodnight and his cowboys were driving a herd through the Pecos country of New Mexico in 1867, where they had been constantly harassed by Indians who stampeded the cattle, shot one of the cowboys, and stole part of the herd. A severe lightning storm added to the difficulties of driving. The herd was in an extremely nervous condition as Goodnight rode along one side of it with "Bose Ikard, an ex-slave and one of the best night riders he ever had." [18]

> The Cattle had been so shot to pieces, [said Goodnight] and so badly spoiled that they continued stampeding, and after we had passed through Buffalo Gap we had a run which I shall never forget. They had been quiet all night, and at daybreak I told Bose, who was on guard with me, to watch them and I would

wake the cook. I reached camp and tied my horse to the wagon wheel, giving him some rope so he could get a little grass. Then I commenced to wake the men who were asleep around the wagon on the side next the herd. Something happened, in an instant the herd stampeded right down on the camp, and it looked as though the men would be trampled to death. There certainly was some scrambling, as most of them had not got out of bed.

I jerked a blanket off one of the beds, jumped in front of the cattle that were coming at full speed, and by waving the blanket and doing all the yelling I could, succeeded in splitting the herd around the wagon and beds. Charlie, powerful, fast and the best trained horse I ever rode in a stampede, was still tied to the wagon. He knew his business, of course, wanted to go, and got to the end of his rope, where the stampede knocked him down and many cattle went over him. I had my belt knife ready, and as the last steer cleared him, I cut the rope and he got up with me on him. I supposed he would be scared out of his wits and run from the cattle, but at once he struck out at full speed with the herd.

By this time it was light enough to see. I kept going up the side of the cattle as fast as possible, wondering why Bose had not turned the front. When I had almost caught up with him, he looked back and saw me, and immediately his horse shot out like lightning and he threw the leaders around. After we got them circled I asked him why he had not turned them sooner.

"I'll tell you sah," answered the cautious Bose. "I wuzn't sartin who had dis herd 'till I saw you. I t'ought mabe de Indians had 'um." [19]

A Negro cowboy who commanded great respect both as a man and as a cowpunch is in "Jack" Thorp's book of the old range days. "Cowmen from Toyah, Texas, to Las Vegas, New Mexico, knew Add, and most of them at different times had worked on round-ups with him." The L F D outfit's range boss, Add, was well liked and was "one of the best hands on the Pecos River." [20] Among other accomplishments, "Nig Add" was a "dictionary on earmarks an' brands," [21] which "in due time [caused him to become the] hero of a cowboy song. . . ." [22] On one occasion, however, Add's popularity created a good deal of embarrassment. "Everybody knew him. When he got married each cow-man wanted to give him a present, no one knowing what the other man had sent him, 'as ranches were far apart.' He received nineteen stoves and ranges for wedding presents." [23]

Perhaps the most interesting of all books dealing with the Negro

cowboy is an autobiography written by one. It is the story of Deadwood
Dick of Deadwood, South Dakota fame, a name well known in Western
lore; the full title reads *The Life and Adventures of Nat Love, Better
Known in the Cattle Country as "Deadwood Dick"—by Himself*. Born
in 1854, sometime in June he thought, in Davidson County, Tennessee,
Nat was the son of slave parents who had positions of responsibility on
a plantation. From Nat Love one must expect some exaggeration, as
one must expect it from every cowboy who wrote his autobiography,
especially after he had left the range and had time to dream through
his experiences, but in his Preface Love writes, "I have tried to record
events simply as they are, without attempting to fill out a chapter at
the cost of the truth." [24] As a boy he had had plenty of riding experience on the plantation, so with his freedom and a growth of fifteen
years he decided to increase his opportunities by going West. Arriving
in a Kansas cattle town, in 1869, Nat sought work from Duval, a Texas
outfit which had just brought in a herd and was preparing to return to
the home ranch. "There were several colored cowboys among them,"
according to Nat, "and good ones too." Before he could be hired he had
to prove his ability, so the boss of the outfit had a colored cowboy
named Bronko Jim get Nat the roughest horse they had, which he rode
and earned the name "Red River Dick." [25]

With his first range outfit Nat Love began a successful and venture-
some career. "By strict attention to business, born of a genuine love of
the free and wild life of the range, and absolute fearlessness, I became
known throughout the country as a good all around cowboy and
splendid hand in a stampede." After three years with Duval, Nat signed
on with the Pete Gallinger Company, "whose immense range was located
on the Gila River in southern Arizona." There he stayed "for several
years and soon became one of their most trusted men, taking an important part in all the big round-ups and cuttings throughout western
Texas, Arizona and other states where the company had interests to be
looked after." [26] And the Gallinger Company eventually made Nat their
chief brand reader.

Love took part in all of the cowboys' activities, and his manner in
relating these events is no different from that found in any other cowboy autobiography. He knew, for example, that the "test of a cowboy's
worth is in his gameness and his nerve." [27] One of the favorite sports
was roping and riding steers, which, thought Nat, "is done more for the
sport's sake than anything else, and the love of showing off, a weakness
of all cowboys more or less." [28] It was not uncommon for them to become involved in shooting trouble over brands, and death was frequently the result. On Christmas Day, 1872,

I and a number of friends were in a place called Holbrook, Ariz. A dispute started over a saddle horse with the following result. Arizona Bob drew his forty-five Colt revolver, but before he had time to fire he was instantly killed by A. Jack. Then a general fight ensued in which five horses and three men were killed.[29]

After delivering a herd, at the end of a trail, Nat was always ready to "see the elephant" with the rest of the boys.

Then we all headed for Dodge City to have a good time, and I assure you we had it. It was our intention and ambition to paint the town a deep red color and drink up all the bad whiskey in the city. Our nearly two months journey over the dusty plains and ranges had made us all inordinately thirsty and wild, and here is where we had our turn, accordingly we started out to do the town in true western style, in which we were perfectly successful until the town had done us, and we were dead broke. . . . While our money lasted we would certainly enjoy ourselves, in dancing, drinking and shooting up the town.[30]

Every old cowhand who has written about his days on the range has included at least one episode of this sort.

During a trip to old Mexico to pick up a herd, Love's outfit had an opportunity to meet Mexican cowboys. "These men were for the most part typical greasers, but they proved to us that they knew a thing or two about the cattle business, and all the things considered they were a jolly companionable sort of an outfit." [31] Along with the other cowboys of the time, Nat went through the usual adventures which appear to have happened to them all. Once, after he had put up a terrific fight, he was captured by Yellow Dog's tribe. They would normally have killed him, he thought, but they did not because there was colored blood in the tribe; "and as I was a colored man they wanted to keep me, as they thought I was too good a man to die." [32] With pride in his ability to more than hold his own among the cowboys, Nat swaggered a bit when he admitted to being "naturally tough," for he "carried the marks of fourteen bullet wounds." He confessed, also, that he had been a "dare devil" cowboy, "wild, reckless, free and afraid of nothing," but he did not want to leave an impression that he was a heartless killer.

It was not with any sense of pride or in bravado that I recount here the fate of the men who have fallen at my hand.

It is a terrible thing to kill a man no matter what the cause. But as I am writing a true history of my life, I cannot leave these facts out. But every man who died at my hands was either seek-

ing my life or died in open warfare, when it was a case of killing
or being killed.[33]

Like other cowboys writing "true life" stories, Nat also happened to
meet the famous men of the plains, including Buffalo Bill, Billy the
Kid, and Bat Masterson, the renowned marshal of Dodge City.

The high point, however, in the career of Nat Love came on July
4, 1876, in Deadwood, South Dakota. In the spring of that year the
home ranch had received an order to drive three thousand head to a
point near Deadwood. After the cattle had been delivered, the boys
headed for town to celebrate. On the morning of the Fourth the gam-
blers and mining men of Deadwood collected a purse of two hundred
dollars as first prize for a roping contest. There were about twelve
contestants, "six of them being colored cowboys." Not only did Nat
win, but he set a record. The morning event had been so successful that
another purse was made up for a shooting contest in the afternoon.
Again Nat won, but with the purse came the biggest prize of all: he was
given the title of "Deadwood Dick," a distinction and honor which he
was still proudly carrying when he wrote his book thirty years later.
Love found freedom and happiness as a cowboy on the Western range,
for he came into his own at a time and place where to be "all man"
was the most important requisite of the West. As Nat expressed it,
"What man with fire of life and youth and health in his veins could not
rejoice in such a life?" [34] Color was no barrier to fame for Nat Love.

At this point these autobiographical data raise a historical question in
Western literature: why did the fame achieved by the Negro cowboy
not carry over into fiction? That the Negro cowboys were on the range
in considerable numbers, and doing a creditable job, is, as has been
pointed out, a historical fact. However, the day of the range cowboy
was over before his fiction began. There is a difference of opinion as
to which is the first Western story, but all students of the genre agree
that it came between 1902 and Zane Grey's *Riders of the Purple Sage*
in 1912.[35] And the comparatively short period of the range cowboy,
approximately thirty-five years, had ended by 1900. We have no cowboy statistics, but the evidence indicates that the greatest percentage of
Negro cowboys were on the Western plains, particularly in Texas, immediately after the Civil War, and that their number was dwindling
rapidly by the end of the century. The Texas Rangers had been dis-
solved during the war, and in 1870 the governor of Texas set up the
state police. Many Negroes were state police officers in a body which
soon became so hated that it was considered a duty to shoot them on
sight, for they were set up to enforce Reconstruction measures. The
state police lasted for only three years, with the Rangers being re-

established in 1874—excluding the Negro. The Negro began moving farther west, into New Mexico and Arizona, and on up into the northern range. Nat Love left Texas for Arizona in 1872. Gradually, as the century moved on, and the West became more populated, the Negro cowboy was forced into other occupations. In 1890 Deadwood Dick became a Pullman porter.

It is possible that the earliest writers of Western stories, during the first decade of this century, attributed the then existing conditions to an earlier period. These writers knew the West only after it had become populated, and they knew but little of those days when a cowboy was paid and valued for skill, not color.

It is quite obvious that the Romantic tradition in fiction laid its heavy hand on the Western story. In Southern fiction the Negro was cast as a "faithful retainer." In the Western story the same attitude prevailed, for the Negro could be a cook but he could not be a cowboy. The earliest Westerns unrealistically included women; the capable but pure, white kind, gracefully riding across the plains, into the sunset and the purple sage, admired from afar by all the cowboys, and won at the end by the hard riding, hard shooting heroes. In the words of a tall puncher called Jess Hill:

> Punchin' cows in these mountains ain't like it is in a book I read before I left the ranch, where all the cute waddie had ter do was ride slick fat horses, sleep on a geese-hair bed, set the boss' daughter en afterwards marry her, en she the prettiest girl in the West. I wonder why some sure-enough cowhand don't write the truth about it, heh? [36]

The fact that truth is stranger than fiction is one of the reasons why the Western romance prevailed in its present form. Fiction was what the East has been brought up on, a romantic concept of the West, and the Western writers saw no reason to write fact when fiction paid. The Negro cowboy did not fit into the romantic concept, and once the Western story stereotype was formed, during its first decade, it became impervious to change.

It is possible, however, because so many of the Westerns were written by people who did not know the West, that these writers were unaware of the contribution of the Negro cowboy to the opening up of the range. When Owen Wister, Bertha Bower, and Zane Grey arrived in the West they saw only the saffron after-glow; had they been in time to witness the West's high noon, the Western story might never have come into existence. Fiction writers could see only a particular kind of man silhouetted against the skyline, and they chose to ignore the fact that "chaps" were worn by men of many nationalities and colors and that these were also included with the "men who made the spirit of the West, who forbade Mason and Dixon's line to extend, who harnessed democracy." [37] But now we know that pioneering, according to tradition, is an Anglo-Saxon job, and the Western myth is sometimes stronger and more important than reality.

In all fairness to those serious novelists of the West who write realistically, it should be said that when their setting and time includes him they can accord the Negro proper treatment. This is in the novel of the West—not the Western story—and two of this type who come to mind are Walter Van Tilburg Clark and Tom Lea.[38] But where is the Negro cowboy in the Western story, in these thousands of books in this multi-million dollar business? The Negro was part of the spirit of the West, but he is not included in its fiction. The early West had a tradition which asked of a man only that he be capable and have courage and loyalty: where he came from and what he looked like was immaterial. That same West is represented in fiction by an Anglo-Saxon tradition which implies that all readers are white and that only a white cowboy can be a hero who is "fearless, fair and square."

NOTES

1. A paper from this article was read before the American Studies Association Group at the Modern Language Association meeting in Chicago on December 28, 1953.

2. Walter Prescott Webb, *The Great Plains* (New York, 1931), p. 467.

3. Charles A. Siringo, *A Texas Cowboy* (New York, 1951), p. 43.

4. *Ibid.*, p. 64.

5. Emerson Hough, *The Story of the Cowboy* (New York, 1927), p. 203.

6. *Ibid.*, p. 91.

7. Philip Ashton Rollins, *The Cowboy* (New York, 1922), p. 22.

8. Charles A. Siringo, *Riata and Spurs* (Boston, 1931), p. 18.

9. *Ibid.*, p. 6.

10. *Ibid.*, p. 145.

11. Frank Eaton, *Pistol Pete* (Boston, 1952), p. 267.

12. J. Frank Dobie, *A Vaquero of the Brush Country, Partly from the Reminiscences of John Young* (Dallas, 1929), p. 1.

13. *Ibid.*, p. 97.

14. *Ibid.*, p. 100.

15. Rollins, *op. cit.*, p. 305.

16. J. Marvin Hunter (ed.), *The Trail Drivers of Texas* (Nashville, 1925), pp. 484-488.

17. Dobie, *op. cit.*, p. 137.

18. J. Everts Haley, *Charles Goodnight, Cowman and Plainsman* (Boston, 1936), p. 166.

19. *Ibid.*, pp. 166-167.

20. N. Howard Thorp, *Pardner of the Wind* (Caldwell, Idaho, 1945), p. 22.

21. N. Howard Thorp, *Songs of the Cowboys* (Boston, 1921), p. 166.

22. Thorp, *Pardner of the Wind*, p. 22.

23. Thorp, *Songs of the Cowboys*, p. 166. See also John A. Lomax, *Adventures of a Ballad Hunter* (New York, 1947), p. 46. Mr. Lomax writes that on the big ranches he had trouble getting the cowboys to sing for him, but with "smaller groups on remote ranches I enjoyed better fortune. Two or three Negro cowboys sang lustily when I got them away from the crowd."

24. Nat Love, *The Life and Adventures of Nat Love* (Los Angeles, 1907), Preface.

25. *Ibid.*, p. 41.

26. *Ibid.*, p. 43.

27. *Ibid.*, p. 50.

28. *Ibid.*, p. 49.

29. *Ibid.*, p. 51.

30. *Ibid.*, pp. 54-55.

31. *Ibid.*, p. 31.

32. *Ibid.*, p. 99.

33. *Ibid.*, p. 105.

34. *Ibid.*, p. 70.

35. Some candidates for the first Western story are Owen Wister, *The Virginian* (1902); Bertha M. Bower, *Chip of the Flying U* (1904); and Zane Grey, *Riders of the Purple Sage* (1912).

36. Thorp, *Pardner of the Wind*, p. 13.

37. Rollins, *op. cit.*, p. 383.

38. Walter Van Tilburg Clark, *The Ox-Bow Incident* (New York, 1940). Tom Lea, *The Wonderful Country* (Boston, 1952).

Index

Abdy, Edward S., 141
Abernethy, Thomas Perkins, 109
Abolitionism, 106, 110-111, 113, 114
Abolitionists and free Negroes, 124, 138-153; and economic views, 148-150; and education, 150-153; and racial myths, 144-148; social relations between, 139-144. *See also* Underground Railroad.
Abraham (Seminole Negro), 332-333, 335, 336-337, 338, 341, 344
Adamic, Louis, 19
Adams, Charles Francis, Jr., 270-271, 283, 286, 287-288
Adams, John, 48
Adams, John Quincy, 316
Addams, Jane, 228, 229, 230
Addeman, J. M., 287
Adler, Henry, 305
Afro-American League, 298
Agassiz, Louis, 100
Aitken, Harry, 226, 229
Akerman, Amos T., 360
Alexander, Will, 385
Allen, Joseph W., 405
Allen, Richard, 20
Alligator, 337, 340, 343-344, 345
Alvord, James W., 146
Ames, Susie M., 62
Anderson, Charles W., 229-230
Anti-slavery societies. *See* Abolitionism; Abolitionists.
Aptheker, Herbert, 79, 87
Arendt, Hannah, 46
Atkinson, W. Y., 206-207, 211
Attwill, Henry, 231
Austin, R. N., 306
Austin, William H., 304, 306

"Back to Africa" movement, 200, 212-214. *See also* Colonization movement.
Bacote, Clarence A., 188, 200-219
Bailey, Joseph, 287-288
Baker, Newton D., 233
Baldwin, James, 46-47
Ballagh, James C., 61-62
Ballard, Bland, 356
Bancroft, Frederic, 173
Barnett, Ross, 55
Bartlett, Charles L., 210-211
Bates, Delevan, 274
Bates, Edward, 321-322
Beale, Howard K., 352

Beard, Charles, 48, 52, 93, 94, 106-107, 112-116
Beckwith, James R., 357
Beckwourth, James, 194
Belknap, B., 77-78
Benezet, Anthony, 192
Bennett, Ned, 74
Bennett, Thomas, 74, 81, 82, 86
Berrien, John, 321
Beveridge, John L., 254
Bird, Dorcas, 194
Bird, Henry, 194
Bird, John, 194
Birney, David, 280, 284
Birney, James, 139-140
Birney, William, 280, 281-283, 290
Birth of a Nation, 176-186; Negro reaction to, 188, 224-234
Bitzer, Billy, 226
"Black laws." *See* Ohio.
Blaine, James G., 99
Blair, Francis P., Jr., 192
Blanchard, Jonathan, 254
Bliss, Z. R., 279
Blue, James, 209
Boas, Franz, 52
Bomley, Francis, 66
Bond, Hugh Lennox, 361
Bonner, C. L., 219
Boston: campaign against *Birth of a Nation* in, 230-233; pre–Civil War school integration in, 150-152
Bower, Bertha, 422
Bradford, Gamaliel, 96
Bradley, Joseph P., 295, 357
Branagan, Thomas, 192
Bridgeman, H. A., 373
Britton, Charles, 128
Brooke, Stopford, 22
Brooks, George W., 362
Brown, Andrew, 401-410
Brown, Andrew, Jr., 402-404
Brown, Daniel P., 298
Brown, George A., 304
Brown, John, 253
Browning, Orville H., 164, 167, 168
Bruce, E. J., 215
Bruce, Philip A., 61, 62
Bryan, Isaac T., 305
Bryan, William Jennings, 207
Buchanan, James, 319
Buffum, Arnold, 146
Bundy, H. S., 169
Burdett, William, 66, 67
Burgess, John W., 107

Burke, Edmund, 48
Burleson, Albert, 369-372
Burnham, Rowland, 66
Burnside, Ambrose E., 276-277, 279
Busteed, Richard, 361
Butler, Andrew Pickens, 258
Butler, Benjamin F., 164, 280, 281, 290
Butler, Marvin B., 246, 247

Caesar, John, 332, 336
Cahn, Edmond, 53
Caldwell, Henry Clay, 362-363
Calhoun, John C., 315, 316
Call, Richard C., 334
Calvert, Leonard, 67
Canby, E. R. S., 270
Cannon, W. S., 218
Carlyle, Thomas, 17
Carter, Everett, 125, 176-186
Carter, J. W., 201, 202, 203
Cash, W. J., 181, 200
Cass, Lewis, 320, 334
Catterall, Helen T., 62
Cavallo, August, 341
Cavallo, John, 337, 338, 339-340, 341, 344, 345
CCC, 383-394
Channing, Edward, 96, 109, 258, 259
Channing, William Emery, 140, 145
Charlton, Stephen, 65
Chase, Salmon P., 164, 170
Chekika, 344-345
Child, Lydia, 144, 242-243
Chisman, John, 65
Cincinnati: Negroes in, 1800-1830, 126-135; "Potter's Field" in, 139; and riot of 1829, 124, 130-133
Cincinnati Colonization Society, 130, 132-133
Civil disobedience, 51
Civil Rights Act of 1875, 212-213, 295
Civil Rights Act of 1957, 354
Civil Rights Act of 1960, 354
Civil Rights Act of 1964, 50
Civil Rights Act, Wisconsin, 239-240, 294-306
Civil War, 112-114; attitude of Northwest toward, 124-125, 159-171; Negro troops in, 239, 266-291
Clansman, The (Dixon), 176-177, 179, 224-225, 228, 231-232
Clark, Thomas D., 195
Clark, Walter Van Tilburg, 423
Clarke, James Freeman, 245, 246, 256
Clay, Cassius M., 149-150
Clayton, John M., 319
Cleveland, Grover, 207, 213

Clinch, Duncan L., 333
Cockrum, William L., 244, 246
Coffin, Addison, 246
Coffin, Levi, 245, 246, 247, 248, 250, 256
Cohen, Jerry, 84
Cohen, Morris R., 29
Coi Hajo, 337, 338
Colfax, Schuyler, 318
Collins, John A., 145-146
Colonization movement, 49, 130, 132-133, 164-166, 170-171, 191-196, 200. *See also* "Back to Africa" movement.
Commager, Henry Steele, 95-96
Compromises of 1820 and 1850, 34
Consensus vs. conformity, 52-53
Constitution, U.S.: as compromise with slavery, 34, 114-116; 14th Amendment to, 295-296, 322; 15th Amendment to, 352-365
Convict-lease system, 208-211
Cook, Samuel DuBois, 15, 27-42
Corbett, Silas H., 305
Cornish, Dudley, 239, 266-291
Coulter, E. Merton, 355, 365
Cowboys, Negro, 399, 413-423
Cox, Samuel S., 161, 162, 170
Craven, Wesley F., 63
Crawford, Lectured, 201, 202, 213
Cressup, Thomas, 132, 133
Crews, H. B., 344
Cripps, Thomas R., 188, 224-234
Crossley, Wallace, 390
Cruden, Robert, 93, 95-103
Curley, James, 230-231
Curtis, Anna L., 257
Curtis, Benjamin, 323
Cushing, Caleb, 321

Dade, Francis L., 333
Daniels, Josephus, 370, 372
Darwin, Charles, 100
Davids, Tice, 247
Davis, Henry Winter, 361
Davis, Hugh, 68
Davis, Jefferson, 108, 113
Davis, Susan, 66
Davis, W. R., 215
Davis, William W., 353, 354
Deadwood Dick. *See* Love, Nat.
Degler, Carl N., 64
Delany, Martin R., 147, 193
Democratic Party, resistance of, to emancipation, 161-163, 168-170
Dennison, William, 167
Dewey, John, 52

Dixon, Thomas, 176, 177, 179-180, 184, 224-228, 232, 233
Dobie, J. Frank, 416
Dodd, William E., 96
Donnan, Andrew, 401, 405-406
Doolittle, James R., 164, 167
Dott, Andrew, 404, 405
Douglass, Frederick, 145, 213, 242, 244, 256, 289, 298, 323
Drake, Daniel, 127
Drayton, Charles, 77, 81-82, 83
Dred Scott decision, 34, 309, 312, 317, 320, 322-324
DuBois, W. E. B., 36, 229, 230, 233, 234, 372, 375, 376, 378-380
Dugan, Thomas, 126
Dumond, Dwight, 79
Dunning, William A., 107, 113, 352, 354-355, 365
Durham, J. J., 205
Durham, Philip, 399, 413-423
DuVal, William P., 330
Dyer, C. V., 248
Dyer, Frederick, 269

Eastman, Zebina, 244
Eaton, Frank, 415-416
Edmunds, Halmor H., 356
Eliot, Charles, 232
Emancipation, white reactions to, 161-171
Enforcement Acts, 310, 352-365
Enslow, John, 83
Erskine, John, 363
Ewing, Thomas, 169
Exclusion laws, 160

Fairbank, Calvin, 247
Farrow, Henry P., 359, 363
Fechner, Robert, 384-393
Fehrenbacher, Don E., 113
Felton, Rebecca L., 207
Ferrero, Edward, 273, 276, 277, 279, 280, 282
Finney, Charles S., 141-142
Firth, Charles Harding, 96
Fishel, Leslie H., Jr., 239, 294-306
Fisher, Babe, 415
Flaherty, Robert, 185
Fleming, Walter L., 230
Follen, Charles, 140
Forrest, Nathan B., 270, 286
Forten, James, 144
Fortune, T. Thomas, 216, 219, 298
Foster, Stephen, 179
Franklin, John Hope, 79
Free Negroes, pre–Civil War, 34, 66; and citizenship, 319-324; and fed-
eral government, 312-324; and "insanity" statistics, 314-316; and issuance of passports, 319-320; and migration to Texas, 190-196; and postal service, 318. *See also* Abolitionists and free Negroes; Cincinnati; Northwest and race issue.
Frissell, Hollis, 231-232, 234
Frontier thesis, 106-112, 187-188, 189-196
Fugitive slave laws, 34
Fulbright, William, 51
Fulkerson, Horace S., 410
Fuller, Edmund, 256

Gaines, Edmund P., 329, 334
Gaines, F. P., 178
Gara, Larry, 239, 241-261
Garbo, Greta, 185
Gardiner, Samuel R., 96
Garrison, William Lloyd, 139, 140, 145, 146, 149, 151, 152, 241-242, 254
Gell, Monday, 77, 83, 86
George, Henry, 48
Georgia: "Back to Africa" movement in, 212-214; and CCC, 384-386, 388; and convict-lease system, 208-211; and "Jim Crow" legislation, 200-205; and lynching, 205-208; and threats to white liberals, 211-212
Gilbert, John, 185
Gilchrist, Charles A., 266
Gish, Lillian, 185
Godkin, Edwin L., 100, 356
Goldwater, Barry, 48, 55
Goodnight, Charles, 417
Goyens, William, 195
Graham, Shirley, 256
Granger, Gideon, 318
Grant, M. B., 272
Grant, Ulysses S., 98, 245, 273, 277, 280, 283, 284, 286, 365
Graves, Bibb, 388
Graves, John Temple, 219
Gray, Simon, 399, 401-410
Gray, Washington, 406
Green, William T., 298, 301, 302-305
Grey, Zane, 421
Griffith, David Wark, 176, 180, 182-184, 225-226, 228-229, 230, 231, 233, 234
Grimké, Sarah M., 143, 144
Groves, Thomas, 66
Grundy, Felix, 313
Gysin, Brion, 256-257

Hackett, Francis, 229
Haig, Harry, 77
Hamilton, Alexander, 116
Hamlin, C. S., 378
Hammett, Bacchus, 77, 83, 84
Hammond, John, 67
Hancock, Winfield Scott, 280
Handlin, Oscar and Mary, 63, 65, 68
Hanna, Mark, 95, 99
Hansberry, Lorraine, 23
Hardin, John Wesley, 415
Hardin, Samuel, 195
Harlan, James, 166, 167
Harlan, John Marshall, 212-213, 295-296, 300
Harney, W. S., 344
Harrington, Michael, 51
Harris, W. H., 384
Harrison, Benjamin, 205
Hart, Albert Bushnell, 96
Harth, Mingo, 74
Hartranft, J. F., 279
Haviland, Laura S., 245
Hawkins, John, 285, 286
Hawley, Joseph R., 271
Hayne, Robert Y., 78, 313
Hazleton, G. W., 300, 305-306
Henry, John, 83
Henson, Josiah, 256
Herick, Eli, 133
Hernandez, J. M., 336, 339
Hill, Jess, 422
Hill, Robert A., 363
Historical tradition, creation of, 17-25
Hixson, William B., Jr., 15, 46-56
Hoar, George F., 97-98
Hoard, William D., 298
Holatoochee, 344, 345
Holden, W. W., 362
Holly, James T., 193
Holmes, Oliver Wendell, Jr., 52, 96
Holsey, Lucius H., 215-216, 219
Holt, Thaddeus, 386
Holzendorf, J. M., 202
Hood, John Bell, 284-285
Hough, Emerson, 414
Houston, Sam, 194
Howard, Jacob M., 163
Howard, Oliver O., 99
Howe, Frederic C., 226, 228, 229
Howell, Owen, 298, 299-300
Hughes, Langston, 23
Humphreys, Gad, 329
Husk, Zylpha, 195
Huskisson, John C., 386
Hutchins, John, 166
Huxley, Thomas, 100

Ikard, Bose, 417-418
Indians, Negroes' relationships with, 194, 310. See also Seminole War.
Inferiority: acceptance of allegations of, 19-20; endeavors to combat allegations of, 20-21. See also Negroes, myths about.
"Insanity" statistics, 314-316
Integration, school, 150-152
Irish, riots against, 124
Irish historical traditions, 17-18

Jack, Gullah, 86
Jackson, Andrew, 109-110, 111, 114
Jackson, James, 318
Jackson, James Caleb, 243
Jackson, John, 410
Jackson, Sam, 210
Jarvis, Edward, 315
Jefferson, Thomas, 192
Jesup, Thomas Sidney, 328, 334-343
Jewish historical traditions, 18-19
"Jim Crow" laws, 200-205
Johnson, Ana Hayes, 75, 76, 80-81
Johnson, Andrew, 352, 363
Johnson, Anthony, 66
Johnson, Daniel H., 299-301, 302, 306
Johnson, Edwina Chavers, 23
Johnson, H. U., 255-256
Johnson, James Weldon, 42
Johnson, Oliver, 254
Johnson, Reverdy, 356
Johnson, S. W., 201
Johnson, William, 80
Jones, Everett L., 400
Jones, Sam, 340
Jones, Thomas H., 304
Jones, Wesley L., 231
Jordan, Michael, 231
Jordan, Winthrop D., 59-60, 61-69
Julian, George W., 164

Kallen, Horace, 52-53
Kavenaugh, Nelson, 195
Kennedy, John F., 48
Key, William I., 403, 404-409
Killens, John Oliver, 56
Kilmer, George L., 278
Kirkham, R. W., 439
Klabunde, Reinhardt, 304
Ku Klux Klan, 352, 355, 356, 358, 359, 361, 362, 363, 364-365

Lafayette, Marquis de, 193
La Follette, Philip, 392
Lane, Henry S., 164
Lanier, Sidney, 179

Lea, Tom, 423
Lecky, W. E. H., 96
Ledlie, James H., 277, 278, 279
Lee, Luther, 246
Lee, Robert E., 266, 286
Legare, Hugh, 321
Lewis, Israel, 132, 133
Lewis, Pierre, 83
Lewis, William, 232, 233
Libby, Oren G., 107, 112, 114
Liberia, conditions in, 214
Lincoln, Abraham, 97, 164, 165-166, 168, 170, 241, 283
Lincoln-Douglas debates, 34, 177-178
Lippmann, Walter, 52
Litwack, Leon, 124, 138-153, 309, 312-324
Livingston, Edward, 321
Logan, John A., 284
Logan, Rayford, 44, 100
Longfellow, Henry Wadsworth, 21-22
Longworth, Nicholas, 132
Lonnon, Ishmael, 209
Loria, Achille, 190
Love, Nat, 419-422
Lowell, James Russell, 139
Ludlow, Thomas, 66
Lundy, Benjamin, 192
Lusk, Virgil S., 363-364
Lynch, John R., 98
Lynching, 205-208
Lynd, Staughton, 94, 106-116, 187

Macauley, Thomas Babington, 24
Maddox, John W., 210
Madison, James, 116, 191, 192
Main, Jackson, 113
Malvin, John, 126
Mann, Horace, 149, 150
Marx, Karl, 113
"Massive resistance," 32-33, 55
Matthews, Jim, 407, 409, 410
Maxwell, L. B., 211
May, Samuel J., 245
Mayer, Louis B., 184
McAdoo, William, 370-372, 375-376
McAfee, Leroy, 177
McBrown, Gertrude Parthenia, 23
McCoy, Joseph, 414
McCullouch, Samuel, 194
McEntee, James, 393
McIntosh, John, 210
McKinley, William, 207
McLean, John, 318, 323
McNeil, Jack, 83
Meade, George G., 277
Merrilies, John, 273

Merrill, Lewis, 358
Merritt, Joe, 336
Mexican War, 309-310
Micanopy, 332-333, 334-335, 336, 337, 338, 339, 340
Miller, Kelly, 98
Miller, Loren, 54
Milner, T. W., 209
Minnis, John A., 362
Miscegenation laws, 68-69, 161
Mitchell, Dean, 83
Mitchell, John P., 229
Mitchell, William, 247
Montgomery, James, 271
Moore, Fred, 228, 229
Moore, John Hebron, 399, 401-410
Morgan, Thomas, 284, 285, 289
Morison, Samuel Eliot, 95-96
Morrill, Amos, 359
Morris, Gouverneur, 116
Morse, John T., Jr., 96, 102
Myrdal, Gunnar, 181

NAACP, 110, 224, 226, 227-229, 233, 234, 372-373, 375, 376, 378-380, 386, 388, 392
National Board of Censorship of Motion Pictures, 226-229
National Negro Business League, 224, 231
National Negro Press Assn., 376
Negro conventions, 20-21, 193
Negro history: and development of traditions, 17-25; as tragedy, 27-42
Negro revolution and intellectuals, 46-56
Negro state, movement for, 215-216
Negroes, myths about, 96-98, 145, 164, 167. See also Free Negroes.
Neshoba community, 192
Nevins, Allan, 258
Noggle, David, 164
Nonviolence campaign, 51
North, post–Civil War conditions in, 215, 218-219
Northen, Governor, 202, 203, 206, 208
Northwest and race issue, 124-125, 159-171

Objectivity, historical, problem of, 95-103
Ohio "black laws," 128-135
Olin, Chauncey C., 253
Operation Heritage, 23
Osceola, 332, 335-336, 338, 339, 340
Otjen, Theobold, 304

Ovington, Mary W., 230
Owen, Robert Dale, 192

Pacheco, Luis, 333, 343
Paine, Charles J., 280, 281
Parker, Isaac C., 364
Parks, Green B., 214
Parrish, Anne, 257
Passports, 319-320
Paul, William, 74-75, 87
Paxson, Frederic L., 96
Peabody, George, 230, 231
Peek, W. L., 206
Pencil, George, 74
Pennington, James W. C., 21
Perez, Leander, 55
Perkins, Frances, 384
Perriere, John de la, 384-385
Perryman, Sandy, 344
Persons, W. Frank, 384-386, 388-393
Pettit, Charles, 415
Pettit, Eber M., 246, 247, 253, 256
Philip, King (Seminole chief), 332-
    333, 334-335, 336, 338, 339
Philip, John, 339
Phillips, Ulrich B., 62, 79, 87, 107,
    111
Piatt, Wykoff, 132
Pierce, James H., 363
Pike, James S., 98-99
Pillsbury, Parker, 245
Pinckney, Thomas, 84-85
"Plantation illusion." See Southern
    illusion.
Platt, H. D., 243
Poinsett, Joel, 78
Pope, Alexander, 32
Pope, John D., 363
Porter, Augustus, 317
Porter, James, 201
Porter, Kenneth W., 309-310, 328-345
Postal service, 319. See also Railway
    Mail Service.
Pott, Francis, 65
Pott, John, 65
Poyas, Peter, 74, 82, 83, 86
Pre-emption Act, 311, 317
Prejudice and slavery, 62-69. See also
    Abolitionists and free Negroes; Ne-
    groes, myths about; Northwest and
    race issue; Ohio "black laws";
    Segregation.
Pressley, Thomas J., 113
Prioleau, Devany, 74, 78, 87
Punch, John, 65
Purvis, Robert, 248, 323
Putnam, Benjamin A., 334

Race as ideology, 33-34
Railway Mail Service, 369-370
Ransome, John Crow, 179
Reconstruction, 34, 38, 97, 98, 100,
    113, 310. See also Enforcement
    Acts.
Red Cloud, 111
Republican Party and abolition, 161-
    171
Revere, Paul, 21-22
Rhodes, Daniel P., 99
Rhodes, James Ford, 93-94, 95-103,
    230, 258, 352
Richardson, William A., 162
Rickard, James A., 280
Riddle, Albert G., 164
Righton, Prince, 84
Robinson, Joseph T., 391
Roche, John P., 52
Rollins, Philip, 415
Rooksbery, William A., 386
Roosevelt, Franklin D., 310-311, 383,
    388, 393
Roosevelt, Theodore, 96, 224, 369,
    379
Rose, Edward, 194
Ross, Alexander M., 247
Royce, Josiah, 41
Russell, John H., 62
Russell, Richard B., 208

Salmond, John A., 311, 383-394
Sawyer, Philetus, 303
Saxton, Rufus, 266
Schiefflin, William Jay, 218
Schiff, Jacob, 228
Schofield, John, 270, 284
Schurz, Carl, 98, 356
Scott, Winfield, 337
Segregation, 124; in government serv-
    ice, 319, 369-380; residential, 38;
    in schools, 37-38, 128, 150-152,
    160
Seminole War, 310, 328-345
Seward, William H., 320
Seymour, Thomas, 272
Shaw, Albert, 96
Sherman, John, 164, 167, 168
Sherman, Thomas W., 287
Siebert, Wilbur H., 243, 244, 251-
    253, 255, 258-260
Sigfried, Joshua, 276, 278
Singleton, "Pop," 216
Siringo, Charles A., 414, 415
Skinner, John, 67
Slavery: as "agrarianism," 106-107,
    112-116; as economic system, 112-

116; minimization of, in works of history, 106-116; origins of, in America, 61-69
Sloane, Rush, 247
Smedley, Robert C., 245, 247, 248
Smith, Benjamin E., 259
Smith, Caesar, 83
Smith, Gerrit, 149
Smith, H. E., 279
Smith, Harry, 233
Smith, Hoke, 204
Smith, John, 62
Smith, William F., 275, 280
Smith, W. W., 333
Snyder, Dean, 391
Sophocles, 42
Southern illusion, 178-182
Spencer, Herbert, 100
Spirituals, 30
Spooner, John C., 299, 302, 303
Stampp, Kenneth M., 63, 178, 181
Stanbery, Henry, 356
Stanton, Edwin M., 283
Starbuck, D. H., 361-362
Steedman, James B., 285
Stephens, Alexander, 113
Stephens, Linton, 358
Stevens, Thaddeus, 177, 179, 225, 254, 361
Stewart, Peter, 248
Still, William, 249-250, 253, 254
Stone, James, 66-67
Stone, Roger, 66
Storey, Moorfield, 230
Story, William, 364
Stowe, Charles Edward, 241
Stowe, Harriet Beecher, 255, 256
Strachey, Lytton, 22
Stuart, Charles, 145
Sumner, Charles, 97, 318, 361
Supreme Court: desegregation decision of, 37-38; as instrument of social change, 54. See also Dred Scott decision.
Swails, Stephen A., 272
Sweet, Robert, 68
Swift, Charles N., 273-274
Swift, Hildegard Hoyt, 257
Swinney, Everette, 310, 352-365

Taft, Alphonso, 360
Taft, William Howard, 369, 379
Talmadge, Eugene, 385
Taney, Roger B., 309, 312, 319, 320, 321, 322-323
Tappan, Arthur, 142-143, 148
Tappan, Lewis, 140, 141-142

Taylor, C. H. J., 214
Taylor, Zachary, 340
Ten Eyck, John C., 166
Texas, migration of free Negroes to, 190-196
Textbooks, Negro in, 23-24
Thacher, Thomas, 232-233
Thackstone, John, 66
Thayer, Eli, 242
Thomas, George H., 266, 284
Thomas, Henry G., 276, 279
Thomas, Jessie O., 385
Thompson, Charles R., 285
Thompson, Pharo, 83
Thompson, William, 233, 410
Thoreau, Henry David, 51
Thorp, Jack, 418
Tillman, Ben, 219
Tocqueville, Alexis de, 111-112
Townes, David, 194
Toynbee, Arnold, 28, 35
Trevelyan, George, 23
Trotter, William Monroe, 230, 232, 233, 373-374
Trumbull, Lyman, 163, 164, 165-166
Tubman, Harriet, 254, 257
Tucker, Dan, 405
Tumulty, Joseph, 227, 232
Turner, Frederick Jackson, 93, 94, 106-112, 115, 116, 187-188, 189-190, 196
Turner, Henry McNeal, 206, 207, 212, 213, 214, 218, 219
Turner, Jonathan B., 253
Turner, Nat, 79, 88
Tyndall, John, 100

Ullmann, Daniel, 267-268
Uncle Tom's Cabin (Stowe), 241, 257
Underground Railroad, 239, 241-261
Upham, W. H., 304
Upshur, Abel, 314
Urban League, 224, 229, 385

Vallandigham, Clement L., 99
Vandiver, John M., 210
Veblen, Thorstein, 52
Vesey, Denmark, 60, 75, 79, 83, 85-86, 88
Vesey "plot," 74-88
Viereck, Peter, 53-54
Villard, Oswald Garrison, 227, 229, 372-373, 374-376, 378
Voegoli, Jacque, 124-125, 159-171
Von Holst, Edward, 108
Von Holst, Hermann, 248
Von Ranke, Leopold, 22

Wade, Benjamin, 149, 150
Wade, Richard C., 60, 74-88, 124, 126-135
Waite, Morrison R., 357
Walker, Charles T., 218
Wallace, George (Governor, Ala.), 55
Wallace, George (Senator, Ga.), 201
Walsh, David Ignatius, 231
Walters, Alexander, 233, 380
Ware, John, 208
Washington, Booker T., 229, 231-232, 233, 234, 305, 306, 372, 373, 376, 378-379
Webb, Walter P., 413
Webber, A. Watson, 266-267
Webster, Daniel, 313
Weisenburger, Francis, 130
Weiss, Julius A., 282
Weitzel, Godfrey, 270, 282-283, 286
Weld, Theodore, 142, 143, 144, 146
Weldon brothers, 410
Wells, G. Wiley, 358
Wesley, Charles H., 14, 17-25
Wharton, Gabriel C., 359
Wheeler, Joe, 284
White, Edward, 227, 232
White, George, 205
White, Horace, 248
White, I. J., 213
White, Walter, 392
Whitfield, James M., 193
Whittington, William, 65
Wiggins, Ben, 194
Wilcox, O. B., 279
Wild Cat, 194, 338, 339-340, 344
Willey, Austin, 245, 246

Williams, George, 355-356, 362, 364
Williams, George Washington, 290
Williams, James, 254
Williams, John Sharp, 208
Williams, Orren T., 301-302
Wilmot, David, 317
Wilson, Henry, 245, 247
Wilson, James, 116
Wilson, Joseph T., 290
Wilson, Woodrow, 96, 176, 224, 227, 229, 230, 231, 232-233, 310, 311; and federal segregation, 369-380
Winans, John, 302
Wirt, William, 319, 320, 321
Wisconsin Civil Rights Act of 1895, 294-306
Wise, Stephen A., 229, 230
Wister, Owen, 422
Wolf, Simon, 19
Wolgemuth, Kathleen, 310, 369-380
Women slaves, taxation of, 67-68
Woods, William B., 357, 362
Woodson, Carter G., 23, 79, 130
Woodward, C. Vann, 123, 159, 200
Woolfolk, George R., 187, 189-196
Worth, W. J., 343
Wright, Frances, 192
Wright, James M., 62

Yaha Hajo, 332
Yates, Adam, 83
Yates, Bellisle, 83
Yates, Napham, 83
Young, John, 417
Young, Joshua, 252-253